Major Problems in
African-American History
Volume II

MAJOR PROBLEMS IN AMERICAN HISTORY SERIES

GENERAL EDITOR

THOMAS G. PATERSON

Major Problems in African-American History

Volume II
From Freedom to "Freedom Now," 1865–1990s

DOCUMENTS AND ESSAYS

EDITED BY

THOMAS C. HOLT
THE UNIVERSITY OF CHICAGO

ELSA BARKLEY BROWN
UNIVERSITY OF MARYLAND, COLLEGE PARK

HOUGHTON MIFFLIN COMPANY
Boston   New York

Editor in Chief: Jean L. Woy
Senior Associate Editor: Frances Gay
Project Editor: Gabrielle Stone
Editorial Assistant: Magdalena Carpenter
Production/Design Coordinator: Jodi O'Rourke
Senior Manufacturing Coordinator: Marie Barnes
Senior Marketing Manager: Sandra McGuire

Series design: Deborah Azerrad Savona

Cover image: *Aspiration,* 1936. Aaron Douglas. Fine Arts Museum of San Francisco.

Printed in the U.S.A.

Library of Congress Catalog Card Number: 99-71961

ISBN: 0-669-46293-4

9-CRS-10 09 08 07

Contents

CHAPTER 3
Renegotiating African-American Life in the New South
Page 87

CHAPTER 4
Rural Exodus and the Growth of New Urban Communities
Page 126

CHAPTER 5

Defining a Race Politics

Page 156

CHAPTER 6

The Culture Wars

Page 186

CHAPTER 7

Opportunities Lost and Found

Page 220

C H A P T E R   8
Origins of the Civil Rights Movement
Page 251

C H A P T E R   9
The Civil Rights Movement
Page 282

C H A P T E R   1 0
After "Freedom Now!"
Page 313

C H A P T E R   1 1
Progress and Poverty: African Americans at the Dawn of the Twenty-First Century
Page 338

Preface

African-American history is, paradoxically, both a very old and a very new field. It is very old in the sense that some of its pioneering works appeared in the middle and late nineteenth century. Moreover, those works—by William Wells Brown, George Washington Williams, and Gertrude Bustill Mossell, among others—addressed some of the field's principal issues, ones that have animated the subject to this day: what contributions blacks have made to building and defending the nation; what role blacks might have had in its cultural development and progress; how blacks might lay claim to equal citizenship. African-American history is also very new, in the sense that its widespread emergence as a formal subject of study in colleges and universities dates from the 1970s.

Whether old or new, however, scholars in this field have generally recognized its intimate connection to the most fundamental and contentious political issues of its day—such as slavery, freedom, equality, and social justice. As such, African-American history has itself been a politically contested field and provides an alternative perspective on the character, formation, and destiny of the American nation. Of course, some of the subjects of African-American history—for example, slavery and emancipation—have long been part of the standard American history curriculum. Outside of a very few predominantly black institutions, these subjects were not studied from the perspective of black Americans themselves. Since the 1970s, historians have focused on developing an African-American historiography that centers on black thought, action, and community. Volume I covers the African-American experience from the beginnings of the Atlantic slave trade to the Reconstruction period; Volume II, from Reconstruction to the present.

As part of the *Major Problems in American History* Series, these volumes are intended to provide students and instructors with a framework for thinking about African-American history and with essential, readable, and provocative documents and essays on the issues raised by African Americans' historical experience. That experience is both intimately linked to American history as a whole and also distinct from that history in innumerable ways. We wanted to acquaint students with the economic, political, and social circumstances in which African Americans have had to function and at the same time to offer students an opportunity to view U.S. history and the African-American experience in the United States through the eyes of African Americans.

As with that of other nonelite groups unable to control the recording of history or the preservation of that record, much of the lived experience of black Americans remains undocumented. In fact, the range and volume of literature and documentation of what has been done to or said about African Americans is much larger than that of the actions and thoughts of African Americans themselves. Even within the records of African Americans, those of men and prominent elites are often more known and available than those of women or of poor and working-class people. This is the reality that has made the choices more difficult for all scholars of the African-American experience; it requires innovation in both the search for and the interpretation of primary sources. In some cases, scholars have found letters and eyewitness accounts by African Americans buried in massive government files, especially those generated at moments of crisis like wars and civil unrest. Others have turned to traditional sources, such as plantation records or the testimony of elite whites, but subjected them to a more searching scrutiny, reading "between the lines." In other cases, scholars have sought out unconventional historical materials, such as folktales, music, photographs, and material objects. The essays and documents in this volume reflect many of these approaches.

A staple of the Civil Rights Movement was the song "They say that freedom is a constant struggle." Volume II explores the varied ways African Americans continuously from Reconstruction to the present day have worked to make for themselves some semblance of freedom in these United States. Chapters 2 and 3 cover the Reconstruction and New South eras. Chapters 4, 5, and 6 focus on black migration in the early twentieth century, the growth of new urban black communities, and the impact of both on black culture and politics. Chapters 7 and 8 focus on the Depression and World War II years. Chapters 9, 10, and 11 cover the Civil Rights Movement and the struggles for political power and economic justice of the 1970s, 80s, and 90s.

Like the other volumes in this series, *Major Problems in African-American History* is made up of both primary sources (textual and visual documents) and essays interpreting some of the major issues in the field. Every chapter opens with a brief introduction that sets the scene and defines the central issues. The documents and essays that follow suggest the differing perspectives from which historians address those issues, either through posing conflicting interpretations of the same events or offering differing angles of vision on a general theme. Our aim in each chapter is to provide materials that suggest ways of thinking about the African-American experience. This will enable readers to develop their own understanding or assessment of the questions scholars have raised and also allow readers to ask their own, perhaps entirely new, questions about the subject. Each chapter closes with a list of books and articles for further reading.

We would like to thank all the people who helped us in compiling this anthology. We have canvassed a large number of scholars of African-American history for suggestions about the appropriate content of these volumes. We are especially indebted to a number of people who provided us with extraordinarily generous replies, including not only helpful advice but in many cases copies of documents and essays: Jerma Jackson and Charlene Regester of the University of North Carolina, Chapel Hill; Robin D. G. Kelley of New York University; Deborah King of Dartmouth College; Marya McQuirter and Michelle Mitchell of the University of Michigan, Ann Arbor; Susan O'Donovan, Leslie Rowland, and Francille Rusan Wilson, of the University of Maryland, College Park; Julie Saville of the University of Chicago; and Stephanie J. Shaw of Ohio State University. We would also like to thank the following people who shared their syllabi with us or reviewed our tables of contents at various stages and provided us with thoughtful commentary and challenges: John D. Baskerville, University of Northern Iowa; Richard J. M. Blackett, the University of Houston; David W. Blight, Amherst College; Margaret Washington Creel, Cornell University; Dennis C. Dickerson, Williams College; Lillie J.

Edwards, Drew University; Patience Essah, Auburn University; V. P. Franklin, Drexel University; Raymond Gavins, Duke University; Robert L. Harris, Jr., Cornell University; Evelyn Brooks Higginbotham, Harvard University; Darlene Clark Hine, Michigan State University; Gerald C. Horne, University of North Carolina, Chapel Hill; James O. Horton, George Washington University; Rhett S. Jones, Brown University; Earl Lewis, the University of Michigan, Ann Arbor; Daniel Letwin, Pennsylvania State University; Daniel C. Littlefield, University of South Carolina; Valinda W. Littlefield, University of South Carolina; Leon F. Litwack and Waldo E. Martin, Jr., University of California, Berkeley; Genna Rae McNeil, the University of North Carolina, Chapel Hill; Peter M. Mhunzi, Pasadena City College; Tiffany L. Patterson, SUNY, Binghamton; Rosalyn Terborg-Penn, Morgan State University; Brenda Gayle Plummer, the University of Wisconsin at Madison; Linda Reed, the University of Houston; Joseph P. Reidy, Howard University; Julius Scott, the University of Michigan, Ann Arbor; Herbert Shapiro, University of Cincinnati; Stephanie J. Shaw, Ohio State University; Gerald Smith, University of Kentucky; Donald Spivey, the University of Miami; Judith Stein, City College of the City University of New York; Brenda Stevenson, University of California, Los Angeles; Jeffrey C. Stewart, George Mason University; Arvarh E. Strickland, University of Missouri-Columbia; Sterling Stuckey, University of California, Riverside; H. Lewis Suggs, Clemson University; Joe W. Trotter, Jr., Carnegie Mellon University; Clarence Walker, University of California, Davis; Juliet E. K. Walker, University of Illinois at Urbana-Champaign; Randolph Walker, LeMoyne-Owen College; Marli Weiner, University of Maine; Robert S. Weisbrot, Colby College; and Francille R. Wilson, the University of Maryland, College Park. Each of us has also incurred debts to student researchers and editorial assistants along the way. Elsa Barkley Brown thanks Marya McQuirter, Kelly Quinn, Jamie Hart, and Doris Dixon not only for library and clerical assistance but also for their useful suggestions regarding the content. Tom Holt is grateful to Hannah Rosen, Laurie Green, and Steven Essig. Elsa Barkley Brown would also like to express her appreciation to everyone in the Women's Studies Department at the University of Maryland for good-naturedly allowing this project to occupy every bit of communal space for way too long. Nataki H Goodall's hand is everywhere in this volume; for her untiring support of all phases of the selection and editing process and especially for her continuously irreverent wit, a very special thank you.

And, finally, the production of these volumes has been immeasurably aided by the staffs of both Houghton Mifflin and its predecessor, D. C. Heath. James Miller and Sylvia Mallory initiated the project. Fran Gay has been indispensably cheerful and determined in seeing that it was completed, and Gabrielle Stone has been thorough in overseeing the production of the project to bound books. Series Editor Thomas G. Paterson has nurtured, cajoled, and driven it forward from start to finish.

E. B. B.
T. H.

Interpreting

African-American History

What has motivated the study of African Americans as a separate topic in American history? What kinds of issues do such studies raise? What, exactly, constitutes the history of people of African descent in the United States? How is the field related to and different from general U.S. history? What are and have been the purposes to which historians and lay people have studied and written this history? What are the material and institutional bases for the development of a study of African Americans?

The question "What is African-American history?" was throughout the nineteenth and twentieth centuries, and continues to be, a political as much as an intellectual question. Most nineteenth- and twentieth-century white historians and social scientists, adopting biological conceptions of racial differences, assumed that black people, in the United States and elsewhere, had no history worth speaking of and no ability to undertake historical or other intellectual scholarship. The very notion that anyone might study the history of black people or that black people themselves might write or teach any subject worth others reading or studying contradicted many of the assumptions of the ordering of human society. Thus the study of African-American history was a contested issue. Additionally, for a people many of whom were newly freed from or only a generation or two removed from slavery, the question of how Americans in general conceptualized the relationship of black people to the national story was crucial in constructing themselves as free people, as citizens with full rights, and as equals. As African Americans, along with allies, struggled to alter their status in U.S. society and in the U.S. academy, history became a battleground.

Throughout the twentieth century various African Americans invested history with the power to transform social institutions. Both whites and blacks, so the argument went, had to overcome ignorance and miseducation about the history of black people. To black men, women, and children, knowledge of African-American history would impart a new sense of themselves and their abilities—an empowerment. To whites, this education would provide an incentive to dismantle the discriminatory legal, educational, economic, and social barriers that have kept black citizens relegated to secondary status or less for the majority of U.S. history. For all Americans, there was, in the arena of African-American history perhaps more than in any other, a recognition of the political power of history. Today we are perhaps less conscious of that, yet contemporary debates about how aspects of African-American experience will be remembered may continue to suggest the political nature of what are often represented as merely intellectual debates.

What are the ways in which and the places where you have been introduced to African-American history? How have your ideas about African-American history in particular and history in general been shaped by the contexts in which you encountered these histories?

D O C U M E N T S

The first three documents reveal the assumptions that many African Americans had about the ways in which the study of history could reshape the status of African Americans in the United States. Writing in 1920 for the first issue of a children's publication, *The Brownies' Book,* edited by W. E. B. Du Bois, Annette Brown addressed a poem to the subject of this lack of information about black achievements in the United States. Implicit in this poem is an assumption that children need to know the history of their people as much as they need to know the dominant national heroes and heroines. Perhaps it also urges children reading it to take responsibility for their own education, to seek out their history. The second document, a speech given at Hampton Institute in November 1922 by Carter G. Woodson, five years after he founded the *Journal of Negro History,* addresses how historical research and writing will help African Americans gain the respect of others. After receiving a Ph.D. in history from Harvard University in 1912, Woodson founded the Association for the Study of Negro Life and History (ASNLH) in 1915 and initiated Negro History Week in 1926. In the third document, Mary McLeod Bethune, then president of the ASNLH, lays out to the 1937 annual meeting her vision of black history as fundamental to the development of black self-esteem.

The fourth and fifth documents, by historians of the African-American experience, suggest how individual scholars, themselves African American, approach their work. John Hope Franklin, perhaps the premiere historian of the African-American experience in the second half of the twentieth century, discusses his experiences working as a historian in a society that denied him many of what might be seen as the basic necessities of work—a place to sit, a place to eat. In the fifth document, Vincent Harding writes what might be called a manifesto for what he and others saw as a new approach to African-American history and to being African American and a historian in the 1970s. Harding, a veteran of the civil rights movement, positions history frankly as a political undertaking and suggests that historians of his generation have viewpoints on history writing, on the experiences of African Americans, and on the United States radically different from the viewpoints of historians of the African-American experience who preceded them.

In the final document, poet Lucille Clifton offers a way of thinking about the development of history and its radical potential. She juxtaposes the acceptance of a history constructed by others, in which she would be portrayed as a victim, to the discovery of a different relationship to history—one that is more empowering.

1. *The Brownies' Book* Encourages Black Children to Know Their History, 1920

We gathered 'round the fire last night,
Jim an' Bess an' me,
And said, "Now let us each in turn
Tell who we'd rather be
Of all the folks that's in our books."
(Of course, we wouldn't want their looks.)

Bess wished that she'd been Betsy Ross,
The first to make the flag.
She said, "I'd like to do some deed
To make the people brag,
And have the papers print my name,—
If colored girls could rise to fame."

An' I stood out for Roosevelt;
I wished to be like him.
Then Bess said, "We've both had our say,
Now tell who you'd be, Jim."
Jim never thinks like me or Bess,
He knows more than us both, I guess.

He said, "I'd be a Paul Dunbar
Or Booker Washington.
The folks you named were good, I know,
But you see, Tom, each one
Of these two men I'd wish to be
Were colored boys, like you and me.

"Sojourner Truth was colored, Bess,
And Phyllis Wheatley, too;
Their names will live like Betsy Ross,
Though they were dark like you."
Jim's read of 'em somewhere, I guess,
He knows heaps more than me or Bess.

2. Carter G. Woodson on His Goals for Black History, 1922

We have a wonderful history behind us. We of the *Journal of Negro History* shall have going the rounds soon a lecture on the ante-bellum period, setting forth the stories of Negroes who did so much to inspire us. It reads like the history of people in an heroic age. We expect to send out from time to time books written for the express purpose of showing you that you have a history, a record, behind you. If

---

Annette Brown, "The Wishing Game," *The Brownies' Book*, 1, no. 1 (January 1920), 7.

Carter G. Woodson, "Some Things Negroes Need to Do," *Southern Workman*, 51 (January 1922), 33–36.

you are unable to demonstrate to the world that you have this record, the world will say to you, "You are not worthy to enjoy the blessings of democracy or anything else." They will say to you, "Who are you, anyway? Your ancestors have never controlled empires or kingdoms and most of your race have contributed little or nothing to science and philosophy and mathematics." So far as you know, they have not; but if you will read the history of Africa, the history of your ancestors—people of whom you should feel proud—you will realize that they have a history that is worth while. They have traditions that have value of which you can boast and upon which you can base a claim for a right to a share in the blessings of democracy.

Let us, then, study this history, and study it with the understanding that we are not, after all, an inferior people, but simply a people who have been set back, a people whose progress has been impeded. We are going back to that beautiful history and it is going to inspire us to greater achievements. It is not going to be long before we can so sing the story to the outside world as to convince it of the value of our history and our traditions, and then we are going to be recognized as men.

3. Mary McLeod Bethune Outlines the Objectives of the Association for the Study of Negro Life and History, 1937

If our people are to fight their way up out of bondage we must arm them with the sword and the shield and the buckler of pride—belief in themselves and their possibilities, based upon a sure knowledge of the achievements of the past. That knowledge and that pride we must give them "if it breaks every back in the kingdom."

Through the scientific investigation and objective presentation of the facts of our history and our achievement to ourselves and to all men, our Association for the Study of Negro Life and History serves to tear the veil from our eyes and allow us to see clearly and in true perspective our rightful place among all men. Through accurate research and investigation, we serve so to supplement, correct, re-orient, and annotate the story of world progress as to enhance the standing of our group in the eyes of all men. In the one hand, we bring pride to our own; in the other, we bear respect from the others.

We must tell the story with continually accruing detail from the cradle to the grave. From the mother's knee and the fireside of the home through the nursery, the kindergarten and the grade school, high school, college and university—through the technical journals, studies and bulletins of the Association,—through newspaper, story-book and pictures, we must tell the thrilling story. When they learn the fairy tales of mythical king and queen and princess, we must let them hear, too, of the Pharoahs and African kings and the brilliant pageantry of the Valley of the Nile; when they learn of Caesar and his legions, we must teach them of Hannibal and his Africans; when they learn of Shakespeare and Goethe, we must teach them of Pushkin and Dumas. When they read of Columbus, we must introduce the Africans who touched the shores of America before Europeans emerged from savagery;

"Clarifying Our Vision with the Facts," by Mary McLeod Bethune. From *Journal of Negro History,* 23, (January 1938), 12–15. Reprinted by permission.

when they are thrilled by Nathan Hale, baring his breast and crying: "I have but one life to give for my country," we must make their hearts leap to see Crispus Attucks stand and fall for liberty on Boston Common with the red blood of freedom streaming down his breast. With the *Tragic Era,* we give them *Black Reconstruction*; with Edison, we give them Jan Matzeliger; with John Dewey, we place Booker T. Washington; above the folk-music of the cowboy and the hill-billy, we place the spiritual and the "blues"; when they boast of Maxfield Parrish, we show them E. Simms Campbell. Whatever man has done, we have done—and often, better. As we tell this story, as we present to the world the facts, our pride in racial achievement grows, and our respect in the eyes of all men heightens.

Certainly, too, it is our task to make plain to ourselves the great story of our rise in America from "less than the dust" to the heights of sound achievement. We must recount in accurate detail the story of how the Negro population has grown from a million in 1800 to almost 12 million in 1930. The Negro worker is today an indispensible part of American agriculture and industry. His labor has built the economic empires of cotton, sugar cane and tobacco; he furnishes nearly 12 per cent of all American bread-winners, one-third of all servants, one-fifth of all farmers. In 1930, we operated one million farms and owned 750,000 homes. Negroes operate today over 22,000 business establishments with over 27 million dollars in yearly receipts and payrolls of more than five million dollars. Negroes manufacture more than 60 different commodities. They spend annually for groceries over two billion dollars, a billion more for clothes, with total purchasing power in excess of 4½ billion dollars. Negro churches have more than five million members in 42,500 organizations, owning 206 million dollars' worth of property and spending 43 million dollars a year. Some 360,000 Negroes served in the World War, with 150,000 of them going to France. Negroes are members of legislatures in 12 states; three or more states have black judges on the bench and a federal judge has recently been appointed to the Virgin Islands. Twenty-three Negroes have sat in Congress, and there is one member in the House at present. Under the "New Deal," a number of well qualified Negroes hold administrative posts.

Illiteracy has decreased from about 95 per cent in 1865 to only 16.3 per cent in 1930. In the very states that during the dark days of Reconstruction prohibited the education of Negroes by law, there are today over 2 million pupils in 25,000 elementary schools, 150,000 high school pupils in 2,000 high schools and 25,000 students in the more than 100 Negro colleges and universities. Some 116 Negroes have been elected to Phi Beta Kappa in white Northern colleges, over 60 have received the degree of Doctor of Philosophy from leading American universities and 97 Negroes are mentioned in *Who's Who in America*. It is the duty of our Association to tell the glorious story of our past and of our marvelous achievement in American life over almost insuperable obstacles.

From this history, our youth will gain confidence, self-reliance and courage. We shall thereby raise their mental horizon and give them a base from which to reach out higher and higher into the realm of achievement. And as we look about us today, we know that they must have this courage and self-reliance. We are beset on every side with heart-rending and fearsome difficulties.

Recently, in outlining to the President of the United States the position of the Negro in America, I saw fit to put it this way: "The great masses of Negro workers are depressed and unprotected in the lowest levels of agriculture and domestic service while black workers in industry are generally barred from the unions and grossly discriminated against. The housing and living conditions of the Negro masses are sordid and unhealthy; they live in constant terror of the mob, generally shorn of their constitutionally guaranteed right of suffrage, and humiliated by the denial of civil liberties. The great masses of Negro youth are offered only one fifteenth the educational opportunity of the average American child."

These things also we must tell them, accurately, realistically and factually. The situation we face must be defined, reflected and evaluated. Then, armed with the pride and courage of his glorious tradition, conscious of his positive contribution to American life, and enabled to face clear-eyed and unabashed the actual situation before him, the Negro may gird his loins and go forth to battle to return "with their shields or on them." And so today I charge our Association for the Study of Negro Life and History to carry forward its great mission to arm us with the facts so that we may face the future with clear eyes and a sure vision. Our Association may say again with Emperor Jean Christophe: "While I live I shall try to build that pride we need, and build in terms white men as well as black can understand! I am thinking of the future, not of now. I will teach pride if my teaching breaks every back in my Kingdom."

4. John Hope Franklin Explains the Lonely Dilemma of the American Negro Scholar, 1963

. . . The dilemmas and problems of the Negro scholar are numerous and complex. He has been forced, first of all, to establish his claim to being a scholar, and he has had somehow to seek recognition in the general world of scholarship. This has not been an easy or simple task, for, at the very time when American scholarship in general was making its claim to recognition, it was denying that Negroes were capable of being scholars. Few Americans, even those who advocated a measure of political equality, subscribed to the view that Negroes—any Negroes—had the ability to think either abstractly or concretely or to assimilate ideas that had been formulated by others. As late as the closing years of the nineteenth century it was difficult to find any white persons in the labor or business community, in the pulpit or on the platform, in the field of letters or in the field of scholarship, who thought it possible that a Negro could join the select company of scholars in America.

The Negro, then, first of all had to struggle against the forces and personalities in American life that insisted that he could never rise in the intellectual sphere. . . .

. . . The world of the Negro scholar is indescribably lonely; and he must, somehow, pursue truth down that lonely path while, at the same time, making certain that his conclusions are sanctioned by universal standards developed and maintained by those who frequently do not even recognize him. Imagine the plight of a Negro historian trying to do research in archives in the South operated by people who cannot conceive that a Negro has the capacity to use the materials there. I well recall my

---

John Hope Franklin, "The Dilemma of the American Negro Scholar," in Herbert Hill, ed., *Soon One Morning: New Writing by American Negroes.* Copyright © 1963 by Alfred A. Knopf, Inc. Reprinted by permission.

first visit to the State Department of Archives and History in North Carolina, which was presided over by a man with a Ph.D. in history from Yale. My arrival created a panic and an emergency among the administrators that was, itself, an incident of historic proportions. The archivist frankly informed me that I was the first Negro who had sought to use the facilities there; and as the architect who designed the building had not anticipated such a situation, my use of the manuscripts and other materials would have to be postponed for several days, during which time one of the exhibition rooms would be converted to a reading room for me. . . .

Many years later, in 1951, while working at the Library of Congress, one of my closest friends, a white historian, came by my study room one Friday afternoon and asked me to lunch with him the following day. I reminded him that since the following day would be a Saturday, the Supreme Court restaurant would be closed, and there was no other place in the vicinity where we could eat together. (This was before the decision in the Thompson restaurant case in April 1953, which opened Washington restaurants to all well-behaved persons.) My friend pointed out that he knew I spent Saturdays at the Library, and he wondered what I did for food on those days. I told him that I seldom missed a Saturday of research and writing at the Library of Congress, [but] that my program for that day was a bit different from other days. On Saturdays, I told him, I ate a huge late breakfast at home and then brought a piece of fruit or candy to the Library, which I would eat at the lunch hour. Then, when I could bear the hunger no longer during the afternoon, I would leave and go home to an early dinner. His only remark was that he doubted very much whether, if he were a Negro, he would be a scholar, if it required sacrifices such as this and if life was as inconvenient as it appeared. I assured him that for a Negro scholar searching for truth, the search for food in the city of Washington was one of the *minor* inconveniences. . . .

5. Vincent Harding on the Differences Between Negro History and Black History, 1971

. . . [M]uch of the story of Negro History is told [in] its attempt to reveal the "contributions" of blacks to the American saga; its emphasis on black heroism in the wars; its call for racial pride and for continued struggle to enter the mainstream of American life; its claim to be primarily interested in objective truth, while writing history through tears. . . .

Much of Negro History took this tack. It did not intend to threaten the established heroes or the basic values of America. . . . Rather it sought only to guarantee that the black presence was properly acknowledged, assuming that blackness could be contained within the confines of the American saga. It was an obvious parallel to the efforts to include a special minority of "ready" Negroes into an American society which would not be basically changed by their presence.

. . . Almost all of [the] proponents [of Black History] have come into their intellectual maturity under the tutelage of the fathers of Negro History, but unlike

---

Vincent Harding, "Beyond Chaos: Black History and the Search for the New Land." Reprinted by permission from Vincent Harding.

them we have lived most of our adult lives since 1954. We have lived through the politics of the sixties, through all of the promises and betrayals, through the discomfiting of the West. . . .

We who write Black History cannot track our "bleeding countrymen through the widely scattered documents of American history" and still believe in America. . . . We cannot—do not wish to—write with detachment from the agonies of our people. We are not satisfied to have our story accepted into the American saga. We deal in redefinitions, in taking over, in moving to set our own vision upon the blindness of American historiography. . . .

Black History does not seek to highlight the outstanding contributions of special black people to the life and times of America. Rather our emphasis is on exposure, disclosure, on reinterpretation of the entire American past. . . . [I]t is clear even now that the black past cannot be remade and clearly known without America's larger past being shaken at the foundations. While Negro History almost never questioned the basic goodness and greatness of American society, while it assumed its innate potential for improvement (provided it was ready to read additional volumes on Negro History), Black History has peeped a different card.

Black History suggests that the American past upon which so much hope has been built never really existed, and probably never will. . . .

. . . Black History is clearly more than the study of exclusively black things, for since the days of our slavery we could not be understood in an exclusively black light. So that Black History which seeks to deal with America begins with its European heritage, assesses the "Rise of the West." It asks how much of this ascendancy came at the expense of the death and degradation of our fathers and other nonwhite peoples of the globe. When it is clear that the "greatness" of Europe was built under the shadow of our ancestors' deaths, how shall we view this Western world and its major child—America? Black History . . . is the exposure of the strange foundations of Western power. . . .

Black History looks upon America with little of the affection and admiration which was obviously carried by our Negro History fathers. We look at the paradox of Black indentured-servitude/slavery being introduced into the colony of Virginia at the same time that the House of Burgesses came into being. So slavery and "representative government" were planted together. . . . From the perspective of Black History, the greater freedom which was gained for local government in the English colonies actually turned out to be freedom to embed the slavery of our forefathers deep into freedom's soil. So we are forced to begin to ask whether it was ever freedom's soil.

. . . [B]lacks must read history with Indian eyes as well, and cannot fail to note that many of the New England "fathers" participated not only in the forced migration and decimation of the original inhabitants, but gave full strength to that trade in men which brought other dark men to these shores. The treatment received by both blacks and Indians cannot fail to shape the black approach to New England history. . . .

Indeed Black History is forced to press on to ask about the meaning of America itself. (This raising of questions did not mark Negro History. Perhaps our fathers lived too close to the brutal experiences of black life to allow such a luxury.) When the spirit and institutions of the nation were so fully formed and defined by the leaders of Massachusetts and the rest of New England—slave traders on the one hand, slaveholders on the other—what indeed is the nation's meaning? Whose founding "fathers" were they, and what does their creation mean for the children of their slaves?

Black History is not satisfied with telling how many black men fought in the Revolutionary War. We are not among those who lift the banner of Crispus Attucks, for we are caught in painful dilemmas. While we recognize their heroism, we recognize too that a revolution which ended with more than 700,000 persons still in slavery was perhaps no revolution at all, but essentially a war among colonialist powers. So the children of the slaves who fought might better mourn rather than rejoice and celebrate, for it is likely that our fathers were no different than the millions of non-white pawns who have been pushed about by the military leaders of the colonizers for centuries. (And we save our energies and our wits for the exposing of this delusion and the encouraging of the heirs of the slaves to refuse to be pawns any longer.) In this way the experiences of our forefathers and the developments of this generation coalesce into a totally different reading of America than is usually known. . . .

Such a reading of America presses us to ask whether it was ever a democracy, demands to know whether it is possible for a democracy to exist where one quarter of the population of the land is either in slavery or being steadily driven off its ancient grounds. Black History is not simply "soul food" and "soul music" as some of its misinterpreters have suggested. Black History is the history of the Black Experience in America, which is the history of black and white—and Indian—inextricably, painfully, rarely joyfully, entwined. So Black History explores Henry Adams concerning the American nation at the beginning of the nineteenth century and hears him say that America in 1800 was a healthy organism. Then in the same work we read that the one major problem in America in 1800 was "the cancer" of slavery. In that set of statements America is diagnosed for black eyes: Healthy—except for cancer.

Black History is the constant demand that the cancerous state of America be seen and known. . . .

Black History cannot help but be politically oriented, for it tends toward the total redefinition of an experience which was highly political. Black History must be political, for it deals with the most political phenomenon of all—the struggle between the master and the slave, between the colonized and the colonizer, between the oppressed and the oppressor. And it recognizes that all histories of peoples participate in politics and are shaped by political and ideological views. . . .

6. Lucille Clifton on the Nurturing of History, c. 1990

> i am accused of tending to the past
> as if i made it,
> as if i sculpted it
> with my own hands. i did not.
> this past was waiting for me

> when i came,
> a monstrous unnamed baby,
> and i with my mother's itch
> took it to breast
> and named it
> History.
> she is more human now,
> learning language everyday,
> remembering faces, names and dates.
> when she is strong enough to travel
> on her own, beware, she will.

 # E S S A Y S

In the first essay, John Hope Franklin, the leading African-American historian in the post–World War II era, sketches the history of the field since the late nineteenth century. He argues that successive generations of African-American scholars struggled to recover their history in the midst of changing but always politically charged circumstances. To reclaim the history of a stigmatized people was, it seems, an inherently political act, even though the character of the politics changed over time. David W. Blight of Amherst College describes the efforts of an earlier generation to reclaim its true historical legacy. On the twentieth anniversary of the Emancipation Proclamation Frederick Douglass struggled passionately against the white southern myth of the "Lost Cause," which appeared to authorize a national reconciliation from which blacks were excluded. An accurate memory of the war and emancipation, Douglass believed, would better sustain the continuing struggle to realize finally the fruits of the destruction of slavery. The continuing mythic power in our own day of the historical myths embodied in monuments, museums, memorials, and rituals is also the subject of the third essay, by Fath Davis Ruffins of the National Museum of American History. The failed effort to win public support for an African-American museum in the nation's capital reflected many of the competing historical visions and political agendas among blacks as well as between blacks and whites. The materialization of African-American history is a form of political recognition, but the debate over the appropriate form and character of that material representation exposes fierce differences over "the politics of memory."

The History of African-American History

JOHN HOPE FRANKLIN

According to my calculation, there have been four generations of scholarship—of unequal length—in Afro-American history. The first generation began auspiciously with the publication in 1882 of the two-volume *History of the Negro Race in America* by George Washington Williams and ended around 1909 with the publication of Booker T. Washington's *Story of the Negro*. Although it is difficult to characterize this first period of serious scholarship in the field, it is safe to say that the primary

John Hope Franklin, "On the Evolution of Scholarship in Afro-American History," in *The State of Afro-American History: Past, Present, and Future,* edited by Darlene Clark Hine, pp. 13–22. Copyright © 1986 by Louisiana State University Press. Reprinted by permission.

concern of the writers was to explain the process of adjustment Afro-Americans made to conditions in the United States. Whether it was the aggressive integrationism of George Washington Williams or the mild accommodationism of Booker T. Washington, the common objective of the writers of this period was to define and describe the role of Afro-Americans in the life of the nation. . . .

There were no trained, professional historians among them, with the exception of W. E. B. Du Bois. . . . They wrote of "The Progress of the Race," "A New Negro for a New Century," and "The Remarkable Advancement of the American Negro." . . . Obviously their concern was with adjustment, adaptation, and the compatibility of Afro-Americans with the white world in which they were compelled to live.

The second generation was marked by no special fanfare until the publication of Du Bois' *The Negro* in 1915, the founding of the Association for the Study of Negro Life and History also in 1915, the launching of the *Journal of Negro History* in 1916, and the publication in 1922 of Carter G. Woodson's *The Negro in Our History*. Woodson was the dominant figure of the period. He was not only the leading historian but also the principal founder of the association, editor of the *Journal,* and executive director of the Associated Publishers. He gathered around him a circle of highly trained younger historians whose research he directed and whose writings he published in the *Journal of Negro History* and under the imprint of the Associated Publishers. Monographs on labor, education, Reconstruction, art, music, and other aspects of Afro-American life appeared in steady succession, calling to the attention of the larger community the role of Afro-Americans, more specifically the contributions they had made to the development of the United States. The articles and monographs reflected prodigious research and zeal in pursuing the truth that had *not* been the hallmark of much of the so-called scientific historical writing produced in university seminars in this country some years earlier.

Woodson provided the intellectual and practical leadership of the second generation. With his strong sense of commitment, he offered the spirit and enthusiasm of a pioneer, a discoverer. He even provided the principal theme for the period when he said—in his writings and on numerous occasions—that it was the objective of him and his colleagues "to save and publish the records of the Negro, that the race may not become a negligible factor in the thought of the world." Nor should the record of Afro-Americans become a negligible factor in their own thought, Woodson contended. Thus he began doing everything possible to keep the history of Afro-Americans before them and before the larger community as well. Every annual meeting of the Association for the Study of Negro Life and History had several sessions devoted to the teaching of Afro-American history in the elementary and secondary schools. In 1926 Woodson began the annual observance of Negro History Week to raise the consciousness of Afro-Americans regarding their own worth and to draw the attention of others to what Afro-Americans had contributed to American civilization. Shortly thereafter he launched the *Negro History Bulletin,* a magazine for students, teachers, and the general public. Forty years before this country began to observe History Day, there was Negro History Week. Fifty years after the beginning of the *Negro History Bulletin,* the American Historical Association was still wrestling with the idea of a popular history magazine for students and the general public.

. . . Perhaps a convenient place to mark the beginning of the third generation is with the appearance in 1935 of W. E. B. Du Bois' *Black Reconstruction*. . . . In his book on Reconstruction, as the subtitle indicates, he was interested in "the part which black folk played in the attempt to reconstruct democracy in America." . . .

The third generation of Afro-American historical scholarship spanned, roughly, a twenty-five-year period that ended with the close of the 1960s. Most of the members of this generation were, like Du Bois, interested in the role that Afro-Americans played in the nation's history. Their training was similar to that of the second generation, but their interests were different. They looked less to Afro-American achievements and more to the interactions of blacks with whites, and more to the frequent antagonisms than to the rare moments of genuine cooperation. They tended to see Afro-American history in a larger context, insisting that any event that affected the status of Afro-Americans was a part of Afro-American history even if no Afro-Americans were directly involved. Mississippi's Theodore Bilbo, reading Rayford Logan's *What the Negro Wants* (1944) to his colleagues in the United States Senate and interpreting it for their benefit, was as much a part of Afro-American history as was Heman Sweatt's seeking admission to the University of Texas Law School.

The third generation experienced the fire and brimstone of World War II. Its predicament was not one that Adolf Hitler created but one created by the racial bigotry within their own government and in the American community in general. While all Afro-Americans were exposed to this special brand of racial perversion in the form of eloquent, if shallow, pronouncements against worldwide racism, Afro-American historians were especially sensitive to the persistent hypocrisy of the United States from the colonial years right down to World War II. Small wonder that they had difficulty maintaining a semblance of balance in the face of studied racial discrimination and humiliation. One of them declared that the United States government was "guilty of catering to the ideals of white supremacy." Another called on the United States to "address herself to the unfinished business of democracy," adding somewhat threateningly that "time was of the essence." If anyone doubts the impatience and anger of Afro-American historians during those years, he or she should examine the proceedings of the annual meetings of the Association for the Study of Negro Life and History or follow the activities of the historians themselves.

A salient feature of this generation was the increasing number of white historians working in the field. Some years earlier the second generation of historians had indicated that there were numerous areas in which work needed to be done. White historians entered the field to share in the work. One of them published the first extensive study of slavery in almost forty years and another wrote an elaborate work on the antislavery movement. Still another presented the first critical examination of Negro thought in the late nineteenth century. Interestingly enough, hostile white critics called these white historians "neo-abolitionists." Others worked on Afro-Americans in the antebellum North, Afro-American intellectual history, racial discrimination in education, and Afro-Americans in urban settings. Meanwhile, university professors began to assign dissertation topics in Afro-American history to white as well as Afro-American students. They also participated in the annual meetings of the Association for the Study of Negro Life and History and contributed to the *Journal of Negro History.* By the end of the 1960s Afro-American history was no longer the exclusive domain of Afro-Americans.

I believe that Carter G. Woodson would have been pleased with this involvement of white historians in the third generation of scholarship. When he founded the *Journal of Negro History* in 1916, he invited white scholars to sit on the editorial board and to contribute articles. He was, nevertheless, a man of shrewd insights, and I am not suggesting for a moment that he would have approved of or even tolerated whites of the third generation whose motives were more political than scholarly. Even so, he would have welcomed papers for publication in the *Journal of Negro History,* whether submitted by whites or blacks, so long as they were the product of rigorous scholarship and were not contaminated by the venom of racial bias. . . .

In the fourth generation, which began around 1970, there emerged the largest and perhaps the best-trained group of historians of Afro-America that had ever appeared. The Afro-Americans in the group were trained, as were the white historians, in graduate centers in every part of the country, in contrast to those of the third generation, who had been trained at three or four universities in the East and Midwest. No area of inquiry escaped their attention. They worked on the colonial period, the era of Reconstruction, and the twentieth century. They examined slavery, the Afro-American family, and antebellum free blacks. Their range was wide, and they brought educational, cultural, and military subjects, among many others, under their scrutiny.

These new approaches as well as the accelerated intensity in the study of Afro-American history were greatly stimulated by the drive for equality that had already begun in the third period. In their insistence that they be accorded equal treatment in every respect, Afro-Americans summoned the history of the United States to their side. They had been here from the beginning, they argued, and had done more than their share in making the country rich and great. Since history validated their claims, it was important that the entire nation should become familiar with the facts of Afro-American history. Consequently, it should be studied more intensely, written about more extensively, and taught more vigorously. Institutions of higher education came under pressure to add courses in Afro-American history and related fields and to employ specialists in the field. Responses were varied. One dean at a leading predominantly white university said that he had no objection to a course in Afro-American history, but it would be difficult in view of the fact that there was not sufficient subject matter to occupy the teachers and students for a *whole* semester. Another rushed out and persuaded one of the leaders in the black community, who happened to be a Baptist minister, to teach a course in Afro-American history. Despite the intellectual, educational, and political considerations affecting their decisions, many colleges and universities incorporated courses in Afro-American history into their curricula.

. . . There was zeal, even passion, in much that they wrote, for [scholars in the field of Afro-American history] were anxious to correct all the errors and misinterpretations of which earlier historians had been guilty. Thus, they undertook to revise not only the racist historians of an earlier day but the Afro-American historians of an earlier generation as well. . . .

In his *History of the Negro Race in America* (1882), George Washington Williams was extremely critical of Frederick Douglass for various positions he took on slavery and freedom in the years before the Civil War. We could excoriate Williams, as did his contemporaries, but that would be unfair without at least first understanding Williams' impatience with a political party that had betrayed not only the freedmen but Frederick Douglass, their chosen spokesman, as well. Likewise, one could be extremely critical of Carter G. Woodson's preoccupation with the achievements of Afro-Americans, but one should remember that Woodson was hurling historical brickbats at those who had said that Afro-Americans had achieved nothing at all. One could likewise be extremely critical of the historians of the third generation for their preoccupation with what may be called "mainstream history." In the process, some claim, they neglected some cherished attributes of Afro-American life and history, such as race pride and cultural nationalism. Such claims overlook the important fact that the historians of the third generation were compelled by circumstances to fight for the integration of Afro-American history into the mainstream of the nation's history. Their fight to integrate Afro-American history into the mainstream was a part of the fight by Afro-American students to break into the graduate departments of history in every predominantly white university in the southern states and in very many such institutions outside the South. It was also a part of the fight of Afro-Americans to gain admission to the mainstream of American life—for the vote, for equal treatment, for equal opportunity, for their rights as Americans. They pursued that course in order to be able to refute those, including our favorite dean—our favorite whipping boy, incidentally—who argued that Afro-Americans had little or no history. They also did so in order to support their argument that Afro-American history should be recognized as a centerpiece—an adornment, if you will—of the history of the United States.

. . . As a relatively new field, at least only recently recognized as a respectable field of intellectual endeavor, [Afro-American history] is alive and vibrant. This is why it can easily attract and excite a large number of graduate and undergraduate students. It provides, moreover, a very important context in which much, if not the whole, of the history of the United States can be taught and studied. It also provides an important context in which much of the history of the United States can be reexamined and rewritten. In its unique position as one of the most recent areas of intellectual inquiry, it invites the attention of those who genuinely seek new avenues to solve some of the nation's most difficult historical problems. And, if it is a valid area of intellectual inquiry, it cannot be segregated by sex, religion, or race. Historians must be judged by what they do, not by how they look.

I like to think that it was more than opportunism that increased the offerings in Afro-American history in the colleges and universities across the land. I like to believe that it was more than the excitement of the late 1960s that provided new opportunities to teach and learn Afro-American history. I prefer to entertain the thought that in addition to those other considerations there was the valid interconnection between the history of a people and their drive for first-class citizenship. The quest for their history, lost and strayed, was a quest in which black and white alike could and did participate, as both teachers and writers of history. The drive for first-class citizenship was a drive whose immediate benefit could be enjoyed only by those who had been denied it or by those others who at least truly understood the loathsome nature that such denial represented.

Some members of the fourth generation, no doubt, will regard this sentiment as optimistic if not maudlin. I would be the first to say that there is some of both in it. I would only add that when one begins a poem, a hymn, a short story, or even a history, one must be optimistic about its completion and about what it seeks to teach. If one believes in the power of his own words and in the words of others, one must also hope and believe that the world will be a better place by our having spoken or written those words.

The Burden of African-American History: Memory, Justice, and a Usable Past

DAVID W. BLIGHT

In the first week of January 1883, on the twentieth anniversary of the Emancipation Proclamation, a distinguished group of black leaders held a banquet in Washington, D.C., to honor the nineteenth century's most prominent Afro-American intellectual, Frederick Douglass. The banquet was an act of veneration for Douglass, an acknowledgment of the aging abolitionist's indispensable role in the Civil War era, a ritual of collective celebration, and an opportunity to forge historical memory and transmit it across generations. The nearly fifty guests comprised a who's who of black leadership in the middle and late nineteenth century. . . . After a sumptuous dinner, numerous toasts were offered to Douglass, and to nearly every major aspect of black life: to "the colored man as a legislator"; to "the Negro press"; to "the Negro author"; to "the Republican Party"; and so forth. Douglass himself finally ended the joyous round of toasts by offering one of his own: to "the spirit of the young men" by whom he was surrounded. Many of the most distinguished guests had come of age only since the Civil War. For them slavery, abolitionism, and even the war itself were the history beyond memory. Douglass had captured an essential meaning of the occasion; the young had gathered in tribute to the old. As they met to celebrate and to understand the pivotal event in their history—emancipation—the meaning of that event was being passed to a new generation of black leaders.

In his formal remarks at the banquet, Douglass demonstrated that during the last third of his life (he lived from 1818 until 1895), a distinguishing feature of his leadership was his quest to preserve the memory of the Civil War as he believed blacks and the nation should remember it. Douglass viewed emancipation as the central reference point of black history. Likewise the nation, in his judgment, had no greater turning point, nor a better demonstration of national purpose. On the twentieth anniversary, Douglass sought to infuse emancipation and the war with the sacred and mythic qualities that he had always attributed to them. . . . Emancipation day, he believed, ought to be a national celebration in which all blacks—the low and the mighty—could claim a new and secure social identity. But it was also an "epoch" full of lessons about the meaning of historical memory. . . . Douglass challenged his fellow black leaders to remember the Civil War with awe. "The day we celebrate," he said, "affords us an eminence from which we may in a measure survey both the past and the future. It is one of those days which may well count for a thousand years." This was more than mere banquet rhetoric. . . .

"'For Something Beyond the Battlefield': Frederick Douglass and the Struggle for the Memory of the Civil War," by David W. Blight. From *Journal of American History,* 75 (March 1989), 1156–1178. Copyright © 1989 by the Journal of American History. Reprinted by permission.

Douglass's effort to forge memory into action that could somehow save the legacy of the Civil War for blacks—freedom, citizenship, suffrage, and dignity— came at a time when the nation appeared indifferent or hostile to that legacy. The richly symbolic emancipation day banquet of 1883 occurred only months before the United States Supreme Court struck down the Civil Rights Act of 1875, sacri- ficing the Civil War amendments, as the dissenting Justice John Marshall Harlan put it, and opening the door for the eventual triumph of Jim Crow laws across the South. The ruling in *United States v. Stanley,* better known as the *Civil Rights Cases,* declared that the equal protection clause of the Fourteenth Amendment applied only to states; a person wronged by racial discrimination, therefore, could look for redress only from state laws and courts. In effect, the decision would also mean that the discriminatory acts of private persons were beyond the safeguards of the Fourteenth Amendment. . . .

Douglass interpreted the *Civil Rights Cases* as a failure of historical memory and national commitment. Reflecting on the Supreme Court decision in his final autobiography, Douglass contended that "the future historian will turn to the year 1883 to find the most flagrant example of this national deterioration." White racism, among individuals and in national policy, he remarked, seemed to increase in proportion to the "increasing distance from the time of the war." Douglass blamed not only the "fading and defacing effects of time," but more important, the spirit of reconciliation between North and South. Justice and liberty for blacks, he maintained, had lost ground from "the hour that the loyal North . . . began to shake hands over the bloody chasm." Thus, Douglass saw the Supreme Court decision as part of a disturbing pattern of historical change. Historical memory, he had come to realize, was not merely an entity altered by the passage of time; it was the prize in a struggle between rival versions of the past, a question of will, of power, of per- suasion. This historical memory of any transforming or controversial event emerges from cultural and political competition, from the choice to confront the past and to debate and manipulate its meaning.

. . . From the early days of Reconstruction, but especially by the 1870s, Douglass seemed acutely aware that the postwar era might ultimately be controlled by those who could best shape interpretations of the war itself. Winning the peace would not only be a matter of power, but also a struggle of moral will and historical consciousness. In the successful rise of the Democratic party, Douglass saw evi- dence that the South was beginning to win that struggle. In 1870 he complained that the American people were "destitute of political memory." But as he tried to reach out to both black and white readers with his newspaper, Douglass demanded that they not allow the country to "bury dead issues," as the Democrats wished. "The people cannot and will not forget the issues of the rebellion," Douglas ad- monished. "The Democratic party must continue to face the music of the past as well as of the present."

Some of Douglass's critics accused him of living in the past. . . . To such criti- cisms Douglass always had a ready answer: he would *not forgive* the South and he would *never forget* the meaning of the war. At the Tomb of the Unknown Soldier in Arlington National Cemetery in 1871, on one of the first observances of Memorial Day, Douglass declared where he stood.

We are sometimes asked in the name of patriotism to forget the merits of this fearful struggle, and to remember with equal admiration those who struck at the nation's life, and those who struck to save it—those who fought for slavery and those who fought for liberty and justice. I am no minister of malice . . . I may say if this war is to be forgotten, I ask in the name of all things sacred what shall men remember?

. . . By intellectual predilection and by experience, Douglass was deeply conscious that history mattered. As the author of three autobiographies by the 1880s, he had cultivated deep furrows into his own memory. In a real sense, the Frederick Douglass who endures as an unending subject of literary and historical inquiry— because of the autobiographies—is and was the creature of memory. Moreover, Douglass deeply understood that peoples and nations are shaped and defined by history. He knew that history was a primary source of identity, meaning, and motivation. He seemed acutely aware that history was both burden and inspiration, something to be cherished and overcome. Douglass also understood that winning battles over policy or justice in the present often required an effective use of the past. He came to a realization that in the late nineteenth-century America, blacks had a special need for a usable past. "It is not well to forget the past," Douglass warned in an 1884 speech. "Memory was given to man for some wise purpose. The past is . . . the mirror in which we may discern the dim outlines of the future and by which we may make them more symmetrical."

. . . [I]n the 1880s, according to Douglass, blacks occupied a special place in America's historical memory, as participants and as custodians. He understood his people's psychological need not to dwell on the horrors of slavery. But the slave experience was so immediate and unforgettable, Douglass believed, because it was a history that could "be traced like that of a wounded man through a crowd by the blood." Douglass urged his fellow blacks to keep *their* history before the consciousness of American society; if necessary, they should serve as a national conscience. . . . But as Douglass learned, such historical consciousness was as out of date in Gilded Age America as the racial justice he demanded.

. . . Douglass hoped that Union victory, black emancipation, and the Civil War amendments would be so deeply rooted in recent American experience, so central to any conception of national regeneration, so necessary to the postwar society that they would become sacred values, ritualized in memory. . . .

Douglass's pledge to "never forget" the meaning of the Civil War stemmed from at least five sources in his thought and experience: his belief that the war had been an ideological struggle and not merely the test of a generation's loyalty and valor; his sense of refurbished nationalism made possible by emancipation, Union victory, and Radical Reconstruction; his confrontation with the resurgent racism and Lost Cause mythology of the postwar period; his critique of America's peculiar dilemma of historical amnesia; and his personal psychological stake in preserving an Afro-American and an abolitionist memory of the war. Douglass never softened his claim that the Civil War had been an ideological conflict with deeply moral consequences. He abhorred the nonideological interpretation of the war that was gaining popularity by the 1880s. The spirit of sectional reunion had fostered a celebration of martial heroism, of strenuousness and courage, perhaps best expressed by Oliver Wendell Holmes, Jr., and later popularized by Theodore

Roosevelt. Holmes experienced and therefore loathed the horror of combat. But to him, the legacy of the Civil War rested not in any moral cause on either side, but in the passion, devotion, and sacrifice of the generation whose "hearts were touched with fire." To Holmes, the true hero—the deepest memory—of the Civil War was the soldier on either side, thoughtless of ideology, who faced the "experience of battle . . . in those indecisive contests." . . . By the 1880s Holmes's memory of the war became deeply rooted in American culture. . . .

Douglass resisted such an outlook and demanded a teleological memory of the war. His Memorial Day addresses were full of tributes to martial heroism, albeit only on the Union side; but more important, they were testaments to the abolitionist conception of the war. The conflict, Douglass insisted in 1878, "was a war of ideas, a battle of principles . . . a war between the old and new, slavery and freedom, barbarism and civilization." After Reconstruction Douglass was one of a small band of old abolitionists and reformers who struggled to sustain an ideological interpretation of the Civil War. . . .

The second source of Douglass's quest to preserve the memory of the Civil War was his refurbished nationalism. At stake for the former fugitive slave was the sense of American nationhood, the secure social identity that he hoped emancipation and equality would one day offer every black in America. Douglass expressed this connection between nationalism and memory in his famous speech at the unveiling of the Freedmen's Memorial Monument at Abraham Lincoln in Washington, D.C., in April 1876. . . . Attended by President Ulysses S. Grant, his cabinet, Supreme Court Justices, and numerous senators, the ceremony was as impressive as the bright spring day, which had been declared a holiday by joint resolution of Congress. After a reading of the Emancipation Proclamation and the unveiling of the statue (which Douglass later admitted he disliked because "it showed the Negro on his knees"), Douglass took the podium as the orator of the day. . . . Through most of the speech he spoke to and for blacks; the monument had been commissioned and paid for almost entirely by blacks. But the monument was not only to Lincoln; rather, it was to the *fact* of emancipation. . . . Douglass was, indeed, trying to make Lincoln mythic and, therefore, useful to the cause of black equality. But the primary significance of Douglass's Freedmen's Memorial address lies in its concerted attempt to forge a place for blacks in the national memory, to assert their citizenship and nationhood. . . .

The third cause of Douglass's concern over the memory of the Civil War was the resurgent racism throughout the country and the rise of the Lost Cause mentality. . . . Historians have defined the Lost Cause in at least three different ways: as a public memory, shaped by a web of organizations, institutions, and rituals; as a dimension of southern and American civil religion, rooted in churches and sacred rhetoric as well as secular institutions and thought; and as a literary phenomenon, shaped by journalists and fiction writers from the die-hard Confederate apologists of the immediate postwar years through the gentle romanticism of the "local color" writers of the 1880s to the legion of more mature novelists of the 1890s and early twentieth century who appealed to a national audience eager for reconciliation. . . . Led by Jefferson Davis, and especially by the prototypical unreconstructed rebel, Gen. Jubal Early, these former Confederate leaders created veterans' organizations, wrote partisan confederate histories, built monuments, made Robert E. Lee into a romantic icon, and desperately sought justification for their cause and explanations for their defeat. . . . During the 1870s and 1880s they forged an organized movement in print, oratory, and granite, and their influence persisted until World War I.

The "national" Lost Cause took hold during the 1880s primarily as a literary phenomenon propagated by mass market magazines and welcomed by a burgeoning northern readership. . . . They wrote about the Old South, about the chivalry and romance of antebellum plantation life, about black "servants" and a happy, loyal slave culture, remembered as a source of laugher and music. They wrote about colonial Virginia—the Old Dominion—as the source of revolutionary heritage and the birthplace of several American presidents. Northern readers were treated to an exotic South, a premodern, preindustrial model of grace. These writers sought, not to vindicate the Confederacy, but to intrigue Yankee readers. Northern readers were not asked to reconcile Jefferson's Virginia with the rebel yell at the unveiling of a Confederate monument. They were only asked to recognize the South's place in national heritage.

The conditioning of the northern mind in popular literature had its counterpart in veterans' reunions, which in the 1880s and 1890s became increasingly intersectional. Celebration of manly valor on both sides and the mutual respect of Union and Confederate soldiers fostered a kind of veterans' culture that gave the Lost Cause a place in national memory. The war became essentially a conflict between white men; both sides fought well, Americans against Americans, and there was glory enough to go around. Celebrating the soldiers' experience buttressed the non-ideological memory of the war. The great issues of the conflict—slavery, secession, emancipation, black equality, even disloyalty and treason—faded from national consciousness as the nation celebrated reunion and ultimately confronted war with Spain in 1898. . . .

In the midst of Reconstruction, Douglass began to realize the potential power of the Lost Cause sentiment. Indignant at the universal amnesty afforded ex-Confederates, and appalled by the national veneration of Robert E. Lee, Douglass attacked the emerging Lost Cause. "The spirit of secession is stronger today than ever . . . ," Douglass warned in 1871. "It is now a deeply rooted, devoutly cherished sentiment, inseparably identified with the 'lost cause.' which the half measures of the Government towards the traitors have helped to cultivate and strengthen." . . .

As for proposed monuments to Lee, Douglass considered them an insult to his people and to the Union. He feared that such monument building would only "reawaken the confederacy." . . .

Douglass never precisely clarified just how much southern "repentance" or "reformation" he deemed necessary before he could personally extend forgiveness. He merely demanded "justice," based on adherence to the Civil War amendments and to the civil rights acts. . . . He lamented the passing of so many of the old abolitionists like Garrison whose services would be needed in what Douglass called "this second battle for liberty and nation."

. . . [T]he aging Douglass never wavered in his critique of racism. "The tide of popular prejudice" against blacks, Douglass said in 1884, had "swollen by a thousand streams" since the war. Everywhere, he lamented, blacks were "stamped" with racist expectations. Douglass expressed the pain of being black in America: wherever a black man aspired to a profession, "the presumption of incompetence confronts him, and he must either run, fight, or fall before it." The alleged rapes by black men of white women were to Douglass manifestations of the South's invention of a new "crime" to replace their old fear of "insurrection." Lynching, therefore, represented a white, southern invention of new means to exercise racial power and oppression. In a speech in 1884, commemorating the rescue of fugitive slaves in the 1850s, Douglass chastised his Syracuse audience for preferring sectional peace over racial justice. "It is weak and foolish to cry PEACE when there is no peace," he cried. "In America, as elsewhere, injustice must cease before peace can prevail."

The fourth source of Douglass's arguments in the debate over the memory of the Civil War was his conviction that the country had been seduced into "national forgetfulness," a peculiar American condition of historical amnesia. In his numerous retrospective speeches in the 1880s, Douglass discussed the limitations of memory. He knew that memory was fickle and that people must embrace an "ever-changing . . . present." Even his own "slave life," he admitted, had "lost much of its horror, and sleeps in . . . memory like the dim outlines of a half-forgotten dream." But Douglass's greater concern was with collective memory, not merely with personal recollection. Douglass was rowing upstream against a strong current in American thought. As a people, Americans had always tended to reject the past and embrace newness. The overweening force of individualism in an expanding country had ever made Americans a future-oriented people, a culture unburdened with memory and tradition. . . . To Douglass, the individualism that bred indifference and the racism that bred oppression were the twin enemies undercutting efforts to preserve an abolitionist memory of the Civil War. . . .

Most assuredly, . . . Douglass was not one of those Americans who rejected the past. . . . He believed that individualism could coexist with social justice, that getting on in the world released no one from the weight of history. "Well it may be said that Americans have no memories," Douglass said in 1888. "We look over the House of Representatives and see the Solid South enthroned there; we listen with calmness to eulogies of the South and of traitors and forget Andersonville. . . . We see colored citizens shot down and driven from the ballot box, and forget the services rendered by the colored troops in the late war for the Union." More revealing still was Douglass's contempt for northern sympathy with the Lost Cause. He believed northern forgiveness toward the South shamed the memory of the war. "Rebel graves are decked with loyal flowers," Douglass declared, "though no loyal grave is ever adorned by rebel hands. Loyal men are building homes for rebel soldiers; but where is the home for Union veterans, builded by rebel hands? Douglass had never really wanted a Carthaginian peace. But he felt left out of the nation's happy reunion; the deep grievances of his people—both historic and current—were no longer to be heard. At the very last, Douglass demanded that the power to forgive should be reserved for those most wronged.

The debate over the meaning of the war was not merely a question of remembering or forgetting. Douglass worried about historical amnesia because his version of the war, his memory, faltered next to the rival memories that resonated more deeply with the white majority in both North and South. Douglass may never have fully appreciated the complexity of the experience of the Civil War and Reconstruction for whites. The overwhelming number of white northerners who voted against black suffrage shared a bond of white supremacy with southerners who rejected the racial egalitarianism of Radical Reconstruction. The thousands of white Union veterans who remembered the war as a transforming personal experience, but not as the crucible of emancipation for four million slaves, had much in common with white Georgians who had found themselves in the path of Gen William T. Sherman's march to the sea. There were many rival memories of the war and its aftermath, and there was much need for forgetting and healing. As Friedrich Nietzsche suggested, personal happiness often requires a degree of forgetting the past. "Forgetting is essential to action of any kind," wrote Nietzsche, "Thus: it is possible to live almost without memory . . . but it is altogether impossible to live at all without forgetting . . . there is a degree of the historical sense which is harmful and ultimately fatal to the living thing, whether this living thing be a man or a people or a culture." Nietzsche captured elements of both truth and danger in human nature. Douglass focused his efforts on the dangers of collective forgetting, not on its personal or cultural necessity. Douglass knew that his people, confined to minority status and living at the margins of society, could rarely afford the luxury of forgetting. Although he may not have thoroughly discriminated between the rival memories he confronted, he became fully aware of their power and their threat. Thus, with ever fewer sympathetic listeners by the late 1880s, Douglass was left with his lament that "slavery has always had a better memory than freedom, and was always a better hater."

Those were not merely words of nostalgic yearning for a vanished past uttered by a man out of touch with changing times. In a sense, Douglass was living in the past during the last part of his life; for him, the Civil War and Reconstruction were the reference points for the black experience in the nineteenth century. All questions of meaning, of a sense of place, of a sense of future for blacks in America drew upon the era of emancipation. Hence, the fifth source of Douglass's pledge to "never forget": a tremendous emotional and psychological investment in his own conception of the legacy of the conflict. As an intellectual, Douglass had grown up with the abolition movement, the war, and its historical transformations. His career and his very personality had been shaped by those events. So, quite literally, Douglass's effort to preserve the memory of the Civil War was a quest to save the freedom of his people and the meaning of his own life.

Douglass embraced his role in preserving an abolitionist memory of the war with a sense of moral duty. In an 1883 speech in his old hometown of Rochester, New York, he was emphatic on that point.

> You will already have perceived that I am not of that school of thinkers which teaches us to let bygones be bygones; to let the dead past bury its dead. In my view there are no bygones in the world, and the past is not dead and cannot die. The evil as well as the good that men do lives after them. . . . The duty of keeping in memory the great deeds of the past, and of transmitting the same from generation to generation is implied in the mental and moral constitution of man.

But what of a society that did not widely share the same sense of history and preferred a different version of the past? Douglass's answer was to resist the Lost Cause by arguing for an opposite and, he hoped, deeper cultural myth—the abolitionist conception of the Civil War, black emancipation as the source of national regeneration.

In trying to forge an alternative to the Lost Cause, Douglass drew on America's reform tradition and constantly appealed to the Constitution and to the rule of law.

Moreover, reversing a central tenet of the Lost Cause—the memory of defeat—Douglass emphasized the memory of victory, the sacrifices of the Union dead, and the historical progress he believed inherent in emancipation. This is what Douglass meant in an 1878 Memorial Day speech in Madison Square in New York, when he declared that "there was a right side and a wrong side in the late war which no sentiment ought to cause us to forget."

In some of his postwar rhetoric Douglass undoubtedly contributed to what Robert Penn Warren has called the myth of the "Treasury of Virtue." He did sometimes imbue Union victory with an air of righteousness that skewed the facts. His insistence on the "moral" character of the war often neglected the complex, reluctant manner in which emancipation became the goal of the Union war effort. In structuring historical memory, Douglass could be as selective as his Lost Cause adversaries. His persistent defense of the Republican party after Reconstruction caused him to walk a thin line of hypocrisy. Indeed, Douglass's millennialist interpretation of the war forever caused him to see the conflict as a cleansing tragedy, wherein the nation had been redeemed of its evil by lasting grace. Douglass knew that black freedom had emerged *from* history more than from policy deliberately created by human agents. Moreover, he knew that emancipation had resulted largely from slaves' own massive self-liberation. But winning the battle over the legacy of the Civil War, Douglass knew, demanded deep cultural myths that would resonate widely in society. He knew that the struggle over memory was always, in part, a debate over the present. In his view, emancipation and black equality under law were the great results of the war. Hence, while urging old abolitionists not to give up their labors in 1875, Douglass contended that "every effort should now be made to save the result of this stupendous moral and physical contest." Moreover, nine years later Douglass warned that unless an abolitionist conception of the war were steadfastly preserved, America would "thus lose to coming generations a vast motive power and inspiration to high and virtuous endeavor." Douglass labored to shape the memory of the Civil War, then, as a skillful propagandist, as a black leader confident of the virtue of his cause, and as an individual determined to protect his own identity.

In his book *The Unwritten War: American Writers and the Civil War,* Daniel Aaron observes that very few writers in the late nineteenth century "appreciated the Negro's literal or symbolic role in the war." Black invisibility in the massive Civil War fictional literature—the absence of fully realized black characters, even in Mark Twain or William Faulkner—is yet another striking illustration that emancipation and the challenge of racial equality overwhelmed the American imagination in the postwar decades. Slavery, the war's deepest cause, and black freedom, the war's most fundamental result, remain the most conspicuous missing elements in the American literature inspired by the Civil War. Black invisibility in America's cultural memory is precisely what Douglass struggled against during the last two decades of his life. Obviously, Douglass was no novelist himself and was not about to write the great Civil War book. But memories and understandings of great events, especially apocalyptic wars, live in our consciousness like monuments in the mind. The aging Douglass's rhetoric was an eloquent attempt to forge a place on that monument for those he deemed the principal characters in the drama of emancipation: the abolitionist, the black soldier, and the freed people. Perhaps the best reason the Civil War remained, in Aaron's words, "vivid but ungraspable" to literary imagination was that most American writers avoided, or were confounded by, slavery and race, the deepest moral issues in the conflict.

The late nineteenth century was an age when white supremacy flourished amid vast industrial and social change. The nation increasingly embraced sectional reunion, sanctioned Jim Crow, dreamed about technology, and defined itself by the assumptions of commerce. Near the end of his monumental work, *Black Reconstruction* (1935), W. E. B. Du Bois declared himself "aghast" at the way historians had suppressed the significance of slavery and the black quest for freedom in the literature on the Civil War and Reconstruction era. "One is astonished in the study of history," wrote Du Bois, "at the recurrence of the idea that evil must be forgotten, distorted, skimmed over. . . . The difficulty, of course, with this philosophy is that history loses its value as an incentive and example; it paints perfect men and noble nations, but it does not tell the truth." As Du Bois acknowledged, it was just such a use of history as "incentive and example" for which Douglass had labored.

Although his jeremiads against the Lost Cause myth and his efforts to preserve an abolitionist memory of the conflict took on a strained quality, Douglass never lost hope in the regenerative meaning of the Civil War. It was such a great divide, such a compelling reference point, that the nation would, in time, have to face its meaning and consequences. In an 1884 speech, Douglass drew hope from a biblical metaphor of death and rebirth—the story of Jesus' raising Lazarus from the dead. "The assumption that the cause of the Negro is a dead issue," Douglass declared, "is an utter delusion. For the moment he may be buried under the dust and rubbish of endless discussion concerning civil service, tariff and free trade, labor and capital . . . , but our Lazarus is not dead. He only sleeps."

Douglass's use of such a metaphor was perhaps a recognition of temporary defeat in the struggle for the memory of the Civil War. But it also represented his belief that, though the struggle would outlast his own life, it could still be won. Douglass gave one of his last public addresses on the final Memorial Day of his life (May 1894) at Mount Hope Cemetery in Rochester, where he would himself be buried some nine months later. The seventy-six-year-old orator angrily disavowed the sectional reconciliation that had swept the country. He feared that Decoration Day would become an event merely of "anachronisms, empty forms and superstitions." One wonders if the largely white audience in Rochester on that pleasant spring afternoon thought of Douglass himself as somewhat of an anachronism. In a country reeling from an economic depression in 1893, worried by massive immigration, the farmers' revolt, and the disorder of growing cities, Douglass's listeners (even in his old hometown) may not have looked beyond the symbolic trappings of the occasion. One wonders how willing they were to cultivate their thirty-year-old memory of the war and all its sacrifice, to face the deeper meanings Douglass demanded. The aged Douglass could still soar to oratorical heights on such occasions. He asked his audience to reflect with him about their "common memory." "I seem even now to hear and feel the effects of the sights and the sounds of that dreadful period," Douglass said. "I see the flags from the windows and housetops fluttering in the breeze. I see and hear the steady tramp of armed men in blue uniforms. . . . I see the recruiting sergeant with drum and fife . . . calling for men, young men and strong, to go to the front and fill up the gaps made by rebel powder and pestilence. I hear the piercing sound of trumpets." These were more than Whitmanesque pictures of bygone peril and glory. In a nation that now acquiesced in the frequent lynching of his people, that shattered their hopes with disfranchisement and segregation, Douglass appealed to history, to what for him was authentic experience, to the recognition scenes that formed personal and national identity. On an ideological level, where Douglass did his best work, he was still fighting the war. By 1894 he was as harsh as ever in his refusal to concede the Confederate dead any equal place in Memorial Day celebrations. "Death has no power to change moral qualities," he argued. "What was bad before the war, and during the war, has not been made good since the war." A tone of desperation entered Douglass's language toward the end of his speech. Again and again he pleaded with his audience not to believe the arguments of the Lost Cause advocates, however alluring their "disguises" might seem. He insisted that slavery had caused the war, that Americans should never forget that the South fought "to bind with chains millions of the human race."

No amount of nationalism, individualism, or compassion could ever change Douglass's conception of the memory and meaning of the Civil War. His pledge to "never forget" was both a personal and a partisan act. It was an assertion of the power of memory to inform, to inspire, and to compel action. Douglass was one of those nineteenth-century thinkers who by education, by temperament, and especially by experience believed that history was something living and useful. Even in the twilight of his life, there was no greater voice for the old shibboleth that the Civil War had been a struggle for union *and* liberty. "Whatever else I may forget," Douglass told those assembled at Mount Hope Cemetery, "I shall never forget the difference between those who fought for liberty and those who fought for slavery; between those who fought to save the Republic and those who fought to destroy it." The jubilee of black freedom in America had been achieved by heroic action, through forces in history, through a tragic war, and by faith. Among Douglass's final public acts, therefore, was to fight—using the power of language and historical imagination—to preserve that jubilee in memory and in reality. In a Rochester cemetery, he stood with the Union dead, waved the last bloody shirts of a former slave, a black leader, and a Yankee partisan, and anticipated the dulling effects of time and the poet Robert Lowell's vision of "the stone statues of the abstract Union soldier" adorning New England town greens, where "they doze over muskets and muse through their sideburns."

Sites of Memory, Sites of Struggle:
The "Materials" of History

FATH DAVIS RUFFINS

Though little noticed by the mainstream press and little discussed within all but a small segment of the museum world, the idea of an African-American museum on the Mall in Washington, D.C., flared and died between 1984 and 1994. Over the course of this decade, there were many debates about the soundness of this concept

"Culture Wars Won and Lost, Part II: The National African-American Museum Project," by Fath Davis Ruffins. From *Radical History Review,* 70 (1998), 78–101. Reprinted with the permission of Cambridge University Press.

within the Smithsonian Institution, within Congress, within professional museum associations such as the American Association of Museums, and within the inbred world of culturally specific Black museums.

Although most Americans are probably unaware of it, museums and archives devoted to what is now called the African-American experience have a long history. The first museum at a historically Black college was founded on paper at Howard University in 1867, and in the flesh at Hampton Institute in 1868. Major collections of archival materials were established before 1900, most famously by Dr. Jesse B. Moorland, a wealthy member of turn-of-the-century Washington's light-skinned elite, at Howard University, and by Arthur Alfonso Schomburg, a Puerto Rican of mixed descent who immigrated to New York City in the 1880s. Both of their collections (with many additions) live in the present as the Moorland-Spingarn Research Center at Howard, and the Schomburg Center for Research in Black Culture, since 1929 part of the vast New York Public Library system. By 1988, the African American Museums Association (AAMA) had documented 108 museums and archives in the U.S. and Canada devoted to the study of African-American life, history, and culture.

Although there have been some significant public and private resources devoted to preserving and interpreting the African experience in America, the larger mythos of Black history is that it has been "lost, stolen, or strayed." This phrase was the title of a widely viewed and well-regarded television special aired in 1968 and narrated by Bill Cosby. Though it seems astonishing today, before about 1970 African Americans were simply missing from most official formulations of American history. The historians who produced the "social history" revolution in scholarship of the 1960s and 1970s wrote to recover the voices of the "voiceless" slaves and put them back into American history in their rightful places. [Their] works . . . changed the landscape of American history and paved the way for more than two generations of inquiry into the lives of many Americans who left neither vast estates nor voluminous letters and diaries, nor were the powerful leaders of their time. In a quite literal way, these scholars recovered some of what had been thought unrecoverable.

How was this possible? When scholars began to ask new questions and search for new sources, they found that actually quite a lot of Black history was there for the analyzing. Church records, court records, published slave narratives, Work Projects Administration oral histories from the 1930s, ethnographic films beginning in the 1890s, photographs, and obscure but published books and articles provided an absolute wealth of material to examine. Although there certainly are important gaps in the nation's collections—such as the relative lack of eighteenth- and nineteenth-century artifacts documenting the lives and world views of rural and enslaved Black folk— there are also many significant resources. Textual, visual, archeological, and, to a lesser extent, artifactual materials have been actively saved for more than a hundred and thirty years, largely by dedicated Afro-American bibliophiles, collectors, and institutions such as the Schomburg Center and Howard, Fisk, and Atlanta Universities. Although much more could have been saved and though many official histories of the U.S. ignore these sources, there actually exist today numerous collections, public and private, which document the diversity of African-American experiences.

It is within this larger climate of the rhetorical loss of Black history, but significant collections holdings, that we must view the initiative for an African-American museum on the Mall. The idea of building a National African-American Museum was not new in 1984. In fact, various proposals to that effect had been circulating around Capitol Hill since the late 1970s at least. In 1981, a National Afro-American Museum was authorized by Congress to be located in Wilberforce, Ohio. Although no federal dollars were ever allocated for the project, the museum was and is largely funded by state resources through the Ohio Historical Society, as part of its general cultural mission within the state thanks to the power of Black state legislators in Ohio. In September 1987 the Wilberforce museum opened to great fanfare. However, that institution clearly did not satisfy the desires of many people to see a national museum in Washington, not in a rural location far from the center of national power and international visibility.

Although numerous people may have discussed the idea of a Black museum on the Mall, Tom Mack was the person who introduced the idea onto the national stage. . . . Mack was and is the president of Tourmobile, Inc., a Washington, D.C., tour bus company with an exclusive contract to ferry tourists along the Mall, past the Smithsonian museums and other monuments. Over the course of doing business, Mack, an African American, became acutely aware of the lack of a Black presence on the Mall. . . . He argued for a clear and positive projection of African Americans in a Black museum on the Mall. Like many Black people, Mack thought that the absence of such a museum represented a tremendous oversight. He felt it was symbolic of the nation's profound and officially sanctioned ignorance of the African-American contribution to U.S. history and culture.

. . . Apparently, Mack first contacted Congressman Mickey Leland (D-Texas) in 1985. Through Leland's work, a *non-binding* House Resolution (H.R. 666) was passed in 1986, which affirmed in principle the idea of an African-American museum on the Mall. . . .

The AAMA is an organization principally comprised of Black museums and, to a lesser degree, Black professionals in the museum world. As a formal organization, AAMA is twenty years old in 1997. . . .

. . . [M]any members of the AAMA were quite opposed to the idea of a Black museum on the Mall. . . .

. . . Many Black museum directors and their staffs feared that an African-American museum on the Mall would suck up all the available public and private funds, leaving nothing for them. Others had similar concerns about collections. Would everyone now wish to donate their collections to the Smithsonian? What would be left for acquisition by smaller institutions without fully up-to-date storage facilities and without the prestige of a Smithsonian connection?

Within the Smithsonian itself, [some] others representing significant centers of Black activity worried that they would be forced to incorporate themselves into the Mall effort, thus risking the hard-won, independent identities of their museums and programs. Still others were concerned that the founding of an African-American museum on the Mall would relieve historically white Smithsonian museums from their responsibilities to include Black people in their narratives. . . .

. . . In 1989, then Smithsonian Secretary Robert McCormick Adams and then Assistant Secretary Thomas Freudenheim hired the well-known New York museum professional Claudine Brown to direct an Institutional Study Project, to investigate the feasibility of a Mall museum. . . .

. . . A key initial question [this committee] had to consider was a sizeable skepticism on the part of a few members of the Smithsonian Board of Regents (and many other Americans) that there were enough artifacts documenting Afro-American experience to justify a museum—on the Mall or anywhere else. The sense that Black history had been lost was enormously powerful. Certainly, many losses in material culture, traditional songs and stories, and documentary evidence have occurred because of the deprivations that slavery and segregation produced. At the same time, an uncounted wealth of historical artifacts, family papers, and the work of self-taught artists remains in private hands, most often those of descendants. In direct contrast to Native peoples, whose artifacts were widely collected from the moment of European contact, most of the objects made and used by Africans in America were routinely discarded or consumed by use. Still, there are two hundred-year-old churches and their records, early manumission papers, nineteenth-century quilts, an abundance of archeological artifacts, and other materials that document the years before about 1890. As for twentieth-century collecting, the process has literally just begun, especially for the years after World War II. Yet there was great doubt in many quarters that the artifactual record was large enough or the artistic production of sufficient quality to justify an entire museum. Eventually, the Institutional Study Project's curator, Deborah Willis, would identify more than 20,000 objects in 150 collections that the Mall museum could acquire. Although her findings silenced critics of the museum, whose doubts were object-based, these findings could not address other, more ideological critics of the museum who had political or pragmatic concerns about issues such as the public financing of the museum.

A second important question had to do with slavery. Would the museum be a memorial to the millions who lived and died in slavery in the way that the Holocaust Museum is a memorial to victims of the Third Reich? Sentiment on behalf of a slavery memorial was particularly reflected in the fact that Tom Mack's original idea was to have a memorial museum on just this subject. Because slavery is "an American holocaust," where more appropriate to have its memorial than among the gleaming white monuments on the Mall?

Though it is little known outside various centers of Afrocentricity, many African Americans interpret their history in the Americas as a holocaust. Focusing extensively on the Atlantic slave trade, this version of American history has replaced nineteenth-century Afro-Americans' biblical millennial claims with twentieth-century claims of intentional genocide and "crimes against humanity." Today, there are multiple interpretations of the "Black Holocaust" far too numerous to detail here. They focus on the horror of capture, the degradation and death of the Middle Passage, and the most brutal aspects of slavery in the United States, and in the American diaspora more generally. For the past decade, Howard University has hosted an annual conference entitled "The Black Holocaust Conference." Indeed, I can recall dozens of conversations with other African-American museum professionals whose "insider" tours of the U.S. Holocaust Museum generated some variant of the following question: "Why can't we have a museum like that, a museum that details what was done to our people and by whom?" This idea did, and still does, have many adherents within African-American museums and cultural institutions.

Further, this interpretation of Africans' history in America as a genocide has become a key aspect of the internal cultural symbolism of most African-American institutions in the 1990s. Just as other communities have their "mythos of origin," most African Americans inhabit a cultural landscape with flags and signposts quite distinct and at odds with many other Americans' views of the national past. A comprehensive cultural history of African Americans since World War II remains to be written. Yet even a cursory look at that subject reveals a set of deep changes that began in the late 1960s and reverberate today. Before 1960, most (though not all) of the positive images of achievement were integration-oriented examples. Afro-American newspapers of the 1950s and 1960s were filled with stories about the "first Negro principal" or the "first fireman" or the "first student" at a locally or nationally known college. But since the 1970s and accelerating in the late 1980s, some African Americans, especially young people, began to turn away from integration as a symbol of success in American society. Increasingly, the symbols of separatism epitomized by Malcolm X for much of his career have become more resonant. Although Malcolm X rejected racial distinctions after a religious trip to Mecca, his longer career flowed back to that of Elijah Muhammad, founder of the separatist Nation of Islam in the 1930s, and eventually back to the crucial work of early Pan-Africanist Marcus Garvey in the 1910s and 1920s. In these versions of African-American history, "doing for self" is the key sign of success. Some examples of this imagery are purely symbolic—such as the flying of a green, black, red, and sometimes gold flag which derives directly from Garveyism. Other examples are the tremendous growth of Black magazines, bookstores, toy companies and other businesses, as well as Afrocentric private schools, publishing companies, and offshoot denominations, such as George Stallings's African-American Catholic Church. Enrollment at historically Black colleges and universities has grown many times over in the 1990s, and the best of them are able to attract some of the best African-American students in the country. It is within this larger African-American cultural framework that the concept of the slave trade and slavery as genocide must be seen. To most African Americans, even those who disagree on political or cultural strategies, this concept is an article of faith, a key element of identity as true as any other clear historical fact.

Yet if we examine the mythos of slavery among other Americans, perceptions immediately shift. From Stone Mountain, Georgia, to Monument Walk in Richmond, from the lovely gardens of Savannah to the white King and Queen of Mardi Gras, the landscape of the South is filled with memorials to the "Lost Cause." From Robert E. Lee and Stonewall Jackson to the Unknown Confederate Soldier, the heroes of, and sacrifices made for, the cause of the Confederacy are still venerated with tremendous zeal in many states. Variations of the Stars and Bars are integral to many southern state flags; and Dixie remains the alternate national anthem in many clubs, schools, and legislatures throughout the South. . . . As is well known to most museum professionals one can tarry a long time in the charming historic houses and beautiful plantation mansions of the antebellum South and hear nary a word about slavery. Though some eighteenth-century sites, such as Mount Vernon and Monticello, have begun to present information about some of the best documented enslaved plantations populations in the early American republic, most of the other historic houses have not done so. In the mid 1980s, Spencer Crew and James Horton surveyed museums across the country and found little change in their presentations of American history. Black participation and contributions were still largely ignored; most museums seemed not to have changed at all.

Affection for the Old South, the Lost Cause, and all of their romantic grandeur and noble tragedy have been a part of American public culture since the late 1870s. From Currier and Ives prints to mass-manufactured greeting cards, from *The Birth of a Nation* to *Gone with the Wind,* from *The Littlest Rebel* to *Jezebel,* the romance of the Old South remains a powerful set of images for many Americans. Of course, Black people are necessary to the scenery of these images. Can a mint julep be as sweet without Old Uncle to serve it? Can the Kentucky Derby be as much fun without a Kentucky colonel and his faithful attendant? Can breakfast pancakes ever be as good without Aunt Jemima's product in our stomachs and our hearts? These images of popular culture are widespread and, unlike direct monuments to the Confederacy, not limited to the South.

From Columbus's era to 1865, slavery was legal in what is now the United States. Although African people were present at the creation of the early colonies and the first states, they could not become citizens until 1868 (with the ratification of the fourteenth amendment to the U.S. Constitution). The end of slavery was seen by many white southerners as a deep attack against the sacred rights of property guaranteed in the Constitution. Southern leaders and intellectuals routinely claimed that emancipation had been the largest confiscation of private property in the history of the world! Unlike the Third Reich, the adherents of slavery never experienced anything like the Nuremberg trials in Germany in the post–World War II years. American slavery was a moot point by the time the United Nations was formed and has never been officially condemned by any international body. Although the Nazis epitomize contemporary visualizations of sadistic criminals and pure evil, the heroes of the American Confederacy remain heroes.

For Americans not from those states where "the Cause" was lost, and especially for that 70 percent of living white Americans who are descendants of turn-of-the-century immigrants from Europe, slavery is not a personal legacy. Indeed, many of these Americans probably view slavery as an unfortunate but distant blot on the land of the free and the home of the brave. Exempt from the pain of the sin of slavery—a pain to which William Faulkner and some other southern novelists gave voice—these northern, midwestern, and western Americans may well view slavery as a historical problem of little direct relevance to them. Indeed, many of the most romantic views of slavery in American popular culture were created by people with no direct ties to the South.

By contrast, the era of legal segregation (1890–1965) is of much greater concern to a wide range of contemporary Americans. Such historical concern seems particularly important to politically emergent groups such as Latinos or Asian Americans whose regional histories also include de jure and de facto segregation. Since the segregated era officially ended only thirty years ago, it is within the living memory of most Americans over forty. In 1944, Swedish sociologist Gunnar Myrdal published his classic two-volume study, *An American Dilemma,* which was commissioned by the Carnegie Foundation of New York. He proposed that segregation and the discriminatory practices that existed throughout American society had produced a functional and essentially emotional problem for many non-Negro Americans. Ambivalent about granting full equality to Afro-Americans, many people also realized that inequality directly violated the essential mythos of America as the land of freedom, where individuals were judged on their own singular terms and merits. Such cultural contradictions were bound, Myrdal felt, to produce a social crisis eventually. Researched and written during America's "Good War," which was fought by segregated armed forces, Myrdal's volumes stand as eloquent testimony to the state of American race relations at the dawning of the modern Civil Rights Movement. The subsequent Supreme Court decisions, demonstrations, boycotts, and marches in the face of massive white Southern resistance, form a central leitmotif in the analysis of the last fifty years of American history. Consequently, the modern era of legal segregation and the movement that dislodged it probably have more emotional salience to many living Americans than the "moonlight and magnolias" of the Confederate South so key to American popular culture in the 1930s and earlier.

This larger, incredibly intricate, and difficult cultural context shaped the work of the Institutional Study Project on the proposed Black museum on the Mall. The advisory committee convened by Claudine Brown was charged with the relatively narrow job of making an internal report to the Smithsonian Board of Regents. Lobbying the board, though difficult, was a lot easier than convincing a majority of white men in the U.S. Congress to agree not only to a piece of legislation but also to the perpetual financial support that is the very foundation of public trusts for national museums. Though the advisory committee struggled with the problem of a new museum on the Mall and made key suggestions regarding the troubling issues of content, its members were unable to resolve questions of control within their own ranks. Preoccupied by a series of internal battles regarding the AAMA National Trust idea, they did not systematically address the perplexing political problems of launching the museum across the bow of some of the most powerful mythos in American life. . . .

There were and still are numerous internal arguments for or against an African-American museum on the Mall. They center on several key issues: Who would control the museum? Who would pay for the museum? Was a free-standing museum necessary? If so, why? These debates permeated the Institutional Study Report. First and perhaps most important, Mack opposed Smithsonian control of the museum. He seemed to feel that the Smithsonian's history of racism and neglect of African Americans made its control inappropriate. Many within the AAMA agreed with him. . . . Mack favored some form of independent control more like that of the National Gallery of Art, or the Kennedy Center. He emphasized the importance of private funding of all or part of the museum. His career as a businessman encouraged him to equate funding with control and management. . . .

. . . However, raising private funds has been quite difficult for Black museums nationwide. Most of the large and successful African-American museums exist today because of city or state allocations, which reflect the political power of Black people in that region. It is no accident that most of these museums are in cities that have had Black mayors for some or all of the past twenty years.

The primary role of public financing in the development of African-American museums is not accidental either. The legacy of twenty generations of slavery and four of segregation has significantly limited the aggregate personal wealth of African Americans. Though currently unfashionable to mention, as it has been for most of American history, slavery and segregation cost Black people the "natural" fruits of their labor that for many white Americans have been the fundamental benefit of the capitalist market economy. This Afro-American history of relative personal poverty is clearly reflected in strategies for funding Black museums—the primary sources are public funds.

... [T]he mood of key members of the 101st and 102nd Congresses was one of budget slashing, especially for hard-to-control cultural projects. . . . [The Institutional Study Report] did not take into account conservative efforts at just that time to do away with the NEA and NEH, entities whose primary responsibility was to give away federal money for culture.

Similarly, proponents of a Mall museum of slavery seemed not to recognize that it would be tantamount to a Holocaust Memorial in Auschwitz, not Washington, D.C. Instead of being removed from the "scene of the crime," the proposed museum would be erected within sight of locations where slave pens stood during the 1850s and the early years of the Civil War. Just as the Holocaust Memorial at Auschwitz has been the subject of international controversy and protest, adherents of a slavery museum on the Mall found themselves embroiled in sophisticated controversies in Congress, in part related to a different, non-African-American version of the history of slavery and the American past. . . . [A] museum of slavery located between the sacred white memorials to Founding Fathers George Washington and Thomas Jefferson, whom we all know to have been slaveholders, would privilege a version of American history important to African Americans but unshared by numerous others.

Although the Lost Cause may be a narrow, regional mythos that most Americans outside the South do not really care much about, there are other, more widespread assumptions that are equally problematic. For example, hip Americans of all backgrounds recognize that Black people have contributed something of importance to American life. After all, jazz is America's classical music! African-American musical traditions can be seen as the "Great Mother" of American music. From the spirituals to the blues, from ragtime to free jazz, from gospel to rhythm-and-blues and rock-and-roll, African Americans have been involved in music and other kinds of performance arts from the earliest days of the republic. At the same time, so have a lot of non–Black Americans. Though ragtime may have emerged from Black jook joints at the turn of the century, many of the most popular ragtime composers were white. In any form of jazz, from Dixieland to swing to bebop and so on, there have been extraordinarily talented musicians and composers who were not Black. Though many African Americans regard jazz as a genre wholly invented and most effectively performed by Black people, many others disagree with that perspective, including a number of well-known jazz artists. In fact, some would argue that what makes jazz so great is that, with the right talent and training, anyone anywhere in the world can play it and even contribute to the body of world jazz music. According to this argument, it is precisely the portable quality of jazz that makes it a classical form. The perception of jazz as a classical music is today almost a cliché. Yet Duke Ellington, who died in 1974, did not live to see this sea change in the musical assessment of jazz; it has largely been achieved over the last fifteen years.

The above analysis of ideas about jazz points to a mythopoetic problem in conjoining internal African-American mythos with wider American mythos, even those that give critical meaning to Black contributions. Is jazz truly great because it demonstrates the achievements of African Americans? Or is jazz truly great because it is a world music that can be played by anyone? In real life, both of these concepts can be true simultaneously. But in official cultural institutions, people must make clear and political choices about which narratives to tell. Debates about jazz exemplify larger debates about the telling of African-American history.

Is the story of Black separation, isolation, and achievement against the odds the primary narrative of meaning? In most African-American museums, some version of this narrative is absolutely central; it fulfills African Americans' need for a validating and distinctive history. However, for other Americans troubled by the history of segregation, the great narrative of African-American life has much more to do with integration into and acceptance by the mainstream of American life. The story of the acceptance of talented, well-qualified, deserving Afro-Americans has a lot to do with the modern Civil Rights Movement between 1945 and about 1970. Many civil rights activists were military veterans, college students, housewives, and ministers. They seemed to be precisely the sort of people who should not be discriminated against; no one epitomized them better than the Reverend Doctor Martin Luther King, Jr.

. . . To many non–African Americans, social integration is *the* important African-American story. In this formulation, recognizing Black separateness seems awfully similar to segregation. Celebrating Black inclusion is essential; that is a story of which *all* Americans can be proud.

Consequently, the notion of an African-American museum on the Mall raised serious questions in the "integration vs. separation" debate. This debate was all too straightforward in the 1940s, when Gunnar Myrdal and his integrated staff of Ph.D.s conducted research for the *American Dilemma* volumes. By 1970, desegregation had become the official law of the land, and full integration was the stated ideal of many governmental and corporate institutions. Yet during the late 1980s and 1990s, a number of Americans, some of them African-American, were re-examining the costs and questioning the value of integration as a goal. . . . Two very different mythos about the American past have collided headlong, and debates about the African-American museum occurred within this context.

By 1992, a number of cultural critics of various ethnic backgrounds had begun to doubt that a Black museum on the Mall was a good idea at all. Articles in a number of publications, especially the *Washington Post,* argued that a separate Black museum would be a step backward. Was this museum idea not just a new form of segregation or even "ghettoization"? Was not Black history really just American history with the "real story" put back in? . . .

In different ways, in two different Congresses, debates about the museum's control and financing, and more general arguments about "ghettoization" and overly zealous spending on "revisionist" cultural interpretation, expressed themselves in legislative difficulties. Such problems served to kill the proposed legislation, first in the House during the 102nd Congress, and in the Senate during the 103rd Congress. . . .

Following this defeat, the push for an African-American museum on the Mall lost momentum. . . .

Although certainly a setback, this legislative defeat does not represent the whole story of the African-American presence on the American cultural landscape in this era. In 1983, Ronald Reagan, under threat of congressional override of a veto, reluctantly signed the Martin Luther King, Jr., holiday into law. No other Americans save for former Presidents have ever had their birthdays celebrated as national holidays. The powerful, bipartisan congressional support for the King Day legislation, though not unanimous, was impressive. Although some states, such as Arizona, refused for a long time to go along with this holiday, today King's birthday is observed in virtually all of the states. Schools, religious institutions, clubs, state governments, many large corporations, and the media all participate in constructing and performing this holiday. The only "new" American holiday declared since World War II, this annual evocation of the memory of King's life, and of others who in modern times gave their lives for freedom and justice helps reinterpret and transform some old American mythos. The symbolic importance of the holiday cannot be overestimated.

The King holiday points unmistakably to the profound meaning of the Civil Rights Movement and its "success" for most living Americans of all ethnic backgrounds. In his profound speeches and sermons, King was uniquely able to articulate a truly mythopoetic version of the American past that could unite people of different colors by calling them to America's highest purpose. During his life, King was a far more controversial figure than young people today may realize. Many, many people did not agree with him. Inside Black communities, some felt that pacifism was a ridiculous position to take in the face of white violence. Many traditionalists within the Baptist Convention and many longtime southern leaders felt that King and his bunch were stirring things up much too much. Others began to follow the lead of Malcolm X, national spokesperson for the Nation of Islam, into a Black separatist vision. Still others abandoned America for a new life in the Caribbean or "returned" to Africa, especially to newly independent nations such as Ghana.

Within white communities, even outside the South, there were many people who opposed desegregation, whether actively or passively. For them, King was an irritant and the epitome of a Black man who had stepped out of his place. Indeed, King and his associates were subjected to relentless surveillance and many "dirty tricks" under at least three presidents. When King began to criticize the Vietnam War as early as 1966, he lost significant support from many Americans who had been brought up during the "Good War" and felt that criticism of the government during wartime was treasonous. . . .

In the face of all this, King . . . continued to voice freedom and justice for all as the nation's highest goal. . . . King articulated a dream of a new America that became the most powerful restatement of the American dream in the twentieth century.

His public assassination made King a martyr. But his crusade for a desegregated America resulted in the Civil Rights Act of 1964 and the Voting Rights Act of 1965. Although we may not yet live in "the promised land" that he saw over the mountaintop, King was clearly a Moses of modern times. Given this powerful overlay of the African-American search for justice and the wider "American Creed" Gunnar Myrdal identified, it is not accidental that King's life and the "success" of the Civil Rights Movement have come to be celebrated in a national holiday.

Over the past ten years, several large and publicly funded museums of African-American history have been built in the South. There is no museum devoted to slavery, but in Memphis, Birmingham, Atlanta, and other cities there are civil rights museums. Clearly, it is this modern freedom movement in which most Americans feel that they can share. As with all mythos, some elements are forgotten or downgraded in importance. . . . Although there may be no African-American museum on the Mall in the foreseeable future, the institution of the King holiday and the widespread celebration of the Civil Rights Movement point to a meeting place between African-American and wider American mythos—perhaps the only meeting place possible today.

. . . The United States exists not only in the North American continent but also in the hearts and minds of its citizens (not to mention those of film and television viewers worldwide). In our minds, however, we do not all live in the same America. In fact, some of our Americas directly contradict one another. For ethnic museums, this dilemma is peculiarly complicated, for it is difficult to reconcile internal ethnic visions with the larger narratives of nationhood that almost inevitably elide culpability in favor of celebration.

At the same time, however, there appear to be some versions of an American dream that can be voiced beyond any specific ethnic experience. . . . Without question, Martin Luther King articulated a complicated but nonetheless pluralistic and inclusive statement of the American dream for which he made the greatest sacrifice. We know the name of King, but we do not know the names of all the others who were murdered trying to vote in the South. . . . To remember them, all nations build memorials and sometimes even museums.

Werner Sollers argues in *Beyond Ethnicity* that the new mythos of America is a narrative about immigration. . . . If Sollers is correct, is it not surprising that the symbolic descendants of John Smith, of Pocahontas, and of some of the millions welcomed by Emma Lazarus's poem have had and will have their narratives celebrated on the Mall. And it is also not surprising that the symbolic descendants of those unknown nineteen Africans taken from a Dutch ship in Jamestown harbor in 1619 do not. The presence of certain buildings, the memorials to certain events, and the absence of others speak eloquently, though with great ambiguity, about the vast structure of national recollection that is mythos.

 F U R T H E R   R E A D I N G

Elsa Barkley Brown, "'What Has Happened Here': The Politics of Difference in Women's History and Feminist Politics," *Feminist Studies,* 18 (Summer 1992), 295–312.
Douglas Henry Daniels, "African American Intellectual and Vernacular History," *Journal of American Ethnic History,* 16 (1997), 69–76.
John Hope Franklin, "Afro-American History and the Politics of Higher Education," *Bulletin of the American Academy of Arts and Sciences,* 40 (1986), 26–42.
John Hope Franklin, *George Washington Williams: A Biography* (1985).
Jesus Garcia and David E. Tanner, "The Portrayal of Black Americans in U.S. History Textbooks," *Social Studies,* 76 (1985), 200–204.
Jacqueline Goggin, *Carter G. Woodson: A Life in Black History* (1993).

Jacqueline Goggin, "Countering White Racist Scholarship, Carter G. Woodson and the *Journal of Negro History," Journal of Negro History,* 68, no. 4. (1983), 355–375.

Lorenzo J. Greene, *Working with Carter G. Woodson, the Father of Black History: A Diary, 1928–1930,* ed. Arvarh E. Strickland (1989).

Vincent Harding, "Power from Our People: The Sources of the Modern Revival of Black History," *Black Scholar,* 18 (1987), 40–51.

Darlene Clark Hine, "Black Women's History, White Women's History: The Juncture of Race and Class," *Journal of Women's History,* 4 (1992), 125–133.

Darlene Clark Hine, ed., *The State of Afro-American History: Past, Present, and Future* (1986).

Kenneth Robert Jankin, *Rayford W. Logan and the Dilemma of the African-American Intellectual* (1993).

Linda McMurry, *Recorder of the Black Experience: A Biography of Monroe Nathan Work* (1985).

August Meier and Elliott Rudwick, *Black History and the Historical Profession, 1915–1980* (1986).

Clarence E. Walker, *Deromanticizing Black History: Critical Essays and Reappraisals* (1991).

Francille Rusan Wilson, "Racial Consciousness and Black Scholarship: Charles H. Wesley and the Construction of Negro Labor in the United States," *Journal of Negro History,* 81, nos. 1–4 (1996), 72–88.

Francille Rusan Wilson, " 'The past was waiting for me when I came': The Contextualization of Black Women's History," *Feminist Studies,* 22 (1996), 345–361.

The Work of Reconstruction

What determined the conditions under which former slaves remade themselves as a free people? What aspirations did they articulate, and what initiatives did they take? What determined their success or failure in those initiatives or in achieving those aspirations?

For 4 million newly freed men, women, and children throughout the South, 1865 was a year of tremendous excitement, hope, and expectation, and, at the same time, a year of enormous effort to make a living, secure families, and protect rights. One former slave, Violet Guntharpe, captured the essence of the terms of emancipation when she said, "Us had no education, no land, no mule, no cow, not a pig, nor a chicken, to set up housekeeping." Three centuries of slavery in the United States had been ended with no compensation to the enslaved. Lacking any economic resources or political power, how could freedpeople remake their lives? In the first days and months after the Confederate surrender, in various ways formerly enslaved people tried on their new freedom. For some this meant removing themselves from the place where they had been enslaved, finding new homes, or just moving about to express or test their freedom. For others it meant staying where they had lived all their lives, claiming as their own the land on which they previously toiled without reward. For still others it meant building their first public church for the congregation of people with whom they had worshiped in secret during slavery or claiming title to the churches they had built with their own monies and labor, the titles to which were held by whites. For most it meant looking for and they hoped, reuniting with family members.

In areas that Union forces had occupied during the war, various experiments with creating free lives and new economics were already underway. There, as elsewhere, former slaves, former masters, Freedmen's Bureau agents, Union army officers, northern missionary teachers, and others brought their own understandings of freedom into the post–Civil War world. Their various antebellum and Civil War experiences fundamentally shaped these understandings. Even so, the Emancipation Proclamation, Union success in the Civil War and ratification of the Thirteenth Amendment to the Constitution, formally terminating slavery, all gave ex-slaves not only the expectation of freedom but also the expectation that the federal government would guarantee their freedom.

Many local and state governments were reorganized as they had been before the war; leading secessionists assumed their former positions in civil life. The Bureau of Refugees, Freedmen and Abandoned Lands (Freedmen's Bureau), authorized by Congress in March 1865, had branches and agents throughout the former Confederacy.

*Ex-slaves' reliance on bureau agents became all the more important after May 1865
when President Andrew Johnson proposed a plan of reconstruction that would pardon
southern rebels and return their confiscated lands if they swore allegiance to the Union.
Buoyed by Johnson's leniency, former Confederates worked to restore as much of the
antebellum social order as possible, including passing a series of restrictive laws aimed
not merely at maintaining a racial hierarchy but also ensuring a dependable supply of
black labor. Historians have collectively named these the Black Codes of 1865 and 1866.*

*In what ways could ex-slaves expect life to be different after emancipation? What
would it take to guarantee real freedom? Who would be their allies in these struggles?*

DOCUMENTS

If ex-slaves thought freedom would immediately accompany emancipation, the events
of the first few weeks and months of Union occupation soon disabused them of such
ideas. In the first two documents, addressed to President Andrew Johnson, ex-slaves set
forth their credentials as loyal citizens, question the restoring of the old order, and call
the question as to which side the federal government would be on. The first document,
delivered directly to the president at the White House in June 1865 by a committee of
freedmen representing the communities of Richmond and Manchester, Virginia, met
with immediate success. Within a week the former Confederate mayor was removed
from office, two of the Freedmen's Bureau agents who had refused to aid the freedpeople were reassigned; and pass laws they objected to were rescinded. The second
document issues from freedmen of Edisto Island, South Carolina, who in January 1865
had taken possession of land confiscated by General William T. Sherman. Learning that
this ownership had been reversed and the land on which they had settled would be
returned to its former owners, they demanded to know what freedom can mean if it is
coupled with economic dependence, especially dependence on the same men who only
days and months previous had held them as slaves. Contrast the understandings of freedom in these two petitions with Captain Charles Soule's characterization in the third
document. Soule, who had captained a black regiment during the war, draws on his very
pessimistic understanding of what it meant to be a free white laboring man in the 1860s
to try to interpret the aftermath of emancipation.

At the heart of ex-slaves' struggles were issues of labor and family. In the fourth
document, a share-wages contract, notice the conditions under which these Arkansas
men and women were to labor and the terms by which they were to be paid. Charles
Raushenberg, a Georgia bureau agent, in the fifth document, argues the need for continued federal oversight. Notice particularly his recounting of the differing interpretations that plantation owners and laborers put on the share-wages contract.

Most enslaved people had known, if not firsthand then certainly through close
acquaintances, the horror of the thousands of sales, migrations, and inheritances that
separated family members. Even for those fortunate enough to locate their loved ones
after the Civil War, the reconstruction of the family was often not easily achieved. In
the sixth document, Martin Lee recounts his struggles during slavery and after to bring
his family together. However, the apprenticeship laws passed as part of the new Black
Codes in many southern states often worked to prevent relatives from laying claim to
their young kin; in this case, Lee asks the Freedmen's Bureau for assistance. In the
seventh document, Elizabeth Botume, a northern schoolteacher working in South
Carolina at the end of the war, recalls the efforts of freedpeople to find their scattered
families and the hard decisions many had to make.

The final two documents suggest the horrors and the possibilities that faced freed-people as they made their way into U.S. citizenship. For many African Americans their assumption of their rights came with the high price of violent recrimination. Harriet Hernandes's testimony in the eighth document is but one of the hundreds of accounts collected by a U.S. Senate committee investigating Ku Klux Klan activities throughout the South; Hernandes offers a view into how family and work decisions were politicized in the Reconstruction era. The ninth document is a portrait of the first men of African descent to be elected to serve in Congress.

1. African Americans in Richmond, Virginia, Petition President Andrew Johnson, 1865

MR. PRESIDENT: We have been appointed a committee by a public meeting of the colored people of Richmond, Va., to make known to your Excellency, as our best friend, the wrongs as we conceive them to be, by which we are sorely oppressed.

We represent a population of more than 20,000 colored people, including Richmond and Manchester, who have ever been distinguished for their good behavior as slaves and as freemen, as well as for their high moral and Christian character; more than 6,000 of our people are members in good standing of Christian churches, and nearly our whole population constantly attend divine service. Among us there are at least 2,000 men who are worth from $200 to $500; 200 who have property valued at from $1,000 to $5,000, and a number who are worth from $5,000 to $20,000. None of our people are in the alms-house, and when we were slaves the aged and infirm who were turned away from the homes of hard masters, who had been enriched by their toil, our benevolent societies supported while they lived, and buried when they died, and comparatively few of us have found it necessary to ask for Government rations, which have been so bountifully bestowed upon the unrepentant Rebels of Richmond.

The law of Slavery severly [sic] punished those who taught us to read and write, but, notwithstanding this, 3,000 of us can read, and at least 2,000 can read and write, and a large number of us are engaged in useful and profitable employment on our own account.

During the whole of the Slaveholders' Rebellion we have been true and loyal to the United States Government; privately and collectively we have sent up our prayers to the Throne of Grace for the success of the Union cause. We have given aid and comfort to the soldiers of Freedom (for which several of our people, of both sexes, have been severely punished by stripes and imprisonment). We have been their pilots and their scouts, and have safely conducted them through many perilous adventures, while hard-fought battles and bloody fields have fully established the indomitable bravery, the loyalty and the heroic patriotism of our race.

We rejoiced with exceeding great joy at the fall of Richmond and the termination of the war, which we supposed broke the last fetter of the American slave. When the triumphant Union army entered the city of Richmond we alone gave it a cordial welcome, receiving it with hearts bursting with joy and thanksgiving; and when our late beloved and martyred President made his *entreé* [sic] into our city

---

New York Tribune, June 17, 1865, p. 1.

we alone hailed his advent with enthusiastic cheers of acclamation, and of all the citizens of Richmond we alone, with a few solitary exceptions, wear the exterior badges of mourning, as truthful expressions of our grief for his untimely death; and it is, therefore, with sorrowing hearts that we are compelled thus to acquaint your Excellency with our sad disappointment, for our present condition is, in many respects worse than when we were slaves, and living under slave law. Under the old system, we had the *protection* of our masters, who were financially interested in our physical welfare. That protection is now withdrawn, and our old masters have become our enemies, who seek not only to oppress our people, but to thwart the designs of the Federal Government and of benevolent Northern associations in our behalf. We cannot appeal to the laws of Virginia for protection, for the old negro laws still prevail, and besides, the oath of a colored man against a white man will not be received in any of our State Courts: so that we have nowhere to go for protection and justice but to that power which made us free. . . .

In the city of Richmond, the military and police authorities will not allow us to walk the streets by day or night, in the regular pursuit of our business or on our way to church, without a *pass*, and passes do not in all cases protect us from arrest, insult, abuse, violence and imprisonment, against which we have thus far had no protection or redress. Men have not only been arrested in the street, but the police, in conjunction with the Provost Guards, have entered our dwellings and workshops, and have taken men from the work-bench and put them into prison because they had no pass, or because they would not recognize the pass presented as genuine or sufficient.

In numerous instances our people have been driven from their old homes, or have sought employment elsewhere, when justice to themselves and their families, demanded that they should make such a change; and many of these people have been rudely arrested, thrust into prison, and hired out by miliary authority for the most insignificant sums. A number of men who have been employed upon plantations have visited Richmond in search of long-lost wives and children, who had been separated by the cruel usages of Slavery. Wives, too, are frequently seen in our streets, anxiously inquiring for husbands who had been sold away from them, and many of these people, who ignorantly supposed that the day of passes had passed away with the system which originated them, have been arrested, imprisoned and hired out without their advice or consent, thus preventing the reunion of long estranged and affectionate families. . . .

. . . [H]owever sad our hearts may be over the present state of our affairs, we have lost none of our faith in or love for the Union, or for yourself as its Chief Magistrate, and therefore, as oppressed, obedient and loving children, we ask your protection, and upon the loyalty of our hearts and the power of our arms you may rely with unbounded confidence; and in conclusion, let us respectfully remind your Excellency of that sublime motto once inscribed over the portals of an Egyptian temple, *"Know all ye who exercise power, that God hates injustice!"*

FIELDS COOK.　　　　　　　　　　　　RICHARD WELLS.
WALTER SNEAD.　　　　　　　　　　　WM. WILLIAMSON.
PETER WOOLFOLK.　　　　　　　　　　T. MORRIS CHESTER.
NELSON HAMILTON.

Richmond, Va., June 10, 1865.

2. Freedmen of Edisto Island, South Carolina, Demand Land, 1865

To the President of these United States. We the freedmen Of Edisto Island South Carolina have learned From you through Major General O O Howard commissioner of the Freedmans Bureau. with deep sorrow and Painful hearts of the possibility of government restoring These lands to the former owners. We are well aware Of the many perplexing and trying questions that burden Your mind. and do therefore pray to god (the preserver of all, and who has through our Late and beloved President (Lincoln) proclamation and the war made Us A free people) that he may guide you in making Your decisions. and give you that wisdom that Cometh from above to settle these great and Important Questions for the best interests of the country and the Colored race: Here is where secession was born and Nurtured   Here is where we have toiled nearly all Our lives as slaves and were treated like dumb Driven cattle. This is our home, we have made These lands what they are. we were the only true and Loyal people that were found in posession of these Lands. we have been always ready to strike for Liberty and humanity yea to fight if needs be To preserve this glorious union. Shall not we who Are freedman and have been always true to this Union have the same rights as are enjoyed by Others? . . . are not our rights as A free people and good citizens of these United States To be considered before the rights of those who were Found in rebellion against this good and just Government (and now being conquered) come (as they Seem) with penitent hearts and beg forgiveness For past offences and also ask if thier lands Cannot be restored to them   are these rebellious Spirits to be reinstated in thier *possessions* And we who have been abused and oppressed For many long years not to be allowed the Privilige of purchasing land But be subject To the will of these large Land owners? God forbid, Land monoploy is injurious to the advancement of the course of freedom, and if Government Does not make some provision by which we as Freedmen can obtain A Homestead, we have Not bettered our condition.

We have been encouraged by Government to take Up these lands in small tracts, receiving Certificates of the same—we have thus far Taken Sixteen thousand (16,000) acres of Land here on This Island. We are ready to pay for this land When Government calls for it, and now after What has been done will the good and just government take from us all this right and make us Subject to the will of those who have cheated and Oppressed us for many years   God Forbid!

We the freedmen of this Island and of the State of South Carolina—Do therefore petition to you as the President of these United States, that some provisions be made by which Every colored man can purchase land. and Hold it as his own. We wish to have A home if It be but A few acres without some provision is Made our future is sad to look upon. yess our Situation is dangerous. we therefore look to you In this trying hour as A true friend of the poor and Neglected race. for

Ira Berlin, Steven Hahn, Steven F. Miller, Joseph P. Reidy, and Leslie S. Rowland, "The Terrain of Freedom: The Struggle over the Meaning of Free Labor in the U.S. South," *History Workshop*, no. 22 (Autumn 1986), 128–129.

protection and Equal Rights. with the privilege of purchasing A Homestead— A Homestead right here in the Heart of South Carolina.

. . . May God bless you in the Administration of your duties as the President Of these United States is the humble prayer Of us all—

In behalf of the Freedmen

Henry Bram

Committee   Ishmael. Moultrie.

yates. Sampson

3. Captain Charles Soule, Northern Army Officer, Lectures Ex-Slaves on the Responsibilities of Freedom, 1865

To the Freed People of Orangeburg District.

You have heard many stories about your condition as freemen. You do not know what to believe: you are talking too much; waiting too much; asking for too much. If you can find out the truth about this matter, you will settle down quietly to your work. Listen, then, and try to understand just how you are situated.

You are now free, but you must know that the only difference you can feel yet, between slavery and freedom, is that neither you nor your children can be bought or sold. You may have a harder time this year than you have ever had before; it will be the price you pay for your freedom. You will have to work hard, and get very little to eat, and very few clothes to wear. If you get through this year alive and well, you should be thankful. Do not expect to save up anything, or to have much corn or provisions ahead at the end of the year. You must not ask for more pay than free people get at the North. There, a field hand is paid in money, but has to spend all his pay every week, in buying food and clothes for his family and in paying rent for his house. You cannot be paid in money,—for there is no good money in the District,—nothing but Confederate paper. Then, what can you be paid with? Why, with food, with clothes, with the free use of your little houses and lots. You do not own a cent's worth except yourselves. The plantation you live on is not yours, nor the houses, nor the cattle, mules and horses; the seed you planted with was not yours, and the ploughs and hoes do not belong to you. Now you must get something to eat and something to wear, and houses to live in. How can you get these things? By hard work—and nothing else, and it will be a good thing for you if you get them until next year, for yourselves and for your families. You must remember that your children, your old people, and the cripples, belong to you to support now, and all that is given to them is so much pay to you for your work. If you ask for anything more; if you ask for a half of the crop, or even a third, you ask too much; you wish to get more than you could get if you had been

Ira Berlin, Steven Hahn, Steven F. Miller, Joseph P. Reidy, and Leslie S. Rowland, "The Terrain of Freedom: The Struggle over the Meaning of Free Labor in the U.S. South," *History Workshop*, no. 22 (Autumn 1986), 120–123.

free all your lives. Do not ask for Saturday either; free people everywhere else work Saturday, and you have no more right to the day than they have. If your employer is willing to give you part of the day, or to set a task that you can finish early, be thankful for the kindness, but do not think it is something you must have. When you work, work hard. Begin early at sunrise, and do not take more than two hours at noon. Do not think, because you are free you can choose your own kind of work. Every man must work under orders. The soldiers, who are free, work under officers, the officers under the general, and the general under the president. There must be a head man everywhere, and on a plantation the head man, who gives all the orders, is the owner of the place. Whatever he tells you to do you must do at once, and cheerfully. Never give him a cross word or an impudent answer. If the work is hard, do not stop to talk about it, but do it first and rest afterwards. . . .

There are different kinds of work. One man is a doctor, another is a minister, another a soldier. One black man may be a field hand, one a blacksmith, one a carpenter, and still another a house-servant. Every man has his own place, his own trade that he was brought up to, and he must stick to it. . . .

You do not understand why some of the white people who used to own you, do not have to work in the field. It is because they are rich. If every man were poor, and worked in his own field, there would be no big farms, and very little cotton or corn raised to sell; there would be no money, and nothing to buy. Some people must be rich, to pay the others, and they have the right to do no work except to look out after their property. It is so everywhere, and perhaps by hard work some of you may by-and-by become rich yourselves.

Remember that all your working time belongs to the man who hires you: therefore you must not leave work without his leave not even to nurse a child, or to go and visit a wife or husband. When you wish to go off the place, get a pass as you used to, and then you will run no danger of being taken up by our soldiers. . . .

Do not think of leaving the plantation where you belong. If you try to go to Charleston, or any other city, you will find no work to do, and nothing to eat. You will starve, or fall sick and die. Stay where you are, in your own homes, even if you are suffering. There is no better place for you anywhere else.

You will want to know what to do when a husband and wife live on different places. Of course they ought to be together, but this year, they have their crops planted on their own places, and they must stay to work them. At the end of the year they can live together. Until then they must see each other only once in a while. . . .

Do not grumble if you cannot get as much pay on your place as some one else, for on one place they have more children than on others, on one place the land is poor, on another it is rich; on one place Sherman took everything, on another, perhaps, almost everything was left safe. One man can afford to pay more than another. Do not grumble, either, because the meat is gone or the salt hard to get. Make the best of everything, and if there is anything which you think is wrong, or hard to bear, try to reason it out: if you cannot, ask leave to send one man to town to see an officer. Never stop work on any account, for the whole crop must be raised and got in, or we shall starve. . . .

. . . Remember that even if you are badly off, no one can buy or sell you . . .

4. A Share-Wages Contract, 1865

State of Arkansas
County of Ouachita

This indenture made and entered into this the 26th day of December AD1865 between H. C Cleaver & Brs of the first part & Isaac Squash; Caroline his wife and Counsel, Cato, Churchill, F[ur]ney, Isah, Epsey and Minerva his children, of the second part witneseth.

Firstly, That the said parties of the first part for and in consideration of twelve (12) months labor to be well and faithfully rendered by the parties of the second part. beginning on the 1st day of January AD1866 & ending on the 31st day of December AD1866. agree to furnish.

1st Land. team and all necessary farming utencels for planting and cultivating the crop for 1866,

2d Good and sufficient rations to be furnished by the week.

3d House rent and fuel free of cost.

4th All necessary attention when sick except when the skill of a physician is necessary.

Secondly, That at the close of the year 1866, the parties of the 1st part are to deliver to the parties of the 2d part one fourth (¼) of the crop of corn and cotton made and saved upon the plantation cultivated by the parties of the 1st part, the parties of the second part agreeing to accept this in lieu of other wages,

Thirdly, That the parties of the 1st part, exempt the old gentleman Isaac and his wife Caroline, of the 2d part from labor in the plantation and furnish the said Isaac with land upon which to make a garden plant potatoes &c but his wife Caroline is to do the cooking and washing for the other seven hands,

Fourthly that no night work be required of the said parties of the second part except such as the necessities of the plantation absolutely demand,

Fifthly, That one hour will be allowed during the winter months for dinner, and two (2) hours and a half during the months of June July and August.

Sixthly, That for and in consideration of one fourth (¼) of the crop of corn & cotton to be delivered to the parties of the 2d part by the said parties of the 1st part at the close of the year 1866, the parties of the 2d part agree,

1st To make good, faithful and obedient servants,

2d To, rise at day break, each one to feed and take care of the stock assigned to him, to eat our breakfast, and be ready for work at the signal to be given at half an hour by sun,

3d To enter into no general conversation during work hours.

4th To have one Dollar deducted for disobedience—neglect of duty and leaving without permission being considered acts of disobedience.

5th To raise no live stock without special contract with the parties of the 1st part of this contract,

---

Labor Contracts, ser. 263, Arkansas Assistant Commissioner, Records of the Bureau of Refugees, Freedmen, and Abandoned Lands, National Archives, Washington, D.C.; filed as A-2493 in Freedmen and Southern Society Project files, University of Maryland, College Park.

6th To be charged with all Apples peaches and Melons and all other products of the farm taken by us without permission of our employers,

7th To receive no visitors during work hours,

8th To suffer dismissal for repeating acts of *insolence, swearing* or *indecent* and *unseemly* language to or in the presence of our employers or their families, or for qurrelling and fighting so as to disturb the peace of the plantation, the like penalty shall be suffered,

9th To be charged for all wilful abuse of stock, breaking of tools and throwing away gear,

10th To render cheerful and willing performance of duty,

11th To feed the stock on sunday,

12th To look after and study the interest of our employers, to inform of anything going amiss, to be peaceable orderly and pleasant, to discourage theft &c

13th In case of any controversy with our employers in regard to contract or to regulations we agree to submit it to the Agent of the Freedmen's Bureau of this county,

In testimony whereof we have herewith set our hands and affixed our seals, day and date above writen

H C Cleaver & Bro.

5. Charles Raushenberg, a Freedmen's Bureau Agent, Reports from Georgia, 1867

Office of Agent Bur. R. F. A Lds.
Division of Cuthbert
Cuthbert, Ga. Novbr. 14, 1867

Lieut O. H. Howard
Sub.Asst Commnr Bur R. F. A. Lds
Albany, Ga.

Sir,

In obedience to the instructions received from you I have the honor to submit this Report on the General Condition of Affairs in my division.

When I entered upon my duties as Agent in this Division the Bureau of R. F. A Lds seemed to be generally considered by the community, a substitute for overseers and drivers and to take up and return run away laborers and to punish them for real or imaginary violations of contract by fines, imprisonment and some times by corporeal punishment. . . .

The idea that a planter or employer of any kind should in case of dissatisfaction with his freedmen, instead of driving him of[f] often without paying him his wages, first establish a complaint before the Bureau and let that tribunal decide wether [sic] a sufficient violation of contract existed to justify the discharge of the

Lawanda Cox and John H. Cox, eds., *Reconstruction, the Negro, and the New South* (New York: Harper & Row, 1973), 339–347.

laborer or not, was then considered quite unreasonable; while every employer thought it perfectly proper that a Bureau agent, when notified of a freedmans leaving his employment should immediately issue an order for the arrest of the same and have him brought back—in chains if possible. The fairness of the principle that either party must submit its complaints to the Bureau for adjustment and that the white man can not decide the case a priori and only use the agent of the bureau as his executive organ and that employer as well as employee must submit to its decision wether [sic] the laborer ought to be discharged or ought to remain is just beginning to gain ground amongst both races. . . . The common bulk of the population is just beginning to suspect that nothing else but what is justice and equity to a white man under certain circumstances would be justice and equity to a negro under the same circumstances. . . .

The number of complaints made at this office is very large and increasing continually as the time of settlements is drawing nearer. The white man complains generally that the freedman is lazy, impudent and unreliable, that he will not fulfill his contract any further than it suits his convenience . . . ; the freedman on the other hand generally complains that the white man has made him sign a contract, which he does not understand to mean what the white man says it does mean. . . .

The majority of complaints that have been made at this Office by both races have found their origin in contracts, where freedmen received as compensation for their labor a certain share in the crop. The majority of the plantations in my division were worked under such contracts. The freedman claims under such contracts frequently that he has no other work to do but to cultivate and gather the crop, that being a partner in the concern he ought to be allowed to exercise his own judgment in the management of the plantation, that he ought to be permitted to loose time, when it suits his convenience to do so and when according to his judgement his labor is not needed in the field, that he ought to have a voice in the manner of gathering and dividing the corn and cotton and in the ginning, packing and selling of the latter product—while the employer claims that the labor of the employee belongs to him for the whole year, that he must labor for him six days during the week and do all kinds of work required of him wether [sic] directly connected with the crop or not, that he must have the sole and exclusive management of the plantation and that the freedman must obey his orders and do all work required as if he was receiving money wages, the part of the crop standing in the place of money, that the laborer must suffer deduction for lost time, that if he does not work all the time for him, he is not bound to furnish him provisions all the time, that the crop must be gathered, divided and housed to suit the convenience and judgement of the employer and that the share of the employee must be held responsible for what he has received in goods & provisions during the year. Taking in consideration that often quite a number of freedmen are employed on one plantation under such a contracts [sic], who frequently not only become discontented with the employer but with each other, accusing each other of loosing time unnecessarily and of not working well enough to be entitled to an equal share in the crop, it is easily understood to what amount of implicated difficulties, and vexatious [sic] questions these contracts furnish the material.

. . . [A]s it is I consider [contracts of that kind] inimical to the maintenance of good order discipline and success on plantations and productive of ill will and hatred between the parties concerned. . . .

My conviction is that plain labor contracts for wages for the year, one half of the wages paid every month or every quarter, the other half to be forfeited if the freedman fails to comply, are the most practicable contracts that can be made. They cause frequent & therefore fairer settlements, showing the freedman oftener what he consumes and how much is left to him, prompting him to economy on the one hand and cheering him up to increased energy if he finds himself saving money and, giving very little cause for difficulties and troubles. . . .

The freedman like other human beings thinks and studies more about his rights and privileges than his duties and obligations and his ignorance and deficient capacity to comprehend and reason cause him to invariably overrate the extent of the former and to underrate that of the later, hence he often claims an independence and freedom of action, which it justly incompatible with the faithful performance of his duties as a laborer and servant. . . .

While the colored people have thus erred, . . . the whites themselves as a mass . . . have failed to treat them with justice, kindness and forbearance. . . . Employers generally are exacting and tyrannical not disposed to forbear, to reason or to exhort but require implicit obedience and unconditional submission and try very frequently to accomplish by revolting harshness and unscrupulous overbearance, what a universally mild and kind but firm and just treatment should accomplish. They yet act the masters.—The freedman in his new condition is not willing to bear that kind of treatment. . . .

The political excitement and the election troubles between the employer and employee have, I am sorrow [sic] to say, perceptibly increased the already existing antagonism between the two races in my division and particularly in Cuthbert. They have no confidence to [sic] each other whatever and the freedpeople generally look almost upon every white man here as an enemy, they are defiant & challenging and many really insulting in their language and conduct. . . . The whites have made threats & have used imprudent language on the streets and every now and then the paper contains an article calculated to hurt feelings. The general voting of the colored people for the colored candidates and their radical ticket has called into existence an association amongst the whites of Randolph undoubtedly for the purpose of controlling hereafter the colored vote. . . . [F]rom all I can learn, they threaten or rather pledge themselves not to employ a colored man, who is not a friend to the white people, which undoubtedly means one that will not vote their way.

The present aspect of the two races in their relations to each other therefore warrants no expectation that they will get along amically with each other for any length of time but insures the belief that after the removal of the military authority the freedmen when allowed to exercise all the rights & privileges of citizens with their want of knowledge and experience in business and law, will generally fail to obtain justice from the hands of the white race in the daily relations of life as well as in the courts. They would generally come out the loosers [sic], factors liens and mortgages being pushed in before their claims, frequently before they even suspected a danger of any loss, would yearly take away thousands of Dollars of their wages, all kinds of frauds would be practiced on them in making contracts, all kinds of impediments and obstacles would be put in the way of their complaints even reaching the courts and when there they would often fail to receive the necessary attention. . . .

The Judges of the County Courts of my counties have, since I have been in office, promptly acted on all cases referred to them and no palpable act of neglect of duty or injustice has come to my knowledge on the part of the officers of the Courts. The causes, why freedmen fail so often to get redress for wrongs practiced on them and are unjustly found guilty appears to me less owing to the conduct of the officers of the courts, then to the indifference and trickery of lawyers and the partial and prejudiced spirit of Juries. The freedmen need friends, who will espouse their cause and who will show them the way to justice, they need attornies [sic] who are not afeared of injuring their popularity by pleading for them and who will conscientiously fulfil their whole duty towards them, when their clients, and they need good and conscientious men of their own race on the Juries. . . .

The educational progress of the colored people in this division is of late origin but of very fair promise. One educational association exists and is in good working order in each one of my counties at Cuthbert, Lumpkin and Georgetown and the people generally seem to be fully aware of the great importance of this subject and have now for some time been contributing regularly for the maintenance of their schools. Young and old are anxious to learn, in some instances almost to the neglect of other duties.

. . . Encouragement and aid in the building of schoolhouses is much needed at all these places. . . .

I apprehend little danger but what the growing generation of the freedpeople will generally have a common education & will be able to read, write and cypher and to take care of themselves pretty well. . . .

As a mass the freedpeople are easier governed by Bureau authority than any other and the large majority of the freedpeople in my division, I am convinced, look upon the Freedmans Bureau as an institution where they will receive full justice. . . .

I have the honor to remain

> Very respectfully
> Your ob'd't serv't
> Ch. Raushenberg
> Agent etc &

6. Martin Lee, a Freedman, Struggles to Reunite His Family, 1866

Florence Ala   December 7[the] 1866

Dear sir   I take the pleashure of writing you A fue lins hoping that I will not ofende you by doing so   I was raised in your state and was sold from their when I was 31 years olde   left wife one childe Mother Brothers and sisters   My wife died about 12 years agoe and ten years agoe I Made money And went back and bought My olde Mother and she lives with Me   Seven years agoe I Maried again

Ira Berlin and Leslie S. Rowland, eds., *Families and Freedom: A Documentary History of African-American Kinship in the Civil War Era* (New York: The New Press, 1997), 231–233.

and commence to by Myself and wife for two thousande dollars and last Christemas I Made the last pay Ment and I have made Some little Money this year and I wish to get my Kinde All with me and I will take it as a Greate favor if you will help me to get them by sending me a order to Carey with me to the agent of Monroe walton County Georgia   I was out their last weeke and Got My daughter And hear children but I could not Get My Sisters Son   She is live and well   there is a Man by the name of Sebe—Burson that ust to one them and he will not let me or his Mother have the boy   he says he has the boy bound to him and the law in our State is that a childe cannot be bounde when the[y] have Mother father brother sistter uncl or Aunt that can take care of them but I went to the Agent and he says the boy has not ben bounde to him his county and if I will Give him 25 dollars he will deliver the boy to me but I think that to harde and I hope you will Sende me a order that I can carry to Mr Arnel so I May be Able to Get him without that much Money   I would not Minde paying him 5 dollars and I think that far [*fair*]   I live 3 hunderde and 25 Miles from Monroe Ande it will cost me 3 hunderde dollars to Get them to Alabma   pleas anser this as soon as you get it and pleas dont sende to Georgia untill I goe   it Might Make it against me   anser this to me and I will let you know the time I will starte and I can get their in 2 days   pleas do the best you can for Me and I remain yours a Servent And will untill death

Martin. Lee

7. Elizabeth Botume, a Northern Schoolteacher, Remembers a Husband and Wife Reunion, c. 1865

Much of our spare time—if by any stretch of the imagination we could be supposed to have spare time—was employed in writing letters for the freed people. . . .

These epistles were sent to every nook and corner of the Confederacy, hunting for lost members of scattered families. . . .

Just after the surrender of Charleston an old woman came to me "fur read one letter" which had just arrived. When I opened these letters I always looked first to see from whom they came. This said, "My dear mother."

"Well, Sarah, who do you think wrote this?"

"I 'spects it's William, ma'am. Him's wid de soldiers in Virginny."

"But have you no other sons?"

"You 'member, ma'am, I bin telling you de oder day de rebels catch my biggest boy an' hang him for a spy. An' Martin, the next boy, been sell off by de secesh, an' de Lord knows where him is ef him living."

"This letter is from Martin, Sarah."

The old woman dropped her head upon her knees, and began to rock forward and back, exclaiming, —

Elizabeth Hyde Botume, *First Days Amongst the Contrabands* (Boston: Lee and Shepard Publishers, 1893), 143–156.

"T'ank ye, good Massa! T'ank ye, good Massa! O blessed Jesus! You is berry good, berry good! . . .

"Oh! I is satisfied, ma'am. Martin is alive. But read de letter, please, missis."

It was the same story, daily and hourly repeated. As soon as our troops took possession of Charleston the slave boy, now a free man, turned with his whole heart and soul to his wife and child and his mother. . . .

These people had a marvellous way of tracing out the missing members of their families, and inflexible perseverance in hunting them up.

"Where is Martin's wife?" I asked.

"Don't you know, ma'am? She is Jane Ferguson."

"Why, Sarah! Jane has taken another husband!" I exclaimed. . . .

"Never mind, ma'am. Jane b'longs to Martin, an' she'll go back to him. Martin been a sickly boy, an' de secesh treat him too bad, an' we never 'specs him to lib t'rough all."

Just then Jane came in.

"Bless de Lord, gal!" said Sarah. "Martin is alive an' coming back to we."

"What will you do now, Jane?" I asked. "You have got another husband."

She drew herself up, and said deliberately,—"Martin Barnwell is my husband, ma'am. I am got no husband but he. W'en de secesh sell him off we nebber 'spect to see each odder more. He said, 'Jane take good care of our boy, an' w'en we git to hebben us will lib togedder to nebber part no more.' You see, ma'am, w'en I come here I had no one to help me."

"That's so," chimed in the mother. "I tell you, missis, it been a hard fight for we."

"So Ferguson come," continued Jane, "an' axed me to be his wife. I told him I never 'spects Martin *could* come back, but if he did he would be my husband above all others. An' Ferguson said, 'That's right, Jane;' so he cannot say nothing, ma'am."

"But supposing he *does* say something, and is not willing to give you up, Jane?"

"Martin is my husband, ma'am, an' the father of my child; and *Ferguson is a man*. He will not complain. And we had an understanding, too, about it. And now, please, ma'am, to write a letter for me to Ferguson,—he was with the Thirty Fourth Regiment. I want to treat the poor boy well."

I wrote the letter word for word as she dictated. It was clear and tender, but decided. Ferguson was not quite so ready to give her up as she expected. He wrote,— "Martin has not seen you for a long time. He *cannot* think of you as I do. O Jane! do not go to Charleston. Come to Jacksonville. I will get a house and we will live here. Never mind what the people say. Come to me, Jane."

I read the letter to her. It was evidently written by the chaplain, who sympathized with *his client*.

"Will you please, ma'am, write a letter yourself for me? Tell him, I say I'm sorry he finds it so hard to do his duty. But as he does, I shall do mine, an' I shall always pray de Lord to bless him."

"Shall I sign your name, Jane?"

"No, ma'am. I shall never write to him no more. But tell him I wish him well."

Soon after this Martin came and claimed his wife and child, who gladly clung to him.

8. Harriet Hernandes, a South Carolina Woman, Testifies Against the Ku Klux Klan, 1871

Spartanburgh, South Carolina, *July* 10, 1871.

Harriet Hernandes (colored) sworn and examined.

Question. How old are you?

Answer. Going on thirty-four years.

Question. Where do you live?

Answer. Down toward Cowpens' Furnace, about nineteen miles from here.

Question. Are you married or single?

Answer. Married.

Question. Did the Ku-Klux come to your house at any time?

Answer. Yes, sir; twice.

Question. Go on and tell us about the first time; when was it?

Answer. The first time was after last Christmas. When they came I was in bed. They hallooed, "Hallo!" I got up and opened the door; they came in; they asked who lived there; I told them Charley Hernandes. "Where is he?" they said. Says I, "I don't know, without he is at the Cowpens; he was beating ore there." Says he, "Have you any pistol here?" Says I, "No, sir." Says he, "Have you any gun?" Says I, "No, sir." He took on, and says he, "Your husband is in here somewhere, and damn him, if I see him I will kill him." I says, "Lord o'mercy, don't shoot in there; I will hold a light under there, and you can look." I held a light, and they looked. They told me to go to bed; I went to bed. Two months after that they came again.

Question. How many men were there at that first visit?

Answer. Eight.

Question. How were they dressed?

Answer. All kinds of form; but the first ones that came would not look me in the face, but just turned their backs to me, for they knew I would know them.

Question. Had they disguises?

Answer. Yes; horns and things over their faces; but still, that did not hinder me from knowing them if these things were off.

Question. Did you know any of them?

Answer. I did not know any of the first ones, to say truthful, but the last ones I did know.

Question. Had the first ones arms—guns or pistols?

Answer. Yes, sir; they had their guns and pistols. They came with a long gun, and told me they were going to shoot my damned brains out if I did not tell where my husband was.

Question. What time of night was it?

Answer. Away between midnight and day.

Question. How long had your husband lived there?

Answer. We have been living there three years, now.

42nd Congress, 2nd Session, S.R. 41, pt. 4, *Testimony Taken by the Joint Select Committee to Inquire into the Condition of Affairs in the Late Insurrectionary States, South Carolina*, Vol. 2 (GPO, 1872), 585–590.

Question. Is he a mechanic or laboring man?

Answer. He is a laboring man.

Question. He was working at the furnace?

Answer. Yes, sir.

Question. Go on to the second time; you say it was two months afterward?

Answer. Yes; just exactly two months; two months last Saturday night when they were at our house. . . . They came in; I was lying in bed. Says he, "Come out here, sir; come out here, sir!" They took me out of bed; they would not let me get out, but they took me up in their arms and toted me out—me and my daughter Lucy. He struck me on the forehead with a pistol, and here is the scar above my eye now. Says he, "Damn you, fall!" I fell. Says he, "Damn you get up!" I got up. Says he, "Damn you get over this fence!" and he kicked me over when I went to get over; and then he went on to a brush pile, and they laid us right down there, both together. They laid us down twenty yards apart, I reckon. They had dragged and beat us along. They struck me right on the top of my head, and I thought they had killed me; and I said, "Lord o'mercy, don't, don't kill my child!" He gave me a lick on the head, and it liked to have killed me; I saw stars. He threw my arm over my head so I could not do anything with it for three weeks, and there are great knots on my wrist now.

Question. What did they say this was for?

Answer. They said, "You can tell your husband that when we see him we are going to kill him." They tried to talk outlandish.

Question. Did they say why they wanted to kill him?

Answer. They said, "He voted the radical ticket, didn't he?" I said "Yes," that very way. . . .

Question. Had your husband any guns or pistols about his house?

Answer. He did not have any there at all. If he had, I reckon they would have got them.

Question. How old is your daughter?

Answer. She is fifteen.

Question. Is that the one they whipped?

Answer. Yes, sir.

Question. Is this all you know about it?

Answer. I know the people that came.

Question. Who were they?

Answer. One was Tom Davis, and there was Bruce Martin and his two sons. There are only four that I knew. There were only six that came that last night.

Question. When did your husband get back home?

Answer. He went back yesterday.

Question. When did he get back home after this whipping? He was not at home, was he?

Answer. He was lying out; he couldn't stay at home, bless your soul!

Question. Did you tell him about this?

Answer. O, yes.

Question. What caused him to lie out?

Answer. They kept threatening him. They said if they saw him anywhere about they would shoot him down at first sight. . . .

Question. Had he been afraid for any length of time?

Answer. He has been afraid ever since last October. He has been lying out. He has not laid in the house ten nights since October.

Question. Is that the situation of the colored people down there to any extent?

Answer. That is the way they all have to do—men and women both.

Question. What are they afraid of?

Answer. Of being killed or whipped to death.

Question. What has made them afraid?

Answer. Because men that voted radical tickets they took the spite out on the women when they could get at them.

Question. How many colored people have been whipped in that neighborhood?

Answer. It is all of them, mighty near. I could not name them all.

Question. Name those you remember.

Answer. Ben Phillips and his wife and daughter; Sam Foster; and Moses Eaves, they killed him—I could not begin to tell all—Ann Bonner and her daughter, Manza Surratt and his wife and whole family, even the least child in the family, they took it out of bed and whipped it. They told them if they did that they would remember it.

Question. You have seen those people that were whipped?

Answer. Yes, sir; and I have seen the marks on them, too.

Question. How do colored people feel in your neighborhood?

Answer. They have no satisfaction to live like humans, no how. . . .

Question. What do the colored people do for their safety?

Answer. They lie out all night.

Question. Is that generally the case?

Answer. Yes, sir; some families down there say they don't think they can get tamed to the house in five years.

Question. Does this fear extend to women and children and whole families?

Answer. Yes, sir; they just whipped all. I do not know how bad they did serve some of them. They did them scandalous; that is the truth—they did them scandalous. . . .

Question. Were those that came the second time the same as those that came the first time?

Answer. No, sir.

Question. How do you know?

Answer. I knew they were not.

Question. How do you know?

Answer. Because those that came the last time lived right at us in about a mile and a half, or worked right in that neighborhood; and ever since we have been there nigh them they can't face me, can't look at me . . . and these here wanted me to work for them a good while, and I could not work for them then. . . .

Question. You say one of the last six was Tom Davis?

Answer. Yes, sir.

Question. Was he disguised?

Answer. Yes, sir.

Question. What had he on?

Answer. His horns and a long blue coat. He was the one that told them to lay us down, and then just jumped right on the top of my head.

Question. Could you see his face?

Answer. Not all of it. I had just seen him the day before. . . .

Question. It was a pretty bold fellow that came that way?

Answer. Yes, sir; that was one of Martin's sons . . . both were along.

Question. What are their names?

Answer. Romeo and Tine.

Question. Which one was it?

Answer. I think it was Romeo. . . .

Question. . . . [W]hat was the reason why you thought it was Romeo?

Answer. Because that family wanted me to work for them and I could not work for them; I was working for another man.

Question. How long was that time when they wanted you to work before this whipping?

Answer. Not more than a month.

Question. Before the last visit?

Answer. Yes, sir.

Question. What took place that you could not work?

Answer. My husband rented some land and I had to come home.

Question. Did they get mad?

Answer. Yes, sir.

Question. What did they say?

Answer. They said they were going to have me Ku-Kluxed. . . .

Question. Who was present?

Answer. Only old Missus Williams, and she said, "Harriet, you'll be Ku-Kluxed for that."

Question. Who is she?

Answer. She is a white woman. It was her son I was to work for. He wanted me to work for him.

Question. What is his name?

Answer. Augustus Williams.

Question. I thought it was the Martins you had the trouble with?

Answer. They were the ones that whipped me. I thought it was Mr. Williams that held the horses.

Question. You said the Martins wanted you to work for them and you could not?

Answer. Yes, sir, all the family; they were all kin.

Question. And when you could not work for them they said they would have you Ku-Kluxed?

Answer. Yes, sir.

Question. Who said that, Bruce Martin?

Answer. Yes, sir.

Question. Was Mrs. Williams there?

Answer. Yes, sir.

Question. She heard them say that?

Answer. Yes, sir.

Question. They were bold enough to say before you and Mrs. Williams that you would be Ku-Kluxed?

Answer. Yes, sir, that I would be Ku-Kluxed. . . .

Question. You think the Martins did this for the reason that they were so mad because you would not work for them, that they Ku-Kluxed you?

Answer. Yes, sir; they got so mad that they could not stand it.

Question. Are they white people?

Answer. Yes, sir.

Question. How did you know Tine Martin?

Answer. By his size and his ways and all. . . .

Question. What did they do, that you knew them?

Answer. Their father was there. . . . One took hold of one arm of my little child and the other took the other arm, and I said, "Lord, don't kill my child;" and he knocked me down with the pistol and said, "Damn you, fall! Damn you, get up!" and I went to get up and he said, "Damn you, get over the fence;" and when I tried to get over he kicked me over, and I knew the horses.

Question. What horses?

Answer. One big black and four big sorrels and a mule. There were two of the Martins, and I reckon they had borrowed a mule of Gus Williams.

Question. Did you talk to him about it?

Answer. No, sir; if I told them I believed it was them they would have come the next night and killed me.

Question. Did you know the mule?

Answer. I knew it; it was Gus Williams's mule. He must have been holding the horses. He must have known that I would have known him if I had touched him almost.

Question. Did not the Martins know that you would recognize the horses?

Answer. I don't know. . . .

Question. Is there any justice of the peace up there? Have you any squires?

Answer. I know there was a squire named Blackwell.

Question. You could have come here and made complaint?

Answer. But I was afraid.

Question. Afraid of what?

Answer. Afraid of the Ku-Klux.

Question. What Ku-Klux?

Answer. Of the Martins.

Question. Why are you not afraid of them now?

Answer. I am; I am afraid to go back home.

Question. Are you going home?

Answer. I don't know whether I shall go back or not.

9. Elected Representatives, 1872

This 1872 Currier and Ives print depicts the black men who served in the Forty-first and Forty-second Congresses of the United States. From left to right they are: Sen. Hiram R. Revels of Mississippi; Rep. Benjamin S. Turner of Alabama; Rep. Robert C. De Large of South Carolina; Rep. Josiah T. Walls of Florida; Rep. Jefferson F. Long of Georgia; Rep. Joseph H. Rainey of South Carolina; and Rep. Robert Brown Elliott of South Carolina.

Library of Congress, Prints and Photographs Division; Eric Foner, *Freedom's Lawmakers: A Directory of Black Officeholders During Reconstruction*, rev. ed. (Baton Rouge: Louisiana State University Press, 1996).

US. Senator H.R.REVELS. of Mississippi   BENJ. S. TURNER, M.C. of Alabama.   JOSIAH T. WALLS, M.C. of Florida.   JOSEPH H. RAINY, M.C. of S.Carolina.   R. BROWN ELLIOT, M.C. of S.Carolina.

ROBERT C. DE LARGE, M.C. of S.Carolina.   JEFFERSON H. LONG. M.C. of Georgia.

THE FIRST COLORED SENATOR AND REPRESENTATIVES.
In the 41ˢᵗ and 42ⁿᵈ Congress of the United States.

These first Congressmen came from a variety of backgrounds. Revels, Elliott, and De Large were born free: Elliott in Boston or England and Revels and De Large in North Carolina and South Carolina respectively. The other four were born enslaved, although Rainey's father purchased their whole family's freedom in the mid-1840s, and Turner, while still enslaved, ran his own hotel and livery stable, accumulating considerable wealth. Their relations to the Confederate and Union forces suggest the range of experiences that black men had during the Civil War. De Large was employed by the Confederate Navy, while Rainey, impressed into work on Confederate fortifications, fled to Bermuda with his wife, returning only at the conclusion of the war. Walls, impressed into labor in the Confederate Army, was captured by Union forces and sent North where he enlisted in the 3d U.S. Colored Infantry, with which he returned South to fight the Confederacy. Revels served the Union forces as an army chaplain.

E S S A Y S

The first essay, by the late historian Herbert G. Gutman, recounts the ways ex-slaves throughout the South took responsibility for providing for their own education and that of their children. Gutman argues against the tendency to view aspirations for education as a middle-class value, noting the ways in which the desires and work for these schools were rooted in black working-class cultural values. In the second essay, Julie Saville, a historian at the University of Chicago, recounts the numerous ways ex-slaves in South Carolina sought to take charge of their economic lives in the post–Civil War era and especially how their struggles to define themselves as free workers were entwined with their struggles for political and family rights. In the final essay, Elsa Barkley Brown, who teaches history, women's studies, and African-American studies at the University of Maryland, explores the little-researched area of black women's political activities after the Civil War. Through the lens of women's activities she argues for understanding how ex-slaves—male and female—developed their understandings of political rights in ways that were profoundly different from those being championed by their white Republican allies. Collectively, what do these essays suggest about the challenges that faced ex-slaves, the resources they could draw on in their struggles, and their prospects for success?

Schools for Freedom

HERBERT G. GUTMAN

"The principle of schools, of education," said James T. White, a black delegate to the 1868 Arkansas Constitutional Convention, "is intended to elevate our families." The role former slaves and other blacks such as White (an Indiana-born minister and Union Army veteran) played in bringing schools to their children offers a rare insight into the values of the black community as it emerged from slavery. Blacks voluntarily paid school tuition, purchased schoolbooks, hired, fed, boarded, and protected teachers, constructed and maintained school buildings, and engaged in other costly (and sometimes dangerous) activities to provide education for their children. To expect such sustained efforts from men and women fresh to freedom, poor by any material standard, and entirely without political power is, perhaps, much to ask. But evidence disclosing such efforts is indeed abundant.

The former slaves themselves, not the schools per se, remain the center of this study. Historians of American (and particularly Southern) education have reconstructed in close detail the work of Northern white schoolteachers and missionaries in the postbellum South. While making it clear that articulate freedmen and freedwomen enthusiastically welcomed education for their children, the existing literature—even by "revisionist" historians of the Reconstruction—emphasizes the energy sympathetic Northern whites expended in helping freedpeople establish schools. In actual fact, the former slaves themselves played the central role in building, financing, and operating these schools, a fact that adds to our understanding of the family sensibilities and parental concerns of these men and women. It also indicates some of the ways in which reciprocal obligations operated beyond the immediate family and bound together former slaves living in rural and urban communities.

Postwar educational efforts by blacks built on a firm base of educational activism during slavery. Scattered but nevertheless convincing evidence reveals that secret slave schools had existed in a number of antebellum Southern cities. A black woman named Deveaux began a secret school in Savannah, Georgia, in 1835 and taught in the same room for the next thirty years. After the war, a visitor talked with her (she still taught in that room but to "the children of the better class of the

Herbert G. Gutman, "Schools for Freedom: The Post-Emancipation Origins of Afro-American Education," in Herbert G. Gutman, *Power and Culture: Essays on the American Working Class,* ed. Ira Berlin (New York: Pantheon Books, 1987), 260–280, 285–293, 296. Reprinted by permission of Donadio & Olson, Inc. Copyright © 1987 by the Estate of Herbert G. Gutman.

colored people") and learned how she had eluded "for more than a quarter of a century the most constant and lynx-eyed vigilance of the slaveholders of her native city." She was not alone in this work. . . .

. . . Southern cities with secret schools included Richmond, Virginia, where an unnamed black woman managed such a place for slaves, and Augusta, Georgia, where Edwin Purdy, a black clergyman, started a school in "a small room of his house" in the middle of the Civil War. Soon discovered, Purdy paid a $50 fine, suffered sixty lashes, and was sentenced to prison for an undisclosed time (friends, apparently whites, won his release after twelve days). . . .

The efforts of blacks to educate themselves expanded greatly during the Civil War, especially in locales that fell to the Union Army. "One of the first acts of the Negroes, when they found themselves free," observed the American Freedmen's Inquiry Commission, "was to establish schools at their own expense." A pay school—the first school for wartime runaways—was opened in Alexandria, Virginia, on September 1, 1861, by two black women. Later that month, one of them joined Mrs. Mary Smith Peake, the daughter of an English father and a free black woman who had taught at an antebellum Hampton, Virginia, school (and had her black stepfather among her pupils), to start a second contraband school at Fortress Monroe, Virginia. White teachers did not work with the Alexandria contrabands until October 1862. By that time, blacks managed three other schools. Before the war's end, at least sixteen other black men and women taught or directed Alexandria schools for runaway slaves. By April 1863, about 2,000 former slaves had congregated in Alexandria and 400 children attended their schools. "The first demand of these fugitives when they come into the place," observed a *New York Evening Post* correspondent, "is that their children may go to school." "Another surprising fact," he went on, "is that the poor negro women had rather toil, earn and pay one dollar per month for their children's education, than to permit them to enter a charity school." The contraband blacks also built, by voluntary labor, a school worth about $500, and later enlarged and improved it, making it "well lathed and plastered."

But there was more to establishing a school than bricks and mortar. At the start, a dispute over whether white or black teachers should be "the superintendents" threatened this Alexandria school's future. The blacks called a meeting. "I wish you could have been at that meeting," reported North Carolina fugitive slave Harriet Jacobs, who had come to Virginia to teach. "Most of the people were slaves until quite recently, but they talked sensibly and . . . put the question to a vote in quite parliamentary style. The result was a decision that the colored teachers should have charge of the school." The school opened in January 1864 with 75 pupils; two months later, it had 225, and the following August it was "the largest school and schoolhouse in the city." Once it had opened, blacks maintained their support. "My table in the school room," an early Hampton teacher reported, "is loaded, morning and noon, with oranges, lemons, apples, figs, candies, and other sweet things too numerous to mention." Such gift-giving was common in many parts of the South. . . .

Schools grew with the arrival of the federal army. . . .

North Carolina contrabands knew their first school in the spring of 1862, taught by a white man in the New Bern African Methodist Episcopal Church. Army officers also gave a Baptist missionary two Beaufort churches in which to teach. He found them "very filthy and sadly out of repair," but Beaufort blacks soon agreed to raise funds for their improvement. A Sabbath collection produced $84.88 ("to my surprise," said the white missionary), and in five weeks the blacks had gathered $200. In the winter and spring of 1863, New Bern blacks also established their own small schools. A *New York Tribune* reporter visited a school near the Camp Trent contraband "huts" built by the former slaves. "In one of the huts," he related, "a school was in progress, kept by a black man. He has thirty scholars, who he told me were learning quite fast. He himself has a fair education; could read, write, and cypher. He had learned all this, while a slave, from a schoolboy." Later that year, New Bern had twenty-four teachers, three blacks among them. James O'Hara, a West Indian mulatto, ran a "self-supported school." O'Hara's institution, New Bern's "most advanced colored school," included among its subjects "Geography, Grammar, and Arithmetic."

In *Rehearsal for Reconstruction,* Willie Lee Rose fully described the schooling given South Carolina Sea Island blacks by Yankee missionaries and schoolteachers. Sea Island blacks contributed mightily to that effort. A white Boston Baptist clergyman started Beaufort's first school in early January 1862. "Both teachers and pupils are negroes," said one report. This school, called "the Billaird Hall school," had four black "assistant" teachers: Paul Johnson, Thomas Ford, Peter Robinson, and Ephraim Lawrence, "themselves not far advanced but able to read and spell one-syllabled words." Missionaries spent an hour each day giving them special instruction, and a weekly contribution of five cents from each pupil (both boys and girls attended the school) helped pay their salary. The five-cent contribution, a white teacher wrote, "is cheerfully made, but not enforced in exceptional cases of orphanage or extreme poverty." Sixteen pupils attended the first day; two months later, school enrollment had reached 101. Indeed, three of every five Beaufort youths regularly attended the wartime schools.

Beaufort was the only town of size on the Sea Islands, but schools also flourished in rural areas, some maintained by Northern benevolent societies like the National Freedmen's Relief Association (which had established twenty-two schools by 1864) and others by the blacks themselves. A former slave woman named Hettie (she had "stolen a knowledge of letters from time to time") began a day school in March 1863 and kept up her work after the Edisto blacks became war refugees on St. Helena's Island. Even before that time, white missionary-teachers arrived at the Smith plantation to find that "the children were all assembled by Cuffy, and he was teaching them when we went in." . . .

In other places, Sea Island parents shared in the supervision of the schools. Northern teachers encouraged St. Helena's blacks to form visiting committees to help manage that island's school. One person from each plantation served on the committee, which Robert Chaplin headed. The school visiting committee did its work every Friday. . . . Chaplin, then seventy-three, composed the report that went North, explaining that the committee visited the schools to "see that everything go regular among the children" and to help the teacher "so far as our understanding goes." All books and property that belong to the school," he added, "is in our charge."

Farther west, blacks exhibited the same concern for wartime schooling. When Union Army recruiters first arrived in Nashville, Tennessee, they found that blacks had started "without any assistance" schools in which more than 800 children "received instruction from teachers paid by their parents—the slaves but just emancipated." . . . A Nashville bookseller remarked that he had "sold more spelling books in a short time than he has done for years." The first school had opened in the fall of 1862 in the First Colored Baptist Church. Its teacher was Daniel Wadkins, an antebellum free black whose school for free black children had twice been closed by worried whites in the 1850s. By the fall of 1863, several schools had "sprung up, taught by colored people who have got a little learning somehow." Students paid between one and two dollars each month. By the summer of 1864, the schools had "become so numerous, and the attendance so large, that all open opposition to them has ceased." That year, more black than white Nashville children attended school, and some black students established "schools on their own as soon as they were able to read." . . .

Between April 1865 and the advent of Radical Reconstruction two years later, educational opportunities for blacks expanded dramatically throughout the South, thanks in part to the work of Northern benevolent societies and the newly established Freedmen's Bureau. But as during the war, initiative often rested with the blacks themselves. The process can best be examined in . . . Virginia, South Carolina . . . and Georgia.

The general public and private policies that affected the education of blacks deserve brief notice. Except for Florida, where the legislature imposed a special education tax on blacks, no Southern state made provision to educate the former slaves. In establishing the Freedmen's Bureau, Congress did not include funds for education in 1865; not until the summer of 1866 did the federal government authorize the bureau to spend half a million dollars for the rental, construction, and repair of schoolhouses. Some additional money for the education of former slaves came from funds appropriated by several Northern states to purchase black substitutes in the South and thereby help to fill draft quotas. Bureau policies and a shortage of funds obliged the former slaves to take the initiative in establishing schools, and in this they were encouraged by the Northern benevolent societies. The New England Freedmen's Aid Society, for example, only offered funds to blacks who erected, repaired, and cared for schools, furnished board for teachers, and paid small tuition fees. Edward Everett Hale explained the guiding assumptions shared by many who managed these benevolent societies: "The policy . . . has not been to make these people beggars. . . . The black people know they must support themselves, as they have always done." Hale admitted that such policies assured "suffering" but went on: "Where is there not suffering in this world? We have never said that the black man's life should be raised above suffering. We have said that he should be free to choose between inevitable hardships. This promise we perform."

In fact, blacks did not wait for state authorization, the advent of the bureau, or the advice of Northern societies to establish schools in 1865 and 1866. In the late fall of 1865, John W. Alvord, superintendent of education for the Freedmen's Bureau, toured the South. Everywhere he traveled, he informed General O. O. Howard, the bureau commissioner, he found "a class of schools got up and taught by colored people, rude and imperfect, but still groups of persons, old and young, *trying* to learn." They lacked "the patience to wait for the coming of a white teacher." Alvord estimated that the South knew "at least five hundred" such schools, many of them never before visited "by any white man." "In the absence of other teaching," he said, "they are determined to be self-taught." . . . "In truth," Alvord added, "these spontaneous efforts of the colored people would start up everywhere if books could be sent them."

Virginia and South Carolina blacks typified the early postwar concern for education. Richmond and Charleston deserve special attention. Quite different in many ways (Richmond, for example, had more black factory workers than any other American city), both cities had fallen to the Union Army just before the war's end. It should be kept in mind that schooling for blacks in these and other Southern places was entirely voluntary. No external compulsion forced the former slaves to attend school or to contribute to the success of educational institutions. A school for Richmond blacks started in mid-April at the First African Baptist Church, and 1,025 students (50 of them sixteen or older) showed up. Their enthusiasm for schooling stunned one observer: "I never before imagined it possible for an uneducated class to have such zeal of earnestness for schools and books. . . ." On a visit to Richmond in 1866, William Hepworth Dixon, the editor of the London *Athenaeum,* agreed, noting that the city had forty black schools. . . . None of this came easily. "Many of our children" explained a Quaker teacher, "have been driven from their homes because they came to school; and, in some instances, *whole families* have been turned into *the streets* because they were represented in the school-room."

In these early months, "by far the largest proportions of Richmond children" paid for "their books, slates, etc." . . . That winter individual black children, most from families living on the edge of poverty, contributed to or collected for a "fuel fund" to heat their schools in sums ranging from two cents to one dollar. When the Second Baptist Church burned in March 1866 (some suspected "rebel malice"), it also meant the destruction of an important school facility. "All were for action," said a leader of the affected blacks. They hired rooms to continue the school and planned to rebuild a brick building. . . .

Charleston blacks took similar initiatives. Schools there opened in early March 1865 and immediately served (in separate rooms and on separate floors) between 200 and 300 white and 1,200 black students. At least that number of black students waited for additional school places. A *New York Tribune* correspondent noted that "the loyal white people—the Irish and German population"—allowed their children to attend school with the freed blacks but would not "tolerate" mixed classes. Five days after the schools opened, James Redpath, their superintendent, counted forty-two teachers, nearly all local residents and twenty-five of them blacks. At first, whites were not permitted to teach the black children. "Some of the colored teachers," said George Newcomb, "passed a good examination, and will, I doubt not, prove excellent." "Colored South Carolinians" also taught in the night schools. These teachers included women "very light in complexion" and members of "the aristocracy of the colored community," who, a white teacher noted, were "advanced enough to pursue intelligently all the common branches of English education." Among them was Miss Weston, an "accomplished and talented colored lady" once jailed "for teaching a little school." Early in 1867, several young Charleston black men ("most of them, though quite well educated, had never taught before") quit that city to spread literacy in "the country districts." A reverse process brought black teachers to Charleston: the Old Zion Church School included on its staff women graduates of the Philadelphia Institute for Colored Youth. . . .

Charleston blacks did not just staff their schools and fill them with their children. They purchased books and, after a time, paid "a school tax." . . .

Letters sent by teachers working for Northern benevolent societies help illuminate Virginia blacks' educational activities. Just after the war, Farmville blacks applied at Petersburg for a teacher, and despite some threats of violence, a school started and remained open two years later. . . . Three teachers started Petersburg schools in May 1865: chased from their first building, they taught 200 students next in a railroad station; when a tobacco company claimed that place, the school was moved to a warehouse. Less than a year later, Petersburg and its vicinity counted twenty-two schools and 2,769 registered pupils. . . .

Official Freedmen's Bureau reports for 1866 and early 1867 fill in the Virginia picture. The bureau took notice of 136 teachers in January 1866 and 225 twelve months later. By March 1867, the number had risen to 278 (81 of them blacks). In January 1866, Rolzo M. Manly, then superintendent of the bureau's Virginia schools, reported: "Every week since the first of October, new schools have been opened in some part of the State. It has been essentially a period of organization." Manly did not give much credit to resident whites, claiming that "practically all our progress, with rare exceptions, is in the face of actual opposition." "Milder modes of resistance" included "refusing the use of all churches or vestries which the whites can possibly control, refusing to rent room or charging exorbitant rates, refusing to board teachers, forbidding colored tenants sending their children to school on pain of being turned out of doors." "The more forcible forms of resistance," Manly felt, "such as mobs and conflagrations, are restrained by occasional hints from the military arms." Later that same year, Manly added that "in more than a score of places, the colored people have erected schoolhouses with their own hands, and employed either some poor white person, or someone of their own people, who has some small attainments, as a teacher. . . . They lack books, and have not a penny of money, their wages of the farm being received in the form of food and clothing." . . .

The detailed letters of two white Quaker teachers in Danville, Eunice Congdon and George Dixon, allow us to examine with greater precision the ways Virginia blacks sustained schools for their children and protected white teachers. Eunice Congdon and another white woman teacher arrived in Danville to teach early in the fall of 1865. . . . By early February 1866, the Danville teachers had enrolled 299 day-school pupils and employed "a young colored girl to assist" in "the lowest division."

The Danville school taught more than reading and writing. In 1866, blacks crowded densely into it to hear the Civil Rights Bill of 1866 read and discussed. Miss Congdon called the discussion "rich and significant beyond description." Another time, the Northern teachers distributed seeds to Danville blacks. And when some black men formed a voluntary association called "The Mechanics' Society for Mutual Aid," they met in the schoolhouse and their president asked Miss Congdon to "send North and get for him the book containing the names of the different *trades*, coming under the head of mechanics." Such community efforts suggest that schools had become more than mere educational institutions. And for that reason, among others, they provoked bitter opposition.

Opposition by whites to the Danville school increased after the Union Army withdrew from the town. The school remained there, however, owing to the courage displayed by Eunice Congdon, George Dixon, and Danville blacks. When Condgon fell ill, Dixon, who was then teaching English in Greensboro, North Carolina, came to help. Soon after his arrival, a white man attacked Eunice Congdon. . . . A Union Army officer later learned that the man had planned to kill Miss Congdon, plunder the place, and then "set fire to the buildings." Threats against Miss Congdon were overheard in the streets. "A white woman," Dixon insisted, "told a colored chid she need not go to school on Monday morning, because Miss Eunice would be dead." Danville blacks protected the teacher and the school. Dixon explained: "The colored men are kind in coming to keep a watch in the dead of night, but we are fearful of their coming in collision with the citizens, and blood being shed, as they will bring firearms with them and feel very desperate." "The colored people are our friends," Congdon confirmed. "They guard us every night." . . . Miss Congdon herself left Danville after the school year ended. "The first day school," she explained, "will be continued by four colored men whom we have initiated." More than this, other blacks promised to protect school property and records. When the Danville school closed for the summer, it had a full enrollment: 237 children had registered for its day classes.

Evidence also abounds of the black zeal for education in rural South Carolina. The Sea Island schools established during the war continued, and still received aid from local blacks. Blacks at Edgerly and Union Point joined together to build a new schoolhouse. "The island has gone wild to have a school on every plantation," reported Laura Towne from Port Royal in November 1865. Enthusiasm did not wane in the next two years. When Elizabeth Botume opened a schoolhouse at the Old Fort Plantation, some men came unannounced to "white-wash the interior of the building." . . .

Throughout South Carolina, blacks pressed for schools and contributed to their success, and their efforts deserve particular notice because, unlike Sea Island blacks, they had not experienced wartime contact with Northern soldiers, missionaries, and school teachers. . . .

. . . [I]n northeastern South Carolina, a rich cotton region that was home to nearly a third of the state's former slave population, Benjamin Franklin Whittemore—an Amherst College graduate, Methodist clergyman, and former Union Army chaplain—supervised education . . . for the Freedmen's Bureau between 1865 and 1867. Despite their economic troubles and local white opposition, he reported that black men and women contributed handsomely to their children's education. They moved an old "Confederate building" ten miles from Florence to Darlington to start the district's first school. By April 1866 six schools existed, and a month later eleven. Northern soldiers had burned a Marion schoolhouse, so its teacher met classes in the woods.

Summerville got its school sometime before July. Two white women offered two acres of land for $200 as school property. Local blacks, many among them poor and destitute, crowded into an army barracks they used as a church to agree that if the Northern societies paid for the land and the government supplied lumber, they would build a school to open in October. "A good carpenter," Dan Meyers, spoke first: "I is a plain man and alers does what I agree, and I say that I will stan' by the good work till it's done finished." Another black man boomed: "I is called a good carpenter; I has no children of my own to send to the school; but I want to see the house build, and I gives two weeks work for it." Others offered their labor, and some, including young boys, gave small sums of money. In all, $60 was raised and twelve weeks of labor pledged. "The women," enthused schoolteacher Esther Hawkes, did "their part, offering to board or lodge the workmen as they best could." "These destitute people," she mused, "living, some of them, in rude huts made of mud and palmetto, one might suppose that all their interest was necessary [just] to keep them from starving. . . ." But this was only the start. By October, the burned Marion school had been rebuilt ($200); Darlington black men and women gave their labor and money for a school ($500); Simmonsville blacks ditched and fenced and then built a home for the teacher ($150); Sumter blacks moved a building forty miles and then reconstructed it ($250). Lynchburg blacks also moved and repaired a building ($150), and so did those in Florence ($350). In Camden, black muscle and money meant a new schoolhouse ($800), and Camden blacks also rented an old building for $30 a month. Schoolhouses also went up on the Mulberry Plantation ($100) and in Springville ($100).

In Camden, most blacks worked crops on contract and saw no cash until they had gathered the full crop. Teachers, however, did not suffer discomfort. "They furnish us with beds, bedding, and furniture for our rooms free, though they do not pay the rent," reported one teacher. "They sell articles to teachers at under price, and bring in gratuitously articles of food. The girls at the night school have made me some presents." "There is no lack of 'a disposition to do all in their power *now*,'" the teacher added. "Indeed I think they *have* done it." The obstacles faced by these former South Carolina slaves seeking education for themselves and their children, however, should not be obscured by this enthusiasm. In June 1867, Darlington residents appealed to Boston's mayor: "We are on the eve of Starvation. . . ." Between September 1866 and January 1867, Camden blacks raised $120 to pay the school rent, heat the school building, and furnish the schoolteachers's rooms. "They have performed *all they have promised*," reported Jane Smith from Sumter. "They were to pay a certain sum toward the erection of their church which they have done. They were to whitewash it, to buy a bell, build a belfry, furnish lamps, lumber for the pulpit, and several comforts for the teachers. All this, *they have done*." Overall, South Carolina blacks had done much to educate themselves. For the entire state in the year starting July 1866, $106,797.73 was expended to educate South Carolina blacks. Northern societies gave $65,087.01, while the Freedmen's Bureau advanced $24,510.72. South Carolina blacks contributed cash to the amount of $17,200.00 (16 percent), and more in kind and labor. Only where poverty prevented such self-help efforts did blacks request assistance. . . .

Still the efforts of [other southern blacks] pale in comparison with those of Georgia blacks. Between 1865 and 1867, black people in Georgia did more to educate their children than those in any other Southern state. When white missionary teachers arrived in Atlanta, they found that two former slaves, James Tate and Grandison Daniels, had started a small school in an old church building. . . . In Augusta, illiterate blacks filled a meeting place and helped pick a committee to aid the white teachers. That committee raised more than $100 and received promises of more money. Augusta blacks also repaired a schoolroom in an old Confederate shoe shop. . . . A school opened on June 12: 500 children showed up the first day and 100 more came in the days that followed . . . Richard R. Wright started learning in a Cuthbert school in 1865. It "scarcely had one of its sides covered or weather-boarded," Wright remembered. "It was about twenty by thirty. . . . The house was packed as tightly with dusky children as a sardine box. . . ." (In Atlanta, Wright's second schoolhouse was "an abandoned box car.") . . . Newton blacks held their first classes in a kitchen.

Georgia blacks made phenomenal advances in educating their children in 1866 and 1867. A March 1866 survey found fifty-two black schools in ten Georgia cities and towns. In a four-month period (December 1865 to March 1866), blacks in seven of these places contributed $5,060 in cash for their schools, causing a Northern missionary to note that "the benevolent efforts among the Freedmen *themselves* for their education are considerable." One of every three Georgia teachers (102 men and women in all) received funds from that state's blacks. Schools existed in out-of-the-way Georgia places. Rome and Marietta had black teachers, and the Rome teacher held his classes "in a church with no windows." Tuition payments supported other black teachers in small Dalton, Deep Valley, Cartersville, and Red Clay schools. . . .

Opposition from hostile whites, especially in 1866, made the work of these blacks and their few white allies especially difficult. Two former Confederate soldiers taught Elberton and McDonough blacks until pressure from white mobs forced them to seek bureau protection. From Henry County came "frequent complaints" to federal officials "that the inhabitants attacked the scholars and teachers of freedom schools—stoned them on the way home and threatened to 'kill every d——d nigger white man' who upheld the establishment and continuation of the 'nigger schools.'" A black teacher in Newman was so harassed that he quit that place. Despite these troubles, twenty-one Georgia schools remained open in the summer of 1866. The Freedmen's Bureau supported three of them, and the freed men and women the rest. More than 2,000 children attended these summer schools. Overall, the number of school[s] increased from 79 in June 1866 to 147 in December 1866 and then to 232 in June 1867. Enrollment jumped from 2,755 to 13,263. Blacks contributed much to these schools; during the 1867 winter quarter, they paid $7,224 in tuition. In June 1867, a bureau report showed that 45 percent of the schools and 23 percent of the pupils were entirely supported by the freedmen themselves. In part, these successes derived from the organization of the Georgia Educational Association in January 1866. But its work cannot be understood without first examining events in Savannah between December 1864 and January 1866.

Prodded by James Lynch, a missionary for the African Methodist Episcopal Church, Savannah blacks entered on a massive program of school organization in the years immediately following the war. Lynch himself deserves notice. Born in 1839 to a Baltimore free black father and a slave mother, Lynch drove a delivery wagon as a boy to help his father's mercantile business, attended a New Hampshire college, preached for a time in Indiana and then in Illinois, and helped to edit the AME's *Christian Recorder.* When Union troops entered the slave South, he followed as one of the African Methodist Episcopal Church's first missionaries. He labored for a time among the South Carolina Sea Island blacks. In late 1864, he taught a St. Helena's Island school sponsored by the National Freedman's Relief Association. . . .

General William T. Sherman's army had conquered the city [of Savannah, Georgia] in December 1864, and Savannah blacks . . . quickly set up their own schools. "I hurried here," Lynch wrote in early January, "expecting much to do, [and] I have not been disappointed." . . . [C]lergy and church officials met on January 12, 1865, with General Sherman and Secretary of War Edwin M. Stanton, to promise their support for the Union, to press for land and protection for the freed-people, and to spark the Savannah educational effort. Twenty men, Lynch among them, talked with Stanton and Sherman. Four had been born free; three each had gained their freedom either through manumission or by self-purchase; and nine had been slaves until Sherman's arrival in Georgia. . . .

Even before they met with Stanton and Sherman, Savannah's "principal colored men" had formed the Savannah Educational Association and started schools for their children. Help came from Lynch and three white missionaries, John Alvord, Mansfield French, and William Richardson. In either late December or early January, Savannah blacks filled Campbell's church to overflowing; hundreds could not gain admission. . . . Lynch, Alvord, and French spoke, calling for the establishment of schools for former slaves. Lynch asked that the local clergy remain afterwards and assured Alvord that "persons could be found among the colored people who would teach [the] schools if organized." He proved true to his word.

Later that day, the cleric Abraham Burke, a Georgia slave who had purchased his freedom sometime in the 1840s, moved that the governing boards and clergy of Savannah's black churches constitute the Savannah Educational Association. A second mass meeting, in early January, heard members propose the names of teachers and saw a constitution adopted requiring all members to pay three dollars a year and twenty-five cents each month in dues. A resolution invited the cooperation and support of the American Missionary Association, and its representative promised such aid. Contributions were then solicited from the crowd, and a white observer reported to the secretary of the American Missionary Association that . . . "Men and women . . . came to the table with a *grand rush*—much like the charge of union soldiers on a rebel battery! Fast as their names could be written by a swift penman, the Greenbacks were laid upon the table in sums from one to ten dollars, until the pile footed up the round sum of *seven hundred* and *thirty dollars* as the cash receipts of the meeting."

Soon after, Lynch and Alvord examined prospective teachers and found fifteen suitable black teachers, ten women and five men. "The teachers," Lynch said, "are the best educated among our people here." . . . Monthly salaries ranged from $35 each for two principals to $15 each for the women teachers, so that the SEA's monthly wage bill came to $300.

Local Union Army officers (Lynch found General John Geary, the federal commander in Savannah, "*sincerely*" willing to encourage anything that will elevate the freed men") gave the Savannah Educational Association four buildings for schoolrooms, including Oglethorpe Medical College and Bryan's Slave Mart, a three-story building that fronted on Market Square and had till nearly that day served as a meeting place for slave traders and owners. . . . A few days later, the schools opened. About 500 children gathered in the First African Baptist Church's lecture room to parade to their new schoolrooms. An observer felt that the street procession excited "feeling and interest second only to that of Gen. Sherman's army." "Such a gathering of Freedmen's sons and daughters that proud city had never seen before," said this same witness. "Many of the people rushed to doors and windows of their houses, wondering what these things could mean! *This* they were told is in *onward march of freedom.*"

. . . Soon after their schools started, they [the Savannah blacks] encountered . . . trouble. . . . It came from the American Missionary Association. S. W. Magill, a missionary, arrived in Savannah to head the association's educational work and schemed to subvert what the local blacks had started. "However good men [they] might be," he said of the Savannah Educational Association leadership clergy, "they know nothing about education." None had "much more in the way of education than [the] ability to read & write & cypher a little." . . . "I fear," he wrote of the Savannah black clergy, "they will be jealous & sullen if I attempt to place t[he] management in t[he] hands of our white teachers. But this must be done in order to make [the] sch[ools] effective for good."

. . . Magill had quite specific complaints. Leaders of the Savannah Educational Association expected to hire white teachers only as "assistants" and hoped the American Missionary Association would lend financial support. "The whole thing in this aspect of it is preposterous," Magill warned. When he first met with the Savannah Educational Association's executive committee, he learned that it controlled four school buildings, had already enrolled 600 pupils, and had appointed fifteen "colored teachers." More than this, his request that the Savannah blacks allow him to start a school for adults did not get a prompt reply. They "gave me the cold shoulder," complained Magill. The entire operation disturbed him: former slaves and free blacks had preempted his mission. "Here," he moaned, "instead of finding a clear field to work in, we find it preoccupied by this radically defective organization."

Magill pressured vigorously for a federal appointment as the head of Savannah's educational work. Even after Savannah blacks allowed him to use a building for his school, he remained dissatisfied and urged the American Missionary Association to withhold promised funds and not to praise the Savannah blacks too excessively in print. A letter dated February 16 (which, incidentally, noted that Savannah's blacks had already raised perhaps $1,000 for their schools) explained that when he took over he would "be obliged to relieve many of their teachers, some of whom are not professors of religion, and are very lavish in the use of the strap & to diminish the salaries of others, some of whom receive from $25 to $35 per month." Magill expected "trouble," but promised to "proceed with great caution and kindness."

The zealous evangelical finally had his way, as Union officials appointed him to supervise the government's educational efforts in the city. Magill soon reported that the executive committee of the Savannah Educational Association had surrendered the principle of "excluding white control." Magill seemed pleased. Managing Savannah's black schools, after all, required "more head than these colored people yet have." Another Northern white cleric, a visitor to Savannah, made the same point somewhat differently. "They have several interesting schools of their own starting and maintaining there," J. W. Fowler reported in June 1865. He found the black clergy and teachers "gifted with a large share of common sense," but worried because "their expression is very bad" and urged that some Savannah black children be sent North to live in the homes of refined whites and study there to become teachers and ministers.

Despite their defeat, Savannah blacks continued to support their own schools. Financial help came from the New England Freedmen's Aid Society after prodding by William C. Gannett, who visited Savannah in the spring of 1865 and thought the Savannah Educational Association's leaders "men of real ability and intelligence" who had "a natural and praiseworthy pride in keeping their educational institutions in their own hands." "What they desire," he observed, "is assistance without control." By late July 1865, Savannah blacks had spent more than $20,000 for salaries and other educational costs. Crude estimates fixed the number of school-age children in Savannah at 1,600, and three-quarters of them were in school. When the schoolteachers Harriet Jacobs and her daughter arrived in mid-December to work in the schools, they found nineteen of them "principally sustained by the colored people." Another visit to Savannah about that same time convinced John Alvord that the Savannah Educational Association had improved over the year. But he worried over its fiscal condition: "Their association is now, with the high price of everything, falling in debt." In March 1866, Savannah still had eight schools, the largest with 300 students. Savannah blacks boasted of their schools, calling them "self-supporting" and insisting that such was "the only true road to honor and distinction." Alvord agreed. He accepted as "fact" that such "self-made efforts may not be perfect" nor "perhaps as good as those taught by men and women from the north." But Alvord pointed out that the Savannah blacks had revealed "a vitality *within themselves*," showed that "*opportunity* will induce *development*," and made it clear that black people "are not always to be dependent on white help and Government charity."

Savannah's blacks did more than start schools on their own in and near their city. In January 1866, together with other Georgia blacks and some friendly whites, they founded the Georgia Educational Association to encourage the state's former slaves to form local associations that would build schools supported "entirely by the colored people." At first the Georgia Educational Association advanced political as well as educational objectives, but at an October 1866 convention attended by blacks from more than fifty counties it renounced its political role and, while defending equal rights under the law, restricted its work to educational matters. By then, the association had established county organizations in different places in the state. Augusta had five subassociations, each with its own officers and a special school committee to "establish the schools and employ and pay the teachers. The scholars pay the expenses. All persons are allowed to attend the schools." The association, however, suffered for want of funds, and John E. Bryant, a Maine-born Union Army officer, and others pleaded for help from the North: $7,000 would sustain its work so well that the Georgia Educational Association would "never need further assistance from friends outside of the State." . . . [The association] helped Georgia blacks organize schools and pressured for a free public school system that would serve whites as well as blacks. When the Radical Constitutional Convention met in 1868, more than half the members of the Georgia Educational Association's state executive board served as delegates. These blacks helped draw up a constitutional provision that assured free public education to black as well as white children. Their work between 1865 and 1868 had prepared them well for this task. . . .

Blacks throughout the South voluntarily built and sustained schools in ways similar to those in Virginia, South Carolina, . . . and Georgia. Although their work cannot be detailed here, John Alvord's published semiannual reports allow a brief summary of that work before 1868. His reports contain serious flaws but nevertheless retain general value. In the fall of 1865, school attendance, as a percentage of all children eligible to attend ranged from 43 percent in New York State to 93 percent in Boston. That same fall, 41 percent of eligible white children and 75 percent of eligible black children attended District of Columbia schools. An equally high percentage of black children attended the Memphis (72 percent) and Virginia (82 percent) schools. In the three years following the war, General O. O. Howard estimated that nearly one-third of black children over the entire South had some formal education. Not all of these former slaves and free blacks studied with Yankee schoolmarms. In December 1866, 37 percent of teachers in the South known to the bureau were blacks. The percentage increased to over 40 in June 1867, and was even higher a year later. The bureau noted in June 1868 that 2,291 men and women were teaching blacks, and that 990 (43 percent) of them were blacks.

In the fall of 1866, moreover, blacks sustained in full or in part the operation of at least half of the Arkansas, Florida, Georgia, Kentucky, Louisiana, Maryland, and Texas schools. In five states (Alabama, North Carolina, South Carolina, Tennessee, and Virginia), between 25 percent and 49 percent of the schools received financial support from resident blacks. Six months later, at least half of the schools in ten Southern states received assistance from black parents and in six states (Arkansas, Delaware, Kentucky, Louisiana, Mississippi, and Texas) at least three of every four schools were partially financed in this way. . . . The significance of these financial payments can best be realized by comparing the dollars paid in by blacks for tuition with the money expended by the Freedmen's Bureau between January 1 and June 30, 1867. . . . In two states, Alabama and Florida, blacks paid in less than $25 for every $100 spent by the bureau, but in seven others, tuition payments ranged between $25.00 and $49.99 for every $100 of federal money. Tennessee blacks paid in $59.20 and Georgia blacks $77.20. In two states, Kentucky ($131.20) and Louisiana ($178.80), resident blacks, nearly all former slaves there as elsewhere, put more money into the schools than the bureau itself.

Innumerable obstacles, which should not be minimized, hampered the voluntary efforts made by former slaves to educate their children before the start of Radical Reconstruction and the coming of free public education to the South. But neither should these difficulties be emphasized so as to divert our attention from the extraordinary energy and social purpose revealed by these men and women. Theirs was a magnificent effort. We study it in detail because of what it tells about important and little-understood historical processes. In examining how men and women fresh to freedom built and sustained schools, we find much more than simply a desire for schooling. It is inconceivable, for example, that former Memphis slaves would have paid more than $5,000 in tuition between November 1864 and June 1865 without preexisting notions of parental . . . responsibility and kin obligation. Yet it is erroneous to find in their quest for education "proof" that the former slaves held "middle-class" values. The ways in which former slaves built and sustained schools, for example, were quite alien to the "middle class." Yankee shopkeepers and successful artisans favored education, but did not move buildings ten miles and then reconstruct them as schoolhouses. Ohio and Indiana farmers paid school taxes, but did not stand guard over teachers threatened with violence. Former slaves did. The freedpeople's early post-emancipation craving for and defense of schooling for themselves, and especially for their children, rested in good part of values and aspirations known among them as slaves. "The daily job of living did not end with enslavement," the anthropologist Sidney Mintz comments, "and the slaves could and did create viable patterns of life, for which their pasts were pools of available symbolic and material resources." That was true for the blacks after emancipation, too. . . .

Not all the schools freedpeople established between 1861 and 1867 succeeded. The poverty of most Southern blacks, the early decline in interest (and in money and teachers) on the part of Northern benevolent societies, the federal government's shifting policies, and white violence closed many schools. Teachers everywhere noticed the strains that poverty caused among schoolchildren and their parents. Near Darlington, South Carolina (where former slaves had done so much to build schools in 1866 and 1867), a teacher said that students came to school "very badly dressed and barefooted, though the winter has been very cold and the ground frozen." Farm laborers there had been offered one-third of the crop (hardly enough "to keep their families from starvation"), and many suffered "for food." "The best of the women get only four or five dollars a month," she added, "and work for nothing but their poor and scanty food." These observations were made by Frances A. Keigh, who had been a student at the new Darlington black school two years before, in 1866. Now she was a teacher.

Another black teacher, Harriet Jacobs, had returned to her Southern birthplace to teach. A single sentence in her narrative, published in 1861, explains why she, a fugitive slave, and so many other Southern blacks had done so much to bring education to their children and those of other former slaves so soon after their emancipation. "There are no bonds so strong," Jacobs insisted, "as those which are formed by suffering." Slaves and freed blacks did not forget the sacrifices they had made for one another. . . . It was because of the daily efforts of many . . . blacks in the American South between 1861 and 1868 that black and white schoolteachers were able to spread literacy among their children.

Defining Free Labor

JULIE SAVILLE

. . . The politicization of former slaves remains a remarkable feature of a politically vibrant era. Underlying the course of Reconstruction was a simultaneous transformation of petty commodity production in the Old North and of slave society in the Old South. In the "old-issue" free states of the North, wage earners mounted their first nationwide movements to redefine the standing of labor in the Republic. In the "new-issue" free states below the Mason-Dixon line, emancipated workers also took into the arena of party politics demands that joined political and economic reconstruction. In South Carolina, the transformation of work under a "free

Julie Saville, "Grassroots Reconstruction: Agricultural Labour and Collective Action in South Carolina, 1860–1868," pp. 173–180, in *Slavery and Abolition, Vol. 12, No. 3* published by Frank Cass & Company, 900 Eastern Avenue, Ilford, Essex, England. Copyright Frank Cass & Co. Ltd. Reprinted by permission.

labor" regimen drove forward local movements of "grassroots reconstruction." Freedpeople reorganized their household and community life in attempts to shape the character of evolving postwar wage relationships. Those concrete struggles were the seeds of the popular movements that coursed through the South Carolina countryside in the wake of emancipation. In them lay the making of a vigorous labor movement ready to seize suffrage rights conferred by Radical Reconstruction in order to bring the terms of agricultural employment under popular control.

Ex-slaves' agrarian movements drew initial force from the outcome of ante-bellum struggles to shape the power relations implicit in daily work routines. In the freedpeople's view, slavery had not died intestate. Rather, they expected to inherit intact whatever improvements of condition their struggles as slaves had garnered. It seems clear that many nineteenth-century slaves produced and independently managed a marketable surplus—comprised of food crops and occasionally of the plantation staple, in addition to barnyard fowl and swine—which their owners did not appropriate outright. Such supplements to the guaranteed, if scant, weekly allowances were the product of combinations of nighttime overwork, Sunday labor, toil on recognized holidays, and exertion to complete assigned tasks in less time than most slaves normally required. In the state's rice and cotton producing regions alike, time for such labor had been augmented when slave-owners set aside certain days during planting season and harvest or portions of Saturdays for all slaves to tend "their" crops. At emancipation, therefore, many slaves claimed ownership of a largely perishable property rooted in a fragile network of customary rights.

Like the mass of servile workers in the age of emancipation, former slaves in South Carolina expected their freedom to be founded on the possession of land. The varying character of ex-slaves' early claims to land reflects the influence of both antebellum circumstance and wartime military events. Freedpeople who had lived as slaves on the sea islands below St. Helena Sound that were early occupied and continuously held be federal forces claimed *particular* lands. Wartime auctions of plantations forfeited for non-payment of taxes under the federal Direct Tax Act of 1862 threatened to sever them from the region's large, quasi-village settlements on which their kinship and networks of social organization converged. The wartime claims to land voiced by Port Royal's longtime residents typically referred to "home land"—land that was, as a former slave and church elder from St. Helena island explained, "rich wid de sweat ob we face and de blood ob we back;" land where "we born" and where rested "we parents" graves. By war's end, it was a steadily dwindling proportion of ex-slaves in the sea islands who still resided on their home plantations. An almost continuous wartime incursion of fugitives climaxed in the winter of 1864–65, when some 15,000 Georgia slaves reached the coast in the wake of Sherman's army. Their arrival forced the Union general to issue his famous Field Order 15, aptly characterized by James S. Allen as "the most far-reaching step taken toward the distribution of land from above."

Sherman's land grants were as singular as they were temporary. In the fall of 1865, an Edisto island freedmen's committee protested President Andrew Johnson's restoration of lands embraced by Sherman's order. Embellishing ex-slaves' wartime claims to land, the Edisto committee delineated a victorious Union's obligations to its supporters in the state where, the committee pointed out, "secession was born and Nurtured." Land, the committee's petition to Andrew Johnson insisted, constituted a franchise by which free men "always . . . true to this Union" rightfully defended themselves against the burden of servitude. On the Carolina coast, ex-slaves' early claims to land were therefore a compound of birthright, indemnification, and enfranchisement.

Freedpeople's desire for land, however ardent, was a landmark of social experience, not an *idée fixe*. For three years, from federal occupation of the entire state to the assembly of the first legislature elected under the Reconstruction acts, the convocation of federal or local assemblies—with the notable exception of the reconvened 1865 legislature—stimulated an endemic hunger for land to assume more open expression. By the onset of congressional reconstruction in 1867, former slaves had also begun to pioneer tactics of collective action premised on grudging acknowledgment that theirs would be a landless emancipation. More than chimera, less than aim, freedpeople's expectation of a government distribution of land came to reside in a murky realm, dimly charted by rumor, grim fear, or faint prospect. By contrast, collective efforts to regulate agricultural employment were clear and direct. Such tactics had, by 1867, begun to supplant expectations of a federal distribution of plantation lands.

Free labor work arrangements constrained, when they did not erode outright, the wide array of localized, idiosyncratic customs by which slaves had gained access to land and created time for domestic production. Owners of men had found that slave workers' production of a marketable surplus complemented their goal to render their plantations self-sufficient. Lords of acres, on the other hand, tried to hold freed employees' non-plantation work to the production of daily necessities. The change was most stark in lowcountry districts. There, antebellum planters' seasonal absenteeism and widespread reliance on drivers to supervise cultivation of the regional staples of rice and long-staple cotton had supported the relative success with which one of the most densely concentrated slave populations in the United States gained intermittently independent management of their working time and community life.

After emancipation, lowcountry planters exploited their possession of land to restrict freedpeople's domestic production. To the approximately forty people working on his Hilton Head island cotton plantation, the Northern planter E. T. Wright in 1865 allowed "one acre [of provision lands] to every *four* [acres of cotton lands] they cultivate for me." Freedmen on the Jehossee island rice plantation of former governor William Aiken, who in 1866 had been permitted to plant as much land as they could tend without interfering with their daily labor, found that in 1867 Aiken's contract allowed them to cultivate but half an acre of rice land and further required that they sow on their supplemental tracts only rice distinct from the plantation's commercially superior golden seed. Some planters attracted workers by initially offering fairly large household plots only to reduce the plots in subsequent planting years. William Hazzard, for example, attracted workers to his Santee river estates in 1867 by offering 5 acres to each household. The next year, Hazzard's contract offered but a single acre of rice land. Such postwar regulations reflect the extent to

which emancipation had transformed the antebellum relationship between plantation labor and domestic production.

Nuances of cultivation colored lowcountry freedmen's responses to the postwar impasse. Workers in rice cultivation, where periodic flooding diminished the
intensity of field cultivation during the growing season, elaborated sexual divisions
of labor in order to expand household production. The men of the household performed the work required by contracts, while women assumed chief responsibility
for tending the supplemental tracts that freedmen exacted in exchange for their
labor on plantation lands. Sea island cotton workers, facing their crops more constant
demands for hoeing throughout the growing season, adopted the classic peasant
tactic of claiming time from obligations to landlords in order to expand household
production. In return for labor on a specified number of "contract days"—usually
two or three in the early postwar period—sea island cotton workers acquired the
right to reside on and cultivate supplemental tracts of plantation lands.

Such alterations gave labor and time devoted to domestic production new political significance. Although ex-slaves in the lowcountry continued to tend the old
provision grounds, few postwar planters mistook the freedpeople's efforts for attempts to retain or restore antebellum practices. From the outset, it was clear that
freedpeople did not seek to work provision grounds and gardens under constraints
that the work loads of slavery had imposed. Edward Barnwell Heyward, who in 1867
planted Combahee river rice lands inherited from his father, found the expanded
domestic production of the new order incompatible with the old labor regimen:

> The women appear most lazy, merely because they are allowed the opportunity. They
> wish to stay in the house, or in the garden all the time. If you chide them, they say
> "Ehch! Massa, ain't I mus mind de fowl, and look a' me young corn aint I must watch
> um," and to do this the best hands on the place will stay at home all day and every day,
> and litterally do nothing.

The independence that ex-slaves in the lowcountry attempted to anchor in household divisions of labor or contractual guarantees of time proved less an alternative
to wage labor than local adjuncts of the wage relationship. Formal restrictions on
provision acreage, an 1866 fence law that prohibited open grazing on the sea
islands, and requirements that workers perform additional labor services for the
use of farm implements and draft animals curtailed domestic production. A committee of freed men in Georgetown district identified contractual requirements that
"they must not have poltry of eny kind a beast or anamal of eny kind, the[y] must
not plant a seed of eny kind for themselves" among features that rendered postwar
work arrangements "to[o] intollarable to comply worst than slavery."

The small slaveholding sector of interior farming districts presented ex-slaves
with circumstances of residence and labor in 1865 that made their agenda upon
emancipation differ from that of freedpeople on coastal plantations. Slaves owned
by the small planters and middling farmers scattered in Piedmont districts had
seldom lived in the same place among all members of their immediate families. The
dispersion of kin among neighboring slaveowners was common. Freedpeople often
needed to reclaim even those family members who lived no more than a few miles
away. Under such circumstances, asserting claims to particular persons preceded
claims to particular lands.

Political overtones attended the reconstitution of families in the wake of emancipation. The consolidation of household animated those challenges to the master's authority which had reposed in slaves' networks of kin associations. Kinship provided the primary means by which freedpeople on small places first articulated resistance to postwar work arrangements.

The reconstitution of families brought to the fore challenges to the master's personal sovereignty that lurked behind abolition. Ties of blood and marriage carried social obligations that ex-slaves readily defended. Family members assumed primary responsibility for defending one of their own against the corporal punishment that freedpeople generally pronounced the most patent violation of their new condition. Heads of reconstituted families served as the chief bargaining agents in negotiating work arrangements with employers; relatives accompanied each other to Freedmen's Bureau posts to demand redress or carried complaints on a relative's behalf. Wielding a solidarity initially expressed in the idiom of kinship, the reconstituted family became an immediate agency for defending common rights.

The reunion of once scattered families introduced into the plantation's work force new residents, who strained ex-masters' personal authority. Masters' dominion over particular slaves was not easily attached to the new arrivals. Into the domain of power that masters had characterized as "my family white and black," newcomers intruded the long suppressed, alien claims or a competing kinship. Where freed men came to work at the "wife place," landowners found them a troublesome presence. John Smith, a farmer in Richland district, was certain that the arrival of the freedman Ephraim, who joined his wife and child on Smith's place sometime during 1865, hastened rejection of the 1866 contract:

> I am influenced to believe that Ephraim was in instrumental [sic] in his Brother in law Simon leaving me as he (Ephraim) told them that they had [not] entered into a written contract and were not bound. To use Ephraims own words to his brother in law Thomas, he Ephraim said to Thomas that he would suck sorrow thro his teeth if he remained on the place.

Emancipation thus intensified the political significance of slaves' extended networks of kinship. Reconstitution of family households was a precondition for the establishment of a domestic economy through whose development freedpeople pursued economic independence. It was their kinship to other ex-slaves that freedpeople customarily tapped in order to forge resistance to postwar work arrangements, reaching for a shield that at times had held at bay the intrusive intimacy of daily contact with a resident owner.

Like their counterparts in coastal plantation districts, ex-slaves in interior cotton districts gained the right to cultivate tracts on their own account in addition to the still undivided arable lands which they most often worked on shares. Such allotments at times antedated emancipation; the practice may have become more widespread in response to slaves' wartime demands. Certainly, by the end of the war, the arrangement appeared widely in the interior. An officer whose command embraced Barnwell and Orangeburg districts noted in November 1865 that crops raised by freedpeople included "produce, on small lots, assigned to them for their benefit."

The postwar allocation of additional plots intensified rather than reconciled contradictions between the regimen of free labor and freedpeople's pursuit of domestic production. Interior cotton planters typically allotted marginal tracts encrusted with usages not compatible with ex-slaves' intent to develop them as the material base of their households. Planters brooked no interference in prior customs which governed the use of marginal lands. Aiken landowner, John Seigler, for example, allotted a tract of land to the freedman Stephen Marshall. The landowner nevertheless refused to turn his hogs out of the field that Marshal had planted in potatoes.

"Open range" grazing and common pasturage rights practiced by landowners on marginal tracts wreaked predictable havoc on freedpeople's crops. Defense of crops planted on marginal tracts drew ex-slaves and landowners into assaults and counterattacks that threatened to engulf all crops, stock, and buildings found on the premises. Freedman Billy Kincaide's determination to protect his corn patch against depredations by the stock of his Fairfield district employer climaxed when he set his dog on the planter's grazing cows and gave the overseer's mare a beating to which Kincaide's employer attributed her death. When the overseer shot the dog, Kincaide's rage coursed through the cotton fields—where he chopped down growing plants, swept up plantation stock—all of which he threatened to kill before the end of the year, and left his employer "afraid to lie Down at night not knowing but [my] house may be on fire before the morning." Conflicting land uses are perhaps most apparent in specialized plantation regions of the Piedmont because the allotments on which ex-slaves staked their production of a marketable household surplus had initially been carved from marginal tracts rather than from improved acreage.

Of course, a deeper antagonism underlay landowners' and ex-slaves' disputes over marginal lands. Their competing land uses were not easily reconciled when freedpeople were attempting to bring marginal tracts into more regular cultivation precisely in order to escape full-time employment on a landowner's more intensively cultivated fields. As wage laborers, freedpeople encountered a form of exclusive use rights even on common lands. Ex-slaves' resistance to the dependent terms to which planters held their employees' use of marginal tracts strained the network of less than absolute property rights in which marginal lands were enmeshed. Pitched battles stemming from competing uses of marginal lands helped push Piedmont planters toward agreements to sub-divide improved arable lands into units for household cultivation.

By the onset of Radical reconstruction, freedpeople in lowcountry and interior districts alike had attempted to expand domestic production in the face of landlessness. The ensuing conflicts were just opening skirmishes in agricultural workers' long postwar efforts to regulate the terms of their employment. Such early disputes did not, however, lack significance for later contests. From early struggles emerged the specific crop mixes, constraints on subsistence production, interposition of landowners' power in freedmen's elaboration of spheres of familial prerogative, and increasingly absolute rights of property with which planters stocked an arsenal to define the social character of wage relations. The planter's measures were also early targets of freedmen's rural associations—the quasi-military marching companies that flowered in the wake of congressional reconstruction to mount public campaigns to regulate wage rates and tenure arrangements. Early postwar reconstructions of work primed freedpeople for the further work of reconstruction.

The Labor of Politics

ELSA BARKLEY BROWN

After emancipation, African American women, as part of black communities throughout the South, struggled to define on their own terms the meaning of freedom. Much of the literature on Reconstruction-era African American women's political history has focused on the debates at the national level over the Fifteenth Amendment, which revolved around the question of whether the enfranchisement of African American men or the enfranchisement of women should take precedence. Such discussions, explicitly or not, contribute to a political framework that assumes democratic political struggles in the late-nineteenth-century United States were waged in pursuit of constitutional guarantees of full personhood and citizenship. A careful investigation of the actions of African American women between 1865 and 1880, however, leads one to question that framework. Historians seeking to reconstruct the post–Civil War political history of African American women have first to determine whether the conceptualizations of republican representative government and liberal democracy, which are the parameters of such a discussion, are the most appropriate ones for understanding southern black women's search for freedom—even political freedom—following the Civil War. . . .

The institutions that ex-slaves developed give testament to the fact that their vision of freedom was not merely an individual one or, as historian Thomas C. Holt has put it, "that autonomy was not simply personal" but "embraced familial and community relationships as well." . . . African Americans throughout the South in the post–Civil War period emphatically articulated their understanding that freedom and autonomy could not be independently achieved. . . .

This understanding of autonomy was shared by those who had been slave and those who had been free. In fact, the whole process of emancipation may have, at least momentarily, reaffirmed the common bonds of ex-slave and formerly free, for, despite their individual freedom in law, "freedom" in actuality did not come to free black men and women until the emancipation of slaves. Thus their own personal experiences confirmed for formerly free men and women as well as ex-slaves the limitations of personal autonomy and affirmed the idea of collective autonomy.

The vision of social relations that [many southern African Americans] articulated was not the traditional nineteenth-century notion of possessive individualism whereby society is merely an aggregation of individuals, each of whom is ultimately responsible for her/himself. In this individual autonomy, "whether one eats or starves depends solely on one's individual will and capacities." According to liberal ideology, it is the self-regulating impersonality of contractual relations that makes social relations just. Such a notion of freedom and social responsibility was diametrically opposed to the one that undergirded [southern] black institutional developments . . . in the post–Civil War period, where the community and each individual in the community were ultimately responsible for every other person.

Elsa Barkley Brown, "To Catch the Vision of Freedom: Reconstructing Southern Black Women's Political History, 1865–1880," in Ann D. Gordon, Bettye Collier-Thomas, John H. Bracey, Arlene Voski Avakian, and Joyce Avrech Berkman, eds., *African American Women and the Vote, 1837–1965* (Amherst: University of Massachusetts Press, 1997), 66, 68–87. Reprinted by permission from Elsa Barkley Brown.

Whether one eats or starves in this setting depends on the available resources within the community as a whole. Individuals must each do their part and are free to make decisions about their lives, but ultimately it is the resources of the whole that determine the fate of the individual. . . .

It is a striking example of the different vision held by white Freedmen's Bureau officials throughout the South that they regarded this ethos of mutuality as one of the negative traits that had to be curtailed in the process of preparing freedpeople for life in a liberal democratic society. One South Carolina bureau agent, John DeForest, lamented the tendency among freedpeople to assume obligations to "a horde of lazy relatives and neighbors, thus losing a precious opportunity to get ahead on their own." A case in point was Aunt Judy, who, though supporting herself and her children on her meager income as a laundress, had "benevolently taken in, and was nursing, a sick woman of her own race. . . . The thoughtless charity of this penniless Negress in receiving another poverty-stricken creature under her roof was characteristic of the freedmen. However selfish, and even dishonest, they might be, they were extravagant in giving." As historian Jacqueline Jones has pointed out, De Forest's notion that the willingness to share constituted a "thoughtless" act was a product of assumptions "that a 'rational' economic being would labor only to enhance her own material welfare." The different vision of African American women, and of freedpeople in general, posed a persistent problem for northern white men and women, who consistently sought to reeducate and assimilate freedpeople . . . by introducing a different cultural world view as a means of imposing a different economic and political world view as well.

Recent historical explorations of the transition from slavery to freedom have provided substantial evidence that the economic vision of many African American women and men differed fundamentally from that imposed even by freedpeople's most supportive white allies. . . .

. . . If an understanding of the different world views from which African Americans and Euro-Americans operated in the post–Civil War South is necessary to analyze work, family, and community behavior, then a similar understanding is also fundamental to an analysis of the political position of African American women in this same time period. Relatively little has been written about southern black women's participation in Reconstruction-era politics. . . . The few efforts . . . have failed to consider the possibility of a radically different political world view in the African American community. . . .

The Reconstruction Act of 1867 required all the former Confederate states, except Tennessee, to hold constitutional conventions. Black men were enfranchised for the delegate selection and ratification ballots. In Virginia, Republican ward clubs elected delegates to the party's state convention, where a platform was to be adopted. On 1 August, the day the Republican state convention opened in Richmond, thousands of African American men, women, and children absented themselves from their employment and joined the delegates at the convention site, First African Baptist Church. Tobacco factories, lacking a major portion of their workers, were forced to close for the day. This pattern persisted whenever a major issue came before the state and city Republican conventions held during the summer and fall of 1867 or the state constitutional convention which convened in Richmond from December 1867 to March 1868. A *New York Times* reporter estimated that "the entire colored population of Richmond" attended the October 1867 local Republican convention where delegates to the state constitutional convention were nominated. Noting that female domestic servants composed a large portion of those in attendance, the correspondent reported: "as is usual on such occasions, families which employ servants were forced to cook their own dinners, or content themselves with a cold lunch. Not only had Sambo gone to the Convention, but Dinah was there also."

It is important to note that these men and women did not absent themselves from work just to be onlookers at the proceedings. Rather, they intended to be active participants. They assumed as equal a right to be present and participate as the delegates themselves, a fact they made abundantly clear at the August 1867 Republican state convention. Having begun to arrive four hours before the opening session, African American women and men had filled the meeting place long before the delegates arrived. Having shown up to speak for themselves, they did not assume delegates had priority—in discussion or in seating. Disgusted at the scene, as well as unable to find seats, the conservative white Republican delegates removed to the Capitol Square to convene an outdoor session. That was quite acceptable to the several thousand additional African American men and women who, unable to squeeze into the church, were now able to participate in the important discussions and to vote down the proposals of the conservative faction.

Black Richmonders were also active participants throughout the state constitutional convention. A *New York Times* reporter commented on the tendency for the galleries to be crowded "with the 'unprivileged,' and altogether black." At issue was not just these men's and women's presence but also their behavior. White women, for example, certainly on occasion sat in the convention's gallery as visitors silently observing the proceedings; these African Americans, however, participated from the gallery, loudly engaging in the debates. At points of heated controversy, black delegates turned to the crowds as they made their addresses on the convention floor, obviously soliciting and relying upon mass participation. Outside the convention hours, mass meetings were held to discuss and vote on the major issues. At these gatherings vote was either by voice or by rising, and men, women, and children voted. These meetings were not mock assemblies; they were important gatherings at which the community made plans for freedom. The most radical black Republican faction argued that the major convention issues should actually be settled at these mass meetings with delegates merely casting the community's vote on the convention floor. Though this did not occur, black delegates were no doubt influenced by the mass meetings in the community and the African American presence in the galleries, both of which included women.

Black Richmonders were, in fact, operating in two political arenas—an internal and an external one. Though these arenas were related, they each proceeded from different assumptions, had different purposes, and therefore operated according to different rules. Within the internal political process women were enfranchised and participated in all public forums—the parades, rallies, mass meetings, and conventions themselves. Richmond is not atypical in this regard.

It was the state constitutional convention, however, that would decide African American women's and men's status in the political process external to the African American community. When the Virginia convention began its deliberations regarding the franchise, Thomas Bayne, a black delegate from Norfolk, argued the inherent link between freedom and suffrage and contended that those who opposed universal suffrage were actually opposing the freedom of African American people. . . . In rejoinder, E. L. Gibson, a conservative white delegate, enunciated several principles of republican representative government. Contending that "a man might be free and still not have the right to vote," Gibson explained the fallacy of assuming that this civil right was an inherent corollary to freedom: If the right were inherent then it would belong to both sexes and to all from "the first moment of existence" and to foreigners immediately. This was "an absurdity too egregious to be contemplated." And yet this "absurd" notion of political rights was in practice in the Richmond black community, where males and females voted without regard to age and the thousands of rural migrants who came into Richmond suffered no waiting period but immediately possessed the full rights of the community. What was absurd to Gibson and most white men—Republican or Democrat—was obviously quite rational to many black Richmonders. Two different conceptions of freedom and public participation in the political process were in place.

Gibson's arguments relied on several assumptions which were by then basic to U.S. democracy. First[,] . . . some persons were not capable, that is, not "fit" to exercise political liberty. . . .

. . . [Second,] even those with political liberty—as indicated by the right of suffrage—were not equally capable of political decision making. Thus the majority of the people, including the majority of those with suffrage, were expected to leave political decision making to those more qualified. Such political assumptions required that an individual, having once achieved freedom, hand over to others the responsibilities and rights of preserving her/his freedom. In fact, late-nineteenth-century assumptions concerning republican representative government required that the majority of people be passive in their exercise of freedom for the proper operation of democracy. Suffrage granted people not the right to participate in political decision making but the right to participate in choosing political decision-makers. Having become accustomed to this political process by now, we often act as if the two are synonymous. Freedpeople knew they were not.

In a frequently noted observation on women in Reconstruction-era politics, Elizabeth Botume, a northern white teacher in Beaufort, South Carolina, made clear that the political view many white northerners tried to impose was consistent with a particular economic view, too:

> Most of the field-work was done by the women and girls; their lords and masters were much interrupted in agricultural pursuits by their political and religious duties. When the days of "*conwentions*" came, the men were rarely at home; but the women kept steadily at work in the fields. As we drove around, we saw them patiently "cleaning up their ground," "listing," "chopping down the old cotton stalks and hoeing them under," gathering "sedge" and "trash" from the riverside, which they carried in baskets on their heads, and spread over the land. And later, hoeing the crops and gathering them in.
>
> We could not help wishing that since so much of the work was done by the colored women—raising the provisions for their families, besides making and selling their own cotton, they might also hold some of the offices held by the men. I am confident they would despatch business if allowed to go to the polls; instead of listening and hanging around all day, discussing matters of which they knew so little, they would exclaim,—
> "Let me vote and go; I've got work to do."

Botume's analysis hinged on several assumptions: that adoption of habits of thrift and diligence were the factors that qualified one for suffrage; that voting equaled political participation; and that "'listening and hanging around all day, discussing matters," were not important forms of political participation. Botume, like so many northern allies, thought free black people were to earn the rights of freedom by adopting the proper habits of responsibility and industry. Her lament was that these African American women, who had been "reconstructed" in that sense, were not rewarded by the franchise. Central to her complaint about African American women's disfranchisement is her exasperation at African American men's assumption that political rights included the right to participate in political discussions (and thereby political decision making). She believed these industrious women, having come to exercise their proper economic role, would also adopt their appropriate role in the political system and would properly exercise the suffrage. They would vote and get on back to work rather than hang around engaging in political issues which, she thought, neither they nor the men had capacity to understand. Botume would leave it to others more capable to make the important political decisions. Thus even the slight support southern black women mustered among white northerners for their enfranchisement came in a context that would have preferred to leave them far less active in the political process than they had been in the most immediate post–Civil War days.

The history of African American women's political involvement in South Carolina and elsewhere leaves one dubious about Botume's predictions regarding how black women would exercise the franchise. Nevertheless, Botume's observations do point to the fact that in the end only men obtained the legal franchise. The impact of this decision is neither inconsequential nor fully definitive. African American women were by law excluded from the political arena external to their community. Yet this does not mean that they were not active in that arena—witness Richmond women's participation in the Republican and the constitutional conventions.

Southern black men and women debated the issue of woman suffrage in both the external and internal political arenas, with varying results. Delegates to the South Carolina convention, 56 percent of whom were black, adopted a constitution that included "male" as a qualification for voting, despite a stirring argument for woman suffrage from William J. Whipper, a black delegate from Beaufort. Nevertheless, a significant proportion of South Carolina's Reconstruction-era black elected officials favored woman suffrage or were at least open to a serious discussion of the issue. It was the South Carolina House of Representative, which was 61 percent black, that allowed Louisa Rollin to speak on the floor of the assembly in support of woman suffrage in March 1869. Several black male representatives argued in favor of the proposal then and again two years later, when Lottie Rollin led a woman suffrage rally at the state capital. In March 1872 Beverly Nash, state senator, and Whipper, then state representative, joined with other delegates to propose a woman suffrage amendment to the state constitution. Alonzo J. Ransier, U.S. congressman from South Carolina and later the state's first black lieutenant governor, presented his argument on the floor of the U.S. House of Representatives in 1874: "until [women as well as men have the right to vote] the government of the United States cannot be said to rest upon the 'consent of the governed.'" According to historian Rosalyn Terborg-Penn, Ransier, who was president of the South Carolina Woman's Rights Association, was widely supported by his black South Carolinian colleagues. In fact, six of the eight black men who represented

South Carolina in the U.S. Congress during the Reconstruction era supported woman suffrage.

The question of woman suffrage was a subject of discussion in other southern legislative chambers as well. It was often raised by white men to demonstrate the absurdity of black delegates' argument for the inherent right of suffrage. Black delegates, even when they rejected woman suffrage, were far more likely to treat it as a matter for serious discussion. If not, as they often did, expressing support, black delegates were far more likely to express at least ambivalence rather than firm conviction of the absurdity of woman electorates . . . [I]t is clear that serious discussion of woman suffrage in southern legislative chambers during the Reconstruction era seemed to depend upon a strong African American representation.

The debate over woman's suffrage occurred in the internal arena as well, with varying results. In Nansemond County, Virginia, a mass meeting held that women should get the legal franchise; in Richmond while a number of participants in a mass meeting held for female suffrage, the majority opinion swung against it. But the meaning of that decision was not as straightforward as it may seem. The debate as to whether women should be given the vote in the external political arena occurred in internal political arena mass meetings where women participated and voted not just before and during *but also after* the negative decision regarding legal enfranchisement. This mass meeting's decision maintained the status quo in the external community; ironically enough, the status quo in the internal community was maintained as well—women continued to have a vote. Both African American men and women clearly operated within two distinct political systems. . . .

Focusing on formal disfranchisement, however, obscures the larger story. . . .

In Richmond and throughout the South exclusion from legal enfranchisement did not prevent African American women from affecting the vote and the political decisions. They organized political societies such as the Rising Daughters of Liberty which actively engaged in the political campaigns by educating the community on the issues, raising funds for the candidates, and getting out the vote. Coal miners' wives living outside Manchester, Virginia, played a similar role through the United Daughters of Liberty. Mississippi freedwomen placed themselves in potentially dangerous positions by wearing Republican campaign buttons during the 1868 election. In some instances the women walked "all the way to town, as many as twenty or thirty miles," to "buy, beg, or borrow one, and thus equipped return and wear it openly in defiance of . . . master, mistress, or overseer" and sometimes of husband as well. Domestic servants also risked job and perhaps personal injury by wearing their buttons to work. "To refuse neglect, or lack the courage to wear that badge . . . amounted almost to a voluntary return to slavery," according to many freedwomen and freedmen.

Black women initially took an active role in the South Carolina political meetings. Those disfranchised women whom Botume imagined would vote and go home, not involving themselves in political discussion, displayed a particular insistence on continued *public* political activity. The assumptions that underlay these women's activities are instructive. Laura Towne, a northern white teacher, tells us it was the white Republicans who first announced to the freedpeople that "women and children ought to stay at home on such occasions." Yet it does not appear to be merely the presence of females that disturbed these white men, for they quickly made it clear that Towne, of course, was welcome. Their announcement was meant to exclude "outsiders who were making some noise." Probably because of protests or disregard of the exclusion notice, the white Republicans modified their initial ban to state that "the *females* can come or not as they choose, . . . but the meeting is for men voters." It was clearly the women's failure to take the position of passive observers that was being censured. Some black men took their cue, one even using the occasion to prompt women to " 'stay at home and cut grass,' that is, hoe the corn and cotton fields—clear them of grass!" while the men were at the political meetings.

Even though they were excluded from further participation in the Republican meetings by the late 1860s, African American women in South Carolina, Louisiana, and elsewhere were still attending the meetings in the 1870s. Although women were never elected delegates, it does appear that occasionally women were sent to the political meetings on behalf of their community. Lucy McMillan, a South Carolina widow, reported that her attendance at a political meeting was the result of community pressure: "They all kept at me to go. I went home and they quizzed me to hear what was said, and I told them as far as my senses allowed me."

Women's presence at these meetings was often anything but passive. In the violent political atmosphere of the last years of Reconstruction, they had an especially important—and dangerous—role. While the men participated in the meeting, the women guarded the guns—thus serving in part as the protectors of the meeting. This was not a symbolic or a safe role in a time when "men are shot at, hunted down, trapped and held till certain meetings are over, and intimidated in every possible way." During the violent times of late Reconstruction, African American women in South Carolina were reported "in arms, carrying axes or hatchets in their hands hanging down at their sides, their aprons or dresses half-concealing the weapons." One clergyman, contending African Americans could defend themselves if necessary, noted that "80,000 black men in the State . . . can use Winchesters and 2000,000 black women . . . can light a torch and use a knife." At times women as well as men actually took up arms. In 1878 Robert Smalls, attacked by redshirts while attempting to address a Republican meeting in Gillisonville, sought refuge and later reported that "every colored man and woman seized whatever was at hand—guns, axes, hoes, etc., and ran to the rescue." Some of these women probably had double incentive as the redshirts had "slap[ped] the faces of the colored women coming to the meeting."

African American women took the political events to heart and took dramatic steps to make their political sentiments known. They also expressed their outrage when the political tide turned against their interests. Alabama women, reportedly, "were converted to Radicalism long before the men and almost invariably used their influence strongly for the purpose of the League." South Carolina Democrats believed African American women to be "the head and fount of the opposition." . . .

African American women in South Carolina and elsewhere understood themselves to have a vital stake in African American men's franchise. The fact that only men had been granted the vote did not mean that only men should exercise that vote. Women reportedly initiated sanctions against men who voted Democratic. One South Carolina witness reported that "no mens were to go to the polls unless their wives were right alongside of them; some had hickory sticks; some had nails—four nails drive in the shape of a cross—and dare their husbands to vote any other than the Republican ticket." In the highly charged political atmosphere of the late 1870s it was no small matter for these women to show up at the election site carrying weapons. Armed Democrats patrolled the polling areas, and Republicans were often "driven from the polls with knives and clubs. Some of them were badly wounded." We might wonder whether the weapons the women carried were for use on their husbands or on the Democratic opponents, but in either case these women very publicly declared their stake in their husband's vote.

Black Republican politicians throughout the South took women's participation seriously and publicly encouraged them to abstain from sexual relations with any man who voted Democratic. Some women left their Democratic husbands. Engaged women were encouraged to postpone the wedding until after the election when they could obtain assurance that their future husband was not a Democrat. In Alabama women banded together in political clubs to enforce these sanctions collectively. Some politicians also endorsed women's use of weapons to influence their husbands' vote. It is likely that, rather than initiating these actions on the part of African American women, Republican legislators merely recognized and endorsed actions initiated by the women themselves. These examples all suggest that African American women and men understood the vote as a collective, not an individual, possession and, furthermore, that African American women, unable to cast a separate vote, viewed African American men's vote as equally theirs. Their belief that the franchise should be cast in the best interest of both was not the nineteenth-century patriarchal notion that men voted on behalf of their wives and children. By the latter assumption, women had no individual wills; rather, men operated in women's best interest because women were assumed to have no right of input. African American women assumed the political rights that came with being a member of the community, even though they were not granted the political rights they thought should come with being citizens of the state.

The whole sense of the ballot as collectively owned is most eloquently presented by Violet Keeling, a tobacco worker who testified in February 1884 before a Senate committee investigating the violence in the previous year's elections in Danville, Virginia. Assenting in her husband's decision not to vote in that election for fear he might be killed, she made it clear that she would not, however, assent in his or anyone else's voting Democratic: "as for my part, if I hear of a colored man voting the Democratic ticket, I stay as far from him as I can; I don't have nothing in the world to do with him. . . . No, sir; I don't 'tallow him to come in my house." Asked why she should "have such a dislike to a colored man that votes the Democratic ticket," she replied:

I think that if the race of colored people that has got no friends nohow, and if they don't hang together they won't have none while one party is going one way and another the other. I don't wish to see a colored man sell himself when he can do without. Of course we all have to live, and I always like to have a man live even if he works for 25 cents a day, but I don't want to see him sell himself away. . . . I think if a colored man votes the Democratic ticket he has always sold himself. . . . If I knew a colored man that voted the Democratic ticket to come to my house, I would tell him to go somewhere else and visit.

Asked "suppose your husband should go and vote a Democratic ticket," she responded: "I would just picke up my clothes and go to my father's, if I had a father, or would go to work for 25 cents a day."

Violet Keeling clearly articulated the notion that a black man could not exercise his vote only in his own behalf. If he sold his vote, he sold hers. The whole issue of the ostracism of black Democrats reveals very clearly the assumptions regarding suffrage that were operative throughout African American communities. Black Democrats were subject to the severest exclusion: disciplined within or quite often expelled from their churches; kicked out of mutual benefit societies; not allowed to work alongside others in the fields of accepted leadership positions at work or in the community. Ministers were dismissed from their churches or had their licenses to preach revoked; teachers who voted Democratic found themselves without pupils. Democrats' children were not allowed in schools. And, perhaps the most severe sanction of all, black Democrats found themselves unaided at time of death of a family member. Women participated in all of these actions as well as in the mobs that jeered, jostled, and sometimes beat black Democrats or rescued those who were arrested for such behavior. In fact, women were often reported to be the leaders of such mob involvements. . . .

From the perspective of liberal democratic political ideology, these activities might be perceived as "unconscionable" "interference with the [individual voter's] expression of . . . political preference." But African Americans in the post–Civil War South understood quite clearly that the actions of one member of the community affected, and in this instance endangered, all others in that community. Thus they understood there was no such thing as an individual action or a "possessive individual," owing nothing to society. . . . It was that sense of suffrage as a collective, not an individual, possession that was the foundation of much of women's political activities.

. . . This is not to suggest that African American women did not desire the vote or that they did not often disagree with the actions taken by some black men. One should, however, be careful about imposing presentist notions of gender equality on these women. Clearly for them the question was not an abstract notion of individual gender equality but rather one of community. That such a vision might over time lead to a patriarchal conception of gender roles is not a reason to dismiss the equality of its inception.

Women's presence at the polls was not just a negative sanction; it was also a positive expression of the degree to which they understood the men's franchise to be a new political opportunity for themselves as well as their children. They reinforced this idea of black men's voting as a new freedom which they had all achieved by turning the occasion into a public festival and celebration, bringing lemonade and gingercakes and spending the day at the polls. Of course, the principal reason for the group presence at the polls was protection. The tendency for "crowds" of freedmen to go to the polls together was seen by their white contemporaries and by some historians as evidence that they were forced to vote the Republican ticket or that they did not take seriously the franchise but instead saw election day as an opportunity for a picnic or other entertainment. Henderson Hamilton Donald, for example, noting that freedmen "always voted in companies," found this behavior "odd and sometimes amusing." Yet his own description suggests the real meaning: "When distances were great, crowds of them under leaders went to the polling places a day in advance and *camped out like soldiers on the march."* Women and children often went along, their presence reflecting their excitement about the franchise but also their understanding of the dangers involved in voting. Women may have gone for additional protection of the voters, like those women in South Carolina who carried weapons, or to avoid potential danger to those left alone in the countryside while the men were gone. But, in any case, the necessity for a group presence at the polls reinforced the sense of collective enfranchisement. What may have been chiefly for protection was turned into festivity as women participated in a symbolic reversal of the meaning of the group presence.

African American women throughout the South in the Reconstruction era assumed *publicly* the right to be active participants in the political process long after they had been formally removed—and they did so, in part, through their husbands. They operated out of an assumption that his vote was theirs. Unlike many northern white middle-class women, southern black women in the immediate post–Civil War era did not base their political participation in justifications of superior female morality or public motherhood. They did not need to; their own cultural, economic, and political traditions provided rationale enough—"autonomy was not simply personal."

One of the ramifications of liberal democratic political theory is that our notion of politics is severely circumscribed. In a context where only certain persons have the rights and abilities to participate fully, the *formal* political process takes on an exclusivity and sanctity all its own. Historians operating from this perspective often ascribe the totality of politics to the formal political arena. . . . But these women's actions were fundamentally *political.* That African American women did not operate inside the formal political process does not negate the intensely political character of their actions. These actions represented a continuous significant political participation on their part. Black women, therefore, were hardly confined (even without the franchise or elective office) to a private sphere. They were certainly not confined to any less bloody sphere.

African American women understood "that freedom meant above all the right to participate in the process of creating it." Being denied this right in the external political arena and having this right increasingly circumscribed in the internal arena as well, these women created their own political expression, thus inventing the power their freedom required. Their actions were not merely a grievance against their own lack of political rights or lack of rights of the black community but, more importantly, a critique of the absence of freedom and democracy, as they understood it, in the society at large. By their actions and assumptions they challenged the fundamental assumptions of the U.S. political process itself. . . .

Ultimately northern and southern white men may have denied African American women the freedom fully to shape their own lives in the post–Civil War era. But we, trapped in our own mental prisons, have denied them their freedom as well, insisting instead that they accept our very limited and pessimistic vision of human possibilities. . . . Just as African American women, as part of black communities throughout the South, struggled in the post–Civil War era to catch, that is, to make real, their vision of freedom, we, as historians, must now struggle to catch, that is, to understand, their vision of freedom. In the process we need not only to refine our base of information but also to reconstruct our frameworks, creating new ones that allow us to interpret these women's lives in ways that do justice to their vision of freedom.

FURTHER READING

James Anderson, *The Education of Blacks in the South, 1860–1935* (1988).

Kathleen C. Berkeley, " 'Colored Ladies Also Contributed': Black Women's Activities from Benevolence to Social Welfare, 1866–1896," in Walter J. Fraser, Jr., R. Frank Saunders, Jr., and Jon L. Wakelyn, eds., *The Web of Southern Social Relations: Women, Family, and Education* (1985).

Ira Berlin, Barbara J. Fields, Steven F. Miller, Joseph P. Reidy, and Leslie S. Rowland, eds., *Free at Last: A Documentary History of Slavery, Freedom, and the Civil War* (1992).

Ira Berlin, Barbara J. Fields, Steven F. Miller, Joseph P. Reidy, and Leslie S. Rowland, eds., *Slaves No More: Three Essays on Emancipation and the Civil War* (1992).

Ira Berlin and Leslie S. Rowland, eds., *Families and Freedom: A Documentary History of African-American Kinship in the Civil War Era* (1997).

W. E. Burghardt Du Bois, *Black Reconstruction in America* (1935).

Eric Foner, *Freedom's Lawmakers: Directory of Black Office Holders During Reconstruction* (1996).

Eric Foner, *Reconstruction: America's Unfinished Revolution, 1863–1877* (1980).

Thavolia Glymph and John Kushma, eds. *Essays on the Postbellum Southern Economy* (1985).

Reginald F. Hildebrand, *The Times Were Strange and Stirring: Methodist Preachers and the Crisis of Emancipation* (1995).

Sharon Ann Holt, "Making Freedom Pay: Freedpeople Working for Themselves, North Carolina, 1865–1900," *Journal of Southern History*, 60 (May 1994), 229–262.

Thomas C. Holt, *Black over White: Negro Political Leadership in South Carolina During Reconstruction* (1977).

Thomas C. Holt, " 'An Empire over the Mind': Emancipation, Race, and Ideology in the British West Indies and the American South," in J. Morgan Kousser and James McPherson, eds., *Region, Race, and Reconstruction: Essays in Honor of C. Vann Woodward* (1982).

Gerald David Jaynes, *Branches Without Roots: Genesis of the Black Working Class in the American South, 1862–1882* (1986).

Jacqueline Jones, *Labor of Love, Labor of Sorrow: Black Women, Work, and the Family from Slavery to the Present* (1985).

Lawrence Levine, *Black Culture and Black Consciousness: Afro-American Folk Thought from Slavery to Freedom* (1977).

Leon F. Litwack, *Been in the Storm So Long: The Aftermath of Slavery* (1979).

Edward Magdol, *A Right to the Land: Essays on the Freedmen's Community* (1977).

Robert C. Morris, *Reading, 'Riting, and Reconstruction: The Education of Freedmen in the South, 1861–1870* (1981).

Donald G. Nieman, *Promises to Keep: African Americans and the Constitutional Order, 1776 to the Present* (1991).

Claude F. Oubre, *Forty Acres and a Mule: The Freedmen's Bureau and Black Landownership* (1973).

Linda M. Perkins, "The Black Female American Missionary Association Teacher in the South, 1861–1870," in Jeffrey J. Crow and Flora J. Hatley, eds., *Black Americans in North Carolina and the South* (1984).

Howard N. Rabinowitz, ed., *Southern Black Leaders of the Reconstruction Era* (1982).

Peter J. Rachleff, *Black Labor in the South: Richmond, Virginia, 1865–1890* (1984).

Armstead L. Robinson, "Plans Dat Comed from God: Institution Building and the Emergence of Black Leadership in Reconstruction Memphis," in Orville Vernon Burton and Robert C. McMath, Jr., eds., *Toward a New South? Studies in Post–Civil War Southern Communities* (1982).

Julie Saville, *The Work of Reconstruction: From Slave to Wage Laborer in South Carolina, 1860–1870* (1994).

James D. Schmidt, *Free to Work: Labor Law, Emancipation, and Reconstruction, 1815–1880* (1998).

Leslie A. Schwalm, *A Hard Fight for We: Women's Transition from Slavery to Freedom in South Carolina* (1997).

Rebecca Scott, "The Battle over the Child: Child Apprenticeship and the Freedmen's Bureau in North Carolina," *Prologue*, 10 (Summer 1978), 101–113.

Alrutheus Ambush Taylor, *The Negro in the Reconstruction of Virginia* (1926).

Allen W. Trelease, *White Terror: The Ku Klux Klan Conspiracy and Southern Reconstruction* (1971).

Theodore Branter Wilson, *The Black Codes of the South* (1965).

CHAPTER
3

Renegotiating African-American Life in the New South

In 1897 the Virginia poet Daniel Webster Davis wrote of the remarkable economic progress some African Americans had made in the post-Reconstruction South: "we kummin' up, yo' kno'/An' sum un us is gittin' rich/Wid do'-bells on de do'/An' got sum lawyers, doctors, too/An' men like dat, fur sho'." As Davis saw it, this economic progress had an unwelcome corollary: "Dey sez de whi' folks mad 'long us/'Cause we kummin' up." Paradoxically both black southerners' cause for hope and their reasons for despair at the turn of the century could, in Davis's estimation, be linked to the fact of their economic and political advancement. Indeed black life in the post-Reconstruction South was marked by increasing access to formal education, the rise of black businesses, and the growth of institutions, such as churches and mutual benefit societies, that proved themselves to be viable vehicles for addressing a number of social, economic, and political situations. At the same time the era was one that the historian Rayford Logan later characterized as the "nadir" in U.S. race relations.

To some degree the 1877 U.S. presidential election, often regarded as the end of Reconstruction, merely sealed a compromise already made by northern and southern white legislators. In 1877, Democrats, who throughout the decade increasingly had gained control of southern legislatures, were able to use the stalemate over the presidential election to force a federal retreat from the protection of southern black peoples' rights and lives—the removal of armed forces from the South and the eventual end of federal marshals and supervisors of elections. By the 1890s the way was clear for white southerners, through the use of constitutional measures, fraud, and violence, to put an end to black men as officeholders and even as voters. Legal segregation, endorsed by the Supreme Court in the 1896 Plessy v. Ferguson decision, soon followed. Assuming that this return of African Americans to their "proper place" in the social hierarchy would mean an era free of northern interference, Henry Grady, editor of the Atlanta Constitution, proclaimed the dawning of a New South, one full of economic and political promise for white southerners.

In what ways did African Americans attempt to renegotiate their positions in the political, economic, and social structures of the New South? To what extent did this effort necessitate a rethinking of their relations with each other as well as with the larger society?

DOCUMENTS

By 1877 a number of black southerners had concluded that the possibilities for a full and productive life did not lie in the South, and they made a commitment to try life elsewhere. Some hoped to emigrate to Africa; more looked expectantly toward life in a different region of the United States. The first document is a handbill circulated by a group of African Americans in Lexington, Kentucky, who have decided to head for Kansas. Twenty-five thousand men, women, and children would soon follow in one of the first mass outmigrations of black southerners.

Most African Americans, however, continued to struggle to make a life in the South. In 1880, 90.5 percent of African Americans in the United States still lived there. By 1910 that percentage had not appreciably changed: 89 percent still resided in the region. And African Americans overwhelmingly (73 percent in 1910) remained a rural population. The second and third documents address the nature of rural labor in the New South. David C. Barrow, Jr., son of a Georgia plantation owner, describes the transition from post–Civil War share-wages agreements, which organized work by squads of laborers, to the emergence of family sharecropping. Nate Shaw (a pseudonym for Alabama farmer Ned Cobb) recalls his first years of trying to make a living at sharecropping. Implicit in Shaw's account is his understanding of his lack of redress for any wrongs committed against him or his family. This was an understanding common to many black southerners, one reinforced by the violence that permeated black-white relations.

During the 1880s and 1890s, large numbers of black southerners were brutally lynched. One of the most graphic examples of this violence came in 1898, however, when Wilmington, North Carolina, was the scene of large-scale postelection attacks on black voters, officeholders, and residents. The fourth document consists of letters to President William McKinley from black southerners requesting, even demanding, federal attention to the destruction of black lives in Wilmington and throughout the South. Federal intervention, however, was not forthcoming.

The 1890s also witnessed the increased use of poll taxes and literacy tests expressly to disfranchise black men. Mississippi led the way by rewriting its state constitution in 1890; other southern states rapidly followed suit. With the loss of black voting strength so too went black officeholding at every level. The fifth document excerpts the final address to Congress by George White, representative from the Second District of North Carolina. Speaking no doubt primarily for the record, White recounts black educational and economic advancement and anticipates a day when Americans of African descent might return in numbers to the U.S. House and Senate.

Southern black men and women, however, did not meekly acquiesce to disfranchisement and segregation. Throughout the South black men, women, and children protested, often drawing on resources provided by the emerging mutual benefit societies and businesses. The sixth document consists of reports about one of a number of boycotts of the newly segregated streetcars in the first decade of the twentieth century—this particular boycott by African Americans in Richmond, Virginia. But in many instances, as the historian Howard N. Rabinowitz pointed out, the alternative to segregation was not integration but exclusion. The seventh document recounts the opening of the first public branch library in the South exclusively for black patrons. Though some black men and women refused to patronize a Jim Crow library, others found it preferable to no library access. In fact when word of this branch opening circulated, some parents from outside the state of Kentucky moved their families to Louisville so that their children could grow up in a place where they had access to a library, even a segregated one.

1. Black Southerners Look Toward Kansas, 1877

All Colored People

THAT WANT TO

GO TO KANSAS,

On September 5th, 1877,

Can do so for $5.00

IMMIGRATION.

WHEREAS, We, the colored people of Lexington, Ky,. knowing that there is an abundance of choice lands now belonging to the Government, have assembled ourselves together for the purpose of locating on said lands. Therefore,

BE IT RESOLVED, That we do now organize ourselves into a Colony, as follows:— Any person wishing to become a member of this Colony can do so by paying the sum of one dollar ($1.00), and this money is to be paid by the first of September, 1877, in instalments of twenty-five cents at a time, or otherwise as may be desired.

RESOLVED, That this Colony has agreed to consolidate itself with the Nicodemus Towns, Solomon Valley, Graham County, Kansas, and can only do so by entering the vacant lands now in their midst, which costs $5.00.

RESOLVED, That this Colony shall consist of seven officers—President, Vice-President, Secretary, Treasurer, and three Trustees. President—M. M. Bell; Vice-President —Isaac Talbott; Secretary—W. J. Niles; Treasurer—Daniel Clarke; Trustees—Jerry Lee, William Jones, and Abner Webster.

RESOLVED, That this Colony shall have from one to two hundred militia, more or less, as the case may require, to keep peace and order, and any member failing to pay in his dues, as aforesaid, or failing to comply with the above rules in any particular, will not be recognized or protected by the Colony.

2. David C. Barrow, Jr., a Georgia Planter's Son, Describes the Emergence of Sharecropping, 1880

. . . In most cases there has been an entire change in the plan upon which our Georgia lands are worked, the change being entirely in favor of "local self-government as opposed to centralization of power." . . .

One of the first planters in Middle Georgia to divide his plantations into farms was Mr. Barrow, of Oglethorpe. . . . This place contains about two thousand acres of land, and with the exception of a single acre, which Mr. Barrow has given to his tenants for church and school purposes, is the same size it was before the war. . . . [T]he plantation, "as it was [before the war]," all the negro houses were close together, forming "the quarter." . . . This has all been so changed that the place would now hardly be recognized. . . .

The transformation has been so gradual that almost imperceptibly a radical change has been effected. For several years after the war, the force on the plantation was divided into two squads, the arrangement and method of working of each being about the same as they had always been used to. . . . The plantation was divided into two equal parts, and by offering a reward for the most successful planting, and thus exciting a spirit of emulation, good work was done, and the yield was about as great as it had ever been. Then, too, the laborers were paid a portion of the crop as their wages, which did much toward making them feel interested in it. . . .

This was the first change made, and for several years it produced good results. After a while, however, even the liberal control of the foremen grew irksome, each man feeling the very natural desire to be his own "boss," and to farm to himself. As a consequence of this feeling, the two squads split up into smaller and then still smaller squads, still working for part of the crop, and using the owner's teams, until this method of farming came to involve great trouble and loss. . . .

[This] led to the present arrangement, which, while it had difficulties in the way of its inception, has been found to work thoroughly well. Under it our colored farmers are tenants, who are responsible only for damage to the farm they work and for the prompt payment of their rent. On the plantation about which I am writing, all of the tenants are colored men, who farm on a small scale, only two of them having more than one mule. Indeed, the first trouble in the way of dividing up the plantation into farms was to provide the new-made tenants with mules. . . . This trouble was met by selling them mules on credit, and though the experiment looked risky at the time, the mules were paid for in almost every case. . . . When the hands all worked together, it was desirable to have all of the houses in a central location, but after the division into farms, some of them had to walk more than a mile to reach their work; then, too, they began to "want more elbow-room," and so, one by one, they moved their houses on to their farms. . . .

The labor of the farm is performed by the man, who usually does the plowing, and his wife and children, who do the hoeing, under his direction. Whenever they have heavy work to do they call on their neighbors, and receive willing aid. Their

David C. Barrow, Jr., "A Georgia Plantation," *Scribner's Monthly,* 21, no. 1 (November 1880), 830–836. Roger L. Ransom and Richard Sutch. From *One Kind of Freedom: The Economic Consequence of Emancipation,* p. 72. © 1977 by Cambridge University Press. Reprinted with the permission of Cambridge University Press.

crops are principally corn and cotton, but they have patches of such things as potatoes, melons, and sorghum-cane, from which they make their sirup. They plant whatever they please, and their landlord interferes only far enough to see that suffi- cient cotton is made to pay the rent. . . . The usual quantity of land planted is be- tween twenty-five and thirty acres, about half of which is in cotton and the rest in corn and patches. An industrious man will raise three times the amount of his rent- cotton, besides making a full supply of corn, sirup, and other provisions, while really good farming would require about five times the rent to be raised in addition to the supply of provisions. Candor compels the admission that only a few tenants reach this standard of good farming; the others work sufficiently well to pay their rent, and make money enough to buy their clothes and spend at Christmas, and let the rainy days of the future take care of themselves. . . .

The slight supervision which is exercised over these tenants may surprise those ignorant of how completely the relations between the races at the South have changed. Mr. Barrow lives on his plantation, and yet there are some of his tenants' farms which he does not visit as often as once a month, and this, too, because they do not need overlooking. Very many negro farmers are capable of directing the working of their own crops, and not a few object to directions. There are, on the other hand, many, in fact a large majority, who, while they know how their crops should be worked, are slow to think and act for themselves, and an occasional visit from the landlord does them much good.

. . . Ben Thomas [is] the old foreman on this plantation, and the best farmer among the negroes on the place. . . . Ben's contract for the past year . . . reads as follows:

By or before the 15th November, 1880, I promise to pay to David C. Barrow, 500 lbs. of white lint cotton, 40 bushels of cotton-seed, 25 bushels of corn and the shucks there- from, and 500 lbs. of good fodder, as rent for land on Syll's Fork, during year 1880.

. . . Ben's contract last year was exactly the same as this, and his crop . . . was as follows:

5 bales	Cotton, 2500 lbs.	@ 11 cts.	$275.00
	Corn, 160 bush.	@ 75 cts.	120.00
	Fodder, 3000 lbs.	@ $1.00 per hun. . .	30.00
	Wheat, 30 bush.	@ $1.00.	30.00
	Total	. . . .	$455.00

This crop was raised by himself, his wife, a son and daughter.

As one of the class who work not so wisely as well, Beckton Barrow is a good specimen . . . a man whose earthly possessions consisted of a wife, two daughters, and a limited supply of provisions. . . . His contract is the same as Ben Thomas's, except that he pays one-fourth of his corn and fodder, instead of a stated amount. . . .

All of these negroes raise hogs, and these, with chickens, of which they raise great numbers, constitute a large portion of their meat food. They generally have to buy some meat during the year, however, for which they pay in the fall.

The land of this plantation is rich, and the tenants are, perhaps, better off than in some other places, but an industrious negro will pay good rent for land and make money for himself almost anywhere in Middle Georgia.

The last census showed three white and one hundred and sixty-two colored people on this plantation. . . .

3. Nate Shaw Aims to Make a Living Farming, 1907–1908

. . . Durin of my correspondin Waldo Ramsey's daughter I had to go right by Mr. Maynard Curtis's house any time I went to her house. Waldo Ramsey and Mr. Curtis owned land joinin—houses didn't set over two hundred yards apart. Mr. Curtis had known of me through I used to work for his daddy—choppin cotton, pullin fodder, strictly day labor. . . . So he knowed who it was correspondin this girl that lived up the road from him. . . .

And so he caught on to me goin over there regular and he figured I was liable to marry over there and I believe he might have heard something about it. So, me and Mr. Curtis agreed—he got at me bout building me a house, before we married, and I traded with him and he went on and built it. . . .

. . . Just a old plantation style house, built for colored folks, no special care took of how it was built. But it'd keep you out the rain, it'd keep you out the cold; just a old common-built house, board cabin. . . . Whenever a white man built a house for a colored man he just run it up right quick like a box. No seal in that house; just box it up with lumber, didn't never box it up with a tin roof. They'd put doors to the house and sometimes they'd stick a glass window in it, but mostly a wood window. Didn't put you behind no painted wood and glass, just built a house for you to move in then go to work. . . .

We moved in the house—and when we moved in I was ready to go to work with Mr. Curtis on halves, 1907. He put me on the sorriest land he had and he took all the best. . . .

I didn't make two good bales of cotton the first year I stayed with Mr. Curtis. Sorry land, scarce fertilize, Mr. Curtis not puttin out, riskin much on me and I a workin little old fool, too. I knowed how to plow—catch the mule out the lot, white man's mule, bridle him, go out there and set my plow the way I wanted—I knowed how to do it. Bout a bale and a half was what I made.

The second year he went out there and rented some piney wood land from Mr. Lemuel Tucker, sixteen acres bout a half mile from his plantation and he put me on it. Well, it was kind of thin but it was a king over Mr. Curtis's land. I worked it all in cotton; what little corn I had I planted on Mr. Curtis's place. Well, I made six pretty good bales of cotton out there for Mr. Curtis and myself. When I got done gatherin, wound up, by havin to buy a little stuff from Mr. Curtis at the start, in 1907—it sort of pulled the blinds over my eyes. It took all them six bales of cotton to pay Mr. Curtis. In the place of prosperin I was on a standstill. Second year I was married it took all I made on Mr. Tucker's place, by Mr. Curtis havin rented it from Mr. Tucker for me, to pay up 1908's debts and also 1907's debts—as I say, by me buyin a right smart to start me off to house-keepin, cleaned me. I had not a dollar left out of the cotton. And also, Mr. Curtis come in just before I moved off his place—I was determined to pay him and leave him straight; in fact, I reckon I just had to do it because he'd a requested it of me, movin from his place, clean up and leave myself clear of him.

Theodore Rosengarten, *All God's Dangers: The Life of Nate Shaw* (New York: Knopf, 1974), 107–108, 112–115.

Mr. Curtis had Mr. Buck Thompson to furnish me groceries. Mr. Curtis knowed all of what Mr. Thompson was lettin me have; kept a book on me. See, he was standin for everything Mr. Thompson gived me; he paid Mr. Thompson and I paid him—the deal worked that way—out of my crop. So he made somethin off my grocery bill besides gettin half my crop when the time come.

Took part of my corn to pay him. He come to my crib, him and Mr. Calvin Culpepper come together to my crib and got my corn, so much of it. And what I had he got the best of it, to finish payin him on top of them six bales of cotton.

Then I moved to Mr. Gus Ames', 1908. Mr. Ames' land was a little better than Mr. Curtis's, but it was poor. Worked his pet land hisself and whatever he made off me, why, that was a bounty for him. I didn't make enough there to help me.

. . . I was eager to get in a position where I could take care of [Hannah, my wife,] and our children better than my daddy taken care of his wives and children.

Mr. Curtis and Mr. Ames both, they'd show me my land I had to work and furnish me—far as fertilize to work that crop, they'd furnish me what *they* wanted to; didn't leave it up to me. That's what hurt—they'd furnish me the amount of fertilize they wanted regardless to what I wanted. I quickly seed, startin off with Mr. Curtis in 1907, it weren't goin to be enough. First year I worked for him and the last year too he didn't allow me to use over twenty-two hundred pounds of guano—it come in two-hundred-pound sacks then—that's all he'd back me up for all the land I worked, cotton and corn. It was enough to start with but not enough to do any more. Really, I oughta been usin twice that amount. Told him, too, but he said, "Well, at the present time and system, Nate, you can't risk too much."

I knowed I oughta used more fertilize to make a better crop . . . but I was a poor colored man, young man too, and I had to go by their orders. It wasn't that I was ignorant of what I had to do. . . . But you had to do what the white man said, livin here in this country. And if you made enough to pay him, that was all he cared for; just make enough to pay him what you owed him and anything he made over that, why, he was collectin on his risk. In my condition, and the way I see it for everybody, if you don't make enough to have some left you aint done nothin, except given the other fellow your labor. That crop out there goin to prosper enough for him to get his and get what I owe him; he's makin his profit but he aint goin to let me rise. If he'd treat me right and treat my crop right, I'd make more and he'd get more. . . .

I worked four years on halves, two with Mr. Curtis. I was just able when I moved from his place to leave him paid. What did I have left? Nothin. Of course, if I'm left with nothin, no cash in my pocket, I can look back and say what I paid for I got. But what little I did get I had to work like the devil to get it. It didn't profit me nothin. . . . You want some cash above your debts; if you don't get it you lost, because you gived that man your labor and you can't get it back.

Now it's right for me to pay you for usin what's yours—your land, stock, plow tools, fertilize. But how much should I pay? The answer ought to be closely seeked. How much is a man due to pay out? Half his crop? A third part of his crop? And how much is he due to keep for hisself? You got a right to your part—rent; and I got a right to mine. But who's the man ought to decide how much? The one that owns the property or the one that works it?

4. Black Southerners Appeal to President William McKinley for Federal Protection, 1898–1900

Please send relief as soon as possible
or we perish.

Wilmington N.C. Nov 13, 1898

Wm. McKinley:—President of the United States of America,

Hon—Sir,

I a negro woman of this city, appeal to you from the depths of my heart, to do something in the negro's behalf. The outside world only knows one side of the trouble here, there is no paper to tell the truth about the negro here in this or any other southern state. The negro in this town had no arms, (except pistols perhaps in some instances) with which to defend themselves from the attack of lawless whites. On the 10th Thursday morning between eight and nine oclock, when all negro men had gone to their places of work. The white men led by Col. A. M. Waddell, Jno. D. Bellamy, & S. H. Fishblate marched from the Light Infantry Armory on market street to seventh down seventh to Love & Charity Hall (which was owned by a society of negroes.) And where the negro daily press was.) and set it afire & burnt it up. And firing Guns Winchesters, they also had a Hotchkiss gun & two Colt rapid fire guns. We the negro expected nothing of the kind as they (the whites) had frightened them from the polls saying they would be there with their shot guns, so the few that did vote did so quietly. And we thought after giving up to them and they carried the state it was settled. . . . After destroying the building they went over in Brooklyn another Negro settlement mostly, and began searching every one and if you did not submit, would be shot down on the spot. They searched all the negro churches. And to day (Sunday) we dare not go to our places of worship. They found no guns or ammunition in any of the places, for there was none. And to satisfy their Blood thirsty appetites would kill unoffending negro men on their way to or from dinner. Some of our most worthy negro men have been made to leave the city. Also some whites, G. Z. French, Deputy Sheriff, Chief of Police Jno R. Melton, Dr. S. P. Wright Mayor and R. H. Bunting United States Comissioner (sic). We dont know where Mr. Chadbourn the Post Master is, and two or three others whites. I call on you the head of the American nation to help these humble subjects. We are loyal we go when duty calls us. And are we to die like rats in a trap? with no place to seek redress or to go with our Grievances? Can we call on any other nation for help? Why do you forsake the negro? who is not to blame for being here. This Grand and noble nation who flies to the help of suffering humanity of another nation? and leave the Secessionists and born Rioters to slay us. . . .When our parents belonged to them, why, the negro was all right now, when they work and accumulate property they are all wrong. The negroes that have been banished are all property owners to considerable extent, had they been worthless negroes, we would not care.

General Records of the Department of Justice, DJ Central Files, Year Files 1887–1903, Folder 1898–17743, National Archives, College Park, Maryland.

Will you for God sake in your next message to Congress give us some relief. If you send us all to Africa we will be willing or a number of us will gladly go. Is this the land of the free and the home of the brave? How can the negro sing my country tis of thee? . . . There seems to be no help for us. No paper will tell the truth about the negro. The men of the 1st North Carolina were home on a furlough and they took a high hand in the nefarious work, also, the companies from every little town came in to kill the negro. There was not any rioting simply the strong slaying the weak. They speak of special police every white man and boy from 12 years up had a gun or pistol, and the negro had nothing, his soul he could not say was his own. Oh, to see how we are Slaughtered, when our husbands go to work we do not look for their return. The man who promises the negro protection now as Mayor is the one who in his speech at the Opera house said the Cape Fear should be strewn with carcasses. Some papers I see, say it was right to eject the Negro editor. That is all right but why should a whole city full of negroes suffer for Manly when he was hundreds of miles away? And the paper had ceased publication. We were glad it was so for our own safety. But they tried to slay us all. To day we are mourners in a strange land with no protection near. God help us. Do something to alleviate our sorrows, if you please. I cannot sign my name and live. But every word of this is true. The law of our state is no good for the negro anyhow. yours in much distress

Wilmington, N.C.

Nov. 15, 1898

Mr. McKinly (sic)

Dear sir, the poor citens of the colored people of north carolina are suffering. there is over four hundred women and children are driven from their home far out into the woods by the dimocrate party. Look out for a letter from Wilmington North Carolina and in that letter that it will be the names of the citens but that letter is not true and if you have ever help the colored people, for God sake help them now that old confradate flage is floating in Wilmington North Carolina. The city of Wilmington is unde the confradate laws, we are over powed with the rapid fire of the guns, and they had cannons, in wagons, and they set fire to almost half of the City. I would give you my name but I am afraid. I am afraid to own my name. it is from a colored citens

San Antonio Tex. (c. 1899)

Dear Mr. President McKinley . . . Will you think once of the barbous act of the *white people* in the south to the poor helpless colored people. Dear President think of the burning of one Sam Hose in Georgia and numbers of other Lynching since that occured (sic). and think of the 7 negroes strung to a limb near Eagle pass on the 20 of May.

Dear President will you as a honest President attend to this Lynch law of the south. . . . I labored hard for you when you was a candidate and I will do the same thing over again. . . . We as colored people are with out protection here   it Seam that we are the off cast race of the earth and yet we are law abiding citizens   But the brutish whites of the south seem to take the law in their own hands. . . . Dear President I hope I'm not out of my place for writing this letter for I mean no harm in this world   I hope you will give this due consideration for we are anxious to have equal rights as American citizen   we dont ask for no more than this consistution demand us to have. And will you see to it that we have it. . . . We have a man in Jail now who was claimed to commit a crime on a Mrs Wilkins and she stated that the negro was a mulatto who committed the act and now the (sic) have a supected one and he is as black as ink and she says he is the one. he does not answer to the first description she gave but just seeked up any just so he is a negro and execute him. . . . Dear President I hope you will see to it that those excuters of Sam Hose will be brought to trial   ex Gov. Atkinson know some of them and they all can be eaisly caught.

P.S. Dear President I often think of when you was a Gov of Ohio when a negro was going to be Lynch and you got in a special car and went to his rescue and save him from that horrible act they was preparing for him. and I never will forget such a worthy man as you   I'm with you both heart and hand   and shall always be for you as long as you are a McKinley. . . .

Please let me hear from you at once. . . . I hope you will work this Lynch law of the south as successfully as you have work the war situation. . . . please urge this matter on.

San Antonio, Texas
Law abiding citizen
W. G. Banks, 650 Soledad st.

Brunswick Ga

July 12 ad 1900

Mr. McKenley (sic)

Dear President it affoards me With much Pleashure to right you to investigate a matter for ous. We are Knights of Pythas of Brunswick Lodge No. 17 Phthagoras   We have had a Worthy Brother K of P By the name of Abe Sebens Lynched By a crowd of White men at nahanta. ga. 2 Weeks a go & L. Keleogg. C.C. & G. Johnson Vice. C. Went up there Last Sunday to investigate the matters & they own Lynching him & it Was all that they could do to get away from there alive them selves Withe out Beaing Killed & it was told to them While Beaing there that they had a Pond over there in the Woods that they called scull Pond & Person could not hardly get through there for the dead Peoples Bornes What they had killed & throwed in there & the White mens of Nahanta. Ga told us to hour face god dam you as many negroes as We have Killed here you arr the first to that Ever came here to investigate a matter god dam your cheeky Sales get away from heare Before some one Will have to come to see about you & did drilled ous away Like We Was dogs & would not Let ous go in the woods & get the Body so i take Pleashure in righting to you to investigate this matter for me   Please oblige ous & come to our Rescue Just as soon as Posible . . .

Pythagras. Lodge. No. 17.
    L. Keleogg. C.C.
    G. Johnson. Vice. C.
        Brunswick. Ga.

5. Representative George White of North Carolina Delivers His Final Speech on the Floor of Congress, 1901

I want to enter a plea for the colored man, the colored woman, the colored boy, and the colored girl of this country. I would not thus digress from the question at issue and detain the House in a discussion of the interests of this particular people at this time but for the constant and the persistent efforts of certain gentlemen upon this floor to mold and rivet public sentiment against us as a people and to lose no opportunity to hold up the unfortunate few who commit crimes and depredations and lead lives of infamy and shame, as other races do, as fair specimens of representatives of the entire colored race. . . .

. . . There never has been, nor ever will be, any negro domination in [North Carolina], and no one knows it any better than the Democratic party. It is a convenient howl, however, often resorted to in order to consummate a diabolical purpose by scaring the weak and gullible whites into support of measures and men suitable to the demagogue and the ambitious office seeker, whose craving for office overshadows and puts to flight all other considerations, fair or unfair. . . .

It is an undisputed fact that the negro vote in the State of Alabama, as well as most of the other Southern States, have been effectively suppressed, either one way or the other—in some instances by constitutional amendment and State legislation, in others by cold-blooded fraud and intimidation, but whatever the method pursued, it is not denied, but frankly admitted in the speeches in this House, that the black vote has been eliminated to a large extent. . . .

. . . Since [slavery] time we have reduced the illiteracy of the race at least 45 per cent. We have written and published near 500 books. We have nearly 300 newspapers, 3 of which are dailies. We have now in practice over 2,000 lawyers and a corresponding number of doctors. We have accumulated over $12,000,000 worth of school property and about $40,000,000 worth of church property. We have about 140,000 farms and homes, valued at in the neighborhood of $750,000,000, and personal property valued at about $170,000,000. We have raised about $11,000,000 for educational purposes, and the property per capita for every colored man, woman, and child in the United States is estimated at $75.

We are operating successfully several banks, commercial enterprises among our people in the Southland, including 1 silk mill and 1 cotton factory. We have 32,000 teachers in the schools of the country; we have built, with the aid of our friends, about 20,000 churches, and support 7 colleges, 17 academies, 50 high schools, 5 law schools, 5 medical schools, and 25 theological seminaries. We have over 600,000 acres of land in the South alone. The cotton produced, mainly by black labor, has increased from 4,669,770 bales in 1860 to 11,235,000 in 1899. All this we have done under the most adverse circumstances. We have done it in the face of lynching, burning at the stake, with the humiliation of "Jim Crow" cars, the disfranchisement of our male citizens, slander and degradation of our women, with the factories closed against us, no negro permitted to be conductor on the railway cars, whether run through the streets of our cities or across the prairies of our great country, no negro permitted to run as engineer on a locomotive, most of the mines

Congressional Record, 56th Cong., 2nd sess., pt. 2, January 29, 1901, pp. 1635–1636, 1638.

closed against us. Labor unions—carpenters, painters, brick masons, machinists, hackmen, and those supplying nearly every conceivable avocation for livelihood have banded themselves together to better their condition, but, with few exceptions, the black face has been left out. The negroes are seldom employed in our mercantile stores. At this we do not wonder. Some day we hope to have them employed in our own stores. With all these odds against us, we are forging our way ahead, slowly, perhaps, but surely. You may tie us and then taunt us for a lack of bravery, but one day we will break the bonds. You may use our labor for two and a half centuries and then taunt us for our poverty, but let me remind you we will not always remain poor. You may withhold even the knowledge of how to read God's word and learn the way from earth to glory and then taunt us for our ignorance, but we would remind you that there is plenty of room at the top, and we are climbing. . . .

Now, Mr. Chairman, before concluding my remarks I want to submit a brief recipe for the solution of the so-called American negro problem. He asks no special favors, but simply demands that he be given the same chance for existence, for earning a livelihood, for raising himself in the scales of manhood and womanhood that are accorded to kindred nationalities. . . .

This, Mr. Chairman, is perhaps the negroes' temporary farewell to the American Congress; but let me say, Phœnix-like he will rise up some day and come again. These parting words are in behalf of an outraged, heart-broken, bruised, and bleeding, but God-fearing people, faithful, industrious, loyal people—rising people, full of potential force.

Mr. Chairman, . . . The only apology that I have to make for the earnestness with which I have spoken is that I am pleading for the life, the liberty, the future happiness, and manhood suffrage for one-eighth of the entire population of the United States. [Loud applause.]

6. *Richmond Planet* Reports a Streetcar Boycott, 1904–1905

[April 9, 1904]: The Virginia Passenger and Power Company of this city announces that it will separate the races in the street-cars in this city. . . . The rear of the street-cars will be for Negroes and the front part for white people and any of its conductors can, whenever they see fit cause a colored person, male or female, to get up and make room for any other person.

We hope that our people will comply with the rule of law, if they ride on the street-cars. To get on there and "jaw" at the conductors will afford some satisfaction, but it will not pay in the long run or the short one either. . . . We are of the opinion that this is a good time to stay off the street-cars. The good Lord has blessed most of us with big feet and we see no reason why we should not start early to work and proceed to use them. If the entire colored population or at least ninety per cent of it would agree to make the sacrifice and walk for a year, the agony produced on the white man's nerve centre, which is his pocket, would tend to cause an amelioration of our condition.

Richmond Planet, April 9, 16, 23, 30, May 14, June 4, July 23, September 24, December 3, 1904; March 18, 1905.

We never believed that such exhibitions of rank race prejudice would take place here and it follows too closely upon our elimination as a political factor. If colored people go on the street-cars, obey the regulations of the company, but our advice is to walk and sweat. Show to this corporation that independence and liberty are sweet and the day of the time-server is past. . . . Walking is good now. Stay off the street-cars!

[April 16, 1904]: The action of the Virginia Passenger and Power Company in adopting rules and regulations for the separation of white and colored people on its street-cars has caused intense feeling among the colored people. For a week, the colored people have studiously applied themselves to walking. The Clay Street line which usually carries a packed crowd of colored people both morning and evening has been avoided and the other lines give the impression that the colored population has left the city.

A conference of colored citizens to discuss the situation took place at Mr. A. D. Price's Hall last Thursday at 5 P.M. A large number of the leading colored men and ladies were present. . . . it was the opinion of the body that the colored people should do all in their power to promote peace and avoid any clash or disorder on the street-cars. It was decided that the best way to do this would be to WALK and STAY OFF the Virginia Passenger and Power Company's cars.

To this end, it was voted to hold a mass-meeting Tuesday night, April 19th, 8 P.M., at the True Reformers' Hall and invite the public to be present to hear the discussion and to take the proper action.

[April 23, 1904]: The True Reformers' Hall was packed last Tuesday night with the colored people, who even lined the aisles and stair ways to attend the mass-meeting of citizens held for the purpose of making a dignified and conservative protest against the action of the Virginia Passenger and Power Company in making racial discrimination upon its lines in Richmond, Manchester and Petersburg.

It was 9 o'clock when Editor John Mitchell, Jr., of the PLANET called the meeting to order. Prayer was offered by Rev. L. A. Carter. . . . A sensation was caused when Chairman Mitchell announced that the Presidents and Cashiers of the four colored Banks, and representing an aggregate capital of $180,000 had met Friday, April 15th, 1904 and pledged their personal and financial support to any movement having for its purpose the transit of the colored people who must ride from one section of the city to the other. . . .

Mr. W. W. Fields arose and made a characteristic address urged the colored people to stay off the cars. . . . He . . . recommended salt water baths for the feet as providing a convenient and satisfactory means of adapting them to the return to the habit of walking. . . . Mrs. Patsie K. Anderson's advice given in terse, explicit language was to do no talking, but walk, walk, walk. She carried the house by storm and sat down amidst great applause. . . . Mr. Geo. St. Julien Stephens called attention to the representative character of the meeting, declaring that there were present Bankers, lawyers, business men, College professors, in fact people from every walk of life.

[April 30, 1904]: The "Jim Crow" street car regulation is in effect in this city and has been since April 20th, 1904. White passengers are ushered up to the front of the car and the colored passengers are seated in the rear. As a result, between eighty and

ninety per cent of the colored people who have used the street-car's are now walking . . . it is a common thing to see street cars with the front part filled and the rear
part empty.

Now and then one or two colored persons may be seen in the "Jim Crow" department. The Clay street line has shown a heavy falling off in travel. Hitherto, it
has been rammed, jammed and packed in the mornings with colored people going
to work. Now at any hour seats can be obtained. Some colored people who pocket
their pride out of respect for their feelings insist upon standing upon the platforms
as there is no discrimination there, and they only move inside when they receive
positive orders from the conductors. Some colored people leave the cars when ordered to take particular seats. . . . Those colored people who ride obey the regulations, but the others prefer to walk. On Sunday, the absence of the colored people
from the cars attracted universal attention. Some colored people are saving 60 cts.
per week and some as much as $1.60 per week as a result of the new rules. . . .

A white gentleman met Editor Mitchell and informed him that he had trouble
with his cook. . . . "Why I told her to bring my dinner to me on the car. She said, 'Yes,
sir, I'll bring it, but I'll walk sir, and bring it.' 'No, you wont,' said he 'your time belongs to me. You bring it on the car.' She said nothing more, but looked worried. She
brought the dinner, and when she was going back, she saw you and some friends
ahead of her. She got off the car at Sixth street and walked the remainder of the way."

[May 14, 1904]: The street-car situation here remains the same. Eighty or ninety
per cent of the colored people are walking. It would require much space to detail
the individual cases, where colored people, both male and female have suffered in
their efforts to emphasize the disapproval of this iniquitous rule made by the street-
car company. One colored female weighing approximately two hundred pounds
has been walking from up-town to Church-hill, although she has been unfit for service when she reached her place of employment. . . .

The officials of the company are of the opinion that the colored people will,
within three months get tired and be back on the cars in full force. The colored
people alone can decide this question. The white gentleman who spoke to us about
his cook says that he has a row with her nearly every day about bringing his dinner
to him on the street-cars. She wants to walk.

[June 4, 1904]: No colored person who resides in this city has as yet been caught in
the "Jim Crow" street-car trap. It would seem to an observer that the cars were being
run for white people only, so few are the number of colored people seen on them. The
morning travel is also very light. Colored laborers are walking and the drays, produce
and delivery wagons haul quite a number down town free of charge. It is a source of
great inconvenience to many, but they heroically walk despite the draw-backs.

[July 23, 1904]: The long expected has happened and the street-car company of
this city has been forced to admit that it is unable to pay its expenses. That this result
in a large measure was brought about by the walking colored people admits of no
question. . . . We were confident that if the colored people would maintain their
self-respect, and walk and sweat that it would result in the financial collapse of the
street-car company. This prediction has been verified.

The Citizens Mass meeting advised the colored people to walk, and to those who would ride, the advice was given that they obey the law. As a result, numbers of white people have been arrested and fined and but only one colored resident of this city has been the victim. This will be an object lesson to the Negro-hating management of the Virginia Passenger and Power Company. The entire electric railway system of Richmond, Manchester and Petersburg is now being operated by the United States District Court, Judge Edmund Waddell, Jr., presiding. The receivers are Mr. William Northrop and Hon. Henry T. Wickham. It remains to be seen whether they will continue a system of operation which has proved injurious to the financial interests of the company, and directly disastrous to the income of the bond-holders of the aggregated railway corporations.

The objectionable card should come down and the rules which are admitted failures should be obliterated from the cars of the street-car company. Colored folks will yet see the red-flag over the street-car system, and until they are properly treated will walk from one end of this city to the other.

The street-car company is "busted." The colored people were instrumental in hastening its down-fall. Walking is good now. We are yet staying off the street-cars.

[September 24, 1904]: The "Jim Crow" streetcars are not patronized by the majority of the colored people here and the great mass of our people are continuing to inconvenience themselves and maintain their self-respect by walking. . . . The corporation has been forced to reduce its force of employees on account of its reduction in revenue. The "Jim Crow" car law should go and the company management should return to a sane and safe platform once more. Many colored people have walked and are still walking. . . .

[December 3, 1904]: The Virginia Passenger and Power Co., better known as the "Jim Crow" Street Car Company continues to have no end of trouble and it now seems that the entire system will be sold at auction. . . .

[March 18, 1905]: Many [colored folks] are yet using "Shank's mare," that is still walking.

7. A Public Library Opens in Louisville, Kentucky, 1908

The new public free library, colored branch, at Tenth and Chestnut streets, was dedicated last night. Mayor James F. Grinstead presiding. In his address he spoke of the opportunities afforded the colored people of the city to secure knowledge and wisdom by Andrew Carnegie and the taxes of the people. He felicitated the race on their progress and said the colored people could live in peace and harmony with their neighbors so long as they obey the laws of the Commonwealth. The opening marked an epoch in the history of the colored people of this city. It was known as "Education Day," yesterday at the Library and thousands visited the new building which was

---

Courier-Journal (Louisville, Kentucky), October 30, 1908, p. 8.

brilliantly lighted and decorated with chrysanthemums, panns and evergreens. Librarian T. H. Blue and his assistants gave every visitor a welcome and took unusual pains to explain the working of the library in detail. The principal feature of the opening was the programme given last night. Over four hundred people were present in the lecture room in the basement to hear addresses made by professional men of the race. Prof. A. E. Meyzeek, principal of the Eastern Colored School, delivered an address on "The Library and the School." He said the library was no longer a myth and that the school children would use it for reference. The Rev. J. C. Anderson of Quinn chapel, A.M.E. Church, spoke on the "Library and the Church." Prof. James E. Simpson, of the Central High School, urged his hearers to remember that the library was for the benefit of the poor man, the workman as well as the professional man; in fact that it was the people's library. The Rev. Leroy Ferguson, of the Church of Our Merciful Saviour, reminded the professional men of the race that books of every nature could be found on the shelves of the library and that they were at their disposal. "The Library and the Business Man," was the subject taken by William H. Steward who spoke on the usefulness of the library to the colored business men of the city. Dr. C. H. Parrish, president of Eckstein-Notton University, delivered a short but pointed address on the subject "Library and the Student." Prof. Joseph Cotter read an original poem and a quartet and other musical selections marked the close of the evening's numbers. This afternoon at 3:30 o'clock will be known as "Children's Day." A programme has been arranged for the occasion. On Saturday the work of issuing books will begin and the library will be open at the usual hours.

E S S A Y S

In the first essay Elsa Barkley Brown of the University of Maryland traces changes in the southern black political landscape in the late nineteenth century. She focuses on the ways in which institutions such as the church were transformed and the ways in which increasing class and gender distinctions developed in black Richmonders' own ideas about political participation. The second essay begins with the case of a little-known strike by washerwomen in Atlanta, Georgia, in 1881 and explores the ways in which black workers in the late nineteenth and early twentieth centuries resisted economic and political exploitation. Tera W. Hunter of Carnegie Mellon University meticulously makes the case for the ways in which many of the increasing restrictions on black economic development and political participation in the New South were precisely responses to black southerners' assertions of their rights.

Renegotiating the Community

ELSA BARKLEY BROWN

On April 15, 1880, Margaret Osborne, Jane Green, Susan Washington, Molly Branch, Susan Gray, Mary A. Soach and "over two hundred other prominent sisters of the church" petitioned the Richmond, Virginia, First African Baptist Church's business meeting to allow women to vote on the pastor:

Elsa Barkley Brown, "Negotiating and Transforming the Public Sphere: African American Political Life in the Transition from Slavery to Freedom," *Public Culture,* 7 (Fall 1994), 107–111, 126–144. Copyright © Elsa Barkley Brown. Reprinted with permission.

> We the sisters of the church feeling that we are interested in the welfare of the same and also working hard to finish the house and have been working by night and day . . . We know you have adopted a law in the church that the business must be done by the male members. We don't desire to alter that law, nor do we desire to have anything to do with the business of the church, we only ask to have a vote in electing or dismissing him. We whose names are attached to this petition ask you to grant us this privilege.

The circumstances surrounding these women's petition suggest the kinds of changes taking place internally in late-nineteenth and early-twentieth century black Richmond and other southern black communities. In the immediate post–Civil War era women had voted in mass meetings and Republican Party conventions held at First African, thus contradicting gender-based assumptions within the larger society about politics, political engagement and appropriate forms of political behavior. Now, women sitting in the same church were petitioning for the right to vote in an internal community institution, couching the petition in terms designed to minimize the request and avoid a challenge to men's authority and position.

Scholars' assumptions of an unbroken line of exclusion of African American women from formal political associations in the late-nineteenth century have obscured fundamental changes in the political understandings within African American communities in the transition from slavery to freedom. Women in First African and in other arenas were seeking in the late-nineteenth century not a new authority but rather a lost authority, one they now often sought to justify on a distinctively female basis. As these women petitioned for their rights within the church and as other women formed voluntary associations in turn-of-the-century Richmond they were not, as often depicted in the scholarly literature, emerging into the political arena through such actions. Rather these women were attempting to retain space they traditionally had held in the immediate post-emancipation period. This essay explores the processes of public discourse within Richmond and other southern black communities and the factors which led to increasingly more clearly gendered and class spaces within those communities to understand why women by the 1880s and 1890s needed to create their own pulpits from which to speak—to restore their voices to the community. This exploration suggests how the ideas, process, meanings and practice of freedom changed within late-nineteenth-century southern African American communities. . . .

After emancipation, African American men, women and children, as part of black communities throughout the South struggled to define on their own terms the meaning of freedom and in the process to construct communities of struggle. Much of the literature on Reconstruction portrays freed African Americans as rapidly and readily adopting a gendered private-public dichotomy. Much of the literature on the nineteenth-century public sphere constructs a masculine liberal bourgeois public with a female counterpublic. This essay, focusing on the civic geography of post–Civil War black Richmond, suggests the problem of applying such generalizations to African American life in the late-nineteenth century South. In the immediate post-emancipation era black Richmonders enacted their understandings of democratic political discourse through mass meetings attended and participated in (including voting) by men, women and children and through mass participation in Republican Party conventions. They carried these notions of political participation into the state Capitol engaging from the gallery in the debates on the constitutional convention floor.

Central to African Americans' construction of a fully democratic notion of political discourse was the church as a foundation of the black public sphere. In the post-slavery era, church buildings also served as meeting halls and auditoriums as well as educational and recreational facilities, employment and social service bureaus and bulletin boards. First African, especially, with a seating capacity of nearly 4000, was the site of large political gatherings. Schools such as Richmond Theological Seminary and Richmond Colored High and Normal School held their annual commencement exercises at First African Baptist, allowing these events to become community celebrations. Other groups, such as the Temperance Union, were regularly granted the church for their meetings or rallies. As a political space occupied by men, women and children, literate and nonliterate, ex-slave and formerly free, church members and nonmembers, the availability and use of First African for mass meetings enabled the construction of political concerns in democratic space. This is not to suggest that official versions and spokespersons were not produced, but these official versions were the product of a fairly egalitarian discourse and, therefore, represented the conditions of black Richmonders of differing classes, ages and genders. Within black Richmonders' construction of the public sphere, the forms of discourse varied from the prayer to the stump speech to the testimonies regarding outrages against freedpeople to shouted interventions from the galleries into the debates on the legislative floor. By the very nature of their participation—the inclusion of women and children, the engagement through prayer, the disregard of formal rules for speakers and audience, the engagement from the galleries in the formal legislative sessions—Afro-Richmonders challenged liberal bourgeois notions of rational discourse. Many white observers considered their unorthodox political engagements to be signs of their unfamiliarity and perhaps unreadiness for politics.

In the decades following emancipation as black Richmonders struggled to achieve even a measured amount of freedom, the black public sphere emerged as more fractured and perhaps less democratic at the end of the nineteenth century, yet even then it retained strong elements of a democratic agenda. This essay examines the changing constructions of political space and community discourse in the post-emancipation era. . . .

Renegotiating Public Life

The 1880 First African women's petition followed three contentious church meetings, some lasting until two or three o'clock in the morning, at which the congregants considered dismissing and/or excluding the pastor, the Reverend James H. Holmes. This discussion was initiated at an April fifth meeting where two women were charged with fighting about the pastor. The April sixth meeting considered charges of "unchristian conduct" on the part of Holmes; those men present voted to exclude Holmes. A meeting on April eleventh endorsed a protest signed by all but two of the deacons against the earlier proceedings. The protest charged the anti-Holmes faction with trying to "dispose of the deacons, take charge of prayer meetings, the Sunday school and revolutionize things generally." The discussions which ensued over the next two months split the congregation; the May and June church business meetings were "disorderly" and "boisterous." Holmes and the deacons called in the mayor, city court judge, and chief of police to support the pastor and the police to remove or arrest those members of the congregation designated as "rebellious." After the anti-Holmes faction was removed from the church, the June meeting expelled forty-six men for "rebelliously attempting to overthrow and seize upon the church government." It also excluded the two women initially charged, one for fighting and the other for tattling; exonerated Holmes "from all false" accusations; and thanked the civil officers who attended the meeting and restored order. Only after these actions did the church consider the women's petition which had been presented in the midst of the controversy more than two months earlier.

First African's records do not adequately reveal the nature of gender relations within the church in the late 1860s and 1870s. We do know that pre–Civil War sex-segregated seating patterns were abandoned by Richmond black Baptist churches immediately after the Civil War and that by the late 1860s women "not only had a voice, but voted in the business meetings" of Ebenezer Baptist Church. Women who voted in political meetings held in First African in the 1860s and 1870s may have carried this participation over to church business meetings. Often in the immediate post–Civil War period, business and political meetings were not clearly distinguishable.

The petition of the women of First African makes clear, however, that by the early 1880s, while women attended and apparently participated in church meetings, the men had "adopted a law in the church that the business must be done by the male members." Whether Margaret Osborne, Jane Green, and others thought that their voices and interests were being inadequately represented, even ignored by the deacons, or wanted to add their voices to those, including the deacons, who were struggling to retain Holmes and control of First African, these women understood that they would have to defend their own rights. The women argued their right to decide on the pastor, justifying their petition by both their work on behalf of the church and the importance of their economic support to the church's ongoing activities and to the pastor's salary. Not until after the matter of Holmes's exclusion was settled were the petitioners granted their request. Since they apparently remained within First African, the petitioners' organization probably indicates that they were not among those dissatisfied with Holmes. It does suggest, however, their dissatisfaction with church procedure and the place of women in church polity. Still, the petition was conservative and the women denied any intention to demand full voting rights in church matters. The petition was not taken as a challenge to church authority, as were the actions of the anti-Holmes faction. When brought up for a vote in the June meeting, the women's petition was adopted by a vote of 413 to 16.

The women's petition and the vote in favor of it suggest the tenuous and ambiguous position that women had come to occupy both within First African and within the internal political arena more generally. They participated actively in church meetings but the authority for that participation and the question of limiting women's role resurfaced throughout the late-nineteenth century. In the 1890s the women of First African would again have to demand their rights, this time against challenges to their very presence at church meetings, when a deacon sought to prohibit women from even attending First African business meetings. The women protested and the church responded quickly by requiring the deacon to apologize to the women and assure them that they were welcome at the meetings. The degree of women's participation and decision-making powers, however, remained ambiguous.

In 1901–1902 during another crisis period in First African, a number of men sought to blame the problems on women. John Mitchell, Jr., a member of First African and editor of the *Richmond Planet,* cited the active participation of women ("ladies who knew nothing of the machinery at work or the deep laid plans on foot") and children ("Sunday School scholars from 8 years of age upward") in church affairs, suggesting that they did not comprehend the proceedings and had been easily misled or manipulated by male factions. Deacon J. C. Farley cited women's active participation in church meetings as the problem, reminding the congregation that "it was the rule of the church" that women were only allowed to vote on the pastor but had extended their participation far past that. And the new minister, the Reverend W. T. Johnson, admonished the women, saying that "the brethren could almost fight in the church meeting and when they went out they would shake hands and laugh and talk. But the sisters would talk about it going up Broad St. and everybody would know what they had done." First African women rejected these assessments of their church's problems. A significant number walked out rather than have their participation censured; those who remained re- portedly refused to be silent but continually "talked out in the meeting." Sister Margaret Hewlett later sought out the editor of the *Richmond Planet* to voice her opposition to the men's denunciation of women's roles and to make clear that the women thought the church's problems lay in the male leadership, saying specifi- cally "the deacons were the cause of all the trouble anyway."

In the early 1890s the *Virginia Baptist* publicized its belief that women, in ex- ceeding their proper places in the church by attempting to preach, and in the commu- nity by their "deplorable" efforts to "exercise the right of suffrage," would lose their "womanliness." The complexity of gender relations within the African American community was such that at the same time First African was debating women's atten- dance at church meetings and the *Virginia Baptist* was advocating a severely re- stricted women's role, other women such as Alice Kemp were known throughout the community as the authors of prominent male ministers' sermons and women such as the Reverend Mrs. Carter were establishing their reputations as "soul-stirring" preachers. The *Richmond Planet* reported these women's activities without fanfare, as if they were commonplace. The debate over women's roles also had become com- monplace. The Reverend Anthony Binga, pastor of First Baptist (Manchester), noted the debate in his sermon on Church Polity; Binga supported women teaching Sunday School, participating in prayer-meetings and voting "on any subject pertaining to the interest of the church" including the pastor; but he interpreted the Bible as forbidding women "throwing off that modesty that should adorn her sex, and taking man's place in the pulpit." The subject received community-wide attention in June 1895 when Ebenezer Baptist Church staged a debate between the ministers of Second Baptist (Manchester) and Mount Carmel, judged by other ministers from Fourth Baptist, First African, First Baptist (Manchester) and others on the subject, "Resolved that a woman has every right and privilege that a man has in the christian church."

The debates within First African and other churches over women's roles were part of a series of political struggles within black Richmond in the late-nineteenth and early-twentieth centuries. As formal political gains, initially secured, began to recede and economic promise became less certain and less surely tied to political advancement, the political struggles over relationships between the working-class and the newly emergent middle-class, between men and women, between literate and nonliterate, increasingly became issues among Afro-Richmonders. Briefly examining how the sites of public discourse changed and how discussions regarding qualifications for and nature of individual participation developed suggests the degree to which debates over space and relationships represented important changes in many black Richmonders' assumptions about freedom itself.

The authority of the church in personal and civil matters decreased over the late-nineteenth and early-twentieth centuries. The church quietly acknowledged these changes without directly confronting the issue of its changed authority. The use of civil authorities to resolve the church dispute, especially since individual members continued to face censure if they relied on civil rather than church sanctions in a dispute with another member, suggests the degree to which First African tried to maintain its traditional authority over its members while acknowledging the limitations of its powers. First African turned outside not only itself but also the black community by inviting the intervention of the mayor, police chief and judge. The decreasing authority of the church, however, accompanied a shrinking sphere of influence and activity for the church and the development of secular institutions and structures to take over, compete for, or share functions traditionally connected to the church as institution and structure. The changing church axis suggests important developments in the structures, nature and understandings of community in black Richmond.

After the Reverend James Holmes and the deacons of First African survived the 1880 challenge to their leadership, one of their first actions was to establish a regulation that church business meetings be closed to all but members. They had argued that it was outside agitators who had instigated and sustained the disorder and opposition. While this reflects concerns about internal church business, the closing off of the church was reflected in other central ways which potentially had more far-reaching consequences, and suggests the particularization of interests, concerns and functions of internal community institutions, and the changed nature of internal community politics. Having completed, at considerable expense, their new edifice, First African worried about avoiding damage and excess wear and tear. In November 1882 the church adopted regulations designed to eliminate the crowds of people attending weddings in the church by requiring guest lists and tickets, and to deny entirely the use of the main auditorium with the largest capacity for "programmes, closing of public schools, political meetings or feasts." In February 1883 when the Acme Lyceum requested use of the main auditorium for a lecture by Frederick Douglass, the church, following its new regulations, refused to grant the request, although it did offer as substitute the use of its smaller lecture room. That same year it denied the use of the church for the Colored High and Normal closing. The paucity of facilities available to black Richmonders meant that these activities now had to be held in much smaller facilities and the possibilities for the large mass meetings which First African had previously hosted were now reduced. Political meetings and other activities moved to other, smaller church sites or to some of the new halls being erected by some of the societies and businessmen. The latter, however, were more expensive to obtain since their rental was a major source of revenue for the group or individual owner; it also often particularized the meeting or occasion to a specific segment of the community. Without the large facility of First African, graduations and school closings could no longer be the traditional community-wide mass celebrations. Denied the use of First African and barred from the Richmond Theatre where the white high school students had their graduation, the 1883 Colored High and Normal graduation class held their exercises in a small classroom where very few could attend.

First African did not initiate and was not singly responsible for the changing nature of Republican Party participation, but its actions reinforced the narrower sense of party politics that white Republicans had already tried to enforce. Disturbed at black influence over Republican meetings, beginning in 1870 white Republican officials had taken steps to limit popular participation and influence in party deliberations. First they moved the party conventions from First African to the United States courtroom, a facility which held many fewer people and was removed from the black community; then they closed the gallery, thus allowing none but official delegates to attend and participate. In such a setting they were able to adopt a more conservative platform. Black Republicans had continued, however, to hold mass meetings, often when dissatisfied with the official Republican deliberations. When they were dissatisfied with Republican nominees for municipal office that came from the 1870 closed party convention, for example, black Republicans agreed to convene their own sessions and make their own nominations.

In increasingly delimiting the church's use, distinguishing more clearly between sacred and secular activities as when it began to disallow certain kinds of entertainments in its facilities or on its behalf, and attempting to reserve the church for what was now designated as the "sacred," First African contributed to the increasing segmentation of black Richmond. With the loss of the largest capacity structure some black Richmonders recognized the need to reestablish a community space. Edward A. Randolph, founder and first editor of the *Richmond Planet,* used Acme Literary Association meetings to argue regularly throughout 1883 and 1884 for the construction of a hall, a public meeting place within the community. His call was reinforced when the Choral Association was denied use of the Richmond Theatre and had to have its production in a small mutual benefit society hall, an inadequate facility for such a production. The construction of a large auditorium on the top floor of the Grand Fountain, United Order of True Reformers' bank and office building when it opened in 1890 was an effort to provide that space. It could hold larger gatherings than the other halls and most churches but still had only a small percentage of the seating capacity of First African. A mass meeting on the scale common in the 1860s and 1870s could be held only outside the community and the facilities for such were often closed to African Americans.

As political meetings moved to private halls rather than church buildings, they became less mass meetings not only in the numerical sense; they also became more gatherings of an exclusive group of party regulars. This signaled not only a change in the role of the church but also a change in the nature of politics in black Richmond. The emerging format gave business and professional men, especially, greater control over the formal political process. First African's prohibitions against mass meetings, school closings, and other programs did not last long; the need and desire of members and other Afro-Richmonders for a space which could truly contain a community-wide activity eventually led members to ignore their prohibition. But instituting the prohibition had not only significantly affected community activities in the early 1880s; it also meant that, even after strict enforcement was curtailed, decisions about using the church for graduation exercises, political meetings and other activities were now subjects of debate. Afro-Richmonders could no longer assume the church as a community meeting place; instead they had to argue such. The church remained an important community institution, but it increasingly shared power with both civil authorities and other community institutions such as mutual benefit and fraternal societies.

The efforts by white Republican officials to limit popular decision-making and the decreased accessibility of First African as a community-wide meeting place affected a politics which had been based in mass participation. Mass meetings were still held throughout the late-nineteenth century, but they were now less regular. These changes were exacerbated by the struggle to retain the vote and office-holding and the necessity, therefore, to counter various tactics of both white Republicans and Democrats. The fraudulent tactics employed to eliminate black voters, for example, led some black Republicans, like John Mitchell, who continued to argue against literacy qualifications for voting, in the 1890s to encourage nonliterate black men to abstain from voting. Difficulty with many of the election officials' questions and with the ballots could not only delay the line but also the nonliterate voter's rights and/or ballot would more likely be challenged. Mitchell thought it important to get those least likely to be challenged or disqualified, and most capable of correctly marking the ballots, through the lines first before polls closed on them. While Mitchell argued for a temporary change in practice—not perspective—regarding the right of all to vote, his and other prominent black Republicans' prioritizing of the literate voter significantly changed the makeup of the presumed electorate.

As the divisions between black and white Republicans became deeper in the 1890s, Mitchell and other black Republicans began to hold small Republican caucuses in selected homes, in essence attempting to control ward conventions by predetermining nominees and issues. The ward conventions themselves were often held in halls rather than the larger churches. The organization in 1898 of a Central Republican League which would oversee black Republican activities through sub-Leagues in all the city's wards reinforced the narrowing party politics framework. Republican party decision-making was now more clearly limited to Party regulars; the mass of black voters and other election activists were expected to support these channels of decision-making. These changes, consistent with democratic politics and republican representative government as practiced in late-nineteenth century United States, served to limit the power and influence of most black Richmonders in the electoral arena. If many black men abandoned electoral politics even before formal disfranchisement, it was in large measure due to the effectiveness of the extra-legal disfranchisement efforts of white men. The exclusion from real decision-making power within the Republican Party and, in this respect within the community, was also decisive.

The increasingly limited notion of political decision-makers which these changes encouraged is also evident in other ways. In 1896 during a factional dispute among black Republicans, John Mitchell challenged the decisions made in one meeting by noting that a substantial portion of those attending and participating were not even "legal voters," that is they were women. Although he espoused feminine dress and comportment, Mitchell supported women's rights and championed Dr. Sarah G. Jones's success as a physician as evidence of women's equality. He also endorsed women's suffrage while advising black women to understand the racism of the white women's suffrage movement and not to align themselves with it. Despite these personal convictions, Mitchell could dismiss or minimize opposing factions by a reference to the participation of women, suggesting the ways in which the meanings and understanding of politics, of appropriate political actors and even of the ownership of the franchise had changed in the late-nineteenth century.

Questions of qualifications for participation in the external political arena and internal community institutions were now frequent. During the conflictual 1901 business meeting at First African, for example, John Mitchell, Jr., questioned his opponents' right to participate even though they were all church members by pointing out their unfamiliarity with parliamentary procedure or their inelegant ways of speaking. The women, who were the targets of much of Mitchell's challenge, refused to accept these as criteria for their participation and even denigrated what he put forth as his formal qualifications by talking out when he got up to speak, saying derisively, "Don't he look pretty." Questions of formal education had already affected the congregation in fundamental ways, most obviously in the late-nineteenth century debate over song, a debate which represented a significant change in the basis of collective consciousness.

The antiphonal nature of the traditional church service at First African and many black churches reinforced a sense of community. The services included spontaneous verbal and nonverbal interaction between minister and prayer, speaker and congregation thus allowing for the active participation of everyone in the worship service. It was this cultural discourse that was carried over into the political meetings. One important element that bound the congregation together was song; as Lawrence Levine has noted, through their collective song churchgoers "meld[ed] individual consciousness into the group consciousness." However, the practice of lining hymns* which was basic to collective song was one which white visitors often referred to when they described what they perceived as the unrefined black church services. Some black churchgoers saw the elimination of this practice as part of the work of uplifting the religious style and uplifting the race. But with the elimination of this practice, those unable to read and follow the lyrics in a song book were now unable to participate, to be fully a part of the community, the collective. It was the equivalent of being deprived of a voice, all the more significant in an oral culture. Daniel Webster Davis, a member of First African and pastor of Second Baptist (Manchester) as well as public school teacher, suggested such in his poem, "De Linin' Ub De Hymns":

---

*The practice of "lining-out" a hymn involved having a song leader read one or two lines of a song's lyrics before the congregation sang them. This was to allow participation in the service by those who could not read.

Dar's a mighty row in Zion, an' de debbil's gittin'
    high,
. . . .
'Twuz 'bout a berry leetle thing–de linin' ub a
    hymn.
De young folks say 'tain't stylish to lin' um out
    no mo';
Dat dey's got edikashun, an' dey wants us all to
    know
Dey likes to hab dar singin'-books a-holin' fore dar
    eyes,
An' sing de hymns right straight along 'to man-
    shuns in de skies.'
. . . .
An' ef de ol' folks will kumplain 'cause dey is ol'
    an' blin',
An' slabry's chain don' kep' dem back frum larnin'
    how to read—
Dat dey mus' take a corner seat, an' let de young
    folks lead.
. . . .
We don' edikate our boys an' gals, an' would do
    de same again;
. . . .
De sarmon's highfalutin', an' de church am mighty
    fin';
. . . .
De ol'-time groans an' shouts an' moans am passin'
    out ub sight—
Edikashun changed all dat, an' we belebe it right,
We should serb God wid 'telligence; fur dis one
    thing I plead:
Jes' lebe a leetle place in church fur dem ez kin not
    read.

The debates about women's roles in the church and in the more formal political arenas, like the debate over lining the hymns, were part of widespread discussions about the nature of community, of participation and of freedom.

The proliferation of scholarly works centered on the flowering of black women's political activity in the late-nineteenth and early-twentieth centuries has perhaps left the impression that this was the inaugural moment or even height of black women's participation in politics. Overt or not, the suggestion seems to be that black women came to political prominence as (because) black men lost political power. In much of this scholarship the reasons for black women's "emergence" are usually tied to external factors. For example, the development of black women's clubs in the late-nineteenth century and their important roles in the political struggles of the twentieth century most often have been seen by historians as the result of the increasing development of such entities in the larger society and as reaction to vitriolic attacks on the morality of black women. Such a perspective explains this important political force solely in terms of external dynamics, but external factors alone cannot account for this development. The internal political arena, which in the immediate post–Civil War era was grounded in the notion of a collective voice which gave men, women and children a platform and allowed them all participation, came increasingly in the late-nineteenth century to be shaped by a narrowing notion of politics and appropriate political behavior.

While mass meetings continued to be held, the more regular forums for political discussions were literary societies, ward meetings, mutual benefit society and fraternal society meetings, women's clubs, labor organizations, newspapers, streetcorners, kitchens, washtubs and saloons. In the development of literary societies as a primary venue for public discussion, one can see the class and gender assumptions that by the turn-of-the-century came to be central to the political organization of black Richmond. While some, as the Langston Literary Association, had male members only, most of the literary societies founded in the 1880s and 1890s had middle-class and working-class men and women members. Despite the inclusive nature of the membership and often of the officers, the form of discussion which developed privileged middle-class males. Unlike mass meetings where many people might take the floor in planned and unplanned expositions and attendees might freely interrupt or talk back to speakers, thus allowing and building mass participation, literary forums announced discussion topics in advance; charged individual members, apparently almost always male, to prepare a paper on the subject; and designated specific, also male, members to reply.

The discussions that then ensued were open to all present but the structure privileged those familiar with the conventions of formal debate. Women, who served as officers and attended in large numbers, may have joined in the discussion but their official roles were designated as the cultural arm of the forum—reading poetry, singing songs, often with political content appropriate to the occasion. The questions under consideration at the meetings often betrayed the class bias of the forum. Even when the discussions centered on some aspect of working-class life and behavior, the conversation was conducted by middle-class men. The purpose of the forums, as articulated by the Acme Literary Society, suggested the passive observer/learner position that most were expected to take: to hold "discussions, lectures, and to consider questions of vital importance to our people, so that the masses of them may be drawn out to be entertained, enlightened, and instructed thereby. Given the exclusionary nature of the discussion in these literary forums, even though welcoming a wide audience, it is understandable that far more working-class black men and women saw the Knights of Labor as their principal political vehicle in the late 1880s.

In the changing circumstances of the late-nineteenth century, working-class men and women and middle-class women were increasingly disfranchised within the black community, just as middle-class black men were increasingly disfranchised in the larger society. Men and women, working-class and middle-class, at the turn-of-the-century were struggling to move back to a political authority they once had—internally and externally. As they did so they each often justified such authority along distinctively gendered and class-based lines.

African American men countered the image of themselves as uncivilized, beastly rapists—an image white southerners used to justify disfranchisement, segregation and violence—with efforts to demonstrate their own manhood and to define white males as uncivilized and savage. While white Richmonders told stories of black barbarity, John Mitchell, Jr., inverted the tale. The *Richmond Planet*, for example, repeatedly focused on the sexual perversions of white men with cases of rape and incest and spoke of white men in terms designed to suggest their barbarism: "Southern white folks have gone to roasting Negroes, we presume the next step will be to eat them." In the process of unmanning white males, however, Mitchell and others developed a narrative of endangered black women. Urban areas, once sites of opportunity for women, became sexually dangerous places for the unprotected female, easy prey to deceitful and barbarous white males. Black men's political rights were essential so that they could do as men should—protect their communities, homes, families, women. The focus on manhood could, initially, be the venue for discussing domestic violence as well. For example, the Reverend Anthony Binga, sermonizing against physical abuse of one's wife drew on the discourse of manhood: "I have never seen a man whip his wife. I mean a *man*. Everyone who wears a hat or a coat is not a *man*. I mean a *man*." And the members of First African took as a serious issue of concern the case of a husband who had infected his wife with syphilis. Concurrent with the narrative of sexual danger in the city and the larger society was an implied corollary narrative of protection within one's own community. Thus the discourse on manhood could keep the concern with violence against women in the public discussion while at the same time setting the stage for issues of domestic abuse and other forms of intraracial violence, which could be evidence of the uncivility of black men, to be silenced as politically dangerous.

In drawing on the new narrative of endangered women, middle-class black women, increasingly disfranchised by the connections between manhood and citizenship in the new political discourse, turned the focus from themselves and on to the working class, enabling middle-class women to project themselves as the protectors of their less fortunate sisters. In this manner they reinserted themselves into a public political role. Autonomous women's organizations, such as the Richmond Women's League (later the Richmond Mothers' Club) or women's divisions within other organizations such as the Standing Committee on Domestic Economy of the Hampton Negro Conference, developed to serve these functions. These associations promulgated class-specific ideas of respectability, in part justifying their public role through the need to impart such protective measures to working-class women. Specific constructions of womanhood, as manhood, thus became central to the arguments for political rights. Through discussions of manhood and womanhood, middle-class men and women constructed themselves as respectable and entitled, and sought to use such constructions to throw a mantle of protection over their working-class brothers and sisters. By increasingly claiming sexual violence as a women's issue, middle-class black women claimed a political/public space for themselves but they also contributed to an emerging tendency to divert issues of sexual violence to a lesser plane and to see them as the specific interest of women, not bound up in the general concerns and struggle for freedom. This set the stage for the masculine conception of liberation struggle which would emerge in the twentieth century.

Collective History/Collective Memory

In July 1895 three black women—Mary Abernathy, Pokey Barnes and her mother, Mary Barnes—were convicted in Lunenberg County, Virginia, of murdering a white woman. When the women were moved to the state penitentiary in Richmond their case became a cause célèbre in the black community there. For over a year black men and women in Richmond struggled to keep the Lunenberg women from being hung or returned to Lunenberg County for a retrial, fearing that a return to Lunenberg would mean death, the women lynched at the hands of an angry white mob. The community succeeded and the three women were eventually released.

The organization of black Richmonders in defense of these women partly illustrates the increasingly gendered nature of internal community politics. Men and women were portrayed as having decidedly different roles in the defense; one avenue of defense was to draw on ideas of motherhood in defending these three women; and the Lunenberg women's release called forth very particular discussions of respectability and womanhood. John Mitchell, Jr., portrayed himself as the militant defender of the women. Women, led by schoolteacher Rosa Dixon Bowser, organized the Richmond Women's League for the purposes of raising funds for the women's defense, visiting them in jail and supporting their husbands and families. Through her column in the *Woman's Era* and her participation in the National Federation of Afro-American Women, Bowser, as did Mitchell, brought the case to national attention. The front page stories in Mitchell's *Planet* emphasized the Lunenberg women as mothers, especially reporting on Mary Abernathy's pregnancy and the birth of her child in her jail cell. While the pictures and stories during the fourteen-month struggle for their release portrayed the women as simply clad, barefoot, farm women the announcement of Pokey Barnes's final victory was accompanied by a photograph of her now transformed into a true Victorian woman with elegant balloon-sleeved dress, a symbol of respectable womanhood. Later descriptions of Barnes, on speaking engagements, emphasized her dress: "a neat fitting, changeable silk gown and . . . a black felt hat, trimmed with black velvet and ostrich plumes." Mitchell emphasized the importance of this transformation: "The picture showing what Pokey Barnes looked like when brought to Richmond the first time and what she appears to-day will be a startling revelation to the public and will fill with amazement the conservative people everywhere when they realize what a terrible blunder the execution of this young woman would have been." He thus suggested that it was her ability to be a respectable woman (signified superficially by a class-based standard of dress) which was the justification for his and others' protection of her.

But the year-long discussion of these women's fates (the front page of nearly every issue of the *Richmond Planet* from July 1895 through early fall 1896 was devoted to these cases and included pictures of the women and sketches of their cabins) occurred alongside stories about lynchings or near lynchings of black men. Importantly, therefore, when black Richmonders spoke of lynching in the late-nineteenth century, they had no reason to assume the victim as male. When a freed Pokey Barnes rode as "mascot" in the 1896 Jackson Ward election rally parade, the idea of Mitchell and other black men as defenders was reinforced. But also affirmed was the underlying understanding that violence, including state repression, was a real threat to African American women as much as men. This meant that the reconstruction of clearly delineated notions of womanhood and manhood as the basis for political activism remained relatively ambiguous in late-nineteenth century black Richmond. But issues of class and gender were increasingly evident, as when Pokey Barnes and Mitchell accepted public speaking engagements—ones in which she was clearly expected to be the silent symbol of oppression and he the vocal proponent of resistance. Barnes, countering that assumption, set forth her own understandings of her role and qualifications, contradicting the class and gender assumptions of Mitchell and of those who invited them: "she said that she was not an educated lecturer and did not have any D.D.'s or M.D.'s to her name, but she was simply Pokey Barnes, c.s. (common sense)." Her two-hour lecture on her ordeal, while giving credit to Mitchell, established herself as not only victim but also heroine.

The rescue of the Lunenberg women by black Richmonders brought women's struggles to the fore of black rights and reaffirmed violence against women as part of their collective history and struggle. At the same time black Richmonders struggled to create a new category of womanhood that would be respected and protected, and of middle-class womanhood and manhood that could protect. The plight of the Lunenberg women reaffirmed the collective history of black men and women at the same time as it invigorated increasingly distinct political vehicles for middle-class black men and women. . . .

The Politics of Labor

TERA W. HUNTER

Washerwomen in Atlanta organized a massive strike in the summer of 1881. Over the course of a two week period in July they summoned 3000 supporters through the neighborhood networks they had been building since emancipation. The strike articulated economic as well as political grievances: the women demanded higher fees for their services and fought to maintain the distinctive autonomy of their trade. When city officials threatened the "washing amazons" with the possibility of levying an exorbitant tax on each individual member of the Washing Society (the group responsible for the strike), the women issued a warning of their own: "We, the members of our society, are determined to stand our pledge . . . we mean business this week or no washing."

Southern household workers, who are often stereotyped as passive victims of racial, sexual, and class oppression, displayed a profound sense of political consciousness through the organization of this strike. Moreover, they initiated it at the dawn of the New South movement, an effort by ambitious businessmen to change the course and fortunes of regional economic development. In order to promote the goals of industrial capitalism and to attract northern capital below the Mason-Dixon Line, proponents of the New South heralded an image of all Southern workers as artless by nature and indifferent to class struggle. But these working-class women stridently scorned this agenda.

The protest in Atlanta was not unique in the post-slavery era. Washerwomen in Jackson, MS, struck in 1866. And on the heels of the Great Strike of 1877, laundresses and other household workers in Galveston stopped work as well. Both of these boycotts articulated goals for a living wage and autonomy, yet neither

Tera W. Hunter, "Domination and Resistance: The Politics of Wage Household Labor in New South Atlanta," *Labor History*, 34, no. 2–3 (Spring/Summer 1993), 205–220. Reprinted by permission from Taylor & Francis, Ltd., P. O. Box 25, Abington, Oxfordshire OX14 3UE, United Kingdom matched the proportions and the affront the Atlanta women posed to the emergent New South ideology. The Atlanta strike was unusual; domestic workers rarely organized strikes. But they did find a multitude of other ways to oppose oppression, usually in the form of surreptitious and quotidian resistance.

Household workers often resorted to covert tactics of resistance because they were frequently the only options available within a system of severe constraints. The magnitude of seemingly unassuming gestures looms large if we realize that workers sometimes transformed them into collective dissent or used them as building blocks for the occasional large-scale outburst. Nonetheless, it is a testament to the potency of the forces dominating women workers in the South that defiance would assume this form and that these forces were powerful enough to cover up the expression of opposition. The importance of strikes such as that by the Atlanta washerwomen in part is that they have generated a precious few documents straight from the mouths of working-class women in the form of letters and petitions to municipal officials and reports from journalists who witnessed mass meetings and rallies. In the main little direct testimony exists from household workers about their activities and the motivations that prompted them. But there is another way to scout out working-class women's discontent and dissent. Evidence from employers and their proxies in public authority positions unwittingly expose the resilience and creativity of African-American household workers' efforts to counter domination.

This article is an effort to understand resistance by looking at the character of domination and the attempts to counter it from Reconstruction to World War I. Domination is defined here as the process of exercising power over the dispossessed by whatever means necessary, but without overt conflict where possible. Conversely, resistance is defined as any act, individual or collective, symbolic or literal, intended by subordinates to deny claims, to refuse compliance with impositions made by superordinates, or to advance claims of their own. This essay outlines examples of African-American women domestics combatting injustice, and it analyzes the responses of employers and public officials. As household workers struggled to negate conditions of abject servitude, their employers worked even harder to repress and contain these workers. The subsequent contests reveal how structures of inequality were reproduced and challenged in daily interactions; their public airing suggest that wage household labor had broader social and political implications beyond its significance to private homes. Atlanta is a fitting place to begin exploring the larger ramifications of wage household labor. Young, white, upwardly mobile businessmen in the years after the Civil War began cultivating an image of the city as the vanguard of a "New South." As the ideas of these urban boosters were instituted, it became all too clear that "modernization" of the social, political, and economic order included racial segregation and political disfranchisement. From this perspective, Atlanta did not simply embody the contradictions of life under Jim Crow, the conscious leadership role it assumed in the region also made it instrumental in creating and perpetuating them.

This self-proclaimed model of the New South held the distinction of employing one of the highest per capita numbers of domestic workers in the nation during the period of this study. Such a repute was not coincidental to the seeming contradiction between the goals of modernization and the advocacy of a retrogressive system such as segregation. One might expect that a modernizing economy would shirk old fashioned manual household labor in favor of up to date mechanized and commercial production. Yet manual household work furthered the goals of the advocates of the New South in restricting black workers' social and economic opportunities. African-American women who migrated to Atlanta following Emancipation were segregated into household labor. Virtually no other options were available to them, yet wage work was essential to the sustenance of their livelihoods from childhood to death. And in Atlanta, as in other Southern cities, the disproportionate sex ratio among blacks made wage work all the more imperative for women, especially for single, divorced, or widowed mothers saddled with the sole responsibility for taking care of their families. And the low wages paid to black men meant that even married women could rarely escape outside employment and worked in far greater numbers than their white counterparts.

Yet despite this occupational confinement, black women managed to assert some preferences for the particular kind of domestic labor they performed. Single and younger women accepted positions as general maids or child-nurses more often, for example, while married women usually chose positions as laundresses. Washerwomen represented the largest single category of waged household workers in Atlanta, and by 1900 their total numbers exceeded all other domestics combined. Laundresses picked up loads of dirty clothes from their patrons on Monday; washed, dried, and ironed throughout the week; and returned the finished garments on Saturday. This labor process encumbered their already cramped living quarters with the accoutrements of the trade, but it exempted workers from employer supervision, yielded a day "off," allowed workers to care for their children and to perform other duties intermittently, incorporated family members into the work routine, and facilitated communal work among adult women.

Regardless of the specific domestic job black women chose, the majority insisted on living in their own homes rather than with their employers. Elsewhere in the country, where immigrant European and native-born white women were more numerous, live-in domestic work predominated; but for recently freed slaves, living with their own families was foremost to approximating independence. Above all, living on their own meant for the former slaves breaking the physical chains of bondage and reestablishing the kinship ties scattered and torn asunder by the caprice of fluctuating fortunes or the ill will of owners. It also meant preventing employers from exercising unmitigated control over their entire lives. Some employers accepted a live-out arrangement; perhaps, because it coincided with their own ambivalence about continuing the intimacy that prevailed between master and slaves. But many employers resented the loss of control that resulted.

Black women's priorities in the post–Civil War years demonstrated that economic motivations alone did not influence their decisions about wage labor. They sought instead to balance wage-earning activities with other needs and obligations. Consequently they moved in and out of the labor market as circumstances in their personal lives demanded and switched jobs frequently. Domestic workers quit in order to buy time off for a variety of reasons; among them participation in special functions, such as religious revivals, or taking care of family members who became ill. The workers also resorted to quitting to make clear their discontent over unfair practices when other efforts to obtain satisfactory redress failed. Quitting did not necessarily guarantee a better situation elsewhere (and often did not), but it

reinforced workers' desire for self-determination and deprived employers of the ascendancy to which they were accustomed as slaveholders.

Consequently, quitting made it difficult for employers to find "good" servants
and, especially, to keep them—the single most oft-repeated complaint from Reconstruction onward. Quitting violated employers' expectations of the ideal worker: one
who conformed to relentless hours of labor, made herself available at beck and call,
and showed devoted loyalty throughout her entire life. In 1866, as the clamor among
employers demanding relief quickly rose to a high pitch, the Atlanta City Council
interceded on their behalf by passing a law to nullify free labor's most fundamental
principle. To obstruct the liberties essential to authentic independence, to hinder the
ease and frequency of workers changing jobs, the law required employers of domestics to obtain recommendations from the previous employer before hiring them.

The 1866 law is instructive of the general crisis of free labor in the South following the Civil War. As African-Americans showed a marked determination to
make their new status live up to their needs and expectations, planters and urban
employers rejected the ideals of the free labor system that conflicted with the safe-
keeping of white supremacy. In 1865, during the brief reign of Presidential Reconstruction under Andrew Johnson, Democrats in state legislatures in the South
instituted the Black Codes, laws designed, among other things, to diminish blacks'
rights in labor contracts. The 1866 law was strongly reminiscent of this mechanism
and its passage signaled the increasing role of the state in relationships formerly
governed entirely by individual masters. Black women workers would still be vulnerable to arbitrary personal power although its exercise would be tempered by the
13th Amendment. Nonetheless employers would try to coerce workers with the aid
of the state. The enactment of the law in 1866 provided concrete evidence that
household workers' refusals to acquiesce to unrelenting physical exertion forced
employers to procure outside intervention.

Employers' augmentation of their authority with municipal power, however,
proved ineffective in part because of their ambivalent attitude towards the law.
Frustrated employers were often willing to employ almost any black woman in
their ever illusive search for individuals whose personal characteristics and occupational behavior coincided with the traits of "good" servants. Despite the employers'
dissatisfaction with the way the system worked, and in defiance of the law passed
for their own protection, they preferred to hire workers without the requisite nod
from former bosses rather than face the unthinkable possibility of no servants at all.

Black women's active opposition to the law also helped to defeat it as they continued to quit work at will. Quitting was an effective strategy of resistance precisely
because it could not be quelled outside a system of bound labor. Though some
women workers may have openly confronted their employer before departing, quitting as a tactic thrived because it did not require such direct antagonism. Workers
who had the advantage of living in their own homes could easily make up excuses
for leaving, or leave without notice at all—permitting small and fleeting victories for
individuals to accumulate into bigger results as domestics throughout Atlanta and
the urban South repeated these actions over and over again. The instability created in
the labor market strengthened the bargaining position of domestic workers since
employers persisted in thinking of the pool as scarce, though, in absolute numbers,
the supply of domestic workers available to the employing population in Atlanta

was virtually endless. The incongruence between the perception of a dearth and the reality of an abundance suggests that black women's self-assertion had indeed created a shortage of workers with the attributes employers preferred.

Quitting and other forms of everyday struggle continued for many decades long after Reconstruction. In 1912 an Atlanta mayoral candidate offered an extreme, if novel, solution to the menacing problem of restraining domestic workers' self-assertions. George Brown, a physician, supported a public health reform that encompassed the concerns of white employers. The candidate promised pure drinking water, free bathing facilities, improved sanitary provisions at railroad stations, and a (white) citizenry protected from exposure to contagious germs. The latter proposal had direct implications for black domestics whom employers and health officials accused of spreading tuberculosis through the food they cooked, the houses they cleaned, and the clothes they washed. Laundry workers were the most vociferously attacked objects of scorn. The freedom they enjoyed from direct white supervision permitted them to operate more as contractors than as typical wage workers, which made them vulnerable to scrutiny of their labor and personal lives.

Brown and like-minded individuals heightened the fear that domestic workers were the primary emissaries of physical contagions and impressed upon white minds that black women were also the harbingers of social disease as well. The attribution of pestilence to domestics unveils deeper frictions that lay bare a central paradox about Jim Crow, which by then was firmly in place. The social and political geography of Atlanta bolstered the exploitation and containment of black bodies and their spatial separation from upper-class whites. African-Americans were segregated in the worst areas of the city and had the least access to the municipal resources essential to good health; services such as street pavings, proper waste disposal, and potable water were provided to Atlantans on the basis of both racial and class privileges. By the late 19th century upper-class whites in large numbers had moved out to ostentatious suburbs and had begun to escape regular interaction with the unattractive sites that the inequitable distribution of city resources typically bred. Yet these white suburbanites continued to hire black household workers from such malodorous neighborhoods. White anxieties about the contaminating touch of black women reflected the ambivalence of a tension between revulsion and attraction to the worker who performed the most intimate labor, taking care, for example, of children.

Brown proposed to wipe out the public health problem and to diminish the ubiquitous "servant problem" in one sweeping measure. He proposed the creation of a city-run servant bureau invested with broad discretionary judiciary powers that would require domestics to submit to rigorous physical examination and to offer detailed personal and employment histories before obtaining prerequisite licenses for work. Brown sought to reinstitute "absolute control" of servants and to relieve white fears by criminalizing presumed carriers of disease; he promised to punish domestics who impeded efforts to keep the scourge away from the door steps of their white bosses.

And the mayoral hopeful went further: he called for disciplinary measures to be used against workers who exercised the conventional liberties of wage work. Quitting for reasons employers did not consider "just" or displaying other forms of recalcitrance would constitute sufficient grounds for arrest, fines, incarceration, or labor on the chain gang. As a candidate outside the inner circle of New South politicos, Brown hardly had a chance to win the election, but his campaign is noteworthy for its dissemination of pejorative images of domestics that further legitimized their subordination as a source of cheap labor.

The Brown campaign is also suggestive about the changing constitution of domination in response to household workers' agency. The prominence of the disease issue, even beyond the mayoral campaign, showed signs of a shift in the "servant problem" discourse from an emphasis on so-called inherent deficiencies of black women, such as laziness and the lack of a proper work ethic, to a more powerful critique of domestic workers as the bearers of deadly organisms. Worker mobility and other acts of defiance undoubtedly took their toll on employers' patience, but the prospects of contracting tuberculosis or other communicable diseases provided new and greater rationalizations for establishing comprehensive mechanisms of control over black females. The ostensible concern with public health, however, falters as an adequate explanation for these exacerbated prejudices, if we consider that proposals like Brown's were based on the faulty assumption that disease traveled solely on one-way tickets from blacks to whites. The servant bureau of Brown's imagination would not have alleviated the propagation of germs, but it would have stripped household workers of important rights. Carried to their logical conclusion, the punitive measures could have conveniently led to a convict labor system for domestic workers, forcing them to work at the behest of employers without compensation and under the threat of physical brutality.

Several of the issues raised in George Brown's run for mayor reverberated in another infamous campaign. Joseph M. Brown, son of the former Confederate governor and unrelated to George, ran for the U.S. Senate against the incumbent Hoke Smith in 1914. The two Brown men shared the view that domestic workers' defiance posed an ample threat to social stability in the New South that justified state intervention. Both men berated the large numbers of household workers who participated in benevolent and mutual aid associations, also known as secret societies, and both believed that it was imperative to dismantle the workers' capacity to bolster clandestine resistance through such institutions.

From Reconstruction onward, black women led and joined secret societies to pool their meager resources to aid the sick, orphaned, widowed, or unemployed, and to create opportunities for personal enrichment as well as broader race advancement. The number of such organizations with explicit labor-related goals were few, but groups that brought working-class women together for other expressed purposes were known to transform themselves on the spur of the moment and operate as quasi-trade unions when necessary.

George Brown had entreated white men to put him in the mayor's seat so that he could direct the cleansing mission of his servant bureau toward eradicating these organizations that debilitated "helpless" white housewives. "Little Joe" Brown followed suit in his bid for the Senate two years later by rebuking African-American domestics for devising "blacklists" in secret societies that deprived errant employers. This tactic was especially unnerving to him (and others) because it shrouded a collective act by relying on individuals to quietly refuse to work, leaving behind perplexed housewives with the sudden misfortune of not being able to find willing workers. Joe Brown preyed on white Southern fears to dramatize the urgent need to eliminate these quasi-union activities and he tried to race-bait his opponent Hoke Smith, no stranger to this ploy himself. Brown accused the black mutual aid groups of conspiring with white labor unions in an interracial syndicate, a charge which white labor leaders quickly rebutted. Brown forewarned the voters against choosing Smith and of the consequences of failing to elect him and neglecting to outlaw the institutional basis of African-American women's dissent: "Every white lady in whose home negro servants are hired then becomes subservient to these negroes," he stated. Brown lost the Senate race, yet his devotion to assailing household workers' resistance had unintended consequences, it acknowledged its effect.

Schemes designed to thwart household workers' agency reached a peak as the Great Migration intensified during World War I. In May 1918, Enoch Crowder, the Selective Service Director, issued a "work or fight" order aimed at drafting unemployed men into the armed forces. The order stressed the nation's need for labor's cooperation in contributing to the war effort through steady gainful work or military service. Trade unions immediately protested the potential abuses that could result from such a directive, having heard of abuses perpetrated against striking British workers under a similar law. Newton D. Baker, the Secretary of War, made assurances to the contrary, but striking machinists in Bridgeport, CT, were threatened with Crowder's order. Southern legislatures and city councils deliberately designed their own "work or fight" laws to break the will of black workers in order to maintain white supremacy in a time of rapid change and uncertainty. Similar to the logic used by white Progressives in anti-vagrancy campaigns during the same period, "work or fight" laws were rationalized as a solution to alleged crime and moral depravity that resulted when blacks filled all or part of their day with pursuits other than gainful work. Atlanta had one of the highest per capita arrest records in the country in the early 20th century, largely because of vagrancy and other misdemeanor convictions; the individuals apprehended were often gainfully employed and always disproportionately black. The relative scarcity of labor produced by the war prompted Southern lawmakers to manipulate Crowder's order and use it to clamp down on African-Americans at the very moment when the war opened new opportunities for employment and increased their bargaining positions in existing jobs.

White Southerners abandoned the original intention of the Federal measure to fill the army with able-bodied men by making the conscription of *women* central to its provisions. As opportunities for black women expanded in the sewing trades, commercial laundries, and less rapidly, small manufacturing plants, the number available for household work declined, giving an edge to those who remained in negotiating for better terms. Employers of domestics resented this new mobility and sought to contain it by using "work or fight" laws to punish black women who vacated traditional jobs.

Individuals arrested under the laws' provisions included black housewives, defined as "idle" and unproductive, and other self-employed black women such as hairdressers. A group of self-described "friends" of the Negro race in Macon, GA, iterated some of the assumptions behind such enforcement. Black women should not withdraw from wage work in general and household labor in particular, no matter what the circumstances; the Macon group argued that patriotic duty required that black women not "sit at home and hold their hands, refusing to do the labor for which they are specially trained and otherwise adapted." Black women's domestic work was essential to the war effort, insisted the Macon group, because it exempted white women "from the routine of housework in order that they may do the work which negro women cannot do." In Atlanta, two 17-year-old girls experienced the encroachment of this notion of patriotism first-hand. "You can not make us work," Nellie Atkins and Ruth Warf protested upon arrest and proceeded to break windows to vent their anger at the injustice, which doubled the sentence to 60 days each in the prison laundry. Warf and Atkins were relatively fortunate, however; other women were tarred and feathered and violently attacked by vigilantes.

African-Americans in Atlanta took the lead in organizing what eventually became a regional assault against racist and sexist implementation of "work or fight" laws. They enlisted the national office of the NAACP, which in turn launched an investigation and supported local chapters in the South in order to stop the passage of the abusive laws. The NAACP discovered that employers not only used the laws to conscript non-domestics; the employers also used the laws against employed household workers who demanded higher wages to meet the rising costs of living, organized protests, quit work because of unfair treatment, or took time out for other activities. Over a half-century after the Jackson washerwomen's strike, for example, all the household workers in that city organized and established a six-day work week, with Sundays off. But employers launched a counter-offensive, forcing the workers to return to an unforgiving seven-day schedule or face prosecution.

Blacks in Atlanta successfully lobbied Governor Hugh Dorsey to veto discriminatory "work or fight" legislation passed by the Georgia House and Senate. Fearing the intensification of the Great Migration and the loss of black laborers, Dorsey responded to their demands. The Atlanta branch of the NAACP similarly appealed to the city council and managed to preempt legislation at the local level, and eliminated de jure discrimination through a war-time measure. Police and vigilantes, however, found other methods of abusing black women with impunity.

The blatantly unjust harassment of household workers during World War I revealed another variation on a familiar theme—the New South's unabashed disdain for the privileges of free labor. Yet the physical brutality and legal coercion rationalized by state "work or fight" laws also signalled the breakdown of the authority of the elite in controlling a work force whose hallmark was supposedly servility. Like similar proposals to regulate domestic workers in previous years, "work or fight" laws uncovered an effort by employers to eliminate black women's ongoing resistance. The abusive legislation also uncloaked the impact of the Great Migration. As African-Americans left the South en masse to pursue freedom in Northern industrial towns, white Southern employers struggled to maintain power over those who stayed.

"Work or fight" laws and the other efforts to control domestic workers are interesting in part because they evidence struggle and contestation that till now had been obscured. While in many of the instances noted above, the household workers' collective consciousness may have been out of sight, it was not out of mind. The washerwomen's strike in the summer of 1881 reveals how working-class women's resistance could and did take a different form, as they openly proclaimed the usually "hidden transcript" of opposition in a profound way. The strike displayed an astute political consciousness among black working-class women who made so-called private labor a public issue and insisted on autonomy and a living wage.

The communal character and self-organization of laundry work proved critical to this mobilization as it facilitated the creation of a relatively autonomous space that had already nurtured the foundation of working-class women's solidarity. The Atlanta laundresses built on this tightly knit system, extended it through an intensive door-to-door recruitment of adherents to their cause, and sustained it through mass or decentralized ward meetings held nightly. Their capacity to arise to this occasion demonstrates why washerwomen were the most outspoken leaders in domestic workers' strikes documented in the South. It is no accident that, as incidents in later years would indicate, employers often combined forces to repress this particular group.

White city leaders put their full weight behind employers' attempts to annihilate a strike. At least one landlord threatened to raise the rent of his washerwoman if she raised the fees for her work. A businessman scoffed "at the colored people's stupidity in not seeing that they were working their own ruin" and warned that if they persisted they would be faced with a harsh winter without white charity. The police arrested several street organizers for "disorderly conduct," charging them with disruptive and violent behavior as they canvassed their neighborhoods. Leading capitalists raised funds for a state-of-the-art steam laundry and offered to employ "smart Yankee girls" to buttress the counter-offensive and requested a tax exemption from the city council to subsidize the costs. Meanwhile, municipal authorities proposed a scheme to regulate the trade and destroy the workers' independence: councilmen suggested that each member of any washerwomen's organization pay an exorbitant business tax of $25.00. In the end, however, the City Council rejected the license fee; the councilmen may have been daunted by the continued determination of women who refused to buckle under to threats and who vowed to reappropriate the license fee and city regulation to gain the benefits of private enterprise. As the women themselves stated in an open letter to the mayor, "We have agreed, and are willing to pay $25 or $50 for licenses as a protection so we can control the washing for the city."

Not only did the washerwomen's spirit of rebellion frustrate the actions of their opponents, it set an example for other black workers. Waiters at the National Hotel followed on the women's coat tails and won demands for better wages and working conditions previously rejected by management. Cooks, maids, and child-nurses also were inspired to begin organizing for better wages. Even the *Atlanta Constitution,* ardent ally of the employers, begrudgingly admitted that the "amazons" had shown remarkable organization.

The most telling piece of evidence about the strike's impact appeared several weeks after the event had apparently subsided, when an unidentified source divulged to the newspaper that the washerwomen were threatening to call a second potentially more perilous general strike of all domestics during the upcoming International Cotton Exposition. While there were no further reports to suggest that this rumor ever came to fruition, the mere threat of a second strike at such a critical moment is quite telling. The laundry workers were clearly conscious of the significance of this event which had been touted as the debut of the New South movement and as a showcase for Atlanta, an upstart metropolis eager to be emulated. A strike held at that particular time not only would have spoiled the image of docile labor that New Southerners were carefully projecting to attract northern capital, it would have wreaked havoc on a city already anxious about its capacity to host the thousands of visitors who would require the services of cooks, maids, child-nurses, and laundresses. The newspaper forewarned white housewives: "prepare for the attack before it is made," and they did.

The actual outcome of the washerwomen's strike is inconclusive, though it is curious that reports on the protest petered out in the medium that had openly flaunted its partisanship against it. Whether or not some or all the washerwomen were able to gain higher wages we may never know; however, they continued to maintain a modicum of independence in their labor not enjoyed by other domestics. The strike speaks volumes symbolically about African-American working-class women's consciousness of their racial, class, and gender position. Domestic work was synonymous with black women in freedom as it was in slavery, and the active efforts by whites to exploit labor clearly circumscribed black lives. Yet black women fought for dignity, to be treated with respect, and for a fair chance to earn the necessary resources for making a decent living. The women identified autonomy as vital to freedom and to making decisions about wage work most commensurate with their non-wage responsibilities as mothers, sisters, daughters, and wives.

The employers could not fathom the motivations that inspired domestic workers to act in these ways. But employers knew they could not afford to take a pacified work force for granted. They used coercion, repression, and violence and sought support from the state to extract compliance to their wishes, which helped to determine the form that resistance would take. Domination and resistance were always defined in dynamic relationship to one another; thus it is not surprising that strikes were atypical events. Domestic workers developed other ways to articulate their grievances and assert their own demands, however, and in return their actions influenced the character of domination itself. The illusive quality of the black women's surreptitious actions made them difficult to control by individual employers and kept them vigilant. Domination was not a project that could be erected in full form and left to operate on its own momentum; it required ongoing efforts of surveillance and reconstitution in order to guarantee its effect. At times this meant that domestic workers won small gains and moments of relief, as when they quit work. At other times their resistance led to greater repression, as during the period of World War I with the implementation of "work or fight" laws.

The contested character of wage household labor between Reconstruction and World War I also highlights another important point. Far from functioning as "separate spheres" the so-called public sphere of politics and business and the private sphere of family and home infiltrated one another in complex ways. It should be noted, however, that employers sometimes displayed an ambivalence about the relationship between their prerogatives as managers of labor and the intervention of public authorities, literally, on their home turfs. Municipalities and legislatures often stopped short of imposing legislation; recall, for example, that the Atlanta City Council failed to impose the business tax on individual laundry workers during the 1881 strike. African-American women's opposition may have thwarted employers' efforts to subdue them, but other factors may have also hindered employers from realizing the optimal balance between compulsion and free labor. In an economy moving toward modernization, even in the constrained version of Southern capitalism, the issue of state power versus individual employer authority was never consistently resolved. Waged household labor played an important role in the economic, social, and political life of the New South. . . .

FURTHER READING

Eric Anderson, *Race and Politics in North Carolina, 1872–1901: The Black Second* (1981).

Eric Arnesen. *Waterfront Workers of New Orleans: Race, Class, and Politics, 1863–1923* (1991).

Edward Ayers, *The Promise of the New South: Life After Reconstruction* (1992).

W. Fitzhugh Brundage, *Lynching in the New South: Georgia and Virginia, 1880–1930* (1993).

Garna L. Christian, *Black Soldiers in Jim Crow Texas, 1899–1917* (1995).

William Cohen, *At Freedom's Edge: Black Mobility and the Southern White Quest for Racial Control, 1861–1915* (1991).

Pete Daniel, *The Shadow of Slavery: Peonage in the South, 1901–1969* (1972).

Miriam DeCosta-Willis, ed., *The Memphis Diary of Ida B. Wells* (1995).

John Dittmer, *Black Georgia in the Progressive Era, 1900–1920* (1977).

Glenda Gilmore, *Gender and Jim Crow: Women and the Politics of White Supremacy in North Carolina, 1890–1920* (1996).

Lawrence C. Goodwyn, "Populist Dreams and Negro Rights: East Texas as a Case Study," *American Historical Review,* 76 (December 1971), 1435–1456.

William Ivy Hair, *Carnival of Fury: Robert Charles and the New Orleans Race Riot of 1900* (1976).

Tera W. Hunter, *To 'Joy My Freedom: Southern Black Women's Lives and Labors After the Civil War* (1997).

Gerald David Jaynes, *Branches Without Roots: Genesis of the Black Working Class in the American South, 1862–1882* (1986).

Jacqueline Jones, *Labor of Love, Labor of Sorrow: Black Women, Work, and the Family from Slavery to the Present* (1985).

Robert C. Kenzer, "Black Businessmen in Post–Civil War Tennessee," *Journal of East Tennessee History,* 66 (1994), 59–80.

Robert C. Kenzer, *Enterprising Southerners: Black Economic Success in North Carolina, 1865–1915* (1997).

Lawrence Levine, *Black Culture and Black Consciousness: Afro-American Folk Thought from Slavery to Freedom* (1977).

Leon Litwack, *Trouble in Mind: Black Southerners in the Age of Jim Crow* (1998).

Rayford W. Logan, *The Betrayal of the Negro, from Rutherford B. Hayes to Woodrow Wilson* (1965).

Neil R. McMillen, *Dark Journey: Black Mississippians in the Age of Jim Crow* (1989).

August Meier and Elliott Rudwick, "The Boycott Movement Against Jim Crow Streetcars in the South, 1900–1906," *Journal of American History,* 55 (March 1969), 756–775.

August Meier and Elliott Rudwick, "Negro Boycotts of Segregated Streetcars in Virginia, 1904–1907," *Virginia Magazine of History and Biography,* 81 (October 1973), 480–487.

Joe A. Mobley, "In the Shadow of a White Society: Princeville, a Black Town in North Carolina, 1865–1915," *North Carolina History Review,* 3 (July 1986), 340–384.

James T. Moore, "Black Militancy in Readjuster Virginia, 1879–1883," *Journal of Southern History,* 61 (May 1975), 167–186.

Nell Painter, *Exodusters: Black Migration to Kansas After Reconstruction* (1976).

Howard Rabinowitz, "From Exclusion to Segregation: Southern Race Relations, 1865–1890," *Journal of American History,* 63 (September 1976), 325–350.

Stewart E. Tolnay and E. M. Beck, *A Festival of Violence: An Analysis of Southern Lynchings, 1882–1930* (1995).

C. Vann Woodward, *The Strange Career of Jim Crow* (1974).

George C. Wright, *Life Behind a Veil: Blacks in Louisville, Kentucky, 1865–1930* (1985).

George C. Wright, *Racial Violence in Kentucky, 1865–1940: Lynchings, Mob Rule, and "Legal Lynchings"* (1990).

Rural Exodus and the Growth of New Urban Communities

Between 1910 and 1930 more than a million African-American men, women, and children left their homes in the South and took up residence in mostly urban areas throughout the country, an estimated half-million of them between 1916 and 1921. This period of rapid population shift is known as the Great Migration. Also between 1910 and 1930 more than one hundred thousand black immigrants, 75 percent from Caribbean countries, entered the United States, going to live principally in New York, Florida, and Massachusetts. Thus by 1930, while the black population of the United States was still overwhelmingly southern (78.7 percent), a number of northern cities had significant black populations, and even within the South over 31 percent of African Americans now lived in urban areas.

What were the causes and patterns of black migration? How did potential migrants make decisions about moving, and how was their movement organized? How did African Americans already living in cities look upon and receive the migrants? To what extent were migrants' expectations for their new lives met? How did this influx of people and cultures change urban areas and institutions? How did it change black life in the cities?

 D O C U M E N T S

The first document shows the population shifts that occurred between 1910 and 1930. The second document consists of letters forwarded north to the Urban League or to the *Chicago Defender,* in anticipation of relocation assistance, and letters that migrants sent south to family members and friends left behind. In these letters the migrants reveal their hopes and expectations as well as their initial assessment of their new homes.

Rapid population growth in a number of cities resulted in the overcrowding of black residents in ethnic enclaves, taxed urban resources, and worried reformers— black and white. Social service and government agencies alike sought professional expertise to guide their social welfare and urban development initiatives. This need provided an opportunity for a small but emerging group of educated black men to carve out careers as social scientists while creating an empirical record of African-American life and presenting themselves as equipped to solve urban problems. Founded in New York City in 1911, the National Urban League (NUL) was the most important of the new social service agencies formed especially to address urban black conditions. By 1919 the NUL had branches in thirty cities, including Atlanta, Richmond, Pittsburgh, Detroit, and Chicago. The third document is an NUL brochure entitled "Helpful Hints" that was passed out to new migrants at the train station or on the streets in Detroit. The fourth is a report and action plan by George Edmund Haynes, a Columbia University sociology Ph.D., cofounder of the National Urban League and director of the Department of Labor's newly formed Division of Negro Economics. Together these documents demonstrate the NUL's dual emphasis on making the migrants fit its ideas of respectability and on creating acceptable economic (as well as housing and recreational) conditions for the newcomers.

The decision to go or stay—in South or North, city or country—was a decision that most individuals made with care, weighing the economic, political, and social costs and benefits for themselves and their families. The fifth document provides insight into how the members of one Georgia farming family adjusted to life in Chicago. This document is revealing in another way as well, for its very existence is the result of a study of black life in the city conducted as a consequence of one of the twenty-five race riots that occurred in the last six months of 1919. Despite all the new freedoms that black southerners transplanted to the North did experience, they had not fully left behind white hostility. Many white northerners perceived the African Americans arriving in northern cities as threats to neighborhoods, jobs, and city resources.

Whatever the unfulfilled expectations or cautionary tales, however, migration remained a central theme in black life and black culture. Migration in general and the railroad in particular became familiar themes in blues lyrics, which, as the lyrics in the sixth document indicate, often presented a very gendered idea of this movement— the idea that women had to watch tearfully as their men moved on to new lives in new places. Lovie Austin composed "Chicago Bound Blues"; both Ida Cox and Bessie Smith recorded it in 1923. In 1934 Memphis Minnie made the Chickasaw train, which ran between Memphis, Tennessee, and St. Louis, Missouri, a central character in one of her recordings. Yet the very lives of these blueswomen contradicted the songs they sang, for they themselves moved about and made new lives for themselves as entertainers and recording artists in Chicago and on the road.

1. Black Population in Selected Cities, 1910–1930

	POPULATION			PERCENTAGE INCREASE	
	1910	1920	1930	1910–1920	1920–1930
South					
Birmingham, AL	52,305	70,230	99,077	34.3	41.1
Washington, DC	94,446	109,966	132,068	16.4	20.1
Jacksonville, FL	29,293	41,520	48,196	41.7	16.1
Tampa, FL	8,951	11,531	21,172	28.8	83.6
Atlanta, GA	51,902	62,796	90,075	21.0	43.4
New Orleans, LA	89,262	100,930	129,632	13.1	28.4
Baltimore, MD	84,749	108,322	142,106	27.8	31.2
Tulsa, OK	1,959	8,878	15,203	353.2	71.2
Charleston, SC	31,056	32,326	28,062	4.1	(-13.2)
Memphis, TN	52,441	61,181	96,550	16.7	57.8
Houston, TX	23,929	33,960	63,337	41.9	86.5
Norfolk, VA	25,039	43,392	43,942	73.3	1.3
North					
Chicago, IL	44,103	109,458	233,903	148.2	113.7
Kansas City, KS	9,286	14,405	19,872	55.1	38.0
Detroit, MI	5,741	40,838	120,066	611.3	194.0
St. Louis, MO	43,960	69,854	93,580	58.9	34.0
New York, NY	91,709	152,467	327,706	66.3	114.9
Cleveland, OH	8,448	34,451	71,899	307.8	108.7
Pittsburgh, PA	25,623	37,725	54,983	47.2	45.7
Milwaukee, WI	980	2,229	7,501	127.4	236.5
West					
Los Angeles, CA	7,599	15,579	38,894	105.0	149.7
Oakland, CA	3,055	5,489	7,503	79.7	36.7
San Francisco, CA	1,642	2,414	3,803	47.0	57.5
Albuquerque, NM	244	213	441	(-12.7)	107.0
Seattle, WA	2,296	2,894	3,303	26.0	14.1

2. Migrants' Letters, 1917

ALEXANDRIA, LA., June 6, 1917.

Dear Sirs: I am writeing to you all asking a favor of you all. I am a girl of seventeen. School has just closed I have been going to school for nine months and I now feel like I aught to go to work. And I would like very very well for you all to please forward me to a good job. but there isnt a thing here for me to do, the wages here is from a dollar and a half a week. What could I earn Nothing. I have a mother and father my father do all he can for me but it is so hard. A child with any respect about her self or his self wouldnt like to see there mother and father work so hard and earn nothing I feel it my duty to help. I would like for you all to get me a good job and as

U.S. Bureau of the Census, *Negroes in the United States, 1920–1932,* prepared under the supervision of Z. R. Pettet, Chief Statistician for Agriculture, by Charles E. Hall, Specialist in Negro Statistics (GPO, 1935); U.S. Bureau of the Census, *Negroes in the United States* (GPO, 1915).

Emmett Scott, "Additional Letters of Negro Migrants of 1916–1918," *Journal of Negro History,* 4, no. 4 (October 1919), 413, 415, 416, 456–462.

I havent any money to come on please send me a pass and I would work and pay every cent of it back and get me a good quite place to stay. My father have been getting the defender for three or four months but for the last two weeks we have failed to get it. I dont know why. . . . I wrote to you all because I believe you will help

PENSACOLA, FLA., April 23, 1917.

Dear Sir: I saw your advice in the Chicago Defender I thought to wright for farther in fermashion I would be glad to now how I can get ther   I am a laborn man want to get where work is plentiful & good wedges i want to get in a Christian nise place   i have a good family and car for them I want to come up there to see the place & then latter on send for family can u send for me or describe me to some one who will send for me.

GREENVILLE, S. C., April 29, 1917.

Dear Sir: I would like for you to write me and tell me how is time up there and jobs is to get. I would like for you to get me a job and my wife. She is a no. 1 good cook, maid, nurse job I am a fireing boiler, steame fitter and experiences mechencs helpc and will do laboring work if you can not get me one off those jobs above that i can do. I have work in a foundry as a molder helper and has lots of experense at that. I am 27 yrs of age. If you can get me job I would like for you to do so please and let me no and will pay for trouble. . . . if you new off any firm that needs a man give them my address please I wont to get out of the south where I can demand something for my work.

ATLANTA, GA., July 4, '17.

Hello Mr. M——: How are you at this time—I arrived here safe and all O. K. and I am well and hope you are the same. Mrs. M—— told me that she reecived the money you sent to her and everybody sends love to you. I found my baby very sick when I come home but he is better now and I am going to try to come back up there in short time. How are times there now since my leaving there. I stopped in Cincinnati Ohio for 4 days then I left for G. but I will be with you some days I hope. Ask J—— W—— did he get my letter I wrote to him. Plenty work here but no money to it $1.50 to $2.00 a day that all I am telling you truly. Have you seen anything of W—— W—— he is there in Chicago If you do tell him to send me his address. I want to here from him. . . .

Tell all the boys Hello. Tell them to write to me and tell me all the news.

Good Bye
YOUR FRIEND.

CHICAGO, ILLINOIS.

My dear Sister: . . . I got here in time to attend one of the greatest revivals in the history of my life—over 500 people joined the church. We had a Holy Ghost shower. . . . It was snowing some nights and if you didnt hurry you could not get standing room. . . . The people are rushing here by the thousands and I know if you come and rent a big house you can get all the roomers you want. . . . I am living with my brother and his wife. My sone is in California but will be home soon. . . . I work in Swifts packing Co. in the sausage department. My daughter and I work for the same company—We get $1.50 a day and we pack so many sausages we dont have much time to play. . . . Tell your husband work is plentiful here and he wont have to loaf if he want to work. . . . Well goodbye from you sister in Christ

P.S. . . . When you fully decide to come write me and let me know what day you expect to leave and over what road and if I dont meet you I will have some one ther to meet you and look after you.

CHICAGO, ILLINOIS, 11/13/17.

Mr. H——
Hattiesburg, Miss.

Dear M——: . . . I was promoted on the first of the month I was made first assistant to the head carpenter when he is out of the place I take everything in charge and was raised to $95. a month. You know I know my stuff.

Whats the news generally around H'burg? I should have been here 20 years ago. I just begin to feel like a man. It's a great deal of pleasure in knowing that you have got some privilege   My children are going to the same school with the whites and I dont have to umble to no one. I have registered—Will vote the next election and there isnt any 'yes sir' and 'no sir'—its all yes and no and Sam and Bill.

Florine says hello and would like very much to see you. All joins me in sending love to you and family. How is times there now? Answer soon, from your friend and bro.

CLEVELAND, OHIO, Aug. 28, 1917.

hollow Dr. . . . i were indeed glad to recieve that paper from Union Springs. . . . i have seval nochants of coming back, yet i am doing well no trouble what ever except i can not raise my children here like they should be this is one of the worst places in principle you ever look on in your life but it is a fine place to make money . . . all kinds of loffers. gamblers pockit pickers you are not safe here to walk on the streets at night you are libble to get kill at eny time . . . yet i have not had no trouble no way. and we are making good money here. i have made as hight at 7.50 per day and my wife $4 Sundays my sun 7.50 and my 2 oldes girls 1.25 but my regler wegers is 3.60 fore 8 hours work. me and my family makes one hundred three darlers and 60 cents every ten days. it don cost no more to live here than it do thir, except house rent. . . .

By By

PHILADELPHIA, PA., Oct. 7, 1917.

Dear Sir: I take this method of thanking you for yours early responding and the glorious effect of the treatment. Oh. I do feel so fine. . . . Well Dr. with the aid of God I am making very good I make $75 per month. I am carrying enough insurance to pay me $20 per week if I am not able to be on duty. I don't have to work hard. dont have to mister every little white boy comes along   I havent heard a white man call a colored a nigger you no now—since I been in the state of Pa. I can ride in the electric street and steam cars any where I get a seat. I dont care to mix with white what I mean I am not crazy about being with white folks, but if I have to pay the same fare I have learn to want the same acomidation. and if you are first in a place here shoping you dont have to wait until the white folks get thro tradeing yet amid all this I shall ever love the good old South. . . . Dr. when you find time I would be delighted to have a word from the good old home state. Wife join me in sending love you and yours.

I am your friend and patient.

3. Helpful Hints for Migrants to Detroit, 1918

HELPFUL HINTS

DON'T carry on loud conversations or use vulgar or obscene language on the street cars, streets, or in public places. Remember that this hurts us as a race.

DON'T go about the streets or on the street car in bungalow aprons, boudoir caps and house slippers. Wear regular street clothes when you go into the streets.

TRY to dress neatly at all times, but don't be a dude or wear flashy clothes. They are as undesirable and as harmful as unclean clothes.

General Disorderly Appearance

DON'T think you can hold your job unless you are on time, industrious, efficient and sober.

DON'T sit in front of your house or around Belle Isle or public places with your shoes off. Don't wear overalls on Sunday.

DON'T stay away from work every time someone gives a picnic or boat ride. Stay on your job. Others do.

DON'T spend all your money for pleasure. Save some of it for extra clothing and fuel for the winter and to take care of your family and yourself when sickness comes.

DON'T forget that cleanliness and fresh air are necessary to good health. Keep your windows open.

DON'T do your children's hair up into alleys, canals and knots if you don't want other children to make fun of them. Keep them clean.

DON'T keep your children out of school. See that they attend the nearest school to you.

DON'T fail to start a savings account with some good bank or building loan association.

DON'T throw refuse and tin cans in your back or front yards. Keep your surroundings as clean as possible. This makes for good health.

Neatly Clothed and Orderly Appearance

DON'T fool with patent medicines in case of sickness. Send for a good doctor. In case you have no money, go to some of the Board of Health clinics.

DON'T be rude and ugly to people on the streets. Be courteous and polite and thereby keep out of trouble.

DON'T fail to meet the teachers of your children. Keep in touch with them. Every hateful thing that your child says about the teacher is not true.

DON'T fail to become connected with some church as soon as you get in the city.

DON'T make lots of unnecessary noise going to and from baseball games. If the parks are taken away from you it will be partly your own fault.

"Helpful Hints" leaflet, Detroit Urban League Papers, Box 1, Folder 9, Bentley Historical Library, University of Michigan.

4. George Edmund Haynes, a Black Social Scientist, Surveys Detroit, 1918

During this migration of the past two years Detroit, the leading center of the automobile industry has been one of the principal points of destination for these migrants, mainly from Alabama, Georgia, Florida, and Tennessee. . . . The industrial demands of Detroit for laborers became imperative [due to the Great War]. Negroes were drawn to the city by the hundreds daily. These new-comers were . . . for the most part unskilled and with little education but were seeking better things. . . . The problem now is not one of Negroes finding work but of doing the work open to them with such efficiency and satisfaction that when the pressing need of the War inflated industry is past their labor will be wanted along with that of other labor groups.

The available evidence that Detroit has removed the barriers from the employment of Negroes in many lines is considerable. Between July 2 and December 23, employers made calls for 5542 male and 317 female Negro workers, thru bonafide requests that came to the employment office run by the Detroit Urban League in co-operation with the Employers Association of Detroit. The large majority of the men were wanted by the automobile factories, the principal industry of the city. These firms demanded mainly unskilled men. About 29.3 per cent of these calls specified unskilled laborers and about 43.9 were miscellaneous calls for men unspecified, mainly unskilled laborers. A large proportion of the calls were for men to work as domestic and personal servants.

But it is significant that there were calls for 336 truckers (automobile), 160 moulders, 109 machinists (unspecified), 45 core-makers and for a number of other miscellaneous skilled and semi-skilled men. Most of the women were wanted in domestic and personal service in private homes. But it should be noted that 32 calls came from a garment factory, 18 from a cigar factory and 19 for ushers in a theatre. . . .

The distribution of Negroes in the various occupations may also be seen in the occupations of 407 heads of families interviewed in a house-to-house canvass made by an investigator for the Board of Health. Of the 362 men who were heads of families, 122 were laborers, 35 were mechanics (unskilled), 11 were porters (unskilled), 5 were automobile and truck drivers, 7 were hostlers, 8 were moulders, 8 machinists. There were 6 barbers, 12 janitors, 1 chauffeur, 3 waiters, 2 cooks, 1 contractor, 1 painter, 3 plasterers, 3 motormen, 1 cooper, 2 carpenters, 3 watchmen, 3 cement finishers, 10 teamsters, 3 garbage, 2 lawyers, 3 ministers, 1 musician, 3 privates in U. S. Army, 19 miscellaneous, 5 unemployed, 79 unknown.

Of the 45 women, there were 12 doing day's work, 10 housekeepers taking roomers, 6 laundresses, 2 hairdressers, 1 nurse (unspecified), 1 seamstress, 1 cook, 1 woman receiving a pension (unspecified), 4 miscellaneous (unspecified) and 7 unknown. . . .

George Edmund Haynes, *Negro New-Comers in Detroit, Michigan: A Challenge to Christian Statesmanship, A Preliminary Survey* (1918; reprint, New York: Arno Press and New York Times, 1969), 8–9, 12–13, 15–20.

As is to be expected for the present and for some time to come, practically all of these workers are unskilled or semi-skilled. Although realizing how dangerous it is to forecast, one may yet reasonably predict that some of these Negroes will gradually work their way into the skilled departments of the industries. . . .

. . . The only available figures on wages were those of the heads of 407 families interviewed in the house-to-house canvass, previously mentioned. . . . [T]he prevailing wages of the men are from about $70 to about $119 per month. For 159 of the 194 men whose wages were ascertained were receiving wages ranging between these amounts. The prevailing wage for women is about that of those doing day work, $2 per day. It is common knowledge that there are very few places in the South where a house-to-house canvass of Negro families would show such a high range of wages. . . .

Another important fact bearing upon the matter of permanence of the Negro's industrial opportunity in Detroit relates to colored women as workers. The A. Krolik Company, large garment manufacturers, have successfully carried thru an experiment that is being watched with interest by other firms in Detroit and elsewhere. They have opened and, so far, successfully operated a pants factory, using colored women entirely in doing the work, including the office work, except the management. . . . The factory conditions under which the work is done are very good. Also, one of the largest theatres has begun to employ colored girls as ushers. They are proving satisfactory. . . .

There is undoubtedly a large industrial opportunity for Negroes in Detroit. . . . What can the churches do to help the new-comers make this great industrial opportunity permanent? . . . First and foremost, they need some provision for training in the processes of the occupations in which so many of them are now entering. This can be done by three means: First, part time arrangements might be made with firms where they are employed for some system of vocational education correlated with the work they are doing. Second, night schools offering an education in skilled and semi-skilled occupations as well as in the English branches might be opened. The community should be led to supply this thru its public school system. Third, special afternoon and evening courses in domestic science for women and girls who must earn their living in domestic and personal service.

On the first item, the churches with the co-operation of the Detroit Urban League might work quietly thru intelligent laymen to lay this matter before foremen, superintendents and owners of factories where these laymen are employed. Thus they could create a sentiment in favor of such a plan. On the second item, the leading members of the churches may unite with the League in securing such provision as mentioned above from the public school officials and if necessary in seeing that public funds were provided. On the third item, the churches could furnish money to start special courses of instruction in domestic science for women and girls.

A second need is stimulation to overcome the industrial ideas and habits brought from the South. The Negro workmen's slowness and irregularity mentioned by those whose opinions were sought are largely due to industrial habits brought from a Southern environment.

The churches could provide lectures, social study classes and intelligent workers for the personal touch in workshop and home to help overcome these faults.

A system of friendly home visitation might be organized. A considerable part of the complaint about Negro workers "quitting" when cold weather comes can be removed by instruction in how to dress and in simple repeated assurances that they need not fear freezing to death if they are properly clad. The churches can give larger support to the "Dress Well Club" which has been already organized. Lectures on food and dress could be supplied by the churches.

Again, every individual Negro needs to have it brought home to him by constant reminder that all the Negro workmen are on trial in the face of unusual industrial opportunities and that individually they must make good for the sake of all their fellow workmen. This is largely the work of preachment from the pulpit and the platform. What a world of service is open here to the Negro churches!

5. A Migrant Family Adjusts to Life in Chicago, 1922

Mr. J——, forty-nine years old, his wife, thirty-eight years, and their daughter twenty-one years, were born in Henry County, Georgia. The husband never went to school, but reads a little. The wife finished the seventh grade and the daughter the fifth grade in the rural school near their home.

They worked on a farm for shares, the man earning one dollar and the women from fifty to seventy-five cents a day for ten hours' work. Their home was a four-room cottage with a garden, and rented for five dollars a month. They owned pigs, poultry, and a cow, which with their household furniture, were worth about $800. The food that they did not raise and their clothing had to be bought from the commissary at any price the owner cared to charge.

They were members of the Missionary Baptist Church and the wife belonged to the missionary society of the church and the Household of Ruth, a secret order. Their sole recreation was attending church, except for the occasional hunting expeditions made by the husband.

Motives for coming to Chicago.—Reading in the *Atlanta Journal,* a Negro newspaper, of the wonderful industrial opportunities offered Negroes, the husband came to Chicago in February, 1917. Finding conditions satisfactory, he had his wife sell the stock and household goods and join him here in April of the same year. He secured work at the Stock Yards, working eight hours at $3 a day. Later, he was employed by a casting company, working ten hours a day and earning $30 a week. This is his present employment and is about forty minutes' ride from his home. Both jobs were secured by his own efforts.

The family stayed in a rooming-house on East Thirtieth Street. This place catered to such an undesirable element that the wife remained in her room with their daughter all day. She thought the city too was cold, dirty, and noisy to live in. Having nothing to do and not knowing anyone, she was so lonely that she cried daily and begged her husband to put her in three rooms of their own or go back home. Because of the high cost of living, they were compelled to wait some time before they had saved enough to begin housekeeping.

Chicago Commission on Race Relations, *The Negro in Chicago: A Study of Race Relations and a Race Riot* (Chicago: University of Chicago Press, 1922), 170–172.

Housing experience.—Their first home was on South Park Avenue. They bought about $500 worth of furniture, on which they are still paying. The wife then worked for a time at the Pullman Yards, cleaning cars at $1.50 a day for ten hours' work. Their house leaked and was damp and cold, so the family moved to another house on South Park Avenue, where they now live. The house is an old, three-story brick, containing three flats. This family occupies the first flat, which has six rooms and bath. Stoves are used for heating, and gas for light and cooking. The house is warm, but dark and poorly ventilated. Lights are used in two of the rooms during the day. The rooms open one into the other, and the interior, as well as the exterior, needs cleaning. There are a living-room, dining-room, and three bed-rooms. The living-room is neatly and plainly furnished.

The daughter has married a man twenty-three years old, who migrated first to Pittsburgh, Pennsylvania, then to Chicago. He works at the Stock Yards. They oc-cupy a room and use the other part of the house, paying half the rent and boarding themselves. A nephew, who was a glazier in Georgia, but who has been unable to secure work here, also boards with Mr. and Mrs. J——, $8 a week. He is now un-employed, but has been doing foundry work. Mrs. J—— occasionally does laundry work at $4 a day.

How they live.—The cost of living includes rent $25; gas $5.40 a month; coal $18 a year; insurance $9.60 a month; clothing $500 a year; transportation $3.12 a month; church and club dues $3 a month; hairdresser $1.50 a month. Little is spent for recreation and the care of the health. The family carries insurance to the amount of $1,700, of which $1,200 is on the husband.

The meals are prepared by the wife, who also does the cleaning. Greens, pota-toes, and cabbage are the chief articles of diet. Milk, eggs, cereals, and meat are also used. Meat is eaten about four times a week. Hot bread is made daily, and the dinners are usually boiled.

Relation to the community.—The whole family belongs to the Salem Baptist Church and attends twice a week. The wife is a member of the Pastor's Aid and the Willing Workers Club, also the Elk's Lodge. The husband is a member of the Knights of Pythias. He goes to the parks, bathing-beaches, and baseball games for amuse-ment. The family spends much of its time in church and helped to establish the "Come and See" Baptist Mission at East Thirty-first Street and Cottage Grove Ave-nue. They have gone to a show only once or twice since they came to the city. During the summer they spend Sunday afternoons at the East Twenty-ninth Street Beach.

Heavier clothes were necessary because of the change of climate, and more fresh meat is used because of the lack of garden space and the high cost of green vegetables.

The wife thinks that northern Negroes have better manners, but are not as friendly as the colored people in the South. She says people do not visit each other, and one is never invited to dine at a friend's house. She thinks they cannot afford it with food so high. She thinks people were better in the South than they are here and says they had to be good there for they had nothing else to do but go to church.

She feels a greater freedom here because of the right to vote, the better treat-ment accorded by white people, the lack of "Jim Crow" laws. She likes the North because of the protection afforded by the law and the better working conditions. "You don't have an overseer always standing over you," she remarked.

Life here is harder, however, because one has to work all the time. "In the South you could rest occasionally, but here, where food is so high and one must pay cash, it is hard to come out even." The climate is colder, making it necessary to buy more clothes and coal. Rent also is very much higher here. They had to sell their two $50 Liberty bonds.

Economic sufficiency.—With all this, Mrs. J—— gets more pleasure from her income because the necessities of life here were luxuries in Georgia, and though such things are dear here there is money to pay for them. Houses are more modern, but not good enough for the rent paid. They had to pay $2 more than the white family that moved out when they moved in.

Sentiments on the migration.—Mrs. J—— says "some colored people have come up here and forgotten to stay close to God," hence they have "gone to destruction." She hopes that an equal chance in industry will be given to all; that more houses will be provided for the people and rent will be charged for the worth of the house; and the cost of living generally will be reduced. She does not expect to return to Georgia and is advising friends to come to Chicago.

6. Migration Blues

Chickasaw Train Blues (Low Down Dirty Thing)

I'm gonna tell everybody, what that Chickasaw have done done for me.
I'm gonna tell everybody, what that Chickasaw have done done for me.
She done stole my man away, and blowed that doggone smoke on me,
She's a low down dirty dog.
I ain't no woman, like to ride that Chickasaw.
Ain't no woman, like to ride that Chickasaw.
Because everywhere she stops, she's stealing some woman's good man off,
She's a low down dirty dog.

I told the depot agent this morning, I don't think he treats me right.
I told the depot agent this morning, I don't think he treats me right.
He done sold my man a ticket, and know that Chickasaw leaving town
     tonight,
He's a low down dirty dog.

I walked down the railroad track, that Chickasaw wouldn't even let me ride
the blinds.
I walked down the railroad track, that Chickasaw wouldn't even let me ride
the blinds.
And she stops, picking up men, all up and down the line,
She's a low down dirty dog.

Hmmm, Chickasaw don't pay no woman no mind.
Hmmm, Chickasaw don't pay no woman no mind.
And she stops, picking up men, all up and down the line.

E S S A Y S

Peter Gottlieb, archivist at the State Historical Society of Wisconsin, lays out the structural factors that shaped the life African Americans might make in North or South
in the first decades of the twentieth century, arguing that family and community
resources were crucial in shaping the decisions that potential migrants made about
relocation—and re-relocation. The second essay reminds us that although conditions
within the United States generated this migration, it was part of a hemisphere-wide
shift in labor demands and transportation networks. Irma Watkins-Owens, who teaches
African-American studies and history at Fordham University, focuses on the forty
thousand immigrants from the British West Indies who relocated to Harlem in the
early twentieth century. She asks how they accommodated themselves to life in this
new country and how their presence remade the black community in New York.

The Great Migration

PETER GOTTLIEB

This essay is a contribution to the historical assessment of black migration. . . . In
particular, . . . it is an attempt to place the Great Migration from 1916 to 1930 in the
context of blacks' northward movement from the 1870s to the 1970s. Drawing on
the example of migration to Pittsburgh, Pennsylvania, and its surrounding industrial
region (Allegheny County), it examines the dynamics of blacks' movement to
northern cities as a way of understanding both the underlying conditions from
which migration sprang as well as the distinctive character of the Great Migration.

Recent studies of African-American migration have demonstrated the migrants' creative role in their geographic movement. Unlike earlier investigations
that primarily concerned the exterior facets of migration—the causes, destinations,
numbers of migrants, and living conditions in origin and destination areas—the
newer studies focus on the experience of geographic movement. Rather than explore only why and where southerners moved, this literature also reconstructs how
they moved. It looks at the structures of group life and the values, attitudes, perceptions, and status that migrants brought to their movement. This view moves the
forces that produce migration into the background and places the migrants themselves closer to the center of the geographic movement. Here the picture is not one
of economic, political, or social conditions shuttling rural peoples from country to
city. The emerging portrayal of African-American migration shows men and
women responding to these conditions on the basis of deep-rooted social practices

Peter Gottlieb, "Rethinking the Great Migration: A Perspective from Pittsburgh," in *The Great Migration
in Historical Perspective: New Dimensions of Race, Class, and Gender,* edited by Joe William Trotter, Jr.,
pp. 68–75, © 1991 by Indiana University Press. Reprinted with permission.

and customs, developing a pattern of movement which reflected both the general causes of migration and their own social organization and aspirations.

Approached in this way, African-Americans' voluntary migration springs from an interplay between socioeconomic structures and the migrants' community and culture. Migrants draw in particular ways on various resources to contend with inducements stemming from socioeconomic structures. The way in which African-Americans engage their resources with the pressures on them to move creates a migration dynamic—the motive force behind their movement. From the end of the Civil War to the 1960s, the structures of southern agricultural backwardness, African-Americans' lack of land, capital, and occupational skills, and racial segregation and discrimination conditioned geographic mobility. But particular inducements to migration changed over time, as did the material and cultural resources that African-Americans deployed in different ways to make their journeys. Thus the dynamic of northward migration shifted from one period to another, marking distinct phases in the 100-year flow of African-Americans out of their native region.

We can begin to explore the dynamics of northward migration by reviewing the genesis of blacks' World War I movement to Pittsburgh, examining factors in both the South and the North that contributed to the particular energy of that migration. . . .

We usually describe the Great Migration in terms of several characteristics that distinguished the movement during World War I and the 1920s. First, there was a rapid growth in the northward migration streams when hundreds of thousands of southern blacks began journeys to eastern and midwestern cities. Behind this sudden increase in the number of migrants were material and social forces that simultaneously encouraged blacks to leave their rural homes and attracted them to the northern destinations. Finally, two results of the wartime migration have seemed most salient: the entry of black migrants to industrial jobs previously closed to them; and the élan of the migrants themselves, which reflected an awareness of a new historical period beginning and their power to enter it on advantageous terms.

Viewed from Pittsburgh, the Great Migration displayed most of these aspects. Black newcomers from the South began flooding into the city and its surrounding industrial district a little after the onset of the general northward movement during World War I. From 1916 to 1919, the Pittsburgh area's workshops, mines, transportation facilities, construction crews, hotels, and private homes badly needed employees to replace men going into the army and women shifting to new and better-paying jobs. The European conflict disrupted the flow of foreign-born workers to Pittsburgh on which the city's employers depended for their labor force and even drew some of Pittsburgh's immigrant workers into the armies of their native countries. The arriving southern blacks wanted the vacant jobs and the wages they paid that were two or three times higher than daily earnings in the South. As news of job openings and comparatively high wages spread through southern communities, African-Americans expressed an eagerness to reach Pittsburgh and to learn more about conditions there. "I have a very large family and would like very much to come north if I could get a good job for all of my folks . . . ," wrote one man from Georgia in 1922. Another prospective migrant stated, " . . . if I can get [an] inside Job for the winter I will get rady [sic] and come in short."

Beneath this tableau of enthusiastic northward movement, powerful inducements to migration were at work. Primary among these was demand for African-
American labor. Its source and its impact on male and female workers differed
according to northern city or industry, but labor demand influenced most aspects
of migrants' journeys and subsequent experiences. The male newcomers in
wartime Pittsburgh were wanted for jobs both where they had customarily been
employed, and, more noticeably, where few had been hired before—in the large,
integrated steel mills and in some of the foundries, machine shops, and electrical
equipment factories. Several large employers who had never before hired African-
Americans enrolled hundreds after 1915, including Oliver Iron and Steel, Pittsburgh Forge and Iron, Duquesne Steel Foundry, and Mackintosh-Hemphill. The
explosive growth during World War I in the number of black laborers in such
Pittsburgh workplaces was an indicator of the demand for their services. By 1920,
black iron and steel laborers alone had increased nearly 500% over the number in
the Pittsburgh area in 1910.

While male migrants could enter jobs in heavy industry, construction, and
transportation, female migrants in Pittsburgh during the war had a much smaller
range of job possibilities. The women could occasionally find temporary places in
the packing and shipping rooms of department stores and in a few industrial plants,
but they most often were limited to the same occupations they had had before the
war: cooking, cleaning, and washing in private homes. Black men had a definite
advantage over black women, both in terms of their expanding work opportunities
and in the wage differential between their new jobs and their old ones.

Labor demand in rural and urban areas of the South also shaped the dynamic
of the Great Migration. Though rural African-Americans faced natural disasters
and threats to cash crop harvests, as a group they were not losing their place on the
land. It is true that flooding of homes and crop lands in 1916 at least temporarily
uprooted families in certain localities of Alabama. More significant was the destruction of cotton crops by boll weevils that had become a fact of agricultural life
since the turn of the century. Dwindling cotton harvests in many areas did make
life precarious for thousands of African-American cultivators, particularly in South
Carolina and the Georgia Piedmont during the early 1920s. Some landowners and
tenants, however, had learned how to use pesticides on weevils or how to grow
other crops until the infestation passed, and rising prices for the smaller total harvest sometimes yielded higher incomes for successful farmers. This was especially
the case during World War I, when demand for American cotton rose sharply.
Despite weevils and natural disasters, agricultural incomes in the South increased
during the War and postwar years, bringing a measure of prosperity to rural
African-Americans as well. This reflected only a trickle from the net gains of the
wartime cotton boom, yet reports from farming districts in 1917–19 refer to
African-American cotton growers purchasing their first cars, buying new clothes
for their families, and refurbishing homes and farm equipment.

There were widening avenues to employment in southern urban areas too,
where African-Americans had moved in search of work for many years. The war
economy generated new jobs in industries throughout the South. Coal and iron ore
mining, dockside labor, railroad and trolley line construction, and the lumber and
turpentine industries all had openings in this period for male laborers. Building and

maintaining military installations in the South provided additional jobs. African-Americans had filled these occupations in the past, moving seasonally from farms to industrial sites to earn extra income before returning to their rural homes. The annual cycle of cotton cultivation, from ground breaking to harvest, included rest periods when men customarily looked for day labor and women tried to find domestic work in white households. Other African-Americans had shifted permanently from agriculture to wage labor, filling the unskilled jobs in extractive industries, construction, transportation, and domestic service throughout the South. Long experience in moving to jobs within their native region gave southern blacks added traction as they began moving toward new job openings during the war.

African-Americans' outlook on this escalating labor demand framed their responses to wartime conditions. Through life-long racial oppression in the South, they regarded work opportunities in the North in a different light from those closer to home. Codes of racial conduct and status had been tightly constricting their lives since the 1880s. Whites had barred access to adequate education, skilled occupations, and the franchise. Segregation and discrimination were often most strictly enforced in the southern towns and cities where African-Americans went in search of wage labor. The most prosperous black landowners and town merchants sometimes attracted whites' resentment and reprisals for lifting their living standards above sanctioned levels. Whites' growing sensitivity to any kind of encroachment on their status, real or imagined, frequently broke out in violence against African-Americans. Middle-aged men and women saw their lives blighted in this atmosphere, but the rising generation of African-Americans, born in the late 1880s or early 1890s and approaching adulthood around 1916, felt especially restless at the prospect of coming of age in such an incubus.

African-Americans' quick departures from the South after 1915 under such popular slogans as "Crossing Over Jordan" and "Going to the Promised Land" was one expression of their engagement with the inducements to northward movement, but the dynamic of the Great Migration arose more directly from other sources. The welling migration streams were fed by myriad kinship and community networks that channeled individuals and small groups toward specific destinations, northern employers, urban residential districts, and even particular boarding houses and private homes. Families carefully rearranged their members' commitments to allow one or more to go on northern scouting expeditions while the others remained at home to cultivate a cash crop or earn wages for the household in nearby towns and work sites. Favorable news about job openings and housing from the dispatched explorers attracted other family members to the North. Though this particular deployment of kinship resources was more feasible for the minority of landowning African-American families, it was similar to strategies that many urban and rural families used.

Community relationships among southerners supported migration in much the same way. Neighbors, friends and workmates passed information and offered assistance to each other. Clubs, churches, and fraternal lodges sponsored migration of their members as well. Personal connections for information and help were preferred to impersonal contacts, but hundreds of letters of inquiry from migrants to public agencies, social welfare organizations, newspaper editors, and employers demonstrated African-Americans' efforts to seek information from a variety of sources.

The kinship and community resources that migrants drew on for their initial journeys to the North also supported return trips to the South that were a prominent feature of the Great Migration in Pittsburgh. In some families, relatives had settled in southern towns and cities; in others, they had retained farms against all odds. More important, the persistence of labor-intensive tenant farming and daywork in cotton cultivation through the 1920s protected the foundations of rural African-American communities. These conditions made it possible for northern migrants to return to their relatives, to birthplaces, to family homes, and to native communities during the Great Migration.

Aside from sheer homesickness or loneliness, there were a variety of reasons for return journeys: illness, injury, loss of work, whites' hostility (especially in crises like strikes and race riots), and family and community celebrations. Walter H. and Laura L. each left Pittsburgh to fulfill obligations to family members who had remained in Virginia. Harrison G. and Charner C. returned to Georgia and South Carolina, respectively, to marry women from their home communities. Trips such as these were temporary returns to the South, but in the aggregate they helped to maintain migrants' links to their origin communities. Visits "down home" for some southerners in Pittsburgh became a regular part of the calendar, scheduled to coincide with the Christmas holidays or the lay-by period in cotton cultivation, when rural blacks held church revivals, barbecues, and homecoming celebrations for former residents. Members of migrants' families reunited in northern cities as well, but southern communities and southern branches of migrants' kinship groups played a crucial nurturing role in the northward movement.

Social structures in Pittsburgh contributed in a number of ways to the constant circulation of migrants between their origin and destination areas. First, southerners found, at best, cramped space in the city for building their northern homes. The unskilled, casual labor to which most of them were confined resulted in frequent layoffs and periods of unemployment. For male migrants in Pittsburgh, the stagnation of the steel industry after the mid-1920s heightened this general lack of job security. Though women's domestic service jobs exposed them to labor market fluctuations somewhat less than men's industrial work did, the low wages paid to all African-Americans were insufficient for supporting homes, even when two adults in a household held jobs.

Second, racial discrimination and whites' resistance to black progress generally withered the hopes for prosperity, equality, and justice that some migrants had cherished. Mortgage lenders and real estate companies prevented them from buying or renting houses outside the deteriorating housing districts, forcing severe overcrowding. Housing conditions in Pittsburgh were worse than some southerners had seen in their home towns. "I never lived in such houses in my life. We had four rooms in my home," fumed a woman from Georgia as she prepared to leave her one-room apartment and return south. Hospitals, police, courts, welfare agencies, and most other public service providers treated African-Americans as inferiors. In Pittsburgh, the Hill District, where most of the city's blacks lived, was subjected to sweeps by police whenever officials detected a public concern over crime.

Finally, migrants in Pittsburgh got little constructive help from long-term residents of their own urban communities as they tried to assimilate to the North.

Arriving in a city whose relatively small African-American community before 1916 derived largely from Virginia, whose black work force included a significant proportion of skilled men, the World War I southern migrants stirred as much alarm as any group of greenhorn newcomers to industrial America ever had. The men and women from Low Country Georgia and South Carolina, quickly distinguished by their speech and other mannerisms, were branded "Geechies" and disregarded by their Pittsburgh brethren and by other migrants alike. Alabama, North Carolina, and Tennessee migrants similarly betrayed their scant education and common labor backgrounds. Some black churches and settlement houses, like the Urban League of Pittsburgh, extended practical assistance, but often with a condescending attitude toward the new arrivals' backgrounds. The migrants found many community institutions that mirrored the scorn of northern-born blacks toward them. Tensions that arose from growing differences of class and culture within the African-American population were not overcome by the rising awareness of a common racial identity, actively promoted by the Pittsburgh *Courier* and by some prominent figures in the community.

Whatever the adverse circumstances that forced migrants to return South during or just after World War I, changing conditions allowed them to move north again and resume their former occupations. Southerners departed from Pittsburgh in droves in 1920–21 when the postwar boom collapsed, causing widespread unemployment. Two-fifths of the entire black population of Allegheny County left the region in that interval. Federal restrictions on foreign immigration, a sharp upswing in the business cycle, and the steel industry's addition of a third shift to accommodate the new eight-hour day in continuous operations elicited a new northward surge in 1922–23. Some of the migrants in this period had clearly awaited the return of prosperity. As labor demand accelerated, they wrote to Pittsburgh contacts to find out if the city's industries would hire them again. "i worked in the Diamond & Corbin iron works & several mills. i boarded in 12 ward on 30th St.," were the bona fides offered by one former resident. Another man inquired about job possibilities in Pittsburgh, though his heart was clearly set on a destination further west. ". . . I prefer Ohio, as I worked at the Firestone Rubber factory and won much fame." Just as the survival of African-American rural communities in the South during the 1920s provided a sheltering base for Pittsburgh migrants, recurring demand for black labor in northern industry helped to make the Great Migration more a circulation of population than a one-way passage.

Evidence from Pittsburgh suggests that the dynamic of the Great Migration arose from conditions in the North and South that strongly induced African-Americans to move, but left them wide options and resources to do so. They met these conditions by rapidly mobilizing family and community relations, converting them to conduits of information and material support for migration. Equally significant, southern blacks quickly adapted their prior experiences in intraregional migration and wage labor to the northward movement. The result was an initial, intense burst of out-migration followed by an energetic flow of population between north and south.

This dynamic, however, was also evanescent. It grew out of an international crisis and lasted only as long as southern blacks had a wide range of choices as well as time, income, and group resources to maximize their chances for successful movement. Before the Great Migration, inducements to move north were compara- tively weak, and relatively few men and women left the South. After the migration, and especially from World War II until the 1960s, changes in southern agriculture and land tenure systems forced blacks to take refuge in urban areas, whether or not they could find employment there. Though these periods of migration preceding and following the 1916–30 era also profoundly influenced the development of African-American communities, their dynamics grew from trends that were very different from those of the Great Migration.

Caribbean Connections

IRMA WATKINS-OWENS

Between 1900 and 1930 some 40,000 immigrants of African descent, most of them from the British-held colonies of the Caribbean, settled in Harlem as it was emerg- ing as a black community in New York City. This settlement converged with that of African American migrants from the states of the southeastern seaboard and elsewhere. The result was the creation of a new ethnic community, unique in the American experience. . . . A 1930s WPA guide to New York City noted, "Negroes blended into their New York environment habits and qualities carried from the southern states, Africa and the West Indies." Yet more recent investigations rarely emphasize Harlem's diverse origins, or explore the intraracial ethnic dimension as an important dynamic in African American community life. . . .

At the scene of their encounter in America, migrating southern and Caribbean blacks found themselves in the midst of a changing New York African American community after 1900. In this year blacks began moving from scattered and crowded downtown Manhattan communities into previously all-white sections of central Harlem. Due to over-building in the 1890s African American real estate agents such as Philip Payton were able to induce a few white landlords to accept black tenants. . . .

When the IRT Lenox Avenue subway line was completed in 1904, central Har- lem became more accessible. In addition the race riots of 1900 and 1905 convinced many that "there is no safety for any Negro in this part of the city at any time." Families and single adults deserted old tenements on crowded West 53rd Street and the San Juan Hill section (West 63rd to 66th Streets, later Columbus Hill), doubled up to pay the rents, and poured into Harlem. Others were displaced by the con- struction of Pennsylvania Station on the site of their old homes around 34th and 35th Streets and sought better housing in Harlem. White tenants and landlords bit- terly resisted this "invasion" at first. But spurred on by ambitious real estate agents like Payton, the migration from downtown took on the character of a crusade. By 1910, African American ministers joined real estate entrepreneurs in spearheading an "On to Harlem" movement.

Irma Watkins-Owens, *Blood Relations: Caribbean Immigrants and the Harlem Community, 1900–1930.* Copyright © 1996 by Indiana University Press. Reprinted with permission.

In 1915 African American Harlem was centered in the 130s. The blocks between 5th and 7th Avenues reflected the diversity of the community. In addition to many migrants from the southeastern seaboard states, residents living in the area came from Jamaica, Barbados, Montserrat, Antigua, Bermuda, the Bahamas, the Virgin Islands, Martinique, Haiti, Guadeloupe, Puerto Rico, Cuba, Panama, Suriname, West Africa, etc. The majority were single and young, lodging with kin or someone from their homeland or southern town. Families, native and immigrant—over 80 percent—were two parent.

Harlem became a desirable community, attracting a new black elite from all over the country and abroad. Intellectual activist W. E. B. Du Bois came there from Atlanta in 1910 as editor of the new NAACP's monthly journal, *The Crisis.* Florida native James Weldon Johnson, later the NAACP's executive director, returned to New York from the diplomatic service and settled in Harlem in 1914. Jamaican poet Claude McKay dropped out of Kansas State College in the same year to move to New York and later lived near the "hub" on 131st Street. In 1916 millionaire hair-care industry pioneer Madame C. J. Walker moved from Indianapolis to Harlem, and Marcus Garvey also arrived that year. Amy Ashwood, who had been a cofounder of the Universal Negro Improvement Association (UNIA) in Jamaica, joined Garvey in 1918. But the vast majority of Harlem's new residents were working-class single women and men from the South and the Caribbean seeking opportunities, if not their fortunes, in the great metropolis. Together they formed the new urban generation.

Native-born African American leaders hoped the masses as well as the poets and business people would help establish a "representative Negro" in a model twentieth-century community. . . . As men and women of color, African American leaders expected black immigrants to conform to the native-born black majority's interests and work toward the race's directed goals. . . .

. . . But who were these newcomers . . . ? Caribbean immigrants were not all peasants coming directly from rural districts. Only 14 percent entering between 1901 and 1935 were classified as agricultural workers according to the *Reports of the Commissioner of Immigration.* A majority had spent some time in small towns or cities before immigrating to the United States. An undetermined number of male and female immigrants were secondary migrants who had traveled to Panama, Central America, or other Caribbean islands in search of work before coming to America. A small but visible educated elite—a Caribbean "Talented Tenth"—were among the immigrants. Other middle-class immigrants possessed a sound grammar school education and often a skilled trade. Thirty-one percent reported occupations in industry and 10 percent in commerce. About 40 percent of those arriving reported occupations as laborers and servants.

Until 1924, Caribbean immigrants entered the United States virtually unrestricted, although previous congressional legislation mirrored Americans' growing intolerance of immigration, foreigners in general, and "undesirable" racial strains in particular. This legislation singled out Asians, particularly Japanese, for exclusion altogether by 1924. The 1924 Act sealed this ban and instituted quotas based on national origin. This law also placed Caribbean colonies under quotas set aside for their mother countries. As subjects of European nations, fewer African Caribbean people qualified for visas after 1924. The bulk of the immigration which helped to shape Harlem's intraracial ethnic character took place before that year. . . . The heaviest years of black immigrants' entry were between 1911 and 1924. The vast majority of these immigrants—82 percent—came from the English-speaking Caribbean. . . .

The ethnic character of New York's black communities evolved with the immigration of increasing numbers of foreign-born black people between 1900 and 1930. Within the city's total African American population of 60,000 in 1900, 5,000 were foreign-born. By 1930 the total African American population was nearly 328,000. Of this number 224,000, including 40,000 foreign-born, resided in Manhattan. The vast majority of these latter individuals lived in Harlem, which possessed the highest concentration of Caribbean-born immigrants in the United States. Miami ranked second, and Boston third.

Caribbean immigrants generally settled in already existing or evolving African American communities. Exclusionary racial and housing practices enforced this pattern. "Unlike others of the foreign born," wrote Jamaican journalist, entrepreneur, and activist W. A. Domingo in 1925, "black immigrants find it impossible to segregate themselves into colonies; too dark of complexion to pose as Cubans or some other Negroid but alien tongued foreigners, they are inevitably swallowed up in black Harlem."

For the immigrants this situation resulted in an inevitable reshaping of identities and raised a number of questions for newcomer and native alike. How would white American society perceive foreign blacks? Would black foreigners become allies with black Americans in the great American race struggle? And how would native blacks and their leaders react to a new expanding ethnic and nonracial dimension to community life? . . .

Initially the presence of significant numbers of dark-skinned immigrants from diverse cultures, speaking a number of European languages or possessing a variety of English accents, disrupted old interpretations of race for white Americans as well as for native-born blacks. One of the earliest observations African Americans made was about the foreign newcomers' reception in places of accommodation or in the workplace. Booker T. Washington reported the following incident in his 1901 autobiography, *Up from Slavery:*

> I happened to find myself in a town in which so much excitement and indignation were being expressed that it seemed likely for a time that there would be a lynching. The occasion of the trouble was that a dark-skinned man had stopped at the local hotel. Investigation, however, developed the fact that this individual was a citizen of Morocco, and that while traveling in this country he spoke the English language. As soon as it was learned that he was not an American Negro, all signs of indignation disappeared. The man who was the innocent cause of the excitement, though, found it prudent after that not to speak English.

. . . Even black American citizens could sometimes avoid being removed to Jim Crow accommodations if mistaken for foreign-born. In 1903 a Florida train conductor asked James Weldon Johnson and a dark-skinned Cuban friend to move to a Jim Crow car, but when he heard them speaking Spanish "his attitude changed; he punched our tickets and gave them back, and treated us just as he did the other passengers in the car."

. . . The *Negro World,* the newspaper of the influential Garvey movement of the 1920s, editorialized in "The Value of Knowing the Spanish Language" that the

Spanish-speaking black enjoyed exceptional freedom and opportunity in travel and accommodations and in employment as bookkeepers, stenographers, and typists. Many were reported to have occupied positions as managers in large importing houses. The writer of the article urged American-born blacks to learn the Spanish language in order to find jobs. But the paper had on other occasions recognized this selective discrimination as "the strange ways of U.S. prejudice." A 1926 article reported that a Kansas City Pullman passenger agent refused a berth to UNIA international organizer Madame Maymie DeMena, a Nicaraguan of African descent, until she produced her passport. The interplay of race with foreign background both in the context of the Harlem community and the larger white American society is important to an investigation of the dynamics in an intraracial ethnic setting. . . .

The backgrounds of Caribbean immigrants just prior to their first massive modern migration into the United States since slavery had a significant impact on the manner in which these newcomers interacted with the emerging Harlem community. The historic waves of migration within the Caribbean and neighboring Central America preceded and continued to affect black immigrant populations in Harlem. Social and cultural patterns institutionalized in the region distinguished immigrant communities from those of southern African Americans. Yet it was no coincidence that Caribbean immigrants and southern migrant blacks arrived in New York at the same time. Both seemingly disparate movements were in part labor displacements influenced by the growth patterns and needs of industry in both regions and the expansion of transportation networks making northern cities more accessible.

Both southern and Caribbean migratory impulses were aided by "myriad kinship and community networks" that directed individual and family groups toward employers and housing. Extended family members and down-South or Caribbean neighbors often lived in the same building or on the same block. These sociofamilial networks formed the basis of community life in Harlem. . . . Indeed community development in Harlem—which is exemplified by the formation of social networks in voluntary associations, political movements, churches, and other organizations—was often the result of cooperation between Caribbean immigrants and native blacks. But it is misleading to define this cooperation too narrowly, for it sometimes emerged even when areas of group friction were not fully ameliorated. . . .

In its first three decades, the evolving Harlem community was comprised of a myriad of social networks linked together by churches, benevolent and fraternal societies, and lodges. It was largely because of these networks that one observer claimed that "inside of six months" immigrants and southern migrants became "pretty good New Yorkers." . . . Alongside and often in cooperation with the church, other voluntary groups promoted the special interests of their members through what can be characterized as homeland societies—more than thirty in number. These were groups formed to maintain contact and preserve traditions of immigrants from the same town or region. There were smaller numbers of these associations among migrants from states along the American southeastern seaboard.

Harlem residents in general also developed a large variety of lodges and social clubs. . . . These associations added interest and vitality to community activity while bringing together influential people to mediate community problems and advance its goals. It is significant that most men in the Harlem community—native or foreign born—who rose to positions of influence at this time were likely to be members of one of the major lodges or fraternal orders. . . . Membership usually conferred a large, automatic constituency for anyone aspiring to leadership. Women's participation in fraternal orders—often women's auxiliaries—also conferred prestige, if not power. Other female-run associations, carried along in the wake of the larger national black women's club movement, sought to elevate the status of black women in the city. Ethnically based women's associations, such as the American West Indian Ladies Aid Society, somewhat reminiscent of the Dorcas societies of the nineteenth century, were insurance associations providing sick and burial benefits and also offering charitable and social-service relief. The activities of all these groups reveal not only the nature of ethnicity in Harlem, but also the context in which disparate social units functioned.

. . . Harlem's fraternal and benevolent associations claimed the membership of a large cross-section of the Caribbean and black American communities. Membership in these associations provided practical mutual aid but also helped to establish an individual's social position and identity in a large, impersonal city. In Harlem, it was often commented, *everyone* belonged to something. An examination of these social networks helps us to learn more about intraracial ethnicity there.

Mutual benefit and relief societies based on place of origin had their roots in late nineteenth-century migrations from the south and the Caribbean. Although the basic purpose of these societies was to provide sick and death benefits for members, acquiring social distinction was an important built-in feature. Many of the early societies restricted their membership to men, prompting the formation of female groups or auxiliaries.

Curiously the northern migration also prompted the formation of an exclusive association based on one's nativity in New York. The Society of the Sons of New York, founded in the 1880s, drew its membership from the "cream" of New York African American society. . . . New York women of comparable social standing formed the Society of the Daughters of New York. According to its public pronouncements, this group [banded] together for "love, mutual protection and elevation."

While the Societies of the Sons and Daughters of New York were clearly organized to reflect status already achieved and to guard against the encroachment of newcomers, the homeland associations organized among southern migrants and Caribbean immigrants helped stabilize life in an evolving community and then promoted upward mobility in it. No official channels—state based or federal—were available to aid either immigrants or southern migrants in their adjustment to the city. . . .

Southern migrants' benevolent associations were formed among individuals migrating from the same state. The Sons and Daughters of Florida's club song captured one of its goals:

> Glory! Glory!
> We are trying to find each other as we travel
>   through the North.

> And we mean to carry out our aim regardless
>   to the cost.
> We hope that they will join us and not a one
>   be lost
> As we go marching on.

There was often more than one association from the same state or island and many of these are still functioning today. The Florida association was formed in 1918, and because many Caribbean immigrants first settled in Florida before coming to New York, the association was comprised of Caribbean and southern migrants. The South Carolina Club was created when twenty-two people met at a party in 1918 and discovered they were all migrants from different towns and cities in South Carolina.

One uniform characteristic of benevolent associations, southern and Caribbean, was their restriction of membership to those born—or having resided a specific number of years—in a particular locality. . . . Critics of the benevolents accused the associations, especially those of Caribbean immigrants, of promoting self-interest ("clannishness") over that of the community. . . .

By 1930 Virginians were the largest southern-migrant group in Harlem. Ten years earlier in November 1920, the Sons and Daughters of Virginia was organized, opening membership to any New York black resident who was a Virginian "by birth or parentage," provided he or she met with other requirements of membership. During the first year of the association's existence, membership grew to 600 and reached its peak of 1,110 in 1927. Picnics and outings as well as regular educational and literary forums were held. Like all other homeland associations, the Virginia association paid death claims and sick benefits.

Ira Reid noted that the foreign-born black groups tended to organize on the basis of three main ideas: (1) mutual benefit and relief; (2) economic and political adjustment in the United States; and (3) the perpetuation of desirable conditions in their homelands. A category not mentioned by Reid was organizational activity that provided a vehicle for self-improvement through educational discussions and debates of various issues. Reid noted that leaders in the first two categories tended to be individuals who had most successfully come to terms—one way or other— with New York's economic, social, and political conditions. Success in these fields automatically conferred prestige on homeland interest groups in which individuals served as the "titular if not the functional leaders." Immigrant organizers of benevolents were also often naturalized citizens—business people or professionals.

The Bermuda Benevolent Association was formed in 1897 by organizers Clarence W. Robinson and George L. Joell, entrepreneurs in the San Juan Hill district. They sent invitations out to forty Bermudians known to be living in the New York area. . . . According to an association history, "The wisdom of including women in the membership was soon recognized." The organization's records indicate that female Bermudians were prime movers within the early association, although the key leadership positions remained male dominated. One woman, Annie Joell, became president but served only one month, from April to May 1901. During the first years of the organization's existence, Rosinia Campbell made her home at 250 West 17th Street available for monthly meetings. She also hosted educational meetings and debates and other special occasions for the association.

The constitutions and bylaws of Caribbean benevolent and native-black benevolent associations were quite explicit. Strict procedures for the conduct of meetings, election of officers, and initiation and acceptance of new members were outlined in the booklets printed and distributed by each society. An "investigating" or admissions committee received all applications at regular meetings and conducted an inquiry into the backgrounds of candidates for membership. A report was submitted at the next meeting. Very carefully worded guidelines relating to the handling and transfer of funds were stated in the constitution. In this regard any member whose dues in arrears exceeded a stated amount was required to forfeit his or her membership.

According to the bylaws of the Bermuda Benevolent Association, when a member in good financial standing became ill and desired to claim a sick allowance, "such member shall cause due notice of this desire in writing to be forwarded to the financial secretary accompanied by a certificate from an authorized medical practitioner stating that member is unable to follow in employment and giving the nature of the complaint." A limited economic safety net was thus available in needy times. A member was eligible for sick or death benefits only after having been a member in good standing for one year. In the event of death, the member's beneficiaries received a stated amount to help defray funeral expenses. But any member who was arrested and convicted of any crime was investigated by the executive committee and, upon its recommendations, suspended or expelled. If expelled no member "shall be reinstated."

As was the case with all such societies, members of the Bermuda Association were required to be of Bermudian birth or parentage or part of the immediate family of a Bermudian and in good health. Any person who had lived continuously in Bermuda for ten years was also eligible. Persons whose reputations reflected "distinction upon the Association" could become honorary members. Membership in the Association never exceeded 250—in part because of careful screening of new members—although the Association's records indicate membership drives were held periodically. In 1898 an initiation fee of two dollars was required and an assessment of twenty-five cents in monthly dues. The Bermudian Association, like other such groups, performed an important service in a period when insurance companies rarely extended coverage to blacks. . . . The benefit program was financed through the assessment of dues and fees. Upon the presentation of a doctor's note, members were eligible for three dollars in sick aid and increments each week during an illness. Members could also expect a visit from the "sick committee." . . .

Prosperity was an underlying goal of all of the benevolents, and the Grenada Mutual Association, formed in 1926, appears to have quickly attracted members. By the mid-1930s it claimed a membership of 425 native Grenadians, a significant number from so small an island. No doubt the Great Depression encouraged cooperative economic efforts. The association charged a membership fee of one dollar, monthly dues of forty to fifty cents, and a tax of fifty cents and provided each member with health and death benefits. Upon the death of any member, one hundred dollars—a very helpful sum for the times—was paid to relatives to assist with funeral expenses. The association held annual affairs and regular musical, literary, and educational functions. It also collected funds to help educate poor students on the island.

Other activities promoted by Caribbean homeland associations regularly brought older and more recent immigrants together at social, educational, and charitable functions. Among these were annual boat rides, picnics, and Thanksgiving programs to which other Caribbean associations were invited to purchase tickets. Aletha Challenor joined the Sons and Daughters of Barbados to find suitable social outlets for her three daughters. Violet Murrell also found the association an important social outlet for picnics, bus rides, and trips to Niagara Falls. Educational forums and musical and literary programs were organized for the mutual improvement of the members and invited guests. Once the Bermuda Association purchased a home on 146th Street, it established its own library. As members became more established, the Association also included charitable programs, including scholarships for students in Bermuda and contributions to community charities in New York. While the Bermudians promoted home traditions, the organization also solidified its links to the larger African American community by purchasing lifetime membership in the NAACP.

As Reid has suggested, cooperative financing was a basic reason for the widespread existence of immigrant (and southern migrant) benevolents. Many things not possible for the individual were made possible together—loans for mortgages, political influence, and general welfare. The Bermuda Benevolent Association began granting mortgages to its members after a forty-year reputation of service to the group. Benevolents were thus significant in not only providing mutual aid to their members but by playing an important role in advancing economic stability in the larger Harlem community.

The financial resources of several associations were aided by contributions of some of their more established or wealthy members. The Trinidad Benevolent Association was founded by Harlem physician Charles Petioni. Petioni also formed the more explicitly political Caribbean Union, which promoted cooperation between the various associations, solidarity with progressive black American causes, and independence for the Caribbean. With economic stability as one of its primary goals, the Montserrat Progressive Society was established in 1914 with businessmen William Roach and Joseph Sweeney and journalist Hodge Kirnon among its founders. A stated purpose was to unite the people from the island of Montserrat in New York, "to assist in uplifting them socially, morally and intellectually, to care for its sick, and those in distress, and to bury its dead." In 1925 the Society had 750 members, contributed $1,200 in sick benefits, and owned a meeting hall at 207 West 137th Street valued at $13,000. Another prominent Montserratan, Helena Benta, a secretary of the Montserrat Progressive Society, was a frequent public speaker in Harlem and an advocate of unity among the Caribbean organizations in their benevolent work as well as in their collective political interest in the Caribbean. She became an organizer of the West Indian Federation and gave talks on the role of women in the development of West Indian nationhood.

In Harlem Caribbean women may have had more opportunities for leadership than at home, although here as in the native communities men dominated the public arena. Still, benevolent associations provided women with a variety of leadership opportunities. In 1915 a group of women from the then Danish West Indies (now the U.S. Virgin Islands) felt women's interests special enough to form their own organization—despite the presence of several other Danish West Indies benevolents in

New York. A group of women connected with the organization known after 1917 as the American West Indian Ladies Aid Society (AWILAS) became Harlem leaders. Male-led Virgin Island Associations frequently communicated with AWILAS for assistance with women's problems. A typical referral was this undated note sent by Ashley Totten, head of the Virgin Islands Industrial Association:

> [A request] comes from a girl of 13 years, Lavinda Urcila March. Her mother's name is Lavinda Cumberbach. She is without support in the islands and [has] not heard from her father since 1919. The name of her father is Archibald Egthebert March, last address 11 West 137th Street. Perhaps someone in your society might help us to locate him.

. . . But in general the Society's records provide evidence of the complex nature of voluntary association among Caribbean women. While the Society maintained a constitution and bylaws like other benevolents and conducted its business by the strict guidelines of most fraternal orders, the leaders of the organization were involved in radical political activity as well as reform movements in the Virgin Islands and in New York. Elizabeth Hendrickson, president of the Society in 1924 and again in the 1930s, was a well-known street corner speaker, involved in rent and landlord struggles of the Harlem Tenants League in the 1920s. The Tenants League was a militant group which attempted to organize residents against unfair treatment—exorbitant rents, increases, evictions, and so on.

The AWILAS was still functioning in the 1950s and was stridently anti-imperialist; it had relationships with similar pro-independence groups during the 1920s and after. During the 1920s AWILAS officers—Redalia Matthews, Antoinette Reubel, Sylvania Smith, and Estelle Williams—were connected to other political movements, particularly of Virgin Islanders in Harlem. The Society participated as part of a network of Harlem community organizations with which the fledgling Brotherhood of Sleeping Car Porters and Maids, led by A. Philip Randolph, sought to cooperate. This link was no doubt facilitated by Ashley Totten, a Virgin Island Pullman porter and a Brotherhood organizer. In the 1930s the International Labor Defense of the American Communist Party also solicited the political support of the Society, probably through Elizabeth Hendrickson, who was by then affiliated with Communist-led activities in Harlem.

Few organizations of this type combined mutual aid with such active politics. The UNIA probably comes closest to this model. The local New York UNIA began with many features of the mutual aid and fraternal orders and at first almost no political agenda. Many native-born and immigrant Harlemites were attracted to the organization because of its provision of sick and death benefits as well as its political program, which matured. . . .

If the benevolent organizations helped institutionalize ethnic presence in Harlem while serving the needs of a larger Caribbean community at home and abroad, other kinds of voluntary associations provided opportunities for interaction between native-born and immigrant groups. In all major African American communities the lodge and fraternal order were popular social anchors for the average nonprofessional middle-class as well as a haven for professionals. Like the benevolents, fraternal orders (Prince Hall Masons, Odd Fellows, Elks, Order of Eastern Star, etc.) were class-defining institutions. One scholar of fraternal organizations has noted that these orders and the "middle-class churches have formed an environ-ment conducive to the creation, maintenance and protection of a self-conscious, socially cohesive black middle-class community." With several exceptions, mem-bership in these orders tended to de-emphasize one's ethnic background while pro-moting racial solidarity, self-help, and self-reliance.

Fraternal orders organized and maintained almost exclusively by black immi-grants were mainly those based in the British-held colonies of the Caribbean and thus unfamiliar to African Americans. For instance, the Ancient Order of Shep-herds, the Mechanics, and the Free Gardeners were all run by Caribbean Har-lemites. In some cases black immigrants found, though ethnically mixed in their homelands, these orders were racially segregated in the States. Such was the case of the Lebanon Foresters, a group consisting of black immigrant men from dif-ferent Caribbean countries who had worked on the Panama Canal and who had an active chapter there. In 1918 they applied for membership in the white New York body and were turned down. They formed their own organization in 1923.

But Caribbean immigrant professionals especially joined native-black-run fraternal orders. Memberships were proudly announced as part of an individual's credentials or list of accomplishments. . . . The Elks were the largest and most powerful fraternal order in Harlem. Membership conferred on an individual access to social, economic, and political influence. The largest order, Manhattan Lodge No. 45 was located at 266 West 139th Street—"a large and imposing structure" with club rooms, assembly hall, and offices. The lodge claimed its own symphony orchestra and band. Its public events included frequent concerts in Harlem parks and public schools. Its membership, according to WPA researcher Baxter Leach, was about 2,000. Another Elks lodge, the Monarch, owned its headquarters at 245 137th Street. The other Elks, the Imperial Lodge, and the Henry Lincoln Johnson Lodge No. 630 had similar holdings. The Henry Lincoln Johnson Lodge had a heavy Caribbean membership. . . . Most of the orders had "ladies auxiliaries" which ran their own affairs and raised their own money as well as funds for the general body.

Caribbean immigrant professionals, while maintaining membership in their own fraternities, often made strategic gestures in joining the American-based orders. Marcus Garvey, whose UNIA had many features of the fraternal orders and drew upon them for membership, became a Mason himself under the influence of John E. Bruce. Many UNIA activities, including elaborate neighborhood parades, were modeled on those of fraternal orders. Other Harlem notables, including mu-nicipal judge James S. Watson, were affiliated with the Masonic Order. Although some immigrants selected lodges in which their groups were heavily represented, fraternal lodges generally reinforced social and political links with the larger African American community. Bibliophile Arthur Schomburg was a high-ranking officer in the Prince Hall Masons and, during the 1920s, considered one of their most distinguished members. He traveled widely as the Grand Secretary of the Prince Hall Grand Lodge of the State of New York and became an associate editor with John E. Bruce of the *Masonic Quarterly Review.* In the 1920s he was better known nationally among African Americans as a fraternal leader than as the founder of the now famous library of black materials that bears his name.

Virgin Islander Casper Holstein was a founder of New York's powerful Monarch Lodge, and in 1929 he nearly gained presidency of the national organization. The 1929 convention was the first at which longtime president J. Finly Wilson faced an effective challenge. Holstein received widespread support from native-black New Yorkers as well as from influential native blacks in other cities. Oscar De Priest of Chicago, the first African American congressman since Reconstruction, supported Holstein's candidacy. Although Holstein was head of the powerful Monarch Lodge in New York, when he ran for president of the national organization, his opponents publicly questioned whether a Caribbean immigrant could become head of a historically African American organization. This was one of the few times Holstein's background was raised as a political weapon against him. The real issue, however, appears not to have been Holstein's foreign birth at all, but the fact that as national president of the Elks and as a powerful and wealthy numbers operator, he could obviously wield influence his rival could not match. His Caribbean birth then became a tool of the opposition, used to split his support among the predominantly native-born membership, and he was defeated. Yet Holstein's attempt to become national head of the Elks was a shrewd political move at a key point in his career as one of the leading businessmen in Harlem.

Churches, benevolent associations, lodges, and fraternal orders comprised the first line of urban accommodation for Caribbean immigrants and southern migrants in Harlem. In important ways they helped to fix Harlem's social, economic, and political agenda by dealing with individual needs from the cradle to the grave. The smaller associations became the training ground of new leaders, who may have found leadership roles in the larger community impossible to acquire at first. Churches and fraternal lodges, through their leaders especially, bonded the newer Caribbean community to larger African American Harlem, although this connection was not always smooth. . . .

F U R T H E R   R E A D I N G

James Borchert, *Alley Life in Washington: Family, Community, Religion, and Folklife in the City, 1850–1970* (1980).

Albert S. Broussard, *Black San Francisco: The Struggle for Racial Equality in the West, 1900–1954* (1993).

Elizabeth Clark-Lewis, *Living In, Living Out: African American Domestics in Washington, D.C., 1910–1940* (1994).

Peter Gottlieb, *Making Their Own Way: Southern Blacks' Migration to Pittsburgh, 1916–1930* (1987).

Robert Gregg, *Sparks from the Anvil of Oppression: Philadelphia's African Methodists and Southern Migrants, 1890–1940* (1993).

Farah Griffith, *"Who Set You Flowin'?": The African-American Migration Narrative* (1995).

James R. Grossman, *Land of Hope: Chicago, Black Southerners, and the Great Migration* (1989).

Winston James, *Holding Aloft the Banner of Ethiopia: Caribbean Radicalism in Early Twentieth Century America* (1998).

Earl Lewis, *In Their Own Interests: Race, Class, and Power in Twentieth-Century Norfolk, Virginia* (1991).

Carole Marks, *Farewell—We're Good and Gone: The Great Black Migration* (1989).

Kimberley L. Phillips, *AlabamaNorth: African-American Migrants, Community, and Working-Class Activism in Cleveland, 1915–1945* (1999).

Milton C. Sernett, *Bound for the Promised Land: African American Religion and the Great Migration* (1997).

Quintard Taylor, *The Forging of a Black Community: Seattle's Central District, from 1870 Through the Civil Rights Era* (1994).

Joe William Trotter, Jr., *Black Milwaukee: The Making of an Industrial Proletariat, 1915–1945* (1985).

Joe W. Trotter, Jr., and Earl Lewis, eds., *African Americans in the Industrial Age: A Documentary History, 1915–1945* (1996).

William H. Tuttle, Jr., *Race Riot: Chicago in the Red Summer of 1919* (1970).

Nancy J. Weiss, *The National Urban League, 1910–1940* (1974).

Lillian Serece Williams, *Strangers in the Land of Paradise: The Creation of an African American Community, Buffalo, NY, 1900–1940* (1999).

Defining a Race Politics

Booker T. Washington's 1895 speech at the Cotton States' Exposition in Atlanta,
Georgia, was probably the best-known public address by a black person in the
nineteenth-century United States. Hailed by northern and southern white conservatives and liberals for its "sensible" approach to black progress, the speech enabled
Washington to gain influence with government officials and wealthy philanthropists and thereby to project himself as national spokesperson for black Americans,
even though he held no elective office and headed no mass-based organization.
Black Americans' responses to Washington were more mixed. Some appreciated his
emphasis on black economic development and thought his appeasement of white
conservatives necessary in an era of increasing racial violence. Others denounced
what they perceived as an abdication of educational and political rights. Recognition of Washington's considerable influence has led some scholars to characterize
the years 1895–1915 as the "Age of Booker T. Washington" and to focus discussions of black politics on him, his supporters such as T. Thomas Fortune, and his
critics, most notably William Edward Burghardt Du Bois. Other historians recognize a wider range of political thought and actors and a more complex array of
issues and debates. Washington's "Tuskegee Machine" was certainly a defining
element in those debates but not the only one.

How might one best understand the factors that shaped the political ideologies
and strategies of black Americans in the late nineteenth and early twentieth centuries? What was at issue in debates over appropriate means of black progress and
appropriate responses to increasing racism? What were the sources of difference
between the various factions? How did persons situated differently—by class, sex,
region, ethnicity—interpret the state of black America? What forms did black political action take? To what degree did black people also have to address exclusionary
practices within black America?

D O C U M E N T S

Several years before Booker T. Washington rose to national prominence, Ida B. Wells
launched a national and international antilynching campaign. The first document is an
excerpt from an 1892 pamphlet reprinting her newspaper columns on the subject, this one

her advice to black southerners. The wide distribution of her columns in this pamphlet was made possible by fundraising efforts of black clubwomen in New York, who also helped to finance Wells's antilynching speaking tour of the United States and the British Isles. The second document is Booker T. Washington's "Speech at the Opening of the Cotton States' Exposition," which projected Washington into the national political arena.

The first truly national black political organization was the National Association of Colored Women (NACW), founded in 1896. The third document reports the resolutions adopted at the 1904 NACW annual convention. Increasingly wary of Booker T. Washington's political stances and resentful of his stranglehold on funding for black educational institutions and on press coverage for competing political views, twenty-nine African-American men—ministers, newspaper editors, educators, physicians—met on the Canadian side of Niagara Falls in July 1905, in response to a call from W. E. B. Du Bois, to organize a political vehicle that would stand strongly for political rights and openly challenge the Tuskegee Machine. They called themselves the Niagara Movement; their statement of principles is the fourth document.

If there was one political strategy common to proponents of accommodation, protest, integration, separatism, nationalism, and even some socialists, it was a focus on economic development, especially black business development. In the fifth document, Maggie Lena Walker, chief executive officer of the Independent Order of Saint Luke mutual benefit society and president of the St. Luke Penny Savings Bank, addresses an audience of black men in Richmond, Virginia, in 1906, seeking their support for the St. Luke Emporium, a department store. Some of those who sought not only economic but also political independence turned to the idea of an all-black town. By 1915 at least sixty-four all-black towns spread from Florida to New Jersey, from North Carolina to California. Scenes from two of them—Eatonville, Florida, and Mound Bayou, Mississippi—constitute the sixth document.

Much of black political activity was initiated on the local level in response to specific community issues. In the seventh document citizens in Charleston, South Carolina, where, by law, no black teacher could be employed in the public schools, demand black teachers for black schools. A 1920 bill rescinded the ban on black teachers. Among those who participated in the petition drive was Septima Clark, who organized schoolchildren to go door to door soliciting signatures for the petition. Decades later Clark organized citizenship classes for both the Highlander Folk School and the Southern Christian Leadership Conference to prepare black people throughout the South to register to vote.

A. Philip Randolph and Chandler Owens criticized black political leaders and civil rights organizations, including the NAACP (founded in 1910), for failing to address the specific conditions of the mass of black workers as workers. In their magazine, *The Messenger,* which they called "The Only Radical Negro Magazine in America," they often focused on organizing black and white workers, were critical of the conservatism of the American Federation of Labor, and voiced support for the socialist Industrial Workers of the World. The eighth document appeared in the August 1919 issue of *The Messenger.*

The largest mass movement of African Americans in the early twentieth century and the first international organization of people of African descent was the Universal Negro Improvement Association, organized by Marcus Garvey. By the early 1920s there were more than eight hundred UNIA branches in the United States and other branches throughout the Caribbean and Africa. In the ninth document, Garvey, writing in 1922, offers his assessment of the state of people of African descent in the United States and throughout the world.

1. Ida B. Wells Urges Self-Defense, 1892

. . . To Northern capital and Afro-American labor the South owes its rehabilitation. If labor is withdrawn capital will not remain. The Afro-American is thus the back-bone of the South. A thorough knowledge and judicious exercise of this power in lynching localities could many times effect a bloodless revolution. The white man's dollar is his god, and to stop this will be to stop outrages in many localities.

The Afro-Americans of Memphis denounced the lynching of three of their best citizens, and urged and waited for the authorities to act in the matter and bring the lynchers to justice. No attempt was made to do so, and the black men left the city by thousands, bringing about great stagnation in every branch of business. Those who remained so injured the business of the street car company by staying off the cars, that the superintendent, manager and treasurer called personally on the editor of the "Free Speech," asked them to urge our people to give them their pa-tronage again. . . . A meeting of white citizens in June, three months after the lynching, passed resolutions for the first time, condemning it. *But they did not pun-ish the lynchers.* Every one of them was known by name, because they had been selected to do the dirty work, by some of the very citizens who passed these resolu-tions. Memphis is fast losing her black population, who proclaim as they go that there is no protection for the life and property of any Afro-American citizen in Memphis who is not a slave.

The Afro-American citizens of Kentucky, whose intellectual and financial im-provement has been phenomenal, have never had a separate car law until now. Delegations and petitions poured into the Legislature against it, yet the bill passed and the Jim Crow Car of Kentucky is a legalized institution. Will the great mass of Negroes continue to patronize the railroad? . . .

. . . [T]he ministers, teachers, heads of secret and other orders, and the head of every family should pass the word around for every member of the race in Kentucky to stay off railroads unless obliged to ride   If they did so, and their advice was fol-lowed persistently the convention would not need to petition the Legislature to re-peal the law or raise money to file a suit. The railroad corporations would be so affected they would in self-defense lobby to have the separate car law repealed. . . .

The appeal to the white man's pocket has ever been more effectual than all the appeals ever made to his conscience. Nothing, absolutely nothing, is to be gained by a further sacrifice of manhood and self-respect. By the right exercise of his power as the industrial factor of the South, the Afro-American can demand and secure his rights, the punishment of lynchers, and a fair trial for accused rapists.

Of the many inhuman outrages of this present year, the only case where the pro-posed lynching did *not* occur, was where the men armed themselves in Jacksonville, Fla., and Paducah, Ky., and prevented it. The only times an Afro-American who was assaulted got away has been when he had a gun and used it in self-defense.

The lesson this teaches and which every Afro American should ponder well, is that a Winchester rifle should have a place of honor in every black home, and it should be used for that protection which the law refuses to give. When the white

Ida B. Wells, *Southern Horrors. Lynch Law in All Its Phases* (New York: New York Age Print, 1892), 22–24.

man who is always the aggressor knows he runs as great risk of biting the dust every time his Afro-American victim does, he will have greater respect for Afro-American life. The more the Afro-American yields and cringes and begs, the more he has to do so, the more he is insulted, outraged and lynched. . . .

The Afro-American papers are the only ones which will print the truth, and they lack means to employ agents and detectives to get at the facts. The race must rally a mighty host to the support of their journals, and thus enable them to do much in the way of investigation. . . .

Near Vicksburg, Miss., a murder was committed by a gang of burglars. Of course it must have been done by Negroes, and Negroes were arrested for it. It is believed that 2 men, Smith Tooley and John Adams, belonged to a gang controlled by white men and, fearing exposure, on the night of July 4th, they were hanged in the Court House yard by those interested in silencing them. Robberies since committed in the same vicinity have been known to be by white men who had their faces blackened. We strongly believe in the innocence of these murdered men, but we have no proof. No other news goes out to the world save that which stamps us as a race of cut-throats, robbers and lustful wild beasts. . . .

. . . The Afro American himself did not know as he should have known as his journals should be in a position to have him know and act.

Nothing is more definitely settled than he must act for himself. I have shown how he may employ the boycott, emigration and the press, and I feel that by a combination of all these agencies [lynch law] can be effectually stamped out . . . , that last relic of barbarism and slavery. "The gods help those who help themselves."

2. Booker T. Washington Promotes Accommodationism, 1895

"Mr. President and Gentlemen of the Board of Directors and Citizens:

"One third of the population of the South is of the Negro race. No enterprise seeking the material, civil, or moral welfare of this section can disregard this element of our population and reach the highest success. . . .

". . . Ignorant and inexperienced, it is not strange that in the first years of our new life we began at the top instead of at the bottom; that a seat in Congress or the State Legislature was more sought than real estate or industrial skill; that the political convention or stump speaking had more attractions than starting a dairy farm or truck garden.

"A ship lost at sea for many days suddenly sighted a friendly vessel. From the mast of the unfortunate vessel was seen a signal: 'Water, water; we die of thirst!' The answer from the friendly vessel at once came back: 'Cast down your bucket where you are.' A second time . . . And a third and fourth signal for water was answered: 'Cast down your bucket where you are.' The captain of the distressed vessel, at last heeding the injunction, cast down his bucket, and it came up full of fresh, sparkling water from the mouth of the Amazon River. To those of my race

Booker T. Washington, *The Story of My Life and Work* (1900; reprint, New York: Negro Universities Press, 1969), 165–171.

who depend on bettering their condition in a foreign land, or who underestimate the importance of cultivating friendly relations with the Southern white man, who is their next door neighbor, I would say: 'Cast down your bucket where you are'— cast it down in making friends in every manly way of the people of all races by whom we are surrounded.

"Cast it down in agriculture, mechanics, in commerce, in domestic service, and in the professions. . . . [W]hatever other sins the South may be called to bear, when it comes to business, pure and simple, it is in the South that the Negro is given a man's chance in the commercial world. . . . Our greatest danger is, that in the great leap from slavery to freedom we may overlook the fact that the masses of us are to live by the productions of our hands, and fail to keep in mind that we shall prosper in proportion as we learn to dignify and glorify common labor, and put brains and skill into the common occupations of life. . . . No race can prosper till it learns that there is as much dignity in tilling a field as in writing a poem. It is at the bottom of life we must begin, and not at the top. Nor should we permit our grievances to overshadow our opportunities.

"To those of the white race who look to the incoming of those of foreign birth and strange tongue and habits for the prosperity of the South, were I permitted I would repeat what I say to my own race, 'Cast down your bucket where you are.' Cast it down among the 8,000,000 Negroes whose habits you know, whose fidelity and love you have tested . . . among these people who have, without strikes and labor wars, tilled your fields, cleared your forests, builded your railroads and cities. . . . Casting down your bucket among my people, helping and encouraging them . . . and to education of head, hand and heart, you will find that they will buy your surplus land, make blossom the waste places in your fields, and run your factories. While doing this, you can be sure in the future, as in the past, that you and your families will be surrounded by the most patient, faithful, law-abiding, and unresentful people that the world has seen. . . . In all things that are purely social we can be as separate as the fingers, yet one as the hand in all things essential to mutual progress.

"There is no defense or security for any of us except in the highest intelligence and development of all. If anywhere there are efforts tending to curtail the fullest growth of the Negro, let these efforts be turned into stimulating, encouraging, and making him the most useful and intelligent citizen. Effort or means so invested will pay a thousand per cent interest. . . .

"Nearly sixteen millions of hands will aid you in pulling the load upwards, or they will pull against you the load downwards. We shall constitute one-third and more of the ignorance and crime of the South, or one-third its intelligence and progress; we shall contribute one-third to the business and industrial prosperity of the South, or we shall prove a veritable body of death, stagnating, depressing, retarding every effort to advance the body politic. . . . ·

"The wisest among my race understand that the agitation of questions of social equality is the extremest folly, and that progress in the enjoyment of all the privileges that will come to us must be the result of severe and constant struggle rather than of artificial forcing. No race that has anything to contribute to the markets of the world is long in any degree ostracized. It is important and right that all privileges of the law be ours, but it is vastly more important that we be prepared for the exercise of those privileges. The opportunity to earn a dollar in a factory just now is worth infinitely more than the opportunity to spend a dollar in an opera house.

". . . I pledge that, in your effort to work out the great and intricate problem which God has laid at the doors of the South, you shall have at all times the patient, sympathetic help of my race. . . ."

3. Resolutions of the National Association of Colored Women, 1904

The National Association of Colored Women's Clubs in the fourth convention assembled . . .

We pledge renewed efforts and loyalty along all lines in this, our national organization, continuing to stand for adherence to our motto "Lifting as We Climb," for we believe that in it lies the future hope of the race.

In view of the fact of the numerous lynchings and the many victims burned at the stake, extending even to women, which have occurred in nearly every section of our country;

Be it Resolved, That we, the representatives of Negro womanhood, do heartily deplore and condemn this barbarous taking of human life, and that we appeal to the sentiment of the Christian world to check and eradicate this growing evil; and be it further

Resolved, That we do all in our power to bring criminals to justice, and that we appeal to all legislative bodies and courts of justice to see that all persons are protected in their rights as citizens.

Whereas, Our people throughout the South are discriminated against by railroads, being compelled to ride in offensive and inadequate cars, after paying first-class fares; and,

Whereas, Some of the Southern cities have introduced separate street cars,

Be it Resolved, That this body condemn such action, and that in all such states and towns the club women unite in trying to induce our people to refrain from patronizing street cars. . . .

Be it Resolved, That we commend the action of the National Republican Convention in the adoption of that part of its platform which asserts that any state disfranchising its voters shall be limited in its Congressional representation.

Be it Resolved, That the women of our Association prepare themselves by the study of civil government and kindred subjects for the problems of city, state and national life, that they may be able to perform intelligently the duties that have come to some and will come to others in the natural progress of the woman's suffrage question.

Be it Resolved, That the Colored Women's Clubs endorse the W.C.T.U. [Women's Christian Temperance Union], and urge that we emphasize more fully the work among the young people, and do all in their power to create a sentiment

Minutes of the Fourth Convention of the National Association of Colored Women, Held at St. Paul's Church, St. Louis, Missouri, July 11 to 16, 1904 (Jefferson City, Mo., n.d.), pp. 23–26. Reprinted in Herbert Aptheker, ed., *A Documentary History of the Negro People in the United States,* vol. 2, *From the Reconstruction to the Founding of the NAACP* (New York: Citadel Press, 1979), 889–890.

against the practice of taking them to places of amusement where intoxicants are sold, and further that we do all in our power to prevent the diffusion of improper and pernicious literature that saps the vitality of the moral life of our young people.

Believing that the mother is the rock upon which the home is built, therefore, be it

Resolved, That we pledge ourselves to hold and encourage mothers' meetings whenever practicable, in order to instruct mothers in all that pertains to home building and child-life.

4. The Niagara Men Pledge Themselves to Persistent Agitation, 1905

The members of the conference, known as the Niagara Movement, assembled in annual meeting at Buffalo, July 11th, 12th and 13th, 1905, congratulate the Negro-Americans on certain undoubted evidences of progress in the last decade, particularly the increase of intelligence, the buying of property, the checking of crime, and uplift in home life, the advance in literature and art, and . . . the conduct of great religious, economic and educational institutions.

At the same time, we believe that this class of American citizens should protest emphatically and continually against the curtailment of their political rights. We believe in manhood suffrage. . . .

We believe also in protest against the curtailment of our civil rights. . . .

We especially complain against the denial of equal opportunities to us in economic life; in the rural districts of the South this amounts to peonage and virtual slavery; all over the South it tends to crush labor and small business enterprises; and everywhere American prejudice, helped often by iniquitous laws, is making it more difficult for Negro-Americans to earn a decent living.

Common school education should be free to all American children and compulsory. High school training should be adequately provided for all, and college training should be the monopoly of no class or race in any section of our common country. . . . We favor well-equipped trade and technical schools for the training of artisans, and . . . adequate and liberal endowment for a few institutions of higher education. . . .

We demand upright judges in courts, juries selected without discrimination on account of color and the same measure of punishment and the same efforts at reformation for black as for white offenders. We need orphanages and farm schools for dependent children, juvenile reformatories for delinquents, and the abolition of the dehumanizing convict-lease system. . . .

We plead for health—for an opportunity to live in decent houses and localities, for a chance to rear our children in physical and moral cleanliness.

We hold up for public execration the conduct of two opposite classes of men: The practice among employers of importing ignorant Negro-American laborers in emergencies, and then affording them neither protection nor permanent employment; and the practice of labor unions in proscribing and boycotting and oppressing thousands of their fellow-toilers, simply because they are black. . . .

We protest against the "Jim Crow" car, since its effect is and must be, to make us pay first-class fare for third-class accommodations, render us open to insults and discomfort and to crucify wantonly our manhood, womanhood and self-respect.

We regret that this nation has never seen fit adequately to reward the black soldiers who, in its five wars, have defended their country with their blood, and yet have been systematically denied the promotions which their abilities deserve. And we regard as unjust, the exclusion of black boys from the military and navy training schools. . . .

We repudiate the monstrous doctrine that the oppressor should be the sole authority as to the rights of the oppressed. . . .

Of the above grievances we do not hesitate to complain, and to complain loudly and insistently. To ignore, overlook, or apologize for these wrongs is to prove ourselves unworthy of freedom. Persistent manly agitation is the way to liberty. . . .

5. Maggie Lena Walker Talks to Black Men About Racial Responsibility, 1906

. . . Hasn't it yet crept into your minds that we are being more and more oppressed each day that we live? Hasn't it yet come to you, that we are being oppressed by the passage of laws which not only have for their object the degradation of Negro manhood and Negro womanhood, but also the destruction of all kinds of Negro enterprises? . . . And yet with the loss of citizenship, . . . the destroying of Negro business enterprises, the refusal of employment to Negroes; the attempt to drive out the Negro barbers, and Negroes from every other occupation, with hostile legislation on the increase—there are those who still believe that we should look to the Lord and keep our mouths shut. . . .

My Friends, come let us put our heads together and run over in our minds and see if we know of *anything* on earth in the whole human family, quite so helpless as the Negro woman. Have you thought of the number of occupations by which she makes her living? She is a domestic in the white man's house, and cooks, cleans, scrubs, washes, nurses and waits. A few are seamstresses, a few teachers, and a very few clerks. . . .

. . . You know too well the condition of affairs in every business house in the city. The white woman is there. . . . You know as to the stores from which you bought your hats, shoes and clothing. The white woman was there. . . . Step into the telegraph office. The white woman is there. . . . Step to the 'phone and by the time you touch it, a white woman is there. The white woman is everywhere. And, my dear friends, she is in many of the places that she is, BECAUSE YOUR MONEY,

---

Maggie Lena Walker, "Benaiah's Valour: An Address for *Men Only*," St. Luke Hall, Richmond, Virginia, March 1, 1906, copy in Maggie Lena Walker Papers, Maggie L. Walker National Historic Site, Richmond, Virginia.

YOUR INFLUENCE, YOUR PATRONAGE keeps *her* there, WHILE YOUR OWN WOMEN, FLESH OF YOUR FLESH, BLOOD OF YOUR BLOOD, ARE LEFT TO SHIFT FOR THEMSELVES, AS BEST THEY CAN. . . . ARE WE NOT AS MUCH TO YOU AS THE WHITE WOMEN YOU ARE SO LOYALLY SUPPORTING by the nickels, dimes and dollars you are spending with them each week? . . .

But, my friends, it is not enough to say, "Yes"—with your lips. If you love these black women—your own women—your own wives, mothers, daughters and sisters, . . . IF YOU LOVE THESE BLACK WOMEN, FEED THEM. . . .

. . . My friends, there is a lion terrorizing us, preying upon us, and upon every business effort which we put forth. The name of this insatiable lion, is PREJUDICE. . . . Even now, at this moment while I am standing here talking to you, that lion is seeking some new plan of attack. The white man's prejudice NEVER sleeps nor slumbers. . . . Is NEVER satisfied. And seeks to crush when it finds that every dollar which the Negro makes does not come into his store and his bank.

Listen to me men of Richmond, listen to me. . . . Some of you have put your money in our hands, in our Bank and in our Store. Some of you are our regular customers, you, your wives and your children—and there are some, I am sorry to say, sitting here looking at me, who have never had your foot across the doorsill of our bank or our store. . . .

. . . It took us two years of dealing under cover to obtain the property in which the St. Luke Bank and the St. Luke Emporium are located now. When it was found out for what purposes the property had been bought there was an attempt made to buy the premises from us at an advance of several thousand dollars more than the purchase price. In addition to this there was a personal offer of TEN THOUSAND DOLLARS in cash if we would not start the Emporium. But nothing changed us: the Bank is there, the store is there and Negro men and women are there earning a living and getting a business education. Women of your race, your own flesh and blood, as polite and capable as any other women on Broad Street. . . .

. . . Those of you who read the papers have doubtless noticed with what activity there has been formed a White Retail Dealers' Association, taking in every white man or woman selling anything at retail: the whiskey dealer, baker, butcher, druggist, milliner, coal dealer, shoe dealer, in short every white merchant regardles[s] of the kind of retail business he conducts, has gone into the association. Now, for what purpose have they done this? Simply to crush out those Negro merchants who are objectionable to them because they compete with them and get a few dollars which would otherwise go to the white merchant.

When the White Retail Dealers' Association decides to crush out a Negro merchant, the wholesale merchants are notified not to sell [to] the Negro, . . . saying if they do, they will not receive the patronage of the white merchants comprising the White Retail Dealers' Association.

A few days ago, as has been our custom, we placed an order with a Richmond wholesale house for several thousand dollars worth of dry goods. After holding the order for several days we were asked to pay cash. Now, if the same order had been given by any reputable white firm, the goods would have been delivered and from sixty to seventy days allowed, as well as a discount, before the date of payment. In short, a white merchant can get his goods, place them upon his shelves and sell them, collect from his customers and pay his bills, while Negro merchants must pay cash for what they buy. This is what the lion of prejudice is doing on Broad Street; and every time you set foot in a white man's store, you are making the lion of Prejudice stronger and stronger, and making it all the more easily for him to devour the Negro merchant. . . .

. . . [A] few months ago we were in New York. Entering a wholesale house we were shown a letter saying that the St. Luke Emporium was underselling the white merchants of Richmond and if our trade was carried by that house, that these Richmond merchants whose names were signed would immediately withdraw their patronage. Now, Friends, just think! There were some of our folks here walking around on the outside, who had never set foot on the inside, saying—"O, they sell everything so dear; they are too *high* for me"—while the white merchants were filing complaints in writing in New York that we were selling too cheap. Now, what do you think of that? . . .

And now my friends, let us lay aside formality and let me appeal to you as sober reasonable men. The St. Luke Emporium has been very largely the work of our women. If we have united and struggled and have gotten to the point which we have, deep down in your heart don't you feel, that you ought to spend your money with us? We have the same kind of shirts, cuffs and collars, underwear, shoes and the other things worn by men as the white stores have. We are not one cent higher and in many instances cheaper in our prices than the other stores. Why then do you pass us by and carry your money and your friends' money to the men who would not give your child employment except as a porter?

If white men are forming combinations and associations for the purpose of crushing us out, is there one single colored man in here, that will now deliberately go and carry his dollars to the white merchant so that he can fight us? Are you really going to feed the lion of prejudice and make him stronger and stronger, so that he can all the more easily devour us? . . .

. . . Listen to me, my friends, the only way we can kill the lion of race prejudice is to stop feeding him. Stop fee[d]ing him every Saturday night and every Monday morning. There are FIFTY THOUSAND Negroes in and around Richmond; you will agree with me that they certainly average NOT LESS THAN $1 per week for food, clothes and medicine. Fifty thousand dollars per week mean $200,000 per month and $2,400,000 per year the lowest possible amount that we are spending. Our white papers, our white pulpits and our legi[s]lature preach but one doctrine and that is the doctrine of separation. Why then does not the "jim crow" car produce the jim crow store? Or are we going to wait until the white man passes a law forcing us to trade in our own store and deposit our money in our own banks?

. . . For the last time, from the very depths of my soul, let me appeal to you to give us your patronage. Spend your money with us. Help us to help ourselves. You are strong, . . . our protection and our refuge. While we can do much ourselves, we can do more with your aid.

The Emporium and the Bank to us is the sprouting acorn—but to your boys and girls, it will be the tall spreading, giant oak, affording shelter and protection for a thousand. Will you come to us? Will you help us?

6. Promoting Black Towns, c. 1907

Photos: Booker T. Washington, *The Negro in Business* (1907; reprint, Chicago: Afro-Am Press, 1969), opp. 78, opp. 91.

Mound Bayou, Mississippi, founded in 1887, was one of the most celebrated all-black towns. Promoters particularly emphasized the town's various business enterprises, including several cotton gins, a saw mill, an oil mill, and the Mound Bayou Bank (see page 166, bottom). Pictured on page 166 (top) is the City Council of Eatonville, Florida, standing in front of the city jail, circa 1907. In her later writings, Zora Neale Hurston, who grew up in Eatonville, recalled the folklore and customs of the town's residents—and the careful monitoring of residents' personal behavior by the bourgeois town leaders.

7. Ten Thousand Charlestonians Petition for Black Teachers in Black Schools, 1919

We the citizens of the negro race and parents of pupils of the aforesaid race in attendance as pupils of the public schools of Charleston, do through our committee, to wit: Thomas E. Miller, John M. Thompson, William H. Johnson, Edwin A. Harleston and Charles C. Jacobs, most respectfully petition for assistance and relief from the uncalled for, unnecessary, unusual, abnormal conditions that surround and control the management, instruction and teaching of the children of the aforesaid race in the public schools of the city of Charleston.

Fifty-six years after freedom, the negroes of the city of Charleston are denied the right to teach negro children by negroes in the free schools of Charleston, and whereas, we need relief from this unnecessary, unusual, abnormal condition, and whereas we have thousands of educated men and women who are prepared and worthy to teach the children of the aforesaid race in the city of Charleston, and whereas under the existing law of the free public schools of the State of South Carolina, it is impossible for teachers of the negro race to teach children of the negro race in the free public schools in the city of Charleston; and whereas negro teachers do teach negro children in every other city of this State and in every city in every one of the 13 old slave-holding States in the Union.

We, therefore, most humbly petition and pray to each and every one of you in authority to have Section 1780 of the civil code of 1912 amended so as to read: "That it shall be unlawful for a person of the white race to teach in the free public schools of South Carolina, provided and set aside for the children of the negro race."

We, the undersigned committee, most respectfully and humbly beg to state that we are not a self constituted committee of a few educated negroes of the city of Charleston, but we are the chosen representatives of the petitioners, namely: Of more than 10,000 adult men and women of the negro race in the city of Charleston, who are petitioning and begging you in authority to use the golden rule toward, for and over them, in the teaching of their children in the free public schools of the State of South Carolina.

"Negroes Petition General Assembly," *The State* (Columbia, South Carolina), January 23, 1919, p. 11, in Tuskegee Clipping News Service, reel 9, frame 615.

8. *The Messenger* Urges Black and White Workers to Organize, 1919

First, as workers, black and white, we all have one common interest, viz., the getting of more wages, shorter hours, and better working conditions.

Black and white workers should combine for no other reason than that for which individual workers should combine, viz., to increase their bargaining power, which will enable them to get their demands.

Second, the history of the labor movement in America proves that the employing class recognize no race lines. They will exploit a white man as readily as a black man. They will exploit women as readily as men. They will even go to the extent of coining the labor, blood and suffering of children into dollars. The introduction of women and children into the factories proves that capitalists are only concerned with profits and that they will exploit any race or class in order to make profits, whatever they be black or white men, black or white women or black or white children.

Third, it is apparent that every Negro worker or non-union man is a potential scab upon white union men and black union men.

Fourth, self-interest is the only principle upon which individuals or groups will act if they are sane. Thus, it is idle and vain to hope or expect Negro workers, out of work and who receive less wages when at work than white workers, to refuse to scab upon white workers when an opportunity presents itself.

Men will always seek to improve their conditions. When colored workers, as scabs, accept the wages against which white workers strike, they (the Negro workers) have definitely improved their conditions. That is the only reason why colored workers scab upon white workers or why non-union white men scab upon white union men.

Every member, which is a part of the industrial machinery, must be organized, if labor would win its demands. . . .

Fifth, if the employers can keep the white and black dogs, on account of race prejudice, fighting over a bone; the yellow capitalist dog will get away with the bone—the bone of profits. . . .

The combination of black and white workers will be a powerful lesson to the capitalists of the solidarity of labor. It will show that labor, black and white, is conscious of its interests and power. This will prove that unions are not based upon race lines, but upon class lines. This will serve to convert a class of workers, which has been used by the capitalist class to defeat organized labor, into an ardent, class conscious, intelligent, militant group. . . .

Sixth: The Industrial Workers of the World commonly termed, the I. W. W., draw no race, creed, color or sex line in their organization. . . . The Negroes are at least giving them an ear, and the prospects point to their soon giving them a hand. With the Industrial Workers Organization already numbering 800,000, to augment it with a million and a half or two million Negroes, would make it fairly rival the American Federation of Labor. . . .

"The Negro and the American Federation of Labor," *The Messenger,* 2, no. 8 (August 1919), 11–12.

. . . The editors of the MESSENGER are not interested in Negroes getting more work. Negroes have too much work already. What we want Negroes to get is less work and more wages, with more leisure for study and recreation.

. . . [W]e urge the Negro labor unions to increase their radicalism, to speed up their organization, to steer clear of the Negro leaders and to thank nobody but themselves for what they have gained. In organization there is strength; and whenever Negroes or anybody else make organized demands, their call will be heeded.

9. Marcus Garvey Assesses the Situation for Black People, 1922

The True Solution of the Negro Problem—1922

As far as Negroes are concerned, in America we have the problem of lynching, peonage and dis-franchisement.

In the West Indies, South and Central America we have the problem of peonage, serfdom, industrial and political governmental inequality.

In Africa we have, not only peonage and serfdom, but outright slavery, racial exploitation and alien political monopoly.

We cannot allow a continuation of these crimes against our race. As four hundred million men, women and children, worthy of the existence given us by the Divine Creator, we are determined to solve our own problem, by redeeming our Motherland Africa from the hands of alien exploiters and found there a government, a nation of our own, strong enough to lend protection to the members of our race scattered all over the world, and to compel the respect of the nations and races of the earth.

Do they lynch Englishmen, Frenchmen, Germans or Japanese? No. And Why? Because these people are represented by great governments, mighty nations and empires, strongly organized. Yes, and ever ready to shed the last drop of blood and spend the last penny in the national treasury to protect the honor and integrity of a citizen outraged anywhere.

Until the Negro reaches this point of national independence, all he does as a race will count for naught, because the prejudice that will stand out against him even with his ballot in his hand, with his industrial progress to show, will be of such an overwhelming nature as to perpetuate mob violence and mob rule, from which he will suffer, and which he will not be able to stop with his industrial wealth and with his ballot.

You may argue that he can use his industrial wealth and his ballot to force the government to recognize him, but he must understand that the government is the people. That the majority of the people dictate the policy of governments, and if the majority are against a measure, a thing, or a race, then the government is impotent to protect that measure, thing or race.

If the Negro were to live in this Western Hemisphere for another five hundred years he would still be outnumbered by other races who are prejudiced against

Amy Jacques Garvey, comp., *Philosophy and Opinions of Marcus Garvey or Africa for the Africans*, vol. 1 (London: Frank Cass, 1967), 38–39.

him. He cannot resort to the government for protection for government will be in the hands of the majority of the people who are prejudiced against him, hence for the Negro to depend on the ballot and his industrial progress alone, will be hopeless as it does not help him when he is lynched, burned, jim-crowed and segregated. The future of the Negro therefore, outside of Africa, spells ruin and disaster.

E S S A Y S

The two essays that follow take up the complex question of what factors shaped black Americans' political consciousness in the late nineteenth and early twentieth centuries. Examining the political ideology and programs of the National Association of Colored Women, Deborah Gray White, of Rutgers University, lays out the ways in which NACW members configured gender in their political analyses. Winston James, of Columbia University, offers an assessment of the possibilities for a radical black politics in the early-twentieth-century United States and argues that ethnicity was a crucial factor in black Americans' political orientations.

Race and Feminism

DEBORAH GRAY WHITE

. . . [T]he National Association of Colored Women [organized in 1896] became the black woman's primary vehicle for race leadership. Its members saw a set of interlocking problems involving race, gender, and poverty, no one of which could be dealt with independently. They believed that if they worked for the poor, they worked for black women, and if they worked for black women they worked for the race. Since, in their minds, "a race could rise no higher than its women," they felt that when they improved the condition of black women, they necessarily improved the condition of the race. When they spoke in defense of black women, they automatically spoke in defense of all black people. They talked about their work as "race work," and their problem as the "race problem." In their minds, though, the problems of the race revolved around the problems of its women. . . .

The clubs of the National Association of Colored Women rose to prominence during [the period in African American history known as the nadir]. Well before any national organization existed, local groups had coalesced throughout the country. The Colored Women's League of Washington, D.C., was among the first of the clubs that would later form the NACW. Organized in 1892 by Mary Church Terrell, Anna Julia Cooper, and Mary Jane Patterson, the Colored Women's League called on a united black womanhood to solve the race's problems. The Women's League soon branched out into the South and as far west as Kansas City, Missouri. A few months after the founding of the League, the Woman's Loyal Union, under the leadership of journalist Victoria Matthews, brought together seventy women from Brooklyn and Manhattan in support of [Ida B.] Wells's antilynching crusade. The

New York–based Union formed sister clubs in Charleston, Memphis, and Philadelphia. Not long afterward, community activist Josephine Ruffin founded the New Era Club in Boston, which provided the prototype for similar clubs in other areas of New England. In Illinois, the Chicago Women's Club organized in late 1893 after Wells appealed to black women to support suffrage and fight lynching. Thereafter, the number of clubs multiplied so rapidly that by the time the National Association of Colored Women pulled them together it was hard to keep count.

While some regional peculiarities existed, the guiding principle behind all the clubs was racial uplift through self-help. Black clubwomen believed they could help solve the race's problems through intensive social service focused on improving home life and educating mothers. Some programs aimed at increasing the skills and intellectual ability of club members, while other sent members into local neighborhoods to assist poor blacks, particularly women and children. Most clubs did both.

. . . [T]he Tuskegee Woman's Club exemplified the spirit and work of black Woman's clubs. With seventy-four members in 1905, the Tuskegee club was larger than average. It was also exclusive. Only female faculty members of Tuskegee College or wives or other female relatives of male faculty could join. Activity went forward on many fronts. In 1905 members made thirty visits to the black men and boys in the town jail, taking food and clean clothing on each visit. In the poor section of town called Thompson's Quarters the club members conducted a Sunday school, ran picnics and parties for the children, assisted in paying the funeral expenses of one child, and helped find new homes for four children. The club sponsored public and private lectures on the virtue of temperance, and organized the senior girls at Tuskegee into a club that taught them the necessity of community service and the basics of how to do it. Younger girls at Tuskegee were likewise organized, and in 1905 they "adopted" an elderly woman, helped her buy a Christmas dinner and basic necessities. Throughout the year the clubwomen assisted a community worker by conducting cooking and sewing classes at the E. A. Russell Settlement House, which club members founded and supported. By 1913, when the Tuskegee club had 102 members it assumed responsibility for a night school that was initially established by Tuskegee College. The club also established a reading room for young boys. Although woman's suffrage fell outside the rubric of community service, Tuskegee women stayed abreast of national developments on the issue and made literature on the subject available to interested members. . . .

In both North and South, mothers' clubs were among the most popular type of club to affiliate with the National Association. . . . [T]he Tuskegee Woman's Club . . . held mothers' meetings at which community women discussed and received instruction in all subjects relating to the care and upbringing of children. The definition of "mother's" responsibilities was wide ranging. The Tuskegee club taught women how to buy land and build houses. In Savannah, members of a mothers' club set up a community watch program. They wore badges so they could be recognized by police and community residents. The black clubwomen of Kingsville, Texas, were likewise organized, and were successful at closing down a gambling house they thought was bad for their neighborhood.

Patrolling their communities, teaching children to read, improving homemaking skills—there were few things that black women's clubs did not do. Everywhere the Phyllis [sic] Wheatley Club of Buffalo, New York, turned they found a task.

Early in the century the club forced the Buffalo police to focus on crimes of vice in Buffalo's black neighborhoods. Mary Talbert, a future president of the NACW, and her club were so demanding that Talbert was invited to join the citywide committee that monitored police enforcement. Through her, the club lobbied for police protection in black neighborhoods. Along with other women's clubs in the city, it established girls' clubs where delicate subjects like personal hygiene and moral improvement were addressed. In the 1920s the Phyllis Wheatley Club helped form a junior YWCA and a Buffalo chapter of the National Association for the Advancement of Colored People. They donated books by black authors to the city's public library, conducted community seminars on the power of the black female vote, and organized political clubs to get the vote out. Like clubs in other parts of the country, Buffalo women regularly visited jails, established kindergartens, and supported homes for aged adults or wayward girls.

Activities like those in Buffalo occurred all over the country. Women's clubs that were part of the Texas Federation of Colored Women's Clubs bought land on which they erected parks and playgrounds. Similarly, the Woman's Musical and Literary Club in Springfield, Missouri, helped raise money for a hospital. . . . While the Phyllis [sic] Wheatley Club of New Orleans established a nurse-training program and raised money to build a hospital, women in Vicksburg, Mississippi, bought a house and established it as a nursing home and orphanage. Following the example of their counterparts across the United States, black women in Indianapolis turned their club into a kind of employment agency, securing work for migrant black women in the canning factories of the city.

Helping rural black women establish themselves in urban areas had special significance for black women's clubs because so many members had made the lonely and dangerous migration themselves. Jane Edna Hunter, for example, was not prepared for the Northern brand of racism that she encountered when she reached Cleveland in 1905. Fresh from her nurse-training courses at Hampton Institute, she fully expected her skills to support her. She found, however, that unlike Southerners, who preferred blacks to take care of them, Northerners preferred white nurses. . . . Unable to secure work as a surgical nurse—her training—Hunter got work in private homes, but only after working at cleaning jobs in office buildings. Finding employment proved as hard as finding decent housing. When Hunter first arrived in Cleveland, she found a room in a boardinghouse that turned out to be a house of prostitution. . . . Alone in the city, Hunter had no place to turn. The YWCA residence accepted only white women, boardinghouses often charged extra for laundry, gas, and use of bathtubs, and their owners preferred male over female boarders. Middle-class black families did not rent to strangers, and most women, even those who were professionals, were compelled to stay in districts filled with gambling houses, dives, and brothels. Forced to settle for the least desirable room, where she paid what was for that time a considerable amount of money, Hunter found the loneliness of the city unbearable. At one point she went looking for peer companionship only to inadvertently find herself in a club that was a recruiting ground for prostitutes.

After this thoroughly alienating and frightening experience, Hunter resolved to remedy the housing problem confronting black women. Six years after arriving in Cleveland she met with seven other black women and together they discussed the indignity of living in boardinghouses where they had to turn lights out at 10 P.M., had no place to entertain friends, and had no access to kitchen facilities. With no social agency to provide or refer services to black women, they resolved that they alone had to initiate the change. After electing Hunter president of the new Working Girls' Home Association, they each pledged to raise a nickel per week and to gather as many new members as they could to increase their funds. From this inauspicious beginning came the Phillis Wheatley Association, a settlement house that provided rooms, recreation, and employment referrals to black women. Similar stories could be told of other homes founded by black women. . . .

As the clubs, and the institutions that they built, grew, so did local federations and the national body they affiliated with. Local federations encouraged coordinated service work and allowed clubs to undertake projects too expensive for a single organization. For example, the Tuskegee Woman's Club had persistently lobbied state officials to provide separate facilities for juvenile delinquents to keep them from coming under the influence of hard-core adult criminals. It was not, however, until the better-financed Alabama State Federation of Colored Women's Clubs took matters into its own hands—by establishing the Mt. Meigs Reformatory for Juvenile Negro Law-Breakers, and later the Mt. Meigs Rescue Home for Girls—that the Tuskegee club's aims were achieved. While the Meigs Reformatory eventually became a state institution, Alabama clubwomen assumed financial responsibility for the Rescue Home. . . .

As time passed, and more and more clubs affiliated with the National Association of Colored Women, the structure of the organization became more complex, and the projects undertaken or supported by clubs more sophisticated. In 1896 the NACW reported a membership of two hundred clubs. By the 1916 national convention there were fifteen hundred affiliates. Over this period, the NACW structure changed to meet women's varied interests. In 1901 the departments of organizational work included kindergartens, mothers' meetings, domestic science, rescue work, religion, and temperance. In 1904, five new departments were added, including art, literature, professional women, businesswomen, and social science. Business and the professions were combined into one department in 1908, the religion department was dissolved, and the departments of parliamentary law, forestry, and humane interest were added. Since the hands-on work of the NACW was done by local clubs, these departments helped the National Association of Colored Women define the needs, set the goals, and voice the concerns of black women. Coordinated activity also came through the process of city, state, and regional federations. By 1909, there were twenty state federations of black woman's clubs, including regional federations in the North, North Central, Northwest, and South.

The philosophy of the black woman's clubs equalled in importance their specific projects. Philosophy, in fact, glued the disparate parts together and impelled the women to take action. Local clubs had, of course, functioned before 1896 and could do so after 1896, effectively carrying forward their community based self-help, racial uplift programs. The NACW, however, was established to say to the nation what black women were saying to their communities. What it said, the philosophy it expounded, was unprecedentedly "feminist" in that NACW leaders insisted that only black women could save the black race. To NACW women, the national organization was not just another narrowly focused woman's organization, but as one of its early presidents, Josephine Silone Yates, claimed, it was "the first step in nationmaking."

Yates's sentiment was echoed by other club leaders. According to Gertrude Culvert, a president of the Iowa State Federation of Colored Women's Clubs, "it is to the Afro-American women that the world looks for the solution of the race problem." The "first step has been the banding of ourselves together . . . putting our heads together, taking counsel of one another." . . .

At the heart of these feelings lay a sad loss of confidence in the ability of most black men to deal effectively with the race problem. Disfranchisement, Jim Crowism, lynching, and race riots seemed to be spreading unchecked. Clubwomen wanted something done, but black men had, as an editorial in the *Woman's Era* claimed, failed "to strengthen the belittling weaknesses which so hinder and retract us in the fight for existence." The editorial called for "timid men and ignorant men" to stand aside. Indeed, Williams ridiculed male attempts to tackle the race problem when she quipped that the black male's "innumerable conventions, councils and conferences during the last twenty-five years have all begun with talk and ended with talk." . . .

If black men could make little headway against the race problem, leaders like [Anna] Cooper believed that black women would prevail. In this they had plenty of support. Like late-nineteenth-century white male and female reformers, Association leaders endorsed the popular belief that women were more nurturing, moral, and altruistic. Women were better suited than men for social welfare work because man's nature was belligerent, aggressive, and selfish. . . . Josephine St. Pierre Ruffin, [f]ounder of the Boston-based New Era Club and later a founding member of the National Association of Colored Women, . . . published the first black woman's newspaper and appropriately titled it *Woman's Era.* Anna Julia Cooper also saw possibilities for women in the period. In 1892, she claimed it was up to women to mold "the strength, the wit, the statesmanship, the morality, all the psychic force, the social and economic intercourse" of the era. It was the "colored woman's office to stamp weal or woe on the history of her people."

Cooper's confidence in her ability to tackle race problems was nourished by her sense of equality with black men. Black women, like black men, had endured incredible hardships during slavery; neither sex had gained any advantage in the nearly two and a half centuries of enslavement. "In our development as a race," argued Fannie Williams, "the colored woman and the colored man started even." She continued:

> The man cannot say that he is better educated and has had a wider sphere, for they both began school at the same time. They have suffered the same misfortunes. The limitations put upon their ambitions have been identical. The colored man can scarcely say to his wife "I am better and stronger than you are," and from the present outlook, I do not think there is any danger of the man getting very far ahead.

Cooper sounded a similar chord when she argued that gender equality grew from the denial of the franchise to the race. Cooper observed that neither black men nor women had the vote. The black man had been driven from the polls by repression, and the black woman had never been given the franchise. Cooper was dismayed but not discouraged by the harsh and exclusionary politics of late-nineteenth-century white America. She thought it might be God's way of preparing the race for something nobler than what white Americans had wrought. Like Williams, she evoked the image of a new and equal beginning for men and women, declaring that "the race is young and full of elasticity and hopefulness of youth, all its achievements are before it."

For Williams, Cooper, and the many women who proclaimed the "woman's era," the fact that black men functioned in a wider arena than black women was clearly inconsequential. Racism severely limited the life chances of black men, but some black men voted, particularly those in the North, and a few held political positions. Black men also dominated the black church, and most, although not all business people, were male. Of course, clubwomen could have pointed to their steadier employment, a few very successful businesswomen, and a host of school founders and educators.

Yet women like Cooper and Williams did not add and then compare the things that black men and women were doing. Their bottom line was the eradication of racism. The economic successes of individual black men, and/or the positions of power a few held in black and white society, mattered less than the ineffectiveness of black men as a group when it came to the race problem. If club leaders considered anything it was the endurance of black women during slavery, their belief in the more humane sensibilities of women, and their acknowledgment of the debilities of black men in white society. For the women who proclaimed the "woman's era," the sum of their equation was the superiority of women in matters concerning the moral welfare of black people, and the equality of black men and women in everything else.

. . . Behind Josephine Yates's insistence that the NACW was the first step in nation-making was the belief that the progress of women marked the progress of the race. According to Yates, "that a nation can rise in the scale no higher than its womanhood, are principles which have come to be looked upon by the sociologist and all students of the development of humanity as self-evident truth." Anna Jones, a University of Michigan alumna, wrote the same thing: "the status of its woman-hood is the measure of the progress of the race."

The most eloquent explanation of this concept came from Oberlin graduate Anna Cooper. In *A Voice from the South,* she argued that "no man can represent the race." Even someone as great as the black nationalist Martin Delany could not, in Cooper's view, speak for black people, because he knew nothing about the lives of "the rank and file of horny handed toiling men and women of the South. . . ." Women, however, were in a position to know because women were at the center, the heart of the family and the community. Black women were also doubly oppressed: as women and as blacks. Therefore, when black women spoke, they spoke for all the masses. Only when black women were totally free would the black race be free. This was the meaning behind one of the most memorable passages in *A Voice from the South*:

> Only the Black Woman can say "when and where I enter, in the quiet, undisputed dignity of my womanhood, without violence and without suing or special patronage, then and there the whole Negro race enters with me."

Not only black clubwomen but many black men also subscribed to the notion that "a race can rise no higher than its women." Dr. Monroe Majors, a Texas physician, made his feelings clear in . . . his 1893 book . . . *Noted Negro Women,* [which] was written not only to put the accomplishments of black women before the world, but to demonstrate how far black people had progressed since slavery. Since the progress of the race was measured by the progress of its women, Majors's . . . four hundred pages of text . . . [were] written as a "signification of Negro progress."

Of course, the issue of progress was not so clear cut. . . . [P]rogress, including the progress of women, meant different things to different people, and not all black women, let alone black men, measured it the same way. While most clubwomen and black men shared the idea that the race would rise as women did, and while most clubwomen believed that the torch of leadership had been passed to them, just how leadership should be exercised was a subject of debate. Not all believed that women ought to exercise leadership by speaking publicly for the race, or by bargaining and mediating with public officials. One of the most fundamental ideological discussions among clubwomen, and one that sometimes put them at odds with each other, was the way that women would lead the race.

Among the leaders it came down to a discussion of a woman's "place." Many believed that a woman exercised her greatest influence on behalf of the race in her role as wife, mother, and teacher. This did not imply notions of woman's inferiority to man. On the contrary, like Alice White, a clubwoman from Montgomery, Alabama, they agreed that "woman is man's equal intellectually." But inasmuch as they also believed in the superiority of women in the sphere of morality they insisted that women did their best work in the home, school, and church. For White, as long as the home was a place of peace, it was woman's source of power. . . . It seemed crucial to women of this bent that blacks, who had for so long under slavery been denied the right and power to establish stable homes, should develop this foundation. They could agree with Yates that the National Association of Colored Women was the first step in nation-making because the NACW did so much in the name of family and community. To build the black home was to build the black nation. . . .

For others the solution to the race problem lay in black women assuming more wide-ranging roles. They had no quarrel with the argument that the home was the first battleground, or that the NACW did important work in making the home and community strong. They just did not believe that a woman's work ended there, or that the Association's role should be confined to coordinating club activity to this end. Nellie Francis, for instance, wrote eloquently about the home as the central source of uplift. She agreed that "neither society nor state can exist without its well-being." She did not, however, believe that a woman's sphere should be confined to the home. Like many white female reformers she believed that the family was best served by women who were involved in politics and public lobbying efforts. Women, in her view, had a responsibility to help improve pure food laws, to shape laws that curbed the high cost of living, and to use the ballot as a way of improving society. . . . Addie Dickerson, a Philadelphia clubwoman and leader in the Northeastern Federation, added her voice to [that] of Francis. . . . Like her conservative counterparts, she believed that women reached their highest function as mother and director of the home. . . . Yet Dickerson also believed that women had to fight vigorously against Jim Crow and join with the progressives of both races to improve the economic opportunities of black women who worked outside the home.

Clubwomen who wanted to expand the black woman's role beyond the traditional spheres were militant supporters of woman's suffrage. Unlike Margaret

Murray Washington [president of the NACW from 1912 to 1918 and Booker T. Washington's third wife], who felt that suffrage did not warrant the full attention of black women, women like Francis . . . and Dickerson insisted that black women needed the vote to do the political work that would bring about reform. . . .

Once again, Anna Cooper's voice most fully expressed the sentiment of activist clubwomen. A supporter of woman's suffrage, Cooper at once believed that the family, with the woman as its guiding force, would be the salvation of the race, and that women had to have the same opportunities as men to develop intellectually in order to "help men tug at the great questions of the world." Intellectual development translated into self-reliance and the "capacity for earning a livelihood." It made women less likely "to look to sexual love as the one sensation capable of giving tone and relish, movement and vim to the life she leads." Education and intellectual development were necessary for all women but they were essential for black women. They could not afford to just "look pretty and appear well in society." Black girls had to learn that "there is a race with special needs which they and only they can help; that the world needs and is already asking for their trained and efficient forces." Like her conservative counterparts, Cooper argued that black women did essential race work in the home as wives and mothers, but she also insisted that the time had come for woman's "personal independence, for intellectual and moral development, for physical culture, for political activity, and for a voice in the arrangement of her own affairs, both domestic and national." . . .

As different as were the opinions of [clubwomen], we must not infer that club leaders were hopelessly divided into ideological camps. They were divided, but they had every reason to hope that their common ground would make their differences insignificant. To begin with, they all suffered humiliating experiences under Jim Crow. They all resented the exclusionary membership policies of white women's clubs. Most were well educated, making their outcast status all the more difficult to accept. Moreover, all believed that it was the "woman's era," that black women could and would solve the race problem. . . .

Race Consciousness and Radicalism

WINSTON JAMES

. . . The fact is that, because of the greater salience of race in America compared to the Caribbean, Afro-Americans have historically been more "race conscious" than Caribbeans. Marcus Garvey reiterated that point time and again, especially during his post-deportation wilderness years. The Negroes in the Caribbean, as he put it, "haven't the racial consciousness possessed by the Negroes of the United States nor those of Africa." They generally have developed "more of the white psychology than of the black outlook." "Though black, he is white" was one of Garvey's descriptions of Caribbean man. But the difference in "race consciousness" between the two groups is hardly surprising given the dissimilarities of the societies in which they were formed. This relatively low level of race consciousness was, in general, transformed by migration to societies such as the United States in the early part of the twentieth century in which racism was a pronounced feature. It is in such an environment that Caribbean people—many for the first time—become self-consciously "black" and thus "race conscious" to a greater degree.

The relatively low level of race consciousness combined with a comparatively high level of educational attainment and class consciousness, made it easier for Caribbeans—Hispanic and non-Hispanic—to work with white people in radical organizations such as the Socialist and Communist Parties in the United States. African Caribbeans in general—but in particular those from the Hispanic territories—because of their experience in the Caribbean, were, clearly, not as prone to view white people with the degree of distrust and suspicion that their African American brothers and sisters were. . . . W. A. Domingo [a 1910 Jamaican immigrant and one of the most subtle and esteemed black socialist thinkers of the 1920s], after nine years of living in the United States, was still dismayed and genuinely shocked by the manner in and the extent to which American racism warps "the ordinary human instincts of both whites and negroes." He wrote:

> They both become indifferent to the sufferings of each other and fail to recognize that most of what they suffer is both preventable and of common origin. So marked is this attitude that it is next to impossible to rouse a white audience of workingmen to the enormity of the crimes committed against society and the black race when the latter is denied elementary justice and fair play. Equally difficult is it to awaken in the breast of negroes any resentment against a vicious system that thrives on the labor of children, the sweating of adults and the robbery of one class by another. Any attempt in that direction among negroes is usually met by them in the same questioning spirit as they meet the tale of any great disaster. If a railroad wreck occurs, or a ship is sunk, the attitude of the average negro is to scan the death list diligently and if none of his race is among the victims, ejaculate "Thank God, they are all white people. There are no colored folks among them." In short, negroes react to prejudice and discrimination by becoming distinctly race conscious, but so far as their class consciousness is concerned, it is not even as much as scratched.

The understandable distrust of white people by black Americans could hardly be overstated. Harry Haywood, one of the pioneering Afro-American members of the Communist Party, vividly recalled some of the difficulties he had in attempting to recruit African Americans to the Party in the 1920s. One of his progressive black friends, whom he thought would be receptive to the idea, told him bluntly: "I'm sorry, [Haywood], but I find being Black trouble enough, but to be Black and red at the same time, well that's just double trouble, and when you mix in the whites, why that's triple trouble."

The Caribbean migrants' relatively low race consciousness but high class consciousness partially explains their "pioneering" role in "white" radical organizations such as the American Communist Party. It is also not insignificant that the longer the early Caribbean Socialists and Communists remained in the United States, the more they became Americanized, the more they moved towards black nationalist positions, the modal Afro-American radical ideology. Indeed, the longer they lived in America, the more they appreciated black America's distrust of white radicals—and white people in general. The pattern began with Hubert Harrison;

Claude McKay and George Padmore followed a similar trajectory. Cyril Briggs and Richard B. Moore were expelled from the CP in 1942 for what was alleged to have been their "Negro nationalist way of thinking." . . .

It is as if there is a hidden and unwritten law of tendency in the United States which states that because of the racism of the labor movement and its organizations, black socialists are almost inexorably pushed to a black nationalist position. This law of tendency may appropriately be called Garvey's Revenge, because it was as if Garvey, from the grave, managed to wreak revenge upon his erstwhile black social-ist opponents by diminishing their belief in and commitment to alliances across racial lines for radical transformation. It is indeed remarkable the way in which, in the 1930s and later, many of Garvey's opponents from the 1920s were to move towards more black nationalist positions, punch drunk and weary from the long years of "beating our brains out against the walls of [white] prejudice," as McKay put it in 1940. . . .

In any event, the historical difference between the strategies adopted by black Americans and black Caribbeans in dealing with the challenges posed by white oppression, in many ways, helps to explain the high profile of Caribbeans in radi-cal movements in the United States in the early part of the twentieth century. Caribbeans also brought to the United States as a component of their cultural inventory tried and tested strategies of struggle—strategies of struggle that had become so routinized they were customary—to a new and different terrain. Thus, to a significant degree, their naïveté about the formidable obstacles erected by the power structure of white America against the fulfilment of black demands and aspirations helps to account for this radical option. "I didn't think that they were as realistic as the American Negro," was George Schuyler's observation of Carib-beans in Harlem in the 1920s. Many of their leaders "seemed given to extremism and flights of fancy and all that." Afro-Americans, in contrast, "had their feet on the ground more. . . ."

The Caribbean modal strategy of frontal and often audacious assaults on the forces of oppression, what Antonio Gramsci would call the "war of maneuvre" (or "war of movement"), was transferred, almost unthinkingly, to a terrain on which African Americans had been used to pursuing—through bitter experience—*their* modal strategy of a more prosaic, incremental ('inchin' along') and cumulative process of struggle, operating on different fronts. Gramsci would call this strategy "war of position," a kind of trench warfare of social and political struggle. It is almost unthinkable, for example, that an African American leader at the time would have adopted the high profile, noisy, confrontational posture adopted by the Garvey movement in the early part of the century—the Universal African Legions, a proto-military wing of the UNIA, even had a cavalry unit which paraded on the streets of New York on horseback, in full military regalia; it is almost unthinkable, because the historical experience of Afro-America would certainly have ruled out such an option. It was too much of an obvious high-risk gamble.

William Monroe Trotter (1872–1934) is the exception that proves the rule. The beloved son of James Monroe Trotter, a veteran of the Civil War who served as an officer in the legendary black regiment, the Massachusetts Fifty-Fifth, William grew up in comfortable surroundings in Boston. His parents instilled pride of race in him from an early age, an abhorrence of racial bigotry, and a willingness to fight it. He excelled at secondary school, went on to Harvard, where he also excelled, graduating *magna cum laude.* After some years working as a successful business-man in real estate in Boston, Trotter felt driven into radical race politics, partly out of his profound disgust with the growing influence of Booker T. Washington and the latter's conservative politics. Trotter regarded Washington and the politics he represented as obsequious, and degrading to black people. In November 1901, with George Forbes, Trotter founded the *Guardian,* a weekly newspaper. He made his intentions clear from the very first issue: "We have come to protest forever against being proscribed or shut off in any caste from equal rights with other citizens, and shall remain forever on the firing line at any and all times in defence of such rights." For the rest of his life, Trotter never wavered from this commitment. "For Every Right With All thy Might," was the motto carried by the *Guardian* on its editorial page. Actively involved in founding the Niagara Movement, formed to ad-vance the cause of civil rights, he attended the launch of the National Association for the Advancement of Colored People, but he loathed the white money that ran the organization and the white people who controlled it. He formed several politi-cal organizations that culminated in the National Equal Rights League, which, under one name or another, could be traced back to 1908. Unlike the NAACP, the National Equal Rights League was "an organization of the colored people and for the colored people and led by the colored people," maintained Trotter.

With the *Guardian* and the League, Trotter maintained a blunt, unbending struggle for his and his people's rights under the Constitution. Fearless, on a visit to the White House in 1914, Trotter told President Woodrow Wilson to his face—in a heated exchange that allegedly lasted some forty-five minutes—exactly what he thought about his segregation policies in Washington. Wilson was shocked by his outspokenness. Trotter's exchange with the president became front page news around the country. Knowing that Trotter intended to expose the chasm between its rhetoric of making the world safe for democracy and its practice of black disen-franchisement, segregation, and other forms of racial oppression, the United States government denied him a passport in order to prevent his attending the Paris Peace Congress in 1919. Hubert Harrison described as "sublimely silly" the UNIA's at-tempt to send a delegation to the Congress, but he sharply identified the reasons why Wilson did not want Trotter and the others in Europe. "How would it look," Harrison asked rhetorically, "to have Negroes telling all Europe that the land which is to make the world 'safe for democracy' is rotten with race-prejudice; Jim-Crows Negro officers on ships coming over from France and on trains run under government con-trol; condones lynching by silent acquiescence and refuses to let its Negro heroes vote as citizens in that part of the country in which nine-tenths of them live. This wouldn't do at all." Undeterred by the denial of a passport, Trotter made his way to Paris, hiding his true identity, working as a cook on a steamer across the Atlantic.

Trotter had in his soul, said Du Bois, "all that went to make a fanatic, a knight errant. Ready to sacrifice himself, fearing nobody and nothing, strong in body, sturdy in conviction, full of unbending belief." But Trotter's relentless and uncom-promising fight along the color line took its toll, defeated, and killed him. On his sixty-second birthday in 1934, lonely, impoverished, his mouthpiece, the *Guardian,* in deep financial trouble, he made his way up to the roof of the three-story building in which he was only a lodger; it was five-thirty in the morning. One of the occupants in the apartment in which Trotter lived heard a noise. Later, Trotter was found unconscious on the sidewalk below. His skull was crushed; he died on the way to the hospital. No one can be sure that Trotter jumped off the roof; his relatives claimed that he accidentally fell. There were no eyewitnesses; but all the evidence suggests that he took his own life. . . . The direct, inflexible assault against the walls of American racism had earlier cost a substantial fortune, and, worse, had taken effectively the life of his beloved wife, Geraldine, in 1918. Kelly Miller, with whom Trotter had crossed swords many times over the years, was generous in his assessment of the fallen fighter. "Trotter is the only Negro, of my knowledge, who has made a sacrifice for his race," said Miller. "Others have had nothing to sacrifice but have gained honor, place and fortune out of the cause which they espoused."

Significantly, and not by accident, the Caribbean radicals admired and loved Trotter. Harrison, Garvey, Briggs, [Grace] Campbell and others worked with him, as did Afro-American radicals such as Randolph and Owen of the *Messenger* magazine. Other Caribbeans joined Trotter's National Equal Rights League and held high office in the organization. Isaac B. Allen, a Barbadian immigrant, served as Secretary of the NERL. Indeed, the president of the League up to his death in 1923 was a Jamaican migrant, the Rev. Dr Matthew A. N. Shaw (1870–1923). Trained as a medical doctor, Dr M. A. N. Shaw, as his contemporaries referred to him, also served for twenty-four years as the pastor for the Twelfth Street Baptist Church in Boston. He was Trotter's closet political ally.

Cyril Briggs referred to Trotter as "this fearless spokesman of the Negro race." And when Woodrow Wilson refused to meet Trotter in Paris in 1919, in Briggs's eyes, this was a positive sign of the type of man Trotter was: "Knowing the kind of Negro that President Wilson and the section of this country he eminently represents are willing to recognize as 'leaders' of the Negro race, we cannot help feeling that Trotter should be mighty proud of the fact that Wilson refused to see him. It is a healthy sign of the character, honor and integrity of a Negro leader when a Bourbon will have nothing to do with him."

In the next, September, issue of the *Crusader*, Briggs honored Trotter by carrying his portrait on the cover of the magazine. . . . In the 1920s, there was in fact an extraordinary degree of collaboration between the [African Blood] Brotherhood and Trotter. Frequent meetings were held at Grace Campbell's house between the leadership of the Brotherhood and William Monroe Trotter. And in 1923, Trotter's National Equal Rights League and the African Blood Brotherhood were the prime movers in calling for a united front of black organizations. The effort eventually materialized in a meeting, dubbed the Sanhedrin, of 1924 in Chicago. However, the differences which emerged at the meeting between the NERL and the ABB, on the one hand, and organizations such as Kelly Miller's National Race Congress, on the other, made sustained co-operation impossible between them. Nevertheless, the relation between Trotter's League and the members of the Brotherhood remained strong. . . .

Strangely, Garvey too, despite Trotter's integrationism—albeit a decidedly militant integrationism—admired the man and worked with him politically. . . .

Why did the Caribbean radicals love Trotter so? In the best and worst senses, he behaved like them. He behaved as if he did not know better, seemingly ignorant of the rules of American racism. He behaved with apparently childish naïveté, expecting America to live up to its vaunted and unrevised creed. "We hold these truths to be self evident. . . ." Unlike Garvey, though, Trotter's politics was predicated upon an unshakeable faith in America's capacity to change and do the right thing by its black citizens. Like Douglass and Du Bois, Trotter intended to remain in America and fight; Garvey also intended to fight, but essentially while in retreat to Africa, protecting his flank and engaging in rearguard action.

Trotter was defeated for a variety of reasons. He was in the wrong place. Boston—genteel, relatively liberal, with its long-established polite black society—was hardly the place where the black revolution would begin at the turn of the century. He too easily made too many unnecessary enemies while being unable to hold on to his friends. He was not a leader of men; he was a maverick, a "free lance," Du Bois rightly called him. He paid insufficient attention to developing a political base. And by the time the Great Migration released new possibilities and energies for black politics favorable to him, Trotter had been superseded by the National Association for the Advancement of Colored People and eclipsed by the meteoric rise of Marcus Garvey and the UNIA. These are important factors that must go into the accounting of Trotter's defeat. But above all, Trotter was defeated because he was too uncompromising, conspicuously walking tall in a land where black men and women were expected to have bent backs—when not invisible. Trotter was a provocation; he . . . enraged his enemies and at the same time, frightened many potential supporters and friends. "Full of unbending belief," he was inflexible to the point of stiffness, tall and politically erect like a magnificent but fragile palm tree, in a land of racist storms. . . .

Trotter was, in essence, an Afro-American aberration. Garvey behaved rather like Trotter: noisily, confrontationally, boldly. But, unlike Trotter, Garvey was naïve; Trotter behaved as if he was naïve, but he knew better and *had* to know better. His behavior was fueled—almost involuntarily—by his capacious reservoir of optimism and valor, and his yearning to keep faith with his father, the Massachusetts Fifty-Fifth, his late wife Geraldine, and the dream of black emancipation.

John Bruce (nicknamed "Bruce Grit"), an old head—born a slave in Maryland in 1856—and respected supporter of Garvey, foresaw danger for the Garvey movement, similar to those which overwhelmed Trotter. In 1920, Bruce was disturbed by Garvey's flamboyant noisiness and wanted him "to bridle his language." Bruce was in fact echoing an observation that he made of Garvey before he became an ardent supporter of the UNIA and of Garvey himself. In 1918, Bruce, in a sketch of Garvey he left unpublished, accused the latter of "perfervid rhetoric mixed with frenzy—and oral gymnastics." The idea of the UNIA, Bruce believed, was all right, "but the method all wrong—all gas." Mr Garvey, said Bruce,

> is *sui generis*. And he is a wonder, really. A good military strategist, wise statesmen, and shrewd politicians always conceal more than they reveal when talking of their plans. But Garvey *tells all* and so we have his number. You won't do, Mr Garvey, too *muchee talkee*.

Nevertheless, it was not for nothing that Afro-American commentators at the time, even some of his harshest critics, refer time and time again to the boldness—in the words of Kelly Miller (hardly a friendly observer) of the man, the "amazing audacity"—of Garvey. One referred to him as being as "brave as a Nubian lion." And he was; but he was perhaps also in equal measure as brave as he was foolhardly and naïve. "He made the mistake," observed James Weldon Johnson, with characteristic astuteness,

> of ignoring or looking with disdain upon the technique of the American Negro in dealing with his problems of race, a technique acquired through three hundred years of such experience as the West Indian has not had and never can have. If he had availed himself of the counsel and advice of an able and honest American Negro, he would have avoided many of the barbed wires against which he ran and many of the pits into which he fell.

But Garvey was not alone; and West Indians were not the only ones to follow him. He had millions of followers around the world and hundreds of thousands of paid-up members (not to mention supporters) in America itself. The conjuncture that prevailed during and in the aftermath of the First World War was such that radical leadership of the type offered by Garvey was made more acceptable to black people in the United States and elsewhere than at any other time since the end of slavery. There was the return of disillusioned and angry black soldiers from Europe whose comrades, in their thousands, had given their lives. President Wilson had told them that the war was about making "the world safe for democracy." And even Du Bois entreatied: "Let us, while this war lasts, forget our special grievances and close ranks with our own white fellow citizens and the allied nations that are fighting for democracy." Uncle Sam, Du Bois had miscalculated, would reward black America with full citizenship for its sacrifice. Trotter, while disagreeing vehemently with Du Bois's "Close Ranks" editorial, supported the war effort and expected, like Du Bois, positive changes with the end of hostilities. But it quickly became clear that America would not be made safe for black people, including those who had traveled over three thousand miles to fight for democracy in Europe. . . .

There was, however, a new spirit of defiance and self-confidence abroad among black people, powerfully demonstrated in the resistance that they mounted in the Red Summer of 1919, when twenty-six American cities—most notably Washington, DC, and Chicago—were consumed by rioting as white mobs attacked black people, and black people, in turn, bravely resisted, with unprecedented resolve. Garvey's frontal posture dovetailed neatly with this new psychology exemplified by the New Negro. So although his tactics departed radically from the American norm, in the post-war conjuncture it nevertheless had mass appeal. For, Garvey had, as one contemporary noted, "leaped into the ocean of black unhappiness at a most timely moment for a savior." The times were ripe for Garveyism; Garveyism was ripe for the times. There was astonishing homology between Garveyism and the conjuncture. Indeed, in a fundamental way, Garveyism was itself a product of the conjuncture.

Garvey, nonetheless, underestimated the antagonistic response his movement aroused among the rulers of America, and the powerful forces that would be unleashed against him and the UNIA. And so, what was remarkable about the Garvey movement, at least in hindsight, was not so much its rapid collapse—the prior historical experience of black America would have predisposed one to suppose that this would have been the most likely final outcome of such a venture—as the fact that it managed to achieve what it did *at all*. For Garvey had transferred from one theater of conflict to another a mode of struggle few thought could succeed to the extent that it did in America.

FURTHER READING

Karen S. Adler, "'Always Leading Our Men in Service and Sacrifice': Amy Jacques Garvey, Feminist Black Nationalist," *Gender and Society* 6, no. 3 (September 1992), 346–375.

James D. Anderson, *The Education of Blacks in the South, 1860–1935* (1988).

Stephen Ward Angell, *Bishop Henry McNeal Turner and African-American Religion in the South* (1992).

Barbara Bair, "True Women, Real Men: Gender, Ideology, and SOcial Roles in the Garvey Movement," in *Gendered Domains: Rethinking Public and Private in Women's History,* ed. Dorothy O. Helly and Susan M. Reverby (1992), 154–166.

Gail Bederman, "'Civilization': The Decline of Middle-Class Manliness, and Ida B. Wells's Antilynching Campaign (1892–94)," *Radical History Review,* 52 (1992), 5–30.

Elsa Barkley Brown, "Womanist Consciousness: Maggie Lena Walker and the Independent Order of Saint Luke," *Signs: Journal of Women in Culture and Society,* 14, no. 3 (1989), 610–633.

W. Fitzhugh Brundage, "The Roar on the Other Side of Silence: Black Resistance and White Violence in the American South, 1880–1940," in Brundage, ed., *Under Sentence of Death: Lynching in the South* (1997), 271–291.

Randall Burkett, *Garveyism as a Religious Movement: The Institutionalization of a Black Civil Religion* (1978).

Rod Bush, *We Are Not What We Seem: Black Nationalism and Class Struggle in the American Century* (1999).

Hazel Carby, "'On the Threshold of Woman's Era': Lynching, Empire, and Sexuality in Black Feminist Theory," *Critical Inquiry,* 12, no. 1 (1985), 262–277.

Mark Ellis, "Closing Ranks and 'Seeking Honors': W. E. B. Du Bois in World War I," *Journal of American History,* 79, no. 1 (1992), 96–124.

Stephen R. Fox, *The Guardian of Boston: William Monroe Trotter* (1971).

Kevin Gaines, *Uplifting the Race: Black Leadership, Politics and Culture in the Twentieth Century* (1996).

Glenda Gilmore, *Gender and Jim Crow: Women and the Politics of White Supremacy in North Carolina, 1896–1920* (1996).

Linda Gordon, "Black and White Visions of Welfare: Women's Welfare Activism, 1890–1945," *Journal of American History,* 78 (September 1991), 559–589.

Kenneth Marvin Hamilton, *Black Towns and Profit: Promotion and Development in the Trans-Appalachian West, 1877–1915* (1991).

Louis Harlan, *Booker T. Washington: The Making of a Leader, 1856–1901* (1972).

Louis Harlan, *Booker T. Washington: The Wizard of Tuskegee, 1901–1915* (1983).

Evelyn Brooks Higginbotham, "Clubwomen and Electoral Politics in the 1920's," in *African American Women and the Vote 1837–1965,* ed. Ann D. Gordon, Bettye Collier-Thomas, et al. (1997), 134–135.

Evelyn Brooks Higginbotham, *Righteous Discontent: The Women's Movement in the Black Baptist Church, 1880–1920* (1993).

William Jordan, "The Damnable Dilemma: African American Accommodation and Protest During World War I," *Journal of American History,* 81, no.4 (1995), 1562–1583.

Elisabeth Lasch-Quinn, *Black Neighbors: Race and the Limits of Reform in the American Settlement House Movement, 1890–1945* (1993).

David Levering Lewis, *W. E. B. Du Bois: Biography of a Race, 1868–1919* (1993).

Linda O. McMurray, *To Keep the Waters Troubled: The Life of Ida B. Wells* (1998).

August Meier, *Negro Thought in America, 1880–1915: Racial Ideologies in the Age of Booker T. Washington* (1963).

William Jeremiah Moses, *The Golden Age of Black Nationalism, 1850–1925* (1978).

Paula E. Pfeffer, *A. Philip Randolph, Pioneer of the Civil Rights Movement* (1990).

Cedric J. Robinson, *Black Marxism: The Making of the Black Radical Tradition* (1983).

Cedric J. Robinson, *Black Movements in America* (1997).

Jacqueline A. Rouse, "Atlanta's African-American Women's Attack on Segregation, 1900–1920," in *Gender, Class, Race, and Reform in the Progressive Era,* ed. Noralee Frankel and Nancy S. Dye (1991), 10–23.

Dorothy Salem, "Black Women and the NAACP, 1909–1922," in *Black Women in America,* ed. Kim Vaz (1995), 54–70.

Dorothy Salem, *To Better Our World: Black Women in Organized Reform, 1890–1920* (1990).

Patricia Schechter, " 'All the Intensity of My Nature': Ida B. Wells, Anger, and Politics," *Radical History Review,* 70 (1998), 48–77.

Stephanie J. Shaw, "Black Club Women and the Creation of the National Association of Colored Women," *Journal of Women's History,* 3, no. 2 (1991), 10–25.

Stephanie J. Shaw, *What a Woman Ought to Be and to Do: Black Professional Women Workers During the Jim Crow Era* (1996).

Judith Stein, *The World of Marcus Garvey: Race and Class in Modern Society* (1986).

Rosalyn Terborg-Penn, *African American Women in the Struggle for the Vote, 1850–1920* (1998).

Emma Lou Thornbrough, *T. Thomas Fortune: Militant Journalist* (1972).

Emory Tolbert, *The UNIA and Black Los Angeles: Ideology and Community in the American Garvey Movement* (1980).

Walter Weare, *Black Business in the New South: A Social History of the North Carolina Mutual Life Insurance Company* (1973).

Judith Weisenfeld, *African American Women and Christian Activism: New York's Black YWCA, 1905–1945* (1997).

Nancy J. Weiss, "From Black Separatism to Interracial Cooperation: The Origins of Organized Efforts for Racial Advancement, 1890–1920," in *Twentieth-Century America: Recent Interpretations,* 2nd ed., ed. Barton J. Bernstein and Allen J. Matusow (1972), 52–87.

Cary Wintz, ed., *African American Political Thought, 1890–1930* (1996).

Victoria W. Wolcott, " 'Bible, Bath, and Broom': Nannie Helen Burroughs's National Training School and African-American Racial Uplift," *Journal of Women's History,* 9, no. 1 (Spring 1997), 88–110.

Nan Woodruff, "African-American Struggles for Citizenship in the Arkansas and Mississippi Deltas in the Age of Jim Crow," *Radical History Review,* 55 (1993), 33–51.

CHAPTER
6

The Culture Wars

Changes in African-American life have not been confined to the realms of politics and economics but also have encompassed broad social and cultural transformations. Migration, urbanization, industrialization, and the commercialization of culture altered relations not only between blacks and whites but also within black communities. While providing greater space for personal and political expression, new cultural forms such as radio, race records, and film also fostered racial conflicts and gender and class tensions among African Americans. African-American cultural developments have, therefore, been not secondary to political and economic transformations but indeed integral to them.

For more than a century, struggles around black life and politics have been accompanied by debates about the nature of black culture and the appropriateness of certain cultural forms. These debates have often centered on the cultural expressions of women, youth, and the working class. Additionally, black men and women at the time and scholars in retrospect often have sought to validate certain expressions as "authentically" black or to denote some cultural forms as "respectable" or "unrespectable" or "black" or "white." Some have sought to protect "black" culture from white appropriation and control.

What, if anything, is distinctive about the cultural forms black Americans have developed? Why has culture been a political battleground? What is at stake in our efforts to understand the nature of black culture?

D O C U M E N T S

Ragtime, blues, gospel, and jazz each were hailed as original American art forms and denounced as degenerative influences in American cultural life. Born in 1868, Scott Joplin was a well-known American composer by the turn of the century. Popularly considered the "King of Ragtime," his association with music that many considered low-brow entertainment denied him professional legitimacy. He hoped his opera *Treemonisha* would enhance his professional reputation. The first document is the highly favorable though racially sensitive review that his self-published opera received in the *American Musician and Art Journal* in 1911. Financial backing to mount a full performance never materialized during Joplin's lifetime.

186

   The classic female blues singers benefited from the growing consumerism of the 1920s and the technological innovations of radio and phonograph records, which allowed them to reach an ever-increasing black audience. The music itself, however, remained controversial. As they had with ragtime, many people associated blues music with saloons and brothels. The lyrics in the second set of documents—Gertrude "Ma" Rainey flaunting lesbian relationships, Bessie Smith denouncing economic inequality—reveal the blues as a personal expression not only of despair but also of defiance, self-assertion, and protest.

   Gospel music, as a religious expression driven by blues rhythms, was from its inception a battleground in the struggle over whether there should be a distinct separation between the sacred and the secular elements of black culture. The late 1930s saw a similar blurring of this boundary as spirituals were set to swing-time and performed in public places of amusement. In the third document a Baptist minister calls for unified race action to end this "sacriligious [sic] desecration."

   In the 1920s and 1930s, a small group of black writers, painters, and sculptors had unprecedented access to white mainstream cultural institutions such as publishing houses and museums. In the period known as the Harlem Renaissance, or New Negro Movement, the recognition these artists received seemed for some a harbinger of the possibility of greater acceptance of all black Americans. Such a possibility brought with it great pressures on the artists themselves. *The New Negro* (1925), edited by Alain Locke, professor of philosophy at Howard University, was a collection of works that both defined and popularized the movement. In his title essay—the fourth document—Locke offered a social context for what he perceived to be an emerging race consciousness that was modern, urban, and pan-African. One of the contributors to the volume was twenty-three-year-old Langston Hughes, whom the Negro literati had embraced four years earlier when his poem "The Negro Speaks of Rivers" was published in the NAACP's *Crisis* magazine. In 1927 those same black cultural conservatives vilified Hughes because in his second book of poetry, *Fine Clothes to the Jew,* he employed the blues idiom to depict the everyday work, street, and night life of the common laboring man and woman. In the fifth document, taken from his 1940 autobiography, Hughes recalls critics' reactions to that earlier book.

   Oscar Micheaux emerged as the most successful and prolific of a handful of black independent filmmakers of an era when white control severely constricted black participation in the burgeoning motion picture industry. Micheaux, whose 1925 *Body and Soul* is advertised in the sixth document, challenged censors both in black communities as well as the film industry by producing films that presented real and not necessarily flattering images of black life in the United States. Micheaux ultimately produced or directed nearly fifty films between 1918 and 1948.

   Even as artists, audiences, critics, and reformers struggled to define and police the parameters of appropriate black cultural expression, increasing numbers of academically trained African Americans were turning their attention to understanding the nature, origin, and meaning of these expressions. Zora Neale Hurston, whose short stories and plays made her a major figure in the Harlem Renaissance, undertook academic study of southern black folk culture in order to counter stereotypical depictions in both scholarly and popular texts. She went home to Florida in the late 1920s, wondering whether her Barnard College education had unprepared her for the task of documenting the authentic black folklore of her native South. She recalls her return to her hometown in the seventh document. Lorenzo Dow Turner, a linguist at Fisk University, focused his studies on connections between African culture and African-American cultural forms. In the eighth document, Turner discusses his work on

African survivals in Gullah language with, among others, sociologist E. Franklin Frazier and white anthropologist Melville Herskovits.

1. A Review of Scott Joplin's Opera *Treemonisha,* 1911

Scott Joplin, well known as a writer of music, and especially of what a certain musician classified as "classic rag-time," has just published an opera in three acts, entitled "Treemonisha," upon which he has been working for the past fifteen years. This achievement is noteworthy for two reasons: First, it is composed by a negro, and second, the subject deals with an important phase of negro life. The characters, eleven in number, and the chorus are also negroes. . . .

A remarkable point about this work is its evident desire to serve the negro race by exposing two of the great evils which have held his people in its grasp, as well as to point them to higher and nobler ideals. Scott Joplin has proved himself a teacher as well as a scholar and an optimist with a mission which has been splendidly performed. Moreover, he has created an entirely new phase of musical art and has produced a thoroughly American opera, dealing with a typical American subject, yet free from all extraneous influence. He has discovered something new because he had confidence in himself and in his mission and, being an optimist, was destined to succeed. . . .

The principal theme of the opera is one of entrancing beauty, symbolic of the happiness of the people when they feel free from the spells of superstition animated by the wiles of the conjurors. . . .

Scott Joplin has not been influenced by his musical studies or by foreign schools. He has created an original type of music in which he employs syncopation in a most artistic and original manner. It is in no sense rag-time, but of that peculiar quality of rhythm which Dvořák used so successfully in the "New World" symphony. The composer has constantly kept in mind his characters and their purpose, and has written music in keeping with his libretto. "Treemonisha" is not grand opera, nor is not light opera; it is what we might call character opera or racial opera. . . .

There has been much written and printed of late concerning American opera, and the American composers have seized the opportunity of acquainting the world with the fact that they have been able to produce works in this line. Several operas by American composers have been produced recently, and there is promise of several others being heard next year, among which will be Professor Parker's "Mona," which won the $10,000 Metropolitan Opera prize. Now the question is, Is this an American opera? And a correlative question is, Are the American composers endeavoring to write American operas? In other words, are they striving to create a school of American opera, or are they simply employing their talents to fashion something suitable for the operatic stage and satisfactory to the operatic management? If so, American opera will always remain a thing in embryo. To date there is no record of even the slightest tendency toward the fashioning of the real American opera, and although this work just completed by one of the Ethiopian race will

"A Musical Novelty," *American Musician and Art Journal,* June 24, 1911, p. 7, reprinted from Edward A. Berlin, *King of Ragtime: Scott Joplin and His Era* (New York: Oxford University Press, 1994), 201–202.

hardly be accepted as a typical American opera for obvious reasons, nevertheless none can deny that it serves as an opening wedge, since it is in every respect indigenous. It has sprung from our soil practically of its own accord. Its composer has focused his mind upon a single object, and with a nature wholly in sympathy with it has hewn an entirely new form of operatic art. Its production would prove an interesting and potent achievement, and it is to be hoped that sooner or later it will be thus honored.

2. Blues Lyrics of the 1920s

Prove It On Me Blues
(as recorded by Gertrude "Ma" Rainey)

Went out last night, had a great big fight
Everything seemed to go on wrong
I looked up, to my surprise
The gal I was with was gone

Where she went, I don't know
I mean to follow everywhere she goes
Folks said I'm crooked, I didn't know where she took it
I want the whole world to know

They say I do it, ain't nobody caught me
Sho got to prove it on me
Went out last night with a crowd of my friends
They must been women, 'cause I don't like no men

It's true I wear a collar and a tie
Make the wind blow all the while
'Cause they say I do it, ain't nobody caught me
They sho got to prove it on me

Say I do it, ain't nobody caught me
Sho got to prove it on me
I went out last night with a crowd of my friends
They must been women, 'cause I don't like no men

Wear my clothes just like a fan
Talk to the gals just like any old man
'Cause they say I do it, ain't nobody caught me
Sho got to prove it on me

Poor Man's Blues
(as recorded by Bessie Smith)

Mister rich man, rich man, open up your heart and mind
Mister rich man, rich man, open up your heart and mind
Give the poor man a chance, help stop those hard, hard times

While you're livin' in your mansion, you don't know what hard
    times means
While you're livin' in your mansion, you don't know what hard
    times means
Poor working man's wife is starvin', your wife's livin' like a queen

Please, listen to my pleading, 'cause I can't stand these hard times
    long
Oh, listen to my pleading, can't stand these hard times long
They'll make an honest man do things that you know is wrong

Poor man fought all the battles, poor man would fight again today
Poor man fought all the battles, poor man would fight again today
He would do anything you ask him in the name of the U.S.A.

Now the war is over, poor man must live the same as you
Now the war is over, poor man must live the same as you
If it wasn't for the poor man, mister rich man, what would you do?

3. Rev. George W. Harvey, Baptist Minister, Denounces Swinging Spirituals, 1939

Braddock, Pa., Mar. 9—"The sacriligious desecration of Spirituals, the only real American music as it is swung in gin shops, dance halls, over the radio and on records in various non-descript amusement places is a disgrace to the whole race," declared the Rev. George W. Harvey, pastor New Hope Baptist church and associate religious editor of *The Courier,* in a stirring address last Monday.

Dr. Harvey asks church people to join in a strong militant protest to stamp out the wanton practice of desecrating the songs of our fathers and mothers.

He declared that ". . . the spirituals, the beloved hymns and songs of our foreparents are being played and sung in swing time. I was told that many of our race bands, artists and orchestras in addition to the records and broadcasting systems are desecrating spirituals. It should be stopped!"

Continuing he said: "I am further informed that there is a Fats Waller record that swings the song, 'When the Saints Go Marching Home.' Further, I understand, that many spirituals may be heard in fast swing time in places of business conducted by or for the race. . . .

"The use of these songs can be heard in cheap dance halls, gin shops, restaurants and other types of amusement places. I think our artists and musicians should use more discrimination in their selections of the places in which they play certain types of music. The use of any spiritual other than for religious, educational, or semi-religious gatherings is strictly sacriligious, disdainful and uncalled for.

"Times are hard, but there are some things a person or a group should not do for love nor money. One is not to be a party to the desecration of that which is held sacred by members of one's group, race or nation. The Bible says: 'There is a time for all things.' And the swinging of spirituals in amusement places is untimely. Jesus said: 'Give not that which is holy unto dogs.'

"I doubt if artists of other groups would use their sacred tunes in such a sinful way. Why would race artists allow others to make them the desecrators of the songs of their own fore-parents? This practice calls for a protest from every church lover and all those who hold dear 'the faith of the Fathers.'

"I remember the storm of protest that went up from the Scotch last year when jazz hounds began to swing 'Loch Lomond.'

"Proprietors of establishments that allow such are also partially guilty of being an accessory to this great racial tragedy. We must put a stop to it in every hamlet, town and city. Won't you help?

"The church should rise up in all of its branches and let the amusement world, shows, taverns, musicians, et al. feel the force of united opposition and protest to this growing evil. Music producers, record makers, electric music box distributors and all concerned need to know that we vehemently disapprove of this practice, that is widely in vogue today.

"I am asking preachers and leaders to raise their voices, pens and influence to eradicate this evil growth as quickly as possible. Make a survey and check up in your town and see how widely this evil has penetrated into our race, business and entertainment world. Preach, write or speak up against it.

"My reader, you have a voice, be like John cry out against this unrighteousness that is growing in such large proportions in this jitter-bug generation. Surely the spirituals, the hymns and songs of our fore-parents that we yet fondly use in most Negro churches should not be used in flagrant and unholy ways by swingsters, jitter-bugs and other nincompoops in places or times that have no semblance of a religious gathering.

"I have yet to hear or know of any Jewish artist, Irving Berlin, et al. using hymns or songs dear to the Synagogue or a Catholic performer desecrating any of the hymns of the Catholic church. You don't hear Rudy Vallee swinging 'Nearer My God to Thee' or 'Faith of Our Fathers.' You seldom hear any celebrated group of artists or producers using that which is held sacred by other large groups using their songs, customs or traditions in an unholy way.

"I do not single Waller out for scorn, perhaps he is or was an unthinking victim of a vicious system. But, I call now for the protests of the faithful, let us unitedly begin a drive to STOP the use of spirituals by jitter-bug bands, swingsters, and singers, on records or over radios, except when these are used in the way that our fore-fathers intended; for the glory of our God."

4. Alain Locke, Philosopher, Defines the "New Negro," 1925

In the last decade something beyond the watch and guard of statistics has happened in the life of the American Negro and the three norns who have traditionally presided over the Negro problem have a changeling in their laps. The Sociologist, the Philanthropist, the Race-leader are not unaware of the New Negro, but they are at a loss to account for him. He simply cannot be swathed in their formulae. For the younger generation is vibrant with a new psychology; the new spirit is awake in the masses, and under the very eyes of the professional observers is transforming what has been a perennial problem into the progressive phases of contemporary Negro life.

Could such a metamorphosis have taken place as suddenly as it has appeared to? The answer is no; not because the New Negro is not here, but because the Old Negro had long become more of a myth than a man. The Old Negro, we must remember, was a creature of moral debate and historical controversy. His has been a stock figure perpetuated as an historical fiction partly in innocent sentimentalism, partly in deliberate reactionism. The Negro himself has contributed his share to this through a sort of protective social mimicry forced upon him by the adverse circumstances of dependence. So for generations in the mind of America, the Negro has been more of a formula than a human being—a something to be argued about, condemned or defended, to be "kept down," or "in his place," or "helped up," to be worried with or worried over, harassed or patronized, a social bogey or a social burden. . . .

. . . A main change has been, of course, that shifting of the Negro population which has made the Negro problem no longer exclusively or even predominantly Southern. Why should our minds remain sectionalized, when the problem itself no longer is? Then the trend of migration has not only been toward the North and the Central Midwest, but city-ward and to the great centers of industry—the problems of adjustment are new, practical, local and not peculiarly racial. Rather they are an integral part of the large industrial and social problems of our present-day democracy. And finally, with the Negro rapidly in process of class differentiation, if it ever was warrantable to regard and treat the Negro *en masse* it is becoming with every day less possible, more unjust and more ridiculous.

In the very process of being transplanted, the Negro is becoming transformed.

The tide of Negro migration, northward and city-ward, is not to be fully explained as a blind flood started by the demands of war industry coupled with the shutting off of foreign migration, or by the pressure of poor crops coupled with increased social terrorism in certain sections of the South and Southwest. Neither labor demand, the boll-weevil nor the Ku Klux Klan is a basic factor, however contributory any or all of them may have been. The wash and rush of this human tide on the beach line of the northern city centers is to be explained primarily in terms of a new vision of opportunity, of social and economic freedom, of a spirit to seize, even in the face of an extortionate and heavy toll, a chance for the improvement of conditions. With each successive wave of it, the movement of the Negro becomes more and more a mass movement toward the larger and the more democratic chance—in the Negro's case a deliberate flight not only from countryside to city, but from medieval America to modern.

Take Harlem as an instance of this. Here in Manhattan is not merely the largest Negro community in the world, but the first concentration in history of so many diverse elements of Negro life. It has attracted the African, the West Indian, the Negro American; has brought together the Negro of the North and the Negro of the South; the man from the city and the man from the town and village; the peasant, the student, the business man, the professional man, artist, poet, musician, adventurer and worker, preacher and criminal, exploiter and social outcast. Each group has come with its own separate motives and for its own special ends, but their greatest experience has been the finding of one another. Proscription and prejudice have thrown these dissimilar elements into a common area of contact and interaction. Within this area, race sympathy and unity have determined a further fusing of sentiment and experience. So what began in terms of segregation becomes more and more, as its elements mix and react, the laboratory of a great race-welding. Hitherto, it must be admitted that American Negroes have been a race more in name than in fact, or to be exact, more in sentiment than in experience. The chief bond between them has been that of a common condition rather than a common consciousness; a problem in common rather than a life in common. In Harlem, Negro life is seizing upon its first chances for group expression and self-determination. It is—or promises at least to be—a race capital.

 . . . [I]nterests are racial but in a new and enlarged way. One is the consciousness of acting as the advance-guard of the African peoples in their contact with Twentieth Century civilization; the other, the sense of a mission of rehabilitating the race in world esteem from that loss of prestige for which the fate and conditions of slavery have so largely been responsible. Harlem, as we shall see, is the center of both these movements. . . . A Negro newspaper carrying news material in English, French and Spanish, gathered from all quarters of America, the West Indies and Africa has maintained itself in Harlem for over five years. Two important magazines, both edited from New York, maintain their news and circulation consistently on a cosmopolitan scale. Under American auspices and backing, three pan-African congresses have been held abroad for the discussion of common interests, colonial questions and the future co-operative development of Africa. In terms of the race question as a world problem, the Negro mind has leapt, so to speak, upon the parapets of prejudice and extended its cramped horizons. In so doing it has linked up with the growing group consciousness of the dark-peoples and is gradually learning their common interests.

 . . . With the American Negro, his new internationalism is primarily an effort to recapture contact with the scattered peoples of African derivation. Garveyism may be a transient, if spectacular, phenomenon, but the possible rôle of the American Negro in the future development of Africa is one of the most constructive and universally helpful missions that any modern people can lay claim to.

Constructive participation in such causes cannot help giving the Negro valuable group incentives, as well as increased prestige at home and abroad. Our greatest rehabilitation may possibly come through such channels, but for the present, more immediate hope rests in the revaluation by white and black alike of the Negro in terms of his artistic endowments and cultural contributions, past and prospective. It must be increasingly recognized that the Negro has already made very substantial contributions, not only in his folk-art, music especially, which has always found appreciation, but in larger, though humbler and less acknowledged ways. For generations the Negro has been the peasant matrix of that section of America which has most undervalued him, and here he has contributed not only materially in labor and in social patience, but spiritually as well. The South has unconsciously absorbed the gift of his folk-temperament. In less than half a generation it will be easier to recognize this, but the fact remains that a leaven of humor, sentiment, imagination and tropic nonchalance has gone into the making of the South from a humble, unacknowledged source. A second crop of the Negro's gifts promises still more largely. He now becomes a conscious contributor and lays aside the status of a beneficiary and ward for that of a collaborator and participant in American civilization. The great social gain in this is the releasing of our talented group from the arid fields of controversy and debate to the productive fields of creative expression. The especially cultural recognition they win should in turn prove the key to that revaluation of the Negro which must precede or accompany any considerable further betterment of race relationships. But whatever the general effect, the present generation will have added the motives of self-expression and spiritual development to the old and still unfinished task of making material headway and progress. No one who understandingly faces the situation with its substantial accomplishment or views the new scene with its still more abundant promise can be entirely without hope. And certainly, if in our lifetime the Negro should not be able to celebrate his full initiation into American democracy, he can at least, on the warrant of these things, celebrate the attainment of a significant and satisfying new phase of group development, and with it a spiritual Coming of Age.

5. Langston Hughes, Poet and Writer, Critiques His Critics, 1940

My second book of poems, *Fine Clothes to the Jew,* I felt was a better book than my first, because it was more impersonal, more about other people than myself, and because it made use of the Negro folk-song forms, and included poems about work and the problems of finding work, that are always so pressing with the Negro people.

I called it *Fine Clothes to the Jew,* because the first poem, "Hard Luck," a blues, was about a man who was often so broke he had no recourse but to pawn his clothes—to take them, as the Negroes say, to "the Jew's" or to "Uncle's." Since the whole book was largely about people like that, workers, roustabouts, and singers, and job hunters on Lenox Avenue in New York, or Seventh Street in Washington or South State in Chicago—people up today and down tomorrow, working this week and fired the next, beaten and baffled, but determined not to be wholly beaten,

Excerpts from "Poetry" from *The Big Sea* by Langston Hughes. Copyright © 1940 by Langston Hughes. Copyright renewed © 1968 by Arna Bontemps and George Houston Bass. Reprinted by permission of Hill and Wang, a division of Farrar, Straus, and Giroux, LLC.

buying furniture on the installment plan, filling the house with roomers to help pay the rent, hoping to get a new suit for Easter—and pawning that suit before the Fourth of July—that was why I called my book *Fine Clothes to the Jew.*

But it was a bad title, because it was confusing and many Jewish people did not like it. I do not know why the Knopfs let me use it, since they were very helpful in their advice about sorting out the bad poems from the good, but they said nothing about the title. I might just as well have called the book *Brass Spittoons,* which is one of the poems I like best:

BRASS SPITTOONS

Clean the spittoons, boy!
    Detroit,
    Chicago,
    Atlantic City,
    Palm Beach.
Clean the spittoons.
The steam in hotel kitchens,
And the smoke in hotel lobbies,
And the slime in hotel spittoons:
Part of my life.
    Hey, boy!
    A nickel,
    A dime,
    A dollar,
Two dollars a day.
    Hey, boy!
    A nickel,
    A dime,
    A dollar,
    Two dollars
Buys shoes for the baby.
House rent to pay.
Gin on Saturday,
Church on Sunday.
    My God!
Babies and gin and church
and women and Sunday
all mixed up with dimes and
dollars and clean spittoons
and house rent to pay.
    Hey, boy!
A bright bowl of brass is beautiful to the Lord.
Bright polished brass like the cymbals
Of King David's dancers,
Like the wine cups of Solomon.
    Hey, boy!
A clean spittoon on the altar of the Lord,
A clean bright spittoon all newly polished—
At least I can offer that.
    Com'mere, boy!

Fine Clothes to the Jew was well received by the literary magazines and the white press, but the Negro critics did not like it at all. The Pittsburgh *Courier* ran a big headline across the top of the page, *LANGSTON HUGHES' BOOK OF POEMS TRASH.* The headline in the New York *Amsterdam News* was *LANGSTON HUGHES—THE SEWER DWELLER.* The Chicago *Whip* characterized me as "The poet lowrate of Harlem." Others called the book a disgrace to the race, a return to the dialect tradition, and a parading of all our racial defects before the public. . . .

Benjamin Brawley, our most respectable critic, later wrote: "It would have been just as well, perhaps better, if the book had never been published. No other ever issued reflects more fully the abandon and the vulgarity of its age." In the Negro papers, I believe, only Dewey Jones of the Chicago *Defender* and Alice Dunbar-Nelson of the Washington *Eagle* gave it a sympathetic review.

The Negro critics and many of the intellectuals were very sensitive about their race in books. (And still are.) In anything that white people were likely to read, they wanted to put their best foot forward, their politely polished and cultural foot—and only that foot. There was a reason for it, of course. They had seen their race laughed at and caricatured so often in stories like those by Octavus Roy Cohen, maligned and abused so often in books like Thomas Dixon's, made a servant or a clown always in the movies, and forever defeated on the Broadway stage, that when Negroes wrote books they wanted them to be books in which only good Negroes, clean and cultured and not-funny Negroes, beautiful and nice and upper class were presented. Jessie Fauset's novels they loved, because they were always about the educated Negro—but my poems, or Claude McKay's *Home to Harlem* they did not like, sincere though we might be.

For every Negro intellectual like James Weldon Johnson, there were dozens like Eustace Gay, who wrote in the Philadelphia *Tribune,* of February 5, 1927, concerning my *Fine Clothes to the Jew:* "It does not matter to me whether every poem in the book is true to life. Why should it be paraded before the American public by a Negro author as being typical or representative of the Negro? Bad enough to have white authors holding up our imperfections to public gaze. Our aim ought to be to present to the general public, already mis-informed both by well-meaning and malicious writers, our higher aims and aspirations, and our better selves."

I sympathized deeply with those critics and those intellectuals, and I saw clearly the need for some of the kinds of books they wanted. But I did not see how they could expect every Negro author to write such books. Certainly, I personally knew very few people anywhere who were wholly beautiful and wholly good. Besides I felt that the masses of our people had as much in their lives to put into books as did those more fortunate ones who had been born with some means and the ability to work up to a master's degree at a Northern college. Anyway, I didn't know the upper class Negroes well enough to write much about them. I knew only the people I had grown up with, and they weren't people whose shoes were always shined, who had been to Harvard, or who had heard of Bach. But they seemed to me good people, too.

So I didn't pay any attention to the critics who railed against the subject matter of my poems, nor did I write them protesting letters, nor in any way attempt to defend my book. Curiously enough, a short ten years later, many of those very poems in *Fine Clothes to the Jew* were being used in Negro schools and colleges.

6. Screening the Race, 1925

Paul Robeson, Mercedes Gilbert, and Julia Theresa Russell in an advertisement for Oscar Micheaux's *Body and Soul*. The 1925 film, which featured a black-on-black rape and depictions of the immorality of a black preacher, met with opposition from both white state film censor boards and black self-appointed guardians of respectability. The *New York Age* refused to run ads promoting the film. Previous Micheaux films depicting white mob violence and sexual assault of African Americans had similarly run afoul of white and black censors afraid of inciting bad feelings, racial animosity, and possibly violence.

Photo: Baltimore *Afro-American,* December 26, 1925, courtesy Charlene Regester, co-editor of the *Oscar Micheaux Society Newsletter,* Film & Video Program, Duke University.

7. Zora Neale Hurston, Writer and Anthropologist, Takes Her University Training Home, 1927

I was glad when somebody told me, "You may go and collect Negro folklore."

In a way it would not be a new experience for me. When I pitched headforemost into the world I landed in the crib of negroism. From the earliest rocking of my cradle, I had known about the capers Brer Rabbit is apt to cut and what the Squinch Owl says from the house top. But it was fitting me like a tight chemise. I couldn't see it for wearing it. It was only when I was off in college, away from my native surroundings, that I could see myself like somebody else and stand off and look at my garment. Then I had to have the spy-glass of Anthropology to look through at that. . . .

First place I aimed to stop to collect material was Eatonville, Florida.

And now, I'm going to tell you why I decided to go to my native village first. I didn't go back there so that the home folks could make admiration over me because I had been up North to college and come back with a diploma and a Chevrolet. I knew they were not going to pay either one of these items too much mind. I was just Lucy Hurston's daughter, Zora, and even if I had—to use one of our downhome expressions—had a Kaiser baby,* and that's something that hasn't been done in this Country yet, I'd still be just Zora to the neighbors. If I had exalted myself to impress the town, somebody would have sent me word in a match-box that I had been up North there and had rubbed the hair off of my head against some college wall, and then come back there with a lot of form and fashion and outside show to the world. But they'd stand flat-footed and tell me that they didn't have me, neither my sham-polish, to study 'bout. And that would have been that.

I hurried back to Eatonville because I knew that the town was full of material and that I could get it without hurt, harm or danger. As early as I could remember it was the habit of the men folks particularly to gather on the store porch of evenings and swap stories. Even the women folks would stop and break a breath with them at times. As a child when I was sent down to Joe Clarke's store, I'd drag out my leaving as long as possible in order to hear more.

Folklore is not as easy to collect as it sounds. The best source is where there are the least outside influences and these people, being usually under-privileged, are the shyest. They are most reluctant at times to reveal that which the soul lives by. And the Negro, in spite of his open-faced laughter, his seeming acquiescence, is particularly evasive. You see we are a polite people and we do not say to our questioner, "Get out of here!" We smile and tell him or her something that satisfies the white person because, knowing so little about us, he doesn't know what he is missing. The Indian resists curiosity by a stony silence. The Negro offers a feather-bed resistance. That is, we let the probe enter, but it never comes out. It gets smothered under a lot of laughter and pleasantries.

---

*To have a child by the Kaiser.

The theory behind our tactics: "The white man is always trying to know into somebody else's business. All right, I'll set something outside the door of my mind for him to play with and handle. He can read my writing but he sho' can't read my mind. I'll put this play toy in his hand, and he will seize it and go away. Then I'll say my say and sing my song."

I knew that even *I* was going to have some hindrance among strangers. But here in Eatonville I knew everybody was going to help me. So below Palatka I began to feel eager to be there and I kicked the little Chevrolet right along.

I thought about the tales I had heard as a child. How even the Bible was made over to suit our vivid imagination. How the devil always outsmarted God and how that over-noble hero Jack or John—not *John Henry,* who occupies the same place in Negro folk-lore that Casey Jones does in white lore and if anything is more recent—outsmarted the devil. Brer Fox, Brer Deer, Brer 'Gator, Brer Dawg, Brer Rabbit, Ole Massa and his wife were walking the earth like natural men way back in the days when God himself was on the ground and men could talk with him. . . .

So I rounded Park Lake and came speeding down the straight stretch into Eatonville, the city of five lakes, three croquet courts, three hundred brown skins, three hundred good swimmers, plenty guavas, two schools, and no jail-house.

8. A Roundtable Discussion on African Survivals in Gullah Language, 1941

Mr. Turner: An interesting situation in Georgia may be mentioned. All the children have nicknames, and I find that 95 per cent of these are African words. Such nicknames are used in their homes and among their associates, but when they go to school they are not allowed to use them, since the teacher, a lady from Charleston, refuses to record those names. When they write to friends off the island they use their English names, but as soon as they return home they use African names. If a field-worker doesn't come into contact with these people in their homes, he will assume, just as some of the writers I mentioned have assumed, that no African names are used, but only English ones.

Mr. Puckett: Do these African words seem to be used more commonly in certain types of group activities than others? Do you find African words especially connected with religion and agriculture, or the family?

Mr. Turner: The largest number would be the proper names, and only a few of these words are used in any other connection. Names of birds and animals would yield the next largest group of African terms. There are a good many religious words, but not as many as for birds and animals and plants. One also finds a group of words that are never used in daily conversation, but only in songs and stories. In their folk tales, the Gullah Negroes sometimes use whole African phrases, though sometimes these phrases will be employed in English translation. But such words,

From Lorenzo Turner, "Linguistic Research and African Survival," *American Council of Learned Societies Bulletin,* 32 (1941), 68–69, 80–81, 84–86, 88–89. Reprinted with permission.

again, are not used in daily conversation. There is, however, a considerable number of African words that figure in everyday usage. For instance, the Kongo word for salt; the word "ninnie," meaning female breast, and the Umbundu word for elephant, "jumba" for the female, and "jumbo" for the male. My list of African words used by the Gullahs comes to approximately five thousand items. . . .

Mr. Herskovits: . . . Mr. Turner's discussion is no less than revolutionary. For, with adequate phonetic training, he has actually gone to African languages in the study of linguistic survivals in this country! . . .

In studying African survivals in the New World we must, of course, exercise great caution at every step. In recognizing the fact that Negroes in this country are descended from Africans whose culture could not immediately be entirely forgotten, we must not overlook the strong influences brought to bear on those people and their descendants by the ways and institutions of the New World. Yet, in taking account of past and present New World influences we should not assume that their historic African past has completely ceased to function in their lives.

Mr. Frazier: I have not found anyone who could show any evidence of survival of African social organization in this country. I may cite a concrete case. You will recall that in reviewing my book, *The Negro Family in the United States,* in *The Nation,* you said the description I gave of the reunion of a Negro family group could, with the change of a few words, be regarded as a description of a West African institution. But it also happens to be equally adequate as a description of a Pennsylvania Dutch family reunion. What are we to do in a case like that? Are we to say it is African?

Mr. Herskovits: Methodologically, it seems to me that if in studying a family whose ancestry in part, at least, came from Africa I found that something they do resembles a very deep-seated African custom, I should not look to Pennsylvania Dutch folk, with whom this family had not been in contact, for an explanation of the origin of such a custom. I may be wrong, but this seems to be elementary.

Mr. Frazier: But where did the Pennsylvania Dutch get their custom that resembles the one I described? Did they get it from Africa, too?

Mr. Herskovits: May I ask if the methodological point at issue is this: is it maintained that if we find anything done by Negroes in this country that resembles anything done in Europe, we must therefore conclude that the Negroes' behavior is derived from the European customs, the inference then being that the traditions of their African ancestors were not strong enough to stand against the impact of European ways?

Mr. Frazier: No, I wouldn't say that, but I believe it should be the aim of the scholar to establish an unmistakable historical connection between the African background and the present behavior of Negroes rather than to rely on *a priori* arguments.

Mr. Herskovits: We will be in agreement, if you will add to your statement of principle that neither should the scholar deny any such connection on *a priori* grounds.

Mr. Frazier: Of course not.

Mr. Bunche: Did I interpret correctly the statement of methodology that was made—I hope I didn't—that if, in a study of social institutions among Negroes in this country a resemblance to African institutions is shown, then the presumption favors African survival?

Mr. Herskovits: I would say if you found traits of American Negro behavior which resembled deep-seated African patterns and certain European customs as well, a European influence is not necessarily indicated.

Mr. Bunche: But would not the task of the social investigator be to attempt to trace the thread with the fullest possible documentation, rather than to jump from an existing trait or institution back to Africa? In general the characteristics of our Negro culture are much more likely to be indigenous to America than to Africa. And unless the thread of contact and correspondence could be carried all the way back, would we not have to regard any assumption of causal relationship to Africa as invalid?

Mr. Herskovits: I agree with you in principle. Naturally, Negroes have experienced different degrees of acculturation over all the New World. Africanisms in the United States are many fewer in number and intensity than in Haiti or Guiana, or even in Brazil or Cuba. But even in Brazil, Cuba or Haiti, some persons are acculturated to European patterns to a far greater degree than others. The matter depends upon the locale, on the group, on the particular historical situation involved. From the point of view of method, it would be as unfortunate if, in discussing the problem of African linguistic survivals, Mr. Turner were to say that Gullah is an African language—as he would not do—as it is for others to claim that Gullah speech is only of English derivation. . . .

Isn't the fundamental point the need in our research to take all possibilities into account? We recognize the complexity of the problem, but if, in trying to explain what we find at the present time in American Negro behavior, we close our eyes to the possibility of some African survivals, no matter how tenuous the form, are we not committing a methodological fault? It seems to me that when we find something in Negro behavior that deviates from the general pattern of American life, we should look elsewhere for a possible explanation, which may be historically substantiated. When among German-Americans we find deviants in behavior that resemble customs existing in Germany, we have no hesitation in asking whether this behavior may not be a survival of German custom. The only difference in the case of Africanisms is that the methodological difficulties in our way are so much greater. That is one reason the West Indies and South America are so important in our research, for here we can utilize the series of diminishing intensities of Africanisms to be found, which, when carefully used, lead to the recognition of relationships in a manner otherwise impossible to achieve when one goes directly from the United States to Africa.

Mr. Frazier: I think there is a mistaken notion that Negro scholars do not wish to recognize Africanisms in American Negro behavior. I do not think that is true; an equally good case could be made out for the opposite point of view. That is, race-conscious Negroes have shown, I think on the whole, a greater disposition to attribute things to African culture than have whites. . . .

Mr. Herskovits: Certainly the problem is not an easy one. It must be studied from all points of view. What Mr. Frazier says is perfectly true; we must look for correspondences all along the line, and I suspect the answer to our problem is going to be cast in terms of the varying degrees of dilution in which African elements will be found in various parts of the New World.

E S S A Y S

In the first essay Tera W. Hunter, Carnegie Mellon University historian, discusses the blues aesthetic in black vernacular dance to illuminate contests over black working-class men's and especially women's bodies and labor. In the second essay Evelyn Brooks Higginbotham, professor of Afro-American studies and history at Harvard University, warns against scholars themselves anointing any one element of African-American culture as the authentic representation of the black working class. Higginbotham notes the interrelationship—in mass media venues such as record companies but also in the leisure lives of the working class—of blues culture and church culture.

The Blues Aesthetic and Black Vernacular Dance

TERA W. HUNTER

Nighttime leisure on Atlanta's Decatur Street was incomplete without a stop in the popular dance halls. Domestic workers were conspicuous among the dedicated dancers in the city who sought pleasure in the "jook joints"—night clubs devoted to dance and music. They contributed to the moment in American history in the 1910s when urban America "danced like mad." But public dance halls were among the most controversial popular amusement sites; they were often associated with crime, drinking, and illicit sex. When Lugenia Burns Hope [prominent clubwoman and founder of Atlanta's Neighborhood Union] and Henry Hugh Proctor [pastor of the First Congregational Church] constructed "wholesome" recreational programs to compete with Decatur Street entertainment, they singled out public dancing as the most egregious activity contributing to the moral decay of the black race. White re-formers and city officials were also strong critics of public dancing and dance halls. The contests that ensued between the opponents of public dancing and the resilient devotees reveal broader tensions and anxieties about race, class, and sexuality.

A central issue at stake was control over black women's and men's bodies. Employers insisted it was their prerogative to limit the physical exertions of black women's bodies to domestic service. Black middle-class reformers tried to mollify white animosity and racial prejudice . . . by insisting that blacks conform to the standards of a chaste, disciplined, servile labor force—on and off the job. African-American wage-earners, however, asserted their own right to recuperate their bodies from exploitation. Their defiance exhibited more than creative release. The substance, style, and form of black vernacular dancing were profound expressions of a cultural aesthetic grounded in an emerging musical form, the blues.

The blues represented the music of post-slavery generations that bore the signs of a historical consciousness, as seen in its borrowings from plebeian art forms such as work songs, spirituals, and field hollers, and in its use of such traditional African-American devices as polyrhythm, falsetto, improvisation, and call and re-sponse. The blues also reflected the changing conditions of black life in its marked departure from the past. The centrality of the singer's individual persona, the highly personalized subject matter of songs, the thematic shifts toward the material world and the pursuit of pleasure were all characteristic of an emergent modern ethos. The philosophical underpinnings of the blues informed and reflected broader African-American working-class self-understandings in the modern world. This is revealed most poignantly in the ongoing battles over dancing.

The popularity and controversy of black dance have a long history. Slaves incorporated dance into their everyday lives to diminish the harsh realities of forced labor. They turned events like corn-shuckings into festive occasions, performing dances that mimicked their routine labor activities such as pitching hay, hoisting cotton bales, and hoeing corn. They also danced for pleasure on Saturdays and holidays and to express sadness in funeral rituals. Slaveholders tolerated dancing, and even enjoyed watching it, as long as it pacified bound labor, enhanced morale, and stayed within the boundaries of acceptable behavior. But dancing sometimes threatened the social order, as when slaves ridiculed masters through song lyrics and dance movement, when slaves defied orders by organizing clandestine dances, or when group solidarity was transformed into insurrections.

Following emancipation, dancing continued to be an important expression of black culture and a source of conflict with white authorities. In the 1870s, African Americans in Atlanta danced in public places near the railroad depot downtown, in halls, bars, and in the privacy of their homes, much to the chagrin of the police. By the 1890s, public officials called for "Negro dance halls" to be outlawed because they were "crime breeders and a disgrace to the city." The ties between drinking, dancing, and the sex trade led moral reformers throughout urban America to advocate regulations or prohibitions against public dance halls as eager working-class patrons flocked to them in droves.

Though there were critics who continued to point out the links between vice and public dance, other reformers sought to grant dance a new sense of respectability and legitimacy at the turn of the century. Although public dance halls of the past had been considered the domain of men and female prostitutes, modern dance halls permitted more social mingling between men and women of good repute. The growing acceptance of heterosexual socializing was also evident in changing attitudes about proper dance etiquette. Previously, dancing had stayed within strict boundaries of patterned movements, disciplined gestures, and formal distance to minimize the possibility of intimacy. In the early 1900s, however, dancing became more inventive, less rigid in style and bodily movement, and encouraged lingering physical contact. Black migration to urban areas (and white "slumming") played a large role in contributing to the sudden popularity of dance in the dominant society in the 1910s and transformed social dancing itself. . . . Controversies over dance during this period reveal the power of dancing as a cultural form and the way it embodied (literally and figuratively) racial, class, and sexual tensions in the urban South.

Domestic laborers and others escaped from their workaday worries through dance in "jook joints" and settings also referred to as "dives." These were among the most important (re)creative sites of black working-class amusements at the turn of the century, where old and new cultural forms, exhibiting both African and European influences, were syncretized. The music and the movements invented there became cultural wares that traveled back and forth via migrants and itinerant entertainers moving from country to town to city and from South to North, forming common ties with people of African descent all over the nation.

"The 'dive' is their evening mecca when they have a few dimes to spend and wish to dance and frolic and give themselves up to hours of uncontrolled pleasure and sport," one source reported. These were places usually located in the basements of storefronts on Decatur, Peters, and Harris Streets. Some dance halls continued to share quarters with saloons, though they were mostly makeshift rooms devoted primarily to music and dance. As Thomas Dorsey said about the dance joints he frequented as a pianist, "Blues would sound better late at night when the lights were low, so low you couldn't recognize a person ten feet away, when the smoke was so thick you could put a hand full of it into your pocket." He described the characteristic odors that lingered in the air as "tired sweat, bootleg booze, Piedmont cigarettes, and Hoyettes Cologne." Dorsey would play, improvising as he went along, for hours on end as the dancers moved gracefully to his music. He prided himself on his ability to play soft but perceptible sounds, in order to keep the police away. But the heat in Atlanta, especially during the summer, would often require windows to be opened, which meant that sounds could be heard on the streets.

The dance halls where Dorsey played were autonomous places, where the patrons refused to be subjected to any rules but their own. Other dance halls were more regulated, however. These establishments often existed with the forbearance of police officers, who tolerated them in exchange for proprietor's cooperation in occasional roundups of wanted criminals. Henry Beattie, a white owner, ran one such dance hall on Decatur Street like an ironfisted "czar" in the early 1900s. He commenced the dancing early in the evening and stopped at 11:00 P.M. sharp. Though the music was continuous, a floor manager, with a billy club in hand to keep order, directed patrons to the floor with the ringing of a bell and collected a nickel per couple for each set. Prior to prohibition, as the couples danced they smoked and drank beer. But Beattie refused to let his patrons drink excessively. He would seize "a person who is over tipsy and shove him from the room and bid him be gone." If a fight broke out, he would lock the doors to hold the culprits hostage until the police could come in and arrest them.

As working-class women and men danced the night away in dark, dingy, public, and, sometimes, shady places, the black elite danced to a different beat in more immaculate surroundings, demonstrating the class privileges they openly embraced. Their gala, private, and formal affairs purposely rejected the African influences conspicuous in the "snake hips" and "buzzard lope" in favor of more European-inspired polkas, waltzes, quadrilles, and pinafore lancers. . . . Perry Bradford recalled well-to-do black Atlantans doing set-dancing. As a youth, around 1905, he had attended dancing school on Wednesday afternoons. For ten cents he received lessons in Euro-American dance and a glass of lemonade. This is not to say, however, that the black elite blindly aped white culture. Despite their statements to the contrary, black elites often incorporated distinctive African-American elements in their dancing, giving novel twists to quadrilles and polkas with improvised breaks, solos, and varied tempos.

It was not dancing per se that the black elites rejected; rather, as their own balls indicated, they disdained dancing of a certain type: they criticized the physical surroundings and social atmosphere of public dance halls, and they condemned the character of working-class body language. In 1905, Proctor distinguished between the virtues of private dance and the sins of public dance. He argued: "A public dance hall [is a place] where anyone may go in and take part for a price," whereas private dancing took place among invited guests who were "socially responsible." The public dance hall was "a stumbling block to the weak and the immature of both sexes," he added; "such a place becomes a center of evil influences, and is a vestibule to the house of shame." . . .

For middle-class blacks throughout the South dedicated to racial uplift, dance halls presented some of their greatest challenges to instilling the virtues that would lead the masses out of the spiral of so-called degradation. Proctor and other elite blacks summed up their position in a petition to the City Council in 1905 in which they denied their support of dance halls: "We resent the statement that there is a demand on the part of the better element of our people for those places." Stating their class biases more bluntly, they added: "The better element does not want them, and the worst element should not be permitted to have them." The self-described elites persistently framed their pejorative descriptions of dancing and dance halls in the language of class. They disparaged people who made scanty livings through wage work as they sought to construct their own identity above the common fray. How one moved one's body constituted one's rank in society.

But despite this evidence of class-based attitudes and social institutions in Atlanta, there is also evidence of cross-over efforts in both directions. Perry Bradford grew up in a working-class family and neighborhoods, yet he gained access to some aspects of bourgeois culture, probably through his high school education at Atlanta University. The dance schools reinforced the view that middle-class status was not hermetically sealed. One could aspire to its stature and achieve its privileges, in part, through proper training and education in the rules of correct bodily carriage. . . .

The seamy reputation of Decatur Street in general and the close proximity of legal and illegal merriment were undoubtedly factors that tainted the reputation of dance halls in the minds of the most vocal members of the black elite. For the patrons of some dance halls, dancing was not the main attraction. The combination of gambling, alcoholic drinks, and excited bodies moving in time to the music was intoxicating, and sometimes the misunderstandings that could occur in festive crowds on any occasion would lead to petty skirmishes or mushroom into spirited melees. Police records in Atlanta are replete with examples of lively partying gone awry, and fights that included women domestic workers were commonplace. Pinkie Chandler, for example, was injured by a beer glass thrown in her face by Helen Henry when she accidentally brushed up against Henry's partner while dancing; Delia Mitchell created trouble when she tried to squeeze onto an already crowded dance floor and another woman pushed her out of the way. . . . Fun and reprieve from hard work may have awaited working-class women and men in dance halls and on the streets, but not without a price; the police made few distinctions in culpability in their indiscriminate raids on "jook joints" and often subjected people to harsh punishments for alleged petty crimes.

Black vernacular dance also generated controversy because of its distinctive physical characteristics, which challenged Euro-American conceptions of proper bodily etiquette. African-American dance emphasized the movement of body parts, often asymmetrically and independent of one another, whereas Euro-American dance demanded rigidity to mitigate its amorous implications. Black dance generally exploded outward from the hips; it was performed from a crouching position with the knees flexed and the body bent at the waist, which allowed a fluidity of movement in a propulsive rhythmic fashion. The facial gestures, clapping, shouting, and yelling of provocative phrases reinforced the sense of the dancer's glee. A woman might shout, for example, "C'mon Papa grab me!" as she danced.

. . . The "slow drag," one of the most popular dances in the 1910s, was described by one observer this way: "couples would hang onto each other and just grind back and forth in one spot all night." The Itch was described as "a spasmodic placing of the hands all over the body in an agony of perfect rhythm." The Fish Tail put the emphasis on the rear end, as the name suggested; the "buttocks weave out, back, and up in a variety of figure eights." The names of other dances had erotic overtones as well: the Grind, Mooche, Shimmy, Fanny Bump, Ballin' the Jack, and the Funky Butt. Skirt lifting, body caressing, and thrusting pelvic movements all conveyed amorous messages that offended moral reformers. . . .

The music that couples enjoyed in the dance halls was varied and fluid, typically characterized as ragtime or "lowdown" blues, performed live before the advent of records and the radio. The blues, which arose toward the end of the nineteenth century, grew to maturity in dance halls, rent parties, and vaudeville theaters and became more formalized in the 1910s and 1920s. In some clubs, the blues were generated by a pianist, a fiddler, or by one or more individuals "patting juba"—a practice dating back to slavery that involved clapping hands, snapping fingers, and patting limbs and armpits rhythmically. In other instances, the piano was the sole instrument driving the rhythmic beat. The dancers themselves would shout and yell as they moved.

. . . Despite the connotations of its name, the blues was "good-time" music that generated a positive rhythmic impulse to divert and drive away depression and resignation among workers whose everyday lives were filled with adversity. The blues served as the call and dance as the response in a symbiotic performance in which ecstatic bodily movements mocked the lyrics and instrumentation that signified pain and lamentation.

The close relationship between the blues and dance was especially evident in Atlanta, where musicians and vernacular dancers had a long-lasting influence on both art forms. "Didn't no dance go on without the blues," Dorsey recalled. This close association was further reinforced by songs that originated in the city with lyrics describing particular steps. Perry Bradford composed tunes with detailed dance instructions, such as "Ballin' the Jack" and "the Original Black Bottom Dance."

This close link between the blues and dance was disconcerting to middle-class and religious people as African Americans renegotiated the relationship between sacred and secular culture. The latter assumed a larger significance as blacks faced the exigencies of a new material, modern, industrial world. The tensions that resulted were most pronounced in the evolution of music and dance and their relationship to religion and the church. The shared pedigree of sacred and secular music and dance complicated matters for the pious, who emphasized the differences between shouting for the Lord and shouting for the Devil. . . .

Dancing was ubiquitous in Atlanta throughout the black neighborhoods, in dance halls, picnics, house parties, and "in the churches, most of all," stated Bradford. "Every prayer meeting of the African Methodist Church ends in a sort of Black Bottom circle dance, with the dancers clapping their hands and crooning, and the preachers calling the steps," he explained further. The circle dance Bradford described was probably very similar to the "ring shout." Dancers formed a circle and shuffled in a counterclockwise direction; they swung their bodies, clapped their hands, and shouted for joy as they became possessed with the Holy Ghost. Some of the most fervent practitioners of the ring shout in Atlanta were members of the Sanctified Churches, derisively called the "Holy Rollers." They were held in nearly as much contempt by middle-class critics as the devotees of secular dance in the "dives." Neighbors and businesses in the vicinity of storefront houses of worship would call the police to arrest the "Holy Rollers" for disorderly conduct and disturbing the peace. The Neighborhood Union helped to remove a group from one area, after circulating a petition.

When hauled into court, the Holy Rollers became spectacles, either through involuntary enactments of their religious fervor or through demonstrations requested by judges. White observers remarked on their failure to comprehend the difference between these sacred shouts and profane gestures such as those used in the "buck dance." Though ignorant of the complex cultural meaning of the "ring shout," these critics were aware of the shifting connotations of black dance, which differed more by its social context than its physical movements. The sacred shout, as musical sound and bodily movement, was indeed a variation of the "lowdown" blues that filled the airwaves of the night clubs and dance halls.

The masses of black worshippers who continued to practice ecstatic religious expression disagreed with middle-class criticisms, though they opposed the sacrilegious uses of dance and music. Black worshippers objected less to the percussive beat of the music and the paroxysmic movements of vernacular dancers, which generated merriment and exhilaration, and more to the fact that secular performances paid homage to the Devil rather than to the Holy Ghost.

Reconciling worldly pleasure and spiritual reverence, however, was not always as simple as choosing right over wrong, or God over the Devil, even for devout church people. . . . Individuals who engaged in popular amusements on Saturday night were among those who attended church on Sunday morning. . . .

The masses of black women and men embraced dancing because it met needs not completely satisfied by the church or other institutions; it countered the debilitating impact of wage labor. As free people, African Americans could pursue entertainment at will—an important distinction from slavery, in which masters largely, though not entirely, controlled and orchestrated both work and leisure. In the unregulated and secluded "jook joints," and even in regulated dance halls such as Beattie's "dive," blacks could reclaim their bodies from appropriation as instruments of physical toil and redirect their energies toward other diversions.

Black women domestic workers were singled out in these attacks against dancing in public halls. The black bourgeoisie lamented the shame and disgrace that befell the entire race when workers failed to live up to the highest expectations of dutiful service. White employers opposed the violation of what they considered their rightful claim to restrict black women's exertions to manual work. Dance halls were a menace, declared Proctor, because "the servant class tried to work all day and dance all night." He warned employers that household laborers would not perform well if they used their leisure unproductively—dancing instead of resting in preparation for the next day of work. Not missing the lesson of subservience proposed in Proctor's counsel, the white newspaper seized the opportunity to offer a reform: "Let the dance halls and places of low resort for the negro give way to schools for the domestic training of the race—schools for cooking and housework." It continued, "instead of dancing and carousing the night away, he (and especially she) will learn to become proficient in the task [for which] he is employed."

White employers also objected to dancing by black domestic workers because they feared that the dance halls bred social contagions that would infect their homes. Some child-nurses were accused of sneaking into the "dives" with white children during the day, exposing the little ones to immorality and vice. . . . It was believed that dancing encouraged sexual promiscuity among black women, who would then taint the white households through their illicit activity. The sexual connotations of black dance exacerbated these anxieties about women's behavior among the black and white middle classes. . . .

Ironically, the castigating remarks made by middle-class blacks and whites had something in common with the meaning conferred by the working class itself. Both sides understood that dancing interfered with wage work, though clearly from antithetical perspectives. The elite saw dancing as a hindrance to the creation of a chaste, disciplined, submissive, and hard-driving labor force—the hallmarks of the Protestant work ethic. Workers saw it as a respite from the deadening sensation of long hours of poorly compensated labor—critical to the task of claiming one's life as one's own.

Black dance itself embodied a resistance to the confinement of the body solely to wage work. The transformation of physical gestures in black dance from slavery to freedom demonstrates the rejection of wage work as the only outlet for physical exertion. Ex-slaves tended to abandon the references and gestures mimicking labor routines in their dances that they had practiced during slavery (such as "pitchin' hay" or "shuckin' corn") as urban freedom gave more meaning to making a living beyond the needs of subsistence alone. Consumption, entertainment, and personal gratification were also vital to working-class livelihoods and essential to an emergent modern ethos or blues aesthetic. . . .

. . . The major underlying principles that informed this [blues] aesthetic and that were embodied in vernacular dance were irreverence, transcendence, social realism, self-empowerment, and collective individualism.

The blues and dance were developed with a fierce sense of irreverence—the will to be unencumbered by any artistic, moral, or social obligations, demands, or interests external to the community which blues and dance were created to serve. While the blues and vernacular dance forms borrowed from traditions of both Euro-America and Afro-America, they ultimately paid homage only to their own interpretations. Despite protests by white authorities or black reformers, black workers persisted in their public dancing to "lowdown" music, continually reaffirming the value that they placed on upholding a collective culture.

The feelings of self-empowerment and transcendence emanating from the blues and dance were evident in the power African Americans invested in sound and bodily movement and in the particular ways in which they generated these forces, especially through the use of polyrhythms. In Euro-American music and dance, the basic pulse was dependent on an evenly partitioned beat. In contrast, the dancer and musician in Afro-American culture were challenged to play and move around the beat, to subvert linear notions of time by playing against it. The complex rhythmic structure and driving propulsive action endowed participants with the feeling of metaphysical transcendence, of being able to overcome or alter the obstacles of daily life. If the sung word was more powerful than the spoken or written word, then the danced song was even more mighty than singing alone. It was the symbiotic relationship between music and dance that made their combination a complex and rich cultural form. Workers used them for personal gratification, to reclaim their bodies from drudgery and exploitation, and actually changed, momentarily, their existential condition. . . .

The blues aesthetic is the key to understanding why African-American vernacular dance was such a contested terrain in Atlanta and the urban South and how it generated conflict over the black body. As an object of discipline and liberation, the body is a site where a society's ideas about race, class, gender, and sexuality are constructed to give the appearance of being mandates of nature while actually conforming to cultural ideologies. The body is the vehicle through which labor produces wealth, although the powerful usually resist acknowledging and rewarding the centrality of labor in the production of wealth. The importance of laboring bodies in the political economy is revealed, however, in the obsession of employers to repress and contain the autonomy of workers in order to reap the maximum benefits of their exertions. The mere sight of African Americans, especially domestic workers, deriving pleasure and expressing symbolic liberation in dance halls by posing alternative meanings of bodily exertion seemed threatening to employers.

The threat was real, since white employers were denied unmitigated control over black labor. Unlike other commercialized recreation, such as the new amusement parks, where one encountered replicas of industrial life in the mechanized, standardized forms of play, dance halls still allowed for a great deal of creativity, imagination, improvisation, and, thereby, change. Dance halls contained a strong element of impulsiveness and unpredictability, as dancers and musicians inspired one another to enact infinite permutations of gestures and sounds. Reformers' efforts to regulate the dance halls or to introduce tame, patterned movements were designed to counteract the forms of free expression that were difficult to suppress when patrons were left to their own devices.

Yet despite the tirades of incensed critics, dancing did have the effect of renewal and recovery, even if on the workers' own terms. It reinvigorated them for the next day of work and enabled them to persevere. It helped to maintain the social order by providing an outlet for workers to release their tensions, to purge their bodies of their travails on the dance floor. Dancing hard, like laboring hard, was consistent with the work ethic of capitalism. Black working-class dance, like the blues, looked back to vernacular roots and forward to the modern world. . . .

Constructing Working-Class Culture

EVELYN BROOKS HIGGINBOTHAM

. . . Black religious culture has played a significant role in the contestation of ideologies in African-American communities. This contestation occurs between the middle class and working class, and it also occurs within the working class itself. Unfortunately, the trend in recent scholarship has not given the religious culture of the working class the attention it deserves. Some of the most imaginative and analytically sophisticated studies tend to privilege the secular life of black working-class communities. Such studies often draw upon the "race records" of the 1920s and 1930s, linking blues records with socioeconomic processes of migration and urbanization. They focus on the lyrics of the blues and the lives of blues singers as emblematic of sexual freedom, iconoclastic values, and an overall culture of resistance to the hegemony of middle-class ideology. Implicitly, if not explicitly, the blues is deemed the "authentic" signifier of African-American culture. Blues culture, working-class culture, and "blackness" become virtually synonymous. The religious culture of the working poor, when visible at all, appears as an anomaly or false consciousness. The blues and church are thus counterposed as cultural icons of class division. . . .

The race records of the 1920s and 1930s are useful for analysis, since they included not only the blues but also the explicitly religious articulations of the black working class. Companies such as Okeh, Victor, Vocalion, and Paramount recorded vernacular discourses of religion in the form of sermons and gospel music, called gospel blues, as eagerly as they recorded the raunchiest blues lyrics. The religious records tapped into the cultural repertoire of storefront Baptist churches and the rising numbers of Holiness and Pentecostal churches in urban ghettos. Langston Hughes recalled his impressions of the Holiness churches in Chicago around the time of World War I: "I was entranced by their stepped-up rhythms, tambourines, hand clapping, and uninhibited dynamics, rivaled only by Ma Rainey singing the blues at the old Monogram Theater." Just as Hughes had juxtaposed the songs of the church with the blues, this odd coupling of the sacred and profane appeared regularly in newspaper advertisements for race records. Paramount Records informed the readers of the *Chicago Defender* that they could "get these Red-Hot Blues and Inspiring Spirituals" through mail order. Okeh included in a single advertisement blues singer Lonnie Johnson and gospel singer Jessie May Hill. Featuring Johnson's "Mean Old Bed Bug Blues," the advertisement read: "Bedbugs big as a jackass bite you and stand and grin. Then drink a bottle of bed bug poison and come and bite you again. The Hottest Blues You Ever Heard." Yet the same advertisement listed "Sister Jessie May Hill and Sisters of the Congregation singing 'Earth Is No Resting Place.'"

If, as some scholars suggest, advertising's juxtaposition of religious and blues records served as an affront to the pious, the coupling nonetheless offers an analytical rubric for disentangling the working class from its exclusive identification with blues culture. Clearly, the church was just as indigenous to the working poor as was the blues. On one level the popularity of the sermons and gospel songs speaks to an emotional folk orality that contested the ethics and aesthetics of the black middle class. Not through the counterculture of the blues, but rather through vernacular discourses of religion, the black poor waged a struggle over cultural authority that ultimately subverted the hegemonic values and aesthetic standards of the traditional Protestantism of the black middle class. On another level the religious race records speak to the existence of multiple and conflicting subcultures within the black working class, indicating differences of consciousness, values, and lifestyle even among the most poor. The religious culture of the poor, as evidenced in the Pentecostal and Holiness churches, for example, embraced a strict moral code that denounced the fast and free lifestyle of blues culture. In the dialect, imagery, and rhythms of the black poor, the religious race records repudiate sexual freedom, gambling, drinking, womanizing, and general defiance of the law. . . .

The religious race records of the 1920s gave a new public dimension to black religion and especially to the working-class churches. The records validated the creative energies of the rural folk, turned urban proletariat, as an alternate, competing voice within African-American communities. At the most prosaic levels, the ascendant voice of southern folk culture challenged the middle-class ideology of racial uplift as pronounced by educated religious leaders of the late nineteenth century. The latter group had defined racial progress not merely in the context of black-white relations but also in the context of a class-based contestation over group beliefs and practices. Educated religious leaders emphasized written texts and rational discourses in the struggle for the advancement of their people. . . . Commitment to collegiate education figured prominently in their belief in an intellectual and professional vanguard. . . .

As time and schooling distanced African Americans further and further from their slave past, many became self-conscious, conflicted, even critical of the culture of their forebears. From gentle persuasion to ridicule and punishment, white and black missionary teachers sought the demise of the older forms of singing and worship. In 1870, Elizabeth Kilham, a white northern teacher among the freedmen, acknowledged the impact of education on the younger generation:

> The distinctive features of negro hymnology, are gradually disappearing, and with another generation will probably be obliterated entirely. The cause for this, lies in the education of the younger people . . . . Already they have learned to ridicule the extravagant preaching, the meaningless hymns, and the noisy singing of their elders. Not perhaps as yet, to any great extent in the country; changes come always more slowly there, but in the cities, the young people have, in many cases, taken the matter into their own hands, formed choirs, adopted the hymns and tunes in use in the white churches. . . .

It is interesting that Kilham, while praising the shift to white hymns, conceded the slowness with which blacks in the countryside assimilated. Bishop Daniel Alexander Payne of the African Methodist Episcopal Church recalled his frustrating experience in a rural church in South Carolina.

> After the sermon they formed a ring, and with coats off sung, clapped their hands and stamped their feet in a most ridiculous and heathenish way. I requested the pastor to go and stop their dancing. At his request they stopped their dancing and clapping of hands,

but remained singing and rocking their bodies to and fro. This they did for about fifteen minutes. I then went, and taking their leader by the arm requested him to desist and to sit down and sing in a *rational* manner. I told him also that it was a heathenish way to worship and disgraceful to themselves, the race, and the Christian name. (my emphasis)

Payne's plea for a "rational manner" of singing formed part of the larger assimilationist project of ridding the black community of sensuality, intemperance, "superstition," and the emotional style of worship practiced in the hush harbors of the slave era. His emphasis on a calm, intellectually oriented religious expression signaled the growing class and cultural differences that would surface prominently as rural southern migrants poured into the northern cities. For Bishop Payne, loud and emotive behavior constituted more than an individual's impropriety or doctrinal error. It marked the retrogression of the entire racial group. . . .

Literacy and published texts came to be linked increasingly to the expression of religious culture. The Reverend Sutton Griggs, a college-educated Baptist minister and novelist, typified the black middle class in its preference for print discourse, thus implicitly devaluing the interpretative authority of illiterate leaders. He proclaimed, "To succeed as a race, we must move up out of the age of the voice. . . ." Educated leaders perceived the medium of print as a source of communication and power. They made continual appeals for the publication of texts that would present the African-American side of history and instill pride in their people. They commonly used the term "distinctive literature," referring to any text that was written and/or published by African Americans. Yet the phenomenal rise in literacy among African Americans in the decades after the Civil War occurred with unsettling consequences for traditions of black worship. Calling attention to the clash between literate and oral traditions in the postbellum South, Elsa Barkley Brown describes the conflict surrounding the introduction of printed songbooks in the First African Baptist Church in Richmond. The adoption of hymnals superseded the older practice of "lining out hymns," a practice increasingly labeled "unrefined" and a vestige of slave culture by educated blacks and whites. Lining out had not required literacy, but only an able song leader to introduce each verse of song, which in turn was followed by the congregation's repetition of the verse. The introduction of hymnals, however, disadvantaged the illiterate, since it reconfigured the collective voice to include the literate only. For the illiterate, asserts Elsa Barkley Brown, "it was the equivalent of being deprived of a voice, all the more significant in an oral culture." . . .

An entire genre of race literature arose in the late nineteenth century for the purpose of "uplifting" the black masses culturally, politically, and economically. The rise of literacy had been foundational to the evolution of a black reading public, and it was this very readership that constituted the race market so crucial to the success of church-based entrepreneurship. Many local religious presses as well as the large denominational ones (the A.M.E. Book Concern, the A.M.E. Sunday School Union Press, the A.M.E. Zion Book Concern, the A.M.E. Zion Publication House, the National Baptist Publishing Board, and the Sunday School Publishing Board of the National Baptist Convention, U.S.A., Inc.) figured significantly in the production of hymnals, church literature, newspapers, and to a lesser extent works of fiction. . . . Literature produced by African Americans strove to negate the pejorative racial images prevalent in film, media, art and scholarly and popular books. Photographs in black-owned periodicals often depicted middle-class men and women in the act of reading. Captions to such photographs made reference to the cultivation of the "higher arts" and sought to convey images of refinement and civility, material comfort and respectability. The conflation of musical taste and literature culture is apparent in the 1904 issue of the *Voice of the Negro,* which featured a photographic series of "representative" black men and women. A caption to a photograph of a young black woman read: "An admirer of Fine Art, a performer on the violin and the piano, a sweet singer, a writer—mostly given to essays, a lover of good books, and a home making girl."

It is no small irony, then, that the newly urbanized southern folk ushered in the "age of the voice" at the height of the renaissance of the black literati. During the 1920s and 1930s the black working class effected the shift to an emotional folk orality that challenged the cultural authority of the black middle class. The migrants built storefront churches, established sects and cults, and "infiltrated" and transformed many of the "old-line" Baptist and Methodist churches with the gospel blues, a twentieth-century musical innovation with roots in the slave past. Historian Lawrence Levine conveys this blend of old and new in the religious culture of the migrants:

> While many churches within the black community sought respectability by turning their backs on the past, banning the shout, discouraging enthusiastic religion, and adopting more sedate hymns and refined concertized versions of the spirituals, the Holiness churches constituted a revitalization movement with their emphasis upon healing, gifts of prophecy, speaking in tongues, spirit possession, and religious dance. Musically, they reached back to the traditions of the slave past and out to the rhythms of the secular black musical world around them. They brought into the church not only the sounds of ragtime, blues and jazz but also the instruments.

The public emergence of a folk orality can be attributed to both the massive migration of southern blacks to northern cities and to a triumphant American commercialism, which during the 1920s turned its gaze upon black consumers. Through advertising, department stores, catalog shopping, and installment buying, the new commercial culture made its impact on the Great Migration. The recently arrived migrants soon became a consuming public, hungry for their own musical styles and for an array of products with a racial appeal. They swelled the ranks of the race market and reconfigured black supply and demand well beyond the small entrepreneur and communities of readership at the turn of the century. . . .

Race-consciousness, creative expression, and the black church itself became implicated in America's growing corporate capitalism. Nowhere is this more evident than in the nexus between working-class religion and the record industry. The record industry tapped into the cultural repertoire of the black working-class churches, drawing upon and promoting the very folk traditions that the middle class had sought to eradicate. While the commodification of black religious culture and the attendant reality of white-controlled profits speak to the problematic aspects of the race records industry, it cannot be denied that this commodification was made possible by the matrix of exchange inherent in the black working-class church. The church was and is at once the producer of musicians and music forms as well as a consumer market with changing tastes. Technological advancement and the consequent rise of the record and broadcast industries, along with mass advertising in the national black press, e.g., the *Chicago Defender,* all worked together to effect the commodification of the religious experience. . . .

If African-American religion succumbed to the commercialism and consumerism of the 1920s, it did so while harnessing new venues for working-class cultural production. A new public voice, indeed a charismatic authority, rivaled the authority of the educated black leadership. The nineteenth century had witnessed the ascendancy of the middle class as the literate public voice of the race. The twentieth century witnessed the ascendancy of the black working class as the oral narrator of modernity. Growing working-class consumerism, coupled with black middle-class disdain for the cultural styles of the poor, had initiated this important shift to working-class orality within the black public sphere. Even the Reverend Sutton Griggs, who had earlier admonished his people to "move up out of the age of the voice," recorded sermons on the Victor label during the 1920s. However, the rise of race records should not imply a false dichotomy between reading and oral/aural constituencies. More often than not, the two constituencies were one and the same, since record consumers looked primarily to black newspapers for the advertisement of new record releases and for coverage on the personal lives and public appearances of recording stars.

Blues scholar Paul Oliver notes that religious records enjoyed a popularity equal to that of the blues, and possibly greater. Produced in three-minute and six-minute sound bites, these records attempt to re-create the black worship experience, presenting highly emotional preaching, moaning, ecstatic audience response, vocal and instrumental accompaniment. Oliver recounts their unrestrained quality: "The preacher develops his subject, often speaking in a direct address at first and moving to a singing tone as he warms to his theme. . . . Urged on by the murmurs, cries, shouts of approval and encouragement from the congregation, he might struggle for the right words, 'straining' with constricted throat . . . 'moaning,' 'mourning,' 'whooping.'"

Building on patterns from the folk tradition and thus rejecting a rational, dispassionate style, the recorded sermons and religious songs were especially appealing to the waves of rural migrants who poured into northern cities, uprooted and in search of cultural continuity. Record companies catered to the migrants' preference for a "down-home," i.e., more rural, southern style by adopting such phrases as "old-fashioned," "real Southern style" and "old-time" in their record titles and advertisements. Paramount proudly announced its "latest new electric method" of record production in its advertisement for *Old Time Baptism* by the Reverend R. M. Massey. Okeh Records invoked similar images of an immediate and authentic black religious experience in its advertisement of two sermons by the Reverend F. W. McGee and his congregation: "They make you feel as if you're right in the church. You hear it all just as it actually happens. The preacher's burning words . . . spontaneous shouts from the congregation . . . and the low-pitched hum of musical instruments." Musical accompaniment in recorded sermons often included the moaning sounds of women in the background, a boogie-woogie piano or the sounds of cornet, guitar, and drums. The sermons met with instant success. The Reverend J. C. Burnett's sermon, the *Downfall of Nebuchadnezzar,* sold eighty thousand records within months of its release in November 1926. Interestingly, the sermon begins in the tradition of the slaves with the lining out of the hymn *I Heard the Voice of Jesus Say.* The sale of Burnett's record quadrupled the normal sale of a Bessie Smith record. By the end of the 1930s, the number of black preachers, male and female, on record had soared from six to seventy, while more than 750 sermons had been recorded.

Also popular during the 1920s and early 1930s were the religious records of male and female singers, especially those identified with the storefront Baptist, Holiness, and Pentecostal churches. The strictly musical records outlived the sermons in their appeal to consumers. Arizona Dranes, the blind vocalist, who sang for Okeh Records, played in a piano style reminiscent of ragtime and boogie-woogie as she rendered the songs of black Pentecostalism to record consumers across the nation. The records of Sanctified singers (Paul Oliver's term for female singers in the Pentecostal and Holiness churches) such as Jessie May Hill, Leora Ross, Bessie Johnson, Melinda Taylor, and Rosetta Tharpe with her gospel hybridization of jazz and swing, were widely distributed in black communities. Sanctified singers did not limit themselves to the piano, but employed secular accompaniment—guitars, jug bands, and tambourines. Oliver notes that blues singers even cut religious records, after record promoters convinced them of the lucrative nature of the religious market. Classic blues queens, such as Bessie Smith, Sara Martin, Clara Smith, and Leola Manning claimed at least one sacred song in their repertoire of otherwise secular recordings.

The standard hymn, with its implicit connotations of order and respectability, yielded ineluctably to improvisation and earthy rhythms. The capitulation of middle-class notions of assimilation and respectability to the new "gospel blues" occurred most glaringly in the black Baptist church. This shifting emphasis is epitomized by the musical styles of Marian Anderson and Mahalia Jackson, both of whose musical talents were discovered and nurtured in the church. During the first two decades of the twentieth century, the talents of the future opera star Marian Anderson grew to maturity under the influence of the musical traditions of Philadelphia's Union Baptist Church. By age thirteen she was promoted to the adult choir, having sung in the junior choir since she was six. Her sense of music and its cultural meaning was informed by traditional hymnody and orchestral performances. Black hymnody in this setting is reminiscent of Houston Baker's discussion of the "mastery of form." Baker identifies such mastery as a strategy efficaciously adopted in the name of group advancement, but clearly based upon the acknowledgment of an appeal to white America's hegemonic cultural styles and values, i.e., the nation's *standards.* The church's annual concerts frequently engaged tenor Roland Hayes who "sang old Italian airs, German Lieder, and French songs exquisitely." Anderson recalls in her autobiography that "even people with little understanding of music knew it was beautiful singing, and they were proud Mr. Hayes was one of their own and world famous."

Mahalia Jackson's talents were cultivated in the musical traditions of the southern black church. She began her singing career in New Orleans, the birthplace of jazz. She performed in an up-tempo rhythm expressive of what Michael W. Harris terms "indigenous black religious song in a down-home manner." Her singing group, while popular in the South, met with initial disfavor after she migrated to Chicago in 1927 at the age of sixteen. In his study of the rise of gospel blues, Harris notes that Jackson was once thrown out of a church—the minister

shouting, "Get that twisting and jazz out of the church." Similar views are expressed in the poem "When Mahalia Sings" by Quandra Prettyman. Although the
poem tells of Prettyman's eventual respect for the emotional religiosity of the
working poor, the excerpt below emphasizes her initial mockery of the "holiness
rhythms" of the storefront churches:

> We used to gather at the high window
> of the holiness church and, on tip-toe
> look in and laugh at the dresses, too small
> on the ladies, and how wretched they all
> looked—an old garage for a church, for pews,
> old wooden chairs. It seemed a lame excuse
> for a church. Not solemn or grand,
> with no real robed choir, but a loose jazz band,
> or so it sounded to our mocking ears.
> So we responded to their hymns with jeers.

Mahalia Jackson's gospel blues appealed greatly to the swelling numbers of
poor, Deep South migrants to Chicago. Jackson gave new voice to an old spirituality
as she regularly performed at storefront churches. By 1932 she was receiving invitations from the established, old-line churches and would soon sing at the annual
meetings of the National Baptist Convention. The gospel blues had subverted the
central, if not hegemonic position of standard hymnody even in these churches. Far
less concerned about the gaze of white America in the projection of an African-
American image, the gospel blues evoked the call and response of blacks themselves.

Nor did church leaders continue to link inextricably racial progress with their
congregants' mastery of Western expressivity and styles of decorum. At issue here
is more than the contestation between middle-class and working-class cultures; it
is rather the interpenetration of the two. While both Marian Anderson and Mahalia
Jackson enjoyed enormous fame throughout their lives, the musical repertoire of
urban black Baptist churches came increasingly to identify (although not without
contestation) the old-line voice with European hymns, while associating the modern with the more spontaneous, emotive style of down-home religious culture. The
transition of black church discourses symbolized the responsive soundings of a
people in transition from an old to a new order. The commodification of black religious culture roared along with the 1920s as a marker of the decade's preoccupation with the black vernacular.

Yet the contestation of cultures occurred not merely between the working class
and the middle class. Division and dispute occurred within the working class itself.
While the musical form of gospel blues incorporated the rhythmic patterns and
sounds of secular blues, ragtime, and jazz, the lyrical content of gospel blues were
embedded in institutions and belief structures that repudiated secular blues themes.
Enjoying a prominence that was not confined to a particular congregation or region,
men such as the Reverends E. D. Campbell, A. W. Nix, J. M. Gates and women such
as the Reverends Leora Ross and Mary Nelson brought messages of doom and salvation to African Americans throughout the nation. Through recorded sermons and
songs they drew upon biblical passages in their denunciation of crime, liquor, dancing, women's fashions, gambling, and fast living in general. In *Better Get Ready for
Judgement* the Reverend Mary Nelson sings in a strong a capella voice, condemning

the hypocrites, drunkards, liars, and adulterers. The recordings constituted vernacular discourses of religion, calling attention to the conditions of ghetto life in the everyday language of the poor and uneducated.

The railroad train figures prominently in the religious race records, just as it does in the blues. In discussing the blues, literary scholars Houston Baker and Hazel Carby point to the train's varied meanings of freedom and loneliness for male and female migrants. However, in the religious race records, the train symbolizes a vehicle of judgment—an image altogether different from its metaphorical usage in the secular blues. For example, the Reverend J. M. Gates's sermon, *Death's Black Train Is Coming,* portrays the train as an instrument of retribution for fast living. The most popular use of the train motif was Reverend A. W. Nix's *Black Diamond Express to Hell.* The Vocalion advertisement announced: "Here she comes! The 'Black Diamond Express to Hell' with Sin, the Engineer, holding the throttle wide open; Pleasure is the Headlight, and the Devil is the Conductor. You can feel the roaring of the Express and the moanin' of the Drunkards, Liars, Gamblers and other folk who have got aboard. They are hell-bound and they don't want to go. The train makes eleven stops but nobody can get off." The route of the train included stops at "Liar's Ave., Dance Hall Depot, and Stealing Town."

Themes of justice to the wicked and proud abound in the recorded sermons. Against the background of moaning voices and cries of amen, Reverend Burnett began his blockbuster hit, the *Downfall of Nebuchadnezzar,* by prophesying the inevitable ruin of people who hold themselves in high estimation and manipulate the weak. Burnett's message serves as a promise to the oppressed: God will bring down the liars, backsliders, and rich men. A similar theme can be found in Reverend J. M. Gates's record, *Samson and the Woman.* Despite the title, the sermon focuses not on gender but on class and race relations. Gates, like Burnett, targets those people who think that their positions of strength, privilege, and power over others will last forever. Those on top will be leveled in time, he proclaims repeatedly in the sermon. Gates was one of the most popular of the recorded preachers, holding contracts with five different record companies during the 1920s. Titles of his recorded sermons reveal concern about rising crime, e.g., *The First Born Was a Murderer, Did You Spend Christmas in Jail?, Death Might Be Your Santa Claus, No Room in the Jailhouse,* and *Dying Gambler.* Whether sung or preached, the religious race records condemned the growing disorder, alienation, and criminal elements in the urban setting, but they did so in the common, everyday language of the black working class. The vernacular discourses of religion constituted a moral idiom for distinguishing the personal and collective identity of the "righteous" from other working-class identities (e.g., blues people). The messages in the recorded sermons and songs articulated shared meanings and constraints for evaluating and interpreting social reality. They sought to establish boundaries around the lives of the black poor in the effort to shield them from dangers that were perceived as emanating from both outside and inside their own communities.

At issue here are not only conflicting value systems but internally generated norms. This latter point is often overlooked by scholars who too readily attribute efforts to restore "moral order" to the intentionality, ideology, and disciplinary mechanisms of the middle class. The middle class certainly played a role in disciplining the poor and in policing black women's bodies, as Hazel Carby perceptively discusses, but so, too, did Pentecostal churches. Nor were notions of "moral panic" situated solely within a 1920s bourgeois ideology. The quest for moral order is replete in the sermons, gospel songs, and religious institutions of the working class. The storefront Baptist, Pentecostal, and Holiness churches along with a variety of urban sects and cults, e.g., Father Divine's Peace Mission movement and Daddy Grace's United House of Prayer, were doubtless more effective than middle-class reformers in policing the black woman's body and demanding conformity to strict guidelines of gender roles and sexual conduct. Within these religious traditions, an impassioned embrace of outward emotion and bodily movement went hand-in-hand with the rejection of sexual contact outside of marriage, secular dancing, and worldly indulgence.

In conclusion, I offer these comments on religion and race records in order to ponder competing values and moral discourses within the black working class. Juxtaposing the sacred and profane forces a rethinking of the oft-rendered image of a working class that is the monolithic and coherent bearer of an "authentic" black consciousness. Black working-class culture, as the generative site of the blues and the zoot suit, produced as well Pentecostalism and the Nation of Islam. Religious culture, like the blues, found expression in the black vernacular.

FURTHER READING

William Barlow, *"Looking Up at Down": The Emergence of Blues Culture* (1989).

Edward A. Berlin, *King of Ragtime: Scott Joplin and His Era* (1994).

Donald Bogle, *Toms, Coons, Mulattoes, Mammies, and Bucks: An Interpretive History of Blacks in America* (1973).

Pearl Bowser and Louise Spence, "Identity and Betrayal: *The Symbol of the Unconquered* and Oscar Micheaux's 'Biographical Legend,'" in *The Birth of Whiteness: Race and the Emergence of U.S. Cinema,* ed. Daniel Bernardi (1996), 56–80.

Hazel V. Carby, "'It Jus Be's Dat Way Sometime': The Sexual Politics of Women's Blues," *Radical America,* 20, no. 4 (1986).

Hazel V. Carby, "Policing the Black Woman's Body in an Urban Context," *Critical Inquiry,* 18 (Summer 1992), 738–755.

Thomas Cripps, *Slow Fade to Black: The Negro in American Film, 1900–1942* (1977).

Angela Yvonne Davis, *Blues Legacies and Black Feminism: Gertrude "Ma" Rainey, Bessie Smith, and Billie Holiday* (1998).

Ann Douglas, *Terrible Honesty: Mongrel Manhattan in the 1920s* (1995).

Martin Bauml Duberman, *Paul Robeson* (1988).

Arthur Huff Fauset, *Black Gods of the Metropolis: Negro Religious Cults of the Urban North* (1944).

Jane Gaines, "Fire and Desire: Race, Melodrama, and Oscar Micheaux," in *Black American Cinema,* ed. Manthia Diawara (1993), 49–70.

Michael W. Harris, *The Rise of Gospel Blues: The Music of Thomas Andrew Dorsey in the Urban Church* (1992).

Daphne Duval Harrison, *Black Pearls: Blues Queens of the 1920s* (1998).

Tony Heilbrut, *The Gospel Sound: Good News and Bad Times* (1971).

Robert E. Hemenway, *Zora Neale Hurston: A Literary Biography* (1977).

Errol Hill, ed., *The Theater of Black Americans: A Collection of Critical Essays* (1980).

Nathan I. Huggins, *Harlem Renaissance* (1971).

Gloria T. Hull, *Color, Sex and Poetry: Three Women Writers of the Harlem Renaissance* (1987).

Lawrence Levine, *Black Culture and Black Consciousness: Afro-American Folk Thought from Slavery to Freedom* (1977).

David Levering Lewis, *When Harlem Was in Vogue* (1981).

Tony Martin, *Literary Garveyism: Garvey, Black Arts, and the Harlem Renaissance* (1983).

Paul Oliver, *Songsters and Saints: Vocal Traditions on Race Records* (1984).

Richard J. Powell, *Black Art and Culture in the 20th Century* (1997).

Arnold Rampersad, *The Life of Langston Hughes* (1986).

Charlene B. Regester, "Oscar Micheaux on the Cutting Edge: Films Rejected by the New York State Motion Picture Commission," *Studies in Popular Culture,* 17, no. 2 (April 1995), 61–72.

Phyllis Rose, *Jazz Cleopatra: Josephine Baker in Her Time* (1989).

Jon Michael Spencer, *The New Negroes and Their Music: The Success of the Harlem Renaissance* (1997).

Jeffrey C. Stewart, ed., *Paul Robeson: Artist and Citizen* (1998).

Ted Vincent, *Keep Cool: The Black Activists Who Built the Jazz Age* (1995).

Margaret Wade-Lewis, "Lorenzo Dow Turner: Pioneer African-American Linguist," *Black Scholar,* 21, no. 4 (Fall 1991), 10–24.

Victoria W. Wolcott, " 'Bible, Bath, and Broom': Nannie Helen Burroughs's National Training School and African-American Racial Uplift," *Journal of Women's History,* 9, no. 1 (Spring 1997), 88–110.

Opportunities Lost

and Found

The Depression and World War II years were times of crisis and loss for black Americans, but at the same time they offered moments of opportunity. High unemployment rates in urban areas accompanied a push off the land for black sharecroppers and tenant farmers. The federal government, which touted the United States as the "arsenal of democracy," continued to organize America's fighting units along segregated lines and to accord German prisoners of war greater respect than it granted black military men and women. And only the threat of mass action prodded the government into providing equal opportunity for African Americans in wartime industries. Yet the Depression opened up the federal government to new programs that benefited black artists in all media, brought unprecedented numbers of African Americans into federal policy-making positions, and focused federal attention more fully on the economic and political plight of black Americans. Nevertheless the government's wartime rhetoric of making the "world safe for democracy" undergirded African Americans' "Double V" campaign—victory at home and abroad—during World War II and became the basis for a broad struggle against the second-class citizenship status of black Americans after the war. Interestingly enough, the first dramatic victory in that struggle came on the baseball field rather than on political or economic terrains. In 1947 Jackie Robinson joined the Brooklyn Dodgers, thus integrating professional baseball. Not only was Robinson's success a harbinger of other breaches in Jim Crow to follow, it undoubtedly reached and inspired African Americans who were missed by other protests and mobilizations.

 D O C U M E N T S

In 1930, 78.7 percent of all black Americans lived in the South. By 1960, only 60 percent resided in that region. The migrations north and, increasingly, west were the result of both the displacement of sharecroppers and other agricultural laborers during and after the Depression and the widening of economic opportunities during and after World War II. Within the South, rural-to-urban migration rose as well. The first document illuminates these population shifts.

Federal initiatives designed to alleviate the economic and social crisis of the 1930s had different and unequal impacts on black and white people. In 1930, more than 40 percent of employed black men worked in agriculture and 90 percent of employed black women did domestic service or agricultural labor. Because both of these occupational categories were exempted from the National Recovery, Social Security, and Fair Labor Standards Acts, the majority of black workers were excluded from new federal minimum wage, maximum hour, unemployment compensation, and Social Security protections. Not all discrimination under the New Deal programs was so indirect. In the second document, Charles Hamilton Houston and John P. Davis expose the "raw deal" black residents received from the Tennessee Valley Authority.

President Franklin Delano Roosevelt focused on gaining broad support for his program of economic recovery. The resulting emphasis on appeasing southern Democrats left civil rights issues on the back burner. The third document is a photograph that shows an NAACP protest of the Roosevelt administration's failure to support publicly an antilynching bill during the president's first term. Nevertheless, at least in part as recognition of their growing voting strength, black Americans gained unprecedented access to the machinery of public policy as they held positions in a variety of federal agencies. Because of their high visibility and collective efforts to influence New Deal policy, these black federal employees were dubbed Roosevelt's "Black Brain Trust" or the "Black Cabinet." The fourth document shows many of the members of the group.

Poor and working-class men and women did not rely solely on federal aid to improve their collective economic lot. Despite organized labor's tradition of indifference at worst—hostility at best—to their interests, increasing numbers of black people in the 1930s affirmed the validity of unionizing to improve their working conditions. Tobacco worker Louise "Mamma" Harris discusses her emergence as a union leader in the fifth document.

The new opportunities for blacks created by the wartime economy—and the limits that continuing racial discrimination imposed on them—were mirrored within the U.S. military. Even as the air and marine corps were opened to black enlistees and African Americans were admitted to officer training programs, persistent Jim Crowism kept black servicemen in low-ranking noncombat positions. In the sixth document, a college-educated marine writes of his frustration to A. Philip Randolph.

In few places was the symbolic leveling of the postwar playing field more visible than on Brooklyn's Ebbets Field, where Jackie Robinson played with the Dodger baseball team from 1947 through 1956. In the seventh document, the *Pittsburgh Courier,* which had spearheaded a campaign to integrate baseball, congratulates Robinson and itself, while at the same time recognizing that the color bar, while lowered, was still a barrier within this and other professional sports.

1. Black Population in Selected Cities, 1940–1960

	POPULATION			PERCENTAGE INCREASE	
	1940	1950	1960	1940–1950	1950–1960
South					
Birmingham, AL	108,938	130,055	135,113	19.4	38.9
Washington, DC	187,266	280,440	411,737	49.8	46.8
Jacksonville, FL	61,782	81,648	105,655	32.2	29.4
Tampa, FL	23,331	27,255	46,244	16.8	69.7
Atlanta, GA	104,533	121,155	186,464	15.9	53.9
New Orleans, LA	149,034	181,120	233,514	21.5	28.9
Baltimore, MD	165,843	223,820	325,589	35.0	45.5
Tulsa, OK	15,151	20,987	22,489	38.5	7.1
Charleston, SC	31,765	19,387	33,522	(–39.0)	72.9
Memphis, TN	121,498	146,830	184,320	21.0	25.5
Houston, TX	86,302	124,760	215,037	44.6	72.4
Norfolk, VA	45,893	63,105	78,806	37.5	24.9
North					
Chicago, IL	277,731	492,635	812,637	77.4	65.0
Kansas City, KS	21,033	26,660	28,134	26.8	5.5
Detroit, MI	149,119	298,875	482,223	100.4	1.3
St. Louis, MO	108,765	153,465	214,377	41.1	9.7
New York, NY	458,444	749,080	1,087,931	63.4	45.2
Cleveland, OH	84,504	147,585	250,818	74.6	69.9
Pittsburgh, PA	62,216	82,255	100,692	32.2	22.4
Milwaukee, WI	8,821	21,910	62,458	148.4	185.1
West					
Los Angeles, CA	63,774	170,880	334,916	168.0	96.0
Oakland, CA	8,462	47,610	83,618	462.6	75.6
San Francisco, CA	4,846	43,460	74,383	796.8	71.2
Albuquerque, NM	547	610	4,672	11.5	665.9
Seattle, WA	3,789	16,734	26,901	341.6	60.8

2. Charles Hamilton Houston and John P. Davis Critique the Lily-White Tennessee Valley Authority, 1934

The Tennessee River drains large parts of seven states: Virginia, North Carolina, Georgia, Alabama, Mississippi, Kentucky and Tennessee. Prior to 1933, little had been done to conserve and harness the vast power potentialities of the river, aside from the construction of a dam, power plant and nitrate factory at Muscle Shoals begun during the World War. Immediately upon the inauguration of President Roosevelt, however, his administration embarked on a Tennessee Valley . . .

U.S. Bureau of the Census, *Sixteenth Census of the United States: 1940. Population. Vol. II. Characteristics of the Population. Part 1* (Washington, D.C.: GPO, 1943), 114; U.S. Bureau of the Census, *Census of Population: 1950. Vol. II. Characteristics of the Population. Part 1,* United States Summary (Washington, D.C.: GPO, 1953), 139–140; U.S. Bureau of the Census, *1970 Census of Population. Supplementary Report. Negro Population in Selected Places and Selected Counties* (Washington, D.C.: GPO, 1971), 8–12.

Charles Hamilton Houston and John P. Davis, "TVA: Lily-White Reconstruction," *Crisis* (October 1934), 290–291, 311.

experiment aimed to rid from economic and social blight the 2,364,000 people of the Valley region, of whom 238,000 are Negroes. More than this, it is intended as a "yardstick" for comparable projects in the development of other sections of the country.

. . . The T.V.A. is spending millions upon millions of dollars in the valley in construction projects. This has suddenly stimulated employment and created a temporary and limited prosperity. But looking beyond the day when this temporary and limited prosperity will peter out as the construction comes to an end, the T.V.A. is attempting to make the valley self-sustaining. It hopes that its hydroelectric development of an ultimate pool of 3,000,000 horsepower of cheap electricity will cause a large scale industrial expansion along its transmission lines, which in turn will start a chain of increased employment at living wages, a rise in purchasing power, more consumption of goods with attendant increase in the standard of living. . . .

The greatest program of regional education ever attempted anywhere is being put in force. Model dairies, poultry farms, tree nurseries, garden farms, woodworking, automotive, metal and electrical shops, and a general agricultural training program either have been, or soon will be started out of public funds, designed to teach the T.V.A. workers and other valley residents how to make an independent living combining industry and agriculture. The whites are being given every encouragement to take advantage of the educational opportunities, but last July when the authors visited the region and asked what provision had been made for the instruction of Negroes the answer was that nothing had been done and nothing definite proposed. There is no rehabilitation for the Negro.

Out of taxpayers' money the T.V.A. is building the model town of Norris, Tennessee, to contain a basic number of 500 families. The town is designed to house the permanent force at Norris Dam and those in charge of adjacent T.V.A. enterprises. No expense has been spared to make and preserve it as the *ideal* American community. . . .

. . . The T.V.A. owns the ground, builds the houses, and then in order to keep the maximum control over the community does not sell the property but only leases it to the workers accepted.

The families admitted to the community are selected by the T.V.A. with the greatest care. They are all white. The authorities told us bluntly no Negroes would be permitted to occupy houses in Norris, "Because Negroes do not fit into the program." Thus their position is that Negroes do not belong in the "ideal American community" built and maintained by public funds, in spite of the fact that there is not a town of 500 families in the entire Tennessee River Basin (except perhaps in the extreme mountain sections) where Negroes and whites do not live side by side. Yet in Norris Negroes are excluded by agents of the federal government.

As one studies the operations of the T.V.A., one is struck by the fact that in almost every activity the Negro is either systematically excluded or else discreetly overlooked. The Authority is bending over backwards not to give any offense to the traditions of the South. The Negro is completely excluded from the social rehabilitation program. In all the public press releases of the T.V.A. the Negro is mentioned only once, and then simply in the capacity of labor. . . . In other words, the only function that the Negro has in the T.V.A., the only recognition which the T.V.A. gives him, is as a labor commodity. And even this function is subject to certain exceptions.

. . . The T.V.A. . . . gave Negroes their "proportionate" share of employment, but not their "proportionate" share of the payroll. When the authors made their visit last July, not a single Negro was employed on the "inside" or in a clerical or office position, except one assistant personnel officer at Norris Dam, Max Bond. Not a single Negro was employed as a foreman or higher. By keeping all Negro employees on the lower levels of employment, the proportionate share of the pay-rolls was less than one per cent of the total.

The authorities were asked if there was discrimination in employment. They first answered no; then they qualified by saying that they would not employ Negro artisans unless they could get enough for a crew; that they would not work a mixed crew of white and colored. But the "mixed crew" objection is simply a bogey to mask discrimination and keep Negroes out of jobs. On the night shift at the Joe Wheeler Dam the authors saw white and Negro drillers working on the same drill. The white worker was the driller: the Negro his helper. When the white worker left the drill for any reason, the Negro helper would run it until he got back. . . .

The authorities next told us that they were employing Negroes according to the trades in which they were customarily found in the valley: such as drillers, powder men, concrete pourers, etc. In short, no attempt is made at educating the Negro or diversifying his skills; the T.V.A. aims to maintain the *status quo*. . . .

Negroes must relentlessly attack and continue to attack discrimination in the T.V.A. with pitiless publicity, politically, at law, and with whatever other means are at their disposal. If they can break discrimination in the T.V.A. and obtain for the Negro population of the Tennessee River Basin its full share of the economic and social rehabilitation of the region, they will have made a great step forward. But only a step. For if the Negro population is to benefit by the cheap electricity produced and distributed by the T.V.A., it means that the fight must go on to in-crease its purchasing power. The fight must go on to get the Negro industrial worker increased recognition and income under the NRA, and the Negro sharecropper and farmer a larger share of his produce under the AAA. The stark truth is that the entire "New Deal" administration must be made to realize that the economic wage slavery and social suppression cursing the South today, are absolutely incompatible with a real return to prosperity.

3. Protesting Lynching: A National Crime, 1934

In December 1934 the Justice Department refused to include lynching as one of the agenda topics at its National Conference on Crime. In response the District of Columbia branch of the NAACP, including a number of Howard University students, organized a protest. To avoid arrest for "parading without a permit," the demonstrators stood in silent rebuke of the conference. A noose hung around the neck of each one.

Photo: Visual Materials from the Records of the National Association for the Advancement of Colored People, Negative Number LC-USZ62-35363, Prints and Photographs Division, Library of Congress, Washington, D.C.

4. A "Black Cabinet" Assembles, 1938

The members of the "Black Cabinet" in 1938 included (front row, left to right) Ambrose Caliver, Department of the Interior; Roscoe C. Brown, Public Health Service; Robert C. Weaver, Housing Authority; Joseph H. Evans, Farm Security Administration; Frank Horne, Housing Authority; Mary McLeod Bethune, National Youth Administration; Lawrence A. Oxley, Department of Labor; William J. Thompkins, Recorder of Deeds; Charles E. Hall, Department of Commerce; William I. Houston, Department of Justice; Ralph E. Mizelle, Post Office; (back row, left to right) Dewey R. Jones, Department of the Interior; Edgar Brown, Civilian Conservation Corps; J. Parker Prescott, Housing Authority; Edward H. Lawson Jr., Works Progress Administration; Arthur Weiseger, Department of Labor; Alfred Edgar Smith, Works Progress Administration; Henry A. Hunt, Farm Credit Administration; John W. Whitten, Works Progress Administration; and Joseph R. Houchins, Department of Commerce.

5. Louise "Mamma" Harris Describes Labor Organizing in Richmond, Virginia, Tobacco Factories, 1940

She was a scrawny hardbitten little woman and she greeted me with that politely blank stare which Negroes often reserve for hostile whites or prying members of their own race. I had been directed to her tenement in Richmond's ramshackle Negro section by another woman, a gray-haired old grandmother whose gnarled hands had been stemming tobacco for five decades.

"The white folks down at union headquarters is all right," she had said, "and we love 'em—especially Mr. Marks. But if you want to know about us stemmers and the rumpus we raised, you better go see Mamma Harris. She's Missus CIO in Richmond."

The blank look softened on the thin dark face when I mentioned this.

"Must've been Sister Jones," she said, still standing near the door. "They all call me Mamma though. Even if I ain't but forty-nine and most of 'em old enough to be my grandmammy." . . .

"I'm a CIO man myself," I remarked. "Newspaper Guild. Our local boys just fixed up *The Times-Dispatch* this morning." . . .

Photo: National Park Service—Mary McLeod Bethune Council House NHS, Washington, D.C.

Ted Poston, "The Making of Mamma Harris," *New Republic*, November 4, 1940, pp. 624–626.

"Bennie!" she called toward the kitchen, "you hear that, Bennie? CIO's done organized *The Dispatch*. Moved right in this morning. What I tell you? We gonna make this a union town yet!"

A hulking overalled Negro appeared in the kitchen doorway. . . .

"Dispatch?" he thundered. "God Amighty, we do come on."

Mrs. Harris nodded in my direction.

"He's a CIO man from up New York. Wants to know about our rumpus out at Export. He's a Guilder too, just like the white 'uns."

Benny limped toward the other chair.

"They give us hell," he said, "but we give it right back to 'em. And it was we'uns who come out on top. The cops was salty. Wouldn't even let us set down and rest. But I told the women, I told 'em 'Sit down' and they did. Right in front of the cops too. Didn't I, Louise?" . . .

"You dead did. And they didn't do nothing neither. They 'fraid of the women. You can outtalk the men. But us women don't take no tea for the fever."

Bennie boomed agreement. "There was five hundred of the women on the picket line and only twenty of us mens. But we sure give 'em hell. I talked right up to them cops, didn't I, Louise? Didn't I?"

Finally Mrs. Harris got around to the beginning.

"I wasn't no regular stemmer at first," she said, "but I been bringing a shift somewhere or other since I was eight. I was took out of school then and give a job minding chillun. By the time I was ten I was cooking for a family of six. And I been scuffling ever since.

"But I don't work in no factory till eight years ago. Then I went out to Export. Well, it took me just one day to find out that preachers don't know nothing about hell. They ain't worked in no tobacco factory." . . .

"Then there was this scab," she went on, "only he ain't no scab then, cause we don't have no union. We ain't even heerd of no union nowhere then, but I knew something was bound to happen. Even a dog couldn't keep on like we was. You know what I make then? Two dollars and eighty cents a week. Five dollars wasn't a too bad week."

"I put in eighty-two and a half hours one week," Bennie said, "and they only give me $18.25. I think about this one day when one of them cops . . ."

Mrs. Harris shushed him.

"Now this scab—only he ain't no scab then—he rides me from the minute I get to Export. He's in solid with the man and he always brag he's the ringtail monkey in this circus. He's a stemmer like the rest of us but he stools for the white folks.

"There's two hundred of us on our floor alone and they only give us four and a half and five cents a pound. We don't get paid for the tobacco leaf, you know. You only get paid for the stems. And some of them stems is so puny they look like horse hair. . . .

"And as if everything else wasn't bad enough, there was this scab. We's cramped up on them benches from kin to can't, and he's always snooping around to see nobody don't pull the stem out the center instead of pulling the leaf down both sides separate. This dust just eats your lungs right out you. You start dying the day you go in. . . .

"Well, I keep this up for six long years. And this scab is riding me ever' single day. He's always riding everybody and snitching on them what don't take it. He jump me one day about singing. Course, a stemmer's bench ain't no place for singing and I ain't got no voice nohow. But I like a song and I gotta do something to ease my mind or else I go crazy.

"But he jump me this morning and tell me to shut up. Well, that's my cup. Six years is six years, but this once is too often. So I'm all over him like gravy over rice. I give him a tongue-lashing what curled every nap on his head. . . .

"I sass him deaf, dumb and blind, and he takes it. But all the time he's looking at me kinder queer. And all at once he says 'You mighty salty all of a sudden; you must be joining up with this union foolishness going on around here.'

"You coulda knocked me over with a Export stem. I ain't even heard nothing about no union. But as soon as he cuts out, I start asking around. And bless my soul if they ain't been organizing for a whole full week. And I ain't heerd a peep. . . .

"Well, I don't only go to the next meeting downtown, but I carries sixty of the girls from our floor. They remember how I sass this scab and they're all with me. We plopped right down in the first row of the gallery. And when they asked for volunteers to organize Export, I can't get to my feet quick enough. . . .

"And it ain't no time . . . before we got seven hundred out of the thousand what works in Export. The man is going crazy mad and the scab is snooping overtime. But they can't fire us. The boom time is on and the warehouse is loaded to the gills."

She paused dramatically.

"And then on the first of August 1938, we let 'em have it. We called our strike and closed up Export tight as a bass drum."

Bennie couldn't be shushed this time.

"The cops swooped down like ducks on a June bug," he said, "but we was ready for 'em. I was picket captain and there was five hundred on the line. And all five hundred was black and evil."

Mrs. Harris was beaming again.

"Then this scab came up with a couple hundred others and tried to break our line," she recalled, "but we wasn't giving a crip a crutch or a dog a bone. I made for that head scab personal—but the cops wouldn't let me at 'im."

"I stayed on the line for twenty-four hours running," Bennie chuckled, "and I didn't take a inch from none of them cops."

"And we wasn't by ourselves neither," Mrs. Harris went on. "The preachers, Dr. Jackson, the Southern Aid Society and all the other union people help us. GWU and them garment ladies give us a hundred dollars right off the bat. Malgamate sent fifty. The ship folks down in Norfolk come through, and your white Guild boys here give ten dollars too."

"It was them white garment ladies what sent the cops," Bennie cut in. "They come out five hundred strong and parade around the factory. They got signs saying, 'GWU Supports Export Tobacco Workers.'

"Them cops jump salty as hell. '*White* women,' they say, '*white* women out here parading for niggers.' But they don't do nothing. Because we ain't taking no stuff from nobody."

"We was out eighteen days," Mrs. Harris said, "and the boss was losing money hand over fist. But you know how much we spend in them eighteen days? Over seven hundred dollars."

Her awed tones made it sound like seven thousand.

"But it was worth it. We win out and go back getting ten, eleven and twelve cents a pound. And better still we can wear our union buttons right out open. We might even have got them scabs fired if we wanted, but we didn't want to keep nobody out of work."

Bennie stopped smiling for the first time.

"We might be better off if we did," he said soberly. "I bet we do next time."

Mrs. Harris explained.

"They been sniping away at us ever since we win. They give the scabs all the breaks and lay off us union people first whenever they can. They give all the overtime to the scabs and even let 'em get away with stripping stem down the center. But we ain't licked yet. We still got two hundred members left and we still got union conditions."

Her face brightened again.

"And we fixed that old scab—even if he is been there nineteen years. We moved him off our floor completely, and he ain't allowed to ride nobody.

"We got a good set of people downtown now and we're reorganizing right along. By the time our new contract comes up in June, we'll probably have the whole thousand." . . .

6. A Marine's Letter to A. Philip Randolph About Discrimination in the Marine Corps, c. 1943

Mr. Randolph:

To start with, please excuse this informal way of addressing you.

My problem is, like 30,000 other colored marines, just this: We want to know why our boys cannot become officers in this our democratic marine corps. Why our boys can only serve in labor or service battalions. . . .

I will start with my entrance in the United States Marines, and try to give an accurate account of the different actions and reactions. I arrived at Camp LeJeyne, New River, North Carolina, the 15th of October 1942. The training was tough, but strictly regulation. We were put into different schools according to our choice and educational qualifications. I stop here to add that up until February of 1943, our colored marines were not draftees, but all enlisted men, and of these men they found Negroes of the highest qualifications.

Out of the first 1500 men, 1000 were college graduates or senior college men, all seeking advancement and adventure like myself. These black marines were an experiment, Eleanor Roosevelt's babies, so we were handled with kid gloves. In February, our first outfit left for overseas. This outfit was made up of the fellows that had doped off in the Marine Corps, consequently meriting shipment over. . . . This first outfit to move over had no special qualification, so they were destined to become a service battalion.

Well, every month from that time on, the least little thing the men did, that was wrong, they found themselves in a service battalion going over. These battalions

The Papers of A. Philip Randolph (microform), introduction by August Meier and John Bracey. Copyright © 1990 by University Publications of America. Reprinted with permission of the A. Philip Randolph Institute.

left at the rate of one a month comprising from 100 to 300. Those that remained were being charmed into the steward's branch or cooks division with the promise of quick ratings. In the meantime, our 1500 men of high educational qualifications were covering up and being shown as the colored Marine Corps. All opposing parties or radicals to these treatments were also sent out with work battalions.

Around April of 43, our first outfit left, not destined for overseas. It was a guard company for Oklahoma. They caught and are still catching hell from the discriminating officers and noncommissioned officers over them. The boys that had their wives there had to stand by and see them abuse to ease the terrific pressure on themselves. The boys were prohibited from wearing their blue uniforms because it gave them a good looking appearance. In that group was a reknown radical "satchel." He was sent back to North Carolina. There he continued to champion our cause. He is now serving time in the naval in Portsmouth, Virginia for five years.

I was working in the Administration Building as a corporal. I heard of an outfit going to Philadelphia and secured for myself a place as second in command of 100 men. When we arrived, we were told that we were to be on the working end of this war, and if we conducted ourselves right, more men would be sent up from North Carolina to Philadelphia. We didn't complain because anything was better than North Carolina or service company somewhere in the Pacific. Philadelphia is one of the largest quartermaster outfits, and for eight hours a day all we see is freight cars and vans and whipcracking crackers worse than the ones that come out and say plain nigger. Yes! We have 400 black stevadors marines, about eleven sergeants, 15 corporals and all the rest are privates first class only to soothe the colored population of Philly to show them that the Negro marines are getting something for their labor (that's a laugh). The majority of the boys live in Philly or nearby states, so like myself bear with this treatment because after 4:30 we can be ourselves and be with our families. This is why we have not beefed before. Half of our sergeants who are supposed to protect us do the opposite to protect their stripes because they, like myself, would get busted for refusing to drive the men and being too radical. We really have no Negro representative within the Corps. This is why we are appealing to you to help us secure our own representatives with power so they cannot be bought or scared. *We want Colored Commissioned Officers in the Marine Corps,* and it is within President Roosevelt's power to see that we get the same treatment as other branches of the armed forces.

Thanks for your help, past, immediate and future.

7. Breaking the Color Bar in Sports, 1947

Equal Opportunity Wins An Inning

An up-standing, clean-living, bright-minded young athlete who happens to be a Negro broke a sixty-year tradition last week when he signed a contract to play with the Brooklyn Club (the Dodgers) of the National League.

Not since 1884 when Moses Fleetwood Walker caught for Toledo of the American Association has an acknowledged colored man played on a major league team, so congratulations are in order for young, 28-year-old Jackie Robinson, the brilliant California athlete, who won his spurs with the Montreal team last season; and for Branch Rickey, president of the Dodgers, who has won a big place in the hearts of all liberty-loving Americans by this final act of liberalism which gained national attention when he gave several young Negro players their chance in the minor leagues.

There is the usual talk about the possibility that young Robinson may not be greeted with enthusiasm or treated with courtesy by some of his teammates, but there was similar talk when Robinson was bought by Montreal.

His Montreal teammates proved to be good sports and comrades, and so will his associates on the Dodgers.

There have been a whole lot of changes in the thinking of Americans on the questions of color, creed and national origin in the past decade, and those who are living mentally in 1927 and physically in 1947, are daily finding their predictions about race relations NOT coming true.

For example, what happened to the wave of race riots supposed to take place immediately after World War II?

Well, having duly recorded the winning of another inning for equal opportunity, The Pittsburgh Courier can now pause and take a bow for the part it played in helping to bring about this victory, the culmination of a long and determined effort to interest baseball moguls, editors and writers in the use of colored players in the major leagues.

We are proud to be able to say that we contributed more than our share to the realization of this goal, but of course we shall not be satisfied until there is not a baseball team or other sporting aggregation in the United States that draws the color line.

E S S A Y S

Robin D. G. Kelley, professor of history at New York University, traces the difficult and dangerous efforts to build a Share Croppers' Union in rural Alabama at the height of the Depression. Kelley argues that southern black farmers readily saw when their interests and objectives coincided with the work of the Communist Party and adapted the party to their needs. Ultimately, however, the economic policies of the federal government, designed to serve the interests of plantation owners, jeopardized many of the farmers' hard-won gains.

World War II created the promise of vast economic opportunity for those willing to seize it. Masses of black migrants, many of them from urban centers in the South, headed west to fill labor needs in booming wartime industries. Following a select group of women migrants to California's East Bay area, Gretchen Lemke-Santangelo, associate professor of history and women's studies at Saint Mary's College (Moraga, California), details the tremendous struggle of these migrants to turn temporary opportunity into permanent homes.

Radical Organizing During the Depression

ROBIN D. G. KELLEY

. . . [Ralph] Gray owned a plot of land but it was hardly enough to survive on. Nevertheless, he managed to remain debt-free and purchased his own automobile, thus earning the respect of his local community. Early in 1931 Gray applied for a low-interest federal loan with which to rent a farm from Tallapoosa merchant John J. Langley. . . . Langley was able to cash the check and withhold Gray's portion, who then retaliated by filing a complaint with the Agricultural Extension Service. . . . Soon thereafter, Ralph began reading the *Southern Worker,* joined the Communist Party, and set out with his brother [Tommy] to build a union.

. . . In April, the Grays' request for an organizer was filled by Mack Coad, an illiterate Birmingham steel worker originally from Charleston, South Carolina, who had joined the Party in 1930. . . .

Coad arrived at the height of an important crisis in rural Tallapoosa. Soon after the cotton had been planted and chopped, several landlords withdrew all cash and food advances in a calculated effort to generate labor for the newly built Russell Saw Mill. The mill paid exactly the same wage for unskilled labor as the going rate for cotton chopping—fifty cents per day for men and twenty-five cents a day for women. By mid-May the *Southern Worker* reported significant union gains in Tallapoosa County and announced that black sawmill workers and farmers in the vicinity "have enthusiastically welcomed Communist leadership." The nascent movement formulated seven basic demands, the most crucial being the continuation of food advances. The right of sharecroppers to market their own crops was also a critical issue because landlords usually gave their tenants the year's lowest price for their cotton and held on to the bales until the price increased, thus denying the producer the full benefits of the crop. Union leaders also demanded small gardens for resident wage hands, cash rather than wages in kind, a minimum wage of one dollar per day, and a three-hour midday rest for all laborers—all of which were to be applied equally, irrespective of race, age, or sex. Furthermore, they agitated for a nine-month school year for black children and free transportation to and from school.

By July 1931 the CFWU [Croppers' and Farm Workers' Union], now eight hundred strong, had won a few isolated victories in its battle for the continuation of food advances. . . . Camp Hill, Alabama, became the scene of the union's first major confrontation with the local power structure. On July 15, Taft Holmes organized a group of sharecroppers near Camp Hill and invited Coad, along with several other union members, to address the group in a vacant house that doubled as a church. In all, about eighty black men and women piled into the abandoned house to listen to Coad. . . . After a black informant notified Tallapoosa County sheriff Kyle Young of the gathering, deputized vigilantes raided the meeting place, brutally beating men and women alike. The posse then regrouped at Tommy Gray's home and assaulted his entire family, including his wife who suffered a fractured skull, in an effort to

Robin D. G. Kelley, *Hammer and Hoe: Alabama Communists During the Great Depression* (Chapel Hill: University of North Carolina Press, 1990), 39–45, 48–56. Used with permission of the publisher and author.

obtain information about the CFWU. Only an agitated Ralph Gray, who had rushed into the house armed, saved them from possible fatal consequences. Union organizer Jasper Kennedy was arrested for possessing twenty copies of the *Southern Worker,* and Holmes was picked up by police the following day, interrogated for several hours, and upon release fled to Chattanooga.

Despite the violence, about 150 sharecroppers met with Coad the following evening in a vacant house southwest of Camp Hill. This time sentries were posted around the meeting place. When Sheriff Young arrived on the scene with Camp Hill police chief J. M. Wilson and Deputy A. J. Thompson, he found Ralph Gray standing guard about a quarter-mile from the meeting. Although accounts differ as to the sequence of events, both Gray and the sheriff traded harsh words and, in the heat of argument, exchanged buckshot. Young, who received gunshot wounds to the stomach, was rushed to a hospital in nearby Alexander City while Gray lay on the side of the road, his legs riddled with bullets. Fellow union members carried Gray to his home where the group, including Mack Coad, barricaded themselves inside the house. The group held off a posse led by police chief J. M. Wilson long enough to allow most members to escape, but the wounded Ralph Gray opted to remain in his home until the end. The posse returned with reinforcements and found Gray lying in his bed and his family huddled in a corner. According to his brother, someone in the group "poked a pistol into Brother Ralph's mouth and shot down his throat." The mob burned his home to the ground and dumped his body on the steps of the Dadeville courthouse. The mangled and lifeless leader became an example for other black sharecroppers as groups of armed whites took turns shooting and kicking the bloody corpse of Ralph Gray.

Over the next few days, between thirty-four and fifty-five black men were arrested near Camp Hill, nine of whom were under eighteen years of age. Most of the defendants were charged with conspiracy to murder or with carrying a concealed weapon, but five union members . . . were charged with assault to murder. Although police chief Wilson could not legally act out his wish to "kill every member of the 'Reds' there and throw them into the creek," the Camp Hill police department stood idle as enraged white citizens waged genocidal attacks on the black community that left dozens wounded or dead and forced entire families to seek refuge in the woods. Union secretary Mack Coad, the vigilantes' prime target, fled all the way to Atlanta. . . .

Outraged middle-class black leaders, clergymen, and white liberals blamed white Communists for the incident, asserting that armed resistance on the part of black sharecroppers and tenants was unnatural. . . .

Hoping to quell black unrest in the area, Robert Russa Moton, superintendent of Tuskegee Institute, dispatched representatives to Tallapoosa in a calculated move to turn blacks away from Communism. Likewise, L. N. Duncan, director of the Agricultural Extension Service based at the Alabama Polytechnic Institute, assured Governor Miller that several black county agents were "making a special effort to quiet the people down, urging them to put away their guns and calling their attention to the fact that they are badly mislead [*sic*] by these communistic representatives." . . . Walter White and local Birmingham NAACP leaders sharply denied any connection to the Communist-led union and accused the Party of using the NAACP's good name to mislead black sharecroppers. . . .

National Communist leadership praised the union's resistance at Camp Hill as vindication of the Party's slogan calling for the right of self-determination. . . . But union organizers found little romance in the bloodletting or in the uprooting of hundreds of poor black farmers that had followed the Camp Hill battle. Moreover, rural conditions in Tallapoosa County had not improved at all. By September, the height of the cotton picking season, landlords again promised to cut off all food and cash advances after the cotton was picked, and many tenants had to pick cotton on other plantations in order to earn enough to survive the winter. The going rate at the time was a meager thirty cents per one hundred pounds, a tiny sum considering the average laborer could only pick about two hundred pounds per day.

The repression and the deteriorating economic conditions stunted the union's growth initially, but the lessons of Camp Hill also provided a stimulus for a new type of movement, reborn from the ashes of the old. On August 6, 1931, the fifty-five remaining CFWU members regrouped as the SCU [Share Croppers' Union] and reconstituted five locals in Tallapoosa County. . . .

Tommy Gray continued to organize, but because he was targeted by landlords and local authorities, escaping at least one attempted assassination, it was difficult for him to maneuver. Instead, Gray's daughter, nineteen-year-old YCL [Young Communist League] leader Eula Gray, held the movement together during this very critical period. . . . [T]he SCU in Tallapoosa County [grew] to 591 members organized in twenty-eight locals, ten youth groups, and twelve women's auxiliaries; sixty-seven members were organized in nine Lee County locals, four of which were based in the town of Notasulga. Chambers and Macon counties each reported thirty members.

. . . Ignoring [Eula] Gray's proven ability and her Tallapoosa roots, district organizer Nat Ross appointed twenty-five-year-old Al Murphy to the position of SCU secretary. . . .

With Murphy in charge, white CP leaders stopped calling on black sharecroppers to "demonstrate in front of the landlord's house [and demand] that the food advances be continued until the crop is taken in." Besides, local blacks had never taken these suicidal directives seriously. Murphy was well aware of the croppers' underground tradition of resistance, and he developed tactics that emphasized self-preservation and cunning. No meetings were to be held in empty houses; SCU members were not to walk in large crowds; and they were not to engage in armed action without notifying Murphy, unless, of course, it could not be avoided. Everything from their actions to their demeanor drew on subterranean forms of everyday resistance. . . . Yet, Murphy's instructions . . . did not mean abandoning armed self-defense. Members such as Lemon Johnson, former secretary of the Hope Hull local, believed armed self-defense distinguished the SCU from other organizations. His own experience informed him that "the only thing going to stop them from killing you, you got to go shooting." When Harry Haywood attended an SCU meeting in Dadeville, he was taken aback by what he described as "a small arsenal." "There were guns," he recalled, "of all kinds—shotguns, rifles and pistols. Sharecroppers were coming to the meeting armed and left their guns with their coats when they came in."

Murphy decentralized the organization by establishing captains for each local, and . . . he kept the locals informed of the situation in other counties. Dues were collected when possible, but most of the funds, never amounting to more than a few cents, were in the hands of the captains. They tended to the day-to-day organizing of the union, the women's auxiliaries, and the youth sections, and those who could write were responsible for sending articles to the Party's press detailing conditions in their respective areas. Murphy warned the captains against becoming tyrannical or egocentric with their power. "No captain is to act as a boss of his local," he frequently advised. Weekly meetings were supposed to be held, always in absolute secrecy to avoid police raids or vigilante attacks. Minutes were rarely kept because of the potential danger of keeping written records, not to mention the problem of literacy in the black belt. Union locals often cloaked their intentions by holding Bible meetings, and some secretaries recorded the minutes by underlining pertinent words or phrases in the Bible. . . .

After a year of rebuilding following Camp Hill, the union emerged stronger than ever. A threatened pickers' strike in 1932 won union members on at least one Tallapoosa plantation the right to sell their own cotton directly as well as a continuation of winter food advances. Days after the victory was announced, organizer Luther Hughley was arrested for vagrancy, but soon after he was placed in police custody, he was accused of kidnapping a white woman from Camp Hill. Before a mass campaign could be initiated, however, Hughley was released and threatened with rope and faggot if he did not leave the county. Aside from Hughley's arrest and the aborted pickers' strike, Camp Hill remained rather quiet and uneventful after the cotton had been picked. . . . The peace did not last very long. . . .

It all started near Reeltown, an area about fifteen miles southwest of Camp Hill. The SCU's armed stand centered around a landlord's attempt to seize the property of Clifford James, a debt-ridden farmer who had been struggling desperately to purchase the land he worked. The story actually dates back to 1926, when James borrowed $950 to purchase the seventy-seven-acre plot he was working from Notasulga merchant W. S. Parker. The full cost of the land was $1,500. In addition to the borrowed money, James paid $250 in cash and sold $450 worth of timber from his property. Parker then absorbed James's debt by taking out a mortgage on the land. After advancing James money, food, and implements in 1927, Parker sold him three mules on credit, which then augmented James's debt to $1,500. . . .

When the SCU reorganized in Tallapoosa County, its approach to debt peonage attracted James and hundreds of other black farmers. . . . SCU added to its core program the abolition of all debts owed by poor farmers and tenants, as well as interest charged on necessary items such as food, clothes, and seed.

. . . Parker asked Deputy Sheriff Cliff Elder to serve a writ of attachment on James's livestock. When Elder arrived on December 19, 1932, about fifteen armed SCU members were already standing outside James's home prepared to resist or avert the seizure. . . . Ned Cobb humbly pleaded with Elder: "Please sir, don't take it. Go to the ones that authorized you to take his stuff, if you please, sir, and tell em to give him a chance. He'll work to pay what he owes em." When Elder and his black assistant officer attempted to seize the animals, humility ceased. James and Cobb warned them against taking the animals, and Elder interpreted their warnings as death threats. Fearing for his life, he left James's farm, promising to return to "kill you niggers in a pile."

Elder returned a few hours later with three reinforcements—Chief Deputy Dowdle Ware, former sheriff J. M. Gaunt, and a local landlord named J. H. Alfred.

Several SCU members barricaded themselves in James's home and others stood poised at the barn. Shots were exchanged almost as soon as the four men stepped onto the property, but when Elder's small posse "seed that crowd of niggers at the barn throw up their guns they jumped in the car" and fled from the vicinity. Unable to persuade Governor Miller to dispatch state troops, Sheriff Young proceeded to form his own posse, gathering men from Lee, Macon, Elmore, and Montgomery counties to scour the area for suspected SCU members.

When the shoot-out was over, SCU member John McMullen lay dead, and several others were wounded, including Clifford James, Milo Bentley, Thomas Moss, and Ned Cobb. Within the next few days, at least twenty union members were rounded up and thrown in jail. Several of those arrested were not involved in the shoot-out, but their names were discovered when the police returned to James's home and uncovered the SCU local membership list along with "considerable Communistic literature." The violence that followed eclipsed the Camp Hill affair of 1931. Entire families were forced to take refuge in the woods; white vigilante groups broke into black homes and seized guns, ammunition, and other property. . . . A blind black woman reported to be nearly one hundred years old was severely beaten and pistol whipped by a group of vigilantes, and one Tallapoosa doctor claimed to have treated at least a dozen black patients with gunshot wounds.

Despite severe injuries to his back, James managed to walk seventeen miles to Tuskegee Institute's hospital. After dressing James's gunshot wounds, Dr. Eugene Dibble of Tuskegee contacted the Macon County sheriff, who then removed James to a cold, damp cell at the Montgomery County jail. Milo Bentley, who reportedly had been shot in the head, back, and arms, was also taken to Montgomery County jail. Observers claimed that Bentley and James received no medical treatment from their jailers. . . . On December 27, James died from infected wounds and pneumonia, both caused by the lack of medical treatment. Ten and one-half hours later, Bentley's lifeless body was found in the same condition.

. . . [A] mass funeral was held for the two martyred union organizers. Pall bearers carrying two caskets draped with banners emblazoned with deep red hammers and sickles led a procession of three thousand people, most of whom were black. The mourners marched six miles through Birmingham to Grace Hills Cemetery on the southern side of the city, cordoned by an additional one thousand people who crowded the sidewalks along the route of the procession.

As more detailed accounts of the shoot-out reached the press, Tuskegee Institute increasingly became a target of criticism. An elderly Alabama black woman, Abbie Elmore Bugg, castigated Moton personally. "Now, if you love your neighbor as yourself," she asked, "why did you not protect those two poor wounded negro farmers? Why did you let them die? A good enimy [*sic*] of all races I should say you be, in a time of real need." . . . Although Moton believed all the attacks directed at him and the institute were Communist-inspired, he refrained from blaming the Communists for Reeltown. "The recent outbreaks of violence," he explained to one inquirer, "between whites and Negroes in that County are primarily the results of the prevailing tenant system in the South that has long since outlived its usefulness." Yet, while the institute was sensitive to black farmers' needs, it rejected unionization as a strategy for change. Tuskegee's statistician and expert on rural affairs, Monroe Work, admitted that the institute's "general policy . . . is to discourage the organization of Negro Farmers."

Like the Camp Hill shoot-out in 1931, white liberals and the Southern press blamed Communists for the Reeltown incident. Although a Birmingham *Post* editorial dissented from other newspapers by discussing the indigenous economic roots of the conflict, the writer still placed considerable blame on Party propaganda and black inferiority: "It is the ignorance of the negro which makes him prey to the incendiary literature with which the mail boxes of both white and negro farmers of Tallapoosa County have been stuffed. It is this literature which transforms him from a law abiding citizen into one who defies the law. . . . The average negro in his normal state of mind does not consider firing on officers seeking to carry out the law."

Many black middle-class leaders agreed that the menace of Communism lurked behind the events at Reeltown. The Atlanta *Daily World* advised blacks to ignore the Communists and instead to "battle for our rights legally in the courts, and economically through mass-owned businesses." But the black elite was not in complete accord. . . . Some respected middle-class blacks even offered support for the union. At the height of the crisis, one relatively wealthy black landlord let Al Murphy hide on his farm and use his barn as an office to produce SCU leaflets.

The trial of the SCU members illustrates the extent of the union's popularity in the eastern piedmont. So many black sharecroppers crowded into the courtroom that Solicitor Sam W. Oliver decided to postpone the trial until the excitement subsided. When proceedings resumed in late April, county officials set up roadblocks outside Dadeville to discourage blacks from attending. Nevertheless, black farmers evaded the roadblocks by traveling through gullies and back roads and filled the courtroom once again. The all-white jury convicted five of the nineteen SCU members indicted for assault with a deadly weapon. Ned Cobb was given twelve to fifteen years; Clinton Moss and Alf White received ten years each; Judson Simpson was sentenced to a maximum of twelve years; and Sam Moss was given five to six years.

The confrontation at Reeltown apparently did not discourage the union's recruitment efforts. By June 1933, Al Murphy reported a membership of nearly 2,000 organized in 73 locals, 80 women's auxiliaries, and 20 youth groups. New locals were formed in Dale and Randolph counties and in the border town of West Point, Georgia. The Communists also established 5 additional rural Party units, each composed of 30 to 35 members. . . .

National Communist leaders regarded the SCU as the finest contemporary example of black revolutionary traditions. . . . But the union's rank-and-file . . . found little to celebrate. Black farmers were organizing primarily for their own survival and for a greater share in the decaying system of cotton tenancy. They might have won the battle to exist, but by late 1933 the SCU faced an additional set of problems when the federal government decided to intervene in the production process.

Congress and President Roosevelt attempted to reinvigorate the country's dying cotton economy with the AAA [Agricultural Adjustment Administration]. Conceived in 1933 as an emergency measure, the AAA was supposed to increase the purchasing power of landowning farmers by subsidizing acreage reduction.

. . . [A]buses were commonplace, and . . . most planters did not have to engage in fraud in order to benefit from New Deal policies. They merely reallocated land, evicted . . . tenants, and applied the cash subsidies to wages rather than sharing it with their tenants. New Deal policies, therefore, indirectly stimulated a structural change in the cotton economy—the mechanization of agriculture. Cotton production remained unmechanized for so long partly because most landlords lacked capital and because the units of production—plots farmed by tenants and sharecroppers—were too small to warrant adoption of expensive technology. Tenancy provided the cheap labor needed to make the transition to mechanization, but it limited production to small, segmented units. By farming larger units of production, landlords could apply the parity payments and savings derived from not furnishing tenants to tractors, fertilizers, and other implements needed for large-scale cotton farming. Local relief administrators helped the landlords by clearing the relief rolls during cotton picking and cotton chopping seasons, thus ensuring an abundant supply of cheap labor. . . .

The SCU adopted a variety of methods to deal with landlords' abuses of the parity program. First, because hundreds of evicted tenants and sharecroppers were simultaneously removed from relief rolls and CWA [Civil Works Administration] projects so that cheap wage labor would be available for cotton chopping, union organizers fought for immediate relief and tried to persuade federal authorities to investigate local CWA administrators. In February 1934, a group of black women organized a "Committee of Action," marched down to the CWA office in Camp Hill, and eventually won partial demands for relief. Tenants and sharecroppers who had not yet been evicted were instructed not to sign the joint parity checks unless the landlords paid their portion in cash rather than use the funds to settle debts. SCU members often refused to give up their rental share of cotton unless they received their portion of the AAA check. The union also convinced some day laborers and cotton pickers to boycott plantations that were considered "vicious in their treatment of tenants and sharecroppers." On one plantation in Chambers County, a boycott of this kind led to the arrests of eleven union members.

Late that summer the SCU prepared for another cotton pickers' strike in Lee and Tallapoosa counties. With a demand of one dollar per hundred pounds, the strike started in mid-September on B. W. Meadows's plantation in Tallapoosa County and soon spread to several large plantations in both counties, involving between seven hundred and one thousand pickers. The landlords' first response was to evict the strikers, but because it was the height of the cotton picking season, planters needed all available labor. With the support of local police, the planters turned to force to break the strike. In Lee County, police arrested seven union members for distributing strike leaflets, and in Tallapoosa vigilantes shot at least three strikers, including a woman Party organizer. Pinned to the doors of several suspected strikers' homes was the following message: "WARNING. TAKE NOTICE. If you want to do well and have a healthy life you better leave the Share Croppers' Union." Hooded night riders in Lee County kidnapped and beat SCU organizer Comit Talbert, and later in the evening two more Lee County sharecroppers were kidnapped, draped in chains, and taken to a nearby swamp where vigilantes threatened to drown them if they remained in the union. The local sheriff intervened but arrested the shackled black sharecroppers and held them on charges of attempted murder.

The Alabama Relief Administration also played a crucial role in undermining the strike. As soon as the SCU announced plans for a cotton pickers' strike. Thad Holt, director of the state relief administration, dropped from the relief rolls all "able bodied" workers who did not volunteer to pick cotton for wages. Even the state reemployment agency in Birmingham relocated several people with "farm experience" to the cotton fields.

In spite of repression, mass evictions, and the expanded pool of cheap labor, the SCU claimed some substantial victories. On most of the plantations affected, the union won at least seventy-five cents per one hundred pounds, and in areas not affected by the strike, landlords reportedly increased wages from thirty-five cents per hundred pounds to fifty cents or more in order to avert the spread of the strike. On Howard Graves's plantation, located on the border of Lee and Tallapoosa counties, union members not only won the sought-after one dollar per hundred pounds, but they forced Graves to raise monthly credit allowances from ten to fifteen dollars. Finally, the SCU claimed a small victory on General C. L. Pearson's plantation when about one thousand sharecroppers and tenants refused to gin their cotton at Pearson's gin. By taking their cotton to an independent gin in Dadeville, they saved money and prevented Pearson from seizing their cotton to cover past debts.

The 1934 cotton pickers' strike marked the SCU's first major victory since its birth three years earlier. As tales of the union's stand in Tallapoosa County spread from cabin to cabin, so did the union's popularity. . . . The celebration ended abruptly, however, as thousands of families found themselves landless during the harsh winter of 1934–1935. The eight-thousand-strong union stood helpless in the face of New Deal–induced evictions, and no . . . demands for self-determination could solve their quandary.

New Lives in the West

GRETCHEN LEMKE-SANTANGELO

. . . Wartime migration to [California's] East Bay Area—by both whites and blacks— greatly exceeded the region's capacity to provide necessary goods and services to its old and new residents. Housing, transportation, schools, social services, and recreation facilities were stretched to the limit, exacerbating racial and class tensions among an increasingly diverse population. Poor white southerners from Oklahoma and Arkansas, skilled tradesmen from the Midwest, and working-class families from throughout the South all came together and competed with existing residents and with each other for scarce resources. John A. Miller, area coordinator of national defense for Contra Costa County—which includes the cities of Richmond and Vallejo—captured the concern of city administrators in his report to the United States House Subcommittee on Congested Areas. "In 1940 Contra Costa County, California, had a population of 100,230 happy souls. . . . Proud, industrious, hard working, prosperous people who paid their bills in advance and laid a little away for a rainy day lived here. Then came the rude awakening. . . . Shipyards required ship

Gretchen Lemke-Santangelo, *Abiding Courage: African American Migrant Women and the East Bay Community* (Chapel Hill: University of North Carolina Press, 1996), 70, 78–95.

workers. Ship workers required homes in which to live. Homes were built. People came to live in homes, trailers, tents, tin houses, cardboard shacks, glass houses, barns, garages, in automobiles, in theaters, or just in fenced off corners with stars for a roof. The population zoomed from 100,000 to 324,000." . . .

Migrants' search for housing typically went through three phases: temporary, transitional, and permanent. Initially, migrants stayed with friends and relatives or found short-term accommodations in crowded boardinghouses, trailer parks, chicken coops, tents, or automobiles. Male migrants who preceded female relatives frequently lived in this type of housing until they found better accommodations. However, many families that migrated as units also lived in these temporary, cramped quarters. Lacey Gray, whose experience was typical of women who came out with their husbands, remembers renting a single room in North Richmond. She, her husband, and two small children shared a single bed, but they felt fortunate to have found anything: "When we came to Richmond, there wasn't much housing at all."

From there, migrants found more spacious housing in government war projects or privately owned apartment buildings. Lacey applied for government housing as soon as she and her family arrived in Richmond. After a month on a waiting list, they moved into a "brand new project." This development, like many in the East Bay, was block-segregated, with white and black residents assigned to separate sections of the project. Although she was disappointed and angry about the segregation, Lacey was delighted to have the additional space. "The project had a living room, one bedroom, and a kitchen. The living room was so big my husband and I slept there and gave our daughters the bedroom. And the rent was only $35 per month. That was water, gas, lights, everything!"

From this transitional housing, migrants moved into permanent rental units or purchased their own homes. By the late 1940s, or sometimes sooner, many migrant families had saved enough to purchase homes. Their choices were severely limited by residential segregation, however. When Lacey Gray and her husband began to look for a home, . . .

> the real estate agents took us out to North Richmond, and I didn't want a place there. So they took us out to Parchester Village and said that it was going to be black and white together. But they had one white lady living in a model home, and when black people had all moved in, she moved out. It was nothing but a black settlement. When they wanted to build a school out there Governor Warren wouldn't let them, because it would have been segregated. But he sent buses out and bused those children into the white community. So we bought a lot in an undeveloped part of Richmond where all the white people had moved out.

The first months in the East Bay, spent in temporary, crowded housing, were the most challenging for migrant women. By 1941, all migrants had difficulty finding housing. Black migrants, however, faced the additional constraint of residential segregation, maintained by restrictive covenants, discriminatory lending and real estate practices, and government financing policies designed to "protect the character" of existing neighborhoods. Long before World War II, these practices had confined the existing black population to aging or undeveloped neighborhoods in the East Bay. These neighborhoods, which were already overcrowded and lacked basic services, accommodated migrants only with great difficulty. . . .

Until migrants found transitional housing in government projects or privately owned apartments, most of them rented rooms in West Oakland in the grand but dilapidated Victorian houses that existing owners or renters had profitably sub-divided. Katherine St. Clair, daughter of a shrewd black entrepreneur, remembers how "father was into buying and selling, and when the war started he bought up property and converted it into apartments . . . all down in West Oakland. He would buy them at low cost and fix them up, converting houses into two or three apart-ments." Katherine Legge, a tenant selection supervisor for the Oakland Housing Authority, found severe overcrowding during her inspections. Reporting to the U.S. House Investigation of Congested Areas, she stated that "you nor anyone has any idea of the living conditions of Negroes working in defense industries. I can take you to see numerous families where 14 people live in one room." Other re-searchers found similar problems, reporting that "new arrivals to the city are taken in trucks to the Negro community and 'peddled out' to rooming houses." They also discovered several trailer camps with inadequate "sanitary provisions." In one West Oakland camp, they observed that "youths and adults, in several cases, are living five to six persons to a room."

In Berkeley, migrants had even more difficulty finding temporary housing. White residents confined black citizens to small geographic areas in West and South Berkeley and, through restrictive covenants and physical intimidation, vigor-ously defended the boundaries between black and white sections of the city. More-over, Berkeley contained only one public housing project, which opened in 1941 over the objections of the Berkeley Chamber of Commerce and the Berkeley Man-ufacturers Association. Their opposition to the project, which mirrored that of most white residents, was based on fears that migrants would take over the city and threaten established patterns of race relations.

Until this project opened, migrants found housing in the existing black com-munities of South and West Berkeley. Before the war, South Berkeley housed middle-class and elite black families that considered its tree-lined streets and single-family homes a step up from Oakland's black neighborhoods. The estab-lished residents of South Berkeley, like the black entrepreneurs of West Oakland, subdivided single-family homes and rented rooms to newcomers. This once-quiet residential area, which became uncomfortably congested within a five-year period, soon threatened to push beyond its traditional boundaries and spill into bordering white neighborhoods. In contrast to the settled residential atmosphere of South Berkeley, West Berkeley contained dilapidated, overcrowded housing stock in close proximity to heavy industry. Migrants who found temporary housing in this neighborhood—Berkeley's oldest and poorest—created an additional burden on an already-blighted section of the city.

Richmond, of all the East Bay cities, provided the least temporary housing for newcomers. Numbering only 270 and inhabiting a marshy four-block section of North Richmond, its prewar black population had few vacancies even when exist-ing housing was subdivided. And white residents, like those in Berkeley, resisted residential integration. Thus, until newcomers advanced to the top of a waiting list

for government housing, they had no alternative but to settle north of the existing black community on unincorporated land near the city dump. There migrants squatted on vacant land, living in tents, shacks, and trailers, without the benefit of running water, electricity, sanitation facilities, paved roads, or garbage collection.
. . . The degree to which women participated in the initial search for housing varied. Women who already had friends or relatives in the East Bay often made housing arrangements well in advance of migration. Even if these relatives were in-laws, women frequently served as housing brokers, securing temporary accommodations prior to migrating. The role of housing broker was an extension of women's unpaid, largely unrecognized family maintenance work; it was migrant women who maintained contact with the fictive and real kin who migrated first and would later house newcomers.
. . . Estelle Peoples maintained a long-distance relationship with cousins who had moved to the East Bay before the war. They . . . wrote of wartime employment opportunities and offered temporary shelter. Estelle's efforts to maintain contact with her cousins paid off. When Estelle's husband moved west while she remained behind in Texas to settle their affairs, her cousins graciously welcomed him as part of the family. By the time Estelle arrived, her husband had a job, and they could afford to rent a place of their own.
. . . Louisa Hall, . . . who lost her home in an Arkansas flood, maintained close ties with a minister who had moved to the East Bay early in the war. When he heard of Louisa's problems, he urged her to come west with her husband. And when they came, the minister provided both temporary housing and spiritual support as Louisa and her husband struggled to retrieve a sense of control over their lives. Ethel Phillips, who came to the East Bay while her husband was fighting in the Pacific, stayed with a young couple she had known back in Minden, Louisiana. These two friends had encouraged Ethel to join them in Oakland, and they shared their home with her until she found her own apartment.
A second group of migrant women came west with husbands, friends, or relatives without prearranging where they would stay. Unless they were underage, these women actively participated in the search for temporary housing. Their concerns— safety, cleanliness, nearness to schools, markets, health services, and laundry and cooking facilities—were infrequently addressed in the East Bay's tight housing market, but they shaped each family's final choice of accommodations. June Williams and her husband left St. Louis for the East Bay in 1942. Arriving in Oakland after a three-day train trip, they went directly to a relative's address. "We just showed up. He was a bachelor with a one-room apartment who gave us the bed and slept on the floor." The following day, June and her husband looked for housing, stopping people on the streets and asking if they knew of any vacancies. In a neighborhood that seemed ideal because it was within walking distance of markets and churches, June stopped a woman who was leaving a corner grocery. "She said she had a room she was going to rent as soon as she cleared it out." Aware of the acute housing shortage, June asked if they "could help, and we cleared it out the same day. And the next day we picked up our luggage and moved right in."
A third group of women, who had no friends or relatives in the East Bay and whose husbands had preceded them, had to trust their spouses' choice of housing. . . . If a man found a single room for his family, he was doing well by wartime

standards. Women who were initially shocked by their surroundings soon learned that all newcomers made similar concessions. . . . Mary Lee's husband . . . migrated first, leaving Shreveport, Louisiana, for a military assignment in Alameda. When Mary arrived, pregnant with their first child, they shared a single room that he had found in South Berkeley. The owners, having converted their single-family home into several units, rented to "young sailors and soldiers and their families." In this noisy, crowded house, where all the residents shared a single bath and kitchen, Mary struggled to create stable and comfortable surroundings.

All migrant women, whether rooming with relatives or living in cramped, rented rooms, experienced physical and emotional hardship during the temporary housing phase. Until women secured more permanent housing—a process that took from one to twelve months—they struggled with minimal resources to care for their families. Bathing, cooking, cleaning, caring for children, and doing laundry required ingenuity, versatility, and additional labor in the absence of proper facilities. Moreover, women had to devote more time and effort to emotional housekeeping—maintaining family peace and mental health—in an environment characterized by its newness and lack of privacy. Along with these household maintenance tasks, migrant women learned to negotiate transportation, and they found jobs, markets, banks, churches, schools, and health services. . . .

. . . Wartime housing investigators documented some of the difficulties migrant women faced. One family, unsuccessful at finding better housing, lived in a basement that contained "no bathroom, no tub, and the whole family seem[s] to wash in the kitchen sink. The place is infested with rats, and when it rains the place is immediately inundated because neither doors nor windows can be shut tightly. . . . The place is unaired and dimly lighted. For these [*sic*] extremely unsanitary, dirty, overcrowded place the family pays weekly $16.25." The migrant woman living there "implored [the researcher] to do something about the situation." Another family occupied a "substandard frame dwelling [with] no bathroom, no toilet or no hot water. They use the next door neighbor's toilet and shower. This toilet is shared by the tenant upstairs over the neighbor." In one rooming house, eight families shared a single kitchen and bathroom. In others, women attempted to create "makeshift kitchen arrangements in their one or two rooms by placing a small gas burner in one corner of the room, using a crate box placed under or outside the window for refrigeration, and having little or no provision for the storage of food commodities." Such conditions were the norm. Over 40 percent of new arrivals lived in buildings without a bathroom. Of those who did have bathrooms, one-fourth lacked showers or tubs. Most dwellings did have kitchens, but "the most characteristic arrangement was for all families . . . to share a common kitchen."

Migrant women creatively transformed these surroundings. June Williams decorated a bleak rented room with her own needlework and with secondhand furniture from nearby thrift stores. Mary Lee made tables and chairs from orange crates and covered the floor with kelly-green linoleum. Then she painted the crates and walls to match the floor, and bought a matching spread for the bed. . . .

From the moment they arrived, migrant women turned to other women for assistance and advice. These early relationships helped recent migrants gather information and resources to create a home base from which they and other family members could search for employment and more permanent housing. Indeed, neighbors, fellow church members, co-workers, and even acquaintances often pro-vided newcomers with information on fair rental rates, landlord obligations, vacan-cies, and how to apply for government housing. For example, one day when Mary Lee was about to give birth to her first child and was depressed at the prospect of bringing her newborn home to a single rented room, she "was walking down the street with tears in my eyes when a lady stopped me and asked me what was wrong." The woman, who became Mary's close friend, was the housing secretary for the government housing project in West Berkeley, and she "told me about an opening there." Olive Blue was sharing a rented room with her child and unmarried sister when she heard about government housing from co-workers at the Kaiser shipyards. They moved in soon and stayed until Olive's husband returned from the service. By then they had enough combined savings to buy their own home.

Most migrants moved from temporary housing into one of several government housing projects in the East Bay. . . . Although they were built and maintained with federal funds, these projects were managed by local housing authorities, whose boards were dominated by conservative businessmen. For example, housing au-thorities placed black migrants in temporary projects slated for demolition after the war. In contrast, they reserved permanent public housing for white applicants who were viewed as "responsible citizens, good workers, healthy, well adjusted fami-lies." Finally, even temporary projects were administered on a segregated basis. Some contained buildings or units reserved for black tenants; others were com-pletely segregated by race, and all-black projects were located far from white neighborhoods and in the least desirable sections of town. Thus, while war housing was an improvement over the substandard, makeshift accommodations in North Richmond or West Oakland, it was also a way of marginalizing and containing the black migrant population.

Oakland housing authorities managed three low-rent housing projects, which had been planned before the war as part of the city's early redevelopment efforts, and eleven temporary wartime projects. Of this total, four were racially integrated, three completely nonwhite, and seven for whites only. Demand greatly exceeded supply. During the first quarter of 1943, Katherine Legge of the Oakland Housing Authority reported that "I have 60 applications per day, 40 of which are Negro, and I can't house one of them." By the end of the 1944 there had been little improve-ment. In December of that year, the housing authority reported 735 applications for housing, but only six placements.

By the end of the war the integrated and nonwhite projects, concentrated in West Oakland, housed approximately 1,500 nonwhite families; all but a few of these families were black. In sum, the housing authority intentionally confined black migrants to West Oakland, complementing the discriminatory housing poli-cies of private citizens and real estate agencies. By 1945, largely because of these policies, the majority of black migrants lived in seven highly congested census tracts. During the postwar years, the city demolished this housing as part of its West Oakland redevelopment plan.

Opposed to any expansion of the city's black population, white citizens of Berkeley resisted a federal plan to construct war housing in West Berkeley. Their efforts failed. In 1944 the Federal Public Housing Agency built Codornices Village, accepting white and black tenants but segregating each group in separate units or blocks. Although they had failed to keep black migrants out of the city entirely, white Berkeleyans could take comfort in the fact that Codornices Village went up in West Berkeley rather than in all-white sections of the city. The project was also designated as temporary, relieving white fears that migrants would become permanent residents.

Richmond's war housing, located in southwest Richmond on vacant tracts of land near the shipyards, was also designated as temporary and administered on a segregated basis. The Richmond Housing Authority assigned black residents to separate buildings within each project, and racial "balance" was maintained through quotas: the ratio of black and white residents was held at one to four, although the authority's own regulations stipulated a quota of "one Negro in every three rentals."

Of all the East Bay cities, Richmond was most successful at containing black migrants within separate, temporary housing developments. By the end of the war, white migrants either secured permanent housing in Richmond, returned home, or relocated within the Bay Area. Black migrants had nowhere to go, but they were determined to stay. By 1952, 90 percent of Richmond's black population still lived in temporary housing.

Public housing allocated to black migrants was flimsily constructed and deteriorated rapidly from overcrowding, lack of maintenance, and under provision of necessary services. Many projects were built on swampy, poorly drained land that was muddy for most of the year and flooded during the winter. Garbage collection was inadequate, contributing to unhealthy conditions and high rates of disease among residents. The west side of Codornices Village, for example, faced the Southern Pacific rail line and the city dump. Housed in the units that faced west, black residents endured fumes from burning trash and the clatter of passing trains, while whites enjoyed the quieter, cleaner portion of the project. Similarly, black migrants in Richmond were concentrated in units built on swampy land adjacent to the shipyards and railroad tracks, while whites lived in those nearest the downtown and white residential neighborhoods. Such disregard for public health and safety signified and reinforced the temporary status of black migrants, placing them outside any system of mutual obligation, although their labor was essential to the war effort.

Despite these deficiencies, migrant women preferred the projects to the single rented rooms they had recently vacated. Women also expressed satisfaction with indoor plumbing, space heat, hot and cold running water, and modern cooking appliances—amenities many black southerners had never had. Indeed, several women commented that the projects were the nicest place they had ever lived. Lacey Gray, whose two-room company house in Louisiana had lacked indoor plumbing, liked her apartment in the projects. For $35 per month, which included utilities, she received more space than she had ever had: a living room, bedroom, kitchen, and full bath. Myrtle Eaton was similarly impressed with her apartment, located only half a mile from Kaiser Yard No. 3, where she worked as a welder. Her wages—$1.20 per hour—easily covered rent and household expenses. This housing was considerably more affordable than the $8 to $17 many families had paid for a single room.

Above all, government housing was woman-centered, spatially conducive to the formation of helping networks. In addition to housing large concentrations of migrants, projects contained recreation centers, laundry facilities, and common yards that women defined as communal. In these common spaces, women assisted each other with orientation tasks like finding markets, churches, and social services. Moreover, transitional housing in government projects also afforded greater stability and facilitated more complex exchanges and joint projects, such as shared child care, common gardens, group celebrations, and loans of food and income. Women also opened up their homes to more recent migrants, providing the same assistance they had received upon arrival. Men undoubtedly used communal space as well, centering their activities on recreation and the exchange of job information, both of which complemented women's efforts to build a sense of community in the projects. . . .

Many migrant women describe their years in the projects as happy and fulfilling. . . . [T]hese years also brought economic prosperity, compared to what migrants had experienced in the prewar South, and an unprecedented amount of disposable income. During the five-year period between the time the first projects were built (1941) and the end of the war (1946), migrants made "good money." Because they came from families that prized economic independence and home ownership, migrants opened savings accounts, and most women continued to be frugal consumers. Ethel Tillman, surprised at the abundant selection of second-hand clothes at the Salvation Army thrift store, bought "beautiful adult clothes and cut them down into dresses, pants, and suits" for her children. For Ethel, this was a luxury. Although migrants continued to observe familiar patterns of saving and thrift, their efforts actually placed them beyond the edge of poverty. For the first time in their lives, many could simultaneously save and afford a higher standard of living. Thus, from a social as well as economic standpoint, life in the projects represented progress. . . .

In the decade following the war, most migrants moved from women-centered projects to permanent housing. Many purchased single-family homes in existing black and racially mixed areas or in formerly white neighborhoods just beyond the prewar black/white residential boundary line. Between 1950 and 1960, the number of black homeowners in Berkeley grew from 1,909 to 4,160. During the same period, Richmond's black homeowning population increased from 329 to 2,191, and Oakland's from 4,133 to 11,552. By 1960, nearly 50 percent of black-occupied homes in Berkeley were owned. In Richmond, this figure was 58 percent, and in Oakland, 42 percent. In Berkeley, a higher percentage of African Americans owned homes than whites. Migrants who could not afford to buy homes found rental housing in permanent low-income projects or in private rental units.

Black renters and homeowners faced a tight housing market in the postwar years. White residents and realtors vigilantly protected white neighborhoods from black encroachment. At the same time, East Bay cities adopted redevelopment plans designed to eliminate temporary war housing. When these units were destroyed, migrants had fewer housing options than they had had during the war. In Oakland, for example, postwar housing construction was most heavily concentrated in white areas, and existing black neighborhoods suffered a net loss of housing units. Whether it was intentionally designed to remove migrants, or simply resulted from poor planning, postwar redevelopment compounded migrants' housing woes. Their tenacity, in the context of forced removal and ongoing housing segregation, certainly confirmed one researcher's conclusion that few migrants ever planned to return to the South. Richmond's total population, for example, declined between 1947 and 1960, from 101,579 to 71,854. However, the number of black residents increased from 13 percent to 20 percent of the total, while the proportion of white residents declined.

By 1950, 78 percent of Richmond's black population lived in temporary war housing slated for demolition by the newly created Richmond Redevelopment Agency. Although the city was legally required to provide replacement housing, few tenants were informed of this obligation. Those who did request replacements were transferred to other temporary projects also slated for demolition. In contrast, the city reserved its permanent, low-rent projects for white tenants. Indeed, as demolition of primarily black projects progressed, the city reclassified an all-white temporary development as permanent. Clearly, Richmond's leadership viewed white migrants as more worthy of permanent citizenship.

Black migrants had fewer options. Those with savings purchased lots in North Richmond or on vacant tracts of land in the southern and western sections of town once occupied by war housing and industry. In the early 1950s, two private developers built a "racially unrestricted" tract of single-family homes in an unincorporated area north of Richmond. This tract, called Parchester Village, became an all-black development—a counterpart of postwar, white, planned suburban communities. The city of Richmond annexed this development in 1963. Those who wished to purchase in white neighborhoods still faced discriminatory real estate practices, although restrictive covenants were no longer legal. Families that circumvented biased realtors confronted violent opposition from white homeowners. One family successfully purchased a home in the all-white Rollingwood neighborhood of Richmond. The night of their move, three hundred white residents gathered outside their house and shouted threats. Although the police provided protection, the family endured threatening phone calls and remarks from hecklers in passing cars for several weeks.

Those who could not afford to buy had to find rental housing, which was even more scarce now than it had been during the war. Contra Costa County built one low-income, integrated project in North Richmond in 1949. And the city built another, Easter Hill Village, in South Richmond. However, the number of families these projects accommodated was insignificant compared with the number of black tenants—10,431—who had been displaced.

Residents of Codornices Village, Berkeley's only war-worker housing project, also faced eviction during the postwar years. In 1954, the federal government notified residents of the village that they had six months to leave. At that time, 88 percent of the village's residents were black. Berkeley, unlike Richmond, had no control over the decision, although the city could have acquired the project from the government and extended its life. But the city in fact welcomed the demolition. Five years earlier, in 1949, the city council had refused to consider the development of low-income housing within its borders, despite the availability of federal aid for that purpose. Had the city built permanent, long-term housing, the residents of Codornices Village would have had an alternative to eviction and displacement.

The only other housing available to migrants was in South and West Berkeley. Those who had savings bought homes in these sections of town, sometimes in white neighborhoods that bordered the black sections. In turn, white residents moved out, gradually expanding the borders of black Berkeley. Profit-minded realtors, black and white, helped migrants purchase homes in bordering white neighborhoods. Katherine St. Clair's father, who during the war had made a living purchasing and subdividing West Oakland Victorians, turned to "block-busting" after the war ended. Working in partnership with a white realtor, Katherine's father found migrants who were willing to buy homes in white neighborhoods. The white realtor would arrange the sale, knowing that neighboring whites would bring him their business as they bought homes elsewhere. Katherine's father then sold vacated houses to other black buyers. Such partnerships were limited to certain sections of Berkeley. Katherine remembers that the white realtor would not have integrated neighborhoods in North Berkeley or the hills. In fact, "he was very prejudiced, but he used Daddy and Daddy used him."

Migrants who could not afford homes found an expanding rental market in South Berkeley and West Berkeley. As building materials became available after the war, white and black housing speculators demolished older, single-family homes and built multifamily units. Katherine and her husband, participating in this postwar housing boom, bought two eight-unit buildings in Alameda that had formerly housed servicemen. "You could buy one for $500, but you had to tear it down from the roof to the foundation." She and her husband took the buildings apart and used the materials to build new apartments in South Berkeley. But the St. Clairs were small-scale landlords who lived in their own building. Other builders engaged in "the worst kind of destructive real estate speculative activity" and thereby undermined the stable character of many historic, all-black neighborhoods in Berkeley. By the time zoning restrictions stopped this process in the early 1970s, whole neighborhoods of small, single-family homes had been replaced with cheap, high-density rental housing. . . .

By the end of the war, 85 percent of Oakland's black population lived in West Oakland, the East Bay's largest black community. There migrants bought or rented homes close to churches, lodges, De Fremery Park, and black business strips along Market and Seventh Streets. Although approximately 11 percent of the city's black population still lived in public housing in 1947, the remainder had either purchased homes or secured permanent rental housing in relatively affordable West Oakland neighborhoods. . . .

However, after World War II, Oakland's city council designated West Oakland as a blighted area and targeted it for redevelopment. At the behest of real estate, construction, and business interests, the city proceeded to demolish existing public housing projects as well as entire neighborhoods of single-family homes, black institutions, and businesses. These were replaced with housing developments designed to lure more affluent residents into the area. During the same period, a freeway divided the neighborhoods of West Oakland and isolated a large section of the community from other sections of the city. Next, half of the black commercial strip along Seventh Street was razed to accommodate a rapid transit system. Finally, hundreds of acres of homes and businesses were demolished to accommodate a new postal complex.

Displaced residents, who numbered well over 10,000, had difficulty finding housing in other sections of the city. It was not until 1966 that East Bay citizens had a legal basis to fight housing discrimination. Most found housing in East Oakland, formerly a white, working-class section of the city. But as one researcher observed, new residents "did not find a system of social organization that existed in West Oakland. East Oakland did not have well established Black neighborhoods that had a history of cooperation and community organization. The Blacks who moved to East Oakland were strangers, and it took time for a community to develop." Thus, migrants who had located permanently in West Oakland, buying or renting homes after moving out of transitional housing, were forced to move yet again. In East Oakland, which had no black businesses or institutions, new residents had to create a community from scratch.

For migrant women, the move from transitional to permanent housing brought a distinct set of challenges. Without the semicommunal spatial design of wartime housing projects, women had greater difficulty meeting friends and engaging in joint projects. Those who bought homes had to literally and figuratively speak over fences. Those who moved into rental housing lived with a high degree of impermanence, seeing neighbors move in and out as their economic fortunes improved or declined. . . .

[However], the process of becoming familiar with one's environment, creating helping relationships, and building enduring, family-supporting institutions is not a product or outgrowth of different types of housing. These tasks were accomplished by people who creatively used the physical resources associated with their surroundings. The women themselves transformed substandard, temporary housing into a relatively stable base from which they could secure better housing and other basic necessities. . . . [I]n the context of mass institutional opposition, women's efforts to create and maintain stable homes must be conceptualized as a form of active resistance against those who tried to prevent them from creating permanent homes in the Bay Area.

FURTHER READING

Jervis Anderson, *A. Philip Randolph: A Biographical Portrait* (1973).

Karen Anderson, "Last Hired, First Fired: Black Women Workers During World War II," *Journal of American History,* 69 (June 1982), 82–97.

Arthur R. Ashe, Jr., *A Hard Road to Glory: A History of the African-American Athlete Since 1946* (1988).

Dominic J. Capeci, Jr., *Race Relations in Wartime Detroit: The Sojourner Truth Housing Controversy of 1942* (1984).

Dan T. Carter, *Scottsboro: A Tragedy of the American South,* rev. ed. (1979).

Melinda Chateauvert, *Marching Together: Women of the Brotherhood of Sleeping Car Porters* (1998).

Lizbeth Cohen, *Making a New Deal: Industrial Workers in Chicago, 1919–1939* (1990).

Herbert Garfinkel, *When Negroes March: The March on Washington Movement in the Organizational Policies for FEPC* (1959).

Nancy Grant, *TVA and Black Americans: Planning for the Status Quo* (1990).

Brenda Clegg Gray, *Black Female Domestics During the Depression in New York City, 1930–1940* (1993).

Cheryl Lynn Greenberg, *"Or Does It Explode?": Black Harlem in the Great Depression* (1991).

Keith P. Griffler, *What Price Alliance: Black Radicals Confront White Labor, 1918–1938* (1995).

William Hamilton Harris, *Keeping the Faith: A. Philip Randolph, Milton P. Webster, and the Brotherhood of Sleeping Car Porters, 1925–37* (1977).

Jacqueline Jones, *Labor of Love, Labor of Sorrow: Black Women, Work, and the Family from Slavery to the Present* (1985).

Robin D. G. Kelley, "The Riddle of the Zoot: Malcolm Little and Black Cultural Politics During World War II," in *Malcolm X: In Our Own Image,* ed. Joe Wood (1992), 155–182.

John B. Kirby, *Black Americans in the Roosevelt Era: Liberalism and Race* (1980).

Steven F. Lawson, *Black Ballots: Voting Rights in the South, 1944–1969* (1976).

Lawrence Levine, *Black Culture and Black Consciousness: Afro-American Folk Thought from Slavery to Freedom* (1977).

August Meier and Elliott Rudwick, *Black Detroit and the Rise of the UAW* (1979).

Shirley Ann Wilson Moore, *To Place Our Deeds: The African American Community in Richmond, California, 1910–1963* (1999).

Mark Naison, *Communists in Harlem During the Depression* (1983).

Bruce Nelson, "Organized Labor and the Struggle for Black Equality in Mobile During World War II," *Journal of American History,* 80 (December 1993), 952–988.

Nell Irvin Painter, *The Narrative of Hosea Hudson: His Life as a Negro Communist in the South* (1979).

Arnold Rampersad, *Jackie Robinson: A Biography* (1997).

Theodore Rosengarten, *All God's Dangers: The Life of Nate Shaw* (1974).

B. Joyce Ross, "Mary McLeod Bethune and the National Youth Administration: A Case Study of Power Relationships in the Black Cabinet of Franklin D. Roosevelt," *Journal of Negro History,* 60 (January 1975), 1–28.

Jeffrey T. Sammons, *Beyond the Ring: The Role of Boxing in American Society* (1988).

Harvard Sitkoff, *A New Deal for Blacks: The Emergence of Civil Rights as a National Issue,* vol. 1, *The Depression Decade* (1978).

Jules Tygiel, *Baseball's Great Experiment: Jackie Robinson and His Legacy* (1997).

Brian Urquhart, *Ralph Bunche: An American Life* (1993).

Margaret Rose Vendryes, "Hanging on Their Walls: An Art Commentary on Lynching, The Forgotten 1935 Exhibition," in *Race Consciousness: African-American Studies for the New Century,* ed. Judith Jackson Fossett and Jeffrey A. Tucker (1997).

David Wiggins, "Wendell Smith, the *Pittsburgh Courier-Journal* and the Campaign to Include Blacks in Organized Baseball, 1933–1945," *Journal of Sport History,* 10, no. 2 (Summer 1983), 5–29.

Raymond Wolters, *Negroes and the Great Depression: The Problem of Economic Recovery* (1970).

Robert L. Zangrando, *The NAACP Crusade Against Lynching, 1909–1950* (1980).

CHAPTER
8

Origins of the
Civil Rights Movement

The roots of the Civil Rights Movement that emerged in the 1950s and 1960s lay in earlier struggles that African Americans waged during the Depression and World War II. During those struggles many African-American activists reevaluated old doctrines and approaches to achieve racial justice, thus laying the ideological, tactical, and institutional foundations for mass direct action campaigns. Indeed, many of the young people involved in the reform movements of the 1930s and 1940s became prominent leaders in the 1950s and 1960s.

The increasing urbanization of black Americans and a corresponding growth in black voting strength, especially in northern but also in southern cities, forced the federal government and national political parties to take notice of the economic and political condition of black Americans. By the late 1940s, African Americans had won a series of legal victories in cases involving educational access, white primaries, residential segregation, and public transportation. These victories provided a constitutional basis for their demands for equality and pushed the Roosevelt and Truman administrations to take civil rights seriously as a political issue. But in the process, black men and women had learned that these hard-won victories would be hollow unless they fought for enforcement; the necessity of direct action was one of the central lessons of the Depression and World War II eras.

D O C U M E N T S

A combination of propaganda and legal efforts had been the hallmark of the NAACP's work from its founding early in the twentieth century. In the early 1930s, however, the organization was forced to respond to sharp challenges to its tactics and strategy from young, radical black activists. In the first document, Ella Baker—who would become an important influence on young civil rights workers in the 1960s—and Marvel Cooke publish in the NAACP's own journal an exposé of conditions among black domestics, a group the organization would not normally deign to notice. Chastened by the Depression's devastating impact on blacks, the NAACP authorized the formation of the Committee on Future Plan and Program, headed by one of the radicals—Abram Harris, an economist teaching at Howard University. The committee's 1935 report, excerpted in the second document, called on the NAACP to redirect its efforts and devote far more of its resources to economic issues important to working-class black Americans. In subsequent years the NAACP began to work closely with labor organizations, but it nevertheless maintained its focus on legal barriers to black equality in the United States. The same year that Harris's committee report was issued, Charles Hamilton Houston, formerly dean of Howard University Law School but in 1935 head of the newly reorganized NAACP Legal Department, set forth what became the NAACP's primary legal strategy for the next two decades, which eventually led to the NAACP victory in *Brown v. Board of Education* in 1954. The third document outlines Houston's plan.

Also in 1935, as the NAACP was debating its future, a number of black intellectuals and political activists, including John P. Davis, A. Philip Randolph, Ralph Bunche, Robert C. Weaver, and Abram Harris, came together to create the National Negro Congress. Delegates from 585 different groups nationwide attended its founding meeting, hoping that collectively they could find ways to improve the economic and civil status of black Americans. In the fourth document the founders set forth the organization's goals.

Drawing on the principles of Mahatma Gandhi in the anticolonial struggle in India, as well as on the successful organization of the Brotherhood of Sleeping Car Porters, A. Philip Randolph in 1941 called for an all-black, nonviolent, mass March on Washington Movement to confront discrimination in defense industries and the armed forces. The fifth document is Randolph's call to the march. In response, President Franklin Delano Roosevelt issued an executive order mandating "full and equitable participation of all workers in defense industries, without discrimination." In the sixth document, James Farmer recalls that he and the other founders of the Committee (later Congress) of Racial Equality drew on Gandhian principles as they organized sit-ins and other demonstrations to desegregate public accommodations in Chicago in the 1940s. The conviction that black Americans had earned the right to equal treatment through their patriotic service at home and abroad during World War II was evident among those who participated in a 1945 boycott of a local department store in Washington, D.C., because of its discriminatory practices. The seventh document comprises letters to the store manager from protesting customers.

1. Ella Baker and Marvel Cooke Describe Exploitation of Black Women Workers During the Depression, 1935

The Bronx Slave Market! . . . the Simpson avenue block exudes the stench of the slave market at its worst. Not only is human labor bartered and sold for slave wage, but human love also is a marketable commodity. But whether it is labor or love that is sold, economic necessity compels the sale. As early as 8 a.m. they come; as late as 1 p.m. they remain.

Rain or shine, cold or hot, you will find them there—Negro women, old and young—sometimes bedraggled, sometimes neatly dressed—but with the invariable paper bundle, waiting expectantly for Bronx housewives to buy their strength and energy for an hour, two hours, or even for a day at the munificent rate of fifteen, twenty, twenty-five, or, if luck be with them, thirty cents an hour. If not the wives

Excerpt from Ella Baker and Marvel Cooke, "The Bronx Slave Market," *The Crisis,* 42 (November 1935): 330–331, 340.

themselves, maybe their husbands, their sons, or their brothers, under the subterfuge of work, offer worldly-wise girls higher bids for their time.

Who are these women? What brings them here? Why do they stay? In the boom days before the onslaught of the depression in 1929, many of these women who are now forced to bargain for day's work on street corners, were employed in grand homes in the rich Eighties, or in wealthier homes in Long Island and Westchester, at more than adequate wages. Some are former marginal industrial workers, forced by the slack in industry to seek other means of sustenance. In many instances there had been no necessity for work at all. But whatever their standing prior to the depression, none sought employment where they now seek it. They come to the Bronx, not because of what it promises, but largely in desperation.

Paradoxically, the crash of 1929 brought to the domestic labor market a new employer class. The lower middle-class housewife, who, having dreamed of the luxury of a maid, found opportunity staring her in the face in the form of Negro women pressed to the wall by poverty, starvation and discrimination.

Where once color was the "gilt edged" security for obtaining domestic and personal service jobs, here, even, Negro women found themselves being displaced by whites. Hours of futile waiting in employment agencies, the fee that must be paid despite the lack of income, fraudulent agencies that sprung up during the depression, all forced the day worker to fend for herself or try the dubious and circuitous road to public relief.

As inadequate as emergency relief has been, it has proved somewhat of a boon to many of these women, for with its advent, actual starvation is no longer their ever-present slave driver and they have been able to demand twenty-five and even thirty cents an hour as against the old fifteen and twenty cent rate. In an effort to supplement the inadequate relief received, many seek this open market.

And what a market! She who is fortunate (?) enough to please Mrs. Simon Legree's scrutinizing eye is led away to perform hours of multifarious household drudgeries. Under a rigid watch, she is permitted to scrub floors on her bended knees, to hang precariously from window sills, cleaning window after window, or to strain and sweat over steaming tubs of heavy blankets, spreads and furniture covers.

Fortunate, indeed, is she who gets the full hourly rate promised. Often her day's slavery is rewarded with a single dollar bill or whatever her unscrupulous employer pleases to pay. More often, the clock is set back for an hour or more. Too often she is sent away without any pay at all. . . .

The real significance of the Bronx Slave Market lies not in a factual presentation of its activities; but in focusing attention upon its involved implications. The "mart" is but a miniature mirror of our economic battlefront.

To many, the women who sell their labor thus cheaply have but themselves to blame. . . .

The exploiters, judged from the districts where this abominable traffic flourishes, are the wives and mothers of artisans and tradesmen who militantly battle against being exploited themselves, but who apparently have no scruples against exploiting others.

The general public, though aroused by stories of these domestics, too often think of the problems of these women as something separate and apart and readily dismisses them with a sigh and a shrug of the shoulders.

The women, themselves present a study in contradictions. Largely unaware of their organized power, yet ready to band together for some immediate and personal gain either consciously or unconsciously, they still cling to that American illusion that any one who is determined and persistent can get ahead.

The roots, then of the Bronx Slave Market spring from: (1) the general ignorance of and apathy towards organized labor action; (2) the artificial barriers that separate the interest of the relief administrators and investigators from that of their "case loads," the white collar and professional worker from the laborer and the domestic; and (3) organized labor's limited concept of exploitation, which permits it to fight vigorously to secure itself against evil, yet passively or actively aids and abets the ruthless destruction of Negroes.

To abolish the market once and for all, these roots must be torn away from their sustaining soil. Certain palliative and corrective measures are not without benefit. Already the seeds of discontent are being sown. . . .

An embryonic labor union now exists in the Simpson avenue "mart." Girls who persist in working for less than thirty cents an hour have been literally run off the corner. For the recent Jewish holiday, habitues of the "mart" actually demanded and refused to work for less than thirty-five cents an hour.

2. Young Radicals Propose an Economic Program for the NAACP, 1935

The work of the Association in the economic field has been conducted as an incidental phase of its civil liberty program. . . . In addition to its persistent protests against discrimination and segregation of Negroes in industry and against the refusal of A.F. of L. unions to organize Negroes, it has the following outstanding accomplishments to its credit. . . . In 1913, it began its fight against the segregation and discrimination of Negro government employees opposing the Aswel-Edwards Bill designed to make this a national policy; in 1917, when the railroads were under Federal control it successfully fought the discrimination against Negro railway employees; in 1919–1920, it obtained, in cooperation with the Association of Colored Railroad Employees, increased pay for colored trainmen; . . . in 1920, it fought the Ku Klux Klan and its attempts to force Negro cotton pickers and domestics into accepting lower rates of pay in many southern states; in 1921, it caused the United States Department of Justice to protect Negro trainmen from the violence and intimidation of white trainmen in the South; and in very recent years its efforts to safeguard the rights of Negro workers in the Mississippi Flood Control area, at Boulder Dam, and in the various national, state and local emergency agencies, relief projects, and in the legislation of the present administration are well known and too numerous for detailed citation.

As significant as is the work typified in the foregoing accomplishments, it reveals the Association's primary objective as being that of securing for the Negro his rights as an American citizen under prevailing economic and social conditions. . . .

. . . [T]he adoption of the economic program contemplated here . . . call[s] for a reformulation of the Association's ultimate objectives. Instead of continuing to oppose racial discrimination on the job and in pay and various manifestations of anti-Negro feeling among white workers, the Association would attempt to get Negroes to view their special grievances as a natural part of the larger issues of American labor as a whole. It would attempt to get white workers and black to view their lot as embracing a common cause rather than antithetical interests. Thus, on one hand, it would show the Negro that his special disadvantages are but the more extreme manifestations of the exploitation of labor; and, on the other hand, it would show white labor that the disadvantages suffered by Negro workmen and frequently supported by white labor not only perpetuate the historic hostility between white and black labor, but also place a reserve of cheap labor at the disposal of employers. . . . It would show that the world which labor would gain is not a white world, nor a black one, and that this world can only be gained through the solidarity of white and black labor.

To this end the following program is proposed for the Association's adoption:

A. It is recommended that the Association:

1. Conduct classes in workers' education designed to create among Negro working men a knowledge of their historic and present role in modern industry and a realization of their identity of interests with white labor; 2. Foster the building of a labor movement, industrial in character, which will unite all labor, white and black, skilled and unskilled, agricultural and industrial; 3. Lay the intellectual basis for united action between white and black workers in local, state and national politics for securing passage of adequate legislation on immediate problems, such as (a) old age pensions, (b) unemployment and sickness insurance, (c) widows' and orphans' pensions, (d) child and female labor, (e) lynching, (f) public discrimination and Jim Crowism; 4. Serve as a basis for national and regional labor conferences to discuss the problems of Negro industrial and agricultural workers and to formulate programs of legislative, political or propaganda activity to be carried out independently or in cooperation with other groups or agencies in sympathy with these objectives; 5. Serve as an opposition force to every manifestation and form of racial chauvinism in the labor movement and among workers everywhere, and to attempt to break down discrimination on the job and in pay, and Jim Crowism in the local and national trade union bodies, by showing the mutually disastrous effects of these conditions upon the interests of white and black labor; 6. Educate Negro industrial and agricultural workers into the practices of the Cooperative Movement in Denmark, Austria, Russia and England as a means of furthering immediate economic relief in employment, credit, housing and consumption on a nonprofit basis, but not as a solution of the "Economic Problem" or as the basis of a separate Negro group economy, an ideal which the Association deems unsound; and, 7. Make its branches centers of education in the use of the ballot, and in local, state and national politics. . . .

3. Charles Hamilton Houston Lays Out a Legal Strategy for the NAACP, 1935

The inequalities and discrimination practiced against the public education of Negroes in this country in every place where there are separate schools and in many places where there are not separate schools, are too well-known for demonstration or argument. These inequalities cover all phases of public education but because of their ramifications and the many chances of officials to shift responsibility from one to another, the N.A.A.C.P. in its attack on these inequalities has had to pick out three glaring and typical discriminations as focal points for legal action, to wit: differential in teachers' pay between white and Negro teachers having the same qualifications, holding the same certificate, and doing the same work; (2) inequalities in transportation facilities which lie at the basis of all problems of consolidation of rural schools; (3) inequalities in graduate and professional education usually offered to white students in universities supported by state funds, while Negro education is cut off with the under-graduate work in college.

Education, in one sense, is a preparation for the competition of life. All elements of American people are in economic competition, one with another. The Negro fundamentally is no exception to this rule, although at the present time, he may seem to escape competition in certain restricted fields, notably dentistry, barbering, undertaking and burial service, and the ministry. Nevertheless, even these fields are dependent for their size and growth upon the economic resources of their Negro clientele, which economic resources of said Negro clientele are themselves derived from competition with whites. In the theatre business, grocery business, drug store business, for a long time Negroes appeared not to have competition when serving Negro neighborhoods, but just as soon as these neighborhoods developed sufficient purchasing power to make business more attractive, white business came in and in most instances, drove Negro business out. Other occupations, such as hotel work and manual labor, are no longer reserved to Negroes.

Since education is a preparation for the competition of life, a poor education handicaps an individual in the competition. For example, in South Carolina, the inequality in school terms alone is such that it takes a Negro child ten years to get as much schooling as a white child gets in seven. In Maryland, the school term for white children is 180 days; for Negroes, 160 days. In other words, the white children in Maryland go to school as many days in eight years as Negro children go in nine years. These inequalities in education must be broken down if the coming generation of Negroes are to receive anything like a fair chance in American life.

The differential in teachers' salaries is selected because the salary scale is usually regulated by law and it presents a definite and concrete issue in which are implicated all the questions of school buildings, physical plant, curriculum, and length of term. Likewise, if and when judgment is obtained, there will be a source

Charles Hamilton Houston, "Tentative Statement Concerning Policy of N.A.A.C.P. in Its Program of Attacks on Educational Discrimination" [July 12, 1935], *Papers of the NAACP, Pt. 3: Campaign for Educational Equality: Legal Dept. & Central Office Records, 1913–1950, Series A: Legal Dept. & Central Office Records, 1913–40* (microfilm), Reel 2, C-197, Subject File—American Fund for Public Service, Frames 293, 294. Copyright © 1935 by NAACP. Reprinted with permission.

from which the money can be secured on execution, which will make the judgment effective and give it teeth.

The transportation inequality is selected for attack because not only is transportation at the basis of all consolidation of rural schools, because it is impossible to consolidate rural schools unless the children are physically able to reach the consolidated school within a reasonable time; but also there is a psychological aspect to white children being transported to school in busses while Negro children plod along the road. An inferiority complex is installed in the Negro children without one word being said about the difference between the races. It does not have to be said to either white children or Negro children, if the white children have ridden to a consolidated brick school for eight years, clean and dry, in busses furnished by the county, while the Negro children have trudged along the road, dirty and sometimes wet, to a little ramshackle, wooden, one-room school house.

The graduate and professional study was selected for attack because a large portion of the leadership of the race should come from Negroes who have had access to the graduate and professional schools. The whites are educating their own children for public leadership through graduate and professional study out of taxes to which Negroes contribute, while Negro students are cut off with under-graduate training. In other words, the white system of education is designed to perpetuate the inferior status of Negroes. Two states, West Virginia and Missouri, make a pretext of equalizing the graduate and professional studies for Negroes by granting so-called out of state scholarships to Negro students who wish graduate courses offered white students in the state universities. But even these two states do not give any real equality because the scholarship covers only tuition. No allowance is made for travel or maintenance outside the state. As a matter of fact, in West Virginia, the maximum amount expended on Negroes for professional and graduate study is about $6,000 a year, which is less than one-half the salary paid the president of the University of West Virginia alone.

Finally, the National Office of the N.A.A.C.P. deems it[s] function in this program to be that of (1) exposing the inequalities and discriminations and (2) wherever requested by the local populace, to render such assistance as it can through its branches and its own staff in making an attack on these evils. . . .

4. Goals of the National Negro Congress, 1935

Today the whole of the United States faces the crisis of mass unemployment, lower standards of living, hunger and misery. For Negroes . . . six terrible years of depression have meant an intolerable double exploitation both as Negroes and as workers.

Negro workers on farms, in factories and in households as servants see their wages fall while prices increase. Discrimination against them has increased on the job. They can no longer be certain that tomorrow will find them employed. . . . [A]n increasing number of barriers are erected against Negroes getting jobs by unions, which, following anti–working class policies, deny Negroes union privileges and union membership. Negro women are being literally driven out of industrial employment. Negro youth find less and less opportunity to earn a living. . . . On government building projects discrimination against employment of Negro artisans continues. Even so-called "Negro" jobs are no longer available. Unemployment spreads, and in every section of the nation the Negro is fast becoming a jobless race.

The Negro farm population in the South is fast becoming landless. We face the fact that within the past fifteen years not only have Negroes not gained in land ownership but they have lost possession of more than four million acres of farm land; and, furthermore, there is a steady decline in the already pitiable farm wage. . . .

Not hunger and poverty alone plague the existence of Black America. The denial of citizenship rights creates a double burden. The ballot, the most elemental right of a citizen, is effectively denied two-thirds of the entire Negro population. In the courts of the land, the Negro is denied justice. He is illegally kept from jury service, and made to face daily unfair trials and inhuman sentences. Negroes are mobbed and lynched while Congress cynically refuses to enact a federal anti-lynching law. They are excluded from public places, even from restaurants in the nation's Capitol. All of these manifestation of injustice have become more severe.

Negroes in America observe with deep indignation the war on Ethiopia by fascist Italy, threatening, as it does, to throw the entire world into a terrible war. . . .

The problems facing the Negro make him more determined to struggle against injustice. . . . [Witness] the struggles of the National Association for the Advancement of Colored People to win for the Negro equal school facilities, to win for the Negro in the South freedom from mob-violence and lynching; . . . the fight of the National Urban Leagues and the International Brotherhood of Sleeping Car Porters to organize Negro workers into militant unions[;] . . . [the] thousands of Negro churches where voices are lifted up in defense of Ethiopia[;] . . . the efforts of hundreds of thousands of Negro citizens to win complete freedom for Angelo Herndon and the Scottsboro Boys. In hundreds of communities Negro citizens have organized in many varied ways, fighting against social and economic oppression. . . .

Every problem presented here calls for greater united action. For this reason we who sign this declaration call for the united action of all organizations and individuals to whom it is addressed, to work for a National Negro Congress to be composed of delegates representing all Negro organizations, and such other organizations— mixed or white—as will take a stand for equal rights for the Negro. This Congress is called to meet in Chicago, Illinois on February 14, 1936, on the historic occasion of the anniversary of the birth of Frederick Douglass.

We believe that this Congress will furnish the opportunity for considering the problems that face the Negro people and that a plan of action—the collective wisdom of all freedom-loving sections of our population—can be intelligently worked out for the solution of these problems. By unity of action we can create a nationwide public opinion which will force real consideration from public officials, such as no single organization can hope to muster. . . .

The NATIONAL NEGRO CONGRESS will be no new organization, nor does it seek to usurp the work of existing organizations. It will seek rather to accomplish unity of action of existing organizations.

It is with these objectives clearly in mind that we propose for discussion and action by the Congress the issues outlined below:

1. The right of Negroes to jobs at decent living wages and for the right to join all trade unions. For the right to equal wages and equal labor conditions with other workers. For the organization of Negro workers with their fellow white workers into democratically controlled trade unions.
2. Relief and security for every needy Negro family; and, for genuine social and unemployment insurance without discrimination.
3. Aid to the Negro farm population, to ease the burden of debts and taxation; for the right of farmers, tenants and sharecroppers to organize and bargain collectively.
4. A fight against lynching, mob violence and police brutality; for enactment of a federal anti-lynching law; for the right to vote, serve on juries and enjoy complete civil liberty.
5. The right of Negro youth to equal opportunity in education and in the economic life of the community.
6. For complete equality for Negro women; for their right, along with all women, to equal pay for equal work; for their right to a suitable environment for themselves and their children—an environment which demands adequate housing, good schools, and recreational facilities; for their right to organize as consumers.
7. To oppose war and fascism, the attempted subjugation of Negro people in Ethiopia, the oppression of colonial nations throughout the world; for the independence of Ethiopia.

5. A Call to March on Washington, 1941

We call upon you to fight for jobs in National Defense.

We call upon you to struggle for the integration of Negroes in the armed forces, such as the Air Corps, Navy, Army and Marine Corps of the Nation.

We call upon you to demonstrate for the abolition of Jim-Crowism in all Government departments and defense employment.

This is an hour of crisis. It is a crisis of democracy. It is a crisis of minority groups. It is a crisis of Negro Americans.

What is this crisis?

To American Negroes, it is the denial of jobs in Government defense projects. It is racial discrimination in Government departments. It is widespread Jim-Crowism in the armed forces of the Nation.

While billions of the taxpayers' money are being spent for war weapons, Negro workers are being turned away from the gates of factories, mines and mills—being flatly told, "NOTHING DOING." Some employers refuse to give Negroes jobs when they are without "union cards," and some unions refuse Negro workers union cards when they are "without jobs."

What shall we do?

What a dilemma!

What a runaround!

What a disgrace!

What a blow below the belt!

'Though dark, doubtful and discouraging, all is not lost, all is not hopeless. 'Though battered and bruised, we are not beaten, broken or bewildered.

Verily, the Negroes' deepest disappointments and direst defeats, their tragic trials and outrageous oppressions in these dreadful days of destruction and disaster to democracy and freedom, and the rights of minority peoples, and the dignity and independence of the human spirit, is the Negroes' greatest opportunity to rise to the highest heights of struggle for freedom and justice in Government, in industry, in labor unions, education, social service, religion and culture.

With faith and confidence of the Negro people in their own power for self-liberation, Negroes can break down the barriers of discrimination against employment in National Defense. Negroes can kill the deadly serpent of race hatred in the Army, Navy, Air and Marine Corps, and smash through and blast the government, business and labor-union red tape to win the right to equal opportunity in vocational training and re-training in defense employment.

Most important and vital to all, Negroes, by the mobilization and coordination of their mass power, can cause PRESIDENT ROOSEVELT TO ISSUE AN EXECUTIVE ORDER ABOLISHING DISCRIMINATIONS IN ALL GOVERNMENT DEPARTMENTS, ARMY, NAVY, AIR CORPS AND NATIONAL DEFENSE JOBS.

Of course, the task is not easy. In very truth, it is big, tremendous and difficult.

It will cost money.

It will require sacrifice.

It will tax the Negroes' courage, determination and will to struggle. But we can, must and will triumph.

The Negroes' stake in national defense is big. It consists of jobs, thousands of jobs. It may represent millions, yes, hundreds of millions of dollars in wages. It consists of new industrial opportunities and hope. This is worth fighting for.

But to win our stakes, it will require an "all-out," bold and total effort and demonstration of colossal proportions.

Negroes can build a mammoth machine of mass action with a terrific and tremendous driving and striking power that can shatter and crush the evil fortress of race prejudice and hate, if they will only resolve to do so and never stop, until victory comes.

Dear fellow Negro Americans, be not dismayed in these terrible times. You possess power, great power. Our problem is to harness and hitch it up for action on the broadest, daring and most gigantic scale.

In this period of power politics, nothing counts but pressure, more pressure, and still more pressure, through the tactic and strategy of broad, organized, aggressive mass action behind the vital and important issues of the Negro. To this end, we propose that ten thousand Negroes MARCH ON WASHINGTON FOR JOBS IN NATIONAL DEFENSE AND EQUAL INTEGRATION IN THE FIGHTING FORCES OF THE UNITED STATES.

An "all-out" thundering march on Washington, ending in a monster and huge demonstration at Lincoln's Monument will shake up white America.

It will shake up official Washington.

It will give encouragement to our white friends to fight all the harder by our side, with us, for our righteous cause.

It will gain respect for the Negro people.

It will create a new sense of self-respect among Negroes.

But what of national unity?

We believe in national unity which recognizes equal opportunity of black and white citizens to jobs in national defense and the armed forces, and in all other institutions and endeavors in America. We condemn all dictatorships, Fascist, Nazi and Communist. We are loyal, patriotic Americans, all.

But, if American democracy will not defend its defenders; if American democracy will not protect its protectors; if American democracy will not give jobs to its toilers because of race or color; if American democracy will not insure equality of opportunity, freedom and justice to its citizens, black and white, it is a hollow mockery and belies the principles for which it is supposed to stand.

To the hard, difficult and trying problem of securing equal participation in national defense, we summon all Negro Americans to march on Washington. We summon Negro Americans to form committees in various cities to recruit and register marchers and raise funds through the sale of buttons and other legitimate means for the expenses of marchers to Washington by buses, train, private automobiles, trucks, and on foot.

We summon Negro Americans to stage marches on their City Halls and Councils in their respective cities and urge them to memorialize the President to issue an executive order to abolish discrimination in the Government and national defense.

However, we sternly counsel against violence and ill-considered and intemperate action and the abuse of power. Mass power, like physical power, when misdirected is more harmful than helpful.

We summon you to mass action that is orderly and lawful, but aggressive and militant, for justice, equality and freedom. . . .

6. James Farmer Recounts CORE's Early Direct Action Strategy, 1942

. . . By the end of the spring of 1942 the first Committee of Racial Equality was a reality.

One evening around this time James R. Robinson, one of the founders of CORE (later its executive secretary), and I, deep in a discussion of CORE, stopped for coffee at a little corner shop called the Jack Sprat, in a middle-class section [of Chicago] near the university. The manager of the place served us with the greatest reluctance and then only after we reminded him that he would be violating state law if he refused. Even so, he tried at first to charge me twenty-five cents for a five-cent doughnut. A few days later our fledgling CORE chapter sent in a small interracial group. The manager had us served, but as we left he raked our money off the counter and threw it after us into the street, screaming, "Take your money and get out!"

At the meeting called to formulate a plan of action we turned down a proposal to parade through the Negro section with signs reading JACK SPRAT SERVES NEGROES FREE OF CHARGE, and still being neophytes, mentally reviewed Shridharani to

discover what our procedure ought to be. We had the facts. The next step: negotiation. Accordingly, we tried to telephone the manager, who hung up on us twice.
Then we wrote him a letter, explaining our position and asking for a conference.
When he did not reply, we wrote a second letter, which also was not answered.
Then we sent four people into the restaurant to try to negotiate on the spot. A different manager was in charge this time; he too refused to talk with us. A few nights
later we sent in another group. This time there was a third person in charge, a
woman, who was somewhat more civil and who explained that they refused service
to Negroes only because they feared the loss of white patrons. The CORE group,
expressing considerably more sympathy with her point of view than a similar
group would today, suggested several ways of proving to her that her fears were
groundless, but she refused to try any of them.

    We wrote the management one more letter, the "ultimatum" of Gandhi's out-
line, saying that if we did not hear from them after seven days, we would regret-
fully be compelled to go into other forms of action. On the eighth day we staged
what I believe to have been the first civil rights sit-in. About twenty-five people,
all pledged to the discipline of non-violence, entered the restaurant at dinnertime
and quietly seated themselves at the counter and in the booths. Several of the
white people were served without question; the Negroes were told that they would
be served only in the basement. After a few minutes the manager realized that
none of the white people had touched their food. They explained that they did not
think it polite to eat until their friends had been served. Growing angry, the manager declared that she would not serve us if we sat there until midnight. Meanwhile, a number of the restaurant's regular patrons had come in, waited for a little
while, and then, finding that no seats were becoming available, had walked out.
Several other customers who had been served before we entered lingered over
their dinners, curious to see the outcome of this novel performance. A girl at the
counter near me caught on to the situation almost immediately, pushed aside her
half-eaten dinner, and spontaneously joined the demonstration.

    The manager, increasingly upset, announced that if the Negroes did not want
to eat in the basement, she would seat them at the two rear booths, where they
would be hidden from view, and have them served very nicely. We declined. Then
she called the police, hoping to have us thrown out on a charge of disorderly conduct, but the two policemen who came in found no sign of disorder at all. In accor-
dance with Gandhi's program, we had telephoned the police captain in advance,
outlined the procedure we intended to follow, and even read him the state's civil
rights law, with which he had apparently been unfamiliar. Consequently, when one
of the officers phoned headquarters at the manager's insistence, he was told that
nothing in the law allowed them to eject us. The police left. A short time later, the
manager had us all served. The test groups sent in during the following weeks were
all served promptly and courteously, without incident.

    When I look back at that first sit-in, I am amazed at our patience and good
faith. We have traveled a great distance since then. No action group today would
prolong the attempts at negotiation for more than a month before finally deciding
to demonstrate. No militant Negro today would dream of trying to persuade a
manager to serve him on the grounds that Negro patronage would not be bad for
business. We have grown too proud for that. But in those days we were childishly

literal-minded. We believed that people meant exactly what they said to us and heard exactly what we said to them. We regarded the sit-in as the successful culmination of a long campaign to reach the heart of the restaurant owner with the truth. What we took to be his conversion was as important to us as the fact that the restaurant had indeed been desegregated. . . .

7. Consumers Boycott Washington, D.C., Department Store, 1945

> Tenth Street Baptist Church
> 10th and R Streets, N.W.
> Washington, D.C.
> Rev. J. L. Henry, A.B., D.D., Pastor
>
> October 19, 1945.

Mr. A. S. Donaldson,
Mgr, Lansburgh Department Store
7th St. Bet. D & E Sts., N.W.,
Washington, D.C.

Dear Mr. Donaldson,

This letter is to protest the discrimination against Negroes at the soda fountain.

The above name Church has a membership of 4,500 on roll, many of whom are customers of your store and have been for a number of years. I regret to say that if the discriminatory policy against Negroes in [*sic*] insisted upon, I will have to advise the membership, of which I am the humble servant, to withdraw their accounts.

Our boys white and black have fought and died together for the cause of Democracy. If that be so, why can't they eat together?

Hoping you will give this matter your early consideration, I am

> Yours for Better Race Relations,
> J. L. Henry

> Wash. D.C.
> Nov. 16 - 1945

Mr. A. S. Donaldson,
420 7th St, N.W.
Wash. D.C.

Sir:

As some of your patrons object to my race drinking at the soda fountain I wish to relieve them of my presence at your counters purchasing merchandise, as I have been for more than thirty years. To do this I am closing the charge account in the name of

> Florence Patterson Clark
> 1532 15 St N.W. 5
>
> 2533 Elvans Road S.E.
> Washington, D.C.
> November 19, 1945

Mr. A. S. Donaldson,
Store Manager
Lansburgh's Department Store

Sir:

I have just been refused service at your soda fountain.

I think it is a disgrace to the United States and a direct show of ingratitude to the men who just died in order to keep this country and its people free from Tyranny.

Just a little while ago, your store had posters urging the sale of War Bonds, now it is Victory Bonds. Evidently you have forgotten why these bonds must be brought [*sic*], just to refresh your memory, it is to insure peace and security for all American citizens who are veterans of the war we have just won.

Would you want the mark on your conscience, that you have denied the right of a sandwich or a piece of pie to a disfigured service man because he happened to be black; then offer the same service to some Japanese or German who has been practicing sabotage against you and your loved ones? There is only one answer to this question, it has to be "NO", or you will be branded as a traitor to America and all that it stands for.

Until the Negro has been offered the right to your soda fountain again, I am withdrawing my patronage and will personally see that any other Negro, I can reach, will withdraw his patronage also.

> Mrs. Beatrice M Short

E S S A Y S

In the first essay Robin D. G. Kelley, professor of history at New York University, discusses the ways in which public transportation became the site of daily contests during and after World War II, as African Americans assumed the right to carve out personal autonomy and equal treatment in public spaces. By implication, Kelley locates the readiness of southern urban black communities for mass direct action in the mid-1950s and 1960s in these earlier expressions of day-to-day resistance. The authors of the second essay, by contrast, locate the site of the wartime fight for civil rights within the workplace, where the progressive politics of organized labor facilitated an aggressive push for civil and economic justice. Historians Robert Korstad of Duke University and Nelson Lichtenstein of the University of Virginia argue that an anti-Communist backlash against the labor movement in the early 1950s weakened the grassroots movement and left in its wake a one-dimensional legal strategy ill equipped to address the full complexity of urban inequality.

Theaters of Resistance

ROBIN D. G. KELLEY

In an address before the Bessemer Kiwanis Club in 1942, Alabama white supremacist leader Horace Wilkinson replayed a conversation he had had in which a Birmingham bus driver pointed to a group of black passengers in the back of the bus and declared, "Right there, mister, is where our next war will break out, and it may start before this one is over." . . . Public spaces were frequently the most embattled sites of black working-class opposition during World War II. . . .

. . . Contrary to the experiences of white workers, for whom public space eventually became a kind of "democratic space" where people of different class backgrounds shared city theaters, public conveyances, streets, and parks, for black people white-dominated public space was vigilantly undemocratic and potentially dangerous. Jim Crow signs, filthy and inoperable public toilets, white police officers, racial epithets, dark bodies standing in the aisles of half-empty busses, were daily visual and aural reminders of the semicolonial status black people occupied in the Jim Crow South. Of course, throughout most of the twentieth century individual African Americans have fought back in an effort to at least ameliorate public accommodations, but their struggles have largely been ignored by historians. While the primary project of civil rights scholarship has been to examine desegregation, the study of black resistance to segregated public space remains one of the least developed areas of inquiry. There are countless studies of well-organized movements with defined goals, spokespersons, and formal organizations behind them, but historians as a whole have not examined in any detail the everyday posing, discursive conflicts, and physical battles that created the conditions for the success of organized, collective movements. . . .

As the wartime economy generated more employment opportunities and rural residents migrated to the city to fill these jobs, the sheer number of people moving to and from work overtaxed an already limited fleet of streetcars and busses. Because public transportation provided limited space that had to be shared—even if racially divided—between blacks and whites, battles over space, as well as the manner in which space was allocated, resulted in intense racial conflict. . . .

In some ways, the design and function of busses and streetcars rendered them unique sites of contestation. An especially apt metaphor for understanding the character of domination and resistance on public transportation might be to view the interior spaces as "moving theaters." Theater can have two meanings: as a site of performance and as a site of military conflict. First, dramas of conflict, repression, and resistance are performed in which passengers witness, or participate in, a wide variety of "skirmishes" that shape their collective memory, illustrate the limitations as well as possibilities of resistance to domination, and draw more passengers into the "performance." The design of streetcars and busses themselves—enclosed spaces with seats facing forward or toward the center aisle—lent a dramaturgical quality to everyday discursive and physical confrontations.

Robin D. G. Kelley, "Congested Terrain: Resistance on Public Transportation," from *Journal of American History,* 80, no. 1, June 1993. Copyright © 1993 by Organization of American Historians. Reprinted with permission.

Theater as a military metaphor is particularly appropriate in light of the fact that all bus drivers and streetcar conductors in Birmingham carried guns and black-jacks, and used them pretty regularly to maintain order. As one Birmingham resident recalls, during the 1940s streetcar conductors "were just like policemans [*sic*]. They carried guns too." African American and some white liberal riders found streetcar conductors and bus drivers to be particularly racist. One leading white progressive noted that "the Klan has picked up a good many members from the street-car and bus operators." And they policed the aisles with a vengeance. Even the mildest act of resistance, from talking too loud to arguing over change, could lead to ejection without a fare refund or, in some cases, arrest. Profanity or physical contest could result in a six-month jail sentence or, in most cases, a substantial fine and court costs.

A transgressive act frequently led to violence, which was surprisingly commonplace on Birmingham's city transit system. In August 1943, for example, when a black woman riding the South East Lake–Ensley line complained to the conductor that he had passed her stop, he followed her out of the streetcar and, in the words of the official report, "knocked her down with handle of gun. No further trouble." Two months later on a North Bessemer streetcar, a black man loaded down with luggage was beaten severely for not moving fast enough for the conductor and for cursing. In the words of the official report, "Operator hit him with his fist and knocked him out of car." Angry but apparently undaunted, the man boarded the car again "and kept talking so operator hit him with [a] black jack." The task of policing public transportation was also taken up by white male *passengers,* many of whom were working-class. There were dozens of incidents in which white men threw African American men and women off the vehicle, slapped black women, or drew guns on black passengers. Rarely were they prosecuted or even charged. . . .

Despite the repressive, police-like atmosphere on public transportation, black passengers still resisted. Over the course of twelve months beginning September 1941, there were at least eighty-eight cases of blacks occupying "white" space on pubic transportation, fifty-five of which were open acts of defiance in which African American passengers either refused to give up their seats or sat in the white section. But this is only part of the story, since the total number of reported incidents and complaints of racial conflict reached 176: including at least 18 interracial fights among passengers, 22 fights between black passengers and operators, and 13 incidents in which black passengers engaged in verbal or physical confrontations over being shortchanged.

What is more striking than the sheer number of incidents is the fact that, in most cases, the racial compartmentalization of existing space was not the primary point of contention. For many black working-class riders, simply getting on the bus was a struggle in and of itself. It was not uncommon, for instance, for half-empty busses or streetcars to pass up African Americans on the pretext that space needed to be reserved in anticipation of additional white riders. . . . Another company policy (the Birmingham Electric Company or BECO owned and operated the public transit system) that had a similar effect was the practice of forcing blacks to pay at the front door and enter through the center doors. On numerous occasions, black passengers paid their fare at the front door but before they had a chance to board the bus drove off. . . .

Public transportation, unlike most forms of public space (e.g., a waiting room or a water fountain) was an extension of the marketplace. Passengers paid for transportation, which if used on a daily basis could add up to a significant portion of the working poor's income. And transportation companies depend on fares for profit (although operators and conductors did not always operate on the basis of economic rationality). . . .

As with the rest of the marketplace, African Americans experienced public transportation as a form of economic exploitation. One source of frustration was the all-too-common cases of black passengers who had been cheated out of their fare or shortchanged. Some unscrupulous drivers and conductors made extra money by returning the wrong change, presuming that black working people could not count. . . .

Unlike in the workplace, where workers entered as disempowered producers dependent on wages for survival and beholden, ostensibly at least, to their superiors, working people entered public transportation as consumers—and with a sense of consumer entitlement. Arguments and fights over being shortchanged were fairly common during the war, and acts of resistance sometimes took on more material than symbolic forms. There were numerous cases in which black passengers in fact refused to pay their fare or attempted to pay only a portion to protest their second-class status. . . .

At the forefront of black resistance were young people who had been radicalized by the war and whose backgrounds ranged from servicemen to zoot suiters, militant female high school students to young household workers. According to an internal report by the Transportation Department of the Birmingham Electric Company, the majority of "racial disturbances" on pubic transportation were "provoked, to a large extent, by younger negroes." It was indeed true that resistance to racist practices on public transportation took place at an especially early age. The evidence suggests that black male children and teenagers not only engaged in verbal and physical confrontations with white authorities, but they tended to direct their attacks on physical property. Groups of black youth spent some summer evenings disengaging trolley cables and escaping into dark Birmingham alley ways, the South Bessemer line being a prime target. One black youth was arrested for throwing rocks at a South East Lake–Ensley streetcar; another was jailed for setting off a "stink bomb" on a Boyles streetcar. Moreover, it wasn't uncommon for black schoolchildren returning home from school to place their hands "in [the] center doors causing [the] signal bell to ring." Some of these forms of behavior could be regarded as playful pranks, but given the repressive, racist atmosphere on the bus and the black youth's sense of alienation and frustration, it is hard to imagine these acts as anything but oppositional. . . .

. . . [B]lack servicemen gained a reputation as militant opponents of Jim Crow. Numerous reports came from Birmingham of black soldiers attempting to move the color boards, sitting or standing in the white section, and fighting with operators as well as white passengers over any act of injustice. In March of 1943, on the Avenue F bus, a black soldier (whom the official report claimed was from New York) refused to move out of the white section, clashed with a knife-wielding white passenger, and was seriously injured. The white passenger was arrested but found not guilty; the black serviceman was taken away by military authorities. A few days later, a black soldier and a female companion boarded the South 15th Street bus late one evening and occupied seats in the white section. When asked to move they complained and then asked for their transfers back. As soon as they stepped off, they began cursing the driver, who then alighted and pulled a gun on them. The solider, who was carrying a "long blade knife," was arrested.

. . . [B]lack men in uniform saw themselves as representing a higher authority and, therefore, felt empowered to act on principle. More importantly, their uniforms signified a clear, active opposition to fascism and Aryan supremacy, which is precisely what African Americans experienced in the South as far as black soldiers were concerned. Occasionally black servicemen tried to turn individual acts of resistance into collective battles, by either drawing other passengers or military personnel into the fray. . . .

. . . [N]ot all of the incidents involving black servicemen could easily translate into demands for collective equity, fairness, and justice. Often the battles were more personal. Issues of personal autonomy, masculinity, dignity, and freedom to transgress the boundaries of accepted behavior—a negation of an assigned "place" as a black "boy" in the Jim Crow South—were the bases for dozens of physical conflicts. . . .

We must not exaggerate the extent to which resistance on busses was initiated by black servicemen. Most of the young men who contested the power of operators to confine blacks to inadequate spaces, who challenged racist remarks and gestures, or who engaged in outrageous acts of rebellion as a means of "testing the limits" of Jim Crow had more in common with the zoot suiters of Los Angeles or Detroit than the upright soldiers who tended to be more acceptable role models. There are clear differences between the two. The soldiers' clothes and style signified an antifascist, pro-democratic message. By contrast, the language and culture of the "hipster" represented a privileging of ethnic identity and masculinity, and a rejection of subservience. . . .

. . . [T]hese young men . . . put on public displays of resistance that left witnesses in awe, though their transgressive acts did not lead directly to improvements in conditions, nor were they intended to. . . . In [one] incident, a black passenger on the Ensley–Fairfield line boarded, moved the color dividers forward to increase space allotted to black passengers, and sat down next to a white man. The operator expelled him, but he reboarded on the return trip and this time "sat between two white men and began to laugh and make a joke about it." He was then moved bodily to the black section, but a few stops later approached the driver with an open knife. Before the police arrived, he jumped out of the window and escaped. When the bus returned later in the evening, he had the audacity to board again. . . .

Nevertheless, . . . the . . . rebel was not always regarded as a hero to other working-class black passengers. Some were embarrassed by his actions; the more sympathetic feared for his life. On the Pratt–Ensley streetcar, for instance, a near altercation took place between the conductor and a black man who had complained loudly of having to board on the "colored side." He was already familiar to the conductor since he had had previous arguments about the color boards. After threatening words were exchanged, the passenger "put hand in pocket and cursed conductor. When he did conductor grabbed his [gun] but did not pull it out of holster, but told the negro if he pulled a knife he was going to kill him." The black passengers, however, told him "to hush before he got killed." A few stops later he decided to disembark.

The large number of incidents involving black women also challenge the myth that most opposition to Birmingham's segregated transit system was waged by black male soldiers. In fact, although the available records are incomplete, it seems that black women outnumbered black men in the number of incidents of resistance on busses and streetcars. Between 1941 and 1942, nearly twice as many black women were arrested as black men, most of them charged with either sitting in the white section or cursing. . . . [B]lack women had a long tradition of militant opposition to Jim Crow public transportation. . . . More significantly, however, black working women in Birmingham generally rode public transportation more often than men. Male industrial workers tended to live in industrial suburbs within walking distance of their place of employment, while the vast majority of black working women were domestics who had to travel to wealthy or middle-class white neighborhoods on the other side of town.

Unlike the popular image of Rosa Parks's quiet resistance, most black women's opposition tended to be profane and militant. In Birmingham, there were dozens of episodes of black women sitting in the white section, arguing with drivers or conductors, and fighting with white passengers, and in most cases the final scene of the "drama" ended with the woman either being ejected, receiving a refund for her fare and leaving of her own accord, moving to the back of the vehicle, or going to jail. Throughout the war, dozens of black women were arrested for merely cursing at the operator or a white passenger. In October of 1943, for example, a teenager named Pauline Carth attempted to board the College Hills line around 8:00 PM. When she was informed that there was no more room for "colored" passengers, she forced her way into the bus anyway, threw her money at the driver, and cursed and spit on him. The driver responded by knocking her out of the bus, throwing her to the ground, and holding her down until police arrived.

Fights between black women and white passengers were also fairly common. In March of 1943, a black woman and a white man boarding the East Lake–West End line apparently got into a shoving match, which angered the black woman to the point where she "cursed him all the way to Woodlawn." When they reached Woodlawn she was arrested, sentenced to thirty days in jail, and forced to pay a $50 fine. On several occasions the violence was worse than simple shoving. One black woman boarded a Lakeview bus and promptly took the closest available seat—next to a white man. The man responded by striking her; blows were exchanged, hers with an umbrella, his including a closed fist upon her jaw. Only the woman was arrested, however. On a North Birmingham bus a fight ensued when a black woman allegedly pushed a white woman out of the way while she was boarding through the front door during a rainstorm. Soaking wet, these two women "went down the aisle . . . fighting with their umbrellas." But the battle did not end there. A white man standing in the aisle who had witnessed the fight walked up to the black woman (who by then had found a seat) and hit her with his own umbrella. She, in turn, "grabbed [his] umbrella and [the] handle came off, and she struck back at man with the part she had. Operator separated them and there was no further trouble." Surprisingly, no one was arrested.

Although black women's actions were no less violent or profane than men's, gender differences did shape black women's resistance. Household workers were in a unique position to contest racist practices on public transportation without significantly transgressing Jim Crow laws or social etiquette. First, company rules permitted domestics traveling with their white employers' children to sit in the section designated for whites. The idea, of course, was to spare white children from having to endure the Negro section. While this was the official policy of the Birmingham Electric Company (owner of the city transit system at the time), drivers and conductors did not always obey it, and a number of employers filed complaints. Nonetheless, the mere existence of the rule enabled black women to challenge the indignity of being forced to move or stand when seats were available.

Second, when employers were willing to intervene on behalf of their domestics, it had the effect of redirecting black protest into legitimate, "acceptable" avenues. Soon after a white employer complained that the Mountain Terrace bus regularly passed "colored maids and cooks" and therefore made them late for work, the company took action. According to the report, "Operators on this line [were] cautioned." Although a few of the reported grievances reflect a genuine concern on the part of white employers for the way domestic workers were treated on the busses and streetcars, most protests were motivated by more utilitarian concerns. Employers complained frequently of vehicles passing their workers, which made them late for work. And when busses continually passed black women late into the night, a few employers grudgingly chose to drive their maids home. . . . [I]t is very possible that black women exaggerated the number of incidents in which public transportation was responsible for tardiness. The unreliability of public transportation provides a plausible excuse for absenteeism, for stealing a few extra hours of sleep, for attending to problems or running errands—all of which were standard resistance strategies, or purely strategies for making ends meet, waged by household workers.

Because most black domestics had to travel alone at night, the fear of being passed or forced to wait for the next vehicle was very real among black women. Standing at a poorly lit, relatively isolated bus stop late at night left them prey to sexual and physical assault by white and black men. . . . Although one might make the argument that open resistance on the busses contradicts the idea that these same women might be afraid in the streets, it misses the crucial point that busses and streetcars, though sites of vicious repression, were occupied, lighted spaces where potential allies and witnesses might be found.

Open black resistance on Birmingham's public transit system conveyed a sense of dramatic opposition to Jim Crow, before an audience, in a powerful way. But discursive strategies, an apparently more evasive form of resistance, carried dramatic appeal as well. No matter how well drivers, conductors, and signs kept bodies separated, black voices could always flow easily into the section designed for whites, serving as a constant reminder that racially divided public space was contested terrain. Black passengers were routinely ejected, and occasionally arrested, for making too much noise, which in many cases turned out to be harsh words directed at a conductor or passenger, or a monologue about racism in general. . . .

Verbal attacks on racism made for excellent theater. Unlike pedestrians passing a street corner preacher, passengers were trapped until they reached their destination.

The official reports reveal a hypersensitivity to black voices from the back of the bus. Indeed, any verbal protest or complaint registered by black passengers was frequently described as "loud"—an adjective almost never used to describe the way white passengers articulated their grievances. One morning in August 1943, during the peak hours, a black man boarded an Acipco bus and immediately began "complaining about discrimination against negroes in a very loud voice." After a failed attempt to have the color boards moved forward, the man "became so loud that operator asked him to leave bus which he did."

Although one could argue that "making noise" was not always a clear-cut act of resistance or protest, even the act of cursing took place in a specific sociohistorical context in which repressive structures and institutions circumscribed black mobility and access to public space. The voices themselves, especially the loud and profane, literally penetrated and occupied white spaces. Moreover, the act of cursing, for which only black passengers were arrested, elicited police intervention, not because the state maintained strict moral standards and would not tolerate profanity but rather because it represented a serious transgression of the racial boundaries. While modern scholars might belittle the power of resistive, profane noise as opposition, Birmingham's entire policing structure did not. Cursing was among the most common crimes for which black passengers were arrested. On the South Bessemer line in 1942, for example, one black man was sentenced to six months in jail for cursing. In most instances, however, cursing was punishable by a $10 fine and court costs, and jail sentences averaged about thirty days. . . .

Some might argue that these hundreds of everyday acts of resistance—from the most evasive to the blatantly confrontational—amounted to very little since they were primarily individual, isolated events which almost always ended in defeat. But such an argument misses the uniquely dramaturgical quality of social intercourse within the interior spaces of public conveyances. Whenever passengers were present, no act of defiance was isolated, nor were acts of defiance isolating experiences. On the contrary, because African American passengers shared a collective memory of how they were treated on a daily basis, both within and without the "moving theaters," an act of resistance or repression sometimes drew other passengers into the fray, thus escalating into collective action, and always impressed itself on other passengers' memories. . . . In some instances, black riders invented collective ways to protest which protected their anonymity. On the College Hills line in August 1943, black riders grew impatient with a particularly racist bus driver who, in the course of a few minutes, twice drew his gun on black passengers, intentionally passed one black woman's stop, and ejected a man who complained on the woman's behalf. According to the report, "the negroes then started ringing bell for the entire block and no one would alight when he stopped."

Resistance to material domination could also take on a collective character, as black passengers attempted to compensate for the daily indignities, losses due to incorrect change, inconveniences caused by passing vehicles, or the many times passengers never reached their destination. When the Airport bus met a large crowd of black and white passengers on their way to work, everything proceeded as normal until someone discovered a way to open the center door, allowing an entire crowd of African-Americans to invade the bus without paying their fare. The back of the bus became so crowded that the startled driver could not get on, "so he asked someone to collect transfers for him. When they refused he made them all alight so that he could collect transfers as they boarded. They refused to board bus the second time." Their collective refusal to reboard the bus was a remarkable show of solidarity, particularly since some of the passengers presumably risked being late for work.

But all oppositional and transgressive acts took place in a context of extreme repression. The occupants sitting in the rear who witnessed or were part of the daily guerrilla skirmishes learned that punishment was inevitable. The arrests, beatings, and ejections were intended as much for the individual transgressor as for all other black passengers on board. The fear of an incident escalating into collective opposition often meant that individuals who intervened in other conflicts received the harshest punishment. On the South Bessemer line early one evening in 1943, a young black man was arrested and fined $25 for coming to the defense of a black woman who was told to move in back of the color dividers. His crime was that he "complained and talked back to the officer." Likewise, the fear of arrest or ejection could persuade individuals who initially joined collective acts of resistance to retreat. Even when a single, dramatic act captured the imaginations of other black passengers and spurred them to take action, there was no guarantee that it would lead to sustained, collective opposition. To take one example, a black woman and man boarded the South East Lake–Ensley line one evening in 1943 and removed the color dividers, prompting all of the black passengers on board and boarding to occupy the white section. When the conductor demanded that they move to their assigned area, all grudgingly complied except the couple who had initiated the rebellion. They were subsequently arrested.

Occasionally specific protests continued long after the incidents that incited them. Sometimes the passengers themselves approached formal civil rights organizations to intercede on their behalf or lead a campaign against the BECO. Following the arrest of Pauline Carth in 1943, a group of witnesses brought the case to the attention of the Birmingham branch of the NAACP, but aside from a perfunctory investigation and an article in the Birmingham *World,* no action was taken. . . . [T]he treatment of African Americans on public transportation was not a high-priority issue for Birmingham's black protest organizations during the war, partly because black middle-class leaders, particularly left-leaning radicals, were more concerned with supporting the war effort, and partly because very few middle-class blacks rode public transportation. Thus working people whose livelihood depended on city transit generally had to fend for themselves.

There are at least three lessons to be learned from examining black working-class resistance on Birmingham's busses and streetcars. First, unorganized, seemingly powerless black passengers made governing public transit more difficult by their acts of transgression. And they brought to the forefront the most hotly contested aspects of Southern regulation of public space. Second, *what* they resisted and the sorts of oppositional practices they adopted serve as a window into the elusive and complex consciousness of African American working people. Sitting with whites, for most black riders, was never a critical issue; rather, African Americans wanted more space for themselves, they wanted to receive equitable treatment, they wanted to be personally treated with respect and dignity, they wanted to be heard and possibly understood, they wanted to get to work on time, and above all, they wanted to exercise power over institutions that controlled them or on which they were dependent.

Finally, the bitter struggles waged by black working people on public transportation, though obviously exacerbated by wartime social, political, and economic transformations, should force us to rethink the meaning of public space as a terrain of class, race, and gender conflict. Although the workplace and struggles to improve working conditions are certainly important, for Southern black workers the most embattled sites of conflict were frequently public spaces. Part of the reason has to do with the fact that policing proved far more difficult in public spaces than in places of work. Not only were employees constantly under the watchful eye of foremen, managers, and employers, but workers could be dismissed, suspended, or have their pay docked on a whim. In the public spaces of the city, the anonymity and sheer numbers of the crowd, whose movement was not directed by the discipline of work (and was therefore unpredictable), required more vigilance and violence to maintain order. Although arrests and beatings were always a possibility, so was escape. Thus, for black workers, public spaces both embodied the most repressive, violent aspects of race and gender oppression and, ironically, afforded more opportunities than the workplace itself to engage in acts of resistance.

Labor and Civil Rights

ROBERT KORSTAD AND NELSON LICHTENSTEIN

. . . The civil rights era began, dramatically and decisively, in the early 1940s when the social structure of black America took on an increasingly urban, proletarian character. A predominantly southern rural and small town population was soon transformed into one of the most urban of all major ethnic groups. More than two million blacks migrated to northern and western industrial areas during the 1940s, while another million moved from farm to city within the South. Northern black voters doubled their numbers between 1940 and 1948, and in the eleven states of the Old South black registration more than quadrupled, reaching over one million by 1952. Likewise, membership in the National Association for the Advancement of Colored People (NAACP) soared, growing from 50,000 in 355 branches in 1940 to almost 450,000 in 1,073 branches six years later.

The half million black workers who joined unions affiliated with the Congress of Industrial Organizations (CIO) were in the vanguard of efforts to transform race relations. The NAACP and the Urban League had become more friendly toward labor in the depression era, but their legal and social work orientation had not prepared them to act effectively in the workplaces and working-class neighborhoods where black Americans fought their most decisive struggles of the late 1930s and

Robert Korstad and Nelson Lichtenstein, "Opportunities Found and Lost: Labor, Radicals, and the Early Civil Rights Movement," *Journal of American History*, 75, no. 3 (December 1988), 786–793, 799–806, 811. Copyright © 1988 Organization of American Historians. Reprinted with permission.

1940s. By the early forties it was commonplace for sympathetic observers to assert the centrality of mass unionization in the civil rights struggle. . . .

This movement gained much of its dynamic character from the relationship that arose between unionized blacks and the federal government. . . . [T]he rise of industrial unions and the evolution of late New Deal labor legislation offered working-class blacks an economic and political standard by which they could legitimate their demands and stimulate a popular struggle. The "one man, one vote" policy implemented in thousands of National Labor Relations Board (NLRB) elections, the industrial "citizenship" that union contracts offered once-marginal elements of the working class, and the patriotic egalitarianism of the government's wartime propaganda—all generated a rights consciousness that gave working-class black militancy a moral justification. . . . During the war the Fair Employment Practices Committee (FEPC) held little direct authority, but . . . it served to expose racist conditions and spur on black activism wherever it undertook its well-publicized investigations. And . . . the mobilization of the black working class in the 1940s [made] civil rights an issue that could not be ignored by union officers, white executives, or government officials.

This essay explores . . . the workplace-oriented civil rights militancy that arose in the 1940s. . . . It analyzes the unionization of predominantly black tobacco workers in Winston-Salem, North Carolina. . . . Similar movements took root among newly organized workers in the cotton compress mills of Memphis, the tobacco factories of Richmond and Charleston, the steel mills of Pittsburgh and Birmingham, the stockyards and farm equipment factories of Chicago and Louisville, and the shipyards of Baltimore and Oakland.

Winston-Salem had been a center of tobacco processing since the 1880s, and the R. J. Reynolds Tobacco Company dominated the life of the city's eighty thousand citizens. By the 1940s whites held most of the highest paying machine-tending jobs, but blacks formed the majority of the work force, concentrated in the preparation departments where they cleaned, stemmed, and conditioned the tobacco. The jobs were physically demanding, the air was hot and dusty, and in departments with machinery, the noise was deafening. Most black workers made only a few cents above minimum wage, and benefits were few. Black women workers experienced frequent verbal and occasional sexual abuse. Reynolds maintained a determined opposition to trade unionism, and two unsuccessful American Federation of Labor (AFL) efforts to organize segregated locals had soured most black workers on trade unionism.

But in 1943 a CIO organizing effort succeeded. Led by the United Cannery, Agricultural, Packing and Allied Workers of America (UCAPAWA), a new union drive championed black dignity and self-organization, employing several young black organizers who had gotten their start in the interracial Southern Tenant Farmers Union. Their discreet two-year organizing campaign made a dramatic breakthrough when black women in one of the stemmeries stopped work on June 17. A severe labor shortage, chronic wage grievances, and a recent speedup gave the women both the resources and the incentive to transform a departmental sit-down into a festive, plant-wide strike. The UCAPAWA quickly signed up about eight thousand black workers, organized a committee to negotiate with the company, and asked the NLRB to hold an election.

The effort to win union recognition at Reynolds sparked a spirited debate about who constituted the legitimate leadership of the black community in Winston-Salem. Midway through the campaign, six local black business and professional men—a college professor, an undertaker, a dentist, a store owner, and two ministers—dubbed "colored leaders" by the *Winston-Salem Journal,* wrote a long letter to the editor urging workers to reject the "followers of John L. Lewis and William Green" and to remain loyal to Reynolds. In the absence of any formal leadership, elected or otherwise, representatives of Winston-Salem's small black middle class had served as spokesmen, brokering with the white elite for small concessions in a tightly segregated society. The fight for collective bargaining, they argued, had to remain secondary to the more important goal of racial betterment, which could only be achieved by "good will, friendly understanding, and mutual respect and co-operation between the races." Partly because of their own vulnerability to economic pressure, such traditional black leaders judged unions, like other institutions, by their ability to deliver jobs and maintain a precarious racial equilibrium.

The union campaign at Reynolds transformed the expectations tobacco workers held of the old community leadership. Reynolds workers responded to calls for moderation from "college-trained people" with indignation. "Our leaders," complained Mable Jessup, "always look clean and refreshed at the end of the hottest day, because they work in very pleasant environments. . . . All I ask of our leaders is that they obtain a job in one of the factories as a laborer and work two weeks. Then write what they think." W. L. Griffin felt betrayed. "I have attended church regularly for the past thirty years," he wrote, "and unity and co-operation have been taught and preached from the pulpits of the various Negro churches. Now that the laboring class of people are about to unite and co-operate on a wholesale scale for the purpose of collective bargaining, these same leaders seem to disagree with that which they have taught their people." Others rejected the influence of people who "have always told us what the white people want, but somehow or other are particularly silent on what we want." "We feel we are the leaders instead of you," asserted a group of union members.

Reynolds, the only major tobacco manufacturer in the country not under a union contract, followed tried and true methods to break the union. Management used lower-level supervisors to intimidate unionists and supported a "no union" movement among white workers. . . . Meanwhile, the white business community organized an Emergency Citizens Committee to help defeat the CIO. In a well-publicized resolution, the committee blamed the recent strikes on "self-seeking representatives of the CIO" and warned that continued subversion of existing race relations would "likely lead to riots and bloodshed."

In earlier times, this combination of anti-union forces would probably have derailed the organizing effort. But during World War II, black workers had allies who helped shift the balance of power. The NLRB closely supervised each stage of the election process and denied the company's request to divide the work force into two bargaining units, which would have weakened the position of black workers. When local judges sought to delay the election, government attorneys removed the case to federal court. In December 1943 an NLRB election gave the CIO a resounding victory. But continued federal assistance, from the United States Conciliation Service and the National War Labor Board, was still needed to secure Reynolds workers a union contract in 1944.

That first agreement resembled hundreds of other wartime labor-management contracts, but in the context of Winston-Salem's traditional system of race relations it had radical implications, because it generated a new set of shop floor rights embodied in the seniority, grievance, and wage adjustment procedures. The contract did not attack factory segregation—for the most part white workers continued to control the better-paying jobs—but it did call forth a new corps of black leaders to defend the rights Reynolds workers had recently won. The one hundred or so elected shop stewards were the "most important people in the plant," remembered union activist Velma Hopkins. They were the "natural leaders," people who had "taken up money for flowers if someone died or would talk to the foreman [even] before the union." . . . The shop stewards transformed the traditional paternalism of Reynolds management into an explicit system of benefits and responsibilities. They made the collective bargaining agreement a bill of rights.

The growing self-confidence of black women, who constituted roughly half of the total work force, proved particularly subversive of existing social relations. To the white men who ran the Reynolds plants, nothing could have been more disturbing than the demand that they negotiate on a basis of equality with people whom they regarded as deeply inferior—by virtue of their sex as well as their class and race. . . .

By the summer of 1944, Local 22 of the reorganized and renamed Food, Tobacco, Agricultural and Allied Workers (FTA) had become the center of an alternative social world that linked black workers together regardless of job, neighborhood, or church affiliation. The union hall, only a few blocks from the Reynolds Building, housed a constant round of meetings, plays, and musical entertainments, as well as classes in labor history, black history, and current events. Local 22 sponsored softball teams, checker tournaments, sewing circles, and swimming clubs. Its vigorous educational program and well-stocked library introduced many black workers (and a few whites) to a larger radical culture few had glimpsed before. "You know, at that little library they [the city of Winston-Salem] had for us, you couldn't find any books on Negro history," remembered Viola Brown. "They didn't have books by Aptheker, Dubois, or Frederick Douglass. But we had them at *our* library."

The Communist party was the key political grouping in FTA and in Local 22. . . . By 1947 party organizers had recruited about 150 Winston-Salem blacks, almost all tobacco workers. Most of these workers saw the party as both a militant civil rights organization, which in the 1930s had defended such black victims of white southern racism as the Scottsboro boys and Angelo Hearndon, and as a cosmopolitan group, introducing members to the larger world of politics and ideas. The white North Carolina Communist leader Junius Scales recalled that the "top leaders [of Local 22] . . . just soaked up all the educational efforts that were directed at them. The Party's program had an explanation of events locally, nationally, and worldwide which substantiated everything they had felt instinctively. . . . It really meant business on racism." The party was an integrated institution in which the social conventions of the segregated South were self-consciously violated, but it also accommodated itself to the culture of the black community. In Winston-Salem, therefore, the party met regularly in a black church and started the meetings with a hymn and a prayer.

The Communist party's relative success in Winston-Salem was replicated in other black industrial districts. In the South a clear majority of the party's new recruits were black, and in northern states like Illinois and Michigan the proportion ranged from 25 to 40 percent. . . . [U]nlike the NAACP, which directed much of its energy toward the courts and Congress, the Communists or their front groups more often organized around social or political issues subject to locally initiated protests, petitions, and pickets. Moreover, the party adopted what today would be called an affirmative action policy that recognized the special disabilities under which black workers functioned, in the party as well as in the larger community. Although there were elements of tokenism and manipulation in the implementation of that policy, the party's unique effort to develop black leaders gave the Communists a special standing among politically active blacks.

Tobacco industry trade unionism revitalized black political activism in Winston-Salem. Until the coming of the CIO, NAACP attacks on racial discrimination seemed radical, and few blacks risked associating with the organization. A 1942 membership drive did increase branch size from 11 to 100, but most new members came from the traditional black middle class: mainly teachers and municipal bus drivers. The Winston-Salem NAACP became a mass organization only after Local 22 conducted its own campaign for the city branch. As tobacco workers poured in the local NAACP reached a membership of 1,991 by 1946, making it the largest unit in North Carolina.

Unionists also attacked the policies that had disenfranchised Winston-Salem blacks for more than two generations. As part of the CIO Political Action Committee's voter registration and mobilization drive, Local 22 inaugurated citizenship classes, political rallies, and citywide mass meetings. Union activists challenged the power of registrars to judge the qualifications of black applicants and insisted that black veterans vote without further tests. The activists encouraged the city's blacks to participate in electoral politics. "Politics IS food, clothes, and housing," declared the committee that registered some seven hundred new black voters in the months before the 1944 elections. After a visit to Winston-Salem in 1944, a *Pittsburgh Courier* correspondent wrote, ". . . One cannot visit Winston-Salem and mingle with the thousands of workers without sensing a revolution in thought and action. If there is a 'New' Negro, he is to be found in the ranks of the labor movement." . . .

By the mid-1940s, civil rights issues had reached a level of national political salience that they would not regain for another fifteen years. . . .

In the South the labor movement seemed on the verge of a major breakthrough. *Fortune* magazine predicted that the CIO's "Operation Dixie" would soon organize key southern industries like textiles. Black workers proved exceptionally responsive to such union campaigns, especially in industries like lumber, furniture, and tobacco, where they were sometimes a majority of the work force. Between 1944 and 1946 the CIO's political action apparatus helped elect liberal congressmen and senators in a few southern states, while organizations that promoted interracial cooperation, such as the Southern Conference for Human Welfare and Highlander Folk School, experienced their most rapid growth and greatest effectiveness in 1946 and 1947.

The opportune moment soon passed. Thereafter, a decade-long decline in working-class black activism destroyed the organizational coherence and ideological elan of the labor-based civil rights movement. That defeat has been largely obscured by the brilliant legal victories won by civil rights lawyers in the 1940s and 1950s, and by the reemergence of a new mass movement in the next decade. But in Winston-Salem . . . and other industrial regions, the time had passed when unionized black labor was in the vanguard of the freedom struggle. Three elements contributed to the decline. First, the employer offensive of the late 1940s put all labor on the defensive. Conservatives used the Communist issue to attack New Deal and Fair Deal reforms, a strategy that isolated Communist-oriented black leaders and helped destroy what was left of the Popular Front. The employers' campaign proved particularly effective against many recently organized CIO locals with disproportionate numbers of black members. Meanwhile, mechanization and decentralization of the most labor intensive and heavily black production facilities sapped the self-confidence of the black working class and contributed to high rates of urban unemployment in the years after the Korean War.

Second, the most characteristic institutions of American liberalism, including the unions, race advancement organizations, and liberal advocacy organizations, adopted a legal-administrative, if not a bureaucratic, approach to winning citizenship rights for blacks. . . .

Finally, the routinization of the postwar industrial relations system precluded efforts by black workers to mobilize a constituency independent of the leadership. Focusing on incremental collective bargaining gains and committed to social change only if it was well controlled, the big unions became less responsive to the particular interests of their black members. By 1960 blacks had formed oppositional movements in several old CIO unions, but they now encountered resistance to their demands not only from much of the white rank and file but also from union leaders who presided over institutions that had accommodated themselves to much of the industrial status quo.

Like most labor intensive southern employers, R. J. Reynolds never reached an accommodation with union labor, although it signed contracts with Local 22 in 1945 and 1946. Minimum wage laws and collective bargaining agreements had greatly increased costs of production, especially in the stemmeries, and the black women employed there were the heart and soul of the union. Soon after the war, the company began a mechanization campaign that eliminated several predominantly black departments. When the factories closed for Christmas in 1945 new stemming machines installed in one plant displaced over seven hundred black women. The union proposed a "share the work plan," but the company was determined to cut its work force and change its racial composition by recruiting white workers from surrounding counties. The black proportion of the manufacturing labor force in Winston-Salem dropped form 44 to 36 percent between 1940 and 1960.

The technological offensive undermined union strength, but by itself Reynolds could not destroy Local 22. When contract negotiations began in 1947, the company rejected union demands for a wage increase patterned after those won in steel, auto, and rubber earlier in the spring. Somewhat reluctantly, Local 22 called a strike on May 1. Black workers and virtually all of the Negro community solidly backed the union, which held out for thirty-eight days until a compromise settlement was reached. But, in a pattern replicated throughout industrial America in those years, Communist influence within the union became the key issue around which management and its allies mounted their attack. The *Winston-Salem Journal* soon denounced Local 22 as "captured . . . lock, stock and barrel" by the Communist party, warning readers that the strike would lead to "open rioting." This exposé brought Local 22 officers under the scrutiny of the House Committee on Un-American Activities (HUAC), which held a highly publicized hearing on the Winston-Salem situation in the summer of 1947.

Communist party members contributed to the volatility of the situation. . . . The party's insistence on the promotion of blacks into public leadership positions sometimes put workers with little formal education into union leadership jobs they could not handle. Moreover, the party's obsession with "white chauvinism" backfired. After the 1947 strike, Local 22 made a concerted effort to recruit white workers. Some young veterans joined the local, although the union allowed most to pay their dues secretly. The party objected, remembered North Carolina leader Junius Scales, "'If they got any guts,' they would say, 'let them stand up and fight,' not realizing, as many black workers and union leaders realized, that for a white worker to just *belong* to a predominantly black union at that time was an act of great courage."

With its work force increasingly polarized along racial and political lines, Reynolds renewed its offensive in the spring of 1948. Black workers remained remarkably loyal to the union leadership, but the anticommunist campaign had turned most white employees against the union and eroded support among blacks not directly involved in the conflict. The company refused to negotiate with Local 22 on the grounds that the union had not complied with the new Taft-Hartley Act. The law required union officers to sign an affidavit swearing they were not members of the Communist party before a union could be certified as a bargaining agent by the NLRB. Initially, all the CIO internationals had refused to sign the affidavits, but by 1948 only Communist-oriented unions such as FTA still held out. When Reynolds proved intransigent, there was little the union could do. FTA had no standing with the NLRB, and it was too weak to win another strike. . . .

Local 22 disappeared from Winston-Salem's political and economic life, and a far more accommodative black community leadership filled the void left by the union's defeat. Beginning in the mid-1940s, a coalition of middle-class blacks and white business moderates had sought to counter the growing union influence within the black community. They requested a study of local race relations by the National Urban League's Community Relations Project (CRP). Largely financed by Hanes Hosiery president James G. Hanes, the CRP study appeared in late 1947 and called for improved health, education and recreational facilities, but it made no mention of workplace issues. The Urban League foresaw a cautious, "step by step approach" and proposed that an advisory committee drawn from the black middle class discuss community issues with their white counterparts and help city officials and white philanthropists channel welfare services to the black community. . . .

The Urban League's program helped make Winston-Salem a model of racial moderation. Blacks continued to register and vote in relatively high numbers and elect a single black alderman. The city high school was integrated without incident in 1957, while Winston-Salem desegregated its libraries, golf course, coliseum, and the police and fire departments. But the dynamic and democratic quality of the black struggle in Winston-Salem would never be recaptured. NAACP membership declined to less than five hundred in the early 1950s, and decision making once again moved behind closed doors. When a grievance arose from the black community, a group of ministers met quietly with Hanes; a few phone calls by the white industrialist led to desegregation of the privately owned bus company in 1958.

A similar story unfolded in the plants of the R. J. Reynolds Tobacco Company. After the destruction of Local 22, the company blacklisted several leading union activists, yet Reynolds continued to abide by many of the wage standards, benefit provisions, and seniority policies negotiated during the union era. The company reorganized its personnel department; rationalized procedures for hiring, firing, and evaluating employees; and upgraded its supervisory force by weeding out old-timers and replacing them with college-educated foremen. To forestall union activity, Reynolds kept its wages slightly ahead of the rates paid by its unionized competitors.

In February 1960, when sit-ins began at segregated Winston-Salem lunch counters, the voices of black protest were again heard in the city's streets. But the generation of blacks who had sustained Local 22 played little role in the new mobilization. College and high school students predominated on the picket lines and in the new protest organizations that confronted white paternalism and challenged the black community's ministerial leadership. NAACP membership rose once again; more radical blacks organized a chapter of the Congress of Racial Equality (CORE). Public segregation soon collapsed.

The subsequent trajectory of the freedom struggle in Winston-Salem was typical of that in many black communities. Heightened racial tensions set the stage for a 1967 riot and a burst of radicalism, followed by the demobilization of the protest movement and years of trench warfare in the city council. The political career of Larry Little, the son of Reynolds workers who had been members of Local 22, highlighted the contrasts between the two generations of black activists. Little moved from leadership of the North Carolina Black Panther party in 1969 to city alderman in 1977, but despite the radicalism of his rhetoric, crucial issues of economic security and workplace democracy were not restored to the political agenda in Winston-Salem. Because black activists of his generation confronted the city's white elite without the organized backing of a lively, mass institution like Local 22, their challenge proved more episodic and less effective than that of the previous generation.

. . . For the black freedom struggle the mid-1940s offered such a time of opportunity, when a high-wage, high-employment economy, rapid unionization, and a pervasive federal presence gave the black working class remarkable self-confidence, which established the framework for the growth of an autonomous labor-oriented civil rights movement. The narrowing of public discourse in the early Cold War era contributed largely to the defeat and diffusion of that movement. The rise of anti-communism shattered the Popular Front coalition on civil rights, while the retreat and containment of the union movement deprived black activists of the political and social space necessary to carry on an independent struggle.

The disintegration of the black movement in the late 1940s ensured that when the civil rights struggle of the 1960s emerged it would have a different social character and an alternative political agenda, which eventually proved inadequate to the immense social problems that lay before it. . . . In retrospect, we can see how greatly [movement activists] were handicapped by their inability to seize the opportunities a very different sort of civil rights movement found and lost twenty years before.

FURTHER READING

Rod Bush, *We Are Not What We Seem: Black Nationalism and Class Struggle in the American Century* (1999).

Richard Dalfiume, "The 'Forgotten Years' of the Negro Revolution," *Journal of American History*, 55, no. 1 (1968), 90–106.

John Egerton, *Speak Now Against the Day: The Generation Before the Civil Rights Movement in the South* (1995).

Herbert Garfinkel, *When Negroes March: The March on Washington Movement in the Organizational Politics for FEPC* (1959).

Joanne Grant, *Ella Baker: Freedom Bound* (1998).

Joseph Harris, *African-American Reactions to War in Ethiopia, 1936–1941* (1994).

Darlene Clark Hine, *Black Victory: The Rise and Fall of the White Primary in Texas* (1979).

Darlene Clark Hine, "The Housewives' League of Detroit: Black Women and Economic Nationalism," in *Visible Women: New Essays on American Activism,* ed. Nancy A. Hewitt and Suzanne Lebsock (1993).

Robin D. G. Kelley, "The Riddle of the Zoot: Malcolm Little and Black Cultural Politics During World War II," in *Malcolm X: In Our Own Image,* ed. Joe Wood (1992), 155–182.

Steven Lawson, *Black Ballots: Voting Rights in the South, 1944–1969* (1975).

Genna Rae McNeil, *Groundwork: Charles Hamilton Houston and the Struggle for Civil Rights* (1983).

August Meier and Elliott Rudwick, *Core: A Study in the Civil Rights Movement, 1942–1968* (1973).

Jesse Thomas Moore, Jr., *A Search for Equality: The National Urban League 1910–1961* (1981).

Aldon Morris, *The Origins of the Civil Rights Movement: Black Communities Organizing for Change* (1984).

Brenda Gayle Plummer, *Rising Wind: Black Americans and U.S. Foreign Affairs, 1935–1960* (1996).

Merl Elwyn Reed, *Seedtime for the Modern Civil Rights Movement: The President's Committee on Fair Employment Practice, 1941–1946* (1991).

William R. Scott, *The Sons of Sheba's Race: African-Americans and the Italo-Ethiopian War, 1935–1941* (1993).

Patricia Sullivan, *Days of Hope: Race and Democracy in the New Deal Era* (1996).

Rosalyn Terborg-Penn, "African-American Women's Networks in the Anti-Lynching Crusade," in *Gender, Class, Race, and Reform in the Progressive Era,* ed. Noralee Frankel and Nancy S. Dye (1991).

Mark V. Tushnet, *The NAACP's Legal Strategy Against Segregated Education, 1925–1950* (1987).

Nan Elizabeth Woodruff, "African-American Struggles for Citizenship in the Arkansas and Mississippi Deltas in the Age of Jim Crow," *Radical History Review,* 55 (1993), 33–51.

CHAPTER

9

The Civil Rights Movement

By the mid-1950s, African Americans in the South and elsewhere had a long-standing tradition of protest. What changed was the intensity and, to some degree, the certainty with which they believed change to be imminent. The FBI estimated that 40 percent of the total African-American population participated in a civil rights demonstration at some time in 1963, a year when there were more than fifteen hundred demonstrations in thirty-eight states.

How do we understand the coming together of people across the South and across the country in daily, organized, mass, public protest? What conditions made this possible—in the state and in individual people's lives? What sustained people and communities throughout the ordeals of violence, retribution, and disillusionment? How were leaders made, determined, and redefined in the midst of social change?

 D O C U M E N T S

When Rosa Parks was arrested on December 1, 1955, for refusing to give up her seat and move to the back of a bus in Montgomery, Alabama, African Americans in that city began a bus boycott that lasted for over a year. The boycott struck many observers at the time and some scholars since as a "spontaneous" reaction. In reality, however, a number of people and organizations, most notably the Women's Political Council (WPC), had been carefully laying plans for such a boycott for more than a year, as is suggested in the first document, a letter from WPC president Jo Ann Robinson to the mayor of Montgomery. It is worth noting that Robinson was writing this letter just four days after the Supreme Court's *Brown v. Board of Education* decision. On September 23, 1957, three black boys and six black girls entered the previously all-white Little Rock Central High School under police escort. Two days later they returned under the protection of troops from the 101st Airborne Division. Melba Pattillo [Beals] was fifteen years old; in the second document she describes a junior year of high school filled with terror but also hope. In the third document sharecropper Fannie Lou Hamer tells an interviewer about her first attempts to register to vote. Hamer later played a central role in the organization of the Mississippi Freedom Democratic Party.

Mass mobilizations involved wide segments of black communities. One of the most controversial strategies was the use of young people in highly violent situations such as existed in Birmingham, Alabama, in 1963, when police used dogs and fire hoses to repel demonstrators. In the fourth document James Bevel, a Southern Christian

Leadership Conference (SCLC) organizer, explains the use of this strategy. In jail for his participation in the Birmingham demonstrations, the Reverend Martin Luther King, Jr., responded to white clergymen who condemned SCLC's direct-action tactics and his participation as a Christian minister. In the fifth document he discusses the nature of morality in a segregated society.

Although much of the old-line civil rights strategy relied on the federal government to serve as both advocate and defender, many activists—particularly younger activists—began to develop doubts about the federal government's commitment to their cause. John Lewis, chair of the Student Nonviolent Coordinating Committee (SNCC), attempted to give voice to this doubt in a defiant speech at the March on Washington on August 28, 1963. The sixth document is from the original text of Lewis's speech, before it was toned down for delivery under pressure from other civil rights leaders.

Change was incremental and often came at great cost, but all across the South black communities began to measure their accomplishments. In 1964, Avon W. Rollins, a SNCC field secretary in Danville, Virginia, prepared a report on the tangible achievements in that city. The seventh document is a listing of those achievements. Increasingly, however, nonviolent protest was being questioned or seen as only one of a variety of acceptable tactics. In 1963, speaking before an audience in Detroit, Michigan, Malcolm X addressed what he saw as the shortcomings in both the goals and the tactics of a nonviolent civil rights movement. The eighth document is an excerpt from his speech.

The final document requires us to think about the exclusions within the civil rights movement and within African-American historical memory. In it Bayard Rustin, who played a central role in Martin Luther King, Jr.'s emergence as a national leader and in the adoption of Gandhian techniques by the southern civil rights movement, announces his resignation from King's staff under pressure from New York congressman Adam Clayton Powell. Rustin planned to hold massive demonstrations at the 1960 Democratic Party Convention, which Powell opposed. He theatened to make a public issue of Rustin's homosexuality. In 1963 Rustin returned to the center of the civil rights leadership when he became one of the principal architects of the March on Washington, but his civil rights work was always constrained by what many civil rights leaders saw as the perils of association with him due to the stigma of his sexuality.

1. Jo Ann Robinson, Women's Political Council President, Hints of a Bus Boycott in Montgomery, Alabama, 1954

Harriet St.
Montgomery, Ala.
May 21, 1954

Honorable Mayor W. A. Gayle
City Hall
Montgomery, Alabama

Dear Sir:

The Women's Political Council is very grateful to you and the City Commissioners for the hearing you allowed our representatives during the month of March, 1954, when the "city-bus-fare-increase case" was being reviewed.

There were several things the Council asked for:

1. A city law that would make it possible for Negroes to sit from back toward front, and whites from front toward back until all the seats are taken.
2. That Negroes not be asked or forced to pay fare at front and go to the rear of the bus to enter.
3. That busses stop at every corner in residential sections occupied by Negroes as they do in communities where whites reside.

We are happy to report that busses have begun stopping at more corners now in some sections where Negroes live than previously. However, the same practices in seating and boarding the bus continue.

Mayor Gayle, three-fourths of the riders of these public conveyances are Negroes. If Negroes did not patronize them, they could not possibly operate.

More and more of our people are already arranging with neighbors and friends to ride to keep from being insulted and humiliated by bus drivers.

There has been talk from twenty-five or more local organizations of planning a city-wide boycott of busses. We, sir, do not feel that forceful measures are necessary in bargaining for a convenience which is right for all bus passengers. We, the Council, believe that when this matter has been put before you and the Commissioners, that agreeable terms can be met in a quiet and unostensible manner to the satisfaction of all concerned.

Many of our Southern cities in neighboring states have practiced the policies we seek without incident whatsoever. Atlanta, Macon and Savannah in Georgia have done this for years. Even Mobile, in our own state, does this and all the passengers are satisfied.

Please consider this plan, and if possible, act favorably upon it, for even now plans are being made to ride less, or not at all, on our busses. We do not want this.

Respectfully yours,

The Women's Political Council

Jo Ann Robinson, President

2. Melba Pattillo Beals Recalls Her First Days at Little Rock Central High School, 1957

The first day [September 23] I was able to enter Central High School, what I felt inside was terrible, wrenching, awful fear. On the car radio I could hear that there was a mob. I knew what a mob meant and I knew that the sounds that came from the crowd were very angry. So we entered the side of the building, very, very fast. Even as we entered there were people running after us, people tripping other people. Once we got into the school, it was very dark; it was like a deep, dark castle. And

Henry Hampton and Steve Fayer, with Sarah Flynn, *Voices of Freedom: An Oral History of the Civil Rights Movement from the 1950s Through the 1980s* (New York: Bantam Books, 1990), 45–46, 48–49. Used by permission of Bantam Books, a division of Random House, Inc.

my eyesight had to adjust to the fact that there were people all around me. We were met by school officials and very quickly dispersed our separate ways. There has never been in my life any stark terror or any fear akin to that.

I'd only been in the school a couple of hours and by that time it was apparent that the mob was just overrunning the school. Policemen were throwing down their badges and the mob was getting past the wooden sawhorses because the police would no longer fight their own in order to protect us. So we were all called into the principal's office, and there was great fear that we would not get out of this building. We were trapped. And I thought, Okay, so I'm going to die here, in school. And I remember thinking back to what I'd been told, to understand the realities of where you are and pray. Even the adults, the school officials, were panicked, feeling like there was no protection. A couple of kids, the black kids, that were with me were crying, and someone made a suggestion that if they allowed the mob to hang one kid, they could then get the rest out. And a gentleman, who I believed to be the police chief, said "Unh-uh, how are you going to choose? You're going to let them draw straws?" He said, "I'll get them out." And we were taken to the basement of this place. And we were put into two cars, grayish blue Fords. And the man instructed the drivers, he said, "Once you start driving, do not stop." And he told us to put our heads down. This guy revved up his engine and he came up out of the bowels of this building, and as he came up, I could just see hands reaching across this car, I could hear the yelling, I could see guns, and he was told not to stop. "If you hit somebody, you keep rolling, 'cause the kids are dead." And he did just that, and he didn't hit anybody, but he certainly was forceful and aggressive in the way he exited this driveway, because people tried to stop him and he didn't stop. He dropped me off at home. And I remember saying, "Thank you for the ride," and I should've said, "Thank you for my life." . . .

[September 25] I went in not through the side doors, but up the front stairs, and there was a feeling of pride and hope that yes, this is the United States; yes, there is a reason I salute the flag; and it's going to be okay.

The troops were wonderful. There was some fear that they were dating the girls in high school, but I don't care what they were doing: they were wonderful, they were disciplined, they were attentive, they were caring. They didn't baby us, but they were there. So for the first time I began to feel like there is this slight buffer zone between me and this hell on the other side of this wall. They couldn't be with us everywhere. They couldn't be with us, for example, in the ladies' bathroom, they couldn't be with us in gym. We'd be showering in gym and someone would turn your shower into scalding. You'd be walking out to the volleyball court and someone would break a bottle and trip you on the bottle. I have scars on my right knee from that. After a while, I started saying to myself, Am I less than human? Why did they do this to me? What's wrong with me? And so you go through stages even as a child. First you're in pain, then you're angry, then you try to fight back, and then you just don't care. You just, you can't care; you hope you do die. You hope that there's an end. And then you just mellow out and you just realize that survival is day to day and you start to grasp your own spirit, you start to grasp the depth of the human spirit and you start to understand your own ability to cope no matter what. That is the greatest lesson I learned.

3. Fannie Lou Hamer's Initiation into the Civil Rights Movement, 1962

Well, we were living on a plantation about four and a half miles east of here. . . . Pap had been out there thirty years, and I had been out there eighteen years, 'cause we had been married at that time eighteen years. And you know, things were just rough. . . . I don't think that I ever remember working for as much as four dollars a day. Yes, one year I remember working for four dollars a day, and I was gettin' as much as the men, 'cause I kept up with the time. . . . But anyway, I just knowed things wasn't right.

So then that was in 1962 when the civil rights workers came into this county. Now, I didn't know anything about voter registration or nothin' like that, 'cause people had never been told that they could register to vote. And livin' out in the country, if you had a little radio, by the time you got in at night, you'd be too tired to listen at what was goin' on. . . . So they had a rally. I had gone to church that Sunday, and the minister announced that they were gon' have a mass meeting that Monday night. Well, I didn't know what a mass meeting was, and I was just curious to go to a mass meeting. So I did . . . and they was talkin' about how blacks had a right to register and how they had a right to *vote*. . . . Just listenin' at 'em, I could just see myself votin' people outa office that I know was wrong and didn't do nothin' to help the poor. I said, you know, that's sumpin' I really wanna be involved in, and finally at the end of that rally, I had made up my mind that I was gonna come out there when they said you could go down that Friday to try to register.

She remembers the date precisely: August 31, 1962. She and seventeen others climbed aboard an old bus owned by a black man from neighboring Bolivar County. SNCC had chartered it for the thirty-mile ride to the county seat in Indianola. Once there, she was the first into the registrar's office.

. . . He brought a big old book out there, and he gave me the sixteenth section of the Constitution of Mississippi, and that was dealing with de facto laws, and I didn't know nothin' about no de facto laws, didn't know nothin' about any of 'em. I could copy it like it was in the book . . . but after I got through copying it, he told me to give a reasonable interpretation and tell the meaning of that section that I had copied. Well, I flunked out. . . .

So then we started back to Ruleville and on our way back to Ruleville, this same highway patrolman that I had seen steady cruisin' around this bus stopped us. We had crossed that bridge, coming over from Indianola. They got out the cars, flagged the bus down. When they flagged the bus down, they told all of us to get off the bus. So at this time, we just started singing "Have a Little Talk with Jesus," and we got off the bus, and all they wanted then was for us to get back on the bus. They arrested Bob [Moses] and told the bus driver he was under arrest. So we went back then to Indianola. The bus driver was fined one hundred dollars for driving a bus with too much yellow in it. Now ain't that ridiculous?

For what?

Howell Raines, *My Soul Is Rested: Movement Days in the Deep South Remembered* (1977; reprint, New York: Penguin Books, 1983), 249–252. Copyright © 1977 Howell Raines. Used by permission of Putnam Berkley, a division of Penguin Putnam, Inc.

Too much yellow. Said the bus looked too much like a school bus. That's funny, but it's the truth. But you see, it was to frighten us to death. This same bus had been used year after year hauling cotton choppers and cotton pickers to Florida to try to make a livin' that winter, and he had never been arrested before. But the day he tried . . . to carry us to Indianola, they fined him a hundred dollars, and I guess it was so ridiculous that they finally cut the fine down to thirty dollars, and all of us *together*—not one, but all us together—had enough to pay the fine. So we paid the fine, and then we got back on the bus and come on to Ruleville.

So Rev. Jeff Summers, who live on Charles Street, just the next street over, he carried me out there on the Marlowe Plantation where I had worked for eighteen years. And when I got out there, my little girl—she's dead now, Dorothy—she met me and one of Pap's cousins, and said that man [who owned the plantation] had been raising a lot of Cain ever since we left, that he had been in the field more times than he usually come a day, because I had gone to the courthouse. See, the people at the courthouse would call and tell it. So they was kinda scared, and quite natural I began to feel nervous, but I knowed I hadn't done nothin' wrong. So after my little girl told me, wasn't too long 'fore Pap got off, and he was tellin' me the same thing that the other kids had told me.

I went on in the house, and I sat down on a little old bed that belonged to the little girl, and when I sat down on the bed, this man [who owned the plantation] he come up and he asked Pap, "Did you tell Fannie Lou what I said?" And Pap said, "Yessir, I sho' did." And I got up and walked to the door, and then he asked me, "Did Pap tell you what I said?" I said, "He told me." And he said, "I mean that. You'll have to go back to Indianola and withdraw, or you have to leave this place." So I said, "Mr. Dee, I didn't go down there to register for you. I went down there to register for myself." And that made him madder, you know.

So he told me, "I want your answer now, yea or nay." And he said, "They gon'"—now, I don't know who the *they* were, whether it was the white Citizens Council or the Ku Klux Klan, 'cause I don't think one is no worse than the other—"they gon' worry me tonight. They gon' worry the hell outa me, and I'm gon' worry hell outa you. You got 'til in the mornin' to tell me. But if you don't go back there and withdraw, you got to leave the plantation."

So I knowed I wasn't goin' back to withdraw, so wasn't nothin' for me to do but leave the plantation. So Pap brought me out that same night and I come to Mrs. Tucker's, a lady live over on Byron Street. I went to her house, and I stayed, and Pap began to feel nervous when he went to the shop and saw some buckshot shells. And they don't have buckshot shells to *play* with in August and September, because you ain't huntin' or nothin' like that.

> On September tenth—again she recalls the date precisely—came the nightrider attack described by Charles Cobb. The riders shot into the McDonald home, where the SNCC workers were staying, and into the Tucker home, where Mrs. Hamer had been given shelter. "They shot in that house sixteen times, tryin' to kill me," she remembers. She fled to the home of a niece in Tallahatchie County when the nighttime terrorism continued on into the fall.

I stayed away, 'cause things then—you could see 'em at night. They would have fires in the middle of the road. . . . You wouldn't see no Klan signs, but just make a fire in the middle of the road. And it was *so dangerous,* I stayed in Talla-hatchie County all of September and then October, and then November I come back to Ruleville. I was comin', I didn't know why I was comin', but I was just sick of runnin' and hadn't done nothin'. . . . I started tryin' to find a place to stay, 'cause we didn't have nothin'.

> *The woman who had been her sixth-grade school teacher put her in touch with a black woman who had a three-room house for rent "for eighteen dollars a month and that was a lotta money." She and her family moved in on December 3.*

That was on a Sunday, and that Monday, the fourth of December, I went back to Indianola to the circuit clerk's office and I told him who I was and I was there to take that literacy test again.

I said, "Now, you cain't have me fired 'cause I'm already fired, and I won't have to move now, because I'm not livin' in no white man's house." I said, "I'll be here every thirty days until I become a registered voter." 'Cause that's what you would have to do: go every thirty days and see had you passed the literacy test. . . . I went back then the tenth of January in 1963, and I had become registered. . . .

4. James Bevel, an SCLC Organizer, Mobilizes Birmingham's Young People, 1963

Up to this point, about five to ten, maybe twelve people would go and demonstrate each day. My position was you can't get the dialogues you need with a few. So the strategy was, Okay, let's use *thousands* of people who won't create an economic crisis because they're off the job: *the high school students.* Besides, most adults have bills to pay, house notes, rents, car notes, utility bills, but the young people— wherein they can think at the same level—are not hooked with all those responsi-bilities. A boy from high school, he can get the same effect in terms of being in jail, in terms of putting the pressure on the city, as his father—and yet there is no eco-nomic threat on the family because the father is still on the job.

We started organizing the prom queens of the high schools, the basketball stars, the football stars, to get the influence and power leaders involved. They in turn got all the other students involved. The black community as a whole did not have that kind of cohesion or camaraderie. But the students, they had a community they'd been in since elementary school, so they had bonded quite well. So if one would go to jail, that had a direct effect upon another because they were classmates.

We held workshops to help them overcome the crippling fears of dogs, and jails, and to help them start thinking through problems on their feet. We also showed the "NBC White Paper" [a network television documentary] about the Nashville sit-ins in all of the schools. Our approach to the students was that you are responsible for segregation, you and your parents, because you have not stood up. In other words, according to the Bible and the Constitution, no one has the power

Henry Hampton and Steve Fayer, with Sarah Flynn, *Voices of Freedom: An Oral History of the Civil Rights Movement from the 1950s Through the 1980s* (New York: Bantam Books, 1990), 131–132. Used by permission of Bantam Books, a division of Random House, Inc.

to oppress you if you don't cooperate. So if you say you are oppressed, then you are also acknowledging that you are in league with the oppressor; now, it's your responsibility to break the league with him.

The first response was among the young women, about thirteen to eighteen. They're probably more responsive in terms of courage, confidence, and the ability to follow reasoning and logic. Nonviolence to them is logical: "You should love people, you shouldn't violate property. There's a way to solve all problems without violating. It's uncomfortable, it's inconvenient to have an immediate threat upon you; however, if you maintain your position, the threat goes away." Then the elementary students, they can comprehend that too. The last to get involved were the high school guys, because the brunt of the violence in the South was directed toward the black male. The females had not experienced that kind of negative violence, so they didn't have the kind of immediate fear of, say, white policemen, as the young men did. So their involvement was more spontaneous and up front than the guys'.

5. Martin Luther King, Jr., Writes from His Jail Cell, 1963

April 16, 1963

My Dear Fellow Clergymen:

While confined here in the Birmingham city jail, I came across your recent statement calling my present activities "unwise and untimely." . . .

You deplore the demonstrations taking place in Birmingham. But your statement, I am sorry to say, fails to express a similar concern for the conditions that brought about the demonstrations. . . . It is unfortunate that demonstrations are taking place in Birmingham, but it is even more unfortunate that the city's white power structure left the Negro community with no alternative. . . .

One of the basic points in your statement is that the action that I and my associates have taken in Birmingham is untimely. . . .

. . . Frankly, I have yet to engage in a direct-action campaign that was "well timed" in the view of those who have not suffered unduly from the disease of segregation. For years now I have heard the word "Wait!" It rings in the ear of every Negro with piercing familiarity. . . .

We have waited for more than 340 years for our constitutional and God-given rights. The nations of Asia and Africa are moving with jetlike speed toward gaining political independence, but we still creep at horse-and-buggy pace toward gaining a cup of coffee at a lunch counter. Perhaps it is easy for those who have never felt the stinging darts of segregation to say, "Wait." But when you have seen vicious mobs lynch your mothers and fathers at will and drown your sisters and brothers at whim; when you have seen hate-filled policemen curse, kick and even kill your black brothers and sisters; when you see the vast majority of your twenty million Negro brothers smothering in an airtight cage of poverty in the midst of an affluent society; when you suddenly find your tongue twisted and your speech stammering as you seek to explain to your six-year-old daughter why she can't go to the public amusement park that has just been advertised on television, and see tears welling up in her eyes when she is told that Funtown is closed to colored children and see ominous clouds of inferiority beginning to form in her little mental sky, and see her beginning to distort her personality by developing an unconscious bitterness toward white people; . . . when your first name becomes "nigger," your middle name becomes "boy" (however old you are) and your last name becomes "John," and your wife and mother are never given the respected title "Mrs."; . . . when you are forever fighting a degenerating sense of "nobodiness"—then you will understand why we find it difficult to wait. . . .

You express a great deal of anxiety over our willingness to break laws. This is certainly a legitimate concern. Since we so diligently urge people to obey the Supreme Court's decision of 1954 outlawing segregation in the public schools, at first glance it may seem rather paradoxical for us consciously to break laws. . . . One has not only a legal but a moral responsibility to obey just laws. Conversely, one has a moral responsibility to disobey unjust laws. . . .

. . . All segregation statutes are unjust because segregation distorts the soul and damages the personality. It gives the segregator a false sense of superiority and the segregated a false sense of inferiority. . . . [S]egregation is not only politically, economically and sociologically unsound, it is morally wrong and sinful. . . .

. . . A law is unjust if it is inflicted on a minority that, as a result of being denied the right to vote, had no part in enacting or devising the law. . . . Throughout Alabama all sorts of devious methods are used to prevent Negroes from becoming registered voters, and there are some counties in which, even though Negroes constitute a majority of the population, not a single Negro is registered. Can any law enacted under such circumstances be considered democratically structured? . . .

. . . You warmly commended the Birmingham police force for keeping "order" and "preventing violence." I doubt that you would have so warmly commended the police force if you had seen its dogs sinking their teeth into unarmed, nonviolent Negroes. . . .

It is true that the police have exercised a degree of discipline in handling the demonstrators. In this sense they have conducted themselves rather "nonviolently" in public. But for what purpose? To preserve the evil system of segregation. . . .

I wish you had commended the Negro sit-inners and demonstrators of Birmingham for their sublime courage, their willingness to suffer and their amazing discipline in the midst of great provocation. One day the South will recognize its real heroes. They will be the James Merediths, with the noble sense of purpose that enables them to face jeering and hostile mobs, . . . They will be old, oppressed, battered Negro women, . . . who rose up with a sense of dignity and with [their] people decided not to ride segregated buses, . . . They will be the young high school and college students, the young ministers of the gospel and a host of their elders, courageously and nonviolently sitting in at lunch counters and willingly going to jail for conscience' sake. One day the South will know that when these disinherited children of God sat down at lunch counters, they were in reality standing up for what is best in the American dream and for the most sacred values in our Judaeo-Christian heritage, . . .

Yours for the cause of Peace and Brotherhood,

Martin Luther King, Jr.

6. John Lewis, SNCC Chairman, Challenges the Federal Government, 1963

We march today for jobs and freedom, but we have nothing to be proud of. For hundreds and thousands of our brothers are not here. They have no money for their transportation, for they are receiving starvation wages . . . or no wages, at all.

In good conscience, we cannot support the administration's civil rights bill, for it is too little, and too late. There's not one thing in the bill that will protect our people from police brutality.

This bill will not protect young children and old women from police dogs and fire hoses, [when] engaging in peaceful demonstrations. . . .

The voting section of this bill will not help thousands of black citizens who want to vote. It will not help the citizens of Mississippi, of Alabama, and Georgia, who are qualified to vote, but lack a 6th Grade education. "One man, one vote," is the African cry. It is ours, too. (It must be ours.) . . .

We are now involved in . . . revolution. This nation is still a place of cheap political leaders who build their careers on immoral compromise and ally themselves with open forms of political, economic and social exploitation. What political leader here can stand up and say, "My party is the party of principles"? The party of Kennedy is also the party of Eastland. The party of Javits is also the party of Goldwater. Where is *our* party?

In some parts of the South we work in the fields from sun-up to sun-down for $12 a week. In Albany, Georgia, nine of our leaders have been indicted not by Dixiecrats but by the Federal Government for peaceful protest. But what did the Federal Government do when Albany's Deputy Sheriff beat Attorney C. B. King and left him half dead? What did the Federal Government do when local police officials kicked and assaulted the pregnant wife of Slater King, and she lost her baby?

It seems to me that the Albany indictment is part of a conspiracy on the part of the Federal Government and local politicians in the interest of expediency.

I want to know, which side is the Federal Government on?

The revolution is at hand, and we must free ourselves of the chains of political and economic slavery. The non-violent revolution is saying, "We will not wait for the courts to act, for we have been waiting for hundreds of years. We will not wait for the President, the Justice Department, nor Congress, but we will take matters into our own hands and create a source of power, outside any national structure that could and would assure us a victory." To those who have said, "Be Patient and

John Lewis, Original text of speech to be delivered at the Lincoln Memorial during the March on Washington, August 28, 1963. Reprinted with permission.

Wait," we must say that, "Patience is a dirty and nasty word." We cannot be patient, we do not want to be free gradually, we want our freedom, and we want it now. We cannot depend on any political party, for both the Democrats and the Republicans have betrayed the basic principles of the Declaration of Independence.

We all recognize the fact that if any radical social, political and economic changes are to take place in our society, the people, the masses, must bring them about. In the struggle we must seek more than civil rights; we must work for the community of love, peace and true brotherhood. Our minds, souls, and hearts cannot rest until freedom and justice exist for *all the people.*

The revolution is a serious one. Mr. Kennedy is trying to take the revolution out of the street and put it in the courts. Listen, Mr. Kennedy, listen Mr. Congressman, listen fellow citizens, the black masses are on the march for jobs and freedom, and we must say to the politicians that there won't be a "cooling-off" period. . . .

We won't stop now. All of the forces of Eastland, Barnett, Wallace, and Thurmond won't stop this revolution. The time will come when we will not confine our marching to Washington. We will march through the South, through the Heart of Dixie, the way Sherman did. We shall pursue our own "scorched earth" policy and burn Jim Crow to the ground—nonviolently. We shall fragment the South into a thousand pieces and put them back together in the image of democracy. We will make the action of the past few months look petty. And I say to you, WAKE UP AMERICA!

7. Avon W. Rollins, an SNCC Field Secretary, Details Progress Made in Danville, Virginia, 1964

I. City Government
   (a) Two social workers.
   (b) One Negro policeman (looking for more qualified applicants).
   (c) Fair Employment Law.
   (d) Chairs have been replaced in City library, which had been taken out previously in an attempt to keep the races separated.
II. Downtown and Surrounding Areas
   (a) Some twenty-five Negroes have been employed in sales positions.
   (b) There are some six lunch counters open to the public in the downtown area.
   (c) And six in the surrounding shopping centers.
III. Dan River Mills
   (a) Dan River Mills has dropped all physical signs of segregation.
   (b) The two previously segregated textile unions have merged.
   (c) The Negro who was previously president of local Negro textile union is now vice-president of the overall union.
   (d) Dan River Mills night high school has opened to Negroes on the same basis as to whites.

    (e) Dan River Mills trade school has now opened to Negroes on an equal basis.

  IV. Milk Dairies employed three Negroes in sales positions.

   V. Coca-Cola Bottling Co. employed one Negro salesman.

  VI. Token Integration of City Schools

    (a) Eleven Negro students enrolled in previously all-white schools.

 VII. Up-Grading in the Tobacco Industry

    (a) Citizenship School.
    For adults to learn how to read and write, how to write checks, and how to apply to become registered voters.

    (b) Scholarships to local youth leaders working in the movement:
    1. Samuel Giler
    2. Howard Logan
    3. Thomas Holt

    (c) Help on home mortgages.

    (d) For those who lost jobs because of their involvement in demonstrations.

    (e) Help to those who lost checks coming from unemployment compensation because of their involvement in demonstrations.

VIII. The Reborn Negro in the Community

    (a) A new sense of dignity for himself and for his fellow man.

    (b) A new sense of civic responsibility.

    (c) The refusal to accept segregation in any form and pride that he is a black man.

  IX. Voter Registration

    (a) We have registered some 1,500 Negroes.

We (S.N.C.C.) are grateful to the Negro community for their assiduous efforts in bringing about these token accomplishments.

8. Malcolm X Defines Revolution, 1963

. . . I would like to make a few comments concerning the difference between the black revolution and the Negro revolution. . . . First, what is a revolution? . . .

Look at the American Revolution in 1776. That revolution was for what? For land. Why did they want land? Independence. How was it carried out? Bloodshed. . . . The French Revolution—what was it based on? The landless against the landlord. What was it for? Land. How did they get it? Bloodshed. Was no love lost, was no compromise, was no negotiation. . . .

The Russian Revolution—what was it based on? Land; the landless against the landlord. How did they bring it about? Bloodshed. You haven't got a revolution that doesn't involve bloodshed. And you're afraid to bleed. . . .

Malcolm X, "Message to the Grassroots," Clayborne Carson, David J. Garrow, Gerald Gill, Vincent Harding, and Darlene Clark Hine, eds., *The Eyes on the Prize Civil Rights Reader: Documents, Speeches, and Firsthand Accounts from the Black Freedom Struggle, 1954–1990* (New York: Viking Penguin, 1991), 251–254. Copyright © 1965, 1989 by Betty Shabazz and Pathfinder Press. Reprinted by permission.

As long as the white man sent you to Korea, you bled. He sent you to Germany, you bled. He sent you to the South Pacific to fight the Japanese, you bled. You bleed for white people, but when it comes to seeing your own churches being bombed and little black girls murdered, you haven't got any blood. . . . How are you going to be nonviolent in Mississippi, as violent as you were in Korea? How can you justify being nonviolent in Mississippi and Alabama, when your churches are being bombed, and your little girls are being murdered, and at the same time you are going to get violent with Hitler, and Tojo, and somebody else you don't even know?

If violence is wrong in America, violence is wrong abroad. If it is wrong to be violent defending black women and black children and black babies and black men, then it is wrong for America to draft us and make us violent abroad in defense of her. And if it is right for America to draft us, and teach us how to be violent in defense of her, then it is right for you and me to do whatever is necessary to defend our own people right here in this country. . . .

. . . There's been a revolution, a black revolution, going on in Africa. In Kenya, the Mau Mau were revolutionary; . . . they believed in scorched earth, they knocked everything aside that got in their way, and their revolution also was based on land, a desire for land. In Algeria, the northern part of Africa, a revolution took place. The Algerians were revolutionists, they wanted land. France offered to let them be integrated into France. They told France, to hell with France, they wanted some land, not some France. And they engaged in a bloody battle.

So I cite these various revolutions, brothers and sisters, to show you that you don't have a peaceful revolution. You don't have a turn-the-other-cheek revolution. There's no such thing as a nonviolent revolution. The only kind of revolution that is nonviolent is the Negro revolution. The only revolution in which the goal is loving your enemy is the Negro revolution. It's the only revolution in which the goal is a desegregated lunch counter, a desegregated theater, a desegregated park, and a desegregated public toilet; you can sit down next to white folks—on the toilet. That's no revolution. Revolution is based on land. Land is the basis of all independence. Land is the basis of freedom, justice, and equality.

The white man knows what a revolution is. He knows that the black revolution is world-wide in scope and in nature. The black revolution is sweeping Asia, is sweeping Africa, is rearing its head in Latin America. The Cuban Revolution—that's a revolution. They overturned the system. Revolution is in Asia, revolution is in Africa, and the white man is screaming because he sees revolution in Latin America. How do you think he'll react to you when you learn what a real revolution is? You don't know what a revolution is. If you did, you wouldn't use that word. . . .

. . . A revolutionary wants land so he can set up his own nation, an independent nation. These Negroes aren't asking for any nation—they're trying to crawl back on the plantation.

When you want a nation, that's called nationalism. . . . All the revolutions that are going on in Asia and Africa today are based on what?—black nationalism. A revolutionary is a black nationalist. He wants a nation. . . . If you're afraid of black nationalism, you're afraid of revolution. And if you love revolution, you love black nationalism. . . .

9. Civil Rights Leader Bayard Rustin Is Forced Out, 1960

NEW YORK—Bayard Rustin has severed his relationships with A. Philip Randolph and the Rev. Martin Luther King.

In handing in his resignations as special assistant to Dr. King and director of the Southern Christian Leadership Conference's New York branch, he challenged Congressman Adam Clayton Powell to "lend his special talents to the building of such a movement and to the support of Dr. King and the other leaders in the South who are on the firing line."

In his statement, Mr. Rustin called attention to the June 25 issue of the *Courier* in which Mr. Powell accused Messrs. Randolph and King of being "captives." . . .

He said, ". . . I can only conclude from the article in the *Courier* that Congressman Powell seeks to weaken, if not destroy, the march on the conventions for his own obvious political reasons. While he on the one hand calls for 'unity,' he on the other hand labels as 'captives' two of the most beloved and respected leaders of the Negro people."

Declaring that Powell had indicated that his association with Dr. King was "divisive," Rustin continued, "I cannot permit a situation to endure in which my relationship to Dr. King and the Southern Christian Leadership Conference is used to confuse and becloud the basic issues confronting the Negro people today. In such a situation I am no longer able to be of effective service."

Mr. Rustin pointed out that he had never sought high position or special privilege, had been arrested 22 times both North and South and had served time on a North Carolina chain-gang during his years of fighting jim crow.

"Nonetheless," he continued, "Congressman Powell has suggested that I am an obstacle to his giving full, enthusiastic support to Dr. King. I want now to remove that obstacle."

He then suggested that Mr. Powell join with Mr. Randolph and Dr. King in urging thousands of people in Los Angeles and Chicago to converge on both political conventions and demand the repudiation of the Dixiecrats in the democratic [sic] party and the racists in the Republican party.

E S S A Y S

The Civil Rights Movement of the 1950s and 1960s was a mass movement precipitated by the lived experiences, and rooted in the culture, of southern African Americans. In the first essay, Clayborne Carson, professor of history at Stanford University and director of the Martin Luther King, Jr., Papers Project, challenges the myth of King as larger-than-life initiator of the era's great social changes. Carson argues that only through understanding that even without King, the southern movement still would have developed in the same ways, we can then begin to grasp King's importance as fully human, struggling with the intellectual and social challenges of leadership. In the second essay, Charles Payne, professor of history at Duke University, examines the unique role of southern black church culture in developing and sustaining the mass orientation of the struggle. Ella Baker's lifetime philosophy and habit of helping people find the resources to lead themselves is the subject of the third essay, also by Charles Payne. All three essays emphasize the Civil Rights Movement as an intellectual as well as a social movement. Taken together, what do they suggest about how social movements are organized, how leaders are defined, and how political traditions are nurtured and sustained?

"A Leader Who Stood Out in a Forest of Tall Trees"

CLAYBORNE CARSON

The legislation to establish Martin Luther King, Jr.'s birthday as a federal holiday provided official recognition of King's greatness, but it remains the responsibility of those of us who study and carry on King's work to define his historical significance. Rather than engaging in officially approved nostalgia, our remembrance of King should reflect the reality of his complex and multifaceted life. Biographers, theologians, political scientists, sociologists, social psychologists, and historians have given us a sizable literature of King's place in the Afro-American protest tradition, his role in the modern black freedom struggle, and his eclectic ideas regarding nonviolent activism. Although King scholars may benefit from and may stimulate the popular interest in King generated by the national holiday, many will find themselves uneasy participants in annual observances to honor an innocuous, carefully cultivated image of King as a black heroic figure.

The King depicted in serious scholarly works is far too interesting to be encased in such a didactic legend. King was a controversial leader who challenged authority and who once applauded what he called "creative maladjusted nonconformity." He should not be transformed into a simplistic image designed to offend no one—a black counterpart to the static, heroic myths that have embalmed George Washington as the Father of His Country and Abraham Lincoln as the Great Emancipator.

One aspect of the emerging King myth has been the depiction of him in the mass media, not only as the preeminent leader of the civil rights movement, but also as the initiator and sole indispensable element in the southern black struggles of the 1950s and 1960s. As in other historical myths, a Great Man is seen as the decisive factor in the process of social change, and the unique qualities of a leader are used to explain major historical events. The King myth departs from historical reality because it attributes too much to King's exceptional qualities as a leader and too little to the impersonal, large-scale social factors that made it possible for King to display his singular abilities on a national stage. Because the myth emphasizes the individual at the expense of the black movement, it not only

Clayborne Carson, "Martin Luther King, Jr.: Charismatic Leadership in a Mass Struggle," *Journal of American History,* 74, no. 2 (September 1987), 448–454. Copyright © 1987. Reprinted with permission.

exaggerates King's historical importance but also distorts his actual, considerable contribution to the movement.

A major example of this distortion has been the tendency to see King as a charismatic figure who single-handedly directed the course of the civil rights movement through the force of his oratory. The charismatic label, however, does not adequately define King's role in the southern black struggle. The term *charisma* has traditionally been used to describe the godlike, magical qualities possessed by certain leaders. Connotations of the term have changed, of course, over the years. In our more secular age, it has lost many of its religious connotations and now refers to a wide range of leadership styles that involve the capacity to inspire—usually through oratory—emotional bonds between leaders and followers. Arguing that King was not a charismatic leader, in the broadest sense of the term, becomes somewhat akin to arguing that he was not a Christian, but emphasis on King's charisma obscures other important aspects of his role in the black movement. To be sure, King's oratory was exceptional and many people saw King as a divinely inspired leader, but King did not receive and did not want the kind of unquestioning support that is often associated with charismatic leaders. Movement activists instead saw him as the most prominent among many outstanding movement strategists, tacticians, ideologues, and institutional leaders.

King undoubtedly recognized that charisma was one of many leadership qualities at his disposal, but he also recognized that charisma was not a sufficient basis for leadership in a modern political movement enlisting numerous self-reliant leaders. Moreover, he rejected aspects of the charismatic model that conflicted with his sense of his own limitations. Rather than exhibiting unwavering confidence in his power and wisdom, King was a leader full of self-doubts, keenly aware of his own limitations and human weaknesses. He was at times reluctant to take on the responsibilities suddenly and unexpectedly thrust upon him. During the Montgomery bus boycott, for example, when he worried about threats to his life and to the lives of his wife and child, he was overcome with fear rather than confident and secure in his leadership role. He was able to carry on only after acquiring an enduring understanding of his dependence on a personal God who promised never to leave him alone.

Moreover, emphasis on King's charisma conveys the misleading notion of a movement held together by spellbinding speeches and blind faith rather than by a complex blend of rational and emotional bonds. King's charisma did not place him above criticism. Indeed, he was never able to gain mass support for his notion of nonviolent struggle as a way of life, rather than simply a tactic. Instead of viewing himself as the embodiment of widely held Afro-American racial values, he willingly risked his popularity among blacks through his steadfast advocacy of nonviolent strategies to achieve radical social change.

He was a profound and provocative public speaker as well as an emotionally powerful one. Only those unfamiliar with the Afro-American clergy would assume that his oratorical skills were unique, but King set himself apart from other black preachers through his use of traditional black Christian idiom to advocate unconventional political ideas. Early in his life King became disillusioned with the unbridled emotionalism associated with his father's religious fundamentalism, and, as a thirteen year old, he questioned the bodily resurrection of Jesus in his Sunday school class. His subsequent search for an intellectually satisfying religious faith conflicted with the emphasis on emotional expressiveness that pervades evangelical religion. His preaching manner was rooted in the traditions of the black church, while his subject matter, which often reflected his wide-ranging philosophical interests, distinguished him from other preachers who relied on rhetorical devices that manipulated the emotions of listeners. King used charisma as a tool for mobilizing black communities, but he always used it in the context of other forms of intellectual and political leadership suited to a movement containing many strong leaders.

Recently, scholars have begun to examine the black struggle as a locally based mass movement, rather than simply a reform movement led by national civil rights leaders. The new orientation in scholarship indicates that King's role was different from that suggested in King-centered biographies and journalistic accounts. King was certainly not the only significant leader of the civil rights movement, for sustained protest movements arose in many southern communities in which King had little or no direct involvement.

In Montgomery, for example, local black leaders such as E. D. Nixon, Rosa Parks, and Jo Ann Robinson started the bus boycott before King became the leader of the Montgomery Improvement Association. Thus, although King inspired blacks in Montgomery and black residents recognized that they were fortunate to have such a spokesperson, talented local leaders other than King played decisive roles in initiating and sustaining the boycott movement.

Similarly, the black students who initiated the 1960 lunch counter sit-ins admired King, but they did not wait for him to act before launching their own movement. The sit-in leaders who founded the Student Nonviolent Coordinating Committee (SNCC) became increasingly critical of King's leadership style, linking it to the feelings of dependency that often characterize the followers of charismatic leaders. The essence of SNCC's approach to community organizing was to instill in local residents the confidence that they could lead their own struggles. A SNCC organizer failed if local residents became dependent on his or her presence; as the organizers put it, their job was to work themselves out of a job. Though King influenced the struggles that took place in the Black Belt regions of Mississippi, Alabama, and Georgia, those movements were also guided by self-reliant local leaders who occasionally called on King's oratorical skills to galvanize black protestors at mass meetings while refusing to depend on his presence.

If King had never lived, the black struggle would have followed a course of development similar to the one it did. The Montgomery bus boycott would have occurred, because King did not initiate it. Black students probably would have rebelled—even without King as a role model—for they had sources of tactical and ideological inspiration besides King. Mass activism in southern cities and voting rights efforts in the deep South were outgrowths of large-scale social and political forces, rather than simply consequences of the actions of a single leader. Though perhaps not as quickly and certainly not as peacefully nor with as universal a significance, the black movement would probably have achieved its major legislative victories without King's leadership, for the southern Jim Crow system was a regional anachronism, and the forces that undermined it were inexorable.

To what extent, then, did King's presence affect the movement? Answering that question requires us to look beyond the usual portrayal of the black struggle. Rather than seeing an amorphous mass of discontented blacks acting out strategies determined by a small group of leaders, we would recognize King as a major example of the local black leadership that emerged as black communities mobilized for sustained struggles. If not as dominant a figure as sometimes portrayed, the historical King was nevertheless a remarkable leader who acquired the respect and support of self-confident, grass-roots leaders, some of whom possessed charismatic qualities of their own. Directing attention to the other leaders who initiated and emerged from those struggles should not detract from our conception of King's historical significance; such movement-oriented research reveals King as a leader who stood out in a forest of tall trees.

King's major public speeches—particularly the "I Have a Dream" speech—have received much attention, but his exemplary qualities were also displayed in countless strategy sessions with other activists and in meetings with government officials. King's success as a leader was based on his intellectual and moral cogency and his skill as a conciliator among movement activists who refused to be simply King's "followers" or "lieutenants."

The success of the black movement required the mobilization of black communities as well as the transformation of attitudes in the surrounding society, and King's wide range of skills and attributes prepared him to meet the internal as well as the external demands of the movement. King understood the black world from a privileged position, having grown up in a stable family within a major black urban community; yet he also learned how to speak persuasively to the surrounding white world. Alone among the major civil rights leaders of his time, King could not only articulate black concerns to white audiences, but could also mobilize blacks through his day-to-day involvement in black community institutions and through his access to the regional institutional network of the black church. His advocacy of nonviolent activism gave the black movement invaluable positive press coverage, but his effectiveness as a protest leader derived mainly from his ability to mobilize black community resources.

Analyses of the southern movement that emphasize its nonrational aspects and expressive functions over its political character explain the black struggle as an emotional outburst by discontented blacks, rather than recognizing that the movement's strength and durability came from its mobilization of black community institutions, financial resources, and grass-roots leaders. The values of southern blacks were profoundly and permanently transformed not only by King, but also by involvement in sustained protest activity and community-organizing efforts, through thousands of mass meetings, workshops, citizenship classes, freedom schools, and informal discussions. Rather than merely accepting guidance from above, southern blacks were resocialized as a result of their movement experiences.

Although the literature of the black struggle has traditionally paid little attention to the intellectual content of black politics, movement activists of the 1960s made a profound, though often ignored, contribution to political thinking. King may have been born with rare potential, but his most significant leadership attributes were related to his immersion in, and contribution to, the intellectual ferment that has always been an essential part of Afro-American freedom struggles. Those who have written about King have too often assumed that his most important ideas were derived from outside the black struggle—from his academic training, his philosophical readings, or his acquaintance with Gandhian ideas. Scholars are only beginning to recognize the extent to which his attitudes and those of many other activists, white and black, were transformed through their involvement in a movement in which ideas disseminated from the bottom up as well as from the top down.

Although my assessment of King's role in the black struggles of his time reduces him to human scale, it also increases the possibility that others may recognize his qualities in themselves. Idolizing King lessens one's ability to exhibit some of his best attributes or, worse, encourages one to become a debunker, emphasizing King's flaws in order to lessen the inclination to exhibit his virtues. King himself undoubtedly feared that some who admired him would place too much faith in his ability to offer guidance and to overcome resistance, for he often publicly acknowledged his own limitations and mortality. Near the end of his life, King expressed his certainty that black people would reach the Promised Land whether or not he was with them. His faith was based on an awareness of the qualities that he knew he shared with all people. When he suggested his own epitaph, he asked not to be remembered for his exceptional achievements—his Nobel Prize and other awards, his academic accomplishments; instead, he wanted to be remembered for giving his life to serve others, for trying to be right on the war question, for trying to feed the hungry and clothe the naked, for trying to love and serve humanity. "I want you to say that I tried to love and serve humanity." Those aspects of King's life did not require charisma or other superhuman abilities.

If King were alive today, he would doubtless encourage those who celebrate his life to recognize their responsibility to struggle as he did for a more just and peaceful world. He would prefer that the black movement be remembered not only as the scene of his own achievements, but also as a setting that brought out extraordinary qualities in many people. If he were to return, his oratory would be unsettling and intellectually challenging rather than remembered diction and cadences. He would probably be the unpopular social critic he was on the eve of the Poor People's Campaign rather than the object of national homage he became after his death. His basic message would be the same as it was when he was alive, for he did not bend with the changing political winds. He would talk of ending poverty and war and of building a just social order that would avoid the pitfalls of competitive capitalism and repressive communism. He would give scant comfort to those who condition their activism upon the appearance of another King, for he recognized the extent to which he was a product of the movement that called him to leadership.

The notion that appearances by Great Men (or Great Women) are necessary preconditions for the emergence of major movements for social changes reflects not only a poor understanding of history, but also a pessimistic view of the possibilities for future social change. Waiting for the Messiah is a human weakness that is unlikely to be rewarded more than once in a millennium. Studies of King's life offer support for an alternative optimistic belief that ordinary people can collectively improve their lives. Such studies demonstrate the capacity of social movements to transform participants for the better and to create leaders worthy of their followers.

Cultural Traditions and the Politicization of Communities

CHARLES M. PAYNE

I once heard a journalist who had covered the movement remark that two decades after its height the civil rights movement had inspired no great works of art—no great novels or films, no great plays. He rather missed the point. The movement was its own work of art, and mass meetings were among the places where that might most easily be seen. Mass meetings, which had the overall tone and structure of a church service, were grounded in the religious traditions and the esthetic sensibilities of the Black South. If the drudgery of canvassing accounted for much of an organizer's time on a day-to-day basis, mass meetings, when they were good, were a part of the pay-off, emotionally and politically.

The Montgomery, Alabama, bus boycott of 1955 is one of the turning points of the modern movement. According to Ralph Abernathy, the first song at the first mass meeting there was "Leaning on the Everlasting Arms": What a fellowship, what a joy divine, leaning, leaning on the everlasting arms. What have I to fear, what have I to dread, leaning on the everlasting arms? It was an appropriate choice. Emile Durkheim wrote:

> The believer who has communicated with his god is not merely a man who sees new truths of which the unbeliever is ignorant; he is a man who is stronger. He feels within him more force, either to endure the trials of existence or to conquer them.

The religious traditions of the Black South were an important part of what empowered members of the movement, especially the older members, allowing them to endure and conquer. In bending Afro-American Christianity toward emancipatory ends the movement took it back to its origins. For much of the twentieth century, the Black church, especially in rural areas, turned people away from this-worldy concerns. The preacherocracy, as one critic termed it, urged patience in the face of suffering. "They saw the church as a way to escape the pains of the world, not as a moral force that could help heal them." This view was a far cry from the Christianity of the slaves. As described by Lawrence Levine among others, slave Christianity was a liberation theology. It is true that those slavemasters who pushed Christianity generally hoped it would make slaves more manageable, but as Herbert Gutman points out, the important question is not just what masters did to slaves but what slaves did with what was done to them. In this case, they were to take what was intended to be a theology of accommodation and fashion from it a theology of liberation. . . .

SNCC had deliberately made a policy of recruiting Mississippi field secretaries from within the state, so many of them were steeped in the religious traditions of the South. Sam Block could slip into his "preacher's air" at will. Many people in Greenwood thought Hollis Watkins was the Reverend Hollis Watkins,

Charles Payne, *I've Got the Light of Freedom: The Organizing Tradition and the Mississippi Freedom Struggle* (Berkeley: University of California Press, 1995), 256–263. Reprinted by permission.

and he did not try to discourage them from thinking so. Willie Peacock grew up in a family that was very involved in the AME church and was able to use his knowledge of its politics to prod reluctant ministers. All of them took pride in their knowledge of the Bible and their ability to find the verses and the parables that made the points they needed to make.

Meetings in Greenwood were frequently opened with a prayer by Cleve Jordan, who had an enviable reputation as a prayer leader. His prayers were part-chant, part-song, with the audience murmuring assent and agreement at the end of every line.

> Oh Father, Oh Lord,
> Now, now, now, Lordie, Oh Lord
> When we get through drinking tears for water
> When we get through eatin' at the unwelcome table
> When we get through shakin' unwelcome hands
> We've got to meet Death somewhere
> Don't let us be afraid to die. . . .
> Father, I stretch my hand to thee
> No other help I know.

Fannie Lou Hamer was such a powerful public speaker that Lyndon Johnson once called a news conference solely to stop television coverage of her. One of the most popular speakers at mass meetings in Greenwood, she stressed that God walks with the courageous. A meeting taped at Tougaloo is a good example of her style. The meeting began with Hollis Watkins leading a vigorous rendition of "Before I'll be a slave, I'll be buried in my grave and go home to my Lord and be free." Mrs. Hamer follows the singing, giving a history of her involvement in the movement, including the kinds of harassment she was subjected to. Lately, the cops in her hometown have taken to coming by late at night with their dogs, letting the dogs bark so she will know she's being watched. They have done it so much she has gotten used to it. "Look like now the dogs help me get to sleep." She the pointed out the need for people to be serious about their religion. There are plenty of people, she says, always talking about "Sure, I'm a Christian," but if you're not doing anything about being a Christian, if you can't stand some kind of test, you need to stop shouting because the 17th chapter of Acts, 26th verse, says that the Lord made of one blood all nations. After giving some examples of how some people in the movement were making their faith concrete, she ends by leading the meeting in a freedom song: "I'm on my way to the freedom land/If you don't go, don't hinder me/I'm on my way, praise God, I'm on my way/If you don't go, let the children go."

The mixture of spirituality and music had a special impact on some of those raised outside the traditions of Afro-Christianity. Jean Wheeler Smith had never so much as heard gospel music before she went to Howard. When she got to Mississippi,

> the religious, the spiritual was like an explosion to me, an emotional explosion. I didn't have that available to me [before]. It just lit up my mind. . . . The music and the religion provided a contact between our logic and our feelings . . . and gave the logic of what we were doing emotional and human power to make us go forward.

Mass meetings partook of the mundane as well as of the sacred. New workers in town might be introduced, internal problems ironed out, tactics debated and explained. They were also educational. At one meeting in February 1963, James Bevel gave what amounted to a lecture on political economy, talking about the separation of Negroes from the land, outmigration to the North, the implications of automation, Negro self-hatred, and the broader purposes of education. Speakers brought news of what was going on in other places. Medgar Evers, for example, a frequent and popular speaker in Greenwood, might bring word of what was happening in Jackson or at the NAACP national office. Meetings broke down the debilitating sense of isolation by bringing local people out so they could see that growing numbers of their neighbors were with them. At the same time, the news from other places reinforced their sense of being part of something larger and more potent than just what was going on in Greenwood.

In some respects, mass meetings resembled meetings of Alcoholics Anonymous or Weight Watchers. Groups like these try to change the behavior of their members by offering a supportive social environment, public recognition for living up to group norms, and public pressure to continue doing so. They create an environment in which you feel that if you stumble, you are letting down not only yourself but all of your friends. One might be afraid to go to a particular demonstration or be tired of demonstrations, period, but not going would mean disappointing those people who were counting on you.

From its inception, SNCC was sensitive to the need to motivate people by giving them public recognition. Ella Baker often stressed the point. At mass meetings in Greenwood, local activists might find themselves sharing a platform with heroes like Medgar Evers or Dick Gregory, or later with Harry Belafonte or Sidney Poitier, or perhaps even with Martin Luther King himself. On one of his trips to Greenwood, King asked to meet Dewey Greene, about whom he had heard so much. Within the movement, the traditional status system was relatively inoperative. Belle Johnson belonged to Strangers Home Baptist Church, which thought itself a high-class church. Not everyone thought she was the kind of person who belonged there. The "dicty" attitude of the church toward her angered her daughter June. In the movement, Belle Johnson was respected for her dedication; her income and education did not matter.

Pressure at mass meetings could be overt or friendly. At one, Hollis Watkins asked for a show of hands from people who had tried to register. Then he asked how they felt about what they had done. People shouted back that they felt good about it. He asked to see the hands of those who had not yet been down ("Don't fool us now") and, after a short pep talk on the importance of what they were trying to do, urged them all to meet him at 8:30 in the morning so they could all go to the courthouse together.

A part of the meeting might be devoted to having people simply recite their life histories, histories inevitably full of deprivation and injustice. At one Greenwood meeting, Cleve Jordan, who had been born near the turn of the century, spoke of how he had spent forty years sawing and hauling logs for a dollar and a quarter a day, working such long days that he only saw his children on Sundays, making forty bales of cotton in a year and having nothing to show for it except the dubious satisfaction of having made some more white people rich. Other speakers continued in the same vein. In his analysis of the Chinese revolution, William Hinton argues that an important element in reconstructing the consciousness of peasants was simply having them publicly recite their biographies. Doing so helped turn private and individual grievances into a collective consciousness of systematic oppression. Mass meetings seem to have served a similar function. They also created a context in which individuals created a public face for themselves, which they then had to try to live up to. In his heart, Reverend Such-and-Such may not feel nearly as militant as the speech he gives at the mass meeting, but once he gives it, he has created an image of himself that he will not want contradicted. After playing the role he has defined for himself for a while—and getting patted on the back for it—he may find that the role becomes natural. Before you know it, he may be shaking his head at how rabbit-hearted these other ministers are. What God can cowards know?

Depending on the situation at a given moment, it might be very easy or very difficult to get people to come to mass meetings. When necessary, canvassers went door to door, passing out handbills. Most people seem to have come initially out of sheer curiosity. The meetings were something new, the regular speakers, including Mrs. Hamer, Medgar Evers, Dick Gregory, and Aaron Henry, could hold an audience, and sometimes the speakers were nationally known celebrities.

Then, too, there was the music. It would be hard to overestimate the significance of the music of the movement. The changing fortunes of the movement and the morale of its participants could have been gauged by the intensity of the singing at the meetings. Music has always been a central part of the Black religious experience. Ministers knew that a good choir was a good recruiting device. In the same fashion, many who came to meetings came just to hear the singing. Bernice Reagon calls the freedom songs "the language that focused the energy of the people who filled the streets." She tells of an incident in Georgia in which a sheriff and his deputies tried to intimidate a mass meeting by their presence. "A song began. And the song made sure that the sheriff and his deputies knew we were there. We became visible, our image was enlarged, when the sounds of the freedom songs filled all the space in that church." When things were hopping in Greenwood, SNCC's Worth Long sometimes brought people over from Little Rock or Pine Bluff to help on the weekends. The mass meetings he saw in Greenwood were different from the ones in Arkansas. Greenwood had more of a singing movement, and the meetings had more of an emotional tone; it was like comparing a Holiness church to a Methodist church. He tried to take some of that feeling back to Arkansas with him.

People in Greenwood were similarly enlarged by the singing and the emotional intensity of the meetings. Among their other talents, Hollis Watkins, Willie Peacock, and Sam Block were all songleaders. Arance Brooks, recalling the period when meetings were always packed, says, "I loved it. I just felt so much better when everybody would go. Looked like I slept better. The singing and everything. I just loved it." In spite of threats to his life, the Reverend Aaron Johnson, during a particularly tense period, opened his church for a meeting after the church that was supposed to have it backed down. People were afraid to come in at first, but when they did "We rocked the church. We rocked that church that night. Ha, Ha, Ha. I said, 'Well, if I die, I had a good time tonight. I had a *good* time tonight.'"

The music operated as a kind of litany against fear. Mass meeting[s] offered a context in which the mystique of fear could be chipped away. At one Greenwood meeting, a speaker noted with satisfaction that at a recent demonstration where it looked as though things might get out of hand, Police Chief Lary was visibly scared; Lary's voice had trembled as he asked demonstrators to break it up. Even the police chief is human. At another meeting a boy who had spent thirty-nine days in jail with Hollis Watkins and Curtis Hayes talked about how jail was not as terrible as most people thought. He had kind of enjoyed it, actually. The community sent them baked chickens and pies and cakes and things, so they just sent the jail food on back.

Much of the humor at mass meetings was an attack on fear. A song could bring the Citizens' Council down to size. To the tune of "Jesus Loves Me, This I Know," they might sing:

> Jesus loves me cause I'm white.
> Lynch me a nigger every night. Hate the Jews and I hate the Pope,
> Jes' me and my rope.
> Jesus loves me, The Citizens' Council told me so.

"We Shall Overcome" could become:

> Deep in my heart, I do believe
> We shall keep the niggers down
> They will never be free—eee—eee
> They will never be registered,
> We shall keep the niggers down.

Mixtures of the sacred and the profane, the mass meetings could be a very powerful social ritual. They attracted people to the movement and then helped them develop a sense of involvement and solidarity. By ritually acting out new definitions of their individual and collective selves, people helped make those selves become real. Informed and challenged by the speakers, pumped up by the singing and the laughing and the sense of community, many of those who only meant to go once out of curiosity left that first meeting thinking they might come once more, just to see.

Challenging the Politics of Spokesmanship

CHARLES M. PAYNE

Ella Jo Baker died in 1986. Her entire adult life was devoted to building organizations that worked for social change by encouraging individual growth and individual empowerment. . . . Few activists can claim a depth and breadth of political experience comparable to Ella Baker's half-century of struggle. She was associated with whatever organization in the Black community was on the cutting edge of the era—the NAACP (National Association for the Advancement of Colored People) in the forties, the Southern Christian Leadership Conference (SCLC) in the fifties, and the Student Nonviolent Coordinating Committee (SNCC) in the sixties. . . .

. . . Exactly how she first became involved in organizing is not clear—she says she left college with conventional notions of personal success—but it is clear that the smorgasbord political environment of New York intrigued her. . . . Subsequently, the economic dislocations of the Depression played an important part in

Charles Payne, "Ella Baker and Models of Social Changes," *Signs: Journal of Women in Culture and Society,* 14, no. 4 (Summer 1989), 885, 887–894, 896–899, University of Chicago Press. Reprinted with permission.

her rejection of "the American illusion that anyone who is determined and persistent can get ahead."

Between 1929 and 1932, she was on the editorial staffs of at least two newspapers, the *American West Indian News* and *Negro National News*. During the Depression, she became national director of the Young Negroes' Cooperative League, which established stores, buying clubs that encouraged poor people to pool their purchasing power, and other cooperative economic ventures in Black neighborhoods. During the same period, she worked with a variety of labor organizations in Harlem, including the Women's Day Workers and Industrial League, which focused on the problems of domestic workers. . . .

Her organizing work in Harlem brought her to the attention of some people active in NAACP circles, and in 1941 she applied to the NAACP for a job as an assistant field secretary. The job involved extensive travel throughout her native South, raising funds, memberships, and consciousness, trying to get people to see the relevance of the organization to their lives and trying to help them work through their very real fears about being associated with the NAACP. She spent about half of each year organizing membership drives and new chapters in the South—Florida, Alabama, Georgia, and Virginia—thus becoming exposed to a wide variety of leadership styles and organizational structures while making innumerable contacts with grassroots leadership, contacts that would become important in her work with the SCLC and SNCC.

In 1943 she became the NAACP's National Director of Branches. In what seems to be the pattern of her life, she was more in the organization than of it. She was a critic—not always a gentle one—of that organization's style of work. By 1941, she was calling the program "stale and uninteresting." She thought the leadership was overly concerned with recognition from whites, overly oriented to a middle-class agenda, unaware of the value of mass-based, confrontational politics, not nearly aggressive enough on economic issues, and too much in the hands of the New York office. She was particularly critical of the organization's tendency to stress membership size without attempting to involve those members more meaningfully in its program. She saw the organization as the victim of its own success. It was successful enough with its program of attacking the legal bases of racial oppression that its very success blinded the organization to its shortcomings. The legal emphasis meant that the huge mass base of the NAACP—400,000 by 1944—could not play a meaningful role in the development of policy and strategy.

She urged the organization to recruit more low-income members by, for example, sending organizers into pool rooms and taverns; her experience had been that some people would join up out of sheer surprise. The branches, she argued, not the national office, should be the focal point of struggle. . . . While many of her recommendations were ignored, she was able in 1944 to initiate a series of regional leadership conferences. The conferences, one of which was attended by Rosa Parks, were intended to help local leaders search for more effective ways to attack local problems and at the same time see how local issues were, inevitably, expressions of broader social issues.

She left the national office in 1946, partly as a result of having accepted responsibility for raising a niece and partly as a result of her conflicts with the organization's viewpoint. She worked for a while as a fund-raiser for the National Urban

League and continued to work with the NAACP at the local level, becoming president of the New York City branch which, in her phrase, she tried to "bring back to the people" by moving the office to a location where it would be more visible to the Harlem community and by developing a program in which Black and Hispanic parents actively worked on issues involving school desegregation and the quality of education. . . .

In the mid-1950s, with Bayard Rustin and Stanley Levison, she helped organize In Friendship, an organization that offered economic support for Blacks suffering reprisals for political activism in the South. This same group helped develop the idea of a mass-based organization to continue the momentum that came out of the Montgomery bus boycott. From that idea, developed by several groups almost simultaneously, grew the Southern Christian Leadership Conference. . . .

Levison and Rustin felt that the fledgling SCLC needed an experienced organizer and were able to talk a reluctant Ella Baker into taking the job. In 1957, she went south, intending to stay only a few weeks. She wound up staying two and a half years, becoming the first full-time executive director. At the beginning, she used to joke, SCLC's "office" was her purse and the nearest phone booth. She was responsible for organizing the voter registration and citizenship training drives that constituted the SCLC program during this period. She did this largely by exploiting the network of personal contacts she had developed while with the NAACP.

As with the NAACP, she had trouble getting her own thinking reflected in the programs of the SCLC. She tried to get the leadership to go into some of the rural counties where Blacks were not voting at all. Prophetically, she tried, also without success, to get the organization to place more emphasis on women and young people, the constituencies that would soon carry much of the movement. Miss Baker's emphasis on women reflected her sense of how southern Black organizations worked. "All of the churches depended, in terms of things taking place, on women, not men. Men didn't do the things that had to be done and you had a large number of women who were involved in the bus boycott. They were the people who kept the spirit going [the women] and the young people." Being ignored was hardly a surprise to her: "I had known . . . that there would never be any role for me in a leadership capacity with SCLC. Why? First, I'm a woman. Also, I'm not a minister. . . . The basic attitude of men and especially ministers, as to . . . the role of women in their church setups is that of taking orders, not providing leadership."

Despite the difficulties, her association with SCLC put her in a position to help create and shape one of the most significant organizations of the sixties, the Student Nonviolent Coordinating Committee (SNCC). When the sit-in movement among Black college students first began, Ella Baker, like several other adult activists, used her extensive contact list to help it spread. The sit-in phenomenon at the time was essentially a series of disconnected local actions. Feeling that the movement might be more effective with some coordination, Ella talked SCLC into sponsoring a meeting of activist students on the campus of her alma mater, Shaw University. From that meeting, held Easter weekend, 1960, evolved SNCC.

Adult civil rights organizations sent representatives to the organizing meeting with hopes of co-opting all that youthful energy. Three organizations—SCLC, the NAACP, and the Congress of Racial Equality (CORE)—wanted in on the action. . . . Miss Baker preferred that the students remain independent. Indeed, at one point she walked out of a staff meeting where strategies to bring the students into the SCLC were discussed. In Raleigh, she reinforced the feelings of those students who saw traditional adult leadership as too accommodating and unimaginative; and SNCC remained independent.

By this time, Miss Baker had been working in the South on and off for almost twenty years. In its early years SNCC, like SCLC previously, had her contact network at its disposal. . . . By 1961 SNCC had become the kind of organization that Ella Baker had been trying to create for some years. It went into the rural areas that other groups were reluctant to enter, it was far more open to the participation of women and young people than the established civil rights groups, and it disdained centralization and bureaucracy and insisted that leadership had to be discovered and developed at the local level. . . .

Miss Baker continued to work with a variety of groups through the sixties and well into the seventies. With SNCC, she helped organize the Mississippi Freedom Democratic Party (FDP), a vehicle to give the poor of that state some political voice. . . . She was involved with attempts to reform urban schools, with South African support groups, with Third World women's organizations, and attempts to organize poor whites in the South. Hers was a wonderfully eclectic style. Whatever the form of the injustice, she was willing to oppose it.

The ideas which undergirded her long activist career do not seem to have changed substantially since the 1930s. If there is one idea that seems central to her approach, it may be the idea of group-centered leadership rather than leader-centered groups. "I have always thought what is needed is the development of people who are interested not in being leaders as much as in developing leadership among other people." In contrast to the more traditional conception of leadership as moving people and directing events, hers was a conception of leadership as teaching, a conception that changes the nature of what it means to be successful. How many people show up for a rally may matter less than how much the people who organize the rally learn from doing so. If the attempt to organize the rally taught them anything about the mechanics of organizing, if the mere act of trying caused them to grow in self-confidence, if the organizers developed stronger bonds among themselves from striving together, then the rally may have been a success even if no one showed up for it. As she said, "You're organizing people to be self-sufficient rather than to be dependent upon the charismatic leader." If growth toward self-sufficiency is the point, then there may be times when people will have to be allowed to make "wrong" decisions, since making decisions and learning from the consequences are necessary to such growth. That was why Ella Baker tried to avoid exerting too much influence on the decision making in SNCC, for example. "Most of the youngsters had been trained to believe in or to follow adults. . . . I felt they ought to have a chance to learn to think things through and to make the decisions."

It follows that she had a poor opinion of centralized leadership, even if skillful and well intentioned.

> I have always felt it was a handicap for oppressed people to depend so largely on a leader, because unfortunately in our culture, the charismatic leader usually becomes a leader because he has found a spot in the public limelight. It usually means that the media made him, and the media may undo him. There is also the danger in our culture

that, because a person is called upon to give public statements and is acclaimed by the establishment, such a person gets to the point of believing that he *is* the movement. Such people get so involved with playing the game of being important that they exhaust themselves and their time and they don't do the work of actually organizing people.

From her perspective, the very idea of leading people to freedom is a contradiction in terms. Freedom requires that people be able to analyze their own social position and understand their collective ability to do something about it without relying on leaders. "Strong people," she said in one interview, "don't need strong leaders." "My basic sense of it has always been to get people to understand that in the long run they themselves are the only protection they have against violence or injustice. . . . People have to be made to understand that they cannot look for salvation anywhere but to themselves."

Whether people develop a sense of their own strength depends partly on the organizational context in which they are working. Ella Baker had misgivings about the common assumption that the bigger the political organization, the better, as well as the parallel assumption that rapid growth is always a sign of organizational vitality. . . . It is easy to forget that during most of the time when SNCC was at the forefront of the southern movement, the organization had only a few hundred very dedicated members. Part of what made that dedication possible, no doubt, was the organization's ability to generate a strong sense of community among its members in the early years. Its scale helped make that community possible, just as it helped each member of the organization to feel that his or her contribution mattered. It also seems that the decline of the organization was related to the sudden growth in the size of its membership after 1964. . . .

Group-centered leadership is leadership in which the ego needs of leaders are placed beneath the developmental needs of the group. It requires leaders who can deal nondestructively with their own need for recognition. Ella Baker held a special fear of the need of leaders for some sort of recognition from the larger society, seeing it as part of the pattern by which initially progressive American movements have traditionally been routinized.

Among Blacks she saw it as a distorting factor across several generations of leadership and across various ideological lines. Black radicals as well as Black moderates have allowed the desire to be recognized to blunt the thrust of their activism. Thus, in the NAACP of the forties and fifties, Ella Baker thought the thirst for recognition was one of the factors leading to accommodationist politics at a time when many of the members were ready for a more militant program. The thirst for recognition was also a problem for the radicals of the late 1960s, some of whom became so enamored of the coverage they were receiving from the press that they began performing for the press. As she saw it: "I think they got caught up in their own rhetoric. . . . To me, it is a part of our system which says that success is registered in terms of, if not money, then how much prestige and how much recognition you have. . . . So these youngsters with their own need for recognition began to respond to the press." It is not difficult to imagine what media recognition must have done to the egos of the leaders involved or how it must have poisoned their relationships with other, less-recognized activists who were working just as hard, risking just as much, as the handful of media celebrities.

The distorting potential of media recognition underscores again the case for groups not being too dependent upon leaders. Part of the reason Ella Baker is not a household name is her conviction that political organizers lose a certain kind of effectiveness when they allow themselves to become media stars. . . .

Miss Baker seems to have viewed the press as more useful in the process of mobilizing than in the process [of] organizing. The distinction between mobilizing and organizing was crucial for her. Organizing, according to Ella Baker, involves creating ongoing groups that are mass-based in the sense that the people a group purports to represent have real impact on the group's direction. Mobilizing is more sporadic, involving large numbers of people for relatively short periods of time and probably for relatively dramatic activities. What SNCC did in rural Mississippi, Alabama, and Georgia was organizing. Activists went into a community committed to staying there for a period of time, trying to identify local leadership, strengthen it, and help it find ways to create organizations and programs that would help local people reach a point of development where they would no longer need to rely on SNCC or anything similar. The intention was to leave behind enduring organizations led by the people in whose name they were created, organizations like the Freedom Democratic Party in Mississippi and the Lowndes County Freedom Organization in Alabama. At least, organizing under this conception involves the creation of stable, ongoing relationships and of ongoing attempts at political education.

By way of contrast, what the SCLC did in Birmingham and Albany and elsewhere was mobilizing—gong in for a matter of weeks or months, leading massive demonstrations aimed at bettering the conditions under which people lived, and then moving on. By its nature, mobilizing is more likely to be public and to be dependent upon generating appropriate publicity. The point is not that one or the other is more important historically—both are clearly necessary—but that they are two different political activities.

The distinction between organizing and mobilizing has become increasingly muddled. Young people looking back at the movement tend to see the mobilizing but not the organizing. They see the great demonstrations and the rallies and take that to be the movement. They do not see the organizing effort, often years of such effort, that made the grand moments possible. They do not see organizers going door to door for months on end trying to win trust, overcome fear, and educate people to the ways the movement might connect with their lives. . . . In general, Deep South organizing was a process of trying to become a part of the lives of the people one was trying to work with, and there was frequently nothing very dramatic about it.

Ella Baker . . . was always dubious about the real value of demonstrations. Lobbying and demonstrations may produce some gains from the powers that be relatively quickly, but the same powers may retract those gains as soon as the political winds shift. What Miss Baker called "real organizing" might mean that results would take longer to achieve, but it might also mean these results would be better protected. . . .

One has to wonder how she sustained her involvement for so long. It is not difficult to imagine how much frustration was built into the work she chose for herself. Nowadays we tend to think that anyone who works for social change for a year or two has made an enormous sacrifice. In the few places I know of where she comments on this, there is a suggestion that she was sustained by the faith that her work was a part of something on-going:

> Every time I see a young person who has come through the system to a stage where he could profit from the system and identify with it, but who identifies more with the struggle of black people who have not had his chance, every time I find such a person I take new hope. I feel new life as a result. . . .

FURTHER READING

Jervis Anderson, *Bayard Rustin: Troubles I've Seen: A Biography* (1997).

Taylor Branch, *Parting the Waters: America in the King Years, 1954–1963* (1988).

George Breitman, *The Last Year of Malcolm X: The Evolution of a Revolutionary* (1968).

Stewart Burns, ed., *Daybreak of Freedom: The Montgomery Bus Boycott* (1997).

Guy Carawan and Candie Carawan, *Freedom Is a Constant Struggle: Songs of the Freedom Movement* (1968).

Clayborne Carson, *In Struggle: SNCC and the Black Awakening of the 1960s* (1981).

Clayborne Carson, *Malcolm X: The FBI File* (1993).

William H. Chafe, *Civilities and Civil Rights: Greensboro, North Carolina, and the Black Struggle for Freedom* (1980).

David Colburn, *Racial Change and Community Crisis: St. Augustine, Florida, 1877–1980* (1985).

Vicki Crawford, Jacquelyn Anne Rouse, and Barbara Woods, eds., *Women in the Civil Rights Movement: Trailblazers and Torchbearers, 1941–1965* (1993).

John D'Emilio, "Homophobia and the Trajectory of Postwar American Radicalism: The Career of Bayard Rustin," *Radical History Review,* 62 (1995), 80–103.

John Dittmer, *Local People: The Struggle for Civil Rights in Mississippi* (1994).

Cynthia Griggs Fleming, *Soon We Will Not Cry: The Liberation of Ruby Doris Smith Robinson* (1998).

David Garrow, *Bearing the Cross: Martin Luther King, Jr., and the Southern Christian Leadership Conference* (1988).

Peter Louis Goldman, *The Death and Life of Malcolm X* (1973).

Joanne Grant, *Ella Baker: Freedom Bound* (1998).

Henry Hampton and Steve Fayer, with Sarah Flynn, *Voices of Freedom: An Oral History of the Civil Rights Movement from the 1950s Through the 1980s* (1990).

Michael K. Honey, *Southern Labor and Black Civil Rights: Organizing Memphis Workers* (1993).

Richard Kluger, *Simple Justice: The History of Brown vs. Board of Education and Black America's Struggle for Equality* (1975).

Steven F. Lawson, *Black Ballots: Voting Rights in the South, 1944–1969* (1976).

Steven F. Lawson and Charles Payne, *Debating the Civil Rights Movement, 1945–1968* (1998).

Chana Kai Lee, *For Freedom's Sake: The Life of Fannie Lou Hammer* (1999).

David L. Lewis, *King: A Critical Biography* (1970).

Aldon Morris, *The Origins of the Civil Rights Movement: Black Communities Organizing for Change* (1984).

Robert J. Norrell, *Reaping the Whirlwind: The Civil Rights Movement in Tuskegee* (1985).

Kenneth O'Reilly, *Racial Matters: The FBI's Secret File on Black America, 1960–1972* (1989).

Charles M. Payne, *I've Got the Light of Freedom: The Organizing Tradition and the Mississippi Freedom Struggle* (1995).

Armstead L. Robinson and Patricia Sullivan, *New Directions in Civil Rights Studies* (1991).

Belinda Robnett, *How Long? How Long? African-American Women in the Struggle for Civil Rights* (1997).

Harvard Sitkoff, *The Struggle for Black Equality, 1954–1980* (1981).

Timothy B. Tyson, *Radio Free Dixie: Robert F. Williams and the Roots of Black Power* (1999).

James M. Washington, ed., *A Testament of Hope: The Essential Writings of Martin Luther King, Jr.* (1986).

Stephen J. Whitfield, *A Death in the Delta: The Story of Emmet Till* (1988).

Youth of the Rural Organizing and Cultural Center, *Minds Stayed on Freedom: The Civil Rights Struggle in the Rural South: An Oral History* (1991).

C H A P T E R
10

After "Freedom Now!"

African-American men, women, and children in the early 1960s manifested their belief that through sit-ins, boycotts, marches, jail-ins, and other forms of literally putting their bodies on the line, they could achieve "Freedom Now!" But even as they met with numerous and unprecedented successes, many came to realize that voter registration, court-ordered desegregated schools, legislation against discrimination in public facilities, the opening up of some jobs, and eventually even a reduction in racist rhetoric and violence were only the opening wedges in black America's freedom struggle. During the 1960s and into the 1970s black Americans more ardently articulated a vision of freedom that linked social justice and economic democracy. This was not a new idea but one that now was often accompanied by little hope that poor housing, health, and other economic resource issues could be susceptible to the kinds of civil rights work that had been successful thus far. These issues called for far-reaching structural changes in wealth and income, a genuine sharing of political power, and full participation in the shaping of public policy.

D O C U M E N T S

In reaction to the 1963 murders of Mississippi NAACP field secretary Medgar Evers and of Addie Mae Collins, Denise McNair, Carole Robertson, and Cynthia Wesley as they attended Sunday School classes at Sixteenth Street Baptist Church in Birmingham, Alabama, pianist-singer Nina Simone composed "Mississippi Goddam." The lyrics from her April 1964 recording are the first document in this chapter. Although banned from radio stations throughout the South, Simone's "incongruously buoyant" rendering freed the song from any sorrowful or even angry tones so that it became a popular anthem that reaffirmed a determined commitment to the freedom struggle. Similarly SNCC's radical vision of political liberty continued to translate into a critique of federal authority, aiming always to transform U.S. politics. SNCC's denunciation of the Vietnam War, the second document, was opposed by the NAACP, the National Urban League, and some SCLC leaders fearful of alienating President Lyndon Johnson.

The Black Panther Party for Self-Defense was founded in Oakland, California, in 1966 by Huey Newton and Bobby Seale. It soon adopted a Ten-Point Program that included full employment, decent housing, an end to police brutality, and exemption from military service. The party rapidly grew to include chapters in thirty cities across the country, many of them engaged in a series of "survival programs" providing vital services within the community. In the third document, nine-year member Jimmy Slater tells political scientist Charles E. Jones about local party programs in Cleveland, Ohio, and subsequent repressive measures by police and by the FBI through its Counter Intelligence Program (COINTELPRO). In the 1970s, black feminists, many of whom grew to political awareness within the civil rights movement, came together to give organized voice to the simultaneous struggles against racism, sexism, classism, and heterosexism. The fourth document outlines the political beliefs of one such group, the Combahee River Collective. This Boston-based group took its name from the region in South Carolina where guerilla campaigns were waged by the Underground Railroad leader Harriet Tubman during the Civil War.

Throughout the late 1960s and 1970s African Americans made progress in the electoral sphere and in educational attainment, but these advances coincided with an economic crisis facing many urban areas in the 1970s and a widening gap in income and in poverty levels between black and white workers. Although the percentage of blacks in poverty declined in the 1960s and 1970s, the relative odds of a black person living in poverty remained more than four times that of a white person. The last two documents look at the extent and nature of black progress in the post–Civil Rights Movement era. The fifth document presents statistics about officeholding, educational attainment, income, and poverty. The sixth document, a list of "collective needs" presented to the governor of Florida by Concerned Black Organizations for Justice of Miami, represents the continuing frustration over police brutality, economic deprivation, and immigration policies that welcomed white Cubans while rejecting black Haitians and led to the Miami Rebellion in May 1980.

1. Nina Simone's Song "Mississippi Goddam," 1964

(The name of this tune is Mississippi Goddam. And I mean every word of it.)

> Alabama's gotten me so upset
> Tennessee made me lose my rest
> And everybody knows about Mississippi Goddam
>
> Alabama's gotten me so upset
> Tennessee made me lose my rest
> And everybody knows about Mississippi Goddam
>
> Can't you see it
> Can't you feel it
> It's all in the air
> I can't stand the pressure much longer
> Somebody say a prayer
>
> Alabama's gotten me so upset
> Tennessee made me lose my rest
> And everybody knows about Mississippi Goddam
>
> > (This is a show tune
> > But the show hasn't been written for it–yet)
>
> Hound dogs on my trail
> School children sitting in jail

Black cat cross my path
I think every day is gonna be my last

Lord have mercy on this land of mine
We all gonna get it in due time
I don't belong here
I don't belong there
I've even stopped believing in prayer

Don't tell me
I'll tell you
Me and my people just about due
I've been there so I know
They keep saying "Go slow!"

But that's just the trouble
                    Too slow
Washing the windows
                    Too slow
Picking the cotton
                    Too slow
You just plain rotten
                    Too slow
Too damn lazy
                    Too slow
Thinking's crazy
                    Too slow
Where am I going
What am I doing
I don't know
I don't know

Just try to do your very best
Stand up be counted with all the rest
Cause everybody knows about Mississippi Goddam

        (I bet you thought I was kiddin' didn't you?)

Picket lines
School boycotts
They try to say it's a Communist plot
All I want is equality
for my sister my brother my people and me

Yes you lied to me all these years
You told me to wash and clean my ears
And talk real fine, just like a lady
And you'd stop calling me Sister Sadie

Oh but this whole country is full of lies
You all gonna die and die like flies
I don't trust you any more

You keep on saying, "Go slow!"
"Go-o-oh slow!"

But that's just the trouble
                    Too slow
Desegregation
                    Too slow
Mass participation
                    Too slow
Reunification
                    Too slow
Do things gradually
                    Too slow
Will bring more tragedy
                    Too slow
Why don't you see it
Why don't you feel it
I don't know
I don't know

You don't have to live next to me,
Just give me my equality
Everybody knows about Mississippi
Everybody knows about Alabama
Everybody knows about Mississippi Goddd dammm

    (That's it!)

2. SNCC Denounces the Vietnam War, 1966

January 6, 1966

The Student Non-Violent Coordinating Committee assumes its right to dissent with United States foreign policy on any issue, and states its opposition to United States involvement in the war in Vietnam on these grounds:

> We believe the United States government has been deceptive in its claims of concern for the freedom of the Vietnamese people, just as the government has been deceptive in claiming concern for the freedom of the colored people in such other countries as the Dominican Republic, the Congo, South Africa, Rhodesia and in the United States itself.
>
> We of the Student Non-Violent Coordinating Committee have been involved in the black people's struggle for liberation and self-determination in this country for the past five years. Our work, particularly in the South, taught us that the United States government has never guaranteed the freedom of oppressed citizens, and is not yet truly determined to end the rule of terror and oppression within its own borders.

Reprinted from *Freedomways Magazine,* 6, no. 1 (Winter 1966), 6–7.

We ourselves have often been victims of violence and confinement executed by U.S. government officials. We recall the numerous persons who have been murdered in the South because of their efforts to secure their civil and human rights, and whose murderers have been allowed to escape penalty for their crimes. The murder of Samuel Younge in Tuskegee, Alabama is no different from the murder of people in Vietnam, for both Younge and the Vietnamese sought and are seeking to secure the rights guaranteed them by law. In each case, the United States Government bears a great part of the responsibility for these deaths.

Samuel Younge was murdered because United States law is not being enforced. Vietnamese are being murdered because the United States is pursuing an aggressive policy in violation of international law. The United States is no respecter of persons or law when such persons or laws run counter to its needs and desires. We recall the indifference, suspicion and outright hostility with which our reports of violence have been met in the past by government officials. We know for the most part that elections in this country, in the North as well as the South, are not free. We have seen that the 1965 Voting Rights Act and the 1964 Civil Rights Act have not yet been implemented with full federal power and concern. We question then the ability and even the desire of the United States government to guarantee free elections abroad. We maintain that our country's cry of "preserve freedom in the world" is a hypocritical mask behind which it squashed liberation movements which are not bound and refuse to be bound by the expediency of the United States cold war policy.

We are in sympathy with and support the men in this country who are unwilling to respond to the military draft which would compel them to contribute their lives to United States aggression in the name of the "freedom" we find so false in this country.

We recoil with horror at the inconsistency of this supposedly free society where responsibility to freedom is equated with responsibility to lend oneself to military aggression. We take note of the fact that 16% of the draftees from this country are Negro, called on to stifle the liberation of Vietnam, to preserve a "democracy" which does not exist for them at home.

We ask: Where is the draft for the Freedom fight in the United States?

We therefore encourage those Americans who prefer to use their energy in building democratic forms within the country. We believe that work in the civil rights movement and other human relations organizations is a valid alternative, knowing full well that it may cost them their lives, as painfully as in Vietnam.

3. An Interview with Black Panther Jimmy Slater

CEJ: Why did you join the Black Panther Party?

JS: I learned about the Black Panther Party from friends and other people who were familiar with the organization. We began to understand the positive

Charles E. Jones, ed., *The Black Panther Party [Reconsidered]* (Baltimore: Black Classic Press, 1998), 147–149, 151–152. Reprinted with permission.

community programs that the Panthers had going on throughout the community. . . . When I became a volunteer worker, I was eighteen. I was between nineteen-and-a-half and twenty years old when I became a full-fledged member of the Party. . . . I became a member of the Black Panther Party in the late sixties, (1968), and I left the Party in the mid-seventies (1977). . . .

We had to go through a procedure that involved serving as volunteers first and then later being accepted as full members of the Party. Practice was the criterion of the troops; and on the basis of practice, we were called upon to become full-time members. . . . I was one of those brothers out on the street, but every one of my leaders was educated. The Party placed an emphasis on education and always tried to persuade every individual around us to pursue higher education. . . . I ended up attending Laney Junior College (Oakland) and going all the way to San Francisco State because of the push from the Black Panther Party. I really didn't have any intention of doing that before I joined the Party.

CEJ: What community programs were offered by your branch?

JS: We had a free health clinic and a free breakfast program in Cleveland. We used to serve out of the Catholic church and a number of the Black churches around. My mother's church was one of those churches. We served breakfast out of the basement. We also had a free clothing program. We utilized the facilities from the churches to set up this program, and we had volunteers—church members, my mother, and a lot of other seniors there who would volunteer to work with us. And they were the ones who really kept the free clothing program going. The free health clinic was blown up. I believe the year was 1969 or somewhere in that area. . . . [W]e would imagine that the police, COINTEL-PRO, [blew it up]. Any positive program that served and mobilized the community was attacked. It was one of the things we had going that served a lot of people who needed free medical aid, and it was attacked to undermine the Party's efforts.

. . . [W]hen the Angela Davis free breakfast program was implemented, they (government officials) weren't giving away free lunch at schools. . . . At one point, we were testing for sickle cell anemia. We found this to be a very vital need in the Black community because at the time no one was testing Black people for sickle cell anemia. . . .

CEJ: What type of COINTELPRO tactics were levied against your particular branch?

JS: Every kind that you could name. From the point of planting people among us to creating friction and divisions among comrades within the organization. There were several examples. Now, we would have a peaceful demonstration, and everything is going okay. And then you have a fool out there hollering and talking about murdering and kill the pig. . . . Another thing was that COINTELPRO played a great part by sending leaders of the East Coast fabricated messages that were supposedly from leaders of the West Coast. In other words, COINTELPRO manipulated contradictions and played upon friction within organization. . . . [W]e had COINTELPRO to deal with on one hand and the police on the other. We had spies sitting all around us and working with us in some cases. We found that out after everything had closed down. . . .

4. Combahee River Collective Statement, 1977

We are a collective of Black feminists who have been meeting together since 1974.
... The most general statement of our politics at the present time would be that we
are actively committed to struggling against racial, sexual, heterosexual, and class
oppression and see as our particular task the development of integrated analysis
and practice based upon the fact that the major systems of oppression are interlocking. The synthesis of these oppressions creates the conditions of our lives. As
Black women we see Black feminism as the logical political movement to combat
the manifold and simultaneous oppressions that all women of color face. ...

   Above all else, our politics initially sprang from the shared belief that Black
women are inherently valuable, that our liberation is a necessity not as an adjunct
to somebody else's but because of out need as human persons for autonomy. This
may seem so obvious as to sound simplistic, but it is apparent that no other ostensibly progressive movement has ever considered our specific oppression a priority
or worked seriously for the ending of that oppression. ... We realize the that the
only people who care enough about us to work consistently for our liberation is
us. Our politics evolve from a healthy love for ourselves, our sisters, and our community which allows us to continue our struggle and work. ... We reject pedestals,
queenhood, and walking ten paces behind. To be recognized as human, levelly
human, is enough.

   We believe that sexual politics under patriarchy is as pervasive in Black
women's lives as are the politics of class and race. We also often find it difficult to
separate race from class from sex oppression because in our lives they are most often
experienced simultaneously. We know that there is such a thing as racial-sexual
oppression which is neither solely racial nor solely sexual, e.g., the history of rape of
Black women by white men as a weapon of political repression.

   Although we are feminists and lesbians, we feel solidarity with progressive
Black men and do not advocate the fractionalization that white women who are sep-
aratists demand. Our situation as Black people necessitates that we have solidarity
around the fact of race, which white women of course do not need to have with
white men, unless it is their negative solidarity as racial oppressors. We struggle
together with Black men against racism, while we also struggle with Black men
about sexism.

   ... We are socialists because we believe that work must be organized for the collective benefit of those who do the work and create the products and not for the profit
of the bosses. Material resources must be equally distributed among those who create
these resources. We are not convinced, however, that a socialist revolution that is not
also a feminist and antiracist revolution will guarantee our liberation. ...

   ... We reject the stance of lesbian separatism because it is not a viable political analysis or strategy for us. It leaves out far too much and far too many people,
particularly Black men, women, and children. We have a great deal of criticism and

The Combahee River Collective, "A Black Feminist Statement," in *Capitalist Patriarchy and the Case
for Socialist Revolution,* ed. Zillah Eisenstein. Copyright © 1978 by Zillah Eisenstein, Monthly Review
Press. Reprinted with permission.

loathing for what men have been socialized to be in this society: what they support, how they act, and how they oppress. But we do not have the misguided notion that it is their maleness, per se—i.e., their biological maleness—that makes them what they are. As Black women we find any type of biological determinism a particularly dangerous and reactionary basis upon which to build a politic. . . .

. . . The inclusiveness of our politics makes us concerned with any situation that impinges upon the lives of women and those of Third World and working people in general. . . . We might, for example, become involved in workplace organizing at a factory that employs Third World women or picket a hospital that is cutting back on already inadequate health care to a Third World community, or set up a rape crisis center in a Black neighborhood. Organizing around welfare or daycare concerns might also be a focus. The work to be done and the countless issues that this work represents merely reflect the pervasiveness of our oppression.

Issues and projects that collective members have actually worked on are sterilization abuse, abortion rights, battered women, rape, and health care. We have also done many workshops on Black feminism on college campuses, at women's conferences, and most recently for high school women. . . .

As Black feminists and lesbians we know that we have a very definite revolutionary task to perform and we are ready for the lifetime of work and struggle before us.

5. A Statistical Portrait of Black America, 1940–1990s

Black Elected Officials, by Selected Office Categories, 1941 – 1997

| Year | U.S. Offices | | State Offices | | | City Offices | | | Total[1] |
	Senate	Representative	Administrator	Senate	Representative	Mayor	Council	School Board	
1941	0	1	0	3	23	0	4	2	33
1947	0	2	0	5	33	0	18	8	66
1951	0	2	0	1	39	0	25	15	82
1965	0	4	1	18	84	3	74	68	280
1970	1	9	1	31	137	48	552	362	1,469
1975	1	17	5	53	223	135	1,237	894	3,503
1980	0	17	6	70	247	182	1,809	1,149	4,890
1985	0	20	4	90	302	286	2,189	1,363	6,016
1997	1	39	6	154	425	387	3,375	1,889	8,656

[1] For 1965 – 1997 total includes all black elected officials, not just those in selected categories.

Sources: David Jaynes and Robin M. Williams, Jr., eds. *A Common Destiny: Blacks and American Society* (D.C.: National Academy Press, 1989), 240; David A. Bositis, *Black Elected Officials: A Statistical Summary, 1993 – 1997* (D.C.: Joint Center for Politcal and Economic Studies, 1998), 9.

Levels of Schooling Completed for 25 to 29 Year Olds: 1940, 1965, 1975, 1985, 1995

Year	Percent Blacks Completing Four Years of High School or More	Percent Blacks Completing Four Years of College or More	Percent Whites Completing Four Years of High School or More	Percent Whites Completing Four Years of College or More
1940	12.3	1.6	41.2	6.4
1965	50.3	6.8	72.8	13.0
1975	71.0	10.7	84.4	22.8
1985	80.6	11.5	86.8	23.2
1995	86.5	15.3	87.4	26.0

Data for 1940, Black and other races. Data for 1995 are high school graduates or more; Bachelor's degree or more.

Source: U.S. Census Bureau, "Percent of People 25 Years Old and Over Who Have Completed High School or College, Selected Years 1940 to 1998;" published 10 December 1998, <http://www. census.gov/population/socdemo/education/tablea-02.txt>

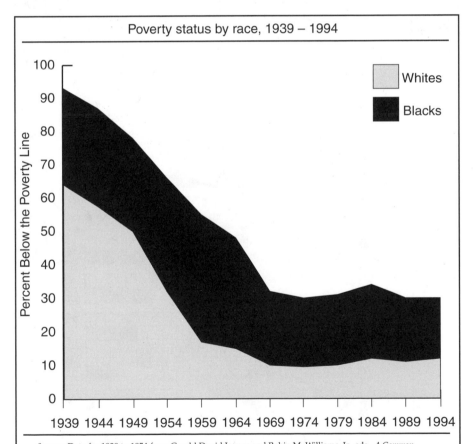

Poverty status by race, 1939 – 1994

Sources: Data for 1939 to 1954 from Gerald David Jaynes and Robin M. Williams, Jr., eds., *A Common Destiny: Blacks and American Society* (D.C.: National Academy Press, 1989), 278. Data from 1959 to 1994 from U.S. Bureau of the Census, "Poverty Status of Persons, by Family Relationship, Race, and Hispanic Origin: 1959 to 1993;" published 1993, <http://www.census.gov/hhes/income/incpov93/povtab2.html> and U.S. Census Bureau, "Age, Sex, Household Relationship, Race, and Hispanic Origin–Poverty Status of Persons in 1994;" published 18 November 1996, <http://ferret.bls.census.gov/macro/031995/pov/1_001.htm>

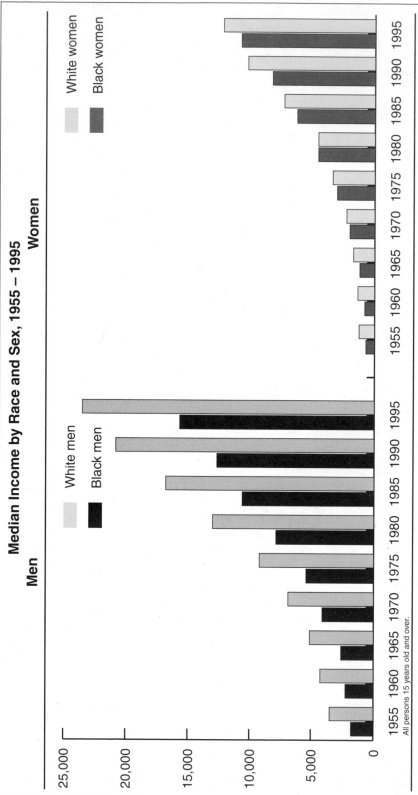

Median Income by Race and Sex, 1955 – 1995

Men

White men
Black men

1955 1960 1965 1970 1975 1980 1985 1990 1995

All persons 15 years old and over.

Women

White women
Black women

1955 1960 1965 1970 1975 1980 1985 1990 1995

25,000

20,000

15,000

10,000

5,000

0

Based on data from U.S. Census Bureau, "Table P-5A. Regions–White People by Median Income and Sex: 1953 to 1998," published 10 November 1999, <http://www.census.gov/hhes/income/histinc/p05a. html> and "Table P-5B. Regions–Black People by Median Income and Sex: 1953 to 1998," published 10 November 1999, <http://www.census.gov/hhes/income/histinc/p05b.html>.

6. Miami's Concerned Black Organizations for Justice Issues a Manifesto of "Collective Needs," 1980

A community-based group, Concerned Black Organizations for Justice, Wednesday asked that Gov. Bob Graham approve a list of "collective needs" for black residents.

The group asks that funds be allocated for black businesses, schools, and a hospital, and for "reinstatement of the Bill of Rights" for black residents.

A spokesman said the list was based on the result of interviews with hundreds of residents in all of Dade's black communities.

"If there is a serious commitment to restore some kind of order to the community, then there must be a serious effort to respond to the needs the masses have voiced," said spokesman Bill Robinson Parks.

"We were born and raised in the community," Parks said. "We work here. We live here. We've been here all our lives. We're not trying to get any grant money."

The group serves as an umbrella organization for several grassroots groups.

Other members of the group said the violence that erupted in Liberty City after the McDuffie verdict was a "spontaneous rebellion" and not a riot.

"We want the white media to immediately discontinue calling our legitimate black rebellion a riot," Parks said. He said the rebellion was not a "planned uprising."

"This is the result of historical neglect," he said. "It has been seething for the past couple of years. A riot is what the police were doing when they slashed tires and vandalized cars."

The group also called the visits of prominent out-of-town blacks "irrelevant . . . We respectfully ask that they return to their own repressed communities," Parks said.

The list of needs included:

• Withdrawal of National Guard troops, FBI agents, plainclothes policemen and special agents.
• Sufficient investment funds to establish black businesses, schools, a hospital, and provide food, medicine and phone services for families and the elderly.
• Reinstatement of the Bill of Rights [in black areas], including freedom of speech and of assembly, an end to illegal search and seizures and the right to bear arms.
• Restitution for cars and property damaged by police and National Guard troops, and an agreement not to use cars marked "looters" as evidence in court.
• A comprehensive job program for blacks over 13 with "minimum living" salaries of $15,000.
• Police surveillance in white communities to protect blacks who live, work and pass through.
• Removal from office of both State Attorney Janet Reno and County Manager Merrett Stierheim and an investigation of the criminal justice system by an "acceptable international organization."
• Refugee status granted to all black immigrants.
• The hiring of black contractors to remove burned-out buildings
• Twenty-four-hour access to radio and television stations.

Reprinted with permission of the *Miami Herald* from Joe Eglesby, "Black Group Sends Graham 'Needs' List," *Miami Herald,* May 22, 1980, p. 2C; permission conveyed through Copyright Clearance Center, Inc.

A number of civil rights activists across the country went to work for the War on Poverty in the mid-1960s. In the first essay, George Lipsitz, professor of Ethnic Studies at the University of California at San Diego, employs a structural analysis of the War on Poverty to show the dilemmas one particular activist faced working within a government bureaucracy. Ivory Perry, the subject of his study, was a Korean War veteran who had been instrumental in CORE actions in St. Louis, New York, and Bogalusa, Louisiana, for more than five years before he began his government job. The second essay draws our attention to transformations in northern black urban life in the late 1960s and early 1970s. Suzanne E. Smith, a historian at George Mason University, analyzes the politics of Motown within a newly emerging black political majority in Detroit.

Civil Rights Activism and the War on Poverty

GEORGE LIPSITZ

. . . Work in the antipoverty campaign brought unprecedented opportunities to Ivory Perry, but it posed some new problems as well. In the past, he had acted on his own or under the auspices of civil rights groups, and he answered to no one but the community he wanted to mobilize. As a paid government official at HDC [St. Louis's Human Development Corporation], he ran the risks of having an entire bureaucratic apparatus passing judgment on his actions. The War on Poverty's enabling legislation specifically called for "maximum feasible participation of the poor" in community action programs, but the poor gained no significant economic or political resources to make that "participation" meaningful. Designed at least in part as a response to the civil insurrections in the ghettos, the structure of the anti-poverty program might just as easily tranquilize as mobilize poor people, depending on its implementation at the local level. Ivory Perry ran the risk of squandering his reputation and prestige in the community on tokenistic efforts to draw poor people into programs with neither the will nor the resources to meaningfully address their grievances. . . .

Antipoverty workers also confronted numerous demands for immediate assistance that conflicted with their own long-range political goal of empowering the poor. People could not participate in the tedious process of improving their communities if they had no jobs or no food. . . . But Perry . . . believed that racism in the North created even more problems than it did in the South. White southerners enacted discriminatory laws and openly proclaimed their commitment to white supremacy, but in the process provided a clear and unambiguous target for those determined to bring about change. Perry found that northerners generally spoke in more conciliatory language but still engaged in discriminatory, exploitative, and repressive actions against black people. Thus when Dr. Martin Luther King, Jr.'s open-housing campaign in Chicago in 1966 attempted to address the

Excerpted and reprinted from the chapter entitled "The War on Poverty: The Emergence of an Organic Intellectual," included in George Lipsitz, *A Life in the Struggle: Ivory Perry and the Culture of Opposition* (Philadelphia: Temple University Press, 1988; rev. ed., 1995), 124, 128–133, 136–142, by permission of Temple University Press. All Rights Reserved.

complex racial problems facing northern cities, his crusade attracted Perry's attention immediately. . . .

The SCLC sent out a call for organizers familiar with the problems of northern ghettos to aid in the Chicago campaign. Excited by King's decision to focus on circumstances confronting black people in the North, Perry spent his vacation time during the summer of 1966 working with the SCLC in Chicago. . . .

. . . Perry felt that the SCLC and Dr. King had understood correctly the need for a new direction in the civil rights movement—to go beyond ending discriminatory laws and to start ending discriminatory practices. Especially in northern industrial cities like Chicago and St. Louis, civil rights issues transcended legal issues and involved concrete acts of economic and political oppression ranging from poor housing to police brutality. Perry felt that the movement had to become more oriented toward what he called the survival issues of jobs, housing, and health.

When he returned to St. Louis, Ivory Perry found one of those issues confronting him in a dramatic way. On Saturday night, September 24, 1966, police officers arrested Russell Hayes, a nineteen-year-old black youth, on suspicion of burglary. According to the police, Hayes made a suspicious movement and appeared to be reaching into his back pocket for a gun, so the arresting officers shot and killed him. To support their contention, the officers produced a tear gas gun they said had been found in Hayes's back pocket. Three days later, a coroner's report endorsed the officers' version of events, ruling the shooting a "justifiable homicide."

Yet some aspects of the police account raised doubts among citizens. The shooting took place in the courtyard of the police station while Hayes sat in the back seat of a squad car with his wrists cuffed behind his back. Police officers generally searched black suspects thoroughly, and it seemed unlikely that they would fail to notice a tear gas gun in the back pocket of a burglary suspect. The back doors of police cars opened only from the outside and a partition divided the front seats from the back. Many wondered how a young man in the back seat with his hands cuffed behind him could pose a threat to police officers sufficient to make them shoot him at close range.

. . . Perry helped plan a march on police headquarters and a demonstration outside the home of the chairman of the board of police commissioners. On September 28, four days after the shooting, another demonstration against the coroner's verdict erupted into violence. At the conclusion of a protest rally, one hundred people roamed through the downtown business district, smashing store windows and damaging parked cars in a violent spree that left ten police officers and two firemen injured. Ivory Perry had no part in the violence, but he understood the anger that lay behind it, and he attempted to channel that anger into political pressure on the police department to secure a change in its policies.

Three weeks after the Hayes shooting, St. Louis police officers killed another suspect, this time a sixteen-year-old white youth named Timothy Walsh. Police spokesmen contended that officers were questioning Walsh inside the police station about a shooting incident when the young man jumped up from his chair, ran through a window, and climbed a fence outside the station. They explained that one of the policemen aimed a shot below the suspect while Walsh stood on top of the fence, but that when Walsh jumped down, the bullet struck him in the back. Perry learned that Timothy Walsh had been enrolled in HDC's Neighborhood Youth

Corps program, and he mobilized the resources of HDC to protest the shooting. He paid a visit to the Walsh home. The youth's mother and brother talked about "being poor and having no one to stand up for you and about their anger at people in power," and Perry pledged to help them. They agreed to organize a picket line that night outside the police station, and to work together to demand an investigation of the incident. . . .

Ivory Perry brought thirty demonstrators, most of them blacks, to the Lucas Avenue police station to protest the Walsh shooting. One week later, two groups of marchers—blacks from the North Side and whites from the South Side—converged on police headquarters where the coroner's inquest was being held. Perry led the demonstrators into the hearing room: some carried cardboard coffins with the names of Walsh and Hayes on them; others held signs reading, "The Police Are Hired to Protect, Not to Shoot." When the coroner declared the shooting a justifiable homicide, Walsh's father pointed to an off-center clock on the wall and said bitterly, "Even the clock is crooked."

From the inquest, the integrated group of marchers accompanied the Walsh family to a City Hall meeting with Mayor A. J. Cervantes. The mayor expressed his regret over the shootings of Walsh and Hayes and threw his support behind moderate proposals to revise police procedures about fleeing suspects. Both St. Louis daily newspapers editorialized about the need for better relations between the police department and the poor, and at least for a time after this demonstration the police did act with more restraint. Perhaps more significantly, for the first time in recent memory, a civil rights issue in St. Louis united poor whites and poor blacks in a common political protest action. . . .

Throughout 1966 and 1967, Ivory Perry used his base at the Union-Sarah Gateway Center as way of intervening in countless disputes and struggles affecting poor people. Housing issues formed the core of his concerns and he instigated a variety of actions designed to address the housing crisis facing poor people. In 1966 he organized the Metropolitan Tenants Organization (MTO) in St. Louis to unite tenants in slum housing in a common effort to secure better housing at affordable rents. The MTO staged Missouri's first rent strike that year, and it encouraged people to think of housing as a community issue rather than a private problem.

On May 8, 1967, Ivory Perry attacked urban renewal as the cause of many housing problems in St. Louis when he testified before the National Commission on Urban Problems. After sitting through optimistic descriptions of St. Louis's urban renewal record by the mayor, civic leaders, and distinguished social scientists, Ivory Perry took the stand and told the commission simply and directly, "This urban renewal is Negro removal. They are knocking down the houses and they have no place to relocate the families. These people can not take too much more." Perry's description contradicted all the previous testimony and it dissented from the assessments of urban renewal presented by architects, urban planners, social scientists, and other traditional intellectuals. But it reflected the things he had learned from daily contact with poor people and from his own research, and he felt confident that he was right and the experts were wrong. . . .

A Gallup poll taken in March 1964 showed that 83 percent of Americans felt that poverty would never be eliminated in the United States. Thirty-three percent claimed that poor people brought misery on themselves through lack of effort,

29 percent blamed circumstances beyond their control, and 32 percent said that laziness and outside circumstances bore equal responsibility for the plight of the poor. Most Americans supported efforts to help individuals victimized by external conditions, but stereotypes about the poor as indolent and immoral worked against a concerted national commitment to eradicate the systemic cause of poverty. Another poll, conducted in October 1964, disclosed that 68 percent of respondents supported government action to guarantee adequate food and shelter to all, but 64 percent also agreed that "welfare and relief make people lazy." . . .

Structural factors clearly played the dominant role in black poverty during the postwar years. At a time when white unemployment hovered between 3 and 6 percent, black unemployment stayed above 10 percent. A survey of selected census tracts in northern ghetto areas in 1960 showed black unemployment ranging from 23 to 41 percent. Black workers came to industrial cities at a time when automation reduced rather than expanded the number of production jobs, when unions and political machines dominated by other ethnic groups dispensed political patronage positions, and when capital flight and deindustrialization began to transform centers of high-paying industrial labor to centers of low-paying service work. Public and private home loan policies denied blacks access to expanding suburbs, while urban renewal programs built up central business districts at the expense of black homeowners and renters. Structural factors explained most of the causes for poverty among whites as well. Trapped in declining rural areas or competing with blacks for unskilled positions in decaying cities, poor whites faced historical and economic transformations similar to those facing many blacks. Sixty percent of poor people could not compete in the labor market because of their age or disabilities, and almost half of the households headed by female or elderly wage earners lived in poverty in the early 1960s. Whatever the quality of their internal moral resources, most poor people faced deprivation because of the nature of jobs open to them in an expanding economy with an inequitable distribution of wealth.

Yet neither the dominant American ideology nor the prevailing American political culture could address these structural inequities. Transfer payments or economic reorganization might have ended poverty, but both demanded sacrifices from the nonpoor. It was easier to blame the victims of this system—the poor people themselves—than to undertake the expense of guaranteed annual income or full-employment policies. A program of self-help aimed at changing the poor themselves by inculcating them with middle-class values required no prohibitive expense, and at the same time helped maintain the fiction that poverty stemmed from the character deficiencies among the impoverished.

Consequently, the War on Poverty emerged as a confused mixture of programs—education, job training, and citizenship instruction, most of which helped prepare poor people for opportunities that did not exist. Low-income people certainly needed literacy, marketable skills, and access to political channels, but without major expenditures on housing, health, transportation, and employment opportunities, the antipoverty program could do little more than raise false hopes for most of the poor.

Even as meliorative self-help, the program spent too little to realize even its own modest goals. Between 1965 and 1970, the Office of Economic Opportunity received only 1.5 percent of the federal budget, a figure amounting to one third of

1 percent of the gross national product. While still large in dollar amount (federal spending on the poor increased from $12 billion to $27 billion in six years, although the War on Poverty itself received only about $1.7 billion per year between 1965 and 1970), spending on the War on Poverty did not even exceed the amount of money the poor paid in taxes, much less approach the size of the massive subsidies and incentives given to middle-class and wealthy citizens through pensions, investment credits, Social Security, or the home mortgage deduction. Had the money spent on poor people during the War on Poverty been parceled out as cash grants, each poor person in America would have received only $50 to $70 per year. As it was, most of the aid came in the form of federal payment for services that actually enriched doctors, school districts, and realtors more than the poor. . . .

Growing Republican voting strength in the South and West threatened traditional electoral support for the Democratic party, and made the Kennedy administration eager to devise programs that would mobilize potential Democratic voters in the rural South and industrial North. Challenges from the civil rights movement and the outbreak of urban riots made government officials sensitive to potential criticisms from the margins of society and posed the specter of a mass movement independent of the control mechanisms of the New Deal coalition. A concerted government program to aid the poor might preempt some of the more radical tendencies of the civil rights movement by drawing activists into government positions where change could be regulated and monitored in ways that prevented radical disruption. Finally, the national Democratic party and pro-growth coalitions coalesced around Democratic big-city mayors depended on an electoral coalition that included poor and black people, and the War on Poverty seemed to offer a vehicle for strengthening those ties.

The diverse political motivations behind the antipoverty program meant that it could succeed in the eyes of its proponents, even if it did nothing to improve the lot of the poor. Yet the measure also created an enhanced opportunity structure for activists and organic intellectuals active in oppositional movements. Social service professionals, civil rights activists, community organizers, and traditional and organic intellectuals viewed the War on Poverty as a vehicle for social change. They understood the limits imposed on OEO by politics, but they also felt that the larger social movement emerging out of the ferment of civil rights activity could exert pressures of its own to turn the antipoverty effort in a more radical direction.

Politicians and social reformers found common, if shaky, ground in the program's legal mandate to encourage the maximum feasible participation of the poor in OEO activities. . . . For politicians, maximum feasible participation held out the promise of fighting poverty at bargain rates by pawning off a lot of antipoverty activity on volunteer boards and committees. Such participation drew poor people into federally funded but locally controlled patronage networks without yielding to them control of existing patronage institutions like school boards, unions, welfare systems, police boards, and housing authorities. In addition, "community" representatives from business, labor, and government also served on OEO boards under the aegis of localism, and they acted as moderating influences on any radical tendencies voiced by the poor themselves.

For their part, the social service professionals and activists that staffed local agencies saw a different potential in maximum feasible participation. In their view, antipoverty organizations could start poor people talking about their problems and

begin drawing them into political activism. Once initiated, that process of involvement might break the hold that fear and pessimism had on the poor, a hold that
often discouraged aggrieved groups from joining social movements. Maximum
feasible participation might mobilize the poor to action, educate them about who
really held economic and political power, and alert them to the possibilities of
social contestation as a cure for their problems. . . .

Ivory Perry stepped into the middle of this complicated historical battle. . . .
His interpretation of "maximum feasible participation" of the poor included rent
strikes, obstructive demonstrations, and a fusing of the antipoverty program with
the civil rights movement. He assumed that disruption worked in his favor, that the
poor would make gains only when they became enough of a nuisance, or enough of
a threat, to make people in power decide that it was less expensive to meet their
demands than to continue to resist them.

Understandably enough, Perry's activist stance made him a focal point of controversy within HDC. Landlords, employers, and realtors wondered why their tax
dollars went to finance obstructive demonstrations against them and their way of
doing business. Politicians questioned the wisdom of a federal program that mobilized poor people around the shortcomings of municipal building inspectors or the
failings of the police review process. Businessmen willing to tolerate an antipoverty program as a necessary antidote to riots and disruptive protests failed to
see why the Human Development Corporation would support an individual who
constantly appeared at the forefront of explosive confrontations.

Even within the agency itself, many felt that Ivory Perry's activities jeopardized their own efforts. With hundreds of jobs and a $35 million budget at stake,
HDC could ill afford powerful enemies, but Perry seemed to specialize in tactics
that antagonized its enemies. . . . Clyde Cahill [director of HDC] . . . felt that Perry
served a useful function, alerting everyone to real grievances that might otherwise be ignored. Yet Cahill had serious disagreements with Perry over tactics and
strategy. From his perspective as an administrator, the poor needed allies from
business, government, and labor; aggressive confrontations turned some of these
potential friends into enemies. . . . [I]t was one thing to organize marches and
demonstrations, but quite another to fashion long-range solutions to structural
social problems. Cahill favored a more disciplined approach, acting in structured
steps to enable the poor to win control over resources. He feared that the antagonisms stirred up by militant direct action might actually retard the progress by isolating the poor from potential friends and the resources they controlled. For his
part, Perry felt that his constituents had no time to wait for phased-in solutions,
that they needed help immediately. In addition, he mistrusted the levels of bureaucracy implicit in Cahill's structured approach because he feared that they would
take on an institutional life of their own and lose contact with the constituency they
presumably served. . . .

Hated outside his community and barraged by constant requests for assistance
from within it, Perry exposed himself to extraordinary pressures working for HDC.
The very perceptions and actions that won him credibility within his community
made him enemies outside of it. The very actions that to him held the most promise
for ending poverty often threatened the institutional survival of the antipoverty program itself. . . . By engaging in confrontational direct-action protests, Ivory Perry

stretched the internal contradictions of the War on Poverty to the breaking point. Every time he took to the streets, every time he organized actions against realtors, building inspectors, or the police, he made a statement about poverty and its causes.

His actions proceeded from the assumption that an unjust system oppressed the poor, and from the belief that specific individuals and institutions profited from poverty. He rejected the idea of poverty as a paradox, as an ironic juxtaposition of deprivation within an affluent society. Instead, he argued for a causal relationship: some people remained poor because the structural systemic workings of the economy benefited the rich. By taking direct action he challenged the idea that poverty stemmed from the character flaws of the poor; he placed the blame instead on the inequitable distribution of wealth and opportunity in American society. In the process, he exposed the deep antagonisms simmering beneath the surface harmony within the coalition supporting the antipoverty programs. . . .

The Political Culture of Detroit

SUZANNE E. SMITH

. . . In October 1970 . . . [a] Langston Hughes and Margaret Danner poetry album . . . became one of the first offerings of Motown's Black Forum spoken-word label. . . . The labels's credo, published on album covers, stated that "Black Forum is a medium for the presentation of ideas and voices of the worldwide struggle of Black people to create a new era. Black Forum also serves to provide authentic materials for use in schools and colleges and for the home study of Black history and culture. Black Forum is a permanent record of the sound of the struggle and the sound of a new era."

Ewart Abner, Junius Griffin, and George Schiffer were in charge of the label and shaped its political orientation. . . . Schiffer, Motown's long-time contract lawyer, worked concurrently as a civil rights attorney for the Congress of Racial Equality in New York City. Each of these men had a commitment to the civil rights struggle that extended beyond the confines of Motown Studios. . . . They perceived the Black Forum project as an opportunity to record subjects and issues often ignored by the musical offerings of the company.

The first Black Forum albums reflected the political agenda and creative interests of the label's producers. Both Abner and Griffin were friends of Stokely Carmichael, and they invited him to come to Motown to record a speech on the subject of his choice. Carmichael accepted and recorded *Free Huey!* in honor of imprisoned Black Panther Huey Newton. The label's second album was a recording of Martin Luther King Jr.'s speech "Why I Oppose the War in Vietnam." Junius Griffin, who had worked closely with King at SCLC, produced the album, which eventually won the Grammy Award for best spoken-word recording in 1970.

Black Forum's literary offerings evolved from George Schiffer's involvement with the black arts movement. . . . The Hughes-Danner album was the first poetry

Reprinted by permission of the publishers from Suzanne E. Smith, *Dancing in the Street: Motown and the Cultural Politics of Detroit* (Cambridge: Harvard University Press, 1999), 230–239, 242–246. Copyright © 1999 by the President and Fellows of Harvard College.

release. . . . Over time, the label also produced *It's Nation Time,* featuring the poetry of Amiri Baraka; *Elaine Brown: Until We're Free,* featuring songs by Black Panther Elaine Brown; and *Black Spirits,* which was recorded live at the Apollo Theater in Harlem and featured the work of Baraka, Clarence Major, the Original Last Poets, and David Henderson, among others.

The Black Forum project never shied away from provocative and politically charged subjects. In February 1972 the label produced *Guess Who's Coming Home: Black Fighting Men Recorded Live in Vietnam,* based on the research audio tapes of Wallace Terry, a black journalist who traveled to Southeast Asia and collected the personal and often brutal stories of black soldiers. Also, in April 1972, Black Forum released *The Congressional Black Caucus,* which featured the keynote speeches of Ossie Davis and Bill Cosby at the first annual banquet of the caucus. . . .

The Black Forum label allowed Motown to engage with political ideas and activities usually not associated with the company. This engagement did not, however, gain much public notice owing to the label's poor distribution and publicity. Martin Luther King Jr.'s recordings achieved more success than the others. Motown mounted special advertising campaigns after King's death, particularly in *Ebony* and *Jet* magazine, to promote these recordings as a memorial to his life. The other Black Forum albums were often forced on record distributors. Berry Gordy told the distributors that they could not receive Motown's latest musical release unless they also agreed to take the Black Forum recordings.

While the Black Forum label failed to attract large audiences, it was nevertheless significant that the company created an outlet for controversial ideas and black poetry. Motown strategically decided, of course, to produce this "forum" of the black struggle on an obscure label clearly separate from the company's popular musical offerings. The separation bespoke the apprehension that existed within the company between its commitment to present "ideas and voices of the worldwide struggle of Black people" and its desire to avoid conflict and maintain its commercial appeal with the widest possible audiences.

Motown's ambivalence about its obligation to record the "sound of the struggle" heightened when several of the company's artists and producers began to create music that addressed social and political issues. Stevie Wonder was the first artist to record such material in his June 1966 release of Bob Dylan's "Blowin' in the Wind." Many listeners embraced Wonder's rendition of the folk song as a poignant commentary about the embattled civil rights movement. He quickly followed the hit single with his album *Down to Earth* in November of 1966, which included the song "A Place in the Sun"—a continuation of some of the sentiments expressed in "Blowin' in the Wind." Theses recordings were quite successful on the music charts, but they did not dramatically alter the content of most Hitsville releases, which continued to be dominated by love songs and dance tunes. Motown remained hesitant in 1966 and 1967 to produce songs that could be interpreted as social commentary or what were later referred to as "message" songs.

By 1968, however, Hitsville, U.S.A., began to experiment with producing songs for the Supremes and the Temptations that addressed social issues. . . . [T]he company's first major "message" song [was] the Supremes' "Love Child," . . . a song that describes the trials of unwed motherhood in the ghetto. The lyrics tell a moral tale that warns listeners to avoid premarital sex and the potential burdens of an unplanned pregnancy ("This love we're contemplating/Is worth the pain of waiting/We'll only end up hating/The child we may be creating"). Motown released "Love Child" in September 1968. The record rapidly went to number one on the pop charts and eventually outsold every Supremes record before it.

The song proved the appeal of social commentary songs and Motown's astute marketing skills. As the single climbed the charts, Motown went to work to produce a follow-up album. The album cover featured a photograph of the three glamorous women in an uncharacteristic setting—leaning on the brick wall of a ghetto alley in sweatshirts and tattered jeans. Stevie Wonder's 1966 album *Down to Earth* had been the first Motown album cover to feature an urban ghetto landscape. With both albums, it was obvious that a change in the visual presentation of the artists accompanied the musical change of addressing social topics. When the Supremes appeared on *The Ed Sullivan Show* to promote the song, they abandoned their glittering ballgowns for new "ghetto" costumes. Their tattered jeans and natural hairdos acted as an effective marketing tool to package and sell the unconventional song. With "Love Child," Motown Records transformed one of the central policy concerns of America's War on Poverty—inner-city unwed mothers—into a profitable musical product.

The Temptations' "psychedelic phase," which coincided with the Supremes' "Love Child" hit, also participated in Motown's new, yet cautious, shift to "message" music. Beginning with the release of "Cloud Nine" in October 1968, the Temptations started performing songs that addressed politically charged subject matter including experimental drug use, racial segregation, and the plight of blacks living in the inner city. Norman Whitfield, Motown's new star producer, masterminded the Temptations' shift from songs such as "My Girl" to "Psychedelic Shack" and "Ball of Confusion (That's What the World Is Today)." These songs also departed musically from the traditional Motown sound. Whitfield had Motown's Funk Brothers experiment with a heavier use of electric guitar, wah-wah pedals, and different rhythms. The Temptations broke down their background vocal arrangements. Each singer sang different lines and parts rather than keeping to their usual unified call-and-response style.

These new styles influenced Whitfield when he began to compose the militant anti-Vietnam song "War!" with Motown songwriter Barrett Strong. The song, with its pounding beat and shouted lyrics (*War—Uh! What is it good for?/Absolutely nothin'!*"), made a militant statement against the Vietnam conflict. Whitfield wrote "War!" for the Temptations, but Motown's management deemed the song too controversial for the famous singing group. As a compromise, Motown gave the song to solo artist Edwin Starr. . . . "War!" quickly reached number one on the pop charts during the summer of 1970. Motown's decision to give Starr, a lesser-known artist, rather than the Temptations the opportunity to sing a song as polemical as "War!" reflected the company's vigilance about its political affiliations. Motown hoped that Edwin Starr's relative obscurity as a singer would keep the contentious song out of the limelight. . . . The popularity of the tune with pop audiences confounded the company's decision to use Starr to detract publicity from the song's angry content. The unexpected success of "War!" did not, however, make Motown more receptive to artistic freedom. The company continued to attempt to control the creative process at Hitsville Studios. This control, however, was about to face its greatest challenge. . . .

Marvin Gaye's career at Motown mirrored the larger ambivalence within the record company about its relationship to the turbulent political milieu of the late 1960s and early 1970s. Gaye first began singing during the mid-1950s, when he performed with the Rainbows and the Marquees at gigs in his hometown of Washington, D.C. . . . . Gaye was one of the first artists to sign on the . . . label and initially worked as a backup musician on several of Motown's first records. . . . Gaye had his first hit with "Stubborn Kind of Fellow" in July 1962. A string of hits soon followed, including "Hitch Hike," "Pride and Joy," and "Can I Get a Witness." . . .

Marvin Gaye enjoyed being on the top of the pop charts but longed to move beyond the teen market. As a young singer he idolized Frank Sinatra and hoped one day to match Sinatra's success as an elegant balladeer. Many of Gaye's solo efforts, such as his tribute album to Nat King Cole in 1965, did not sell well, but his romantic duets with Mary Wells, Kim Weston, and Tammi Terrell, including "Your Precious Love" and "You're All I Need to Get By," proved his talent with ballads. By the late 1960s, however, Gaye found it increasingly difficult to perform music that seemed utterly removed from the social concerns of the day. He struggled to reconcile his artistic and commercial success as a singer with his political ideas and beliefs. . . .

In 1966 Gaye's brother, Frankie, returned from serving in Vietnam. Frankie Gaye had a difficult time finding work and eventually had to accept a job as a hotel doorman. Marvin, moved by his brother's courage and sacrifice, vowed that he would one day write a song in honor of him. In 1971 he fulfilled his promise with the poignant song "What's Happening, Brother?" one of the movements in Gaye's masterwork: the *What's Going On?* album. Marvin Gaye composed the album over the course of several years. When completed, the work addressed not only the senselessness of the Vietnam war, but also ecology, racism, and urban violence. Berry Gordy initially resisted the project. Gordy felt Gaye's subject matter had little, if any, commercial potential and would damage Gaye's image as a balladeer. Moreover, Gordy wanted to maintain a clear division of labor within Motown's creative process and continued to believe that performers should not be given much artistic freedom. Despite these obstacles, Gaye pursued the project and was encouraged by friends and Motown songwriters such as James Nyx, who cowrote "What's Happening, Brother?"

Musically, *What's Going On?* broke new ground. The recording refined the idea of a concept album in which all the songs on a long-playing record are interwoven and unified by a cohesive theme. On *What's Going On?* nine individual and highly textured songs, among them "What's Going On?" "What's Happening, Brother?" "Save the Children," "Mercy Mercy Me (The Ecology)," and "Inner City Blues (Make Me Wanna Holler)," were presented as a seamless whole. As the lyrics of one song ended, the instrumental backup melted into the subsequent song with no sound breaks or fade-outs between sets. This continuity gave the recording a musical unity and thematic completeness that had never been attempted before in popular music. Gaye layered the musical arrangements in a lush, orchestrated, yet improvisational style. The finished songs offered a stark contrast to the regulated structure, rhythm, and syncopation of standard Motown hits such as the Temptations' "My Girl."

These musical innovations heightened the political impact of Gaye's lyrics. The music created a spiritual atmosphere and stage on which Gaye could portray his drama about poverty, violence, racial discrimination, and social injustice. The combination captivated audiences and music critics—contrary to all of Berry Gordy's initial misgivings about the project. The "What's Going On?" single was released in January 1971, and by early March the song had reached number two on the pop charts and number one on *Billboard*'s "Soul" chart. When audiences embraced the album, the company had to acknowledge that there was, in fact, a market for socially conscious music and that this music should not be delegated to lesser-known artists, such as Edwin Starr, or released on a more obscure label like Black Forum.

The astonishing success of Marvin Gaye's *What's Going On?* also renegotiated the terms on which Motown music participated in political organizing. In September 1972 the album inspired the theme of Jesse Jackson's first Operation PUSH (People United to Save Humanity) Expo in Chicago. Jackson founded Operation PUSH in December 1971. The expo . . . brought together black political leaders, businesses, community activists, and entertainers to share ideas, participate in workshops, organize grass-roots efforts, and celebrate black culture and music. Jackson entitled the first annual fund-raiser "Save the Children," quoting the title of Gaye's song from *What's Going On?* Motown artists including Gladys Knight and the Pips, the Temptations, and Gaye came to the four-day event and performed in support of the expo. Paramount Pictures filmed the festivities and released *Save the Children* as a feature film to the general public. At most charity benefits, Motown artists performed their hit songs as entertainment. In Chicago, Marvin Gaye's music did more that entertain when it inspired the entire theme of the Operation PUSH Expo. *What's Going On?* and specifically "Save the Children," poetically captured the gathering's political agenda, which sought to address the concerns facing black America—particularly in the urban North. . . .

In his song "Inner City Blues (Makes Me Wanna Holler)," Marvin Gaye sings about how "crime is increasing" and laments that because of "[t]rigger-happy policing / panic is spreading / God knows where we're heading." At the time of the song's release in 1971, tensions between the Detroit police force and the city's black citizens were high. Police brutality or "trigger-happy policing" against black Detroiters had been a volatile political issue since the Detroit Police Department was first founded after the race riot of 1863. In the late 1960s and early 1970s, police-community relations were perhaps the most contentious issue in Detroit city politics. . . . For black Detroit, law and order came at a high price, and many felt that only a black mayor could ease the tensions between the city's primarily white police force and its black citizens. . . .

Local political organizers knew that they needed a strong candidate and a sound platform to elect Detroit's first black mayor. Coleman Young and Detroit's continuing struggles with police-community relations provided the last pieces in the puzzle. Young, a Michigan state senator, had built his political reputation as a radical leader. As a young man, Young worked at Ford, but he was fired after an altercation with a white racist foreman. He flew as a second lieutenant with the Tuskegee Airmen and fought against Jim Crow segregation within the military. In 1951 he participated in the founding of the National Negro Labor Council (NNLC), the most radical black labor organization of its time, and was eventually elected executive director. Because of his involvement with NNLC, Young was ordered to testify about his relationship to the Communist Party before the House

Committee on Un-American Activities in 1952. When he appeared before the committee, Young boldly defied his accusers. In his testimony he proclaimed: "I am part of the Negro people . . . I am now in the process of fighting against what I consider to be attacks and discrimination against my people. I am fighting against un-American activities such as lynchings and denial of the vote. I am dedicated to that fight, and I don't think I have to apologize or explain it to anybody." Young's bravado won him many fans in Detroit. Local supporters circulated phonograph recordings of his testimony throughout the city's black community.

. . . Young's militant approach was well suited to the issues that came to dominate the 1973 election—most notably, the continuing struggle over police brutality. In January 1971 Detroit's police commissioner, John Nichols, formed a new elite undercover police operation called STRESS, which stood for "Stop the Robberies, Enjoy Safe Streets." The majority of the officers assigned to the STRESS squads were white and were trained to use decoy techniques to entrap criminals in Detroit's "high-crime" neighborhoods—most often black neighborhoods. The STRESS units quickly became a notorious and violent presence in black Detroit. By the end of 1971 Detroit's Police Department was leading the country in the number of civilian killings per capita—at a rate of 7.17 civilians per 1,000 officers. More than one-third of the killings were committed by STRESS officers, who represented only 2 percent of the entire police force. Public protests against STRESS began as early as September 1971, when over 5,000 people attended a rally to abolish the unit, and continued throughout 1972 and into the election year of 1973.

Coleman Young used the STRESS controversy as the focal point of his campaign platform. With Police Commissioner John Nichols as his main opponent, the issue was difficult to avoid. Nichols beat Young in the primary election winning 33.8 percent of the vote to Young's 21.1 percent. In the final election both candidates had to win voters across racial lines. Nichols attempted to capitalize on white fears of black crime by emphasizing his law-and-order approach. Young, an experienced politician, broadened his platform to include economic redevelopment and won the support of several business organizations. Young's combination of a forceful attack against STRESS, a promise to increase minority hiring in the Detroit Police Department, and economic revitalization plans won the election. On November 6, 1973, Detroit voted in its first African American mayor. . . .

Motown Records had already left Detroit for Los Angeles when Coleman Young won the mayoral election. Coincidentally, however, the record company released Stevie Wonder's single "Living for the City" during the election month of November 1973. Wonder's song, inspired by the success of Marvin Gaye's *What's Going On?* album, directly engages with social issues as it tells the tale of a young black man who migrates from the South to the urban North. Once in the city, the protagonist confronts the struggles, temptations, and despair of urban life in the ghetto. In the song's closing refrain Wonder makes an urgent plea for change—a plea that had particular relevance to Detroit, which was on the verge of black political control. Coleman Young's election, by its very uniqueness, created tremendous excitement and speculation about what this "new" era could bring to an increasingly enervated city.

By 1973 Detroit's economic base had deteriorated, as many companies and white citizens left the city for the suburbs after the devastation of 1967. Motown's departure for California in 1972 participated in this trend, and the cultural loss to the black community was equally difficult. J. L. Hudson, founder of the original New Detroit committee and corporate leader, commented on the possibility of black political rule in Detroit on the fifth anniversary of the uprising in 1972. Hudson remarked, "The black man has the feeling he is about to take power in the city . . . but he is going to be left with an empty bag." Coleman Young somewhat similarly admitted, "I knew that this had only happened to me because, for once in my life, I was in the right place at the right time, and that my fortune was the direct result of my city's misfortune—of the same fear and loathing that had caused all my problems and Detroit's problems in the first place. I was taking over the administration of Detroit because the white people didn't want the damn thing anymore. They were getting the hell out, more than happy to turn over their troubles to some black sucker like me."

The Motor City's economy was also hit hard in 1973 as a result of the OPEC oil embargo. . . . The national energy crisis reverberated with particular intensity in Detroit. The city's entire identity and economic base revolved around the automotive industry—an industry completely dependent on the international oil market.

With all of these pressing concerns, Young's inauguration in January 1974 became a critical moment for the new mayor to proclaim his agenda and for his supporters to celebrate their victory. . . .

. . . Young's immediate agenda involved fulfilling campaign promises such as his vow to dismantle the STRESS unit in an effort to combat police brutality. Yet the new mayor did not want to appear "soft" on criminals in a city with a serious crime problem. In his inaugural speech Young boldly announced his intentions: "I issue a warning to all dope pushers, rip-off artists and muggers. It's time to leave Detroit—hit the road. Hit Eight Mile Road. I don't give a damn if they are black or white, or if they wear Superfly suits or blue uniforms with silver badges. Hit the road." Young believed that his comments would reassure his constituents that he could promote law and order and also eliminate police brutality. But his brazen language and his reference to Eight Mile Road, the dividing line between the city and its surrounding, primarily white suburbs led many people to wonder if the new black mayor was going to agitate rather than calm the racial tensions that plagued Detroit's entire metropolitan area.

Coleman Young's "hit the road" remark unfortunately tapped into dominant fears that a black mayor would increase racial polarization between blacks and whites in Detroit and between the city and its suburbs. The long-fought struggle to elect a black mayor did not appear to ensure that Detroit was any closer to becoming a model of harmonious race relations than it was in 1963. The dream of black political power, like the myth of black capitalism, was more elusive in practice than in the imagination. In Detroit Young's election did lead to the end of the STRESS unit and an increase in minority hiring in the city's police force. But it did not bridge Detroit's entrenched racial divides or alter the basic configuration of economic power in the city, which was still maintained by white-owned private corporations.

Only Motown Records, which was the most profitable black business in America in 1973, could have reconfigured the racial composition of Detroit's corporate economy, but this possibility disappeared when the company left the city in 1972.

In the end, black political control ascended in the Motor City only to be defined and circumscribed by its relationship to white corporate power. Motown's music—Stevie Wonder's "Living for the City" or Marvin Gaye's "What's Going On?"—did make eloquent statements about the plight of black Americans left with the "empty bag" of urban America. Yet, without Motown's cultural presence and financial profits invested in the city, the songs could only passively speak about, not actively participate in, Detroit's continuing struggle to create itself anew.

 FURTHER READING

Herb Boyd, *Black Panthers: For Beginners* (1995).

Rod Bush, ed., *The New Black Vote: Politics and Power in Four American Cities* (1984).

Clayborne Carson, David J. Garrow, Gerald Gill, Vincent Harding, and Darlene Clark Hine, eds., *The Eyes on the Prize Civil Rights Reader* (1991).

Ward Churchill and Jim Vander Wall, *Agents of Repression: The FBI's Secret War Against the Black Panther Party and the American Indian Movement* (1988).

Henry Hampton and Steve Fayer, with Sarah Flynn, *Voices of Freedom: An Oral History of the Civil Rights Movement from the 1950s Through the 1980s* (1990).

Gerald Horne, *The Fire This Time: The Watts Uprising and the 1960s* (1995).

Gerald David Jaynes and Robin M. Williams, Jr., eds., *A Common Destiny: Blacks and American Society* (1989).

Charles E. Jones, ed., *The Black Panther Party [Reconsidered]* (1998).

Steven F. Lawson, *In Pursuit of Power: Southern Blacks and Electoral Politics, 1965–1982* (1985).

George Lipsitz, *A Life in the Struggle: Ivory Perry and the Culture of Opposition* (1988).

Manning Marable, *Race, Reform, and Rebellion: The Second Reconstruction in Black America, 1945–1990,* 2nd ed. (1991).

Kenneth O'Reilly, *Racial Matters: The FBI's Secret File on Black America, 1960–1972* (1989).

Francis Fox Piven and Richard A. Cloward, *Poor People's Movements: Why They Succeed, How They Fail* (1979).

Jerald E. Podair, "'White' Values, 'Black' Values: The Ocean Hill–Brownsville Controversy and New York City Culture, 1965–1975," *Radical History Review,* 59 (1994), 36–59.

Karen Brodkin Sacks, *Caring by the Hour: Women, Work, and Organizing at Duke Medical Center* (1988).

Suzanne E. Smith, *Dancing in the Street: Motown and the Cultural Politics of Detroit* (1999).

Ricki Solinger, *Wake Up Little Susie: Single Pregnancy and Race Before Roe v. Wade* (1992).

James D. Sullivan, *On the Walls and in the Streets: American Poetry Broadsides from the 1960s* (1997).

Wallace Terry, ed., *Bloods, an Oral History of the Vietnam War* (1984).

William L. Van Deburg, *New Day in Babylon: The Black Power Movement and American Culture, 1965–1975* (1992).

James Westheider, *Fighting on Two Fronts: African Americans and the Vietnam War* (1997).

Progress and Poverty: African Americans at the Dawn of the Twenty-First Century

By the dawn of the twenty-first century more than a generation had passed since the high tide of the Civil Rights Movement of the 1960s. Everywhere there was evidence that that movement had made a difference in the lives of most African Americans and had changed—perhaps permanently—the face of America. In entertainment, sports, media, politics, government, and the economy, blacks were more present and visible than at any point in their previous history. No longer bound by the structural prisons of slavery and sharecropping, many black Americans experienced phenomenal economic progress and witnessed the growth of a substantial middle class. But it was equally evident that large segments of black communities remained impoverished and frustrated and had no real prospects of sharing in or benefiting from that progress. Contrary to Martin Luther King's dream that one day Americans would be judged solely by the content of their characters, at the beginning of the twenty-first century it still very much mattered whether one was born black.

How, then, are we to understand and assess the legacy of the Civil Rights Movement? Does the racial backlash of the Reagan-Bush years suggest a fixed limit to racial progress—fixed, that is, by white racial prejudice—or the need for new tactics, strategies, targets, and coalitions? Does the fact that the movement's political successes came at precisely the moment that the American economy was dramatically deindustrializing and radically restructuring suggest the need to study African-American experience within a broader framework? What would such a framework look like, structurally and geographically? What issues would define it?

Finally, what does all of this suggest about the future of African Americans in the twenty-first century? A more globalized, technology-driven economy has enhanced class inequities, while at the same time a money-driven, heavily mediated political system makes insurgent mobilizations difficult. Meanwhile, the immigration of new groups with different histories and potentially different cultural, social, political, and economic interests further complicates issues of racial identity and mobilization. Some of these developments pose issues—albeit in new forms—as old

*as African-American history itself. As at Jamestown in 1619, the new black immi-
gration poses the problem of forming an African-American people out of peoples of
disparate cultural elements who may share only the color of their skins. As in the
antebellum period, the new Asian and Cuban immigration poses the problem of
how to confront or make allies of peoples whose history and interests may diverge
from those of blacks born in America. And, finally, it must be remembered that
slavery, too, was a global economic system, with global pressures and demands.
The ultimate question, perhaps, is what the previous four centuries of African-
American history might teach us as we prepare for the fifth century of that saga.*

D O C U M E N T S

In the first document, the late Leanita McClain, a *Chicago Tribune* editorial writer,
describes the personal cost of the economic success achieved by the new black middle
class, suggesting some of the unexpected internal fissures that racial progress promoted.
In the second document, a speech to the 1988 Democratic Convention, presidential
aspirant Jesse Jackson reminds us that success for some need not lead to forgetting those
left behind. The legacy of the Civil Rights Movement that Jackson envisioned was one
that inculcated values and models for a more just and democratic America. The third
document, the Children's Defense Fund's statistical catalog of the life chances of the
typical black child more than thirty years after Martin Luther King's "I Have a Dream"
speech, dramatically qualifies any presumptions of economic and political progress.
The three graphs constituting the fourth document show the relative economic condition
of African Americans thirty years after the March on Washington as well as changes over
the previous twenty years. The fifth document, consisting of excerpted congressional
testimony on the dangers of rap music, shows the continuing political and historical
resonance of cultural issues in the African-American experience.

The widespread practice of racial profiling, the subject of the sixth document,
reflects one of the new forms of racial discrimination and abuse that emerged as other
more overt abuses receded. The discriminatory response to Haitian immigrants in the
1990s described in the seventh document suggests still another of the new faces and
terrains of racism. With renewed and more diverse sources of immigration the American
nation is in the process of recreating itself. A significant proportion of the new immigrants are physically black and thus counted among the African-American population.
But, as the eighth document shows, this black immigrant presence can further compli-
cate issues of race, culture, and nation. Thus issues raised at the very inception of the
African presence in the Americas continue to be relevant in the twenty-first century.

1. Leanita McClain on Being Black, Successful, and Middle Class, 1980

I am a member of the black middle class who has had it with being patted on the
head by white hands and slapped in the face by black hands for my success.

Here's a discovery that too many people still find startling: when given equal
opportunities at white-collar pencil pushing, blacks want the same things from life

---

"Leanita McClain on Being Black, Successful, and Middle Class," from Leanita McClain, "My Turn,"
Newsweek, October 13, 1980, p. 21. Reprinted by permission of Northwestern University Press.

that everyone else wants. These include the proverbial dream house, two cars, an above-average school and a vacation for the kids at Disneyland. We may, in fact, want these things more than other Americans because most of us have been denied them so long.

Meanwhile, a considerable number of the folks we left behind in the "old country," commonly called the ghetto, and the militants we left behind in their antiquated ideology can't berate middle-class blacks enough for "forgetting where we came from." We have forsaken the revolution, we are told, we have sold out. We are Oreos, they say, black on the outside, white within.

The truth is, we have not forgotten; we would not dare. We are simply fighting on different fronts and are no less war weary, and possibly more heartbroken, for we know the black and white worlds can meld, that there can be a better world.

It is impossible for me to forget where I came from as long as I am prey to the jive hustler who does not hesitate to exploit my childhood friendship. I am reminded, too, when I go back to the old neighborhood in fear—and have my purse snatched—and when I sit down to a business lunch and have an old classmate wait on my table. I recall the girl I played dolls with who now rears five children on welfare, the boy from church who is in prison for murder, the pal found dead of a drug overdose in the alley where we once played tag.

Attaché Case: My life abounds in incongruities. Fresh from a vacation in Paris, I may, a week later, be on the milk-run Trailways bus in Deep South backcountry attending the funeral of an ancient uncle whose world stretched only 50 miles and who never learned to read. Sometimes when I wait at the bus stop with my attaché case, I meet my aunt getting off the bus with other cleaning ladies on their way to do my neighbors' floors.

But I am not ashamed. Black progress has surpassed our greatest expectations; we never even saw much hope for it, and the achievement has taken us by surprise.

In my heart, however, there is no safe distance from the wretched past of my ancestors or the purposeless present of some of my contemporaries; I fear such a fate can reclaim me. I am not comfortably middle class; I am uncomfortably middle class.

I have it made, but where? Racism still dogs my people. There are still communities in which crosses are burned on the lawns of black families who have the money and grit to move in.

What a hollow victory we have won when my sister, dressed in her designer everything, is driven to the rear door of the luxury high rise in which she lives because the cab driver, noting only her skin color, assumes she is the maid, or the nanny, or the cook, but certainly not the lady of any house at this address.

I have heard the immigrants' bootstrap tales, the simplistic reproach of "why can't you people be like us." I have fulfilled the entry requirements of the American middle class, yet I am left, at times, feeling unwelcome and stereotyped. I have overcome the problems of food, clothing and shelter, but I have not overcome my old nemesis, prejudice. Life is easier, being black is not.

I am burdened daily with showing whites that blacks are people. I am, in the old vernacular, a credit to my race. I am my brothers' keeper, and my sisters', though many of them have abandoned me because they think I have abandoned them.

I run a gauntlet between two worlds, and I am cursed and blessed by both. I travel, observe and take part in both; I can also be used by both. I am a rope in a tug of war. If I am a token in my downtown office, so am I at my cousin's church tea. I assuage white guilt. I disprove black inadequacy and prove to my parents' generation that their patience was indeed a virtue.

I have a foot in each world, but I cannot fool myself about either. I can see the transparent deceptions of some whites and the bitter hopelessness of some blacks. I know how tenuous my grip on one way of life is, and how strangling the grip of the other way of life can be.

Novelty: Many whites have lulled themselves into thinking that race relations are just grand because they were the first on their block to discuss crab grass with the new black family. Yet too few blacks and whites in this country send their children to school together, entertain each other or call each other friend. Blacks and whites dining out together draw stares. Many of my co-workers see no black faces from the time the train pulls out Friday evening until they meet me at the coffee machine Monday morning. I remain a novelty.

Some of my "liberal" white acquaintances pat me on the head, hinting that I am a freak, that my success is less a matter of talent than of luck and affirmative action. I may live among them, but it is difficult to live with them. How can they be sincere about respecting me, yet hold my fellows in contempt? And if I am silent when they attempt to sever me from my own, how can I live with myself?

Whites won't believe I remain culturally different; blacks won't believe I remain culturally the same.

I need only look in a mirror to know my true allegiance, and I am painfully aware that, even with my off-white trappings, I am prejudged by my color.

As for the envy of my own people, am I to give up my career, my standard of living, to pacify them and set my conscience at ease? No. I have worked for these amenities and deserve them, though I can never enjoy them without feeling guilty.

These comforts do not make me less black, nor oblivious to the woe in which many of my people are drowning. As long as we are denigrated as a group, no one of us has made it. Inasmuch as we all suffer for every one left behind, we all gain for every one who conquers the hurdle.

2. Jesse Jackson Addresses the Democratic National Convention, 1988

Tonight, we pause and give praise and honor to God for being good enough to allow us to be at this place, at this time. When I look out at this convention, I see the face of America: Red, Yellow, Brown, Black and White. We are all precious in God's sight—the real rainbow coalition.

Frontline website on Jesse Jackson at www.pbs.org/wgbh/pages/frontline/jesse. "Address by The Reverend Jesse Louis Jackson, July 19, 1988," in *The Pilgrimage of Jesse Jackson.* http://www.pbs.org/wgbh/pages/frontline/jesse/speeches/index.jesse88speech.html. Copyright 1998 PBS and WGBH/Frontline.

All of us—all of us who are here think that we are seated. But we're really stand-ing on someone's shoulders. Ladies and gentlemen, Mrs. Rosa Parks. The mother of the civil rights movement. [*Mrs. Rosa Parks was brought to the podium.*] . . .

My right and my privilege to stand here before you has been won, won in my lifetime, by the blood and the sweat of the innocent.

Twenty-four years ago, the late Fannie Lou Hamer and Aaron Henry—who sits here tonight from Mississippi—were locked out into the streets in Atlantic City; the head of the Mississippi Freedom Democratic Party.

But tonight, a Black and White delegation from Mississippi is headed by Ed Cole, a Black man from Mississippi; 24 years later.

Many were lost in the struggle for the right to vote: Jimmy Lee Jackson, a young student, gave his life; Viola Liuzzo, a White mother from Detroit, called nigger lover, had her brains blown out at point blank range; [Michael] Schwerner, [Andrew] Goodman and [James] Chaney—two Jews and a Black—found in a common grave, bodies riddled with bullets in Mississippi; the four darling little girls in a church in Birmingham, Alabama. They died that we might have a right to live.

Dr. Martin Luther King Jr. lies only a few miles from us tonight. Tonight he must feel good as he looks down upon us. We sit here together, a rainbow, a coali-tion—the sons and daughters of slavemasters and the sons and daughters of slaves, sitting together around a common table, to decide the direction of our party and our country. His heart would be full tonight.

As a testament to the struggles of those who have gone before; as a legacy for those who will come after; as a tribute to the endurance, the patience, the courage of our forefathers and mothers; as an assurance that their prayers are being an-swered, their work [has] not been in vain, and hope is eternal; tomorrow night my name will go into nomination for the Presidency of the United States of America.

We meet tonight at the crossroads, a point of decision. Shall we expand, be in-clusive, find unity and power; or suffer division and impotence?

We've come to Atlanta, the cradle of the old South, the crucible of the new South. Tonight, there is a sense of celebration, because we are moved, fundamen-tally moved from racial battlegrounds by law, to economic common ground. Tomor-row we will challenge to move to higher ground.

Common ground! Think of Jerusalem, the intersection where many trails met. A small village that became the birthplace for three religions—Judaism, Christian-ity and Islam. Why was this village so blessed? Because it provided a crossroads where different people met, different cultures, different civilizations could meet and find common ground. When people come together, flowers always flourish—the air is rich with the aroma of a new spring.

Take New York, the dynamic metropolis. What makes New York so special? It's the invitation of the Statue of Liberty, "Give me your tired, your poor, your huddled masses who yearn to breathe free." Not restricted to English only. Many people, many cultures, many languages—with one thing in common, they yearn to breathe free. Common ground!

Tonight in Atlanta, for the first time in this century, we convene in the South; a state where Governors once stood in school house doors; where Julian Bond was denied a seat in the State Legislature because of his conscientious objection to the

Vietnam War; a city that, through its five Black Universities, has graduated more black students than any city in the world. Atlanta, now a modern intersection of the new South.

Common ground! That's the challenge of our party tonight. Left wing. Right wing. . . .

Tonight I salute [my opponent] Governor Michael Dukakis [of Massachusetts]. . . . His foreparents came to America on immigrant ships; my foreparents came to America on slave ships. But whatever the original ships, we're in the same boat tonight. Our ships could pass in the night—if we have a false sense of independence—or they could collide and crash. We could lose our passengers. But we can seek a high reality and a greater good.

Apart, we can drift on the broken pieces of Reaganomics, satisfy our baser instincts, and exploit the fears of our people. At our highest we can call upon noble instincts and navigate this vessel to safety. The greater good is the common good.

As Jesus said, "Not My will, but Thine be done." It was his way of saying there's a higher good beyond personal comfort or position.

The good of our Nation is at stake. Its commitment to working men and women, to the poor and the vulnerable, to the many in the world.

With so many guided missiles, and so much misguided leadership, the stakes are exceedingly high. Our choice? Full participation in a democratic government, or more abandonment and neglect. And so this night, we choose not a false sense of independence, and our capacity to survive and endure. Tonight we choose interdependency, and our capacity to act and unite for the greater good.

Common good is finding commitment to new priorities to expansion and inclusion. A commitment to expanded participation in the Democratic Party at every level. A commitment to a shared national campaign strategy and involvement at every level. . . .

Common ground! Easier said than done. Where do you find common ground? At the point of challenge. This campaign has shown that politics need not be marketed by politicians, packaged by pollsters and pundits. Politics can be a moral arena where people come together to find common ground.

We find common ground at the plant gate that closes on workers without notice. We find common ground at the farm auction, where a good farmer loses his or her land to bad loans or diminishing markets. Common ground at the school yard where teachers cannot get adequate pay, and students cannot get a scholarship, and can't make a loan. Common ground at the hospital admitting room, where somebody tonight is dying because they cannot afford to go upstairs to a bed that's empty waiting for someone with insurance to get sick. We are a better nation than that. We must do better.

Common ground. What is leadership if not present help in a time of crisis? So I met you at the point of challenge. In Jay, Maine, where paper workers were striking for fair wages; in Greenville, Iowa, where family farmers struggle for a fair price; in Cleveland, Ohio, where working women seek comparable worth; in McFarland, California, where the children of Hispanic farm workers may be dying from poisoned land, dying in clusters with cancer; in an AIDS hospice in Houston, Texas, where the sick support one another, too often rejected by their own parents and friends.

Common ground. America is not a blanket woven from one thread, one color, one cloth. When I was a child growing up in Greenville, South Carolina, my grandmama could not afford a blanket, she didn't complain and we did not freeze. Instead she took pieces of old cloth—patches, wool, silk, gabardine, crockersack—only patches, barely good enough to wipe off your shoes with. But they didn't stay that way very long. With sturdy hands and a strong cord, she sewed them together into a quilt, a thing of beauty and power and culture. Now, Democrats, we must build such a quilt.

Farmers, you seek fair prices and you are right—but you cannot stand alone. Your patch is not big enough. Workers, you fight for fair wages, you are right—but your patch of labor is not big enough. Women, you seek comparable worth and pay equity, you are right—but your patch is not big enough.

Women, mothers, who seek Head Start, and day care and prenatal care on the front side of life, relevant jail care and welfare on the back side of life—you are right—but your patch is not big enough. Students, you seek scholarships, you are right—but your patch is not big enough. Blacks and Hispanics, when we fight for civil rights, we are right—but our patch is not big enough.

Gays and lesbians, when you fight against discrimination and [for] a cure for AIDS, you are right—but your patch is not big enough. Conservatives and progressives, when you fight for what you believe, right wing, left wing, hawk, dove, you are right from your point of view, but your point of view is not enough.

But don't despair. Be as wise as my grandmama. Pull the patches and the pieces together, bound by a common thread. When we form a great quilt of unity and common ground, we'll have the power to bring about health care and housing and jobs and education and hope to our Nation.

We, the people, can win!

We stand at the end of a long dark night of reaction. We stand tonight united in the commitment to a new direction. For almost eight years we've been led by those who view social good coming from private interest, who view public life as a means to increase private wealth. They have been prepared to sacrifice the common good of the many to satisfy the private interests and the wealth of a few.

We believe in a government that's a tool of our democracy in service to the public, not an instrument of the aristocracy in search of private wealth. We believe in government with the consent of the governed, "of, for and by the people." We must now emerge into a new day with a new direction.

Reaganomics. Based on the belief that the rich had too little money and the poor had too much. That's classic Reaganomics. They believe that the poor had too much money and the rich had too little money so they engaged in reverse Robin Hood—took from the poor and gave to the rich, paid for by the middle class. We cannot stand four more years of Reaganomics in any version, in any disguise.

How do I document that case? Seven years later, the richest 1 percent of our society pays 20 percent less in taxes. The poorest 10 percent pay 20 percent more. Reaganomics.

Reagan gave the rich and the powerful a multibillion-dollar party. Now the party's over, he expects the people to pay for the damage. I take this principal position, convention, let us not raise taxes on the poor and the middle-class, but those who had the party, the rich and the powerful must pay for the party.

I just want to take common sense to high places. We're spending $150 billion a year defending Europe and Japan 43 years after the war is over. We have more troops in Europe tonight than we had seven years ago. Yet the threat of war is ever more remote.

Germany and Japan are now creditor nations; that means they've got a surplus. We are a debtor nation. It means we are in debt. Let them share more of the burden of their own defense. Use some of that money to build decent housing. Use some of that money to educate our children. Use some of that money for long-term health care. Use some of that money to wipe out these slums and put America back to work!

I just want to take common sense to high places. If we can bail out Europe and Japan; if we can bail out Continental Bank and Chrysler—and Mr. Iaccoca, makes $8,000 an hour, we can bail out the family farmer.

I just want to make common sense. It does not make sense to close down 650,000 family farms in this country while importing food from abroad subsidized by the U.S. Government. Let's make sense.

It does not make sense to be escorting all our tankers up and down the Persian Gulf paying $2.50 for every $1 worth of oil we bring out, while oil wells are capped in Texas, Oklahoma and Louisiana. I just want to make sense.

Leadership must meet the moral challenge of its day. What's the moral challenge of our day? We have public accommodations. We have the right to vote.

We have open housing. What's the fundamental challenge of our day? It is to end economic violence. Plant closings without notice—economic violence. Even the greedy do not profit long from greed—economic violence.

Most poor people are not lazy. They are not black. They are not brown. They are mostly White and female and young. But whether White, Black or Brown, a hungry baby's belly turned inside out is the same color—color it pain, color it hurt, color it agony.

Most poor people are not on welfare. Some of them are illiterate and can't read the want-ad sections. And when they can, they can't find a job that matches the address. They work hard every day. I know, I live amongst them. They catch the early bus. They work every day. They raise other people's children. They work every day.

They clean the streets. They work every day. They drive dangerous cabs. They change the beds you slept in in these hotels last night and can't get a union contract. They work every day.

No, no, they're not lazy. Someone must defend them because it's right and they cannot speak for themselves. They work in hospitals. I know they do. They wipe the bodies of those who are sick with fever and pain. They empty their bedpans. They clean out their commodes. No job is beneath them, and yet when they get sick they cannot lie in the bed they made up every day. America, that is not right. We are a better Nation than that!

We need a real war on drugs. . . .

We are spending $150 billion on drugs a year. We've gone from ignoring it to focusing on the children. Children cannot buy $150 billion worth of drugs a year; a few high-profile athletes—athletes are not laundering $150 billion a year—bankers are.

I met the children in Watts who unfortunately, in their despair, their grapes of hope have become raisins of despair, and they're turning on each other and they're self-destructing. But I stayed with them all night long. I wanted to hear their case.

They said, "Jesse Jackson, as you challenge us to say no to drugs, you're right; and to not sell them, you're right; and to not use these guns, you're right." And by the way, the promise of CETA; they displaced CETA—they did not replace CETA. "We have neither jobs nor houses nor services nor training; no way out.

"Some of us take drugs as anesthesia for our pain. Some take drugs as a way of pleasure, good short-term pleasure and long-term pain. Some sell drugs to make money. It's wrong, we know, but you need to know that we know. We can go and buy the drugs by the boxes at the port. If we can buy the drugs at the port, don't you believe the Federal government can stop it if they want to?"

They say, "We don't have Saturday night specials anymore." They say, "We buy AK47's and Uzi's, the latest make of weapons. We buy them across and along these boulevards."

You cannot fight a war on drugs unless until you're going to challenge the bankers and the gun sellers and those who grow them. Don't just focus on the children, let's stop drugs at the level of supply and demand. We must end the scourge on the American Culture! . . .

America, let us expand, When Mr. Reagan and Mr. Gorbachev met there was a big meeting. They represented together one-eighth of the human race. Seven-eighths of the human race was locked out of that room. Most people in the world tonight—half are Asian, one-half of them are Chinese. There are 22 nations in the Middle East. There's Europe; 40 million Latin Americans next door to us; the Caribbean; Africa—a half-billion people.

Most people in the world today are Yellow or Brown or Black, non-Christian, poor, female, young and don't speak English in the real world.

This generation must offer leadership to the real world. We're losing ground in Latin America, Middle East, South Africa because we're not focusing on the real world. That's the real world. We must use basic principles, support international law. We stand the most to gain from it. Support human rights; we believe in that. Support self-determination, we're built on that. Support economic development, you know it's right. Be consistent and gain our moral authority in the world. I challenge you tonight, my friends, let's be bigger and better as a Nation and as a Party!

We have basic challenges—freedom in South Africa. We have already agreed as Democrats to declare South Africa to be a terrorist state. But don't just stop there. Get South Africa out of Angola; free Namibia; support the front line states. We must have a new humane human rights consistent policy in Africa.

I'm often asked, "Jesse, why do you take on these tough issues? They're not very political. We can't win that way."

If an issue is morally right, it will eventually be political. It may be political and never be right. Fanny Lou Hamer didn't have the most votes in Atlantic City, but her principles have outlasted the life of every delegate who voted to lock her out. Rosa Parks did not have the most votes, but she was morally right. Dr. King didn't have the most votes about the Vietnam War, but he was morally right. If we are principled first, our politics will fall in place. "Jesse, why do you take these big bold initiatives?" A poem by an unknown author went something like this: "We mastered the air, we conquered the sea, annihilated distance and prolonged life, but we're not wise enough to live on this earth without war and without hate."

As for Jesse Jackson: "I'm tired of sailing my little boat, far inside the harbor bar. I want to go out where the big ships float, out on the deep where the great ones are. And should my frail craft prove too slight for waves that sweep those billows o'er, I'd rather go down in the stirring fight than drowse to death at the sheltered shore."

We've got to go out, my friends, where the big boats are.

And then for our children. Young America, hold your head high now. We can win. We must not lose to the drugs, and violence, premature pregnancy, suicide, cynicism, pessimism and despair. We can win. Wherever you are tonight, now I challenge you to hope and to dream. Don't submerge your dreams. Exercise above all else, even on drugs, dream of the day you are drug free. Even in the gutter, dream of the day that you will be up on your feet again.

You must never stop dreaming. Face reality, yes, but don't stop with the way things are. Dream of things as they ought to be. Dream. Face pain, but love, hope, faith and dreams will help you rise above the pain. Use hope and imagination as weapons of survival and progress, but you keep on dreaming, young America. Dream of peace. Peace is rational and reasonable. War is irrational in this age, and unwinnable.

Dream of teachers who teach for life and not for a living. Dream of doctors who are concerned more about public health than private wealth. Dream of lawyers more concerned about justice than a judgeship. Dream of preachers who are concerned more about prophecy than profiteering. Dream on the high road with sound values.

And then America, as we go forth to September, October, November and then beyond, America must never surrender to a high moral challenge.

Do not surrender to drugs. The best drug policy is a "no first use." Don't surrender with needles and cynicism. Let's have "no first use" on the one hand, or clinics on the other. Never surrender, young America. Go forward.

America must never surrender to malnutrition. We can feed the hungry and clothe the naked. We must never surrender. We must go forward.

We must never surrender to inequality. Women cannot compromise ERA or comparable worth. Women are making 60 cents on the dollar to what a man makes. Women cannot buy meat cheaper. Women cannot buy bread cheaper. Women cannot buy milk cheaper. Women deserve to get paid for the work that you do. It's right and it's fair.

Don't surrender, my friends. Those who have AIDS tonight, you deserve our compassion. Even with AIDS you must not surrender.

In your wheelchairs. I see you sitting here tonight in those wheelchairs. I've stayed with you. I've reached out to you across our Nation. Don't you give up. I know it's tough sometimes. People look down on you. It took you a little more effort to get here tonight. And no one should look down on you, but sometimes mean people do. The only justification we have for looking down on someone is that we're going to stop and pick them up.

But even in your wheelchairs, don't you give up. We cannot forget 50 years ago when our backs were against the wall, Roosevelt was in a wheelchair. I would rather have Roosevelt in a wheelchair than Reagan and Bush on a horse. Don't you surrender and don't you give up. Don't surrender and don't give up!

Why I cannot challenge you this way? "Jesse Jackson, you don't understand my situation. You be on television. You don't understand. I see you with the big people. You don't understand my situation."

I understand. You see me on TV, but you don't know the me that makes me, me. They wonder, "Why does Jesse run?" because they see me running for the White House. They don't see the house I'm running from.

I have a story. I wasn't always on television. Writers were not always outside my door. When I was born late one afternoon, October 8th, in Greenville, South Carolina, no writers asked my mother her name. Nobody chose to write down our address. My mama was not supposed to make it, and I was not supposed to make it. You see, I was born of a teen-age mother, who was born of a teen-age mother.

I understand. I know abandonment, and people being mean to you, and saying you're nothing and nobody and can never be anything.

I understand. Jesse Jackson is my third name. I'm adopted. When I had no name, my grandmother gave me her name. My name was Jesse Burns until I was 12. So I wouldn't have a blank space, she gave me a name to hold me over. I understand when nobody knows your name. I understand when you have no name.

I understand. I wasn't born in the hospital. Mama didn't have insurance. I was born in the bed at [the] house. I really do understand. Born in a three-room house, bathroom in the backyard, slop jar by the bed, no hot and cold running water.

I understand. Wallpaper used for decoration? No. for a windbreaker. I understand. I'm a working person's person. That's why I understand you whether you're Black or White.

I understand work. I was not born with a silver spoon in my mouth. I had a shovel programmed for my hand.

My mother, a working woman. So many of the days she went to work early, with runs in her stockings. She knew better, but she wore runs in her stockings so that my brother and I could have matching socks and not be laughed at at school. I understand.

At 3 o'clock on Thanksgiving Day, we couldn't eat turkey because momma was preparing somebody else's turkey at 3 o'clock. We had to play football to entertain ourselves. And then around 6 o'clock she would get off the Alta Vista bus and we would bring up the leftovers and eat our turkey—leftovers, the carcass, the cranberries—around 8 o'clock at night. I really do understand.

Every one of these funny labels they put on you, those of you who are watching this broadcast tonight in the projects, on the corners, I understand. Call you outcast, low down, you can't make it, you're nothing, you're from nobody, sub-class, underclass; when you see Jesse Jackson, when my name goes in nomination, your name goes in nomination.

I was born in the slum, but the slum was not born in me. And it wasn't born in you, and you can make it.

Wherever you are tonight, you can make it. Hold your head high, stick your chest out. You can make it. It gets dark sometimes, but the morning comes. Don't you surrender. Suffering breeds character, character breeds faith. In the end faith will not disappoint.

You must not surrender. You may or may not get there but just know that you're qualified. And you hold on, and hold out. We must never surrender. America will get better and better.

Keep hope alive. Keep hope alive. Keep hope alive. On tomorrow night and beyond, keep hope alive!

I love you very much. I love you very much.

3. The Children's Defense Fund Assesses the Life Chances of a Black Child in America, 2000

For Black children:

Every Day in America

     24 babies die
    723 babies are born into poverty
    247 babies are born without health insurance
    114 babies are born to women who had late or no prenatal care
     49 babies are born at very low birthweight (less than 3 lbs. 4 oz.)
    212 babies are born at low birthweight (less than 5 lbs., 8 oz.)
    372 babies are born to teen mothers
    450 babies are born to mothers who are not high school graduates
  1,138 babies are born to unmarried mothers
  1,426 children are arrested
    105 children are arrested for violent crimes
    143 children are arrested for drug abuse
  1,009 public school students are corporally punished**
  5,725 public school students are suspended**
    500 high school students drop out**
      2 young persons under 25 die from HIV infection
      6 children and youths under 20 die from accidents
      5 children and youths under 20 die from firearms
      1 youth under 20 commits suicide
      6 children and youths under 20 are homicide victims

**Based on calculations per school day (180 days of seven hours each)

Children's Defense Fund, "Every Day in America for Black Children." Retrieved from the Internet at http://www.childrensdefense.org/everyday.html on April 17, 2000.

4. The Relative Economic Condition of Black Youths, 1973 and 1993

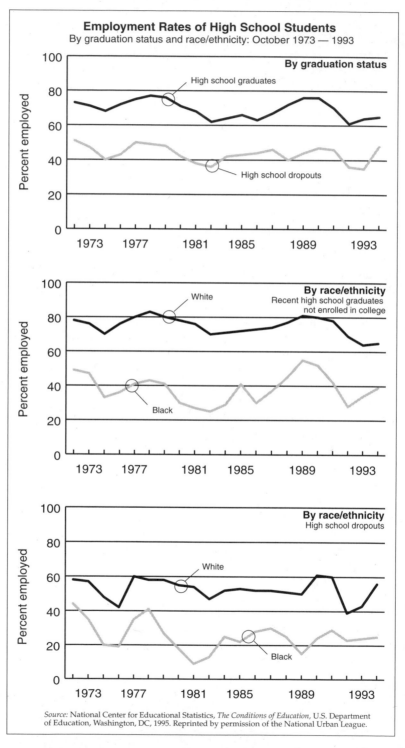

Employment Rates of High School Students
By graduation status and race/ethnicity: October 1973 — 1993

Source: National Center for Educational Statistics, *The Conditions of Education*, U.S. Department of Education, Washington, DC, 1995. Reprinted by permission of the National Urban League.

5. The United States Congress Investigates Rap Music, 1994

Statement of C. DeLores Tucker, Chair, National Political Congress of Black Women

The Honorable Cardiss Collins and members of the Subcommittee on Commerce Consumer Protection and Competitiveness, I thank you for the opportunity to testify and to raise my concerns for the welfare of the young people of this Nation. I speak as the chair of the National Political Congress of Black Women, a nonprofit, nonpartisan organization for the political and economic empowerment of African-American women and their families.

As I prayerfully prepared my testimony for this important congressional hearing, . . . I was consumed by a penetrating thought. The thought was this. If Dr. Martin Luther King, Jr., the moral leader and conscience of this Nation, were alive today he would be leading a nationwide crusade to restore the deteriorating moral values of this Nation.

Again, it would be Dr. King who would be marching and demonstrating against the glamorization of violence and its corrupting influence, which has now become a part of our culture in the name of freedom. This freedom, freedom from responsibility and accountability, is not the kind of freedom that Dr. King, Medgar Evers, John Lewis, James Farmer, Rosa Parks and so many others risked their lives for.

Indeed, Dr. King would be deeply saddened by those in our community who abuse and misuse the freedom of speech by dehumanizing, demeaning and degrading our own women. Dr. King would take offense to have African Americans who for decades fought against stereotypical "Amos and Andy" and "Aunt Jemima" images, now be the subject of public disrespect as a result of the messages heralded by gangsta rap.

So, Congresswoman Collins and members of this congressional subcommittee, I come to you in the spirit of Dr. King and on behalf of millions of African American women, women who should not be seen as objects of disdain, but rather as grandmothers, mothers, sisters, aunts and daughters who demand respect and who demand that the human decency and dignity that is defended and protected for other members of American society should not be so freely compromised in our case.

Yes, images that degrade our dignity and insult our children and families concern us too, as any other self-respecting member of society. Even if it comes out of our own mouths, the gangsta rap and misogynist lyrics that glorify violence and denigrate women is nothing more than pornographic smut. And with the release of Snoop Doggy Dogg's debut album, *Doggystyle,* that includes the graphic artwork that is in the room here today that is sold with it.

Because this pornographic smut is in the hands of our children, it coerces, influences, encourages and motivates our youth to commit violent behavior, to use drugs and abuse women through demeaning sex acts. The reality of the 1990s is that

---

Excerpts from testimony on "Music and Commerce," Hearings before the Subcommittee on Commerce, Consumer Protection, and Competitiveness, Committee on Energy and Commerce, House of Representatives, 103rd Congress, February 11 and May 5, 1994, Serial No. 103–112 (Washington, D.C.: U.S. Government Printing Office, 1994), 4–6, 38–39, 40–41, 144–145.

the greatest fear in the African American community does not come from earth-quake, floods or fires, but from violence, the kind of violence that has already trans-formed our communities and schools into war zones where children are dodging bullets, instead of balls, and planning their own funerals.

This explains why so many of our children are out of control and why we have more black males in jail than we have in college. As an illustration of this, let me share with you excerpts from a letter that I received from a prisoner in Lorton, Virginia.

He said, "Rappers make it sound so good and look so real that I would drink and smoke drugs just like on the video, thinking that was the only way that I could be somebody. My hood girls became ho's and bitches. What is so bad is, they accepted it, and you know why? Because they put themselves in the video, too, and the guns, money, cars, drugs and men became reality. But look where this kind of thinking has gotten me—facing 25 years to life in jail."

Enough is enough. I am here today to put the Nation on notice that the pro-liferation of violence and unacceptable sexual messages in our youth's music is due in large part to the avarice of the record industry. The record industry is now demanding in many of their contracts that these messages of degradation be in the music of the artist. The record industry is out of control.

Something must be done to stop the financing and promoting of this cultural plague that is infecting the minds of our most valuable asset, our children. I am saying that principle must come before profit. . . .

Statement of David Harleston

Good morning, Madam Chairwoman. My name is David Harleston and I am presi-dent of Rush Associated Labels, or R.A.L., which has as its largest and most prolific division Def Jam Recordings, Incorporated.

Def Jam Recordings or Def Jam was founded in 1983 by Russell Simmons who has been widely recognized as the individual who brought hip hop music to the cul-tural fore. Russell Simmons currently serves as our chief executive officer.

R.A.L. is engaged primarily in the creation, marketing, promotion, and distri-bution of the spectrum of music that is known as hip hop. In 1993, hip hop music in all its forms accounted for approximately 7.8 percent of the estimated $10.2 billion of music in the United States. Without question, hip hop has evolved into a major contributor to the music industry.

This music and this culture have achieved a level of creative energy which justifies our corporate commitment to the genre. Hip hop has provided an extraor-dinary avenue of artistic expression for African-American youth and it has eco-nomically empowered a generation of artists, producers and others who have imported hip hop culture and music into areas such as fashion, film, advertising, comedy, television, and publishing.

Madam Chairwoman, I would be less than candid if I did not acknowledge my concerns about this hearing. During the past year, the hip hop community has been the subject of intense scrutiny concerning the role of rap music in our culture. Some critics have suggested, for example, that rap music glorifies violence, de-grades women, and erodes community values.

I do not question the sincerity of those who have expressed those views. However, I strongly believe that those views are myopic.

Let's be clear. Like all artists, hip hop artists are products of their environment. Their environments have influenced who they are and the kinds of music that they make. Accordingly, hip hop artists frequently relate experiences which many find unsettling or uncomfortable. That is precisely the point that certain artists are trying to make.

However, it is increasingly apparent that certain opponents of hip hop music are of the misguided view that if we do not hear about the issues raised and addressed in the music then those issues will not exist.

In fact, one could argue that efforts to suppress hip hop artists are efforts to ignore unpleasant realities that exist in America's backyard. Such a view simply denies reality. Silencing the messenger will not extinguish the problem. . . .

Statement of Yolanda "Yo Yo" Whitaker

Hello, it is a pleasure to be here, Madam Chairwoman, the subcommittee. My name is Yolanda Whitaker, I am known as Yo Yo. I am on East West Records.

I am out of south central Los Angeles, born and raised. I am very involved in the music business. I have been for 5 years. Along with that, I am involved in an organization entitled the Intelligent Black Women's Coalition, which I have formed for many years now, 4 years, and we have 9 chapters in different States, which help boost the self-esteem for young black teenagers. We also deal with voting, teenage pregnancy, and education.

We deal with non—this is a nonprofit organization. We do have fund-raisers. We donate to black women, battered women shelters, little league football teams that are brought up in the neighborhoods. We donate to premature babies, mainly from Martin Luther King Hospital, drug babies.

On behalf of the rappers, we ask, where does it end? We see and hear violent acts every day, whether it may be through the eyes of the media, movie producers, or businesses. There was violence before rap and there will continue to be violence after rap.

For example, how many times do we see the Rodney King beating, the Lorena Bobbitt story, Tonya Harding, the Menendez trial? I can go on and on, but where does it end? Violence permeates our every day life.

I am here to help you understand that there is a thing called context. When our lyrics are taken out of context, they take on a whole new meaning that you interpret as violence. There is a language difference from 20 years ago to now. Words change. We have a totally different meaning for the language we speak.

That is why, if you don't understand, ask, and we will take the time to explain. You take the time to listen to the whole story.

If you don't, our generation is lost. Those who block our music and refuse to take the whole story will never understand. Saying one is to respect our ancestors for what they have worked for is one thing, but saying that rap causes violence is another.

People choose to point the finger on us and censor our right to freedom of speech, but is that constitutional?

Why is the so-called negative rap so popular? It is because negativity is what surrounds us. The true rap listeners are surrounded by the negativity in the neighborhood and until you can help our situation, don't criticize the way we feel.

Rap artists cannot be held accountable for why people are in jail. These jails have been filled with our black males and females since slavery, and yet, where does it end?

This is the time for more autonomy. This is a time for each individual to take responsibility of their own actions. Rap cannot be the scapegoat. If we fail as a whole to acknowledge the real problems that we face, then we will never resolve the problems. Jobs, education, home discipline, teen pregnancy, AIDS, homelessness is something that we all should focus on, not rap.

Being from the hood, neighborhood, I can tell you that violence didn't start from a cassette tape that might have been popped into a home or car stereo system. Whitney Houston sells more records than any rapper. Why isn't that man's kids emulating her? Why is it our fault? We are the product of America your generation created. Don't shut us down. Hear us out.

Now is the time to focus on real villains, not the rap artists. I ask you, Madam Chairwoman, where does it end and when will it end?

Statement of Robin D. G. Kelley

My name is Robin D. G. Kelley, and for the record I just made a couple of corrections. It is Robin D. G. Kelley. "Kelley" is spelled with an "ey," and I am not an associate professor, I am a full professor at the University of Michigan.

While I do agree that sexism and sexist language is a serious problem among African Americans and in U.S. society as a whole, to begin to deal with this issue, we need to establish at least three things: One, rap music in particular draws on much older traditions of sexist vernacular culture that has to be [understood] historically; two, that misogynistic language in popular music is a symptom of the culture and circumstances we live in rather than the cause of sexist behavior; and, three, that censorship will not alleviate sexism.

First, like virtually all of American culture, African American vernacular tradition has a very long history of sexism evidenced in oral forms such as toasting, the blues, and the age old "baaadman tales." Some of the older toasts are more venomous in their use of sexist profanity than much of what we find today in hip hop.

Although it wasn't marketed like rap is today, vulgar oral traditions have been in circulation. Indeed, one finds scholarly books of such vernacular poetry edited by leading scholars in public and university libraries and even the Library of Congress has sexist, profanity-ridden recordings by artists like Jelly Roll Morton in its own collection.

The historic characters from the "baaadman tales" of the late 19th and early 20th centuries such as Stagolee and Railroad Bill were intended to be thoroughly bad, rebels against anyone who stood in their way—the white man, the law, the community, and women—and, in a context where lynching was seen by whites and blacks as acts of racial class and gender domination, as a means of keeping so-called "niggers" in their place and stripping black men of any sense of manhood or sexual assertiveness. Black communities who heard these stories derived both pleasure and fear from these horrific tales of transgression and nihilism. That they were profoundly sexist goes without saying, but they were never intended to be mirrors of actual gender relations nor prescriptions for how to live.

These characters were aesthetically compelling precisely because their transgressions were so total, so complete, and hence so mythic. Many, not all, rap artists draw on this tradition because they too find the mythic baaadman compelling not only for its sexism but for its resistance to police, to racism, to government, and other embodiments of authority.

Yet we also need to ask why these sexist traditions are so compelling to so many young men of all ethnic groups. Children are raised in a world where men are expected to dominate, to control, to be the main breadwinner, and women are expected to be weaker and dependent.

Despite the limited successes of the feminist movement, men and women who don't fall within these roles are often treated as strange exceptions. Indeed, as Susan Faludi points out in her book *Backlash,* TV shows like *Married with Children,* and the so-called new men's movement represent an adult male counterattack on challenges to traditional gender roles.

Similarly, backlash has taken place among poor inner city men, but with a twist. The very things associated with male power are more difficult for these men to achieve. Permanent unemployment and the constant threat of violence and incarceration has made it difficult for men to be the primary wage earner, achieve financial security, and establish patriarchal families. The shift to a post-industrial economy in which young urban African Americans have fewer and fewer prospects has shaped rap music narratives about sexual relationships and, as in the past, women have been the target of young men's frustrations. Indeed, except for the use of profanity, some of these young men's attacks on African American women sound very much like that of conservative critics. Young women are portrayed as welfare queens making babies merely to stay on public assistance, or so-called "skeezers" who use their sexuality to take black men's meager wages. So many young men see heterosexual conquest as a key element in achieveing masculinity. Of course, we must not apologize for or condone this behavior, but if we want to eradicate sexism, we need to understand its roots. . . .

6. The New Face of Racism: Racial Profiling, 1999

Robert L. Wilkins, a Harvard-educated Washington attorney, was traveling along Interstate 68 a few years ago, returning from his grandfather's funeral, when a Maryland state trooper pulled the family's rented Cadillac over for speeding. When the trooper asked to search the car and its contents, Wilkins refused. But the trooper set loose a drug-sniffing dog to comb the car's exterior, including the windshield, the hubcaps, and the taillights. No drugs were found. Says Wilkins: "We were completely humiliated."

Wilkins is among hundreds of American motorists who claim to be victims of "racial profiling," the police practice of stopping and searching African-American and Hispanic drivers at rates far disproportionate to their numbers on the road.

Angie Cannon, "DWB: Driving While Black," *U.S. News & World Report,* March 15, 1999, p. 72. Copyright 1999, U.S. News & World Report, Inc. Visit us at our web site at www.usnews.com for additional information.

"Driving while black," as the phenomenon has come to be known, flared anew last week when New Jersey Gov. Christine Todd Whitman fired the state police superintendent, Carl Williams, for saying that while he did not condone racial profiling, minorities were responsible for most of the country's illegal drug trade. The Williams incident gave momentum to a grassroots campaign by civil rights groups to make minority motorists more aware of their rights.

Statistics on racial profiling are controversial, but in a recent study, Temple University Prof. John Lamberth determined that about 75 percent of the motorists and traffic violators along one stretch of Interstate 95 were white, but 80 percent of searches were of minorities.

Grateful Dead. Anecdotal evidence of racial profiling has been accumulating for years. Prominent African-Americans, including actors Blair Underwood and Wesley Snipes and former Los Angeles District Attorney Christopher Darden, have been stopped by police, allegedly for no other reason than the color of their skin. Even white youths with long hair, beards, or Grateful Dead stickers are targeted, lawyers say.

Police insist they don't engage in profiling, but Williams, in the remarks that got him fired, cited disproportionately high drug arrests for minorities. While blacks comprise only about 13 percent of the population, statistics show they make up 35 percent of all drug arrests and 55 percent of all drug convictions. Nevertheless, civil rights advocates say Williams's remarks reflect a pattern of stereotyping by police. When police look for minorities, critics say, it is minorities they will arrest.

Increasingly, targets of racial profiling are challenging the practice in court— and winning. Sgt. David Smith, an Indiana state trooper, won a legal settlement from the Carmel, Ind., police department after he was pulled over while driving an unmarked car. Wilkins, the Washington lawyer, won $95,000 from the Maryland State Police, as well as an agreement by the agency to keep records to help prevent discrimination.

On the national level, the American Civil Liberties Union and other grassroots groups, such as Citizens Opposing Profiled Police Stops, are pushing for legislation that would require the federal government to study traffic stops and to note the race and ethnicity of motorists detained. In the meantime, they are soliciting motorists' complaints. You can call COPPS at (757) 624-6620 or visit its Web site (www.copps.org).

7. The New Face of Racism: The Ordeal of Haitian Immigrants, 1998

During the past four decades, from the beginning of the dictatorial regime of François "Papa Doc" Duvalier in 1957 to the end of the term of the first democratically elected president of the republic, Jean Bertrand Aristide, in 1996, tens of thousands of Haitians left the island and resettled in New York, Miami, Chicago, Boston, Los Angeles, Washington, D.C., New Orleans, and other American cities.

Michael S. Laguerre, "Refugees and Immigrants," in *Diasporic Citizenship: Haitian Americans in Transnational America* (New York: St. Martin's Press, 1998) 75–76, 80–83. Reprinted with permission of St. Martin's Press, LLC.

Three major factors explain the mass immigration into the United States during this period. The first relates to the iron-fist rule of the dictatorial regime of François Duvalier. As a result of political persecution and state violence, several politicians and members of the elite left after Duvalier named himself president for life in 1964, and they sent for the members of their immediate and extended family. With President Duvalier's transfer of power to his son, Jean-Claude Duvalier, in 1971, large numbers of Haitians, both urban and rural, boarded sailboats to reach the shores of Florida. While the earlier migration had relied mostly on air transport, a very large portion of the later migration consisted of "boat people."

The second factor concerns the change of government in Cuba. Up until the late 1950s, several hundreds of Haitians made the yearly trip to Cuba during the sugar cane harvest to work. With the installation of the Castro administration, however, that window of opportunity was closed off to potential migrants because the socialist regime did not want to give the impression that it was in the business of exploiting foreign labor. This Cuban policy had a detrimental impact on the economic conditions in Haiti because the government could no longer rely on the hard currency earned through contractual arrangements and the taxable money that workers brought back to their local communities.

The third factor has to do with the Civil Rights Act of 1964, which eventually relaxed racial tensions in the United States. For black Haitians, the civil rights movement was a signal that the United States was making an effort toward national antidiscrimination, pro-integration policies.

Furthermore, immigration of Haitians into the United States was tolerated, but not encouraged or welcomed, as a way to prevent the friendly "maroon republic" from following the "bad" example of neighboring socialist Cuba, that is from placing itself in the arms of then communist Russia. . . .

Beginning in the late 1950s the policy of the US government was to welcome the white Cubans who were fleeing a socialist state and to deport black Haitians who were escaping from a right-wing dictatorial regime. The unequivocal welcome of the Cubans remained a practice until the Refugee Act of 1980. While cold war ideology was often invoked to justify the recognition of Cubans fleeing a communist country and to distinguish them from the Haitians, many analysts have concluded that racial discrimination has been a major factor in the way in which Haitian refugees were deported to the island. In the 1980s, as more black and brown Cubans began to migrate to the United States, the open door policy was revised.

Since the early 1970s, when boatlifts of refugees began to seek asylum in the US, Haitians have been incarcerated in various detention centers in Florida and other states. The gist of US policy was to jail Haitian refugees upon their arrival and deport them to Haiti. To deal with the backlog of applicants for asylum and to prevent more from coming to the US, the State Department and INS established in 1978 their "Haitian Program," which evolved into the wholesale deportation of Haitian refugees. . . .

For several reasons, 1980 was a turning point in the history of Haitian refugees in the United States. First, the Refugee Act issued in March 1980 provided a more inclusive definition of "refugee." Fleeing a Communist country was no longer the central feature of the definition, and therefore there was no legal ground to separate the Cubans from the Haitians. The Cubans, however, remained better organized in terms of lobbying political allies in Washington, DC and inside the Republican Party, and this continued to make a difference in practice in how Haitians and Cubans are treated by INS.

The second crucial event of 1980 came in July, when Judge James L. King ruled that the State Department's Haitian program was unconstitutional. This was the first major victory of Haitian refugees in the US court system, and its timing— during a presidential election year—gave national visibility to their plight. According to the decision of the court, "the manner in which INS treated the more than 4000 Haitian plaintiffs violated the Constitution, the immigration statutes, multinational agreements, INS regulations and INS operating procedures. It must stop." At the heart of the decision was the finding that the federal government had no legal basis to undermine the human rights of the plaintiffs or their ability to seek asylum in the United States.

Spring and summer of 1980 saw a flood of refugees from Cuba (130,000) and Haiti (11,000) arriving at the same time and at the same Florida port. The Haitian Program was under attack by human rights lawyers, church associations and the congressional black caucus. With the presidential election only a few months away, President Carter attempted a damage-control effort. On 20 June 1980, he established a new program, the *Cuban-Haitian entrant* status. This was a preemptive measure to soften the blow and embarrassment of Judge King's forthcoming decision. The new classification "allowed members of both groups who had arrived prior to 20 June to remain in the United States until their status is resolved. The Carter administration, in effect, granted parole to the Cuban-Haitian entrants." On 10 October 1980, a month before the presidential election, this privilege was extended to those who arrived after 20 June perhaps in an effort to sway black voters.

The decade 1970–1980 was a disaster for Haitian refugees who sought asylum in the United States. For example, "approximately 50 000 Haitians sought asylum in the United States between 1972 and 1980; only twenty-five succeeded." The situation was even worse during the first Reagan administration: "From September 1981 to March 1985, some 3000 Haitians had been intercepted by the US Coast Guard. Not one Haitian was found by US authorities to have presented a valid claim to asylum, and not one Haitian was taken to the US to have his claim more carefully examined.

The treatment of the Mariel Cubans and Haitians arriving in Florida, despite President Carter's attempt to provide a provisional solution, exemplified the double standard of US policy *vis-à-vis* the Haitian refugees. At a congressional hearing in 1980, Senator Dennis De Concini bluntly summarized the disparity: "If you are a boat refugee from Cuba, INS automatically considers you a refugee. If you are a boat refugee from Baby Doc's Haiti, INS automatically considers you an illegal alien coming to the United States for economic purposes."

President Carter's attempt to resolve the issue before the elections failed, and President Reagan inherited the problem. On 29 September 1981, he issued an executive order directing the US Coast Guard to patrol the waters between Haiti and Florida and prevent boatlifts of refugees from entering the US. The Coast Guard were supposed to intercept the boats, interview the passengers to evaluate whether they had a justifiable claim for asylum, send those who were ineligible back to Haiti, and bring to the US those who passed this first interview test.

This interdiction program, carried out on the high seas, precluded applicants from any access to legal advice. During the first ten years of the program—up until the September 1991 coup in Haiti—over 24 000 Haitians were interviewed but only twenty-eight were brought to the United States to pursue claims for political asylum.

After the September 1991 coup, the large number of refugees overwhelmed the Coast Guard's ability to intercept boats at sea. At this juncture, the Bush administration, hoping to prevent the refugee crisis from influencing the outcome of the presidential elections, established a tent city at the Guantanamo Bay naval base. From November 1991 on, the refugees were to be sent there for screening interviews. Guantanamo ended up being used as a detention camp for both Haitian and Cuban refugees.

Several attempts by the Bush administration to place refugees in various Anglophone Caribbean islands and Central American countries were not successful. In the meantime, the interdiction program and the detention at Guantanamo became a headache for the Bush administration, as more refugees from Cuba and Haiti continued to attempt to come to the United States. Guantanamo was very overcrowded, and the specter of violence by angry refugees was not what Bush wanted in an election year.

So, on 24 May 1992, President Bush issued the so-called Kennebunkport Order authorizing the Coast Guard to return to Haiti—without any screening—boatlifts of Haitian refugees found on the high seas. Haitians desiring asylum in the United States were told that all applications for asylum would have to be initiated at the US Consular Office in Port-au-Prince, where they would be screened by US immigration officers.

The plight of Cubans and Haitians at Guantanamo became a hot issue during the Bush-Clinton presidential campaign. Candidate Clinton repeatedly decried Bush's policy toward the refugees as cruel and vowed to provide a humanitarian solution to the dilemma. Once elected, however, Clinton changed his mind and continued the policy he had so eloquently deplored during the campaign.

Much of the Clinton administration efforts were directed at disaggregating the Cubans from the Haitian issue. After the United States occupied Haiti in 1994 (for the second time in this century) and brought Aristide back, the majority of Haitians at Guantanamo were sent back to Haiti. In contrast, the Cubans at Guantanamo were allowed to come to the United States and were given refugee status. The last Haitians were returned from Guantanamo to Haiti in November 1995, while the last Cubans left Guantanamo for the United States in January 1996. The old policy of bringing the Cubans in and returning the Haitians to Haiti had not changed.

8. The Borders of Black America: The New "Black" Immigrants, 1999

NEW YORK—He passes for an African American teenager, easily. The talk, the poise, the posture, even the cornrows. He is dressed in the trademark style of the urban teen: Baggy jeans, Timberland boots, Versace sunglasses, baseball cap. At 17, José Mendoza is visibly and inescapably black. He brings up Martin Luther King Jr. and Rosa Parks, race and its tribulations. "Why do white people gotta hate black people?" he asked. "Know what I'm saying?"

Gabriél Escobar, "Dominicans Face Assimilation in Black and White," *Washington Post,* May 14, 1999, pp. A3, A22. Reprinted with permission.

He once played a joke at George Washington High School, home to upper Manhattan's immigrants since the early 1920s. Fluent in English and fluent in "street," Mendoza fooled everyone by pretending he was a bona fide American black. But this American-born, Spanish-speaking Dominican was simply too good. Some Dominicans, not keen on African Americans, thought he was too African, too American, *too black.*

One day he surprised two Dominican girls derisively talking about him in Spanish. *"Que fue lo que tu dijiste?"* he asked. "What did you say?" His Spanish made him suddenly Dominican. From then on, he said recently, "they treated me with respect."

This is Mendoza's world, the complex and conflicted world of black Latinos. He is at once very black but not quite black enough for many African Americans, very Latino but not light enough to matter to most Hispanics, American in every way but at the same time inexorably foreign. "From the inside we're Dominicans. From the outside we're black," is how he described it.

Dominicans account for eight in every 10 students at George Washington, reflecting the enormous migration of islanders to New York City. Dominicans have been the largest immigrant group in the city every decade since 1970, and this historical influx has altered the face of the immigrant population here and introduced an entirely new culture. To assimilate, or even to fit in, the black Latinos must adapt not only to white America and black America but to Latino America.

Their strong ties to the island make them citizens of both countries and, it seems, citizens of neither. "They are here and there and in between. Yet they are perceived as foreigners in both locations," noted Luis E. Guarnizo, a sociologist at the University of California at Davis and an authority on the Dominican migration.

Nowhere is the assimilation of black Latinos more evident than in New York, where Dominicans have flocked in such great numbers. Throughout the early 1990s, the Dominican Republic accounted for one in five immigrants to the city, an average of 22,000 annually, according to the most current figures. By next year, the Dominican population in New York City may reach 700,000, the equivalent of many middle-sized cities.

Between 1990 and 1994, an astonishing 35,657 Dominicans settled in Washington Heights, Inwood and Hamilton Heights, contiguous neighborhoods in upper Manhattan that have been dramatically altered by the legal migration from the Caribbean. Dominicans, skilled at grass-roots organization, already are a force on the New York school board and have elected two judges, a city councilman and a state assemblyman. Politically they have fit in better and faster than most immigrant groups. New York City Council member Guillermo Linares, the country's first elected official born in the Dominican Republic, said Dominicans like to refer to themselves as "300 percenters—100 percent Dominican Republic, 100 percent Dominican American and 100 percent American."

But on the street and in school, what is skin deep is often what matters. While those with Mendoza's skin color will be automatically identified as black, many lighter-skinned Dominicans are not so easily pegged. In his writings, the Dominican writer Junot Diaz uses the term "halfie" to describe this significant group. One consequence is that many in the community define themselves less by color than by cultural identity. "Where you gravitate to speaks so loudly," Linares said, reflecting the unusual position many Dominicans are in because so many can literally choose their race.

Of course, black Dominicans like Mendoza don't have that choice. And while his comfortable identification with African Americans shows he has answered a central question faced by Dominicans—black like who?—hundreds of thousands must still reconcile their very nuanced views on race with the stark black-white reality of their adopted country.

Finding a place for themselves, much less assimilating, has not been easy. Afro-Latinos are largely ignored by leaders of African American national groups. "We have to go there and give them evidence that we are black, which doesn't mean they will believe us," Silvio Torres-Saillant, the director of the Dominican Studies Center at the City College of New York, said of African American civil rights groups.

Diaz, whose short fiction has been lauded for capturing the varied landscape of the Dominican diaspora, said America's dialogue between blacks and whites is so narrow that it leaves out this large and new migration. African Americans "are allowed to be black because they don't speak Spanish," he said, "but I'm not allowed to be black because I speak Spanish."

Afro-Latinos are ignored even by some fellow Latinos. And when they're not, they are often depicted in ways no longer tolerated by African Americans. While national Hispanic groups bitterly complain about how they are portrayed in the English-speaking media, a small group of Afro-Latinos has fought, largely in vain, to remove stereotyping in the Spanish-language media. Roland Roebuck, an Afro-Latino from Puerto Rico, last year wrote a bitter letter about the portrayal of black Latinos to Henry Cisneros, a former Clinton administration Cabinet member and now president of the powerful Univision network.

"Imagine for a moment, Mr. Cisneros, how an Afro-Latino family viewing your station feels when our people are portrayed in your news, novelas and programs as criminal, savage, lazy, slick, sex-driven, violent, superstitious, uneducated, undependable and untrustworthy," wrote Roebuck, who works for the District government.

If Afro-Latinos are sometimes ignored by their own kind, they are practically invisible in America. The black Latino, so visible on the streets of upper Manhattan and especially in major league baseball, still does not register in the collective American definition of who a Hispanic is.

As if this were not challenge enough, Dominican migrants must also reconcile their island's complex racial code with America's historically contentious one. In the Dominican Republic, the oppressors have generally been mulattoes and light-skinned blacks. One of the worst insults for a black Dominican is to call him a Haitian. Haiti invaded and occupied the Dominican Republic twice and these seminal events heavily influenced the island's view on race. "You are what you appear to be," said Torres-Saillant, "which is very different from the generic racial definition here."

Which is, in essence, what happened to Mendoza when he pulled off his joke. Dominican students, seeing his black skin, "dissed" him because he was black and seemingly foreign to them. The African American he pretended to be became the hated Haitian of the island. In a group of light- and brown-skinned students and teachers, the island's racial sensibilities hold sway. Parents' preference is for sons and daughters to marry "light," according to some teenagers.

For Dominicans, particularly teenagers, sorting out their racial identity can be confusing. Teenagers choose their race, going white or black, depending on their own skin tone. "Some of the kids who are darker more readily accept the African Americans, and they look to that kind of music," said Thomas Garcia, a Dominican who teaches at the school.

"You see that black guy? He's Dominican," Albert Bonilla, 17, said one day between classes, when the hallways were crowded. The student Bonilla singled out, like Bonilla himself, was a light-skinned black who was "thugged out," their term for hip-hop getup that defines the group.

"My grandmother be like, put your pants up! *Subate el pantalon!*" said Bonilla. "You see the way we talk?" he asked. "You don't hear white people talking like that."

Mendoza and other black Dominicans identify with African American culture—their game, for example, is basketball and not baseball. They talk in what is best described as "black spanglish," a mixture of English and Spanish with a decidedly hip-hop accent.

"I used to be a decent boy," Mendoza said, cracking up the kids around him. Now, he said, he filters race through the African American experience. "If white people are going to hate me," he said, "I'm going to hate back."

Mendoza fulfills the prediction of one study that said the longer black Dominicans are in this country the likelier they are to identify with American blacks. But after all his talk and posturing, Mendoza steps back just a little and, like Linares, plays the percent game. He announces that he still prefers rice and beans over American food. He calls it "a Dominican plate. The grub."

"I'm still part Dominican," he said, suddenly serious. "That's my nationality. If you become African American, you give your nationality away. That's like saying you're betraying your country."

ESSAYS

The three essays that conclude this volume offer strongly argued perspectives on themes that run through African-American historical experience: political-economic status and participation, cultural creativity and autonomy, and the problem of constituting the very boundaries of African America and of African-American issues. Though differing in subject matter, each of these essays also shows how all of these themes are interrelated and cross-cutting.

Lani Guinier, a Harvard Law School professor, assesses the political situation of African Americans who, having won formal access to political power, find themselves all too often excluded still from real influence on legislation and its enforcement. In situations where the majority's interests are historically and structurally at odds with the minority, how does one reconcile the democratic principle of majority rule with the equally compelling principle of substantive justice?

Tricia Rose, who teaches history and Africana studies at New York University, examines an issue of cultural creativity and political expression that is as decisive among African Americans as in the larger society. In modern consumer societies access to tools for cultural creativity and to an audience for that creativity is mediated by the market and shaped by forces and interests external to African-American communities. Rejecting simplistic solutions, Rose shows the need to recognize the links between cultural, social, and political struggles.

Narrating a local struggle over the siting of a toxic waste dump, Temma Kaplan, professor of history and women's studies at the State University of New York at Stony Brook, raises important questions about how and when an issue becomes one of race or civil rights. At the same time she reveals the deep imprint that the midcentury freedom movement has left on ordinary citizens, white and black. The methods of mobilization, tactics of struggle, and the language of rights and wrongs drew on still vivid memories of that prior history.

Rethinking Constitutional Rights

LANI GUINIER

When President Ronald Reagan left office in January 1989, many of us within the black community collectively sighed with relief. For eight years the Reagan Administration had sowed conflict and division between itself and civil rights groups, and had contributed to an increasing sense of isolation among African-Americans.

The Reagan legacy has directly affected the role of blacks in the political process. On the one hand, black registration and turnout has increased in response to Reagan's perceived anti–civil rights agenda. As blacks begin to vote at levels approximating their numerical strength in the community, they see the ballot as an important tool for preserving a traditional civil rights agenda. Electing Democrats, or moderate Republicans, is the most obvious way for blacks to assure their community of some voice in the public debate, especially since Ronald Reagan gave blacks no public forum and made no effort to seek out or appoint traditional civil rights leaders.

On the other hand, many blacks have felt particularly stifled by the traditional two-party approach to black political participation. One party has taken blacks for granted; the other, at best, ignored them. Mainstream Democrats do not accept black Democrats, such as Jesse Jackson, as legitimate party spokespersons, and too often only whites are allowed to run for office on the Democratic ticket. On the other hand, Republicans have refused to court the black vote at all. Blacks may vote, but it is whites who will govern. It is this dilemma, exacerbated by the Reagan success in polarizing the electorate, which presently challenges black voters. Can we keep the faith?

This chapter attempts to spotlight the Reagan civil rights legacy by examining, through the prism of black political participation, both the Reagan Administration's record in voting rights enforcement and its success in polarizing the electorate. It then examines the importance of vigorous voting rights enforcement to the empowerment of the black community, and offers recommendations . . . on inclusionary ways to address the racial divisions of the body politic. The chapter suggests that we should reclaim the Voting Rights Act for those it was intended to benefit, along with eliminating all barriers to universal voter registration. Finally, it stresses that we should make a concerted effort to promote black political clout through actual, and not simply virtual, representation. . . .

Lani Guinier, "Keeping the Faith: Black Voters in the Post-Reagan Era," in *Tyranny of the Majority: Fundamental Fairness in Representative Democracy* (New York: Free Press, 1994), 21–40. Reprinted with permission of The Free Press, a division of Simon & Schuster, Inc.

The polarizing philosophy of the Reagan years affected more than the Administration's enforcement activities. Its legacy, engrafted upon Reconstruction era stereotypes about black elected officials, has perpetuated and accentuated a racially skewed reality in which blacks vote but do not govern, at least not in majority white jurisdictions.

In the effective pursuit of political empowerment, black voters have begun to relinquish the presumption that a Democratic White House is necessarily the ticket to a better future. Management by good people with excellent credentials will not alone lead America into the twenty-first century.

Political euphoria about the possibility of a Democratic presidential victory in 1988 was neither justified nor shared by the black community. In 1986, Democrats gained a majority in the United States Senate on the strength of four predominantly southern victories; these triumphs were built on the solid base of black Democratic support. Black political activity also figured decisively in the Democrats' greatest symbolic success in recent years—the defeat of Robert Bork. Even Governor Dukakis' early lead in the 1988 presidential race was provided largely by African-Americans. On election day, Dukakis received almost 90% of the black vote while Bush polled nearly 60% of the white vote nationwide, and more than 70% in the deep South. Yet, the vision Democrats offered in 1988 hardly mentioned, even indirectly, problems of race, and it deliberately ignored connections between racism and poverty. Similarly, Jesse Jackson's second place showing in the primaries did not secure blacks a place at the bargaining table.

Snubbing its loyal black constituency, the Democratic Party has responded to racial polarization by distancing itself from black interests. Thus, many white Democratic Party candidates have not actively sought black allies, nor have they aggressively supported black leaders who are Democrats. While the Democratic Party . . . elected Ronald H. Brown as its first black national chair, Mr. Brown's ties to the Jackson wing of the party were generally perceived as a disadvantage. Indeed, the events surrounding Ron Brown's election may signal recognition of the Jackson "problem," not the Jackson "program."

Some Democrats asserted that Mr. Jackson's high profile in the party contributed to the November 1988 election defeat. Thus, despite their consistent loyalty to the Democrats, African-Americans have not been able to protect themselves with a "voice and a vote." Democrats, who control both houses of Congress, seem unaware that reciprocity in bargaining requires the active promotion of black interests, not just the occasional subvention and authorization of civil rights enforcement. In other words, black legislative issues can be ghettoized from the Left as well as the Right.

The Democrats' policy of benign neglect toward African-Americans has not gone unnoticed. Where racial concerns should properly be a campaign issue, to mask controversial stands in euphemism easily offends if white decisionmakers have demonstrated in the past that they do not take into account minority interests. Consequently, when Governor Dukakis "snubbed" Jesse Jackson, who learned from a reporter of his being passed over for the vice-presidency, blacks took affront. It reemphasized that white politicians have not demonstrated fairness, and that blacks have reason to feel abandoned and unprotected without someone in a leadership role with whom they can identify and who identifies with their interests.

Although black voters are frustrated with the Democratic Party's response to their interests, they are hardly convinced of the sincerity of the Republican Party's nascent and token outreach. Republican Party leaders, including President Bush, now claim that they want to attract black voters to the party ranks. Despite the racially offensive tactical choices which they have made in recent campaigns, these same leaders now repudiate the racial views of white supremacists who also proclaim themselves to be GOP leaders. While the condemnation of racism is minimally appropriate, the Bush Administration has rejected important opportunities to enforce its rhetorical approach to public policy with substantive evidence of the "Republican outreach."

The evolution in black priorities from a civil rights protest agenda to electoral politics carries with it the continued need for opportunities for mass mobilization, in which the governed systematically give their consent to their government. However, blacks cannot mobilize to participate in the political process unless candidates offer an inclusionary vision of the future. This is essentially an instrumental formulation of the causes of political activity. People participate "where, when and how" they think it matters. If the political system is unresponsive, people "tend to withdraw or seek nonsystemic means of pursuing their demands."

How then are blacks to mobilize to participate in the political process without a vision of the future that reaches out to include them broadly and not just euphemistically? Certainly, part of the answer for African-Americans is to push for the removal of existing barriers to voter participation, to make voting and registration a one-step process. The United States still permits a variety of state-erected barriers to simple and convenient registration. Most voter registration requirements in the United States were enacted in the late 1800's to exclude blacks in the South and new immigrants in the North from voting. Although such requirements have been rationalized by the need to prevent voter fraud, most election fraud actually occurs in voting, not in registration, and is typically committed by election officials. Whatever the arguable justification, these requirements primarily serve to reduce voter participation among all citizens, especially minorities.

First, registration rules require that the citizen make an affirmative effort to enter the voting rolls rather than allowing automatic inclusion: enrolling citizens by social security number, for example. Believing individual initiative to register is a legitimate voting requirement, many local officials treat the franchise as a privilege which the voter must earn. Whereas other democratic governments assume the responsibility, both financial and administrative of canvassing eligible voters to enroll them on the registration list, in the United States, only volunteers and private individuals perform this task.

Second, rules which require the initiative of individual voters make it difficult for blacks who are more likely to be without cars or telephones, or who may hold a notion of political participation which pre-dates the passage of the Act, to register. Restrictive local registration practices still exist that are both burdensome and discriminatory. They are burdensome because they make voting a two-step process that must occur during working hours. They discriminate because private resources such as cars and telephones, which are critical to functioning in this two-step process, are unavailable to poor people, especially racial and language minorities. This is especially true in the South where most registration occurs at the county courthouse and where there is no public transportation. In rural Arkansas, for example, according to the 1980 census, 42% of blacks (compared with 9% of whites) have no access to a car, truck or van; 30% of blacks (compared with 10% of whites) have no telephone. Without these politically relevant private resources, poor blacks are effectively excluded from both registering and voting.

Many rural counties in the South have only one place to register and that location is typically closed weekends, evenings and at lunchtime. Some county officials refuse to appoint blacks as volunteer deputy registrars who could go door to door to register blacks. By relying on blacks' unequal access to private resources, incumbent politicians effectively exclude eligible black voters from the electorate. As a result, large numbers of blacks remain unregistered and thus are outside the political process. For example, in *Operation PUSH v. Allain,* a federal district court found that census survey figures routinely over-estimate the number of registered blacks because they are based solely on reports of a respondent's unverified past activity. Unlike questions of present fact that do not require much thought, such as the number of vehicles available, or indoor plumbing, census questions that call for specific past information are often answered inaccurately, due to the self-image that the respondent wishes to project. This leads, for blacks more than whites, to over-reporting. The court found a twenty-five percent gap between white and black registration rates, a clear sign that even rudimentary statistical parity had not been realized. . . .

The election of more black representatives proves a second important opportunity for substantive rather than rhetorical outreach. At present the electoral process is permeated by a subtle, yet pervasive, racial atmosphere that deters black candidates from running, that dismissed *prematurely* Jesse Jackson's presidential aspirations (on the basis of his race) and that permits jurisdictions not to recognize members of a sizeable minority as part of the governing coalition. Indeed, a recent survey indicated that the higher the office in question, the less whites are inclined to vote for a qualified black candidate.

Predictably, black voters seek more candidates, with more responsive programs, from which to choose. They seek both to overcome the deep-seated prejudice many whites harbor against black office-holders and to share political power through their ability to choose their own representatives. Blacks cannot enjoy equal dignity and political status until black representatives join the council of government.

Of course, not all minority-sponsored candidates are selfless public servants, but at least through "actual" representation, the mechanism exists for improving accountability. The black community can demonstrate its displeasure at the next election if black voters have a right to elect representatives of their choice, a right enforced through the drawing of district lines or alternative remedies which lower the threshold of exclusion to permit minority group representation. The enforcement of this representational right does not require legislative set-asides, color coded ballots, electoral quotas, or "one black, two votes" remedies which some might argue are also justified. Thus, many of the worries implicit in opposition to affirmative action in employment are inapposite. Moreover, black electoral success does not mean the displacement of "innocent whites" who are being forced to bear society's burdens at the ballot box unless whites have a right to be represented only by whites. Indeed, the whites being displaced are not voters but incumbent politicians who may not get re-elected in a reconfigured, racially fair, single member district plan. These incumbents, however, are usually direct beneficiaries of prior discrimination, who have no particular right to their position. The rights at stake are those of the voter, not the candidate.

Blacks have thus been attempting, through federal litigation under Section 2 of the Voting Rights Act, to exercise real legislative and executive power, not merely imagined electoral influence. They want the option of nominating, and being represented by, other black representatives. They are no longer satisfied with automatically choosing the Democratic candidate or with the ephemeral role of "the swing vote," in elections between two moderate-to-conservative white candidates. Black voters, want, and need, aggressive advocates, not momentarily concerned opportunists.

For a group that has been excluded as long as blacks, aggressive advocacy is essential to ensure that black interests are taken seriously. Technical, formal access to the political process may not be enough to guarantee even good faith representation. This is a particular problem where black voters are less likely to engage in the "extended political process" of post-election day accountability with white representatives.

The obvious role that black lawmakers perform within a legislative body was expressly endorsed by Congress when it amended Section 2 of the 1965 Voting Rights Act in 1982. In recent interviews, members of the House of Representatives acknowledged that regarding questions concerning blacks, black representatives "exert special influence on their colleagues," providing "internal leadership" to which people defer. Scholars and experienced observers of the political process have found that minority candidates "enhance minority turnout, especially where they have a realistic chance of winning." For blacks, black representation is a "crucial lever for obtaining the benefits—patronage, contracts, public services— that must be bargained for in the public arena." Moreover, diversity of representation that promotes political activity is in itself a collective good. Minority officeholding increases political consciousness and signals to constituents that the system is legitimate and ought to be supported. Thus, it promotes values of "civic inclusion," meaning a "sense of connectedness to the community and of equal political dignity, greater readiness to acquiesce in governmental decisions and hence broader consent and legitimacy, and more informed, equitable and intelligent governmental decisionmaking."

The question for the immediate future is whether blacks will have the opportunity to elect other blacks to advocate their interests and aggressively articulate their muted voices in the legislative hall.

The courts have recognized the importance for blacks of the opportunity to "elect candidates of their choice, . . . to have their ideas on political matters afforded the recognition to which they are entitled on their merits and by virtue of their individual citizenship and their numerical strength in the community." The importance of this opportunity derives from fundamental assumptions about representative democracy: that the government's authority depends on the consent of the governed and that the interests of those who are bound by governmental actions cannot be arbitrarily ignored in the legislative process. But, this notion of "opportunity" has been transformed into one of "right" to empower a historically disenfranchised and politically despised group. The most notable example of institutional vindication of this right is the enactment of the Voting Rights Act.

The courts have recognized that creating a minority group "right to representa-tion" may be appropriate in the political arena for several reasons. First, the funda-mental nature of the right to vote stems from its role in preserving all other rights. Other rights, even the most basic, are illusory if the right to vote is undermined. The franchise gives status to the individual voter but derives its vitality from its exercise by a "politically cohesive" group of citizens who elect representatives to promote consideration of group interests in public policy. A voice in the process of self-government is heard only through the medium of elected representatives; the oppor-tunity to vote is the vital means of affecting representation. Unlike other government benefits, the right to vote is therefore a *meaningful* entitlement. For the minority, the meaningful right to vote must include the correlative opportunity to elect a represen-tative of that group's choice. Even if, as Reaganism posits, blacks are merely another "special interest," it is important that they be represented. In a racially polarized sit-uation, this means creating districts or electoral opportunities in which such a repre-sentative can be elected.

Second, equal status as participants within the political sphere is possible only if members of the group are allowed to participate at all stages of the process. . . . A meaningful right to vote contemplates minority participation in post-election legisla-tive policymaking as well as pre-election coalition building and deliberation. This ideal is obviously frustrated if racial status is a consistent disqualification for such participation simply because whites refuse to work with or vote for a black candidate.

Nevertheless, some commentators argue that judicially imposed remedies to create electoral opportunities for "black representatives" constitute electoral "affirmative action" and disable black voters. The argument is that since whites can, and do, represent black voters, blacks should pursue instead an "integrative" electoral strategy in which white politicians compete for black votes. As long as blacks enjoy formal access to the polling place and intentionally discriminatory statements are suppressed, some commentators contend, blacks should have no special rights to affect an election outcome, even where no black candidate can win because of bloc voting by the white majority. Abigail Thernstrom has advocated a theory of "virtual" representation, in which black interests are taken into account to some extent, but are not actively promoted. Under this rationale, "one can be represented in a political regime in which one has no actual participatory role . . . through the participation of another who is one's likeness."

Virtual representation, which assumes surrogate representation based on com-mon interests, is rooted in the defense by the English Whigs in the eighteenth cen-tury of a franchise system in which industrial towns with no representatives in the House of Commons were considered "virtually" represented by members from similar cities. Recent commentators, including Thernstrom, have revived that theory in an attempt to justify monochromatic legislatures on the premise that whites can represent black interests.

Where interests between those "actually represented" are in fact comparable to those "virtually represented," the concept has contemporary relevance. For example, during the 1950's and 1960's, as a young black boy growing up in North Carolina, Frank Ballance, now a member of the North Carolina General Assembly, knew he had a congressman even though no black had been elected to Congress from North Carolina since Reconstruction. His "representative" was Harlem Congressman

Adam Clayton Powell, Jr. Ballance did not expect actual representation from the North Carolina congressman elected from his district. Similarly, where majority black single member districts are created within a formerly at-large electoral system to remedy vote dilution, blacks outside the majority black district are considered "virtually" represented.

However, virtual representation theory is not appropriate if the interests of a racial minority are not necessarily fungible with those of the "actual" representatives or of their white constituents. For example, blacks, as a poor and historically oppressed group, are in greater need of government sponsored programs and solicitude, which whites often resent and vigorously oppose. Even a mildly sympathetic white official will not dependably consider black interests if that individual must also accommodate the more dominant views of white constituents.

The theory that white politicians who compete in a majority white district for minority votes also take minority demands seriously is not generally supported by the immediate empirical evidence of the 1988 presidential campaign. To the extent that it has merit, the virtual representation theory requires the active advocacy of minority interests by at least one of the competing parties. Like the swing vote theory, virtual representation presumes inter-party competition. When minority interests are not only distinct but antagonistic to those of the white majority, and when one political party presumes black loyalty while the other panders to racial hostility, such representation is merely symbolic. Thus, black interests are neither actually nor virtually represented.

Blacks are still the pariah group: systematic losers in the political marketplace. Despite visible gains, legislative and executive policy is dominated by white males who lack a sustaining link to black concerns. While commentators critique the representation-reinforcing view of pluralist society, blacks should be supported in their struggle to elect representatives who will advocate a vision which includes their experience. It is unreasonable to expect blacks to allow others to name their reality, especially in the absence of visible reciprocity.

Inflamed racial polarization during the Reagan years rekindled de facto separate and unequal political, economic and social status for African-Americans. The Reagan years have left blacks geographically more concentrated and isolated. Seven states currently have black populations that are over twenty-two percent, yet until 1993 there were no blacks in the United States Senate. Before Douglas Wilder there were no black governors elected by either party in this century, and 1.5% of the elected officials nationwide are black (mostly mayors from majority-black towns with populations under 1000). The potential political influence which concentrations of blacks could wield at the local level has not been combined with a willingness by state and national governments to democratize the voting process. A majority of white voters, in general, has been reluctant to support or contribute to black candidates. In light of the Reagan record of voting enforcement, racial polarization of the electorate and white politicians' limited response, both political parties must affirmatively give black voters a reason to "keep the faith." . . .

Twenty-nine years ago President Johnson anticipated that overcoming the "crippling legacy of bigotry and injustice" was necessary, not just for blacks, but for all Americans. In the wake of passage of the Civil Rights Act of 1964, and while the Voting Rights Act was being considered by Congress, President Johnson set the tone for a country with an unfinished political agenda: "We seek not just legal equity but human ability, not just equality as a fact but equality as a result. And we shall overcome."

Twenty-nine years later we have not yet overcome. The promise of our political system has yet to reach beyond symbols to commitments, beyond token appointments to representative black advocates, beyond electing black candidates to mainstreaming black issues. To keep the faith, blacks expect political fairness. At this moment in history, political fairness for blacks means a fair opportunity to choose their representatives, a fair shake in administrative enforcement that protects minority voting rights, and a fair share of substantive, legislative policy outcomes.

To implement an electoral agenda, African-Americans face the dual challenge of encouraging vigorous enforcement of existing law and the structuring the political process to reflect more fundamentally the sobering reality of inequality. While it is true that under our constitutional system laws have removed most formal barriers to black electoral participation, the Reagan and Bush Administrations did not enforce many of these laws. Blacks do not yet fully participate in the system, even as contemplated by federal statute.

If the voting rights laws are vigorously enforced and the immediate barriers to political fairness are crossed, blacks can obtain a greater degree of actual representation. Even after blacks reach this goal, however, new questions regarding political fairness will certainly arise if blacks remain seen, and not heard. But first, our political system must redress its historical insult to African-Americans by fostering actual representation whenever possible, and thoughtfully considering race issues whenever relevant.

Twenty-First Century Cultural Politics

TRICIA ROSE

African-American history is paradoxical. It can be characterized as one in which black people's sustained and heroic struggle for freedom, equality, and justice has resulted in both greater and lesser degrees of each. Various struggles for and against parity for African Americans have produced uneven and contradictory forms of black political and social progress and new forms of isolation and economic fragility. Much has been achieved, but great hurdles remain. As we approach the next century, what strategies can we imagine for responding to what will likely be newly figured and less visible means of social, political, ideological, and material oppression for black people? How can we be most flexible, creative, forward-thinking, and resilient in our ability to create new communities, adopt and adapt technologies, and respond to future crises, attacks, and defeats; and how can we do this without erasing crucial historical knowledge, links, and patterns of cultural expression?

Tricia Rose, "Cultural Survivalisms and Marketplace Subversions: Black Popular Culture and Politics into the Twenty-First Century," in *Language, Rhythm, and Sound: Black Popular Cultures into the Twenty-First Century,* ed. Joseph K. Adjaye and Adrianne R. Andrews (Pittsburgh: University of Pittsburgh Press, 1997), 259–272. Reprinted by permission of the University of Pittsburgh Press.

The economic, political, and cultural spheres are all crucial locations for establishing strategies of resistance against oppression and for developing visions of community and democracy. Few observers would question the importance of the first two; but the last, the cultural sphere, has been questioned as a location for resistance—especially now, in these times of heavily commodified culture. Why is the cultural realm so important? And why and how should our struggles for equity and freedom privilege the sphere of black cultural production, especially cultural forms that are a prominent part of the global capitalist economy?

Cultural expression is an important site of social and political reproduction. How we imagine, reproduce, and define ourselves, and how we are imagined, reproduced, and defined through culture, are critically linked to (and often sustain) struggles for change and freedom. For black people, popular culture has long provided rich and complex opportunities for expression in which pleasure, pain, vision, desire, and the politics of racial resistance, identity, community, and historical memory converge. As we design and implement forward-thinking strategies, we must seriously consider the close links between black popular cultural representations and the history of black people's struggles for social and economic equality and dignity.

Cultural forms, expressions, and representations continue to be deployed, directly and indirectly, in the service of political agendas, not always those of our choosing. The present political moment is no exception. The political-cultural rhetoric of the Republican Right about family values, morality, and fighting crime supports draconian policies fueled by profoundly patriarchal, homophobic, and racist ideologies. Support for the expanding prison-building economy in the 1990s has been achieved by a politics of fear that systematically criminalizes and dehumanizes black and brown male adolescents and adults through racialized languages of cultural deprivation and primitivism. These criminalizing discourses very often tap into long-standing fears of dark-skinned men that overshadow collective narratives that might encourage other forms of institution building, such as schools, recreation, and political action centers, drug treatment facilities, sex education, and conflict resolution seminars—not just for troubled young people of color, but for all Americans.

Such nationally fanned, historically resonant fears are reworked, exaggerated, and reclaimed by young black men who feel trapped by them and are manipulated by an industry that has marketed blacks as exotic and dangerous subject matter. Hip-hop's maniacal gangstas are products of the white imagination *and* of the prisons, projects, and the subcultures of desperation these big business and government institutions help make. Gangstas serve two related purposes: they buttress white fears of black men and justify building more prisons to house them, and they fuel the proliferation of outlaw fantasies of power among black males in the face of extraordinary social, economic and political marginalization. As hip-hop's gangsta-laden fantasies absorb more and more of the social and creative space for young black males, conservative gangsta-laden policies take up more of our political and social space. Black cultural attempts to find prestige, pleasure, and power in exile are converted into fuel for social warehousing policies.

Black political actors have also participated in this public political exchange over culture. Under the (sometimes heartfelt) guise of "protecting our youth" from cultural expressions of violence and sexism, black leaders such as Sen. Carol Mosley-Braun, Rev. Calvin Butts, and others have encouraged antirap movements and coordinated antirap music hearings in the House and Senate. These hearings are in no way suited to serious and much-needed cross-racial, public dialogue on violence, sexism, patriarchy, and how some young people are reproducing these entrenched, multigenerational patterns in new and disturbing ways.

Such hearings and other strategic cultural-political outbursts cannot be expected to dismantle complex structures of sexual, racial, and economic oppression, nor are they designed to. At best, they are political sound bites for uncourageous, symbolic political action; at worst, they are the nation's way of deflecting attention from the state-generated forms of structural oppression and focusing attention on sometimes destructive responses to these conditions. While rap music and our most troubled young people remain in the spotlight as the cultural carriers of sexism and moral decline, global and local cultures of gender, class, and racial oppression (the family, corporations, schools, religious institutions, the workplace) are shadowy figures in the national landscape.

For example, in the heated mainstream focus on vulgar and mean-spirited sexism against black women, a whole range of systematic erasures and quiet forms of degradation of women in both black and white patriarchal narratives go relatively unnoticed. Actually, more to the point, they are affirmed. Expressions of shock and outrage at examples of vulgar and extreme sexism are frequently silently anchored by an affirmation of the underlying everyday structures of patriarchy. It is much more difficult to stir up heated public dialogue about the deeply oppressive, less sexually vulgar forms of marginalization and objectification of black women.

Andre Willis's essay on Leslie Harris's film *Just Another Girl on the IRT,* speaks eloquently to this problem. It highlights the fact that Harris's mere narrative-centering of a young, urban black woman's experiences is a significant break from the body of contemporary, often hip-hop inspired films. Vulgarity notwithstanding, most black popular cultural forms and film have fully marginalized black women's points of view and all but erased young black women's subjectivity and agency in favor of presenting their value only as showpieces of male power. Both "positive" and "negative" tales from the 'hood share this mode of representing black females. Active and passive approval of the symbolic domination, erasure, and marginaliza-tion of young black women in contemporary American culture reproduces the common assumption of black patriarchy itself.

A similar problem exists in the national debates about welfare. These debates frequently center on black women's "sexual irresponsibility" and "matriarchal power," which have resulted in their economic dependence on the state instead of their "proper" dependence on black men. Slavery-derived narratives about black breeding, now supposedly out of control (and, more important, no longer to the economic advantage of white people), are revised and reinvoked in the popular phrase "having babies for welfare." Again, black women stand at the symbolic center of narratives about cultural decline and excesses that are primarily designed to affirm an oppressive norm (and to support punitive economic policies), which in this case is a "normal" patriarchal family in which black women's dependence is shifted from the state to men.

Culture—most especially that produced and consumed by the least powerful—is central, therefore, to contemporary debate and policy on domestic budget issues and American values. More specifically, commodified mass-market culture is on the hot seat because many critics and activists from across the political spectrum believe that mass culture diminishes, intervenes in, and manipulates everyday and traditional cultures and rituals. Most critics begin with the assumption that mass culture has done substantial damage and consider responses to this condition.

Allow me to make some gross generalizations to illustrate the point. On the political and cultural right, mass culture is often understood as a morally debased, corporate-sponsored site in need of Christian policing. Here, a possibility for so-called good mass culture exists as long as it expresses better values. On the political and cultural left (except for those who also call for leftist, nonreligious versions of corporate cultural policing), the central question is whether the marketplace, the field of commodified culture, is an appropriate location for expressions of political and cultural resistance and organization. Those who answer no, or who believe that it is only rarely possible, see real politically progressive or radical work almost by definition taking place outside the market, a fundamental site of oppression itself.

Those who dismiss the idea of mass market–based culture as resistance are not a monolithic group. Two camps from the political left—black cultural survivalism folks and those who like their politics "uncut," or those who advocate so-called real (noncommodified) black politics—frequently reject the possibility of black resistance in commodified spaces and in information technologies generally, as well as their potential for radical critique or politically subversive activity. These seemingly similar positions, especially on market-based culture, are less in agreement on the relationship between nonmarket culture and politics. The cultural survivalists are comfortable with culture as a form of racial, political resistance, while the others often see it as less important than traditional, direct political activism.

This theme—the role of the market or commodified culture in sustaining subversive or resistant cultural practices—is what most interests me here. I suggest that commodified cultural production is a *deeply dangerous but crucial* terrain for developing politically progressive expression at this historical moment. In other words, whatever counterhegemonic work is done outside the market, work that takes place inside it is also very important. In a way, *inside* and *outside* are fictions, since market forces and market logic, to one degree or another, pervade all American culture and politics. Still, the impact of the market varies significantly across social and cultural arenas, and it is critically important to distinguish between them. Market-based cultural politics, though, are not an easy space to manipulate from "below." It is often difficult or impossible to resist these market-driven spaces, especially as cultural workers confront very powerful corporate interests. Further, information-based technology is not neutral; it is pivotal in cultivating or discouraging resistance among African Americans and oppressed people generally. Even so, the cultural and political terrain in which we live demands close attention to these possibilities and a consideration of market spaces, modes of mass communication and the access they provide, and the popular pleasures they construct and serve.

Black people and other oppressed people have cultivated cultural strategies of collective countermemory and cultural survivals to sustain links and rework lost traditions, and these strategies are some of the most innovative elements in black music, languages, and literature. Black dances, drumming, music, slang, and creolizations of European languages and religious practices are also major sources of pleasure and affirmation, a powerful necessity, especially under difficult social conditions.

Cultural survivalism and collective countermemory are not only sources of pleasure; they increase collective vocabularies and the sense of collective history that is so very much under siege. . . .

At the same time, black social and cultural survivalist strategies are not always productive, nor should they always be celebrated. This is true not only of rap music's sustained tendency to perform and celebrate historically familiar aggressively sexist narratives, but also of less obviously deleterious forms of expression. The scholarly erasure of black women's contributions to oral and other popular cultural games and practices, especially in the areas of ethnographic research, is a less shocking but no less vulgar means of obliterating the role of black females. . . . Similarly, celebrations of canonized artists and musical and cultural movements rarely, if ever, consider the fact that these forms are sustained in deeply male-dominated and male-cultivated spaces that actively sustain the creative marginality of black females. The more we wax eloquent about great geniuses, who are virtually all male, the more blinded we may become to black female creative privilege and to what degree collective community resources have been allocated to producing and reproducing this gross gender imbalance in the name of black excellence.

While knowledge and interpretation of recent and distant cultural traditions, forms of cultural production, and resistance are absolutely necessary to future political and cultural work, such knowledge can sometimes obscure how changes and ruptures *enable* rather that *disable*. A frequently nostalgic call for authentically black expressions, rooted in premodern African histories and myths, can contribute to stagnation in the name of historical reclamation. The popular Akan word *sankofa,* which means that one must look backward before one can move forward, is often used, in contemporary black American culture, to buttress a desire to look backward rather than confronting how to move forward. This tension between survivalism and a need for fierce commitment to incorporation and change places black Americans at a crucial and dangerous crossroads as we make the transition to the next century.

The cogent phrase coined by Amiri Baraka about the relationship between continuity and improvisation in black music, "the changing same," speaks to the tension between retention and hybridity. What if we further emphasize the elements of change and draw attention to black cultural changes that are so layered, so much concerned with multiple incorporations of the new that survivalism is not the driving point of analysis or creation, but a kernel from which radical cultural formations emerge? Perhaps then the "sources" of blackness, as it were, can be housed in the future as well as the past.

This attempt to doubly emphasize *historically* and *culturally literate change and transformation*—not just newness for its own sake or for the sake of the market, or newness admired out of ignorance, but informed, critical deployment of cultural knowledge—emerges partially from my suspicions about the conservative tendencies in black retentionist thinking and black canon building. Cultural conservatism is problematic not only because it tends toward rigid (sometimes suffocating), very often nostalgic notions of "truly black expression" located in another, mythically glorious time; it is troubling because it places excessive emphasis on cultural survivalism and the issues of purity and authenticity that seem destined to tag along with it. Thus it dehistoricizes black cultural formation and deemphasizes the degree of incorporation and vision that so often accompany new black expressions.

These tendencies are especially ill-suited to this moment, one of unprecedented and profound technological growth and change. In the face of current and future technologies of domination and dispersion, cultural survivalism has to be coupled with fearless acts of incorporation. These fearless acts are already present in some of the richest and most highly amalgamated black cultural forms; I am calling for a heightened awareness of the importance of these transformative moves. Some of these creative moves that break with tradition are crucial to mobility, flexibility, and rejuvenation. These breaks are not diversions from "tradition" that should be curtailed; they are occasions for creativity, experimentation, and transformation. I want to problematize facile understandings of continuity and survivalism as necessarily equal to progressive acts of sustenance and interrogate similarly reactive notions of rupture and change as signs of loss and crisis.

Cultural incorporation is not necessarily antithetical to cultural survivalism. The widely held scholarly notion that cultural forms have multiple simultaneous meanings and uses presupposes a mobility of cultural practices that reflect some degree of cultural incorporation. Incorporation sometimes involves the retention or reclamation of previous meanings (an act that presupposes rupture and change) and a sort of desire for reclamation under new conditions. In other moments, incorporation of new materials and technologies is privileged rather than reclaimed. These dynamics are most hotly contested when changes or new materials or technologies associated with the marketplace, or products of the market, are the basis of cultural incorporation or meaning making.

[Cultural historian Joseph Adjaye has shown us] that the uses and meanings of kente cloth over the past five centuries have changed not only as a result of aggressive capitalist-driven forms of European colonization; the transition from the production of two-color (blue and white) cotton cloth to multicolored silk kente cloth "was made possible by a combination of indigenous Asante creativity and external influences," including the ecological difficulty of growing cotton in the Asante forest and the creative adaptation of weaving designs and patterns found in Fulani blankets. At the same time, however, the move from a slow, collective process of weaving kente cloth by hand, which enables the transmission of highly codified meanings and spiritual values, to a faster, more alienated machine process entails obvious losses. Yet, this change has also enabled Ghanaians with meager economic resources to have much greater access to the cloth. In this transformation from hand weaving to machine processing, kente cloth moves from being a fabric available only to an African elite to one that poorer Africans and other diasporan peoples are more likely to obtain. Kente moves not only from being a "pure," richly symbolic Ghanaian fabric to mass commodity, but also from haute couture to a collective text with new and diverse meanings and uses.

This easily disparaged marketing and mass production of kente cloth ("we've lost the true, important meanings of kente cloth") involves more than a masked but important celebration of elite control over important symbolic rituals; it also denies the possibility that mass market access can provide new contexts for collective consumption. The market circulates a fabric formerly virtually inaccessible to African Americans and British and Jamaican blacks, as well as the collective and multiple meanings and uses that come from such circulation. A collective meaning for kente cloth becomes possible in this global context, in Harlem, Watts, Brixton, and Kingston, not despite multinational commodity exchanges, but *because of* them.

. . . The global circulation of hip-hop music and culture has produced new black diasporan links. In 1992, I was asked to participate in a panel discussion on hip-hop sponsored by the French Embassy and held at the Apollo theater in Harlem. The audience was a small, highly attentive group of French teachers and cultural and government officials interested in the American roots of hip-hop and its role as a prominent symbol of rebellion among North African immigrants in Paris. The French could not explain why young black immigrant males had adopted hip-hop as a sign of racial resistance, notwithstanding the sustained racist and nationalist exclusions and abuses to which they were subjected. After a brief discussion regarding the racialized conditions of economic oppression and social isolation endured by these recent immigrants, the French representatives reached a partially irrational but familiar conclusion: the demonstrations do not reflect any racial tension in France; instead, hip-hop is a vehicle for exporting America's race problem.

In part, this interpretation is correct: America's export muscle clearly produces U.S.-centered lines of cultural exchange and global racial narratives. But this does not fully explain the attraction of hip-hop's themes of social protest to marginalized North African youth in lower-class Paris suburbs. Through hip-hop, these people are linked to a market-mediated collective discourse that allows them to create a local race-based critique of French society. It names their condition in ways that reject France's racially repressive dominant nationalist narratives while linking them to other similarly oppressed communities of color in the neocolonial diaspora.

Similarly, Chuck D's famous sound bite, "Rap music is black people's CNN," is correct on at least two counts; rap music is a highly accessible, quickly incorporative cultural form that gathers and presents information from multiple, black (usually inaccessible) sources, *and* it is a highly mediated corporate-dominated product that tends to produce homogenized and deeply problematic representations. The mass media market is a dangerous place; in it we spin narratives and narratives are spun around us. As narratives are more and more easily and quickly reproduced, and pressure to be on the cutting edge of these contortions grows more intense, our response skills must be continually sharpened in order to survive. This is the double-edge sword of the information game as we approach the end of the twentieth century.

These examples of international, hip-hop related meaning making are intertwined with the use of hip-hop by global capitalist advertisers to sell Campbell soup, Coca-Cola, clothing, and all brands of athletic shoes to children of all ages, black women's attempts to negotiate hip-hop's profoundly abusive narratives that float atop highly compelling beats, white males' voyeuristic love of gangsta profiling, and the many other means by which folks make sense of hip-hop. We must be sensitive to these multiplicities; without such sensitivity, we may accept monolithic understandings that either overly celebrate hip-hop's cultural survivalism or overly condemn hip-hop's use of technology and its reckless investment in getting paid, leaving us locked in a fruitless battle between equally one-sided, disabling interpretations of late twentieth-century cultural circulations. . . .

It is crucial that we press for a more intricate understanding of how popular expression and resistance works within and in relation to market forces. We must look closely at the pernicious effects of the market, the fissures and pockets within the market where critical counterhegemonic work can take place, and think carefully about how to sustain and enlarge these fissures and pockets. The marketplace, its effects on our modes of communication, expressions, and political systems, are too vast, too diverse to be denied consideration as an environment in which resistance and/or sub-version can take place. It simply takes up much too much cultural, political, and dis-cursive space to be rejected out of hand. This is not to say that we should limit our imagination or our quest for counterhegemonic work to this space. We must imagine and foster spaces that can be sustained outside these market conditions, nurture what Cornel West refers to as the nonmarket values of love, support, and nurturance. And yet we must be honest in representing the ways in which we all work within this mar-ket system and are profoundly shaped and influenced by it, whether we like it or not.

The information superhighway and its potential as a completely corporate-dominated and government-dominated vehicle of information gathering, policing, and dissemination of culture must be resisted by our taking up these spaces—especially as they are in formation—and making politically informed demands on them, carving out spaces that resist such controls, fighting the legal and ideological battles that might force important reconceptualizations of cyberspace. Avoiding, rejecting, refusing, or conceding these spaces—most crucially while the cyberink is still wet—is close to political and cultural suicide.

Black people have always made creative and interesting uses of technology, not only in unconventional ways, but in ways that make the environment resonate with black cultural ideas, traditions, and sounds. Blacks' use of musical instruments, elec-tronic equipment, film, and other new technologies have figured prominently in the transformation of Western cultural ideas and forms. Given the speed with which con-temporary technologies are introduced and dominated by the most powerful, exclu-sion based on gender, race, and class will have a profound impact on black creativity.

This is especially true of information and visual technologies. The explosion of video technology in the 1980s had the most significant impact in African-American communities through black musical creativity. The simultaneous occurrence of hip-hop and the introduction of music videos to market popular music has produced a quantity of black directors, camera operators, and other black production crew members versed in film and video technology. Access to these fields, the white male unions that control them, and the apprenticeship systems that sustain them was all but denied to African Americans, especially women. Low-budget music videos offered low-risk, high-yield environments for untrained but motivated teenagers and young adults. The hip-hop film business is completely indebted to the creative energy of a technologically skilled population that emerged vis-à-vis black music video. The fight for access to these and more cutting-edge, computer-based tech-nologies paves the way for transforming visual representations and therefore assists in waging war against a well-funded battery of racist, sexist, and elite-dominated cultural representations. Of course, if we consider the marketplace to be fundamen-tally antithetical to progressive subversions, or if we imagine these technologies as valuable only insofar as they provide means of cultural documentation and survival (for example, black encyclopedias on CD-ROM), then black people will be further marginalized from affecting the processes that will surely work upon us.

Resistance to these diverse processes of domination is exhausting and frag-mented work; it is not always progressive; it is not absolutely resistant. African-American history is packed with understandably romantic and heroic collective memories of struggles that highlight tenacious acts of cultural survival against daunt-ing odds. However, romancing resistance, either within or outside market forces or technologies encourages the reproduction of strategies that rely on organizational structures based on gender and class oppression. Buried beneath well-defended heroic narratives we find pervasive sexism in various black resistance struggles, black scholarship, subversive cultural forms, and "traditional" politics. Any one of these is a prime location in which to begin unpacking the complexities of unproblematized cultural survivalism and honoring of tradition. This is not a call to halt one kind of race/gender/class work in favor of another; it is a call for internal reconfiguration and collective self-critique, for sorting out what to keep and what to discard through honest self-examination and critical dialogue.

There are both passive and active modes of sexism and homophobia in much cultural survivalism and the resistance work that binds us to one another; at the same time, these tendencies blind us to the diversity and power struggles within our own communities. This tension often binds us to models of community and protest that ironically perpetuate many of the most problematic forms of oppression that black people face. These intragroup forms of oppression also blind us to the rich cultural expressions that take place in those marginalized sites. For example, black gay dance and cultural form-voguing are extraordinary revisions of sexual and racialized identities and fantasies as articulated through the white high-fashion industry. This example of how black people use the black body in relation to racialized, gendered, and class-stratified market forces, as well as black surversive pleasures, aesthetics, and style is underexamined by black cultural critics for many reasons, not the least of which is the systematic marginalization of black lesbians and gay men.

As we move into the next century, racism, sexism, homophobia, and class oppression seem well placed to follow us there and perhaps in some places may lead the way. Caribbean peoples, Afro-Europeans, African-Americans, Africans, and others have to forge ahead and fight the way in which global and postindustrial capitalism are transforming our mutual relations. The modes of oppression that we all face will likely be familiar and yet promise to be fundamentally transformed and transforming. If we are to respond to new systems of domination as quickly as we must, then we must grapple with technologies and the spaces they occupy as swiftly and creatively as possible. We have to look carefully and creatively at market-driven spaces as well as imagine and produce new social spaces for community building. I hope that we can sustain and remake the past while fearlessly fighting for access to, and to transform, the cutting edge. Nothing less will do as we move swiftly into the next century.

The Changing Face of the Continuing Struggle

TEMMA KAPLAN

When I finally reached Dollie Bullock Burwell at about 10:30 at night, we'd already been playing telephone tag for weeks. She'd just returned home after campaigning with Eva Clayton, who, one month later, in November 1992, became one of the first two African-Americans elected to the United States Congress from North Carolina since Reconstruction.

Temma Kaplan, "'When It Rains, I Get Mad and Scared': Women and Environmental Racism," in *Crazy for Democracy: Women in Grassroots Movements* (New York: Routledge, 1997), 47–61, 65–69. Reprinted with permission.

Exhausted, Dollie spoke relatively slowly over the phone, with a refinement and ease common to people from the northern borders of North Carolina. Despite the time and the fact that Dollie had been campaigning for months, her voice was energetic and enraged remembering how 40,000 cubic yards of PCB-laced soil had been dumped three miles from her backyard ten years earlier. "I was ticked off. I couldn't believe they'd dump that dirt on us—the landfill's a mile away from the school my daughter Kim went to and down the road from the Baptist Church," she said. "Everybody around here knows everyone's business. How did they get the land?" Like a person slowly waking from a nightmare, she stopped for a moment and recalled, "I became registrar of deeds in 1988; I never wanted to be surprised like that again."

We arranged to meet in person in her office in Warrenton in late January 1993. Having driven up from Durham on a blustery day and arriving way too early, I wandered around town before going to see Dollie. I'd done a stint in Mississippi in the mid-sixties, teaching at Tougaloo College outside Jackson. Despite the terror of those times, walking around small southern towns always conjures in me a sense of possibility from a time and place when interracial victory over white supremacy seemed possible—even inevitable.

With a population of scarcely more than five thousand, Warrenton is the county seat of one of the poorest, blackest regions in the state. Downtown consists of two city blocks along a main street. In front of the post office, there is the usual monument to white Civil War dead vying for attention with historic markers, pointing to the houses of Revolutionary War heroes and senators from the slave South.

The local stationery store, which sells the *Warren Record,* a weekly newspaper, also stocks books on local history, self-help studies, and the latest offerings of conservative Republicans. Postcards in black and white fill the racks with three scenes of downtown Warrenton at the turn of the century. But around the corner from the shop, opposite the library and the single-story county office building, is the Taste Paradise health-food store on whose front door is the motto "Cleanse your body with herbs." A few doors down is the Hercules Fitness Center. The sign out front has a black muscle man and a white couple dancing, seemingly indicating that, despite racial stereotypes, the center is integrated. If the war monument and historic homes look back to a sectional past, certainly health food and a sexually and racially integrated fitness center indicate that never before has American culture been so unified. For better and worse, there's a national culture, and the media have a lot to do with it.

Television aerials and even a satellite dish or two stood out along the country roads I'd taken between Durham and Warrenton. Thirty years ago, more naive and purist, I'd been shocked by the presence of television sets in the shacks of even the most abject sharecroppers in Mississippi. When I returned to Tougaloo after one weekend in the Delta and expressed my indignation to the campus minister, he countered by saying, "Hey, you've seen the schools. And Negro kids here can't even get into this new Head Start. What's better than TV to show your kid a world outside of Mississippi?" Talking about television recently to a friend who has lived in another small southern town for twenty years made me take stock again. He said, "It's not just television but cable that's changed the outlook of the South. When you can get thirty channels, local people no longer control what you know. You begin to make your own connections."

I was thinking about this when I first walked into Dollie Burwell's office. She told her male assistant she'd be talking to me, and we went to her ground-floor office, which opens onto a lawn and the street. Dieting after months of living on doughnuts and fried chicken on the campaign trail, she suggested we skip lunch and talk. A soft-spoken woman in her mid-forties, dressed in a long blue skirt, high black boots, and a heavy, cable-knit white sweater, Dollie seemed younger and more vulnerable than I had imagined. I wouldn't have picked her out as a prophet whose views about the connection between civil rights and the degradation of the environment are changing the way people around the country are thinking. Vernice Miller, co-founder of the West Harlem Environmental Action, and herself a force to reckon with, says when Dollie speaks even male civil rights leaders stop to listen. Among women, that is high praise.

Dollie Burwell is a shrewd political leader, filled with confidence but also a little shy. It's hard to envision her giving way to anyone, but it's easy to imagine her cultivating the political opinions of people who usually don't know what views they have until they speak. When an opponent in North Carolina, exasperated with Dollie said, "She's a professional agitator—that's her profession. She just goes around making trouble," Dollie responded, explaining patiently, "Yes, I'm an agitator. Soap and water just don't do the job. Without the agitator, the clothes in the washing machine remain soiled."

Like many American radicals, Dollie believes in the American system. So in 1978 she discounted rumors about secret, state plans to build a large toxic-waste dump near her house in rural Afton, a town outside of Warrenton. . . .

. . . In 1978 Dollie fervently believed that the courts would protect her and her neighbors against pollution. She couldn't imagine why the governor would allow a landfill to be built in Afton. The sandy soil and poor drainage made that land a particularly dangerous place for a dump. . . .

Confident that the law would protect her and her neighbors, Dollie was nonetheless outraged in 1978 when she first learned that nearly 31,000 gallons of transformer oil filled with PCB had been dumped along two hundred miles of road in fourteen counties in central North Carolina some time around July 28, 1978. Robert J. Burns and his sons, Randall James Burns and Timothy P. Burns, owners of a trucking company in Jamestown, New York, had been hired by the Ward Transformer Company in Raleigh, North Carolina, to dispose of the oil. The New Yorkers "obtained a 750-gallon tank and installed it in back of a truck . . . [V]alves were run from the tank through the wall of the truck so that fluid could be drained at will." Then the truck simply drove along at about 20 miles per hour, dribbling the contaminated oil along the highway. In a similar case, the driver of a tanker revealed how, by leaving his valve open, he could go along a road in the rain, dropping a slick of oil filled with toxic wastes. According to that driver, "The only way I can get caught is if the windshield wipers or the tires of the car behind me start melting."

The Burns family pleaded guilty in federal court to technical violations of the Toxic Substances Control Act and the Clean Water Act. The father got three to five years, and his sons received suspended sentences in return for testifying against Robert E. "Buck" Ward Jr. and Robert E. "Bob" Ward III of Raleigh. The judgment against the Burns family, rare as it was, did not make the problem go away. Despite a civil suit for $12.5 million filed by the federal government and the state of North Carolina against both companies, the state showed its own shortsightedness. Instead of incinerating and thus neutralizing the 40,000 cubic yards of contaminated soil resulting from the oil dumping, the state decided on the cheaper method of simply disposing of it in a landfill, disregarding the health of the largely black population destined to receive the contaminated soil.

Little was done with the dirt for four years while the courts tried to decide how to dispose of it. A sixty-eight-year-old woman, Mame Stansbury, who lived with her sister near the small town of Arlie along Rural Road 1308, described what life was like after the dumping: "There was a brown streak along the highway" and the smell was "so strong that we had to roll our glasses up, and even with the glasses up it would get in your eyes and burn." They "rode by this stuff for months and months with [their] glasses rolled up, and it was awfully strong," she said. The area around NC 43, NC 561, NC 5, and Rural Road 1308 in Halifax County remained polluted for four years.

Miscarriages increased and children were born with defects all along the roads where the toxic liquids had been dumped. In 1980, a local physician, Dr. Brenda Armstrong, claimed to see an increased incidence of congenital illnesses among her patients. Three weeks after the spill, Vicky Jordan, who lived about thirty feet away from one of the rights of way where soil was contaminated, had a stillbirth. A year later, she had a child with heart defects who lived only eight months.

Then in the fall of 1982, twelve women who came in contact with the spill were found to have suffered contamination of their breast milk with Aroclor 1260, the exact form of PCB that was in the transformer oil. Most of the women lived along the road; one, Diane Griffen, 34, of Raleigh, had been looking at some land to buy and had noticed a "black, oily substance" on the road in October 1978, when she was two weeks pregnant. All of this was what experts considered anecdotal evidence, but local people, calculating the increased threat, got worried.

The question was how to dispose of the tainted soil. Dollie, a legal secretary, had confidence that the state would find a safe way to dispose of it. Little could she imagine that the EPA would approve a 142-acre site near her home. The county Board of Supervisors, with a single black official, at first opposed the site, and with good reason. Although the U.S. Environmental Protection Agency recommended that dumps be located at least fifty feet from the water table in dense clay soil, the site where 20 acres were targeted for the landfill at Afton was within fifteen feet of water, and the soil was sandy. But, to the horror of local residents, on June 4, 1979, when the state requested a waiver, the EPA waived requirements for clay soil in the case of Warren County. More than any case that had come to light earlier, the case of potential PCB pollution in Afton opened the eyes of the nation, if only for a quick blink, to the relationship between seemingly powerless, poor, and isolated people of color and the pollution of the soil and water supply.

According to sociologist Robert Bullard, Afton was chosen for suspicious reasons, among which is the fact that "Warren County has the highest percentage of blacks in the state," and 84 percent of Afton was African-American. Although blacks constituted barely one-quarter of the state population, they were 63.7 percent of the county population. Local people lived at two-thirds the per capita income of the rest of the state. Descended from slaves who became tenants and sharecroppers, even the 13 percent of the population who were unemployed and sought work outside the county had roots going back at least a century in this part of the world. Many people had grown up without running water so that, unlike city dwellers, they knew where their water came from and how fragile life was without it. All local drinking water comes from wells, into which the PCB linked to benzene would almost certainly leach.

The state's blueprint for the landfill included covering the hole with plastic, pouring in the contaminated soil, covering the soil with more plastic, and planting grass above it. As one manager of landfills explained, "A hazardous-waste landfill can be described as a bathtub within a bathtub with an umbrella over it." What he failed to say was that the "bathtubs" were made of garbage bags.

When the Environmental Protection Agency refused to take action by testing those along the highway to see how the chemicals may have affected them, and when the state moved inexorably to deposit the contaminated soil in Afton, local residents organized. The state, required to hold public hearings, scheduled them at Christmastime for early January 1979. Dollie Burwell alerted all the women and local ministers she knew, including the Reverend Luther G. Brown, paster of Coley Springs Baptist Church, down the road from the proposed dump. She also got word to Henry Pritford, head of the local NAACP chapter.

Before rumors of the dump, few blacks paid much attention to the oil spill, but seven hundred local people, mostly women, came to the hearings in Warren County. "Most of the folks had not even been involved in the integration," Dollie Burwell remembers. Like her, they were frightened for themselves and their families. No one automatically connected experiences in the civil rights movement with local determination to prevent Afton from becoming home to a toxic-waste dump. Though Dollie first remembers hearing about the federal government's dump in Emelle, Alabama, in a private conversation with a woman at a SCLC meeting, Dollie now says "We were just talking. We didn't really know any of the people from those parts. We hadn't yet heard about the rashes and nervous diseases, of the miscarriages and suffering. We never thought about the fact that most of those folks were black."

She later learned more than she wanted when she helped spawn an investigation into the connection between toxic-waste dumping and race, which revealed that race was the most significant determinant of uncontrolled hazardous-waste sites. Forty-one states send waste to Emelle, Alabama, where 86 percent of the population is African-American. Of the five largest disposal areas in the country, the Emelle site in Sumpter County represents 25 percent of the U.S. capacity for toxic-waste landfills. According to a report issued by the Commission for Racial Justice of Dollie's church, the United Church of Christ, "Three out of five African Americans or Hispanics in the United States live in a community with one or more uncontrolled hazardous waste sites. This represents more than 15 million African Americans and eight million Hispanic Americans."

Dollie and her neighbors, none of whom regarded themselves as community activists, did not even begin to suspect the magnitude of the problem when they prepared themselves to ask questions at the January 1979 hearings. A mixed-race group of homeowners led by Ken and Deborah Ferruccio joined Dollie in forming the Warren County Citizens Concerned About PCBs. Now convinced that Governor Jim Hunt didn't really intend to stop with the 40,000 cubic yards of contaminated soil, but planned to turn the 142 acres in Afton into an East Coast Emelle, Dollie credits the Ferruccios and local women with making that impossible.

Ken Ferruccio, who grew up on the outskirts of Boston and still retains a thick Kennedyesque accent, and Deborah, who was raised in Ohio, were dissatisfied in their jobs as school teachers in the Midwest in the seventies. By chance, they met a couple from northern North Carolina. Seemingly on impulse, they decided to move to the town of Afton.

Ken Ferruccio is a philosopher by training. He likes to take ideas apart and con- sider them piece by piece. Few grassroots activists speak about the epistemology of this or the phenomenology of that, but Ken does when discussing choices the state and federal governments have made about where to site landfills. He also speaks in catchy phrases such as "The landfill puts Rosa Parks right in the back of the bus again" or "Justice is a living organism." Although in the struggle to save Warren County, Ken Ferruccio emerged as one of the most visible leaders, he prefers to hover behind the scenes deliberating, working out his arguments, establishing his facts, writing position papers. Ken's wife and partner is as much an activist as he.

At the time of the public meeting in January 1979, neither Ken nor Deborah had ever engaged in any political activities, and Ken had largely missed the domes- tic political turmoil of the early sixties while serving in Vietnam. They were most definitely not political activists looking for a cause. As white, seemingly middle- class outsiders among largely poor black and white rural people, the Ferruccios simply did what they thought was right, and their neighbors welcomed them.

Dollie Burwell and Ken and Deborah Ferruccio joined forces. Dollie, deter- mined at all costs to keep her neighborhood from becoming a dump, never thought of herself as a leader until this time. But she turned to her church and to the civil rights groups of which she had been a part since her childhood. Sharing expe- riences of racial oppression and a history of fighting against it, SCLC, the United Church of Christ, and the local people of Warren County set out to make their plight known. The United Church of Christ was born when white northern Congre- gationalists merged with black southern Evangelicals in the late fifties. Although African-Americans make up only 4 percent of its membership, the leaders of the church uphold a commitment to racial justice rare among religious denominations. Dollie's pastor, the Reverend Leon White, is a leading force in the United Church in North Carolina, and someone she treats as a wise and beloved uncle.

At the time of the toxic-waste landfill, Dollie and White called on other allies, the Reverend Dr. Joseph Lowery, president of SCLC, and Floyd McKissick, former president of the Congress of Racial Equality. McKissick, a civil rights activist who had led the efforts to integrate the schools in Durham, about one hour's drive from Warren County, also had had a long history in the northern part of the state. . . .

Dollie, Deborah, and Ken roused their neighbors and fellow parishioners, most of whom were women concerned with their family's welfare. Before the first act of attempted waste deliveries and demonstrations against them began, however, on August 21, 1982, a vandal slashed the plastic liner of the dump every twenty-five feet in twenty-foot incisions. Rather than replace it, officials just glued it together, Dollie remembers with a sigh. The local newspaper claimed that after the damage, estimated at about $8,000, was repaired, the contractor would re-stretch the plastic above a large portion of sand. Then they would layer in five feet of clay above which the contaminated soil would rest. The state presumed that the five feet of clay would act as a filter, leaching out and collecting the PCB in the soil above it, all of this only fifteen feet above the water table. An additional two feet of compacted clay was to go above the soil, then an artificial liner, then protective material, then several feet of topsoil, which would be seeded. Downhill from the pit, authorities dug a hole to catch drainage water and keep it from filling a nearby stream. Before all this could begin, Ken Ferruccio and others from the Warren County Citizens Concerned About PCBs had unsuccessfully tried to convince EPA officers in Washington to try a new method being tested at that time in South Carolina. There, bacteria that consumed the PCB was released in a contaminated pond and then was eaten by microorganisms, thus restoring the balance of nature; the government claimed this technology was untried and that the material had to be buried.

The government scheduled the first dumping in Afton for Wednesday, September 15, 1982. Ken Ferruccio knew the movement needed publicity, and he got press releases to a journalist he knew in New York who thought events in Warren County newsworthy. Since by the early eighties, demonstrations occurred infrequently, and the connection between civil rights and environmental issues was a novelty, some TV stations and news media turned their attention to how events were unfolding.

The Sunday before the trucks were scheduled to roll, the Citizens Concerned About PCBs rented a flatbed truck to serve as a stage for a rally at the Afton school. Marching under signs saying "EPA Landfills Leak" and "Stop Toxic Aggression," demonstrators moved from the school, a mile away from the proposed dump, to the top of the road leading to the landfill. Choirs came from all of the surrounding churches and, as in the civil rights movement, music became a source of strength and solidarity, helping to prevent the violence that would certainly have occurred without the participation of the clergy and their commitment to nonviolence. Reverend White suggested that demonstrators practice civil disobedience by resisting arrest and preparing to go to jail. And though many people objected, the strategy of nonviolent resistance that had been so successful during the civil rights movement prevailed.

When the first of seven thousand truckloads of contaminated soil rolled down the road, four hundred to five hundred demonstrators, mostly women, tried to stop it in front of Coley Springs Baptist Church, a short distance from the proposed dump. Highway patrol officers dressed in riot gear descended on the demonstrators, many of whom were too young to have ever seen the police in full battle dress earlier in the civil rights movement. Chanting "Oh Lord, don't let 'em drop that PCB on me," fifty-five people moved onto the paddy wagons. The protesters, who were also singing "We Shall Overcome," recalled civil rights demonstrators of decades earlier. Yet, the arrests themselves were notable: never before had authorities treated protesters against a hazardous waste facility so forcefully—and never before had large numbers of environmental activists been black women.

When I asked Dollie Burnwell why there were so many women in the demonstrations, she replied, "More women participate. Even in the hearings, you have more women. . . . You have more women at church. . . . More women saw the need to do something. . . . For black folk, it was the first time they really got involved. They saw it as someone destroying what my community is, destroying black folk and poor people.

"Before, when people spoke about the environment, they were talking about animals and trees. When you come in and say, 'We gotta save our lives or we gotta save our children's lives or we've gotta save our homes from this poison,' black folks can relate." Dollie herself had always viewed the Sierra Club and other environmental organizations as far removed from "what would affect my everyday living. I should've been concerned with the whales and birds, but I wasn't." When the need to resist became clear, "people in Warren County didn't really consider it as an environmental movement. People talked about their land, their surroundings, their health, the fact that they are poor would mean they have no health[care]."

One reason Dollie and her neighbors were able to resist is that their land belongs to them, even if that's all they own. According to sociologist Robert Bullard, "More than 78 percent of the whites and 64 percent of the blacks [in Warren County] own their homes (nationally only 45 percent of blacks are home owners)." Like the homeowners in Love Canal, the people of Warren County have mortgage investments that make it impossible to pick up and go elsewhere. All the families in Afton except Dollie's and one other family have lived there for generations since Emancipation, and Dollie grew up in the neighboring county.

With the median income for Afton residents under $10,000 a year in 1982, people couldn't afford simply to leave. "And that's why," says Dollie, "I get scared and mad every time it rains. . . . The government is haphazard. To put that plastic in is not safe. It won't even be safe if it meets EPA standards. It certainly won't be safe when it doesn't."

During the fist week of demonstrations, between September 15 and 22, 1982, the highway patrol arrested more than 268 people. According to one newspaper, they "included teenagers, housewives with their hair in curlers and middle-aged men." People knelt down in the road in front of the trucks and prayed. The fifty-five people arrested the first day included Dollie and the Ferruccios. Thirty or so arrests were made the next day. Dollie was released on her own recognizance the first day, but she had to post $500 in bond the second day. Nevertheless, she and many others kept returning to the demonstrations. It was clear, however, that such disruption only delayed the trucks a little while and did not make the point the protesters hoped for.

At the time the dump was scheduled to open in September 1982, Dollie's older daughter, Kim, was ten. She had been hearing lots of talk about how PCB causes cancer and liver damage. Because she knew that Dollie already had had Hepatitis A, which affects the liver, she was worried and clung closely to her mother.

When the first demonstration to stop the trucks carrying the PCB-laced soil was set for September 15, Dollie presumed that people who knelt to pray in front of the trucks would face arrest. Because she was prepared to go to jail at least the first day, she was reluctant to permit Kim to join the march, but Kim insisted. Finally making sure that Kim had her father's and aunt's phone numbers, Dollie warned her daughter that they would be separated. She worried about what Kim would do when the police began to carry her mother and other women off to the vans.

When, in fact, the highway patrolmen arrested Dollie, Kim began to scream and cry hysterically. She wanted to go with her mother. The CBS evening news as well as the local news media were on the scene that day, perhaps because of the press release to the Associated Press. The national news caught Kim crying for her mama and explaining that she was "not afraid to go to jail, but I'm afraid of what this PCB is going to do to my people in Warren County," beaming an image reminiscent of children in earlier civil rights struggles and of the children gunned down in 1976 in Soweto, South Africa.

At the end of the second week of the demonstrations, a group of women, Dollie Burwell among them, decided that they had to remain in jail to dramatize their commitment. Joining Dollie in refusing to pay bail were Ann Shepherd Turner, a longtime civil rights activist; Martha Nathan, widow of a Communist Workers' Party member slain in 1979 in Greensboro, North Carolina, in a confrontation with the Ku Klux Klan and the Nazis; Joycelyn McKissick of CORE; and Evelyn Lowery of SCLC. They spent several days in jail. Burwell recalls the women having plenty of time in jail to talk about their public struggles and their difficulties in the movement making their voices heard. They thought their concerns about their children's health were being submerged in more general political rhetoric. And as women, they sometimes seemed to be ornaments rather than leaders. . . .

Though other environmental activists had carried on demonstrations in various places in the United States, the largely poor African-American demonstrators in Afton became, according to anthropologist Harriet Rosenberg, the first people arrested "in relationship to grass-roots anti-toxic movements. Not since the civil rights movements had African-American people in the South mobilized in such large numbers to demonstrate that they had reached the end of their rope and wouldn't have their human dignity and their very lives discounted because they were black and poor." Two hundred mothers marched three to four miles every day and stayed in jail to protest against what was happening to them, transforming their struggle into one for "environmental justice" and against "environmental racism." . . .

When I asked Dollie whether she had immediately drawn a connection between civil rights politics and the new environmental threat, she said she never thought of the dump as political—by which she meant holding office; she thought it was about people's lives. That's why she devoted most of her attention to making sure the women of the neighborhood and fellow parishioners came out to the meetings.

A commitment to life and service has, however, led Dollie Burwell to consider the importance of electoral politics. She thinks that had there been more than one black person on the county Board of Supervisors, they might have kept up the pressure on the governor through legal means and would have prevented or at least delayed the landfill. Others seem to have agreed that black representation would make a difference because later in 1982, Eva Clayton, a fifty-eight-year-old business woman from Littleton, North Carolina, ran for and won a seat on the board. Several blacks joined the school board, and one became sheriff. Since that time, more than 50 percent of local black people have voted in the elections, and sometimes their numbers rise to 75 percent.

Dollie says she wanted to become registrar of deeds because even though the state promised that there would be no other landfill within a fifty-mile radius of the dump at Afton, she wanted to make sure herself that no land was deeded to people for suspicious reasons. Her move into politics has not come without its price. Her opponent in 1988, a white racist, repeatedly referred to Dollie as "that darkie."

Because Jesse Jackson was running in the Democratic primary, held in April of 1988, agitated white voters were turning out in droves to defeat him—and possibly other black candidates. Dollie knew that if the white people in Warrenton voted in large numbers, she had to turn out the much less numerous rural vote, including the four hundred Native Americans who lived around Hollister.

Dollie calls that campaign a lesson in humility since, as an African-American person whose whole life had been defined in relationship to whites, she had scarcely known or dealt with issues of concern to Native Americans. What seems to have stuck in her mind is that in North Carolina historically, white undertakers embalmed Native Americans, although blacks had to have separate funeral parlors. Dollie's brother told her, "Whoever gets your body says who you are." But, as in everything, she made up her own mind and decided to find out about Native Americans. She regards her first campaign as a period of intensive self-education, one that helped her make friends and win the vote of Native Americans, who cast the 350 votes by which she won over her opponent.

In 1992, various blacks decided to run for two newly created congressional seats, one of which went from the northeast of the state to Wilmington in the south. Representing 552,386 people, of whom about 52 percent were black, the congressional seats ran over twenty-eight counties. Having succeeded in getting districts established where blacks could win for the first time since Reconstruction, the local black caucus of the Democratic Party chose its candidates from among five black men. Against them, Dollie supported Eva Clayton. Active in civic affairs, Clayton won the primary and the election with help from Dollie and other women whose political experience lay in the community.

Dollie attributes the victory to changes in the South few have recognized. "It took a lot of educating. . . . It took a lot of hard work. Folks looked at what [Clayton] had been involved in. She had run for Congress in 1968. . . . She got 30 percent of the vote. She was also assistant secretary to Howard Lee for Community Development in the Department of Human Resources [in North Carolina], bringing sewage and water to small communities. It took a lot of work making people realize.

"The biggest thing was what happened to Anita Hill. A lot of women got mad. A lot of women didn't believe Anita Hill, but they didn't like the way she was treated. Everyone was glued to the screen during the Clarence Thomas hearings. Eva Clayton, in smaller groups, talked about how women had to be in government. She talked about Queen Esther and how she saved her people. When Carol Moseley-Braun won the Democratic nomination, it cleared the way for Eva. The media's proclamation that this was the year of the woman helped her. She got more press than any of her male opponents. Press followed her extensively, but she did not get the support of the black caucus. They treated her as if she were the spoiler. [At first] even the women were for the men," Dollie sadly recalled.

In one of her campaign speeches, Clayton assumed a deliberately feminized position, using her sex to emphasize her uniqueness among a field of men. She claimed to "care about people. . . . I care about the quality of their lives. I care about whether they have good jobs, education and health care, whether their families can be secure in their communities." Dollie believes that Clayton showed women's commitment to improving everybody's life.

For Dollie, there is no contradiction between saying women are more capable of fulfilling human needs in the public sphere than men and saying women deserve equality. Dollie, who happily admits to being a feminist, sees continuity between feminism and other civil rights activities. Unwilling to argue for women's community activism as an extension of female self-sacrifice, Dollie and many other female African-American grassroots leaders have assumed special positions as spokes-women for women's rights as human rights. They are linking feminism, civil rights, welfare reform, and environmentalism. . . .

FURTHER READING

Lucius J. Barker, Mark H. Jones, and Katherine Tate, eds., *African-Americans and the American Political System,* 4th ed. (1999).

Lucius J. Barker, and Ronald W. Walters, eds. *Jesse Jackson's 1984 Presidential Campaign: Challenge and Change in American Politics* (1989).

C. Anthony Broh, *A Horse of a Different Color: Television's Treatment of Jesse Jackson's 1984 Presidential Campaign* (1987).

Cathy J. Cohen, *The Boundaries of Blackness: AIDS and the Breakdown of Black Politics* (1999).

Angela Davis, "Race and Criminalization: Black Americans and the Punishment Industry," in *The House That Race Built: Black Americans, U.S Terrain,*" ed. Wahneema Lubiano (1997).

Angela Davis et. al., *If They Come in the Morning: Voices of Resistance* (1971).

Michael C. Dawson, *Behind the Mule: Race and Class in African-American Politics* (1994).

Larry M. Gant, "When Silence Equals Death: Advocacy and Policy Perspectives in AIDS and African Americans," in *Social Workers Speak Out on the HIV/AIDS Crisis: Voices from and to African-American Communities,* ed. Larry M. Gant, Patricia A. Stewart, and Vincent J. Lynch (1998).

Robert Gooding-Williams, ed., *Reading Rodney King/Reading Urban Uprising* (1993).

Patricia Gurin, Shirley Hatchett, and James S. Jackson. *Hope and Independence: Blacks' Response to Electoral and Party Politics* (1989).

Penn Kimball, *"Keep Hope Alive!": Super Tuesday and Jesse Jackson's 1988 Campaign for the Presidency* (1992).

Toni Morrison, ed., *Race-ing Justice, En-gendering Power: Essays on Anita Hill, Clarence Thomas, and the Construction of Social Reality* (1992).

Melvin Oliver and Thomas Shapiro, *Black Wealth/White Wealth: A New Perspective on Racial Inequality* (1995).

Adolph L. Reed, Jr., *The Jesse Jackson Phenomenon: The Crisis of Purpose in Afro-American Politics* (1986).

Dorothy Roberts, *Killing the Black Body: Race, Reproduction, and the Meaning of Liberty* (1997).

Tricia Rose, *Black Noise: Rap Music and Black Culture in Contemporary America* (1994).

Barbara Smith, *The Truth That Never Hurts: Writings on Race, Gender, and Freedom* (1998).

Sarah White, "Change in a Closed Little Town," *Southern Exposure* (1997), 44–46.

Kristal Brent Zook, *Color by Fox: The Fox Network and the Revolution in Black Television* (1999).